9/11
REPORT

THE
9/11
REPORT

The National Commission on
Terrorist Attacks Upon
the United States

Thomas H. Kean, Chair, and
Lee H. Hamilton, Vice Chair

With reporting and analysis by

The New York Times

St. Martin's Paperbacks

THE 9/11 REPORT

Copyright © 2004 by St. Martin's Press.

Reporting and analysis © 2004 by *The New York Times*.

The Report of The National Commission on Terrorist Attacks Upon the United States is in the public domain and no copyright is claimed therein.

All rights reserved. No part of this book that is not in the public domain may be used or reproduced in any manner whatsoever without written permission except in the case of brief quotations embodied in critical articles or reviews. For information address St. Martin's Press, 175 Fifth Avenue, New York, NY 10010.

ISBN: 0-312-93554-4
EAN: 80312-93554-2

Printed in the United States of America

St. Martin's Paperbacks edition / August 2004

St. Martin's Paperbacks are published by St. Martin's Press, 175 Fifth Avenue, New York, NY 10010.

10 9 8 7 6 5 4 3 2 1

Contents

Background on the 9/11 Commission   vii
Times **Coverage of the Report**   xxxv
Executive Summary of *The 9/11 Report*   lxxix

List of Illustrations and Tables   cxiii
Member List   cxv
Staff List   cxvii
Preface   cxxi

The 9/11 Report   1
  1. "We Have Some Planes"   3
  2. The Foundation of the New Terrorism   71
  3. Counterterrorism Evolves   104
  4. Responses to al Qaeda's Initial Assaults   158
  5. Al Qaeda Aims at the American Homeland   210
  6. From Threat to Threat   251
  7. The Attack Looms   311
  8. "The System Was Blinking Red"   365
  9. Heroism and Horror   400
10. Wartime   465
11. Foresight—and Hindsight   485
12. What to do? A Global Strategy   516
13. How to do it? A Different Way of Organizing   570
    the Government

Appendices   609

Coming in March 2006 from Avon Books...
Four amazing love stories, by four
outstanding authors!

Portrait of a Lover by Julianne MacLean

An Avon Romantic Treasure

She met a stranger on a train . . . and suddenly Annabelle Lawson was swept away by a passion she could not control. But Magnus Wallis is a scoundrel—a man who would seduce a young lady and then leave her to face the consequences. And when the two meet again, Annabelle is the lady scorned, while Magnus is determined to show her that he has reformed. And everyone knows there is no better lover than a reformed rake.

Running for Cover by Lynn Montana

An Avon Contemporary Romance

Cole Bannon is handsome, rugged—and perhaps unscrupulous . . . but Lexie Chandler needs this dangerous man. She's on a mission that threatens her life...and she's not about to let anything go wrong. Cole is her best bet when it comes to facing a small army and a tiger or two—but even if she makes it out alive, she faces a greater danger than mere gunfire: seduction by Cole himself!

A Study in Scandal by Robyn DeHart

An Avon Romance

Lady Amelia Watersfield is over twenty, very unwed...and longing for adventure. So when a priceless family heirloom is stolen, she is determined to retrieve it. And the help of the breathtakingly handsome inspector, Colin Brindley, is most certainly welcome! Not only is he sharp-witted and brave, but he's unleashed a wild desire in Amelia . . . a desire she has no intention of taming!

The Bewitching Twin by Donna Fletcher

An Avon Romance

Aliss is being held against her will—by Rogan, a strong, sexy Scotsman who insists she use her bewitching healing powers to save his people. He swears to return her home once her task is complete, but he doesn't want to let her go. And when it comes to being captured in a game of seduction, Aliss begins to wonder just *who* has captured *whom*!

BACKGROUND ON THE 9/11 COMMISSION

What follows is a chronology of major developments in the work of the 9/11 commission, as they have been reported in The New York Times *since the fall of 2002; the articles have been abridged. They are followed by two complete stories that appeared in the paper on July 22, 2004.*

HOUSE GIVES WAY ON A SEPT. 11 COMMISSION; CONGRESS IS SET TO CREATE IT

By DAVID FIRESTONE

WASHINGTON, Friday, Nov. 15 [2002]

Yielding to intense pressure from families of Sept. 11 victims, the White House agreed last night to a Congressional compromise that would create an independent commission to investigate the terrorist attacks. The House immediately approved a bill to establish the commission on a 366-to-3 vote before adjourning for the year early this morning. The Senate was expected to pass it later today.

The 10-member commission will be charged with providing the nation the most comprehensive examination of the vulnerabilities that made the attacks possible. It will have up to 18 months to hold hearings and prepare a report on topics that include intelligence agencies, diplomacy and immigration controls, and is intended to be unflinching in assigning blame for specific government failures.

The agreement puts an end to several months of wrangling between Congress and the Bush administration, which had objected to details of the commission's makeup. Senator Tom Daschle, the Democratic leader, said earlier Thursday that the administration was stalling on the plan because it could not control the commission's eventual findings.

But the White House had said for a month that Mr. Bush supported a commission, and after intense pressure from victims' families, the administration agreed to a plan tonight that is similar to the one originally proposed by members of Congress and family representatives.

The panel of private citizens will be evenly divided between appointees of Republicans and Democrats. Congressional negotiators conceded two points to the administration, allowing it to choose the chairman and agreeing that any subpoenas would have to be issued by at least six commission members. The White House had feared that the five Democrats on the panel could turn it into a political witchhunt.

The key to the compromise was allowing Senator John McCain, Republican of Arizona, to appoint one of the Republican slots. Mr. McCain had fought zealously for the commission for months, leveling bitter criticism at the White House as stalling it, and family representatives as well as Democrats said he would appoint someone who would be aggressive in questioning public officials. At the same time, the White House was satisfied that Mr. McCain's appointment would not be partisan in nature.

PRESIDENT NAMES KISSINGER TO LEAD 9/11 COMMISSION

By RICHARD W. STEVENSON

WASHINGTON, Nov. 28 [2002]

President Bush today named Henry A. Kissinger, a Republican who has been one of the most respected but polarizing figures in foreign policy and Washington for more than three decades, to lead an independent investigation into the Sept. 11 terrorist attacks.

In choosing Mr. Kissinger, 79, the president selected a person whose reputation as a towering intellect in foreign policy is matched by the passions he has aroused among critics of his role in the Vietnam War, relations with the Soviet Union and the exercise of American power in Latin America. Mr. Bush made the appointment as he signed legislation creating the commission, a step he came to support after opposing the bill for much of the year partly on the ground that it could divert attention from the war on terrorism.

Democratic leaders in Congress, who will appoint half of the 10 members of the commission, immediately named George J. Mitchell, the former Senate majority leader and peace envoy to Northern Ireland and the Middle East, as vice chairman.

The commission's mandate is to conduct a wide-ranging inquiry into the causes of the attacks, whether they could have been averted and what changes are needed to prevent a similar occurrence.

The commission is required to complete its work within 18 months—a timetable that would have it issue its final report in the middle of a presidential election year—though Mr. Bush said he hoped it would finish sooner. The leaders of the two parties in Congress must appoint the rest of the members by Dec. 15.

The commission will have the power to issue subpoenas by majority vote, and lawmakers have urged that it cast its net widely and interview current and former government officials, including Mr. Bush and his predecessor, Bill Clinton.

KISSINGER PULLS OUT AS CHIEF OF INQUIRY INTO 9/11 ATTACKS

By DAVID FIRESTONE

WASHINGTON, Dec. 14 [2002]

Henry A. Kissinger abruptly resigned today as chairman of the commission intended to investigate the Sept. 11 attacks, informing President Bush that he decided to step down because resolving potential conflicts of interest would have meant liquidating his consulting firm, Kissinger Associates, a step that he said would have unduly delayed the commission's work.

President Bush, who aides said was surprised by the decision, vowed to find a replacement quickly.

"His chairmanship would have provided the insights and analysis the government needs to understand the methods of our enemies and the nature of the threats we face," Mr. Bush said. "My administration will work quickly to select a new chairman whose mission will be to uncover every detail and learn every lesson of Sept. 11, even as we act on what we have learned so far to better protect and defend America."

Mr. Kissinger, who was appointed by Mr. Bush, is the second prominent figure on the panel to resign this week over a personal conflict. His decision seemed to underscore how difficult it is proving to fill a commission intended to find out about the government's inability to prevent the attacks. On Wednesday, former Senator George J. Mitchell, who had been selected by Congressional Democrats to be the vice chairman, resigned from the panel, citing time pressures and an unwillingness to sever ties with his law firm.

Congressional Democrats immediately appointed former Representative Lee H. Hamilton as vice chairman. But Republicans have still not announced three of their appointments, two days before a Sunday deadline set in the law that created the 10-member commission. Five members are appointed by Congressional Democrats, four by Congressional Republicans and the chairman is chosen by the president. No confirmation of the appointees is needed.

Mr. Kissinger's appointment last month revived memories over his contentious service in the Nixon administration and his role in the war in Vietnam. But more immediately, it set off an argument between Congressional Democrats, who said he had to disclose his financial ties, and the White House, which said there was no need for him to do so. Mr. Kissinger did not return a message left at his New York office tonight, but his letter to President Bush said he feared such arguments would soon engulf his firm, Kissinger Associates.

BUSH NAMES FORMER NEW JERSEY GOVERNOR TO 9/11 PANEL

By PHILIP SHENON

WASHINGTON, Dec. 17 [2002]

President Bush named Thomas H. Kean, a former Republican governor of New Jersey, to replace Henry A. Kissinger as chairman of an independent commission to investigate the Sept. 11 attacks.

Mr. Kean, a political moderate who served on White House commissions in the Clinton administration and is the president of Drew University in New Jersey, said he did not believe he faced the potential business conflicts that led Mr. Kissinger to abruptly withdraw last week as chairman.

"I have no clients except the students," Mr. Kean said at the university today, vowing "to get to the bottom of every question and give the nation whatever answers are required."

He acknowledged that he lacked expertise in many areas that will be examined by the bipartisan, 10-member commission, which is being asked to determine why law enforcement and intelligence agencies were unable to predict or prevent the attacks.

"I am not a Washingtonian," Mr. Kean said. "I am going to learn."

In announcing the selection, President Bush described Mr. Kean as "a leader respected for integrity, fairness and good judgment."

9/11 COMMITTEE MEMBERS ESTABLISH RULES ON FINANCIAL DISCLOSURES AND RECUSALS

By PHILIP SHENON

WASHINGTON, Jan. 28 [2003]

A federal commission investigating the terrorist attacks of Sept. 11, 2001, met today for the first time and agreed that all of its members would file full financial disclosure statements and that panelists would remove themselves from any part of the inquiry that could pose a financial conflict of interest, the panel's chairman said.

The chairman, Thomas H. Kean, the former governor of New Jersey, said in an interview that the meeting, which was closed to the public, focused on the scope and logistics of the $3 million inquiry, which is expected to last 18 months. Public hearings are expected this winter.

Mr. Kean, a Republican who is now the president of Drew University in New Jersey, said the financial disclosure and conflict-of-interest rules that the 10-member panel had imposed on itself reflected a desire to remove any possibility of taint from its deliberations.

"Our only interest is to get to the bottom of this," he said in the telephone interview, referring to the terrorist attacks. "I don't think anybody on the commission has any other purpose in mind."

Although Mr. Kean did not specify which panelists might face a conflict of interest, the rules would appear to force at least three members of the panel with business ties to the airline industry to recuse themselves on issues involving airline liability.

The White House named Mr. Kean to lead the bipartisan commission last month after its original chairman, Henry A. Kissinger, the former secretary of state, abruptly resigned. Family members of victims of the attacks had protested Mr. Kissinger's appointment because of his ties to corporations and foreign governments that would come under scrutiny in the inquiry.

9/11 COMMISSION SAYS U. S. AGENCIES SLOW ITS INQUIRY

By PHILIP SHENON

WASHINGTON, July 9 [2003]

The federal commission investigating the Sept. 11 terror attacks said today that its work was being hampered by the failure of executive branch agencies, especially the Pentagon and the Justice Department, to respond quickly to requests for documents and testimony.

The panel also said the failure of the Bush administration to allow officials to be interviewed without the presence of government colleagues could impede its investigation, with the commission's chairman suggesting today that the situation amounted to "intimidation" of the witnesses.

In what they acknowledged was an effort to bring public pressure on the White House to meet the panel's demands for classified information, the commission's Republican chairman and Democratic vice chairman released a statement, declaring that they had received only a small part of the millions of sensitive government documents they have requested from the executive branch.

While praising President Bush and top aides for their personal commitment to the panel's work, the commission's leaders—the chairman, Thomas H. Kean, the former Republican governor of New Jersey, and Lee H. Hamilton, the former Democratic member of the House from Indiana—said that federal agencies under Mr. Bush's control were not cooperating quickly or fully.

"The administration underestimated the scale of the commission's work and the full breadth of support required," they said. "The coming weeks will determine whether we will be able to do our job within the time allotted. The task in front of us is monumental."

Claire Buchan, a White House spokeswoman, said today in response to the statement from the panel, known formally as the National Commission on Terrorist Attacks Upon the United States: "The president is committed to ensuring that the commission has all the information it needs. The president has directed federal agencies to cooperate and to do so quickly."

9/11 COMMISSION COULD SUBPOENA OVAL OFFICE FILES

By PHILIP SHENON

MADISON, N.J., Oct. 26 [2003]

The chairman of the federal commission investigating the Sept. 11, 2001, terror attacks says that the White House is continuing to withhold several highly classified intelligence documents from the panel and that he is prepared to subpoena the documents if they are not turned over within weeks.

The chairman, Thomas H. Kean, the former Republican governor of New Jersey, also said in an interview on Friday that he believed the bipartisan 10-member commission would soon be forced to issue subpoenas to other executive branch agencies because of continuing delays by the Bush administration in providing documents and other evidence needed by the panel.

"Any document that has to do with this investigation cannot be beyond our reach," Mr. Kean said on Friday in his first explicit public warning to the White House that it risked a subpoena and a politically damaging courtroom showdown with the commission over access to the documents, including Oval Office intelligence reports that reached President Bush's desk in the weeks before the Sept. 11 attacks.

"I will not stand for it," Mr. Kean said in the interview in his offices here at Drew University, where he has been president since 1990.

"That means that we will use every tool at our command to get hold of every document."

He said that while he had not directly threatened a subpoena in his recent conversations with the White House legal counsel, Alberto R. Gonzales, "it's always on the table, because they know that Congress in their wisdom gave us the power to subpoena, to use it if necessary."

PANEL REACHES DEAL ON ACCESS TO 9/11 PAPERS

By PHILIP SHENON

WASHINGTON, Nov. 13 [2003]

The commission investigating the Sept. 11 attacks said on Wednesday that it had reached agreement with the White House to give the panel access to copies of the daily intelligence briefings sent to President Bush's desk shortly before the attacks.

The accord was reached after months of talks over the reports, known as the President's Daily Brief, which the Central Intelligence Agency presents to Mr. Bush and his senior aides every morning. The bipartisan commission had threatened to subpoena the reports.

"We believe this agreement will prove satisfactory and enable us to get our job done," the panel said in a statement that lacked details on the agreement.

Although panel officials said the pact imposed substantial limits on access, it still appeared to establish a precedent for outside access to some of the most highly classified intelligence reports in the executive branch, a precedent that the White House had not been eager to set.

Administration officials acknowledge that they fear that information in the reports might be construed to suggest that the White House had clues before Sept. 11, 2001, that Al Qaeda was planning a catastrophic attack. The White House acknowledged last year, in response to news reports, that an intelligence briefing in August 2001 suggested that Al Qaeda might be planning hijackings.

Commission officials said that under the accord two members of the 10-member commission would have access to the full library of daily briefings prepared in the Bush and Clinton administrations and that two other members would be allowed to read just the copies of the briefings that the White House deemed relevant to the inquiry.

MAYOR AGREES TO ALLOW PANEL TO EXAMINE SEPT. 11 RECORDS

By RAYMOND HERNANDEZ

WASHINGTON, Dec. 4 [2003]

In an abrupt reversal, Mayor Michael R. Bloomberg of New York City announced on Wednesday that he had agreed to release records of emergency 911 calls and other materials sought by the federal commission investigating the Sept. 11 terrorist attacks.

Mr. Bloomberg's action comes nearly two weeks after the commission announced that it had issued a subpoena to New York City for records related to the attacks. The panel said that the city's refusal to turn over the information had "significantly impeded" its investigation.

Initially, Mr. Bloomberg said he intended to challenge the federal subpoena, arguing that the request was ghoulish and that complying with it would invade the privacy of the victims' families.

But with the deadline for complying with the subpoena looming, the Bloomberg administration reached a deal with the commission that seemed to address the privacy concerns even as it gave the commission access to the materials it has been demanding. The city had until Wednesday to comply.

Under the deal, the city secured the right to block out information identifying specific people from any records that city officials hand over to the commission. In return, however, city officials agreed to allow panel members on their premises seven days a week, from 8 a.m. to 10 p.m., to review the unedited versions of those records.

The commission's investigators are also permitted to take extensive notes when they review unedited documents or tapes, under the terms of the agreement. And the commission's final report may include statements by people taken from the 911 tapes and transcripts, provided the commission receives permission from those people or their family members, according to the agreement.

BUSH, IN REVERSAL, SUPPORTS MORE TIME FOR 9/11 INQUIRY

By PHILIP SHENON

WASHINGTON, Feb. 5 [2004]

The White House reversed itself on Wednesday and said it would support a request from the independent commission investigating the Sept. 11 attacks to extend its deadline until late July, even though that would mean the panel's final report would be released closer to the height of the presidential campaign.

The White House, which had previously opposed any extension of the May 27 deadline, said it had come to accept the commission's judgment that an additional two months was needed to complete the report.

"The president is pleased to support the commission's request, and we urge Congress to act quickly to extend the timetable," said Scott McClellan, the White House press secretary.

Congressional Democrats and members of the commission suggested that the White House was acting to pre-empt a move in Congress to extend the life of the panel into next year, allowing the commission to continue digging through Election Day. Republican political advisers worry that the inquiry could embarrass President Bush and harm his re-election chances by cataloging intelligence and law enforcement blunders before the Sept. 11 attacks.

The White House announcement on Wednesday was welcomed by the commission. At the same time, though, the panel moved closer to a showdown with Mr. Bush and his lawyers in a dispute over access to information included in highly classified Oval Office intelligence briefings given to the president in the months before the Sept. 11 attacks.

Panel members say they could vote as early as next week to serve a subpoena on the White House for access to the intelligence reports, which are known as the President's Daily Brief and are presented to Mr. Bush each morning by the Central Intelligence Agency.

BUSH ALLOWS RICE TO TESTIFY ON 9/11 IN A PUBLIC SESSION

By PHILIP SHENON and ELISABETH BUMILLER;
Philip Shenon reported from Washington
for this article and Elisabeth Bumiller
from New York. Richard W. Stevenson
contributed reporting from Washington.

WASHINGTON, March 31 [2004]

President Bush bowed to growing political pressure on Tuesday and agreed to allow Condoleezza Rice, his national security adviser, to testify in public and under oath before the independent commission investigating the Sept. 11 attacks.

The decision was a major reversal for the White House after weeks of insisting that public testimony by an incumbent national security adviser would erode the president's

constitutional authority and set a dangerous precedent. It
came as the White House also agreed to drop the strict terms
it sought on the panel's private interviews with Mr. Bush and
Vice President Dick Cheney.

"I've ordered this level of cooperation because I consider
it necessary to gaining a complete picture of the months and
years that preceded the murder of our fellow citizens on
Sept. 11," Mr. Bush said in a brief appearance before reporters at the White House.

The president, who took no questions, said, "Our nation
must never forget the loss or the lessons of Sept. 11, and we
must never assume that the danger has passed."

Aides to the president said he decided over the weekend
to compromise with the commission in light of the furor created by the White House refusal to allow Ms. Rice to testify
in public and by sworn testimony to the same panel last
week by Richard A. Clarke, the president's former counterterrorism chief.

The White House sent a letter on Tuesday to the panel
setting forth the conditions for Ms. Rice's testimony. [Ex-
cerpts, Page A20.]

Ms. Rice has been the principal spokeswoman for a
White House effort to discredit Mr. Clarke, who said in his
testimony and in his new, best-selling memoir that the Bush
administration, and Ms. Rice in particular, largely ignored
terrorism threats before Sept. 11, 2001.

9/11 WIDOWS SKILLFULLY APPLIED THE POWER OF A QUESTION: WHY?

By SHERYL GAY STOLBERG

WASHINGTON, April 1 [2004]

Kristen Breitweiser was at home in Middletown, N.J., cleaning out closets. Patty Casazza of Colts Neck was dashing to
the dry cleaners. Lorie Van Auken of East Brunswick was

headed out to do grocery shopping. Her neighbor Mindy Kleinberg had just packed her children off to school.

Then came word, Tuesday morning, that President Bush had agreed to allow his national security adviser, Condoleezza Rice, to testify publicly about the Sept. 11 terrorist attacks. All at once, the cellphones started ringing and the e-mail started flying and "the Jersey girls," as the four women are known in Washington, were getting credit for chalking up another victory in the nation's capital.

Americans just tuning in to the work of the commission investigating the attacks may not have heard of Ms. Breitweiser and the rest. But on Capitol Hill, these suburban women are gaining prominence as savvy World Trade Center widows who came to Washington, as part of a core group of politically active relatives of Sept. 11 victims, and prodded Congress and a recalcitrant White House to create the panel that this week brought official Washington to its knees.

"They call me all the time," said Thomas H. Kean, the commission's chairman and a former Republican governor of New Jersey. "They monitor us, they follow our progress, they've supplied us with some of the best questions we've asked. I doubt very much if we would be in existence without them."

The families have spent months pressing for Ms. Rice's public testimony; when the White House failed to send her to last week's hearings, they walked out in silent protest. On Tuesday, two Democratic senators, Edward M. Kennedy of Massachusetts and Charles E. Schumer of New York, suggested that the families think about asking Mr. Bush and Vice President Dick Cheney to testify publicly as well.

Ms. Van Auken said that had always been their preference. "Of course we would like them to testify publicly," she said Wednesday.

PANEL MEMBERS TALKING FREELY
(SOME CRITICS SAY TOO FREELY)

By JIM RUTENBERG

WASHINGTON, April 15 [2004]

As President Bush was appearing at a news conference on Tuesday night, the two leaders of the independent commission investigating the Sept. 11 attacks were not behind closed doors dissecting intelligence documents. They were sitting at a CNN studio here waiting to go on "Larry King Live."

One of them, Thomas H. Kean, the former New Jersey governor who is the commission's chairman, said he and his colleagues were so determined to be credible with Americans that they decided early on to conduct themselves in a very public manner.

"We made a conscious decision, and part of it was under strong pressure from the families, to make this commission as transparent and as visible as possible," Mr. Kean said in an interview.

But Democrats and Republicans alike have raised concerns about the degree to which commission members are discussing their deliberations on television and, even, in newspaper columns—to the point that they are spinning their views like the politicians that many of them are.

Americans can hardly turn on a television or pick up a newspaper these days without seeing or reading about a member of the commission. From the Fox News Channel to ABC to newspapers including The Wall Street Journal, panel members have been providing a running commentary about the investigation as it unfolds, sometimes drawing blunt conclusions months before the final report is to be published in late July.

The accessibility of the commissioners to the news media, not to mention the openness of their views, is a departure from similar independent commissions of the past. Its members' openness troubles some officials here, who say they worry that it is giving the panel an edge that will taint its conclusions—especially when coupled with what some have called a partisan tone to members' questions at the hearings here.

QUIET BUT AGGRESSIVE STAFF AT CENTER OF 9/11 INQUIRY

By JENNIFER LEE and ERIC LICHTBLAU

April 29 [2004]

When Dietrich Snell first felt his office shake on the morning of Sept. 11, 2001—the reverberations from the first jetliner crashing into the World Trade Center down the street—he ran into the office of his boss, the attorney general of New York, Eliot L. Spitzer.

Mr. Snell, who was a federal prosecutor in the 1993 World Trade Center bombing case, had a feeling that this was no accident. Gazing through the windows at the burning tower, Mr. Snell told his co-workers, Mr. Spitzer said, that one of the defendants convicted in a terrorism case had warned as he was being led away: "We're going to get them. We're going to get them."

In the spring of 2003, Mr. Snell again walked into Mr. Spitzer's office, this time after he received an offer to be an investigator on the independent commission looking into government actions before the Sept. 11 attacks. "Well, you have no choice," Mr. Spitzer recalled telling Mr. Snell, who was a deputy attorney general. "You can't say no to that request."

Mr. Snell is one of more than 80 commission staff members who have become the silent center of the political maelstrom that has enveloped Washington in the last few weeks. In contrast to the bright-light personas of the 10 commissioners, the staff members do not have biographies or faces that are instantly recognizable in a city that churns on television appearances.

With the commission scheduled to plow over much of the same ground covered by a 2002 Congressional inquiry, many doubted the panel would break much new ground when it was created 17 months ago. But in a series of stinging reports, the staff has produced fresh evidence of intelligence failures at the F.B.I. leading up to the Sept. 11 attacks, miscommunication and poor coordination at the C.I.A., and signs of political inertia by the Bush and Clinton administrations in confronting Al Qaeda. Although the panel's final report is not due until July, its findings have already prompted President Bush to consider intelligence overhauls that he once resisted as unnecessary.

Thomas H. Kean, the commission's chairman, said in an interview last week that the staff had been asked to draw up "questions that are essential for both the president and vice president" when Mr. Bush and Dick Cheney testify in closed session today. "We have to have the answers to those questions," particularly those dealing with exactly what took place on Sept. 11, Mr. Kean said.

BUSH AND CHENEY TALK STRONGLY OF QAEDA LINKS WITH HUSSEIN

By DAVID E. SANGER and ROBIN TONER;
David E. Sanger reported from New York for
this article, and Robin Toner from Detroit.

June 18 [2004]

President Bush and Vice President Cheney said yesterday that they remain convinced that Saddam Hussein's government had a long history of ties to Al Qaeda, a day after the commission investigating the Sept. 11 attacks reported that its review of classified intelligence found no evidence of a "collaborative relationship" that linked Iraq to the terrorist organization.

Mr. Bush, responding to a reporter's question about the report after a White House cabinet meeting yesterday morning, said: "The reason I keep insisting that there was a relationship between Iraq and Saddam and Al Qaeda" is "because there was a relationship between Iraq and Al Qaeda."

He said: "This administration never said that the 9/11 attacks were orchestrated between Saddam and Al Qaeda. We did say there were numerous contacts between Saddam Hussein and Al Qaeda. For example, Iraqi intelligence officers met with bin Laden, the head of Al Qaeda, in the Sudan. There's numerous contacts between the two."

He repeated that Mr. Hussein was "a threat" and "a sworn enemy to the United States of America."

Last night Mr. Cheney, who was the administration's most forceful advocate of the Qaeda-Hussein links, was more pointed, repeating in detail his case for those ties and saying that The New York Times's coverage yesterday of the commission's findings "was outrageous."

"They do a lot of outrageous things," Mr. Cheney, appearing on "Capital Report" on CNBC, said of The Times, referring specifically to a four-column front page headline that read "Panel Finds No Qaeda-Iraq Tie." Mr. Cheney added, "The press wants to run out and say there's a fundamental split here now between what the president said and what the commission said."

He said that newspapers, including The Times, had confused the question of whether there was evidence of Iraqi participation in Sept. 11 with the issue of whether a relationship existed between Al Qaeda and Mr. Hussein's government.

CHAIRMAN, UNIFIER OF
PARTISAN COMMISSION MEMBERS

By PHILIP SHENON

WASHINGTON, July 21 [2004]

Mr. Kean went to Washington.

But unlike Frank Capra's Hollywood vision of a naïve Boy Scout leader drafted into politics who triumphs over the evils of Washington, Thomas H. Kean is ultimately no Mr. Smith. The former two-term Republican governor of New Jersey is a politician through and through, though the sort of sunny old-fashioned consensus-builder that this embittered capital is not used to seeing anymore.

"This city is so divided that I just don't see how government works anymore, how Washington works anymore," said Mr. Kean, who has for 19 months led—and to a remarkable degree, held together—the independent bipartisan panel that investigated the 2001 attacks.

"This commission has been unified," he said, his distinctly patrician accent a legacy of a childhood of wealth and privilege in New Jersey and Washington, where his father served 20 years in the House of Representatives. "We are unified by a sense of history, by our friendships and by our responsibility to the American people."

On Thursday, the panel of five Democrats and five Republicans is scheduled to release a book-length final report that will show how virtually every element of national security failed on Sept. 11 and why Osama bin Laden was able to dispatch 19 Arab terrorists across American borders undetected, murder 3,000 people in a matter of hours and change the course of the nation's history.

In what other commission members describe as a signal achievement that they credit to Mr. Kean and the deputy chairman of the panel, Lee H. Hamilton, the report will be unanimous. It will call for an overhaul of the way the government collects and shares intelligence, including establishing a cabinet-level post of national intelligence director to coordinate spy agencies that the panel will say are nearly dysfunctional.

The report arrives at the end of an investigation that has made history by forcing the White House to turn over—and sometimes make public—documents taken from the nation's most closely guarded intelligence files and by demanding public testimony from senior leaders who would otherwise never be required to answer for themselves under oath, most importantly Condoleezza Rice, President Bush's national security adviser.

"There are folks out there who wanted to see this commission devolve into a partisan food fight, but we were determined not to have that happen," said Richard Ben-Veniste, a Democrat on the panel who was a Watergate prosecutor. "There has been a tremendous spirit of cooperation and camaraderie that is in large part attributable to the leadership of Governor Kean and Congressman Hamilton."

Another Democratic member, Jamie S. Gorelick, deputy attorney general in the Clinton administration, said Mr. Kean and Mr. Hamilton had forged such a close partnership that "most people can't tell who is the D and who is the R."

"Tom Kean is a lovely, sweet, smart man, a really strong leader who is extremely principled and probably the single biggest reason that we have hung together," Ms. Gorelick said. "And Lee brings decades of experience and perspective that have been invaluable."

Since he was drafted for the position a week before Christmas 2002, Mr. Kean has often said the commission, formally the National Commission on Terrorist Attacks Upon the United States, was "set up to fail."

The panel was created over the initial objections of the White House. The administration warned that an independent investigation would distract from its so-called war on terrorism. Republican strategists worried that it might do damage to Mr. Bush's re-election hopes.

Mr. Kean, who left the governor's office in 1990 to become president of Drew University in Madison, N.J., and who has since turned down Republican Party pleas to return to politics, was selected to lead the panel only after Mr. Bush's first choice, former Secretary of State Henry A. Kissinger, resigned, he said, because resolving potential conflicts of interest would have meant liquidating his consulting firm.

Similarly, Mr. Hamilton, a 34-year House veteran considered one of the Democrats' wise men on foreign policy and intelligence, took over as vice chairman after the first choice of Congressional Democrats, George J. Mitchell, the former Senate majority leader, resigned for similar reasons involving his legal clients.

Panel members say it was the partnership of Mr. Kean and Mr. Hamilton, both political veterans known for centrist politics, personal civility and an ability to work across party lines, that explained why the panel has remained unified in the face of showdowns with the White House and bitter, often partisan, attacks from elsewhere.

"It's tough when you're getting attacked, when the attacks are unfair," said Mr. Kean, who won 70 percent of the vote in 1985 in his re-election as governor of New Jersey, a mostly Democratic state. "Everybody told me when I started this thing that with commissioners appointed by the two parties, the chances of having a partisan split on this thing were clearly very strong." He suggested that the spirit of bipartisan unity had been forged by the pressure, and by the weight of history.

"I didn't think anybody on this commission was going to cave into pressure from anywhere," he said. "When you run for elective office in New Jersey, you're pretty prepared for anything they want to throw at you."

As for the other members, he said: "I believe I'm talking about a commission where we respect each other, like each other. And I think all of us recognized that if we allowed partisan differences to upset this commission at any point, we would have wasted our time. The American people are sick of politics, frankly."

He described Mr. Hamilton as a "remarkable individual whose bottom line is always to do what is right."

"There isn't any other bottom line," he added.

"And his courtesy is old-fashioned," said Mr. Kean, who adds that he has spent as much time talking with Mr. Hamilton over the last 19 months as he has with his family members. "I go back a long way with Congress. My father was in Congress for 20 years. So I remember those days of courtesy and friendship. And that is what describes Lee Hamilton."

FAMILIES FORCED A RARE LOOK AT GOVERNMENT SECRECY

By JIM DWYER

July 22 [2004]

With the release this morning of the Sept. 11 commission's final report, not quite three years after the attacks, the country will receive an account of the day no longer anchored in the shock of the moment, but one that peels open layers of the federal government that are rarely glimpsed, much less scrutinized.

The version of events that evolved from those secret records reflects a profound shift. The inquiry established that the attacks, rather than being bolts from the blue, were preceded by a rising tide of unheard, ignored or mishandled warnings of pending trouble. The hearings and interim reports revealed years of troubling entanglements with other countries and evidence of a fractured national intelligence system of squabbling, uncommunicative agencies.

The commission has cut more quickly and deeply into the secrets of two presidential administrations than did earlier commissions that studied national calamities, such as Pearl Harbor, the John F. Kennedy assassination and the Iran-contra affair, according to scholars on the presidency and secrecy.

Often, the scholars said, this kind of historical overhaul takes years or decades, but the pressures of a presidential election year and the persistent inquiries of victims' families meant that closely guarded secrets and embarrassing lapses were revealed with remarkable speed.

"The commission has been given pretty extraordinary free rein, particularly in the area of national security, an area that past presidents have been most vigilant in claiming the right to withhold information," said Mark J. Rozell, a professor of public policy at George Mason University and an authority on presidential secrecy. "They had access to presidential policy directives, to information that is normally for the president's eyes only, and documents that political scientists and historians normally would not be able to get for years."

President Bush promised that his administration would cooperate with any inquiry that had the goal of making the country safer. From the outset, though, the White House had a difficult relationship with the commission, and in one confrontation after another the administration and its allies were forced to retreat. The victims' families, it turned out, were a rare force in Washington, with leverage that was not negotiable in ordinary political terms.

Their status gave them general—though hardly absolute—immunity from accusations that they were seeking partisan advantage, or that by asking questions about what went wrong they were subverting a president leading a war in one country and preparing for an invasion in a second one.

The families were "a huge factor, they were present every day in the hearings," said Louis Fisher, a scholar of executive privilege who works for the Congressional research service of the Library of Congress.

Patricia Casazza, whose husband, John, was killed at the World Trade Center, said that she and others had been moved by the families of people killed in the terrorist bombing of Pan Am Flight 103 over Lockerbie, Scotland, in 1988. "When they met with us, they said that on 9/11 they felt that they had failed us," Ms. Casazza said. "They had been pushing to have the cockpit doors hardened for 13 years, and they had not gotten it done. I, in turn, felt we had failed in not supporting them. I didn't want to turn around to the next victims and say we didn't try."

Even before the commission was formed, a joint committee of the Senate and the House issued a report on the Sept. 11 attacks for the first anniversary, but that investigation encountered rigid limits on access to intelligence information.

Sixty years earlier, similar problems confounded the first inquiries into the attack on Pearl Harbor, said Donald M. Goldstein, a professor of public and international affairs at the University of Pittsburgh and an authority on those investigations. Because President Franklin D. Roosevelt had immediately declared war, many details of America's prewar intelligence—including intercepted messages that appeared, in retrospect, to provide warning of an attack—were not revealed until a definitive Congressional study in 1946, a year after the war ended, Mr. Goldstein said. More information has trickled out over the years.

The terms for the Sept. 11 commission—bipartisan, 10 members, subpoenas issued on a majority vote, and an appointment that was to end in 18 months—were not finally settled and signed into law by the president until Nov. 27, 2002. While the commission began hearings and collecting information quickly, some agencies were slow to respond. The delay galled families who saw months run out during the wait for records.

"They did not use the subpoena power early enough and often enough," said Bill Harvey, whose wife, Sara Manley, was killed at the trade center.

The families agitated for the use of subpoenas, resisting the notion that independent commissions were a waste of time, said Kristen Breitweiser, whose husband, Ronald, also died in the trade center. Nearly a year into the commission's term, subpoenas were issued to the Federal Aviation Administration, the Department of Defense and the City of New York.

Early this year, against the wishes of J. Dennis Hastert,

the speaker of the House of Representatives, they lobbied for an extension of the term of the commission and won an additional two months.

In the spring, the administration at first refused to permit the national security adviser, Condoleezza Rice, to testify, saying the president was entitled under the Constitution to confidential advice. Then the administration retreated. The unanimity of the commission was important, Mr. Fisher said, in affecting the administration's change of heart, as was the determination of the families.

Mr. Rozell, the author of "Executive Privilege: Presidential Power, Secrecy, and Accountability" (second edition, University Press of Kansas, 2002), said it would be hopeless for the president to undertake any broad effort at secrecy during an election year, particularly with a vocal group like the families monitoring the administration's cooperation. "The fact that the family members were well organized and demanded the commission be able to fully investigate was very powerful," Mr. Rozell said. "It made it doubly hard for the president to put up any roadblocks in this area."

Even so, the commission's success may not be known for years, said Michael Beschloss, a presidential historian. "What you don't know is what Americans will learn 20 years from now about where the commission may not have had access to important information, and other areas where they might have been shortsighted," Mr. Beschloss said.

For her part, Ms. Breitweiser said that the commission had provided enough details on needed reforms, and that she and other victims' relatives would seek a meeting with the White House in early August to push for them. "The clock is ticking on the next attack," she said.

TIMES COVERAGE
OF THE REPORT

9/11 REPORT CALLS FOR A SWEEPING OVERHAUL OF INTELLIGENCE

By PHILIP SHENON

WASHINGTON, July 22 [2004]—The bipartisan commission that investigated the Sept. 11 attacks concluded in its unanimous final report on Thursday that the attacks "were a shock but they should not have come as a surprise." It warned that without a historic restructuring of the nation's intelligence agencies and a new emphasis on diplomacy, the United States would leave itself open to an even more catastrophic attack.

After a 19-month investigation that laid bare the failures of the Central Intelligence Agency, the Federal Bureau of Investigation, the Pentagon, the National Security Council and virtually every other government agency responsible for defending the nation on that brilliantly sunny September morning in 2001, the 10-member panel offered a detailed proposal for reorganizing the way the country gathers and shares intelligence. "Because of offensive actions against Al Qaeda since 9/11, and defense actions to improve homeland security, we believe we are safer today," the commission wrote in an executive summary of its long-awaited report, praising in particular the United States invasion that toppled the Taliban in Afghanistan, ending its sanctuary for Al Qaeda. "But we are not safe."

Thomas H. Kean, the panel's chairman and a former Republican governor of New Jersey, said at a news conference to release the report that the commission had been repeatedly warned during its investigation that "an attack of even greater magnitude is now possible and even probable—we do not have the luxury of time."

In a package of recommendations for overhauling intelligence operations, the commission called for a cabinet-level national intelligence director within the White House who would control the budgets of all 15 federal intelligence agencies.

The intelligence director's office would take substantial

power away from the C.I.A., the F.B.I. and the Pentagon, and it would essentially strip the National Security Council of its role in coordinating the actions of intelligence agencies.

Under the commission's proposals, the C.I.A. would cede authority to the Defense Department for control over paramilitary operations, another effort by the panel to end fragmentation among agencies in the government's war on terrorism. The panel also urged lifting the shroud of secrecy about how much money is spent for national intelligence operations.

"A critical theme that emerged throughout our inquiry was the difficulty of answering the question: Who is in charge?" said Lee H. Hamilton, the panel's vice chairman and a former Democratic House member from Indiana.

"Who oversees the massive integration and unity of effort necessary to keep America safe?" Mr. Hamilton asked. "Too often, the answer is no one."

In a report that reflected remarkable bipartisan unity on issues that often result in sharp divisions along party lines, the five Democrats and five Republicans on the commission called for broad changes elsewhere in the federal government, including Congress, which the commission harshly criticized for having failed in its role as watchdog over intelligence agencies, and at the State Department. The panel suggested that the State Department had faltered in diplomatic efforts since the Sept. 11 attacks, especially in support of vital Muslim allies, especially Pakistan and Afghanistan.

"Our efforts here should be as strong as they were in combating closed societies during the cold war," the commission said in what seemed to be an indirect attack on the Bush administration for failing to match its military effort against terrorism since Sept. 11 with an equally aggressive diplomatic campaign, leaving the United States unnecessarily isolated from its allies.

The commission's report did not offer a judgment on whether the invasion of Iraq had made terrorist attacks against the United States more or less likely, although it warned that if "Iraq becomes a failed state, it will go to the top of the list of places that are breeding grounds for attacks against Americans at home."

The 567-page report and its list of dozens of policy recommendations drew immediate, if tentative, praise from the White House and Republican Congressional leaders, with President Bush and lawmakers eager to demonstrate their support of the commission while withholding judgment on its specific proposals.

After receiving a copy of the report, Mr. Bush, who had initially opposed creation of the commission, told reporters that the panel had done a "wonderful job" and had produced "very solid, sound recommendations about how to move forward, and I have assured them that where government needs to act, we will."

Republican leaders in the House and Senate have vowed to study the report closely but say there is little time to act on legislation before the general election in November.

Senator John Kerry of Massachusetts, who is set to accept the Democratic Party's nomination for president next week, praised the report, noting his longstanding support for creation of the post of national intelligence director.

"It is absolutely vital to have somebody of cabinet level who is going to help coordinate both domestic and international efforts so we have the right standards, the right sharing of information," Mr. Kerry said. "That's overdue. And when I'm president, it's going to happen."

Although the commission did not place special blame for intelligence failures on either the Bush or Clinton administration, Mr. Kerry's political advisers have seized on the report's findings as proof that Mr. Bush was inattentive in the spring and summer of 2001 to warnings of an imminent catastrophic terrorist attack.

This year the commission pressured the White House to make public a copy of an Aug. 6, 2001, intelligence report presented to Mr. Bush that was entitled: "Bin Laden Determined to Strike in the U.S." While the White House has insisted that the briefing was a "historical" document, the commission's final report on Thursday disclosed that two C.I.A. analysts involved in its preparation had said that it represented "current and serious" threats.

• • •

In assessing the performance of Congress, the commission said that lawmakers "responded slowly to the rise of transnational terrorism as a threat to national security" in the years before Sept. 11 and that oversight of intelligence and counterterrorism issues was "dysfunctional" and divided among too many committees.

The panel recommended that Congress either create a joint House-Senate committee on intelligence, with budget authority over all of the nation's intelligence agencies, or provide that authority to a single committee in each house.

At a joint news conference on Thursday that was clearly meant to signal their unity on the issues, the 10 commissioners vowed to bring pressure on the White House and Congress to adopt their recommendations. They said that unlike blue-ribbon commissions that have disbanded as soon as a final report is delivered, they would lobby throughout the summer and fall on behalf of their report.

James R. Thompson, a Republican commissioner and a former governor of Illinois, suggested that if Mr. Bush and Congress did not act, it would be at their political peril.

"Our reform recommendations are urgent," Mr. Thompson said. "We have come together with the families to agree on that. If these reforms are not the best that can be done for the American people, then the Congress and the president need to tell us what's better. But if there is nothing better, they need to be enacted and enacted speedily. If something bad happens while these recommendations are sitting there, the American people will fix political responsibility for failure—and that responsibility may last for generations."

His comments were met by applause from several family members of victims of the Sept. 11 attacks, who had been invited to attend the news conference.

After reading the report, several of those family members said they felt vindicated by the commission's scathing criticism of the government's intelligence and law enforcement agencies, and they vowed to pressure Congress and the White House to adopt the long list of recommendations, much as they lobbied for creation of the commission two years ago.

"This report lays out a very active plan to make sure something gets done," said Kristen Breitweiser of Middletown, N.J, whose husband, Ronald, was killed in the World Trade Center and who has emerged in her grief as a leading advocate for victims' families.

"I think without a doubt this commission has shattered the ceiling on access," Ms. Breitweiser said after a briefing by the commission, a newly dog-eared copy of the report under her arm. "I think this is proof positive that democracy is alive and working."

The commission's report called for change in virtually every part of the federal government that deals with terrorist threats, from the Federal Aviation Administration and the Transportation Security Administration to the immigration and border security agencies, which have been criticized for allowing the 19 hijackers to enter the United States undetected.

The report did not dwell on questions of how civil liberties might be affected by tightened antiterrorism efforts, although it called for the government to be sensitive to the issue and to the need for humane treatment of foreign citizens detained in counterterrorism operations abroad.

In a response to the scandal over the abuse of detainees held in American military prisons in Iraq, the commission urged the United States to "engage its friends to develop a common coalition appropriate toward the detention and humane treatment of captured terrorists."

"Allegations that the United States abused prisoners in its custody make it harder to build the diplomatic, political and military alliances the government will need," it said.

The commission said that the Bush administration, which has determined that captured terrorists are not entitled to the full protection of the Geneva Conventions, should draw on the treaty in developing new detention policies.

"Its minimum standards are generally accepted throughout the world as customary international law," the panel said. "America should be able to reconcile its views of how to bal-

ance humanity and security with our nation's commitment
to these same goals."

REPORT CITES LAPSES ACROSS GOVERNMENT AND 2 PRESIDENCIES

By DAVID JOHNSTON and DOUGLAS JEHL

WASHINGTON, July 22—The Clinton and the Bush administrations failed to grasp the gravity of the threat from Al
Qaeda before the Sept. 11, 2001, attacks and left counterterrorism efforts to a disparate collection of uncoordinated, un-
derfinanced and dysfunctional government agencies, the
commission on the attacks said in its final report published
on Thursday.

"Across the government, there were failures of imagination, policy, capabilities and management," the panel said in
its report, which was harshly critical of how the intelligence,
law enforcement and military branches performed before the
attacks.

In a series of findings that were searing in tone, sweeping
in judgment and backed by voluminous reporting, the report
said senior officials were repeatedly warned about Osama
bin Laden's intentions, but failed to respond with an aggressive sense of national purpose.

"Terrorism was not the overriding national security concern for the U.S. government under either the Clinton or the
pre 9/11 Bush administration," the report said.

In contrast to most government reports, the findings were
presented in a dramatic, often gripping narrative style with
chapter headings like "We Have Some Planes" and the "The
System Was Blinking Red."

In a tone that sometimes resembled a paperback thriller,
the report chronicled Mr. bin Laden's rise as a global terrorist leader and the agonizingly slow recognition by the Clinton and Bush administrations of the danger that his network
represented.

The account described in authoritative detail how the plot, despite setbacks, gathered shape and direction and how it finally struck with four nearly simultaneous hijackings even as the national security experts here continued to ponder a counterterrorism strategy and the agencies responsible for protecting the country were completely blindsided.

Many findings were foreshadowed in the 17 staff reports previously made public, but the new report had new information about the Sept. 11 attacks, including a detailed account of how passengers on Flight 93 tried to gain control of their hijacked plane.

The report did not address directly whether the attacks might have been prevented.

"Since the plotters were flexible and resourceful, we cannot know whether any single step or series of steps would have defeated them," the commissioners wrote in the executive summary. "What we can say with confidence is that none of the measures adopted by the U.S. government, from 1998 to 2001, disturbed or even delayed the progress of the Al Qaeda plot."

Senior officials in both administrations, the report said, regarded an invasion of Afghanistan before Sept. 11 as "practically inconceivable." The ambivalent attitude continued up to the attacks. In one internal memorandum on Sept. 4, 2001, Richard A. Clarke, who was the White House counterterrorism adviser, sought to protest what he regarded as foot dragging in the Pentagon and C.I.A.

"Are we serious about dealing with the al Qida threat?" Mr. Clarke asked. "Is al Qida a big deal?"

In the end, the commissioners reached no definitive verdict on whether Mr. Clinton or Mr. Bush deserved greater blame for the lapses and inaction. The report seemed to portray Mr. Clinton as better informed and more intensely engaged than Mr. Bush. In contrast to Mr. Bush, the report said, Mr. Clinton and his national security adviser, Samuel R. Berger, had "a special daily pipeline of reports feeding them the latest updates on bin Laden's reported location."

But neither administration received much praise. Accord-

ing to the report, Mr. Clinton, Mr. Bush and their advisers
said in interviews with the panel that "they understood bin
Laden was a danger."

"But given the character and pace of their policy efforts,"
the study said, "we do not believe they understood just how
many Al Qaeda might kill and how soon it might do it."

Different sections give contrasting accounts of responses
by national security advisers under Mr. Clinton and Mr.
Bush. It describes how Mr. Berger, under Mr. Clinton, took
the lead in December 1999 in mobilizing the F.B.I. and other
domestic agencies to address the so-called millennium plot,
in which attacks planned in Jordan and Los Angeles were
disrupted. By contrast, the report describes Condoleezza
Rice and her deputy, Stephen Hadley, as not having regarded
the coordination of domestic agencies as part of their responsibility after they took office in 2001, even as warnings
of a possible attack continued to grow.

The report said of the Bush White House before Sept. 11:
"The domestic agencies never mobilized in response to the
threat. They did not have direction, and did not have a plan
to institute."

The report found no evidence that Iraq, Iran or Saudi Arabia provided operational or financial support to Al Qaeda as
part of the Sept. 11 attacks. In contrast to the Bush administration, the panel singled out as most worthy of further investigation not Al Qaeda's pre-Sept. 11 ties to Iraq, but its
links to Iran.

The lapses, mistakes and bureaucratic inefficiencies that
hobbled the government were apparent in every agency investigated, although the report did not fault any individuals
for specific mistakes. The military had no plans to defeat Al
Qaeda or kill or capture Mr. bin Laden or his chief lieutenants. Diplomatic efforts failed to dislodge Mr. bin Laden
from Afghanistan. Border authorities failed to detect false
passports or recognize passports that had been fraudulently
manipulated. Aviation security officials failed to expand lists
of people to be excluded from flying or impose thorough
passenger screening.

The C.I.A., responding to rapidly expanding priorities, and the F.B.I., bogged down by its case-oriented reactive approach, failed to share crucial information with each other and in some instances failed to follow up potentially important leads.

Immigration and aviation agencies were largely left outside the efforts. The emergency response by federal, state and local authorities on Sept. 11 was often "improvised and ineffective," the report said, "even as extraordinary acts of heroism saved countless lives."

"Our failures took place over many years and many administrations," the panel chairman, Thomas H. Kean, said at a news conference. "There's no single individual who is responsible for our failures. Yet individuals and institutions cannot be absolved of responsibility. Any person in a senior position within our government during this time bears some element of responsibility for our government's actions."

Specifically, in the years before the attacks, the report found, the intelligence agencies tried to combat the problems posed by Al Qaeda with tools and tactics that were inadequate and misdirected, principally those developed against the Soviet Union late in the cold war.

The report singled out the Central Intelligence Agency for serving at the forefront of counterterrorism, saying no agency did more to attack Al Qaeda before Sept. 11. But the report also described its response and those of other intelligence agencies as insufficient and hamstrung by a lack of resources, competing priorities and internal rivalries.

At no point after 1995, the report noted, did the intelligence agencies produce a new formal National Intelligence Estimate to sum up in a fully developed assessment the Qaeda threat. Even in summer 2001, it said, counterterrorism analysts were slow to perceive a broader threat. Before Sept. 11, the report said, the Clinton and Bush administrations limited the C.I.A. primarily to disrupt terrorism abroad and efforts via proxies. The operations tried to capture Mr. bin Laden and his aides in Afghanistan rather than kill him. Officials of the Counterterrorist Center at the intelligence agency and the National Security Council staff, the report notes, grew more frustrated. At a briefing for reporters on Wednesday, senior C.I.A. officials acknowledged that its performance before Sept. 11 had flaws. But they also said the panel had underestimated the degree to which the agency had warned senior policy makers and shared information with other agencies about the terrorist threat.

THE NEXT HARD STEP POLITICS AND RESISTANCE TO CHANGE MAKE SWIFT ACTION ON 9/11 PANEL'S ADVICE UNLIKELY

By TODD S. PURDUM

WASHINGTON, July 22—Months of unsparing study by the Sept. 11 commission and the Senate Intelligence Committee have now produced a broad consensus about two colossal intelligence failures: the missed opportunities that left the United States open to attack from Al Qaeda and the misread clues on unconventional weapons that sent American troops to attack Iraq.

Together, those lapses amount to nothing less than the gravest dysfunctions in the national security apparatus of the United States since the modern Defense Department and the Central Intelligence Agency were created at the dawn of the cold war, and the commission has proposed perhaps the most extensive overhaul of those functions since then.

But achieving consensus on adopting the commission's recommendations will almost certainly be much harder. The partisan wrangling of a presidential election and the capital's entrenched resistance to change make swift action unlikely—despite the persistent threats that the commission's chairman, Thomas H. Kean, said make another attack not only possible but probable.

"On that beautiful September day, we felt great hurt," Mr. Kean said, recalling the attacks, as he presented the panel's final report on Thursday. "But we believed and we acted as one nation. We united as Americans have always united in the face of any common foe." Now, he added, "We must unite to make our country safer. Republicans and Democrats must unite in this cause."

The likelihood of that happening, or of either party or the public embracing all the costly, complicated steps the commission believes are needed to make the country safer is by no means assured—assuming all the recommendations even make sense. There is reason to doubt whether the government, let alone the public, has fully embraced the uncertain realities that many commentators were so quick to describe in the aftermath of the attacks as the "new normal." Ports, power grids, water supplies, rail hubs and many private buildings remain vulnerable in a society that remains open by its essence, and some of the initial political and bureaucratic response to the commission's findings and recommendations sounded suspiciously like business as usual.

The Pentagon and the C.I.A., Secretary of Homeland Security Tom Ridge and some in Congress already oppose the commission's call for a new National Intelligence Director to supplant some of the functions of the Director of Central Intelligence. President Bush himself praised the report as "very constructive" but top White House officials remained coolly noncommittal on specifics.

Mr. Bush initially opposed creation of the commission, and acceded only under pressure from Congress and 9/11 families. Only concerted action by Mr. Bush and Congressional leaders seems likely to produce big changes in the coming months. On Thursday, the sponsors of the original legislation creating the commission, Senators John McCain, Republican of Arizona, and Joseph I. Lieberman, Democrat of Connecticut, said they were constituting an informal "bipartisan Congressional caucus" to press to enact the panel's recommendations, as Mr. Lieberman put it.

The commission members themselves vowed to take no active role in the fall election, but instead to press for enactment of their recommendations through an aggressive public lobbying campaign. At least one of them, James R. Thompson, the former Republican governor of Illinois, warned sharply of the practical and political consequences of inaction.

"If I were the president of the United States, I would want sitting next to me in a cabinet meeting a national director of intelligence so that I could fix responsibility in one person for issues of this sort," Mr. Thompson said. "And if I were in the Congress of the United States, I would want to make sure that I was protected from the accusation that oversight funding authorization and appropriations were not adequate."

"Everyone was caught unawares by Sept. 11," Mr. Thompson added, "the president, the Congress, the American people, law enforcement agencies. Blame, if there's blame, has to be spread all across the board because the American people never demanded more or better. But now we've been warned, specifically warned. And now we've been told by everyone, from the president of the United States on down, it's going to happen again. And if it happens, and we haven't moved, then the American people are entitled to make very fundamental judgments about that."

Gaddis Smith, a retired diplomatic historian at Yale University, noted that the investigation after World War II into the Japanese attack on Pearl Harbor led to the National Security Act of 1947, which established the C.I.A., consolidated the rival Army and Navy Departments into a single Defense Department, created an independent Air Force and created the National Security Council to coordinate policy.

"Pearl Harbor had a very salutary effect," Mr. Smith said. "It created a national security establishment, and an intelligence establishment which was not perfect but in fact served the nation well. Whether the 9/11 commission proposals will lead to such a sweeping change remains to be seen. I tend to think not. The biggest potential change is the melding of internal threats to security with international ones. It's going to be very difficult, and as a civil libertarian, I'm disturbed at the potential for going far beyond the Patriot Act in curtailing civil liberties."

Doris Kearns Goodwin, the presidential biographer, said

the Pearl Harbor and Sept. 11 investigations grappled with similar problems.

"The problems that led up to Pearl Harbor, and this, are in a certain sense intractable human problems: bureaucracies, people being unwilling to share," Ms. Goodwin said. "At certain moments, those things can be overcome"

But absent an all-out feeling of urgency like the one that prevailed in World War II, it remains to be seen whether this is such a moment.

It may be tempting to imagine that no disaster quite like the hijackings of Sept. 11 could ever recur, but there are too many anecdotal examples of Swiss Army knives eluding airport metal detectors to inspire confidence that it could not. What are the clues, which some day may seem so portentous, that are being missed today?

The commission's report quotes the historian Roberta Wohlstetter, whose 1962 study on Pearl Harbor remains highly regarded, on the handicaps of hindsight. She wrote that it is always "much easier *after* the event to sort the relevant from the irrelevant signals. After the event, of course, a signal is always crystal clear; we can now see what disaster it was signaling since the disaster has occurred. But before the event it is obscure and pregnant with conflicting meanings."

REPORT URGES NEW STRATEGY ON MUSLIMS

By DAVID E. SANGER

WASHINGTON, July 22—The final report of the Sept. 11 commission includes a call for a broad rethinking of American foreign policy toward the Arab and Muslim world, declaring that the United States needs "a preventive strategy that is as much, or more, political as it is military," and that reshapes its approach to Pakistan and Saudi Arabia.

Crucial to the strategy, the commission said, is ensuring that terror groups cannot find sanctuary in what it called "the least governed, most lawless places in the world." It listed places from western Pakistan to Afghanistan to Saudi Arabia, Yemen, West Africa and Southeast Asia, particularly the hard-to-police islands of the Philippines and Indonesia.

Suggesting that the United States has yet to come up with a comprehensive strategy that uses "all elements of national power" to ensure that those areas do not become terrorist breeding grounds, the commission recommends that "the U.S. government must identify and prioritize actual or potential terrorist sanctuaries," and "have a realistic strategy to keep possible terrorists insecure and on the run."

White House officials appeared somewhat surprised by the scope of the commission's foreign policy recommendations, which went far beyond the expected recommendations to revamp the intelligence agencies and security measures. They are contained in a chapter of the report that calls for "a global strategy" to get at the roots of terrorism that—while never directly challenging President Bush's 2002 "National Security Strategy"—makes it clear that the commission concludes that the Bush administration's efforts so far are inadequate.

It is particularly blistering about American public diplomacy, declaring that "the U.S. government must define what its message is, what it stands for." It goes on to argue that "we should offer an example of moral leadership in the world," which Mr. Bush often declares in his campaign speeches is already a central tenet of American policy.

Mr. Bush also maintains that Iraq had been a "central front" in the war on terror, a point that the report treats with stony silence. Instead, it warns of what could happen if the American experiment in Iraq goes bad, declaring, "If, for example, Iraq becomes a failed state, it will go to the top of the list of places that are breeding grounds for attacks against Americans at home."

In contrast, the commission was admiring of Mr. Bush's accomplishments in Afghanistan, saying he and Congress "deserve praise for their efforts in Afghanistan so far," but urging "long-term commitments" to helping a country that has been abandoned before, in the early 1990's.

Meeting with reporters in her office at the White House on Thursday afternoon, Mr. Bush's national security adviser, Condoleezza Rice, characterized the commission's call as an extension of the administration's current policy. "The hearts and minds issues are back," she said, using a term from the Vietnam era, "maybe in an even more real way than they were in the cold war."

But when pressed, she took issue with the commission's conclusion that America's message to the world is muddled. She argued that "no president in 60 years" has been clearer than Mr. Bush in calling for democratization in the Arab world, or in offering a clear alternative to Al Qaeda's ideology.

As recently as Tuesday, Mr. Bush has been arguing to crowds of supporters at campaign rallies that during his tenure, Pakistan and Saudi Arabia have been turned into allies in the war against terror.

The commission report draws a far more shaded picture, calling the Saudis "a problematic ally in combating Islamic terrorism," though acknowledging that they are now "locked in mortal combat with Al Qaeda."

"The problems in the U.S.-Saudi relationship must be confronted, openly," the report concludes, and a relationship must be "about more than oil." But it said it was an open question whether Saudi Arabia and Pakistan could develop "a shared commitment to political and economic reform, as Saudis make common cause with the outside world."

The commission did not find any Saudi government involvement in the Sept. 11 attacks or in financing Al Qaeda, contrary to charges made popular by books and films.

It was more critical of Pakistan, saying that in the two years after Sept. 11, "the Pakistani government tried to walk the fence, helping against Al Qaeda while seeking to avoid a larger confrontation with Taliban remnants and other Islamic extremists." But the commission report concluded that attempts late last year to assassinate Gen. Pervez Musharraf, the Pakistani president, had hardened the general's approach and made him realize that he was literally in a life-or-death struggle.

ANTITERRORISM PROPOSALS CONFRONTING
AN ARRAY OF OBSTACLES

By RICHARD W. STEVENSON
and SHERYL GAY STOLBERG

WASHINGTON, July 22—The Sept. 11 commission's detailed recommendations for overhauling the way the United States battles terrorism at home and abroad ran into issues of turf, politics and money on Thursday, even as the White House and members of Congress pledged to be open-minded in studying them.

Some of the commission's proposals would require legislation from Congress at a time when it is deeply divided along partisan lines. Some would require wholesale bureaucratic reorganization that would wrest power from individuals and institutions. Others would call for new commitments of money at a time of substantial budget deficits. And however much the recommendations were a product of a bipartisan consensus within the commission, they landed in the highly charged atmosphere of a tight presidential campaign.

"I would call myself hopeful, but not optimistic, that these changes will be enacted prior to another terrorist attack on the United States, regrettable though that may be," said Bob Kerrey, the former Democratic senator from Nebraska who is a member of the commission.

While acknowledging the political and practical difficulties of putting the recommendations into effect, other commission members said that political leaders would find themselves in an even more difficult situation if they did nothing and terrorists struck again.

"If these reforms are not the best that can be done for the American people, then the Congress and the president need to tell us what's better," said former Gov. James R. Thompson of Illinois, a Republican member of the commission. "But if there is nothing better, they need to be enacted, and enacted speedily, because if something bad happens while these recommendations are sitting there, the American people will quickly fix political responsibility for failure, and that responsibility may last for generations."

The White House expressed support for calls for change in general but remained noncommittal about the commission's main recommendations.

"I don't think anyone believes the answer is the status quo," said Condoleezza Rice, the national security adviser. But Ms. Rice added that there were no quick fixes, particularly when it came to overhauling the intelligence services.

"These are pretty fundamental recommendations for fundamental change," and would require a lot of legislative action, she said. "Whatever we end up doing on intelligence reform, it is not going to have an impact tomorrow. It is not going to have an impact a month from now."

The recommendations include a call for the establishment of a national intelligence director, who would oversee all the intelligence agencies, as well as a national counterterrorism center. The proposals also seek a fresh approach to elements of American foreign policy, including more effective efforts to sell American ideals around the world.

The proposals also urge that the highest priority be given to protecting New York and Washington. They also urge development of new technology to identify travelers through biometric measurements, and the allocation of more radio spectrum for public safety agencies to improve their communications.

There is deeply entrenched opposition to some of the recommendations, especially those that would change the structure of the nation's intelligence services and Congressional oversight of intelligence activities. The acting director of central intelligence, John McLaughlin, has publicly questioned the need for a national intelligence director.

On Capitol Hill, leaders of the two parties said that they would begin studying the recommendations. But they suggested that their efforts would not proceed on a particularly fast track. J. Dennis Hastert of Illinois, the Republican speaker of the House, said that he would ask committee chairmen to hold hearings "over the next several months" to begin looking at the need for change.

But some members of Congress said the commission had at least forced lawmakers to confront their shortcomings in overseeing intelligence gathering, and to contemplate changes that previously would have been unthinkable, especially to the extent that they would reshape the committee structure, the source of power for most senior legislators.

At a news conference Thursday afternoon, Senators Joseph I. Lieberman, Democrat of Connecticut, and John McCain, Republican of Arizona, who cosponsored the legislation that created the Sept. 11 commission, said that they would work quickly to translate the recommendations into legislative language. Mr. Lieberman called for a special session after the election to consider the changes.

Still, it did not take long for the report to spark partisan recriminations. Senate Democrats, led by Charles E. Schumer of New York, held a news conference to assert that Mr. Bush and Republicans in Congress have given short shrift to various spending measures for seaport security, aviation security, chemical plant security and other domestic security programs.

"If we can spend almost $200 billion to protect the people of Iraq," said Senator Barbara Boxer, Democrat of California, "then we can spend $15 billion to protect the people of America."

Among the commission's recommendations was either creating a joint House-Senate intelligence committee or giving existing intelligence committees the power of the purse, which would strip the appropriations committees of that authority.

Senator Pat Roberts, Republican of Kansas and chairman of the Senate Intelligence Committee, said it "heretofore probably would have been impossible" even to think about such changes. Mr. Roberts said he would soon convene hearings.

But with the country immersed in a bitter election battle, he said he did not envision legislation this year.

Representative Porter Goss, Republican of Florida and chairman of the House Intelligence Committee, was equally noncommittal. "There will be some reforms, but I don't know what they will be," Mr. Goss said.

Some experts said it would be a good idea for Congress to resist a rush to pass legislation. They said the last major piece of antiterrorism legislation to be sped through Congress, the USA Patriot Act, prompted widespread criticism.

"Actually having a good discussion about the report's recommendations will be a good idea," said James M. Lindsay, a fellow at the Council on Foreign Relations. "It's not at all clear that the report's recommendations will necessarily produce the results the commission members have in mind."

LOOKING BACK AND LOOKING AHEAD, PANEL ASSESSES THE OPPORTUNITIES FOR PREVENTION

COVERT OPERATIONS

By THOM SHANKER

The commission's most far-reaching recommendation for the military is that the Defense Department take charge of "directing and executing paramilitary operations, whether clandestine or covert," a set of tasks that routinely have fallen under the C.I.A.'s domain.

The language of the proposal appears to go further than current directives to the military's Special Operations Command to not only organize, train and equip the nation's elite commando force, but also to plan and execute its own missions against terrorists.

In the years before the Sept. 11 attacks, the C.I.A. "did not invest in developing a robust capability" in this area, the report says, but relied on proxy forces organized by agency officers. "The results were unsatisfactory," it states.

Rather than invest the money and personnel in both the C.I.A. and in the military to create and enhance capabilities for paramilitary counterterrorist operations, "the United

States should concentrate responsibility and necessary legal authorities in one entity," the report says.

The war in Afghanistan showed the effectiveness of joint C.I.A.-military teams for covert operations, even as it illustrated that the spy agency was agile and that the Pentagon remained both methodical and cumbersome, the report states. It says the C.I.A. should integrate its expert personnel into the training, exercises and planning done by the Defense Department, which it calls "the behemoth among federal agencies."

The idea is not new. The report cites discussions dating to 1998 about how best to attack Al Qaeda leaders and their training infrastructure in Afghanistan, and quotes Gen. Peter J. Schoomaker, then the Special Operations Command's senior officer, urging that his organization take the lead in planning and executing such missions.

The proposal was not adopted. General Schoomaker retired, but was invited back into service by Defense Secretary Donald H. Rumsfeld to be the current Army chief of staff.

The report goes into detail about how the C.I.A. developed a plan to capture or kill Osama bin Laden in 1997 and 1998, when intelligence was deemed especially good about his residence at Tarnak Farms on the outskirts of Kandahar, Afghanistan.

Complete rehearsals were run in the United States and across three international time zones. Although the report says that "no capture plan before 9/11 ever again attained the same level of detail and preparation," the mission was viewed as too risky, and not approved by senior Clinton administration national security officials.

DOMESTIC INTELLIGENCE

By ERIC LICHTBLAU

The Federal Bureau of Investigation came under sharp criticism in the report for failing to piece together leads before the Sept. 11 attacks, but it dodged one bullet when the commission rejected the widely discussed idea of creating a domestic intelligence agency in place of the F.B.I.

Instead, the panel said the F.B.I. must make "an all-out effort to institutionalize change" internally in combating terrorism.

It recommended that the president, by executive order, direct the F.B.I to create an internal intelligence cadre that would better foster the training and development of counterterrorism agents, linguists, analysts and surveillance specialists. The aim, the commission said, should be to "ensure the development of an institutional culture imbued with a deep expertise in intelligence and national security."

The F.B.I. said Thursday that it agreed with the bulk of the commission's recommendations. "We agree with the commission that much work remains to be done, and their findings and recommendations will certainly guide and help us refine our continuing transformation efforts," said Robert S. Mueller III, the F.B.I. director.

The commission cited nine "operational failures" that allowed the Sept. 11 plot to proceed without disruptions, four of which involved the F.B.I.'s either not receiving needed information about terror suspects or failing to properly act on it.

In the case of Zacarias Moussaoui, now awaiting trial in connection with the Sept. 11 plot, F.B.I. officials failed to link his arrest in the summer of 2001 to broader concerns about a terrorist attack, the report says. "A maximum U.S. effort to investigate Moussaoui" could conceivably have brought investigators to the core of the Sept. 11 plot, the report concludes.

The commission found that under Mr. Mueller, the bureau "has made significant progress in improving its intelligence capabilities," as it has sought to move since the Sept. 11 attacks from a criminal investigative mind-set to a more pre-emptive approach. But the 20-month investigation "also found gaps between some of the announced reforms and the reality in the field," the report says. In particular, the commission was concerned that the F.B.I.'s 56 field offices still retain the power to reallocate agents and resources to local concerns that diverge from national security.

Nonetheless, the commission's explicit rejection of a separate domestic intelligence agency was an important victory for the F.B.I. The commission said it ultimately rejected the idea in part because adding a new agency to the bureaucratic mix could exacerbate information-sharing problems.

TRACING CONNECTIONS

By DOUGLAS JEHL

The Sept. 11 commission said that it had found no evidence that Iraq, Iran or Saudi Arabia knowingly provided operational or financial support to Al Qaeda in advance of the attacks, but it called for further investigation of the relationship between Iran and Al Qaeda.

For the most part, the conclusion effectively absolves all three governments from allegations of complicity in the attacks. In particular, it finds no indication that contacts between Iraq and Al Qaeda in the 1990's "ever developed into a collaborative operational relationship," a conclusion very different in tone from assertions by Vice President Dick Cheney and other Bush administration officials.

The commission also said it found no evidence that the Saudi government as an institution or senior Saudi officials individually had financed Al Qaeda, though it did say that charities sponsored by the government had probably diverted money to Al Qaeda.

Those conclusions essentially reiterated findings spelled out in staff reports issued by the committee in May. Similarly, the final report by the commission repeats the staff conclusion that available evidence "does not support" a claim initially made by Czech intelligence that the hijacker Mohammed Atta met with a senior Iraqi official in Prague in April 2001.

Between Iran and Al Qaeda, however, the ties described in the report are more extensive than has previously been made public. At least eight of the Sept. 11 hijackers passed through Iran on the way to or from Afghanistan between October 2000 and February 2001, the report says, though it says there is "no evidence" that Iran was aware of the planning for the attack.

The hijackers' passports were not stamped by Iranian authorities, the report says, but it leaves unresolved the question of whether that reflected a deliberate effort to provide assistance to Al Qaeda. It says that Khalid Shaikh Mohammed, believed to be the mastermind of the attacks, has said only that the hijackers were taking advantage of a well-known Iranian practice of not stamping Saudi passports.

A senior C.I.A. official, at a briefing on Wednesday, said, "I don't think we know that this was a deliberate Iranian policy." The official said Iran's strong antipathy at the time toward the Taliban government of Afghanistan, which was playing host to Al Qaeda, would suggest that "it's a little hard to see Iran as an ally of Al Qaeda."

American officials have said there is evidence that senior members of Al Qaeda have stayed for a time in Iran since Sept. 11, but the senior C.I.A. official said it was not clear whether the government was supporting them.

TRANSPORTATION SECURITY

By MATTHEW L. WALD

The nation's investment in improving transportation security has been too focused on passenger airlines, the commission said, arguing that the Transportation Security Administration was trying "to fight the last war."

"Opportunities to do harm are as great, or greater" in maritime or surface transportation, or cargo aviation or general aviation, the report says.

Over 90 percent of the agency's $5.3 billion budget goes to airline security, the report says, and it is time to make hard choices in allocating limited resources.

It says that defending mass transit is very difficult and

that "perfection is unattainable," but that spending should be based on a systematic analysis of risks, costs and benefits. "Terrorists should perceive that potential targets are defended," the report says. "They may be deterred by a significant chance of failure."

And the aviation security system still has shortcomings, the commission said. One is that the United States has a comprehensive list of terrorists and terrorism suspects, the commission said, but is afraid to share it with the airlines, which carry out the current security system, called the Computer Assisted Passenger Prescreening System, known as Capps. The Transportation Security Administration is trying to develop a more advanced system, called Capps 2, which it would operate directly. But Capps 2 would involve extensive use of computerized databases and has raised civil liberties concerns. The commission said that switching to a more extensive list for screening "should not be delayed while the argument about a successor to Capps continues."

Capps relies on facts about passengers including how the ticket was paid for and whether the trip is one-way. Homeland Security officials have said that Capps is antiquated, but in the report's history of the events of Sept. 11, Capps identified eight of the 19 hijackers as suspicious.

But at the time, Capps was intended only to foil suitcase bombers, and was used to assure that no baggage was loaded on a plane unless its owner was on board.

IMMIGRATION CONTROLS

By RACHEL L. SWARNS

With thousands of agents patrolling the borders and scrutinizing foreign visitors, the nation's immigration service could have helped deter the attacks, the commission said. But it said that time and time again, the dysfunctional and poorly resourced agency failed to detect the hijackers as they presented fraudulent passports at airports, lied to border agents and violated immigration laws in the months before the attacks.

Efforts have been made to strengthen the nation's border controls and immigration enforcement since the attacks, but the system remains inadequate to prevent terrorists from entering the United States and hiding here, the commission said.

The report criticizes a program started this year to improve the screening of foreign visitors by fingerprinting and photographing them at the nation's busiest airports. The program, called U.S. Visit, screens travelers who need visas to visit the United States and will expand in September to include travelers from 27 industrialized nations, including European countries, who do not need visas now.

The commission said those visitors constitute only about 12 percent of the noncitizens who regularly cross the borders. It recommended that Mexicans and Canadians, who make up the bulk of foreign travelers to the United States and remain exempt from the program, should be required to carry passports that enable them to be identified using face recognition, fingerprinting or other technology.

The report also notes that data on foreigners who enter the country is still not fully automated and that U.S. Visit still does not uniformly collect departure data on visitors.

The report recommends that the Department of Homeland Security "properly supported by Congress," institute a broader "entry-exit screening system" as soon as possible. It also calls for federal standards governing the issuance of driver's licenses and birth certificates; several of the hijackers obtained driver's licenses in the United States. It also recommends sharing more information with allied governments.

At the time of the attacks, the commission reported, immigration inspectors did not believe their role was to focus on terrorists and often lacked the information needed to determine admissibility. The commission said 15 of the 19 hijackers were potentially vulnerable to interception by border officials.

Consequently, the commission urged the government to combine terrorist travel intelligence, operations and law enforcement to prevent terrorists from entering the United States.

THE PLOT AND MISSED OPPORTUNITIES—TIMELINE

AL QAEDA LEADERSHIP

May 1996 Osama bin Laden leaves Sudan for Afghanistan.

Mid-1996 Khalid Shaikh Mohammed pitches a plan to use airplanes as weapons to Mr. bin Laden, who listens, but does not commit.

August 7, 1998 Car bombings by Al Qaeda of American embassies in Kenya and Tanzania kill more than 200.

Early 1999 Mr. bin Laden tells Mr. Mohammed to go ahead with his plans to use airplanes as weapons in both the United States and Southeast Asia, and suggests four hijackers, including **Nawaq Alhazmi** and **Khalid al-Midhar**.

Spring 2000 Mr. bin Laden cancels the Southeast Asia part of the plan, deciding it would be too hard to coordinate.

Mid-2000 When it becomes clear than Mr. Alhazmi and Mr. Midhar are not learning how to fly, Mr. Mohammed adds **Hani Hanjour** to the operation.

October 12, 2000 In Yemen, 17 American sailors are killed in an attack by Al Qaeda on the warship *Cole*.

September 11, 2001 Attacks on the World Trade Center and the Pentagon kill almost 3,000 people.

MOVEMENT OF THE HIJACKERS

1998 Mohamed Atta, a student in Hamburg, Germany, who would become the lead hijacker, moves into an apartment with **Ramzi bin al-Shibh** and **Marwan al-Shehhi**. They meet **Ziad al-Jarrah**.

Fall 1999 The four Al Qaeda members suggested by Mr. bin Laden attend a training camp in Afghanistan.

November-December 1999. The Hamburg students travel to Afghanistan and join Al Qaeda and the September 11 plot.

January 2000 Mr. Alhazmi and Mr. Midhar meet in Kuala Lumpur with **Khallad**, who later becomes a suspect in the Cole bombing, before arriving in California on January 15. They soon take a few flying lessons.

May-June 2000 Mr. Atta, Mr. Shehhi and Mr. Jarrah enter the U.S. and begin flight training in Florida. Mr. bin al-Shibh is unable to obtain a visa and remains overseas.

December 2000 Mr. Hanjour arrives in San Diego and soon begins taking flight lessons.

February 2001 Zaccarias Moussaoui who may have been considered to replace one of the hijackers, arrives and starts flight school in Oklahoma.

August 2001 Mr. Moussaoui begins training on a 747 simulator at a school in Minnesota. A suspicious instructor alerts the authorities.

INTELLIGENCE COMMUNITY

[The report from the 9/11 Commission detailed 10 opportunities, numbered below, that intelligence agencies missed to thwart the September 11 plot.]

1996 The C.I.A.'s Counterterrorist Center creates a special "issue station" devoted exclusively to Mr. bin Laden, considered to be a terrorist financier.

Early 1997 The issue station is aware that Mr. bin Laden is not just a financier but an organizer of terrorist activity.

May 1998 A plan to use Afghan tribal groups to capture Mr. bin Laden is scrapped.

August 1998 After the embassy bombings, cruise missile strikes are launched against terrorist sites in Sudan and Afghanistan. Covert operations using tribal groups to capture or kill Mr. bin Laden are planned.

December 1998-May 1999 Several times after receiving intelligence on Mr. bin Laden's whereabouts, missile strikes are considered but never carried out because of concerns about the intelligence and the casualties.

Summer 1999 Staff changes at the counterterrorism center and the bin Laden issue station shift its focus toward developing the C.I.A.'s own sources in Afghanistan, rather than relying on the Afghan groups.

December 1999 The arrests of a terrorist cell in Jordan and of a terrorist at the U. S.-Canadian border lead to warnings of a millennium terrorist attack.

January 2000 Surveillance teams watch the meeting in Kuala Lumpur but do not know the identity of all the members and lose the trail.

1. The C.I.A. does not place Mr. Midhar on a watch list or notify the F.B.I. when it learns he has a U.S. visa.
2. The C. I. A. does not develop a plan to track Mr. Midhar's movements.

March 2000
   3. The C.I.A. does not place Mr. Alhazmi on a watch
      list or notify the F. B. I. when it learns he has a U.S.
      visa and had flown to Los Angeles.

September 2000 The C.I.A. flies unmanned reconnaissance
aircraft over Afghanistan to look for Mr. bin Laden. During
the fall, 16 missions are flown, twice possibly spotting him.
The program is halted in 2001 to wait for an armed version
of the drone to be developed.

January 2001
   4. The C.I.A. does not inform the F.B.I. that a source
      had identified Mr. Khallad as having attended the
      meeting in Kuala Lumpur.

Spring 2001 Reports of terrorist threats reach the highest
level since the millennium plots.

May 2001
   5. A C.I.A. official does not inform the F.B.I. about
      Mr. Midhar's visa, Mr. Alhazmi's U.S. travel or Mr.
      Khallad's presence at the meeting.

June 2001
   6. F.B.I. and C.I.A. officials do not ensure that all rele-
      vant information regarding the Kuala Lumpur meet-
      ing is shared with Cole investigators.

Summer 2001 Threat reports surge, and disruption operations are launched in 20 countries.

August 2001
   7. The F.B.I. does not recognize the significance of
      Mr. Midhar's and Mr. Alhazmi's arrival.
   8. The F.B.I. does not recognize the significance of

Mr. Moussaoui's flight training.

9. The C.I.A. does not focus on information that Mr. Mohammed is a key Al Qaeda lieutenant.

10. The C.I.A. and F.B.I. do not connect the presence of Mr. Midhar, Mr. Alhazmi, and Mr. Moussaoui to general reports about imminent attacks.

A VIGOROUS, IMPROVISED RESPONSE IN A CITY THAT REMAINS A PRIME TARGET

By JIM DWYER and KEVIN FLYNN

In its chronicle of the blunders, lapses and shortsightedness that permitted hijackers to attack New York, the Sept. 11 commission found that the city's emergency response was plagued by many of the same failures of imagination and preparedness that it cited in the nation's antiterrorism policies.

Yet that cascade of systemic failures and institutional weaknesses, while leading to its awful toll in human life, was overcome in part by the vigorous, improvised response in New York, where thousands of people escaped from the World Trade Center, the commission found.

Those who worked in the trade center, and those who came to help them, "did their best to cope with an unimaginable catastrophe—unfolding furiously over a mere 102 minutes—for which they were unprepared in terms of both training and mind-set," the commission said.

The commission warned that New York and Washington remain prime targets of even bigger terrorist attacks that not only are possible, but probable. Those cities, the 10 commissioners said in their unanimous report, should receive the bulk of federal homeland security money. They urged Congress to drop the current system of spreading the funds across the country based on population. "Congress should not use this money as a pork barrel," the commission recommended.

The panel also recommended that federal money be

granted only when cities routinely trained their emergency response personnel to work together, using a command system designating one agency as the leader at a particular emergency. Elsewhere in the report, the commission said that New York's current emergency system, revised in May, "falls short of an optimal response plan."

A spokesman for Mayor Michael R. Bloomberg said the city's plan was still being refined and had not yet been submitted to federal authorities. Mayor Bloomberg, who made a presentation to the commission in May urging that the city get a bigger share of homeland security money, said, "This commission agrees with us that we've got to get homeland security funds in this country allocated based on where the risks are."

In the commission's final report, the chapter on the emergency response, titled "Heroism and Horror," describes the high-velocity events at the trade center, revisiting shortcomings that have been well documented before, either in news accounts or management studies.

Many people who called the city's 911 system for help were told by operators to stay where they were, even though fire commanders had ordered an evacuation. The report found that the city had no way to get valuable information to 911 operators, who are employees of the Police Department, or fire dispatchers, who also handled some 911 calls.

As a result, people on the 83rd floor in the north tower, and the 77th floor in the south, were advised to stay put, even though both buildings were already in flames and their floors were below the fire. The commission obtained the tapes and records of those calls and others from the Bloomberg administration only after the commission had issued a subpoena and accused the city of "seriously impeding" the investigation.

The mayor said yesterday that 911 operators would now be given useful information from the scenes of emergencies.

For most of those below the floors struck by the planes, the evacuation was a great success, the commission found.

The panel said that a tide of human effort carried many to safety, much faster than when the buildings were bombed in

1993. "As a result of the efforts of first responders, assistance from each other, and their own good instincts and good will, the vast majority of civilians below the impact zone were able to evacuate the towers," the report said.

One central lesson, the commission said, was the importance of people finding out how to get out of their workplaces. Preparation by tenants in the trade center was uneven, the report noted, with some companies rigorously conducting drills, but many companies and individuals not taking the practice sessions seriously. It noted that the Port Authority of New York and New Jersey, the owner of the trade center, had no plan for people trapped above a fire, and had not specifically instructed tenants during drills not to go to the roof.

Many people tried to go to the roof on Sept. 11, the report noted, only to find the doors locked—they were controlled by a computer that failed. The report suggested that those trips upstairs diverted them from their only realistic prospect of escape, particularly in the south tower, where a stairway remained open.

Many apparently hoped to be rescued by helicopter, which was how a few dozen people left the towers after the 1993 bombing, the report said. They were unaware, as were the 911 operators, that roof rescues had been ruled out by a police commander. The Port Authority police were poorly prepared, the commission found, with officers responding from the agency's airports, tunnels and bridges but unable to find a common radio frequency or a command post for instructions. Individual sergeants, lieutenants and captains tried to organize on the fly.

The commission said that there had been "a lack of communication and coordination among responding agencies," but that this had not hurt the evacuation; it said it was unclear whether it had contributed to the casualties among the rescue workers.

"Information that was critical to informed decision-making was not shared among agencies," the commission said. Rescuers from the Police, Fire and Port Authority Police Departments often searched the same floors over and over.

Firefighters did not know what police helicopter pilots were seeing.

The commission offered a number of explanations for one of the day's most enduring mysteries: why scores of firefighters did not escape from the north tower before it collapsed, 29 minutes after the south tower fell. The report said the evacuation order did reach many firefighters, even if it was second-hand, from others who had heard that it was time to leave.

Technical difficulties with radios were only one factor that slowed the communication of the order; the commission said the system was overloaded, firefighters were tuned to the wrong channel, and others were without radios. Some firefighters who were told to get out simply refused, the report said, citing several incidents in which they stayed behind with slow moving civilians.

The report related the accounts of police officers who said that as they scrambled out of the north tower, they met firefighters who did not seem to want to hear orders delivered by a police officer.

"At least one firefighter who was in the north tower," the report continued, "has supported that assessment, stating that he was not going to take an evacuation instruction from a cop."

FAMILIES SAVOR THEIR VICTORY OVER GRIEF AND A RELUCTANT GOVERNMENT

By LYDIA POLGREEN

WASHINGTON, July 22—More than two wrenching years after she began agitating for an independent commission to investigate the terrorist attack that killed her husband, Kristen Breitweiser finally had the fruits of that labor in her hand, all 567 pages of it, and seemed a little surprised to find herself fairly satisfied.

"This report lays out a very active plan to make sure something gets done," Ms. Breitweiser said after a briefing by the commission, her copy of its report tucked under her arm, already underlined. "I think without a doubt this commission has shattered the ceiling on access. I think this is proof positive that democracy is alive and working."

In the nearly three years since the attacks of Sept. 11, 2001, the families of those who died have become a formidable political force. Fueled by their grief, they forced the 9/11 commission into existence, using the moral authority granted them by their loss to force a reluctant government to submit to close examination.

Some had said that their questions would never be answered and that their demands to know whom to blame could never be met. But on Thursday, as they thumbed through the report, many relatives said the commission had been a success.

"I came here pessimistic," said April Gallop, who along with her 2-month-old son, Elisha, suffered brain and spine injuries in the attack on the Pentagon. "But I am leaving here optimistic."

The release of the report was a huge victory for the families, many of whom had pushed hard against bureaucracy, partisanship and government agencies to get the commission established and force it to act.

From the telegenic "Jersey girls," as the four New Jersey widows who agitated and cajoled the commission into being were known, to the relatives of those who died on Flight 93 and demanded to hear the tapes from that flight before it crashed in southwestern Pennsylvania, the families quickly learned the ways of Washington and the news media, demanding and getting much of what they wanted.

There seemed to be little appetite for rest Thursday, as the families faced the task ahead of making sure the president and Congress act on the report's recommendations.

"This isn't the end," said Theresa M. McGovern, whose mother, Ann, died at the World Trade Center. "This can't be the end. No other American should have to go through this. This is no longer about that day. It is about the security of the people living in America today."

The families are bitterly divided on many issues—how to list the names of their loved ones on the memorial, whether the families of rescue workers should have received greater compensation than other victims, whether the war in Iraq has made them any safer from future attacks—but they were all but unanimous on the need for the 9/11 commission to be created.

Still, on Thursday, if there was widespread satisfaction with the panel's work, there was not complete acceptance, despite a report that produced a damning portrait of a government ill-informed, uncoordinated and unprepared. Some relatives said the report would leave some key questions unanswered, some dots unconnected, some lapses unaccounted for.

"No one has been punished," said Abraham Scott, whose wife, Janice, died at the Pentagon. "They don't name names. No one takes the blame."

Mr. Scott said he was disappointed that aside from the director of central intelligence, George Tenet, there have been no high-level resignations, and that aside from the apology offered by the former counterterrorism official Richard A. Clarke, which was dismissed by Republican critics as grandstanding, there has been no admission of the government's failure to guard against terror adequately.

Others found fault with corners of the report on which they had become expert. Sally Regenhard, whose son, Christian, a first-year firefighter, died in the trade center, has been one of the most vocal family members criticizing New York City's emergency response and the city's lack of coordination. She said the report did not focus enough on the response to the attack in New York, and she vehemently disputed the report's conclusion that the failure of the firefighters' radios was not the main reason so many firefighters died that day.

"I am quite shocked by this," Ms. Regenhard said. "I expected to read a thorough, insightful analysis, but this is very weak. I am very disappointed."

Other families had tuned out entirely. Talat Hamdani's son, Salman, died at the trade center, and her life since then has been a spiral of despair. Interviewed earlier this week in New York, she said her husband's health has failed, and that he has terminal cancer.

"After Salman was gone, my husband had no will to fight

this," Mrs. Hamdani said, standing at her husband's hospital bed at New York University Hospital, his limbs jaundiced and puffy, his eyes wild in his head. "No report, no commission can take all of this away. I just pray that tragedy will not strike us again."

Despite the victory the report represents, the families are girding for yet another battle, this one with the executive and legislative branches of government, where they say they will apply the same pressure that brought results with the commission.

NEW DETAILS IN BATTLE OF HIJACKERS AND PASSENGERS TO CONTROL PLANE

By MATTHEW L. WALD

WASHINGTON—In the last minutes of United Airlines Flight 93, as the passengers mounted their assault on the cockpit, the hijackers struggled to maintain control.

The man piloting the plane rolled it from side to side, trying to knock the passengers off balance. He warned another hijacker to block the cockpit door. He pitched the nose of the plane up and down violently. Finally, when it seemed as if the passengers might be seconds from overcoming the terrorists, the hijacker turned the control wheel hard to the right, rolling the plane onto its back and, the report appears to say, intentionally crashed it into a Pennsylvania field as a hijacker shouted "Allah is the greatest."

The report from the 9/11 Commission on Thursday provided new, chilling details about what happened in the cockpit of Flight 93 in its last minutes. It provides a gripping account of the battle to gain control of the aircraft by passengers who knew that terrorists had seized the plane and were determined to prevent them from using it as a missile. It also discloses that the phrase "Let's roll," previously reported as a rallying cry for those passengers, may have been misinterpreted.

At 9:24 a.m. on Sept. 11, Capt. Jason Dahl was flying over eastern Ohio when a text message flashed on his computer screen: "Beware any cockpit intrusion—two a/c [aircraft] crashed into World Trade Center." Apparently puzzled, Captain Dahl fired back a message to Ed Ballinger, the Chicago dispatcher who sent the warning: "Ed, confirm latest mssg plz—Jason."

Two minutes later, terrorists stormed his cockpit. The plane, bound from Newark, N.J., to San Francisco, was the last of the four to be hijacked that morning. Unlike the other three planes, Flight 93 continued transmitting over the radio during the struggle in the cockpit.

The captain or first officer declared "Mayday," the report said, and 35 seconds later, one of them shouted, "Hey, get out of here—get out of here—get out of here." Later, passengers in phone calls to relatives and others reported seeing two bodies outside the cockpit, injured or dead, probably the pilots.

At 9:57, about seven minutes before the end, one of the passengers ended her phone conversation saying: "Everyone's running up to first class. I've got to go. Bye."

Soon after, Ziad Jarrah, sitting at the controls, began rolling the plane to thwart the passengers. Just after 10 a.m., he is heard on the cockpit voice recorder saying: "Is that it? Shall we finish it off?"

But another hijacker responds: "No. Not yet. When they all come, we finish it off."

The voice recorder captured sounds of continued fighting, and Mr. Jarrah pitched the plane up and then down. A passenger is heard to say: "In the cockpit. If we don't we'll die!"

Then a passenger yelled, "Roll it!" While earlier accounts reported the phrase as "Let's roll," which was repeated in speeches by President Bush and became the title of a bestseller, some aviation experts have speculated that this was actually a reference to a food cart, being used as a battering ram.

Mr. Jarrah "stopped the violent maneuvers" about 10:01, according to the report.

"He then asked another hijacker in the cockpit, 'Is that it?

I mean, shall we put it down?' to which the other replied, 'Yes.'" Eighty seconds later, a hijacker is heard to say: "Pull it down! Pull it down!"

Soon after, the plane plunged into a field in Shanksville, Pa., about 20 minutes flying time from Washington.

FOR BUSH AND KERRY, DIFFERENT LESSONS

By MICHAEL JANOFSKY and DAVID M. HALBFINGER

GLENVIEW, Ill., July 22—President Bush staunchly defended his administration's antiterrorism policies on Thursday, the day that a bipartisan panel called for the nation's intelligence apparatus to be restructured, while his Democratic challenger, Senator John Kerry, called such changes "long overdue" and criticized Mr. Bush for failing to carry out such an overhaul.

"This report carries a very simple message for all of America about the security of all Americans: We can do better," Mr. Kerry said in Detroit after speaking at the National Urban League convention. "We must do better, and there's an urgency to our doing better. We have to act now."

He added, "If I am elected president and there still has not been sufficient progress rapidly in these next months on these issues, then I will lead."

While generally embracing the recommendations of the panel, Mr. Bush used his appearance here at a training facility north of Chicago to underscore one of his major campaign themes, that the nation was better protected as a result of his administration's policies.

One example, he said, was the medical and emergency workers called first responders; he praised several hundred attending his speech at the Northeastern Illinois Public Safety Training Academy.

Mr. Bush congratulated them and strongly defended his

actions since the Sept. 11 attacks, saying "Because of these achievements, America and the world are safer."

"If an attack should come," he said, "American will be prepared."

Mr. Bush referred several times to the commission report, characterizing it as an important tool in mapping future strategies to combat terrorist activities. He called it "a serious and comprehensive report with thoughtful recommendations," and said, "We will carefully study all their proposals, of course."

Mr. Bush, who was introduced by Tom Ridge, the secretary of homeland security, also said that the report affirmed many steps his administration had already taken. He used much of his speech to review those steps, recalling military efforts in Afghanistan and Iraq, disruptions of financial networks used by terrorists and changes that eased the sharing of information by law enforcement agencies.

"I agree with their conclusion that the terrorists were able to exploit deep institutional failings in our nation's defenses that developed over more than a decade," he said. "The commission's recommendations are consistent with the strategy my administration is following to address these failings and to win the war on terror."

"But the job is not done," Mr. Bush said. "This report will help our country identify even more steps we can take to better defend America."

Mr. Kerry used the report to challenge Mr. Bush's leadership and priorities, blaming him for the conflicts among agencies that have been cited as impediments to more efficient intelligence gathering and response.

"Unfortunately, this administration has had an ongoing war between the State Department, the Defense Department, the White House," Mr. Kerry said. "People have been at odds, everybody knows it, they'll deny it, but everybody does know. And the fact is that it has created a struggle that has delayed our ability to move forward."

Mr. Kerry aimed only veiled criticism of former President Bill Clinton, saying some changes in the nation's intelligence-gathering efforts should have been made before Mr. Bush took office. And he said he agreed with the commission's finding that Congress had given terrorism too little attention and had responded slowly and inadequately in the years before the attacks.

But he focused much more of his criticism on Mr. Bush.

"Sure, Congress shares some responsibility," Mr. Kerry said, "But as you know, the watchdog role is a role of proposal, a role of scrutiny."

He added: "The bottom line is, the executive is the implementer. The executive department proposes the budget, the executive department has the ability to lead."

Mr. Kerry's running mate, Senator John Edwards, was more circumspect in his response to the report, interrupting a fund-raising trip to Hartford to speak to reporters after telephone conversations with the commission's leaders, Thomas H. Kean, the former Republican governor of New Jersey, and Lee H. Hamilton, the former Democratic representative from Indiana.

Mr. Edwards praised the "bipartisan nature" of the commission's work, then called on Mr. Bush to act immediately on those recommendations that could be accomplished by executive order, and for Congress to work on the rest.

"We had thousands of Americans who lost their lives on Sept. 11," Mr. Edwards said, "and it is very important for us, those of us in positions of responsibility, to pay the greatest tribute we can pay to them, which is to take action and reform our intelligence operations."

Mr. Kerry's remarks about the Sept. 11 report came after he addressed the National Urban League, vowing to expand loans, contracting and other business opportunities for minorities and to crack down on gang violence, not just by prosecuting it but by offering alternatives like job training and drug treatment.

President Bush is to address the group on Friday, an appearance the White House scheduled after it rejected an invitation from the National Association for the Advancement of Colored People to speak at its convention last week. A

Bush campaign official said Thursday that Mr. Bush would "speak directly to the African-American community" about how his agenda was helping cities. The official said Mr. Bush would also highlight the increases in minority home ownership and drops in drug use and crime under his administration.

Mr. Kerry, who did address the N.A.A.C.P., alluded to the tiff after he was introduced by Vernon Jordan, a former Urban League president who heads his debate negotiation team.

"As president of the United States, I will show up—not just at national meetings during election season," Mr. Kerry said. "I want you at the table with me, in a full partnership to build a stronger America at home and an America more respected in the world again."

EXECUTIVE SUMMARY OF THE 9/11 REPORT

Executive Summary

We present the narrative of this report and the recommendations that flow from it to the President of the United States, the United States Congress, and the American people for their consideration. Ten Commissioners—five Republicans and five Democrats chosen by elected leaders from our nation's capital at a time of great partisan division—have come together to present this report without dissent.

We have come together with a unity of purpose because our nation demands it. September 11, 2001, was a day of unprecedented shock and suffering in the history of the United States. The nation was unprepared.

A NATION TRANSFORMED

At 8:46 on the morning of September 11, 2001, the United States became a nation transformed.

An airliner traveling at hundreds of miles per hour and carrying some 10,000 gallons of jet fuel plowed into the North Tower of the World Trade Center in Lower Manhattan. At 9:03, a second airliner hit the South Tower. Fire and smoke billowed upward. Steel, glass, ash, and bodies fell below. The Twin Towers, where up to 50,000 people worked each day, both collapsed less than 90 minutes later.

At 9:37 that same morning, a third airliner slammed into

the western face of the Pentagon. At 10:03, a fourth airliner crashed in a field in southern Pennsylvania. It had been aimed at the United States Capitol or the White House, and was forced down by heroic passengers armed with the knowledge that America was under attack.

More than 2,600 people died at the World Trade Center; 125 died at the Pentagon; 256 died on the four planes. The death toll surpassed that at Pearl Harbor in December 1941.

This immeasurable pain was inflicted by 19 young Arabs acting at the behest of Islamist extremists headquartered in distant Afghanistan. Some had been in the United States for more than a year, mixing with the rest of the population. Though four had training as pilots, most were not well-educated. Most spoke English poorly, some hardly at all. In groups of four or five, carrying with them only small knives, box cutters, and cans of Mace or pepper spray, they had hijacked the four planes and turned them into deadly guided missiles.

Why did they do this? How was the attack planned and conceived? How did the U.S. government fail to anticipate and prevent it? What can we do in the future to prevent similar acts of terrorism?

A Shock, Not a Surprise

The 9/11 attacks were a shock, but they should not have come as a surprise. Islamist extremists had given plenty of warning that they meant to kill Americans indiscriminately and in large numbers. Although Usama Bin Ladin himself would not emerge as a signal threat until the late 1990s, the threat of Islamist terrorism grew over the decade.

In February 1993, a group led by Ramzi Yousef tried to bring down the World Trade Center with a truck bomb. They killed six and wounded a thousand. Plans by Omar Abdel Rahman and others to blow up the Holland and Lincoln tunnels and other New York City landmarks were frustrated when the plotters were arrested. In October 1993, Somali tribesmen shot down U.S. helicopters, killing 18 and wounding 73 in an incident that came to be known as "Black Hawk down." Years later it would be learned that those Somali tribesmen had received help from al Qaeda.

In early 1995, police in Manila uncovered a plot by Ramzi Yousef to blow up a dozen U.S. airliners while they were flying over the Pacific. In November 1995, a car bomb exploded outside the office of the U.S. program manager for the Saudi National Guard in Riyadh, killing five Americans and two others. In June 1996, a truck bomb demolished the Khobar Towers apartment complex in Dhahran, Saudi Arabia, killing 19 U.S. servicemen and wounding hundreds. The attack was carried out primarily by Saudi Hezbollah, an organization that had received help from the government of Iran.

Until 1997, the U.S. intelligence community viewed Bin Ladin as a financier of terrorism, not as a terrorist leader. In February 1998, Usama Bin Ladin and four others issued a self-styled fatwa, publicly declaring that it was God's decree that every Muslim should try his utmost to kill any American, military or civilian, anywhere in the world, because of American "occupation" of Islam's holy places and aggression against Muslims.

In August 1998, Bin Ladin's group, al Qaeda, carried out near-simultaneous truck bomb attacks on the U.S. embassies in Nairobi, Kenya, and Dar es Salaam, Tanzania. The attacks killed 224 people, including 12 Americans, and wounded thousands more.

In December 1999, Jordanian police foiled a plot to bomb hotels and other sites frequented by American tourists, and a U.S. Customs agent arrested Ahmed Ressam at the U.S. Canadian border as he was smuggling in explosives intended for an attack on Los Angeles International Airport.

In October 2000, an al Qaeda team in Aden, Yemen, used a motorboat filled with explosives to blow a hole in the side of a destroyer, the USS *Cole*, almost sinking the vessel and killing 17 American sailors.

The 9/11 attacks on the World Trade Center and the Pentagon were far more elaborate, precise, and destructive than any of these earlier assaults. But by September 2001, the executive branch of the U.S. government, the Congress, the news media, and the American public had received clear warning that Islamist terrorists meant to kill Americans in high numbers.

Who Is the Enemy?

Who is this enemy that created an organization capable of inflicting such horrific damage on the United States? We now know that these attacks were carried out by various groups of Islamist extremists. The 9/11 attack was driven by Usama Bin Ladin.

In the 1980s, young Muslims from around the world went to Afghanistan to join as volunteers in a jihad (or holy struggle) against the Soviet Union. A wealthy Saudi, Usama Bin Ladin, was one of them. Following the defeat of the Soviets in the late 1980s, Bin Ladin and others formed al Qaeda to mobilize jihads elsewhere.

The history, culture, and body of beliefs from which Bin Ladin shapes and spreads his message are largely unknown to many Americans. Seizing on symbols of Islam's past greatness, he promises to restore pride to people who consider themselves the victims of successive foreign masters. He uses cultural and religious allusions to the holy Qur'an and some of its interpreters. He appeals to people disoriented by cyclonic change as they confront modernity and globalization. His rhetoric selectively draws from multiple sources—Islam, history, and the region's political and economic malaise.

Bin Ladin also stresses grievances against the United States widely shared in the Muslim world. He inveighed against the presence of U.S. troops in Saudi Arabia, which is the home of Islam's holiest sites, and against other U.S. policies in the Middle East.

Upon this political and ideological foundation, Bin Ladin built over the course of a decade a dynamic and lethal organization. He built an infrastructure and organization in Afghanistan that could attract, train, and use recruits against ever more ambitious targets. He rallied new zealots and new money with each demonstration of al Qaeda's capability. He had forged a close alliance with the Taliban, a regime providing sanctuary for al Qaeda.

By September 11, 2001, al Qaeda possessed

- leaders able to evaluate, approve, and supervise the planning and direction of a major operation;
- a personnel system that could recruit candidates, indoctrinate them, vet them, and give them the necessary training;
- communications sufficient to enable planning and direction of operatives and those who would be helping them;
- an intelligence effort to gather required information and form assessments of enemy strengths and weaknesses;
- the ability to move people great distances; and
- the ability to raise and move the money necessary to finance an attack.

1998 to September 11, 2001

The August 1998 bombings of U.S. embassies in Kenya and Tanzania established al Qaeda as a potent adversary of the United States.

After launching cruise missile strikes against al Qaeda targets in Afghanistan and Sudan in retaliation for the embassy bombings, the Clinton administration applied diplomatic pressure to try to persuade the Taliban regime in Afghanistan to expel Bin Ladin. The administration also devised covert operations to use CIA-paid foreign agents to capture or kill Bin Ladin and his chief lieutenants. These actions did not stop Bin Ladin or dislodge al Qaeda from its sanctuary.

By late 1998 or early 1999, Bin Ladin and his advisers had agreed on an idea brought to them by Khalid Sheikh Mohammed (KSM) called the "planes operation." It would eventually culminate in the 9/11 attacks. Bin Ladin and his chief of operations, Mohammed Atef, occupied undisputed leadership positions atop al Qaeda. Within al Qaeda, they relied heavily on the ideas and enterprise of strong-willed field commanders, such as KSM, to carry out worldwide terrorist operations.

KSM claims that his original plot was even grander than those carried out on 9/11—ten planes would attack targets on both the East and West coasts of the United States. This plan was modified by Bin Ladin, KSM said, owing to its scale and complexity. Bin Ladin provided KSM with four initial operatives for suicide plane attacks within the United States, and in the fall of 1999 training for the attacks began. New recruits included four from a cell of expatriate Muslim extremists who had clustered together in Hamburg, Germany. One became the tactical commander of the operation in the United States: Mohamed Atta.

U.S. intelligence frequently picked up reports of attacks planned by al Qaeda. Working with foreign security services, the CIA broke up some al Qaeda cells. The core of Bin Ladin's organization nevertheless remained intact. In December 1999, news about the arrests of the terrorist cell in Jordan and the arrest of a terrorist at the U.S.-Canadian border became part of a "millennium alert." The government was galvanized, and the public was on alert for any possible attack.

In January 2000, the intense intelligence effort glimpsed and then lost sight of two operatives destined for the "planes operation." Spotted in Kuala Lumpur, the pair were lost passing through Bangkok. On January 15, 2000, they arrived in Los Angeles.

Because these two al Qaeda operatives had spent little time in the West and spoke little, if any, English, it is plausible that they or KSM would have tried to identify, in advance, a friendly contact in the United States. We explored suspicions about whether these two operatives had a support network of accomplices in the United States. The evidence is thin—simply not there for some cases, more worrisome in others.

We do know that soon after arriving in California, the two al Qaeda operatives sought out and found a group of ideologically like-minded Muslims with roots in Yemen and Saudi Arabia, individuals mainly associated with a young Yemeni and others who attended a mosque in San Diego. After a brief stay in Los Angeles about which we know little, the al Qaeda operatives lived openly in San Diego under their true names. They managed to avoid attracting much attention.

By the summer of 2000, three of the four Hamburg cell members had arrived on the East Coast of the United States and had begun pilot training. In early 2001, a fourth future hijacker pilot, Hani Hanjour, journeyed to Arizona with another operative, Nawaf al Hazmi, and conducted his refresher pilot training there. A number of al Qaeda operatives had spent time in Arizona during the 1980s and early 1990s.

During 2000, President Bill Clinton and his advisers renewed diplomatic efforts to get Bin Ladin expelled from Afghanistan. They also renewed secret efforts with some of the Taliban's opponents—the Northern Alliance—to get enough intelligence to attack Bin Ladin directly. Diplomatic efforts centered on the new military government in Pakistan, and they did not succeed. The efforts with the Northern Alliance revived an inconclusive and secret debate about whether the United States should take sides in Afghanistan's civil war and support the Taliban's enemies. The CIA also produced a plan to improve intelligence collection on al Qaeda, including the use of a small, unmanned airplane with a video camera, known as the Predator.

After the October 2000 attack on the USS *Cole*, evidence accumulated that it had been launched by al Qaeda operatives, but without confirmation that Bin Ladin had given the order. The Taliban had earlier been warned that it would be held responsible for another Bin Ladin attack on the United States. The CIA described its findings as a "preliminary judgment"; President Clinton and his chief advisers told us they were waiting for a conclusion before deciding whether to take military action. The military alternatives remained unappealing to them.

The transition to the new Bush administration in late 2000 and early 2001 took place with the *Cole* issue still pending. President George W. Bush and his chief advisers accepted that al Qaeda was responsible for the attack on the *Cole*, but did not like the options available for a response.

Bin Ladin's inference may well have been that attacks, at least at the level of the *Cole*, were risk free.

The Bush administration began developing a new strategy with the stated goal of eliminating the al Qaeda threat within three to five years.

During the spring and summer of 2001, U.S. intelligence agencies received a stream of warnings that al Qaeda planned, as one report put it, "something very, very, very big." Director of Central Intelligence George Tenet told us, "The system was blinking red."

Although Bin Ladin was determined to strike in the United States, as President Clinton had been told and President Bush was reminded in a Presidential Daily Brief article briefed to him in August 2001, the specific threat information pointed overseas. Numerous precautions were taken overseas. Domestic agencies were not effectively mobilized. The threat did not receive national media attention comparable to the millennium alert.

While the United States continued disruption efforts around the world, its emerging strategy to eliminate the al Qaeda threat was to include an enlarged covert action program in Afghanistan, as well as diplomatic strategies for Afghanistan and Pakistan. The process culminated during the summer of 2001 in a draft presidential directive and arguments about the Predator aircraft, which was soon to be deployed with a missile of its own, so that it might be used to attempt to kill Bin Ladin or his chief lieutenants. At a September 4 meeting, President Bush's chief advisers approved the draft directive of the strategy and endorsed the concept of arming the Predator. This directive on the al Qaeda strategy was awaiting President Bush's signature on September 11, 2001.

Though the "planes operation" was progressing, the plotters had problems of their own in 2001. Several possible participants dropped out; others could not gain entry into the United States (including one denial at a port of entry and visa denials not related to terrorism). One of the eventual pilots may have considered abandoning the planes operation. Zacarias Moussaoui, who showed up at a flight training school in Minnesota, may have been a candidate to replace him.

Some of the vulnerabilities of the plotters become clear in retrospect. Moussaoui aroused suspicion for seeking fast-track training on how to pilot large jet airliners. He was arrested on August 16, 2001, for violations of immigration regulations. In late August, officials in the intelligence community realized that the terrorists spotted in Southeast Asia in January 2000 had arrived in the United States.

These cases did not prompt urgent action. No one working on these late leads in the summer of 2001 connected them to the high level of threat reporting. In the words of one official, no analytic work foresaw the lightning that could connect the thundercloud to the ground.

As final preparations were under way during the summer of 2001, dissent emerged among al Qaeda leaders in Afghanistan over whether to proceed. The Taliban's chief, Mullah Omar, opposed attacking the United States. Although facing opposition from many of his senior lieutenants, Bin Ladin effectively overruled their objections, and the attacks went forward.

September 11, 2001

The day began with the 19 hijackers getting through a security checkpoint system that they had evidently analyzed and knew how to defeat. Their success rate in penetrating the system was 19 for 19. They took over the four flights, taking advantage of air crews and cockpits that were not prepared for the contingency of a suicide hijacking.

On 9/11, the defense of U.S. air space depended on close interaction between two federal agencies: the Federal Aviation Administration (FAA) and North American Aerospace Defense Command (NORAD). Existing protocols on 9/11 were unsuited in every respect for an attack in which hijacked planes were used as weapons.

What ensued was a hurried attempt to improvise a defense by civilians who had never handled a hijacked aircraft that attempted to disappear, and by a military unprepared for the transformation of commercial aircraft into weapons of mass destruction.

A shootdown authorization was not communicated to the NORAD air defense sector until 28 minutes after United 93 had crashed in Pennsylvania. Planes were scrambled, but ineffectively, as they did not know where to go or what targets they were to intercept. And once the shootdown order was given, it was not communicated to the pilots. In short, while leaders in Washington believed that the fighters circling above them had been instructed to "take out" hostile aircraft, the only orders actually conveyed to the pilots were to "ID type and tail."

Like the national defense, the emergency response on 9/11 was necessarily improvised.

In New York City, the Fire Department of New York, the New York Police Department, the Port Authority of New York and New Jersey, the building employees, and the occupants of the buildings did their best to cope with the effects of almost unimaginable events—unfolding furiously over 102 minutes. Casualties were nearly 100 percent at and above the impact zones and were very high among first responders who stayed in danger as they tried to save lives. Despite weaknesses in preparations for disaster, failure to achieve unified incident command, and inadequate communications among responding agencies, all but approximately one hundred of the thousands of civilians who worked below the impact zone escaped, often with help from the emergency responders.

At the Pentagon, while there were also problems of command and control, the emergency response was generally effective. The Incident Command System, a formalized management structure for emergency response in place in the National Capital Region, overcame the inherent complications of a response across local, state, and federal jurisdictions.

Operational Opportunities

We write with the benefit and handicap of hindsight. We are mindful of the danger of being unjust to men and women who made choices in conditions of uncertainty and in circumstances over which they often had little control.

Nonetheless, there were specific points of vulnerability in the plot and opportunities to disrupt it. Operational failures—opportunities that were not or could not be exploited by the organizations and systems of that time—included

- not watchlisting future hijackers Hazmi and Mihdhar, not trailing them after they traveled to Bangkok, and not informing the FBI about one future hijacker's U.S. visa or his companion's travel to the United States;
- not sharing information linking individuals in the *Cole* attack to Mihdhar;
- not taking adequate steps in time to find Mihdhar or Hazmi in the United States;
- not linking the arrest of Zacarias Moussaoui, described as interested in flight training for the purpose of using an airplane in a terrorist act, to the heightened indications of attack;
- not discovering false statements on visa applications;
- not recognizing passports manipulated in a fraudulent manner;
- not expanding no-fly lists to include names from terrorist watchlists;
- not searching airline passengers identified by the computer-based CAPPS screening system; and
- not hardening aircraft cockpit doors or taking other measures to prepare for the possibility of suicide hijackings.

GENERAL FINDINGS

Since the plotters were flexible and resourceful, we cannot know whether any single step or series of steps would have defeated them. What we can say with confidence is that none of the measures adopted by the U.S. government from 1998 to 2001 disturbed or even delayed the progress of the al Qaeda plot. Across the government, there were failures of imagination, policy, capabilities, and management.

Imagination

The most important failure was one of imagination. We do not believe leaders understood the gravity of the threat. The terrorist danger from Bin Ladin and al Qaeda was not a major topic for policy debate among the public, the media, or in the Congress. Indeed, it barely came up during the 2000 presidential campaign.

Al Qaeda's new brand of terrorism presented challenges to U.S. governmental institutions that they were not well-designed to meet. Though top officials all told us that they understood the danger, we believe there was uncertainty among them as to whether this was just a new and especially venomous version of the ordinary terrorist threat the United States had lived with for decades, or it was indeed radically new, posing a threat beyond any yet experienced.

As late as September 4, 2001, Richard Clarke, the White House staffer long responsible for counterterrorism policy coordination, asserted that the government had not yet made up its mind how to answer the question: "Is al Qida a big deal?"

A week later came the answer.

Policy

Terrorism was not the overriding national security concern for the U.S. government under either the Clinton or the pre-9/11 Bush administration.

The policy challenges were linked to this failure of imagination. Officials in both the Clinton and Bush administrations regarded a full U.S. invasion of Afghanistan as practically inconceivable before 9/11.

Capabilities

Before 9/11, the United States tried to solve the al Qaeda problem with the capabilities it had used in the last stages of the Cold War and its immediate aftermath. These capabilities were insufficient. Little was done to expand or reform them.

The CIA had minimal capacity to conduct paramilitary operations with its own personnel, and it did not seek a large-scale expansion of these capabilities before 9/11. The CIA also needed to improve its capability to collect intelligence from human agents.

At no point before 9/11 was the Department of Defense fully engaged in the mission of countering al Qaeda, even though this was perhaps the most dangerous foreign enemy threatening the United States.

America's homeland defenders faced outward. NORAD itself was barely able to retain any alert bases at all. Its planning scenarios occasionally considered the danger of hijacked aircraft being guided to American targets, but only aircraft that were coming from overseas.

The most serious weaknesses in agency capabilities were in the domestic arena. The FBI did not have the capability to link the collective knowledge of agents in the field to national priorities. Other domestic agencies deferred to the FBI.

FAA capabilities were weak. Any serious examination of the possibility of a suicide hijacking could have suggested changes to fix glaring vulnerabilities—expanding no-fly lists, searching passengers identified by the CAPPS screening system, deploying federal air marshals domestically, hardening cockpit doors, alerting air crews to a different kind of hijacking possibility than they had been trained to expect. Yet the FAA did not adjust either its own training or training with NORAD to take account of threats other than those experienced in the past.

Management
The missed opportunities to thwart the 9/11 plot were also symptoms of a broader inability to adapt the way government manages problems to the new challenges of the twenty-first century. Action officers should have been able to draw on all available knowledge about al Qaeda in the government. Management should have ensured that information was shared and duties were clearly assigned across agencies, and across the foreign-domestic divide.

There were also broader management issues with respect to how top leaders set priorities and allocated resources. For instance, on December 4, 1998, DCI Tenet issued a directive to several CIA officials and the DDCI for Community Management, stating: "We are at war. I want no resources or people spared in this effort, either inside CIA or the Community." The memorandum had little overall effect on mobilizing the CIA or the intelligence community. This episode indicates the limitations of the DCI's authority over the direction of the intelligence community, including agencies within the Department of Defense.

The U.S. government did not find a way of pooling intelligence and using it to guide the planning and assignment of responsibilities for joint operations involving entities as disparate as the CIA, the FBI, the State Department, the military, and the agencies involved in homeland security.

SPECIFIC FINDINGS

Unsuccessful Diplomacy

Beginning in February 1997, and through September 11, 2001, the U.S. government tried to use diplomatic pressure to persuade the Taliban regime in Afghanistan to stop being a sanctuary for al Qaeda, and to expel Bin Ladin to a country where he could face justice. These efforts included warnings and sanctions, but they all failed.

The U.S. government also pressed two successive Pakistani governments to demand that the Taliban cease providing a sanctuary for Bin Ladin and his organization and, failing that, to cut off their support for the Taliban. Before 9/11, the United States could not find a mix of incentives and pressure that would persuade Pakistan to reconsider its fundamental relationship with the Taliban.

From 1999 through early 2001, the United States pressed the United Arab Emirates, one of the Taliban's only travel and financial outlets to the outside world, to break off ties and enforce sanctions, especially those related to air travel to Afghanistan. These efforts achieved little before 9/11.

Saudi Arabia has been a problematic ally in combating

Islamic extremism. Before 9/11, the Saudi and U.S. governments did not fully share intelligence information or develop an adequate joint effort to track and disrupt the finances of the al Qaeda organization. On the other hand, government officials of Saudi Arabia at the highest levels worked closely with top U.S. officials in major initiatives to solve the Bin Ladin problem with diplomacy.

Lack of Military Options

In response to the request of policymakers, the military prepared an array of limited strike options for attacking Bin Ladin and his organization from May 1998 onward. When they briefed policymakers, the military presented both the pros and cons of those strike options and the associated risks. Policymakers expressed frustration with the range of options presented.

Following the August 20, 1998, missile strikes on al Qaeda targets in Afghanistan and Sudan, both senior military officials and policymakers placed great emphasis on actionable intelligence as the key factor in recommending or deciding to launch military action against Bin Ladin and his organization. They did not want to risk significant collateral damage, and they did not want to miss Bin Ladin and thus make the United States look weak while making Bin Ladin look strong. On three specific occasions in 1998–1999, intelligence was deemed credible enough to warrant planning for possible strikes to kill Bin Ladin. But in each case the strikes did not go forward, because senior policymakers did not regard the intelligence as sufficiently actionable to offset their assessment of the risks.

The Director of Central Intelligence, policymakers, and military officials expressed frustration with the lack of actionable intelligence. Some officials inside the Pentagon, including those in the special forces and the counterterrorism policy office, also expressed frustration with the lack of military action. The Bush administration began to develop new policies toward al Qaeda in 2001, but military plans did not change until after 9/11.

Problems within the Intelligence Community

The intelligence community struggled throughout the 1990s and up to 9/11 to collect intelligence on and analyze the phenomenon of transnational terrorism. The combination of an overwhelming number of priorities, flat budgets, an outmoded structure, and bureaucratic rivalries resulted in an insufficient response to this new challenge.

Many dedicated officers worked day and night for years to piece together the growing body of evidence on al Qaeda and to understand the threats. Yet, while there were many reports on Bin Laden and his growing al Qaeda organization, there was no comprehensive review of what the intelligence community knew and what it did not know, and what that meant. There was no National Intelligence Estimate on terrorism between 1995 and 9/11.

Before 9/11, no agency did more to attack al Qaeda than the CIA. But there were limits to what the CIA was able to achieve by disrupting terrorist activities abroad and by using proxies to try to capture Bin Ladin and his lieutenants in Afghanistan. CIA officers were aware of those limitations.

To put it simply, covert action was not a silver bullet. It was important to engage proxies in Afghanistan and to build various capabilities so that if an opportunity presented itself, the CIA could act on it. But for more than three years, through both the late Clinton and early Bush administrations, the CIA relied on proxy forces, and there was growing frustration within the CIA's Counterterrorist Center and in the National Security Council staff with the lack of results. The development of the Predator and the push to aid the Northern Alliance were products of this frustration.

Problems in the FBI

From the time of the first World Trade Center attack in 1993, FBI and Department of Justice leadership in Washington and New York became increasingly concerned about the terrorist threat from Islamist extremists to U.S. interests, both at home and abroad. Throughout the 1990s, the FBI's counterterrorism efforts against international terrorist organizations included both intelligence and criminal investigations. The FBI's approach to investigations was case-specific, decentralized, and geared toward prosecution. Significant FBI resources were devoted to after-the-fact investigations of major terrorist attacks, resulting in several prosecutions.

The FBI attempted several reform efforts aimed at strengthening its ability to prevent such attacks, but these reform efforts failed to implement organization-wide institutional change. On September 11, 2001, the FBI was limited in several areas critical to an effective preventive counterterrorism strategy. Those working counterterrorism matters did so despite limited intelligence collection and strategic analysis capabilities, a limited capacity to share information both internally and externally, insufficient training, perceived legal barriers to sharing information, and inadequate resources.

Permeable Borders and Immigration Controls

There were opportunities for intelligence and law enforcement to exploit al Qaeda's travel vulnerabilities. Considered collectively, the 9/11 hijackers

- included known al Qaeda operatives who could have been watchlisted;
- presented passports manipulated in a fraudulent manner;
- presented passports with suspicious indicators of extremism;
- made detectable false statements on visa applications;
- made false statements to border officials to gain entry into the United States; and
- violated immigration laws while in the United States.

Neither the State Department's consular officers nor the Immigration and Naturalization Service's inspectors and agents were ever considered full partners in a national counterterrorism effort. Protecting borders was not a national security issue before 9/11.

Permeable Aviation Security

Hijackers studied publicly available materials on the aviation security system and used items that had less metal content than a handgun and were most likely permissible. Though two of the hijackers were on the U.S. TIPOFF terrorist watchlist, the FAA did not use TIPOFF data. The hijackers had to beat only one layer of security—the security checkpoint process. Even though several hijackers were selected for extra screening by the CAPPS system, this led only to greater scrutiny of their checked baggage. Once on board, the hijackers were faced with aircraft personnel who were trained to be nonconfrontational in the event of a hijacking.

Financing

The 9/11 attacks cost somewhere between $400,000 and $500,000 to execute. The operatives spent more than $270,000 in the United States. Additional expenses included travel to obtain passports and visas, travel to the United States, expenses incurred by the plot leader and facilitators outside the United States, and expenses incurred by the people selected to be hijackers who ultimately did not participate.

The conspiracy made extensive use of banks in the United States. The hijackers opened accounts in their own names, using passports and other identification documents. Their transactions were unremarkable and essentially invisible amid the billions of dollars flowing around the world every day.

To date, we have not been able to determine the origin of the money used for the 9/11 attacks. Al Qaeda had many sources of funding and a pre-9/11 annual budget estimated at $30 million. If a particular source of funds had dried up, al Qaeda could easily have found enough money elsewhere to fund the attack.

An Improvised Homeland Defense

The civilian and military defenders of the nation's airspace—FAA and NORAD—were unprepared for the attacks launched against them. Given that lack of preparedness, they attempted and failed to improvise an effective homeland defense against an unprecedented challenge.

The events of that morning do not reflect discredit on operational personnel. NORAD's Northeast Air Defense Sector personnel reached out for information and made the best judgments they could based on the information they received. Individual FAA controllers, facility managers, and command center managers were creative and agile in recommending a nationwide alert, ground-stopping local traffic, ordering all aircraft nationwide to land, and executing that unprecedented order flawlessly.

At more senior levels, communication was poor. Senior military and FAA leaders had no effective communication with each other. The chain of command did not function well. The President could not reach some senior officials. The Secretary of Defense did not enter the chain of command until the morning's key events were over. Air National Guard units with different rules of engagement were scrambled without the knowledge of the President, NORAD, or the National Military Command Center.

Emergency Response

The civilians, firefighters, police officers, emergency medical technicians, and emergency management professionals exhibited steady determination and resolve under horrifying, overwhelming conditions on 9/11. Their actions saved lives and inspired a nation.

Effective decisionmaking in New York was hampered by problems in command and control and in internal communications. Within the Fire Department of New York, this was true for several reasons: the magnitude of the incident was unforeseen; commanders had difficulty communicating with their units; more units were actually dispatched than were ordered by the chiefs; some units self-dispatched; and once units arrived at the World Trade Center, they were neither comprehensively accounted for nor coordinated. The Port Authority's response was hampered by the lack both of standard operating procedures and of radios capable of enabling multiple commands to respond to an incident in unified fashion. The New York Police Department, because of its history of mobilizing thousands of officers for major events requiring crowd control, had a technical radio capability and protocols more easily adapted to an incident of the magnitude of 9/11.

Congress

The Congress, like the executive branch, responded slowly to the rise of transnational terrorism as a threat to national security. The legislative branch adjusted little and did not restructure itself to address changing threats. Its attention to terrorism was episodic and splintered across several committees. The Congress gave little guidance to executive branch agencies on terrorism, did not reform them in any significant way to meet the threat, and did not systematically perform robust oversight to identify, address, and attempt to resolve the many problems in national security and domestic agencies that became apparent in the aftermath of 9/11.

So long as oversight is undermined by current congressional rules and resolutions, we believe the American people will not get the security they want and need. The United States needs a strong, stable, and capable congressional committee structure to give America's national intelligence agencies oversight, support, and leadership.

Are We Safer?

Since 9/11, the United States and its allies have killed or captured a majority of al Qaeda's leadership; toppled the Taliban, which gave al Qaeda sanctuary in Afghanistan; and severely damaged the organization. Yet terrorist attacks continue. Even as we have thwarted attacks, nearly everyone expects they will come. How can this be?

The problem is that al Qaeda represents an ideological movement, not a finite group of people. It initiates and inspires, even if it no longer directs. In this way it has transformed itself into a decentralized force. Bin Ladin may be limited in his ability to organize major attacks from his hideouts. Yet killing or capturing him, while extremely important, would not end terror. His message of inspiration to a new generation of terrorists would continue.

Because of offensive actions against al Qaeda since 9/11, and defensive actions to improve homeland security, we believe we are safer today. But we are not safe. We therefore make the following recommendations that we believe can make America safer and more secure.

RECOMMENDATIONS

Three years after 9/11, the national debate continues about how to protect our nation in this new era. We divide our recommendations into two basic parts: What to do, and how to do it.

WHAT TO DO? A GLOBAL STRATEGY

The enemy is not just "terrorism." It is the threat posed specifically by Islamist terrorism, by Bin Ladin and others who draw on a long tradition of extreme intolerance within a minority strain of Islam that does not distinguish politics from religion, and distorts both.

The enemy is not Islam, the great world faith, but a perversion of Islam. The enemy goes beyond al Qaeda to include the radical ideological movement, inspired in part by al Qaeda, that has spawned other terrorist groups and violence. Thus our strategy must match our means to two ends: dismantling the al Qaeda network and, in the long term, prevailing over the ideology that contributes to Islamist terrorism.

The first phase of our post-9/11 efforts rightly included military action to topple the Taliban and pursue al Qaeda. This work continues. But long-term success demands the use of all elements of national power: diplomacy, intelligence, covert action, law enforcement, economic policy, foreign aid, public diplomacy, and homeland defense. If we favor one tool while neglecting others, we leave ourselves vulnerable and weaken our national effort.

What should Americans expect from their government? The goal seems unlimited: Defeat terrorism anywhere in the world. But Americans have also been told to expect the worst: An attack is probably coming; it may be more devastating still.

Vague goals match an amorphous picture of the enemy. Al Qaeda and other groups are popularly described as being all over the world, adaptable, resilient, needing little higher-level organization, and capable of anything. It is an image of an omnipotent hydra of destruction. That image lowers expectations of government effectiveness.

It lowers them too far. Our report shows a determined and capable group of plotters. Yet the group was fragile and occasionally left vulnerable by the marginal, unstable people often attracted to such causes. The enemy made mistakes. The U.S. government was not able to capitalize on them.

No president can promise that a catastrophic attack like that of 9/11 will not happen again. But the American people are entitled to expect that officials will have realistic objectives, clear guidance, and effective organization. They are entitled to see standards for performance so they can judge, with the help of their elected representatives, whether the objectives are being met.

We propose a strategy with three dimensions: (1) attack terrorists and their organizations, (2) prevent the continued growth of Islamist terrorism, and (3) protect against and prepare for terrorist attacks.

Attack Terrorists and Their Organizations

- Root out sanctuaries. The U.S. government should identify and prioritize actual or potential terrorist sanctuaries and have realistic country or regional strategies for each, utilizing every element of national power and reaching out to countries that can help us.

- Strengthen long-term U.S. and international commitments to the future of Pakistan and Afghanistan.
- Confront problems with Saudi Arabia in the open and build a relationship beyond oil, a relationship that both sides can defend to their citizens and includes a shared commitment to reform.

Prevent the Continued Growth of Islamist Terrorism

In October 2003, Secretary of Defense Donald Rumsfeld asked if enough was being done "to fashion a broad integrated plan to stop the next generation of terrorists." As part of such a plan, the U.S. government should

- Define the message and stand as an example of moral leadership in the world. To Muslim parents, terrorists like Bin Ladin have nothing to offer their children but visions of violence and death. America and its friends have the advantage—our vision can offer a better future.
- Where Muslim governments, even those who are friends, do not offer opportunity, respect the rule of law, or tolerate differences, then the United States needs to stand for a better future.
- Communicate and defend American ideals in the Islamic world, through much stronger public diplomacy to reach more people, including students and leaders outside of government. Our efforts here should be as strong as they were in combating closed societies during the Cold War.
- Offer an agenda of opportunity that includes support for public education and economic openness.
- Develop a comprehensive coalition strategy against Islamist terrorism, using a flexible contact group of leading coalition governments and fashioning a common coalition approach on issues like the treatment of captured terrorists.
- Devote a maximum effort to the parallel task of countering the proliferation of weapons of mass destruction.

- Expect less from trying to dry up terrorist money and more from following the money for intelligence, as a tool to hunt terrorists, understand their networks, and disrupt their operations.

Protect against and Prepare for Terrorist Attacks

- Target terrorist travel, an intelligence and security strategy that the 9/11 story showed could be at least as powerful as the effort devoted to terrorist finance.
- Address problems of screening people with biometric identifiers across agencies and governments, including our border and transportation systems, by designing a comprehensive screening system that addresses common problems and sets common standards. As standards spread, this necessary and ambitious effort could dramatically strengthen the world's ability to intercept individuals who could pose catastrophic threats.
- Quickly complete a biometric entry-exit screening system, one that also speeds qualified travelers.
- Set standards for the issuance of birth certificates and sources of identification, such as driver's licenses.
- Develop strategies for neglected parts of our transportation security system. Since 9/11, about 90 percent of the nation's $5 billion annual investment in transportation security has gone to aviation, to fight the last war.
- In aviation, prevent arguments about a new computerized profiling system from delaying vital improvements in the "no-fly" and "automatic selectee" lists. Also, give priority to the improvement of checkpoint screening.
- Determine, with leadership from the President, guidelines for gathering and sharing information in the new security systems that are needed, guidelines that integrate safeguards for privacy and other essential liberties.
- Underscore that as government power necessarily expands in certain ways, the burden of retaining such

powers remains on the executive to demonstrate the value of such powers and ensure adequate supervision of how they are used, including a new board to oversee the implementation of the guidelines needed for gathering and sharing information in these new security systems.

- Base federal funding for emergency preparedness solely on risks and vulnerabilities, putting New York City and Washington, D.C., at the top of the current list. Such assistance should not remain a program for general revenue sharing or pork-barrel spending.
- Make homeland security funding contingent on the adoption of an incident command system to strengthen teamwork in a crisis, including a regional approach. Allocate more radio spectrum and improve connectivity for public safety communications, and encourage widespread adoption of newly developed standards for private-sector emergency preparedness—since the private sector controls 85 percent of the nation's critical infrastructure.

HOW TO DO IT? A DIFFERENT WAY OF ORGANIZING GOVERNMENT

The strategy we have recommended is elaborate, even as presented here very briefly. To implement it will require a government better organized than the one that exists today, with its national security institutions designed half a century ago to win the Cold War. Americans should not settle for incremental, ad hoc adjustments to a system created a generation ago for a world that no longer exists.

Our detailed recommendations are designed to fit together. Their purpose is clear: to build unity of effort across the U.S. government. As one official now serving on the front lines overseas put it to us: "One fight, one team."

We call for unity of effort in five areas, beginning with unity of effort on the challenge of counterterrorism itself:

- unifying strategic intelligence and operational planning against Islamist terrorists across the foreign-domestic divide with a National Counterterrorism Center;
- unifying the intelligence community with a new National Intelligence Director;
- unifying the many participants in the counterterrorism effort and their knowledge in a network-based information sharing system that transcends traditional governmental boundaries;
- unifying and strengthening congressional oversight to improve quality and accountability; and
- strengthening the FBI and homeland defenders.

Unity of Effort: A National Counterterrorism Center

The 9/11 story teaches the value of integrating strategic intelligence from all sources into joint operational planning— with *both* dimensions spanning the foreign-domestic divide.

- In some ways, since 9/11, joint work has gotten better. The effort of fighting terrorism has flooded over many of the usual agency boundaries because of its sheer quantity and energy. Attitudes have changed. But the problems of coordination have multiplied. The Defense Department alone has three unified commands (SOCOM, CENTCOM, and NORTHCOM) that deal with terrorism as one of their principal concerns.
- Much of the public commentary about the 9/11 attacks has focused on "lost opportunities." Though characterized as problems of "watch-listing," "information sharing," or "connecting the dots," each of these labels is too narrow. They describe the symptoms, not the disease.
- Breaking the older mold of organization stovepiped purely in executive agencies, we propose a National Counterterrorism Center (NCTC) that would borrow the joint, unified command concept adopted in the 1980s by the American military in a civilian agency,

combining the joint intelligence function alongside the operations work.

- The NCTC would build on the existing Terrorist Threat Integration Center and would replace it and other terrorism "fusion centers" within the government. The NCTC would become the authoritative knowledge bank, bringing information to bear on common plans. It should task collection requirements both inside and outside the United States.

- The NCTC should perform joint operational planning, assigning lead responsibilities to existing agencies and letting them direct the actual execution of the plans.

- Placed in the Executive Office of the President, headed by a Senate-confirmed official (with rank equal to the deputy head of a cabinet department) who reports to the National Intelligence Director, the NCTC would track implementation of plans. It would be able to influence the leadership and the budgets of the counterterrorism operating arms of the CIA, the FBI, and the departments of Defense and Homeland Security.

- The NCTC should *not* be a policymaking body. Its operations and planning should follow the policy direction of the president and the National Security Council.

Unity of Effort:
A National Intelligence Director

Since long before 9/11—and continuing to this day—the intelligence community is not organized well for joint intelligence work. It does not employ common standards and practices in reporting intelligence or in training experts overseas and at home. The expensive national capabilities for collecting intelligence have divided management. The structures are too complex and too secret.

- The community's head—the Director of Central Intelligence—has at least three jobs: running the CIA, coordinating a 15-agency confederation, and being the intelligence analyst-in-chief to the president. No one person can do all these things.

- A new National Intelligence Director should be established with two main jobs: (1) to oversee national intelligence centers that combine experts from all the collection disciplines against common targets—like counterterrorism or nuclear proliferation; and (2) to oversee the agencies that contribute to the national intelligence program, a task that includes setting common standards for personnel and information technology.
- The national intelligence centers would be the unified commands of the intelligence world—a long-overdue reform for intelligence comparable to the 1986 Goldwater-Nichols law that reformed the organization of national defense. The home services—such as the CIA, DIA, NSA, and FBI—would organize, train, and equip the best intelligence professionals in the world, and would handle the execution of intelligence operations in the field.
- This National Intelligence Director (NID) should be located in the Executive Office of the President and report directly to the president, yet be confirmed by the Senate. In addition to overseeing the National Counterterrorism Center described above (which will include both the national intelligence center for terrorism and the joint operations planning effort), the NID should have three deputies:
  - For foreign intelligence (a deputy who also would be the head of the CIA)
  - For defense intelligence (also the under secretary of defense for intelligence)
  - For homeland intelligence (also the executive assistant director for intelligence at the FBI or the under secretary of homeland security for information analysis and infrastructure protection)
- The NID should receive a public appropriation for national intelligence, should have authority to hire and fire his or her intelligence deputies, and should be able to set common personnel and information technology policies across the intelligence community.

Unity of Effort in Managing Intelligence

Executive Office of the President

POTUS

National Intelligence Director

National Counterterrorism Center

Staff

National Intelligence Centers
(conduct "joint" collection and analysis – *illustrative*)

WMD Proliferation

Int'l Crime & Narcotics

China / East Asia

Middle East

Russia / Eurasia

Hire, Train, Acquire, Equip & Field
(agencies support / staff the Nat'l Intel Centers)

Deputy NID Foreign Intelligence (CIA Dir.)
- CIA
  - Clandestine Services
  - All-Source Analysis
  - Open Source Agency (new)

Deputy NID Defense Intelligence (USD Intelligence)
- DIA
- NSA
- NGA
- NRO
- Other

Deputy NID Homeland Intelligence (FBI/Intel Dir.)
- FBI
  - Intel & CT / CI
- DHS / IAIP
  - Other DHS (e.g. CBP, TSA, Nat'l Labs, Coast Guard, etc.)

- The CIA should concentrate on strengthening the collection capabilities of its clandestine service and the talents of its analysts, building pride in its core expertise.
- Secrecy stifles oversight, accountability, and information sharing. Unfortunately, all the current organizational incentives encourage overclassification. This balance should change; and as a start, open information should be provided about the overall size of agency intelligence budgets.

Unity of Effort: Sharing Information

The U.S. government has access to a vast amount of information. But it has a weak system for processing and using what it has. The system of "need to know" should be replaced by a system of "need to share."

- The President should lead a government-wide effort to bring the major national security institutions into the information revolution, turning a mainframe system into a decentralized network. The obstacles are not technological. Official after official has urged us to call attention to problems with the unglamorous "back office" side of government operations.
- But no agency can solve the problems on its own—to build the network requires an effort that transcends old divides, solving common legal and policy issues in ways that can help officials know what they can and cannot do. Again, in tackling information issues, America needs unity of effort.

Unity of Effort: Congress

Congress took too little action to adjust itself or to restructure the executive branch to address the emerging terrorist threat. Congressional oversight for intelligence—and counterterrorism—is dysfunctional. Both Congress and the executive need to do more to minimize national security risks during transitions between administrations.

- For intelligence oversight, we propose two options: either a joint committee on the old model of the Joint Committee on Atomic Energy or a single committee in each house combining authorizing and appropriating committees. Our central message is the same: the intelligence committees cannot carry out their oversight function unless they are made stronger, and thereby have both clear responsibility and accountability for that oversight.

- Congress should create a single, principal point of oversight and review for homeland security. There should be one permanent standing committee for homeland security in each chamber.

- We propose reforms to speed up the nomination, financial reporting, security clearance, and confirmation process for national security officials at the start of an administration, and suggest steps to make sure that incoming administrations have the information they need.

Unity of Effort: Organizing America's Defenses in the United States

We have considered several proposals relating to the future of the domestic intelligence and counterterrorism mission. Adding a new domestic intelligence agency will not solve America's problems in collecting and analyzing intelligence within the United States. We do not recommend creating one.

- We propose the establishment of a specialized and integrated national security workforce at the FBI, consisting of agents, analysts, linguists, and surveillance specialists who are recruited, trained, rewarded, and retained to ensure the development of an institutional culture imbued with a deep expertise in intelligence and national security.

At several points we asked: Who has the responsibility for defending us at home? Responsibility for America's national defense is shared by the Department of Defense, with its new Northern Command, and by the Department of Homeland Security. They must have a clear delineation of roles, missions, and authority.

- The Department of Defense and its oversight committees should regularly assess the adequacy of Northern Command's strategies and planning to defend against military threats to the homeland.
- The Department of Homeland Security and its oversight committees should regularly assess the types of threats the country faces, in order to determine the adequacy of the government's plans and the readiness of the government to respond to those threats.

We call on the American people to remember how we all felt on 9/11, to remember not only the unspeakable horror but how we came together as a nation—one nation. Unity of purpose and unity of effort are the way we will defeat this enemy and make America safer for our children and grandchildren.

We look forward to a national debate on the merits of what we have recommended, and we will participate vigorously in that debate.

List of Illustrations and Tables

FAA Air Traffic Control Centers   24

Reporting structure, Northeast Air Defense Sector   25

Flight paths and timeline   50-53

The World Trade Center Complex as of 9/11   402

The World Trade Center radio repeater system   409

The World Trade Center North Tower stairwell   415
with deviations

Unity of effort in managing intelligence   589

COMMISSION
MEMBERS

Thomas H. Kean
CHAIR

Lee H. Hamilton
VICE CHAIR

Richard Ben-Veniste

Bob Kerrey

Fred F. Fielding

John F. Lehman

Jamie S. Gorelick

Timothy J. Roemer

Slade Gorton

James R. Thompson

Commission Staff

Philip Zelikow, *Executive Director*
Christopher A. Kojm, *Deputy Executive Director*
Daniel Marcus, *General Counsel*

Joanne M. Accolla
Staff Assistant
Alexis Albion
Professional Staff Member
Scott H. Allan, Jr.
Counsel
John A. Azzarello
Counsel
Caroline Barnes
Professional Staff Member
Warren Bass
Professional Staff Member
Ann M. Bennett
Information Control Officer
Mark S. Bittinger
Professional Staff Member
Madeleine Blot
Counsel
Antwion M. Blount
Systems Engineer

Sam Brinkley
Professional Staff Member
Geoffrey Scott Brown
Research Assistant
Daniel Byman
Professional Staff Member
Dianna Campagna
Manager of Operations
Samuel M. W. Caspersen
Counsel
Melissa A. Coffey
Staff Assistant
Lance Cole
Consultant
Marquittia L. Coleman
Staff Assistant
Marco A. Cordero
Professional Staff Member
Rajesh De
Counsel

Douglas J. MacEachin
Professional Staff Member &
Team Leader
Ernest R. May
Senior Adviser
Joseph McBride
Intern
James Miller
Professional Staff
Member
Kelly Moore
Professional Staff Member
Charles M. Pereira
Professional Staff Member
John Raidt
Professional Staff Member
John Roth
Senior Counsel & Team
Leader
Peter Rundlet
Counsel
Lloyd D. Salvetti
Professional Staff Member
Kevin J. Scheid
Professional Staff Member &
Team Leader

Kevin Shaeffer
Professional Staff Member
Tracy J. Shycoff
Deputy for Administration &
Finance
Dietrich L. Snell
Senior Counsel & Team Leader
Jonathan DeWees Stull
Communications Assistant
Lisa Marie Sullivan
Staff Assistant
Quinn John Tamm, Jr.
Professional Staff Member
Catharine S. Taylor
Staff Assistant
Yoel Tobin
Counsel
Emily Landis Walker
Professional Staff Member &
Family Liaison
Garth Wermter
Senior IT Consultant
Serena B. Wille
Counsel
Peter Yerkes
Public Affairs Assistant

Preface

We present the narrative of this report and the recommendations that flow from it to the President of the United States, the United States Congress, and the American people for their consideration. Ten Commissioners—five Republicans and five Democrats chosen by elected leaders from our nation's capital at a time of great partisan division—have come together to present this report without dissent.

We have come together with a unity of purpose because our nation demands it. September 11, 2001, was a day of unprecedented shock and suffering in the history of the United States. The nation was unprepared. How did this happen, and how can we avoid such tragedy again?

To answer these questions, the Congress and the President created the National Commission on Terrorist Attacks Upon the United States (Public Law 107-306, November 27, 2002).

Our mandate was sweeping. The law directed us to investigate "facts and circumstances relating to the terrorist attacks of September 11, 2001," including those relating to intelligence agencies, law enforcement agencies, diplomacy, immigration issues and border control, the flow of assets to terrorist organizations, commercial aviation, the role of congressional oversight and resource allocation, and other areas determined relevant by the Commission.

In pursuing our mandate, we have reviewed more than 2.5 million pages of documents and interviewed more than 1,200 individuals in ten countries. This included nearly every senior official from the current and previous administrations who had responsibility for topics covered in our mandate.

We have sought to be independent, impartial, thorough, and nonpartisan. From the outset, we have been committed to share as much of our investigation as we can with the American people. To that end, we held 19 days of hearings and took public testimony from 160 witnesses.

Our aim has not been to assign individual blame. Our aim has been to provide the fullest possible account of the events surrounding 9/11 and to identify lessons learned.

We learned about an enemy who is sophisticated, patient, disciplined, and lethal. The enemy rallies broad support in the Arab and Muslim world by demanding redress of political grievances, but its hostility toward us and our values is limitless. Its purpose is to rid the world of religious and political pluralism, the plebiscite, and equal rights for women. It makes no distinction between military and civilian targets. *Collateral damage* is not in its lexicon.

We learned that the institutions charged with protecting our borders, civil aviation, and national security did not understand how grave this threat could be, and did not adjust their policies, plans, and practices to deter or defeat it. We learned of fault lines within our government—between foreign and domestic intelligence, and between and within agencies. We learned of the pervasive problems of managing and sharing information across a large and unwieldy government that had been built in a different era to confront different dangers.

At the outset of our work, we said we were looking backward in order to look forward. We hope that the terrible losses chronicled in this report can create something positive—an America that is safer, stronger, and wiser. That September day, we came together as a nation. The test before us is to sustain that unity of purpose and meet the challenges now confronting us.

We need to design a balanced strategy for the long haul, to attack terrorists and prevent their ranks from swelling while at the same time protecting our country against future attacks. We have been forced to think about the way our government is organized. The massive departments and agencies that prevailed in the great struggles of the twentieth century must work together in new ways, so that all the instruments of national power can be combined. Congress needs dramatic change as well to strengthen oversight and focus accountability.

As we complete our final report, we want to begin by thanking our fellow Commissioners, whose dedication to this task has been profound. We have reasoned together over every page, and the report has benefited from this remarkable dialogue. We want to express our considerable respect for the intellect and judgment of our colleagues, as well as our great affection for them.

We want to thank the Commission staff. The dedicated professional staff, headed by Philip Zelikow, has contributed innumerable hours to the completion of this report, setting aside other important endeavors to take on this all-consuming assignment. They have conducted the exacting investigative work upon which the Commission has built. They have given good advice, and faithfully carried out our guidance. They have been superb.

We thank the Congress and the President. Executive branch agencies have searched records and produced a multitude of documents for us. We thank officials, past and present, who were generous with their time and provided us with insight. The PENTTBOM team at the FBI, the Director's Review Group at the CIA, and Inspectors General at the Department of Justice and the CIA provided great assistance. We owe a huge debt to their investigative labors, painstaking attention to detail, and readiness to share what they have learned. We have built on the work of several previous Commissions, and we thank the Congressional Joint Inquiry, whose fine work helped us get started. We thank the City of New York for assistance with documents and witnesses, and the Government Printing Office and W.W. Norton & Company for helping to get this report to the broad public.

We conclude this list of thanks by coming full circle: We thank the families of 9/11, whose persistence and dedication helped create the Commission. They have been with us each step of the way, as partners and witnesses. They know better than any of us the importance of the work we have undertaken.

We want to note what we have done, and not done. We have endeavored to provide the most complete account we can of the events of September 11, what happened and why. This final report is only a summary of what we have done, citing only a fraction of the sources we have consulted. But in an event of this scale, touching so many issues and organizations, we are conscious of our limits. We have not interviewed every knowledgeable person or found every relevant piece of paper. New information inevitably will come to light. We present this report as a foundation for a better understanding of a landmark in the history of our nation.

We have listened to scores of overwhelming personal tragedies and astounding acts of heroism and bravery. We have examined the staggering impact of the events of 9/11 on the American people and their amazing resilience and courage as they fought back. We have admired their determination to do their best to prevent another tragedy while preparing to respond if it becomes necessary. We emerge from this investigation with enormous sympathy for the victims and their loved ones, and with enhanced respect for the American people. We recognize the formidable challenges that lie ahead.

We also approach the task of recommendations with humility. We have made a limited number of them. We decided consciously to focus on recommendations we believe to be most important, whose implementation can make the greatest difference. We came into this process with strong opinions about what would work. All of us have had to pause, reflect, and sometimes change our minds as we studied these problems and considered the views of others. We hope our report will encourage our fellow citizens to study, reflect—and act.

Thomas H. Kean
chair
Lee H. Hamilton
vice chair

THE 9/11
COMMISSION
REPORT

CHAPTER ONE

"We Have Some Planes"

Tuesday, September 11, 2001, dawned temperate and nearly cloudless in the eastern United States. Millions of men and women readied themselves for work. Some made their way to the Twin Towers, the signature structures of the World Trade Center complex in New York City. Others went to Arlington, Virginia, to the Pentagon. Across the Potomac River, the United States Congress was back in session. At the other end of Pennsylvania Avenue, people began to line up for a White House tour. In Sarasota, Florida, President George W. Bush went for an early morning run.

For those heading to an airport, weather conditions could not have been better for a safe and pleasant journey. Among the travelers were Mohamed Atta and Abdul Aziz al Omari, who arrived at the airport in Portland, Maine.

1.1 INSIDE THE FOUR FLIGHTS

Boarding the Flights
Boston: American 11 and United 175.
Atta and Omari boarded a 6:00 A.M. flight from Portland to Boston's Logan International Airport.[1]

When he checked in for his flight to Boston, Atta was selected by a computerized prescreening system known as CAPPS (Computer Assisted Passenger Prescreening System), created to identify passengers who should be subject to special security measures. Under security rules in place at the time, the only consequence of Atta's selection by CAPPS was that his checked bags were held off the plane until it was confirmed that he had boarded the aircraft. This did not hinder Atta's plans.[2]

Atta and Omari arrived in Boston at 6:45. Seven minutes later, Atta apparently took a call from Marwan al Shehhi, a longtime colleague who was at another terminal at Logan Airport. They spoke for three minutes.[3] It would be their final conversation.

Between 6:45 and 7:40, Atta and Omari, along with Satam al Suqami, Wail al Shehri, and Waleed al Shehri, checked in and boarded American Airlines Flight 11, bound for Los Angeles. The flight was scheduled to depart at 7:45.[4]

In another Logan terminal, Shehhi, joined by Fayez Banihammad, Mohand al Shehri, Ahmed al Ghamdi, and Hamza al Ghamdi, checked in for United Airlines Flight 175, also bound for Los Angeles. A couple of Shehhi's colleagues were obviously unused to travel; according to the United ticket agent, they had trouble understanding the standard security questions, and she had to go over them slowly until they gave the routine, reassuring answers.[5] Their flight was scheduled to depart at 8:00.

The security checkpoints through which passengers, including Atta and his colleagues, gained access to the American 11 gate were operated by Globe Security under a contract with American Airlines. In a different terminal, the single checkpoint through which passengers for United 175 passed was controlled by United Airlines, which had contracted with Huntleigh USA to perform the screening.[6]

In passing through these checkpoints, each of the hijackers would have been screened by a walk-through metal detector calibrated to detect items with at least the metal content of a .22-caliber handgun. Anyone who might have set off that detector would have been screened with a hand wand—a procedure requiring the screener to identify the metal item or items that caused the alarm. In addition, an

X-ray machine would have screened the hijackers' carry-on belongings. The screening was in place to identify and confiscate weapons and other items prohibited from being carried onto a commercial flight.[7] None of the checkpoint supervisors recalled the hijackers or reported anything suspicious regarding their screening.[8]

While Atta had been selected by CAPPS in Portland, three members of his hijacking team—Suqami, Wail al Shehri, and Waleed al Shehri—were selected in Boston. Their selection affected only the handling of their checked bags, not their screening at the checkpoint. All five men cleared the checkpoint and made their way to the gate for American 11. Atta, Omari, and Suqami took their seats in business class (seats 8D, 8G, and 10B, respectively). The Shehri brothers had adjacent seats in row 2 (Wail in 2A, Waleed in 2B), in the first-class cabin. They boarded American 11 between 7:31 and 7:40. The aircraft pushed back from the gate at 7:40.[9]

Shehhi and his team, none of whom had been selected by CAPPS, boarded United 175 between 7:23 and 7:28 (Banihammad in 2A, Shehri in 2B, Shehhi in 6C, Hamza al Ghamdi in 9C, and Ahmed al Ghamdi in 9D). Their aircraft pushed back from the gate just before 8:00.[10]

Washington Dulles: American 77.

Hundreds of miles southwest of Boston, at Dulles International Airport in the Virginia suburbs of Washington, D.C., five more men were preparing to take their early morning flight. At 7:15, a pair of them, Khalid al Mihdhar and Majed Moqed, checked in at the American Airlines ticket counter for Flight 77, bound for Los Angeles. Within the next 20 minutes, they would be followed by Hani Hanjour and two brothers, Nawaf al Hazmi and Salem al Hazmi.[11]

Hani Hanjour, Khalid al Mihdhar, and Majed Moqed were flagged by CAPPS. The Hazmi brothers were also selected for extra scrutiny by the airline's customer service representative at the check-in counter. He did so because one of the brothers did not have photo identification nor could he understand English, and because the agent found both of the passengers to be suspicious. The only consequence of their selection was that their checked bags were held off the plane until it was confirmed that they had boarded the aircraft.[12]

All five hijackers passed through the Main Terminal's west security screening checkpoint; United Airlines, which was the responsible air carrier, had contracted out the work to Argenbright Security.[13] The checkpoint featured closed-circuit television that recorded all passengers, including the hijackers, as they were screened. At 7:18, Mihdhar and Moqed entered the security checkpoint.

Mihdhar and Moqed placed their carry-on bags on the belt of the X-ray machine and proceeded through the first metal detector. Both set off the alarm, and they were directed to a second metal detector. Mihdhar did not trigger the alarm and was permitted through the checkpoint. After Moqed set it off, a screener wanded him. He passed this inspection.[14]

About 20 minutes later, at 7:35, another passenger for Flight 77, Hani Hanjour, placed two carry-on bags on the X-ray belt in the Main Terminal's west checkpoint, and proceeded, without alarm, through the metal detector. A short time later, Nawaf and Salem al Hazmi entered the same checkpoint. Salem al Hazmi cleared the metal detector and was permitted through; Nawaf al Hazmi set off the alarms for both the first and second metal detectors and was then hand-wanded before being passed. In addition, his over-the-shoulder carry-on bag was swiped by an explosive trace detector and then passed. The video footage indicates that he was carrying an unidentified item in his back pocket, clipped to its rim.[15]

When the local civil aviation security office of the Federal Aviation Administration (FAA) later investigated these security screening operations, the screeners recalled nothing out of the ordinary. They could not recall that any of the passengers they screened were CAPPS selectees. We asked a screening expert to review the videotape of the handwanding, and he found the quality of the screener's work to have been "marginal at best." The screener should have "resolved" what set off the alarm; and in the case of both Moqed and Hazmi, it was clear that he did not.[16]

At 7:50, Majed Moqed and Khalid al Mihdhar boarded the flight and were seated in 12A and 12B in coach. Hani Hanjour, assigned to seat 1B (first class), soon followed. The Hazmi brothers, sitting in 5E and 5F, joined Hanjour in the first-class cabin.[17]

Newark: United 93.

Between 7:03 and 7:39, Saeed al Ghamdi, Ahmed al Nami, Ahmad al Haznawi, and Ziad Jarrah checked in at the United Airlines ticket counter for Flight 93, going to Los Angeles. Two checked bags; two did not. Haznawi was selected by CAPPS. His checked bag was screened for explosives and then loaded on the plane.[18]

The four men passed through the security checkpoint, owned by United Airlines and operated under contract by Argenbright Security. Like the checkpoints in Boston, it lacked closed-circuit television surveillance so there is no documentary evidence to indicate when the hijackers passed through the checkpoint, what alarms may have been triggered, or what security procedures were administered. The FAA interviewed the screeners later; none recalled anything unusual or suspicious.[19]

The four men boarded the plane between 7:39 and 7:48. All four had seats in the first-class cabin; their plane had no business-class section. Jarrah was in seat 1B, closest to the cockpit; Nami was in 3C, Ghamdi in 3D, and Haznawi in 6B.[20]

The 19 men were aboard four transcontinental flights.[21] They were planning to hijack these planes and turn them into large guided missiles, loaded with up to 11,400 gallons of jet fuel. By 8:00 A.M. on the morning of Tuesday, September 11, 2001, they had defeated all the security layers that America's civil aviation security system then had in place to prevent a hijacking.

The Hijacking of American 11

American Airlines Flight 11 provided nonstop service from Boston to Los Angeles. On September 11, Captain John Ogonowski and First Officer Thomas McGuinness piloted the Boeing 767. It carried its full capacity of nine flight attendants. Eighty-one passengers boarded the flight with them (including the five terrorists).[22]

The plane took off at 7:59. Just before 8:14, it had climbed to 26,000 feet, not quite its initial assigned cruising altitude of 29,000 feet. All communications and flight profile data were normal. About this time the "Fasten Seatbelt" sign would usually have been turned off and the flight attendants would have begun preparing for cabin service.[23]

At that same time, American 11 had its last routine communication with the ground when it acknowledged navigational instructions from the FAA's air traffic control (ATC) center in Boston. Sixteen seconds after that transmission, ATC instructed the aircraft's pilots to climb to 35,000 feet. That message and all subsequent attempts to contact the flight were not acknowledged. From this and other evidence, we believe the hijacking began at 8:14 or shortly thereafter.[24]

Reports from two flight attendants in the coach cabin, Betty Ong and Madeline "Amy" Sweeney, tell us most of what we know about how the hijacking happened. As it began, some of the hijackers—most likely Wail al Shehri and Waleed al Shehri, who were seated in row 2 in first class—stabbed the two unarmed flight attendants who would have been preparing for cabin service.[25]

We do not know exactly how the hijackers gained access to the cockpit; FAA rules required that the doors remain closed and locked during flight. Ong speculated that they had "jammed their way" in. Perhaps the terrorists stabbed the flight attendants to get a cockpit key, to force one of them to open the cockpit door, or to lure the captain or first officer out of the cockpit. Or the flight attendants may just have been in their way.[26]

At the same time or shortly thereafter, Atta—the only terrorist on board trained to fly a jet—would have moved to the cockpit from his business-class seat, possibly accompanied by Omari. As this was happening, passenger Daniel Lewin, who was seated in the row just behind Atta and Omari, was stabbed by one of the hijackers—probably Satam al Suqami, who was seated directly behind Lewin. Lewin had served four years as an officer in the Israeli military. He may have made an attempt to stop the hijackers in front of him, not realizing that another was sitting behind him.[27]

The hijackers quickly gained control and sprayed Mace, pepper spray, or some other irritant in the first-class cabin, in order to force the passengers and flight attendants toward the rear of the plane. They claimed they had a bomb.[28]

About five minutes after the hijacking began, Betty Ong contacted the American Airlines Southeastern Reservations Office in Cary, North Carolina, via an AT&T airphone to report an emergency aboard the flight. This was the first of several occasions on 9/11 when flight attendants took action outside the scope of their training, which emphasized that in a hijacking, they were to communicate with the cockpit crew. The emergency call lasted approximately 25 minutes, as Ong calmly and professionally relayed information about events taking place aboard the airplane to authorities on the ground.[29]

At 8:19, Ong reported: "The cockpit is not answering, somebody's stabbed in business class—and I think there's Mace—that we can't breathe—I don't know, I think we're getting hijacked." She then told of the stabbings of the two flight attendants.[30]

At 8:21, one of the American employees receiving Ong's call in North Carolina, Nydia Gonzalez, alerted the American Airlines operations center in Fort Worth, Texas, reaching Craig Marquis, the manager on duty. Marquis soon realized this was an emergency and instructed the airline's dispatcher responsible for the flight to contact the cockpit. At 8:23, the dispatcher tried unsuccessfully to contact the aircraft. Six minutes later, the air traffic control specialist in

American's operations center contacted the FAA's Boston
Air Traffic Control Center about the flight. The center was
already aware of the problem.[31]

Boston Center knew of a problem on the flight in part because just before 8:25 the hijackers had attempted to communicate with the passengers. The microphone was keyed,
and immediately one of the hijackers said, "Nobody move.
Everything will be okay. If you try to make any moves,
you'll endanger yourself and the airplane. Just stay quiet."
Air traffic controllers heard the transmission; Ong did not.
The hijackers probably did not know how to operate the
cockpit radio communication system correctly, and thus inadvertently broadcast their message over the air traffic control channel instead of the cabin public-address channel.
Also at 8:25, and again at 8:29, Amy Sweeney got through to
the American Flight Services Office in Boston but was cut
off after she reported someone was hurt aboard the flight.
Three minutes later, Sweeney was reconnected to the office
and began relaying updates to the manager, Michael Woodward.[32]

At 8:26, Ong reported that the plane was "flying errati-
cally." A minute later, Flight 11 turned south. American also
began getting identifications of the hijackers, as Ong and
then Sweeney passed on some of the seat numbers of those
who had gained unauthorized access to the cockpit.[33]

Sweeney calmly reported on her line that the plane had
been hijacked; a man in first class had his throat slashed; two
flight attendants had been stabbed—one was seriously hurt
and was on oxygen while the other's wounds seemed minor;
a doctor had been requested; the flight attendants were unable to contact the cockpit; and there was a bomb in the
cockpit. Sweeney told Woodward that she and Ong were trying to relay as much information as they could to people on
the ground.[34]

At 8:38, Ong told Gonzalez that the plane was flying er-
ratically again. Around this time Sweeney told Woodward
that the hijackers were Middle Easterners, naming three of
their seat numbers. One spoke very little English and one

spoke excellent English. The hijackers had gained entry to the cockpit, and she did not know how. The aircraft was in a rapid descent.[35]

At 8:41, Sweeney told Woodward that passengers in coach were under the impression that there was a routine medical emergency in first class. Other flight attendants were busy at duties such as getting medical supplies while Ong and Sweeney were reporting the events.[36]

At 8:41, in American's operations center, a colleague told Marquis that the air traffic controllers declared Flight 11 a hijacking and "think he's [American 11] headed toward Kennedy [airport in New York City]. They're moving everybody out of the way. They seem to have him on a primary radar. They seem to think that he is descending."[37]

At 8:44, Gonzalez reported losing phone contact with Ong. About this same time Sweeney reported to Woodward, "Something is wrong. We are in a rapid descent . . . we are all over the place." Woodward asked Sweeney to look out the window to see if she could determine where they were. Sweeney responded: "We are flying low. We are flying very, very low. We are flying way too low." Seconds later she said, "Oh my God we are way too low." The phone call ended.[38]

At 8:46:40, American 11 crashed into the North Tower of the World Trade Center in New York City.[39] All on board, along with an unknown number of people in the tower, were killed instantly.

The Hijacking of United 175

United Airlines Flight 175 was scheduled to depart for Los Angeles at 8:00. Captain Victor Saracini and First Officer Michael Horrocks piloted the Boeing 767, which had seven flight attendants. Fifty-six passengers boarded the flight.[40]

United 175 pushed back from its gate at 7:58 and departed Logan Airport at 8:14. By 8:33, it had reached its assigned cruising altitude of 31,000 feet. The flight attendants would have begun their cabin service.[41]

The flight had taken off just as American 11 was being hijacked, and at 8:42 the United 175 flight crew completed

their report on a "suspicious transmission" overheard from
another plane (which turned out to have been Flight 11) just
after takeoff. This was United 175's last communication
with the ground.[42]

The hijackers attacked sometime between 8:42 and 8:46.
They used knives (as reported by two passengers and a flight
attendant), Mace (reported by one passenger), and the threat
of a bomb (reported by the same passenger). They stabbed
members of the flight crew (reported by a flight attendant
and one passenger). Both pilots had been killed (reported by
one flight attendant). The eyewitness accounts came from
calls made from the rear of the plane, from passengers originally seated further forward in the cabin, a sign that passengers and perhaps crew had been moved to the back of the
aircraft. Given similarities to American 11 in hijacker seating and in eyewitness reports of tactics and weapons, as well
as the contact between the presumed team leaders, Atta and
Shehhi, we believe the tactics were similar on both flights.[43]

The first operational evidence that something was abnormal on United 175 came at 8:47, when the aircraft changed
beacon codes twice within a minute. At 8:51, the flight deviated from its assigned altitude, and a minute later New York
air traffic controllers began repeatedly and unsuccessfully
trying to contact it.[44]

At 8:52, in Easton, Connecticut, a man named Lee Hanson received a phone call from his son Peter, a passenger on
United 175. His son told him: "I think they've taken over the
cockpit—An attendant has been stabbed—and someone else
up front may have been killed. The plane is making strange
moves. Call United Airlines—Tell them it's Flight 175,
Boston to LA." Lee Hanson then called the Easton Police
Department and relayed what he had heard.[45]

Also at 8:52, a male flight attendant called a United office
in San Francisco, reaching Marc Policastro. The flight attendant reported that the flight had been hijacked, both pilots
had been killed, a flight attendant had been stabbed, and the
hijackers were probably flying the plane. The call lasted

about two minutes, after which Policastro and a colleague tried unsuccessfully to contact the flight.[46]

At 8:58, the flight took a heading toward New York City.[47]

At 8:59, Flight 175 passenger Brian David Sweeney tried to call his wife, Julie. He left a message on their home answering machine that the plane had been hijacked. He then called his mother, Louise Sweeney, told her the flight had been hijacked, and added that the passengers were thinking about storming the cockpit to take control of the plane away from the hijackers.[48]

At 9:00, Lee Hanson received a second call from his son Peter:

> It's getting bad, Dad—A stewardess was stabbed—They seem to have knives and Mace—They said they have a bomb—It's getting very bad on the plane—Passengers are throwing up and getting sick—The plane is making jerky movements—I don't think the pilot is flying the plane—I think we are going down—I think they intend to go to Chicago or someplace and fly into a building—Don't worry, Dad—If it happens, it'll be very fast—My God, my God.[49]

The call ended abruptly. Lee Hanson had heard a woman scream just before it cut off. He turned on a television, and in her home so did Louise Sweeney. Both then saw the second aircraft hit the World Trade Center.[50]

At 9:03:11, United Airlines Flight 175 struck the South Tower of the World Trade Center.[51] All on board, along with an unknown number of people in the tower, were killed instantly.

The Hijacking of American 77

American Airlines Flight 77 was scheduled to depart from Washington Dulles for Los Angeles at 8:10. The aircraft was a Boeing 757 piloted by Captain Charles F. Burlingame and

First Officer David Charlebois. There were four flight attendants. On September 11, the flight carried 58 passengers.[52]

American 77 pushed back from its gate at 8:09 and took
off at 8:20. At 8:46, the flight reached its assigned cruising
altitude of 35,000 feet. Cabin service would have begun. At
8:51, American 77 transmitted its last routine radio communication. The hijacking began between 8:51 and 8:54. As on
American 11 and United 175, the hijackers used knives (reported by one passenger) and moved all the passengers (and
possibly crew) to the rear of the aircraft (reported by one
flight attendant and one passenger). Unlike the earlier
flights, the Flight 77 hijackers were reported by a passenger
to have box cutters. Finally, a passenger reported that an announcement had been made by the "pilot" that the plane had
been hijacked. Neither of the firsthand accounts mentioned
any stabbings or the threat or use of either a bomb or Mace,
though both witnesses began the flight in the first-class
cabin.[53]

At 8:54, the aircraft deviated from its assigned course,
turning south. Two minutes later the transponder was turned
off and even primary radar contact with the aircraft was lost.
The Indianapolis Air Traffic Control Center repeatedly tried
and failed to contact the aircraft. American Airlines dispatchers also tried, without success.[54]

At 9:00, American Airlines Executive Vice President
Gerard Arpey learned that communications had been lost
with American 77. This was now the second American aircraft in trouble. He ordered all American Airlines flights in
the Northeast that had not taken off to remain on the ground.
Shortly before 9:10, suspecting that American 77 had been
hijacked, American headquarters concluded that the second
aircraft to hit the World Trade Center might have been Flight
77. After learning that United Airlines was missing a plane,
American Airlines headquarters extended the ground stop
nationwide.[55]

At 9:12, Renee May called her mother, Nancy May, in
Las Vegas. She said her flight was being hijacked by six individuals who had moved them to the rear of the plane. She

asked her mother to alert American Airlines. Nancy May and her husband promptly did so.[56]

At some point between 9:16 and 9:26, Barbara Olson called her husband, Ted Olson, the solicitor general of the United States. She reported that the flight had been hijacked, and the hijackers had knives and box cutters. She further indicated that the hijackers were not aware of her phone call, and that they had put all the passengers in the back of the plane. About a minute into the conversation, the call was cut off. Solicitor General Olson tried unsuccessfully to reach Attorney General John Ashcroft.[57]

Shortly after the first call, Barbara Olson reached her husband again. She reported that the pilot had announced that the flight had been hijacked, and she asked her husband what she should tell the captain to do. Ted Olson asked for her location and she replied that the aircraft was then flying over houses. Another passenger told her they were traveling northeast. The Solicitor General then informed his wife of the two previous hijackings and crashes. She did not display signs of panic and did not indicate any awareness of an impending crash. At that point, the second call was cut off.[58]

At 9:29, the autopilot on American 77 was disengaged; the aircraft was at 7,000 feet and approximately 38 miles west of the Pentagon.[59] At 9:32, controllers at the Dulles Terminal Radar Approach Control "observed a primary radar target tracking eastbound at a high rate of speed." This was later determined to have been Flight 77.

At 9:34, Ronald Reagan Washington National Airport advised the Secret Service of an unknown aircraft heading in the direction of the White House. American 77 was then 5 miles west-southwest of the Pentagon and began a 330-degree turn. At the end of the turn, it was descending through 2,200 feet, pointed toward the Pentagon and downtown Washington. The hijacker pilot then advanced the throttles to maximum power and dove toward the Pentagon.[60]

At 9:37:46, American Airlines Flight 77 crashed into the Pentagon, traveling at approximately 530 miles per hour.[61]

All on board, as well as many civilian and military personnel in the building, were killed.

The Battle for United 93

At 8:42, United Airlines Flight 93 took off from Newark (New Jersey) Liberty International Airport bound for San Francisco. The aircraft was piloted by Captain Jason Dahl and First Officer Leroy Homer, and there were five flight attendants. Thirty-seven passengers, including the hijackers, boarded the plane. Scheduled to depart the gate at 8:00, the Boeing 757's takeoff was delayed because of the airport's typically heavy morning traffic.[62]

The hijackers had planned to take flights scheduled to depart at 7:45 (American 11), 8:00 (United 175 and United 93), and 8:10 (American 77). Three of the flights had actually taken off within 10 to 15 minutes of their planned departure times. United 93 would ordinarily have taken off about 15 minutes after pulling away from the gate. When it left the ground at 8:42, the flight was running more than 25 minutes late.[63]

As United 93 left Newark, the flight's crew members were unaware of the hijacking of American 11. Around 9:00, the FAA, American, and United were facing the staggering realization of apparent multiple hijackings. At 9:03, they would see another aircraft strike the World Trade Center. Crisis managers at the FAA and the airlines did not yet act to warn other aircraft.[64] At the same time, Boston Center realized that a message transmitted just before 8:25 by the hijacker pilot of American 11 included the phrase, "We have some planes."[65]

No one at the FAA or the airlines that day had ever dealt with multiple hijackings. Such a plot had not been carried out anywhere in the world in more than 30 years, and never in the United States. As news of the hijackings filtered through the FAA and the airlines, it does not seem to have occurred to their leadership that they needed to alert other aircraft in the air that they too might be at risk.[66]

United 175 was hijacked between 8:42 and 8:46, and

awareness of that hijacking began to spread after 8:51. American 77 was hijacked between 8:51 and 8:54. By 9:00, FAA and airline officials began to comprehend that attackers were going after multiple aircraft. American Airlines' nationwide ground stop between 9:05 and 9:10 was followed by a United Airlines ground stop. FAA controllers at Boston Center, which had tracked the first two hijackings, requested at 9:07 that Herndon Command Center "get messages to airborne aircraft to increase security for the cockpit." There is no evidence that Herndon took such action. Boston Center immediately began speculating about other aircraft that might be in danger, leading them to worry about a transcontinental flight—Delta 1989—that in fact was not hijacked. At 9:19, the FAA's New England regional office called Herndon and asked that Cleveland Center advise Delta 1989 to use extra cockpit security.[67]

Several FAA air traffic control officials told us it was the air carriers' responsibility to notify their planes of security problems. One senior FAA air traffic control manager said that it was simply not the FAA's place to order the airlines what to tell their pilots.[68] We believe such statements do not reflect an adequate appreciation of the FAA's responsibility for the safety and security of civil aviation.

The airlines bore responsibility, too. They were facing an escalating number of conflicting and, for the most part, erroneous reports about other flights, as well as a continuing lack of vital information from the FAA about the hijacked flights. We found no evidence, however, that American Airlines sent any cockpit warnings to its aircraft on 9/11. United's first decisive action to notify its airborne aircraft to take defensive action did not come until 9:19, when a United flight dispatcher, Ed Ballinger, took the initiative to begin transmitting warnings to his 16 transcontinental flights: "Beware any cockpit intrusion—Two a/c [aircraft] hit World Trade Center." One of the flights that received the warning was United 93. Because Ballinger was still responsible for his other flights as well as Flight 175, his warning message was not transmitted to Flight 93 until 9:23.[69]

By all accounts, the first 46 minutes of Flight 93's cross-country trip proceeded routinely. Radio communications from the plane were normal. Heading, speed, and altitude ran according to plan. At 9:24, Ballinger's warning to United 93 was received in the cockpit. Within two minutes, at 9:26, the pilot, Jason Dahl, responded with a note of puzzlement: "Ed, confirm latest mssg plz—Jason."[70]

The hijackers attacked at 9:28. While traveling 35,000 feet above eastern Ohio, United 93 suddenly dropped 700 feet. Eleven seconds into the descent, the FAA's air traffic control center in Cleveland received the first of two radio transmissions from the aircraft. During the first broadcast, the captain or first officer could be heard declaring "Mayday" amid the sounds of a physical struggle in the cockpit. The second radio transmission, 35 seconds later, indicated that the fight was continuing. The captain or first officer could be heard shouting: "Hey get out of here—get out of here—get out of here."[71]

On the morning of 9/11, there were only 37 passengers on United 93—33 in addition to the 4 hijackers. This was below the norm for Tuesday mornings during the summer of 2001. But there is no evidence that the hijackers manipulated passenger levels or purchased additional seats to facilitate their operation.[72]

The terrorists who hijacked three other commercial flights on 9/11 operated in five-man teams. They initiated their cockpit takeover within 30 minutes of takeoff. On Flight 93, however, the takeover took place 46 minutes after takeoff and there were only four hijackers. The operative likely intended to round out the team for this flight, Mohamed al Kahtani, had been refused entry by a suspicious immigration inspector at Florida's Orlando International Airport in August.[73]

Because several passengers on United 93 described three hijackers on the plane, not four, some have wondered whether one of the hijackers had been able to use the cockpit jump seat from the outset of the flight. FAA rules allow use of this seat by documented and approved individuals, usually air carrier or FAA personnel. We have found no evidence indicating that one of the hijackers, or anyone else, sat there on this flight. All the hijackers had assigned seats in first class, and they seem to have used them. We believe it is more likely that Jarrah, the crucial pilot-trained member of their team, remained seated and inconspicuous until after the cockpit was seized; and once inside, he would not have been visible to the passengers.[74]

At 9:32, a hijacker, probably Jarrah, made or attempted to make the following announcement to the passengers of Flight 93: "Ladies and Gentlemen: Here the captain, please sit down keep remaining sitting. We have a bomb on board. So, sit." The flight data recorder (also recovered) indicates that Jarrah then instructed the plane's autopilot to turn the aircraft around and head east.[75]

The cockpit voice recorder data indicate that a woman, most likely a flight attendant, was being held captive in the cockpit. She struggled with one of the hijackers who killed or otherwise silenced her.[76]

Shortly thereafter, the passengers and flight crew began a series of calls from GTE airphones and cellular phones. These calls between family, friends, and colleagues took place until the end of the flight and provided those on the ground with firsthand accounts. They enabled the passengers to gain critical information, including the news that two aircraft had slammed into the World Trade Center.[77]

At 9:39, the FAA's Cleveland Air Route Traffic Control Center overheard a second announcement indicating that there was a bomb on board, that the plane was returning to the airport, and that they should remain seated.[78] While it apparently was not heard by the passengers, this announcement, like those on Flight 11 and Flight 77, was intended to deceive them. Jarrah, like Atta earlier, may have inadvertently broadcast the message because he did not know how to operate the radio and the intercom. To our knowledge none of them had ever flown an actual airliner before.

At least two callers from the flight reported that the hijackers knew that passengers were making calls but did not seem to care. It is quite possible Jarrah knew of the success of the assault on the World Trade Center. He could have learned of this from messages being sent by United Airlines to the cockpits of its transcontinental flights, including Flight 93, warning of cockpit intrusion and telling of the New York attacks. But even without them, he would certainly have understood that the attacks on the World Trade Center would already have unfolded, given Flight 93's tardy departure from Newark. If Jarrah did know that the passengers were making calls, it might not have occurred to him that they were certain to learn what had happened in New York, thereby defeating his attempts at deception.[79]

At least ten passengers and two crew members shared vital information with family, friends, colleagues, or others on the ground. All understood the plane had been hijacked. They said the hijackers wielded knives and claimed to have a bomb. The hijackers were wearing red bandanas, and they forced the passengers to the back of the aircraft.[80]

Callers reported that a passenger had been stabbed and that two people were lying on the floor of the cabin, injured or dead—possibly the captain and first officer. One caller reported that a flight attendant had been killed.[81]

One of the callers from United 93 also reported that he thought the hijackers might possess a gun. But none of the other callers reported the presence of a firearm. One recipient of a call from the aircraft recounted specifically asking her caller whether the hijackers had guns. The passenger replied that he did not see one. No evidence of firearms or of their identifiable remains was found at the aircraft's crash site, and the cockpit voice recorder gives no indication of a gun being fired or mentioned at any time. We believe that if the hijackers had possessed a gun, they would have used it in the flight's last minutes as the passengers fought back.[82]

Passengers on three flights reported the hijackers' claim of having a bomb. The FBI told us they found no trace of explosives at the crash sites. One of the passengers who mentioned a bomb expressed his belief that it was not real. Lacking any evidence that the hijackers attempted to smug-

gle such illegal items past the security screening checkpoints, we believe the bombs were probably fake.[83]

During at least five of the passengers' phone calls, information was shared about the attacks that had occurred earlier that morning at the World Trade Center. Five calls
described the intent of passengers and surviving crew members to revolt against the hijackers. According to one call,
they voted on whether to rush the terrorists in an attempt to
retake the plane. They decided, and acted.[84]

At 9:57, the passenger assault began. Several passengers
had terminated phone calls with loved ones in order to join
the revolt. One of the callers ended her message as follows:
"Everyone's running up to first class. I've got to go. Bye."[85]

The cockpit voice recorder captured the sounds of the
passenger assault muffled by the intervening cockpit door.
Some family members who listened to the recording report
that they can hear the voice of a loved one among the din.
We cannot identify whose voices can be heard. But the assault was sustained.[86]

In response, Jarrah immediately began to roll the airplane
to the left and right, attempting to knock the passengers off
balance. At 9:58:57, Jarrah told another hijacker in the cockpit to block the door. Jarrah continued to roll the airplane
sharply left and right, but the assault continued. At 9:59:52,
Jarrah changed tactics and pitched the nose of the airplane
up and down to disrupt the assault. The recorder captured
the sounds of loud thumps, crashes, shouts, and breaking
glasses and plates. At 10:00:03, Jarrah stabilized the airplane.[87]

Five seconds later, Jarrah asked, "Is that it? Shall we finish it off?" A hijacker responded, "No. Not yet. When they
all come, we finish it off." The sounds of fighting continued
outside the cockpit. Again, Jarrah pitched the nose of the aircraft up and down. At 10:00:26, a passenger in the background said, "In the cockpit. If we don't we'll die!" Sixteen
seconds later, a passenger yelled, "Roll it!" Jarrah stopped
the violent maneuvers at about 10:01:00 and said, "Allah is
the greatest! Allah is the greatest!" He then asked another hi-

jacker in the cockpit, "Is that it? I mean, shall we put it down?" to which the other replied, "Yes, put it in it, and pull it down."[88]

The passengers continued their assault and at 10:02:23, a hijacker said, "Pull it down! Pull it down!" The hijackers remained at the controls but must have judged that the passengers were only seconds from overcoming them. The airplane headed down; the control wheel was turned hard to the right. The airplane rolled onto its back, and one of the hijackers began shouting "Allah is the greatest. Allah is the greatest." With the sounds of the passenger counterattack continuing, the aircraft plowed into an empty field in Shanksville, Pennsylvania, at 580 miles per hour, about 20 minutes' flying time from Washington, D.C.[89]

Jarrah's objective was to crash his airliner into symbols of the American Republic, the Capitol or the White House. He was defeated by the alerted, unarmed passengers of United 93.

1.2 IMPROVISING A HOMELAND DEFENSE

The FAA and NORAD

On 9/11, the defense of U.S. airspace depended on close interaction between two federal agencies: the FAA and the North American Aerospace Defense Command (NORAD). The most recent hijacking that involved U.S. air traffic controllers, FAA management, and military coordination had occurred in 1993.[90] In order to understand how the two agencies interacted eight years later, we will review their missions, command and control structures, and working relationship on the morning of 9/11.

FAA Mission and Structure.

As of September 11, 2001, the FAA was mandated by law to regulate the safety and security of civil aviation. From an air traffic controller's perspective, that meant maintaining a safe distance between airborne aircraft.[91]

Many controllers work at the FAA's 22 Air Route Traffic *Control Centers*. They are grouped under regional offices and coordinate closely with the national Air Traffic Control System *Command Center*, located in Herndon, Virginia, which oversees daily traffic flow within the entire airspace system. FAA headquarters is ultimately responsible for the management of the National Airspace System. The *Operations Center* located at FAA headquarters receives notifications of incidents, including accidents and hijackings.[92]

FAA Control Centers often receive information and make operational decisions independently of one another. On 9/11, the four hijacked aircraft were monitored mainly by the centers in Boston, New York, Cleveland, and Indianapolis. Each center thus had part of the knowledge of what was going on across the system. What Boston knew was not necessarily known by centers in New York, Cleveland, and Indianapolis, or for that matter by the Command Center in Herndon or by FAA headquarters in Washington.

Controllers track airliners such as the four aircraft hijacked on 9/11 primarily by watching the data from a signal emitted by each aircraft's transponder equipment. Those four planes, like all aircraft traveling above 10,000 feet, were required to emit a unique transponder signal while in flight.[93]

On 9/11, the terrorists turned off the transponders on three of the four hijacked aircraft. With its transponder off, it is possible, though more difficult, to track an aircraft by its primary radar returns. But unlike transponder data, primary radar returns do not show the aircraft's identity and altitude. Controllers at centers rely so heavily on transponder signals that they usually do not display primary radar returns on their radar scopes. But they can change the configuration of their scopes so they can see primary radar returns. They did this on 9/11 when the transponder signals for three of the aircraft disappeared.[94]

FAA Air Traffic Control Centers
Graphics courtesy of ESRI

Reporting structure, *Northeast Air Defense Sector*

Graphics courtesy of ESRI

Otis Air Force Base

Langley Air Force Base

Northeast Air Defense Sector (NEADS)

Continental Aerospace Command Region (CONR)

NORAD Headquarters

Before 9/11, it was not unheard of for a commercial aircraft to deviate slightly from its course, or for an FAA controller to lose radio contact with a pilot for a short period of time. A controller could also briefly lose a commercial aircraft's transponder signal, although this happened much less frequently. However, the simultaneous loss of radio and transponder signal would be a rare and alarming occurrence, and would normally indicate a catastrophic system failure or an aircraft crash. In all of these instances, the job of the controller was to reach out to the aircraft, the parent company of the aircraft, and other planes in the vicinity in an attempt to reestablish communications and set the aircraft back on course. Alarm bells would not start ringing until these efforts—which could take five minutes or more—were tried and had failed.[95]

NORAD Mission and Structure.

NORAD is a binational command established in 1958 between the United States and Canada. Its mission was, and is, to defend the airspace of North America and protect the continent. That mission does not distinguish between internal and external threats; but because NORAD was created to counter the Soviet threat, it came to define its job as defending against external attacks.[96]

The threat of Soviet bombers diminished significantly as the Cold War ended, and the number of NORAD alert sites was reduced from its Cold War high of 26. Some within the Pentagon argued in the 1990s that the alert sites should be eliminated entirely. In an effort to preserve their mission, members of the air defense community advocated the importance of air sovereignty against emerging "asymmetric threats" to the United States: drug smuggling, "non-state and state-sponsored terrorists," and the proliferation of weapons of mass destruction and ballistic missile technology.[97]

NORAD perceived the dominant threat to be from cruise missiles. Other threats were identified during the late 1990s, including terrorists' use of aircraft as weapons. Exercises were conducted to counter this threat, but they were not based on ac-

tual intelligence. In most instances, the main concern was the
use of such aircraft to deliver weapons of mass destruction.

Prior to 9/11, it was understood that an order to shoot down
a commercial aircraft would have to be issued by the National
Command Authority (a phrase used to describe the president
and secretary of defense). Exercise planners also assumed
that the aircraft would originate from outside the United
States, allowing time to identify the target and scramble interceptors. The threat of terrorists hijacking commercial airliners
within the United States—and using them as guided missiles—was not recognized by NORAD before 9/11.[98]

Notwithstanding the identification of these emerging
threats, by 9/11 there were only seven alert sites left in the
United States, each with two fighter aircraft on alert. This
led some NORAD commanders to worry that NORAD was
not postured adequately to protect the United States.[99]

In the United States, NORAD is divided into three sectors. On 9/11, all the hijacked aircraft were in NORAD's
Northeast Air Defense Sector (also known as NEADS),
which is based in Rome, New York. That morning NEADS
could call on two alert sites, each with one pair of ready
fighters: Otis Air National Guard Base in Cape Cod, Massachusetts, and Langley Air Force Base in Hampton, Virginia.[100] Other facilities, not on "alert," would need time to
arm the fighters and organize crews.

NEADS reported to the Continental U.S. NORAD Region (CONR) headquarters, in Panama City, Florida, which
in turn reported to NORAD headquarters, in Colorado
Springs, Colorado.

Interagency Collaboration.
The FAA and NORAD had developed protocols for working
together in the event of a hijacking. As they existed on 9/11,
the protocols for the FAA to obtain military assistance from
NORAD required multiple levels of notification and approval at the highest levels of government.[101]

FAA guidance to controllers on hijack procedures assumed that the aircraft pilot would notify the controller via

radio or by "squawking" a transponder code of "7500"—the universal code for a hijack in progress. Controllers would notify their supervisors, who in turn would inform management all the way up to FAA headquarters in Washington. Headquarters had a hijack coordinator, who was the director of the FAA Office of Civil Aviation Security or his or her designate.[102]

If a hijack was confirmed, procedures called for the hijack coordinator on duty to contact the Pentagon's National Military Command Center (NMCC) and to ask for a military escort aircraft to follow the flight, report anything unusual, and aid search and rescue in the event of an emergency. The NMCC would then seek approval from the Office of the Secretary of Defense to provide military assistance. If approval was given, the orders would be transmitted down NORAD's chain of command.[103]

The NMCC would keep the FAA hijack coordinator up to date and help the FAA centers coordinate directly with the military. NORAD would receive tracking information for the hijacked aircraft either from joint use radar or from the relevant FAA air traffic control facility. Every attempt would be made to have the hijacked aircraft squawk 7500 to help NORAD track it.[104]

The protocols did not contemplate an intercept. They assumed the fighter escort would be discreet, "vectored to a position five miles directly behind the hijacked aircraft," where it could perform its mission to monitor the aircraft's flight path.[105]

In sum, the protocols in place on 9/11 for the FAA and NORAD to respond to a hijacking presumed that

- the hijacked aircraft would be readily identifiable and would not attempt to disappear;
- there would be time to address the problem through the appropriate FAA and NORAD chains of command; and
- the hijacking would take the traditional form: that is, it would not be a suicide hijacking designed to convert the aircraft into a guided missile.

On the morning of 9/11, the existing protocol was unsuited in every respect for what was about to happen.

American Airlines Flight 11
FAA Awareness.

Although the Boston Center air traffic controller realized at an early stage that there was something wrong with American 11, he did not immediately interpret the plane's failure to respond as a sign that it had been hijacked. At 8:14, when the flight failed to heed his instruction to climb to 35,000 feet, the controller repeatedly tried to raise the flight. He reached out to the pilot on the emergency frequency. Though there was no response, he kept trying to contact the aircraft.[106]

At 8:21, American 11 turned off its transponder, immediately degrading the information available about the aircraft. The controller told his supervisor that he thought something was seriously wrong with the plane, although neither suspected a hijacking. The supervisor instructed the controller to follow standard procedures for handling a "no radio" aircraft.[107]

The controller checked to see if American Airlines could establish communication with American 11. He became even more concerned as its route changed, moving into another sector's airspace. Controllers immediately began to move aircraft out of its path, and asked other aircraft in the vicinity to look for American 11.[108]

At 8:24:38, the following transmission came from American 11:

> AMERICAN 11: We have some planes. Just stay quiet, and you'll be okay. We are returning to the airport.

The controller only heard something unintelligible; he did not hear the specific words "we have some planes." The next transmission came seconds later:

> AMERICAN 11: Nobody move. Everything will be okay. If you try to make any moves, you'll endanger yourself and the airplane. Just stay quiet.[109]

The controller told us that he then knew it was a hijacking. He alerted his supervisor, who assigned another controller to assist him. He redoubled his efforts to ascertain the flight's altitude. Because the controller didn't understand the initial transmission, the manager of Boston Center instructed his quality assurance specialist to "pull the tape" of the radio transmission, listen to it closely, and report back.[110]

Between 8:25 and 8:32, in accordance with the FAA protocol, Boston Center managers started notifying their chain of command that American 11 had been hijacked. At 8:28, Boston Center called the Command Center in Herndon to advise that it believed American 11 had been hijacked and was heading toward New York Center's airspace.

By this time, American 11 had taken a dramatic turn to the south. At 8:32, the Command Center passed word of a possible hijacking to the Operations Center at FAA headquarters. The duty officer replied that security personnel at headquarters had just begun discussing the apparent hijack on a conference call with the New England regional office. FAA headquarters began to follow the hijack protocol but did not contact the NMCC to request a fighter escort.[111]

The Herndon Command Center immediately established a teleconference between Boston, New York, and Cleveland Centers so that Boston Center could help the others understand what was happening.[112]

At 8:34, the Boston Center controller received a third transmission from American 11:

> AMERICAN 11: Nobody move please. We are going back to the airport. Don't try to make any stupid moves.[113]

In the succeeding minutes, controllers were attempting to ascertain the altitude of the southbound flight.[114]

Military Notification and Response.

Boston Center did not follow the protocol in seeking military assistance through the prescribed chain of command. In addition to notifications within the FAA, Boston Center took the initiative, at 8:34, to contact the military through the FAA's Cape Cod facility. The center also tried to contact a former alert site in Atlantic City, unaware it had been phased out. At 8:37:52, Boston Center reached NEADS. This was the first notification received by the military—at any level—that American 11 had been hijacked:[115]

> FAA: Hi. Boston Center TMU [Traffic Management Unit], we have a problem here. We have a hijacked aircraft headed towards New York, and we need you guys to, we need someone to scramble some F-16s or something up there, help us out.
>
> NEADS: Is this real-world or exercise?
>
> FAA: No, this is not an exercise, not a test.[116]

NEADS ordered to battle stations the two F-15 alert aircraft at Otis Air Force Base in Falmouth, Massachusetts, 153 miles away from New York City. The air defense of America began with this call.[117]

At NEADS, the report of the hijacking was relayed immediately to Battle Commander Colonel Robert Marr. After ordering the Otis fighters to battle stations, Colonel Marr phoned Major General Larry Arnold, commanding general of the First Air Force and NORAD's Continental Region. Marr sought authorization to scramble the Otis fighters. General Arnold later recalled instructing Marr to "go ahead and scramble them, and we'll get authorities later." General Arnold then called NORAD headquarters to report.[118]

F-15 fighters were scrambled at 8:46 from Otis Air Force Base. But NEADS did not know where to send the alert fighter aircraft, and the officer directing the fighters pressed for more information: "I don't know where I'm scrambling these guys to. I need a direction, a destination." Because the hijackers had turned off the plane's transponder, NEADS personnel spent the next minutes searching their radar scopes for the primary radar return. American 11 struck the

North Tower at 8:46. Shortly after 8:50, while NEADS personnel were still trying to locate the flight, word reached them that a plane had hit the World Trade Center.[119]

Radar data show the Otis fighters were airborne at 8:53. Lacking a target, they were vectored toward military-controlled airspace off the Long Island coast. To avoid New York area air traffic and uncertain about what to do, the fighters were brought down to military airspace to "hold as needed." From 9:09 to 9:13, the Otis fighters stayed in this holding pattern.[120]

In summary, NEADS received notice of the hijacking nine minutes before it struck the North Tower. That nine minutes' notice before impact was the most the military would receive of any of the four hijackings.[121]

United Airlines Flight 175
FAA Awareness.
One of the last transmissions from United Airlines Flight 175 is, in retrospect, chilling. By 8:40, controllers at the FAA's New York Center were seeking information on American 11. At approximately 8:42, shortly after entering New York Center's airspace, the pilot of United 175 broke in with the following transmission:

UAL 175: New York UAL 175 heavy.

FAA: UAL 175 go ahead.

UAL 175: Yeah. We figured we'd wait to go to your center. Ah, we heard a suspicious transmission on our departure out of Boston, ah, with someone, ah, it sounded like someone keyed the mikes and said ah everyone ah stay in your seats.

FAA: Oh, okay. I'll pass that along over here.[122]

Minutes later, United 175 turned southwest without clearance from air traffic control. At 8:47, seconds after the impact of American 11, United 175's transponder code changed, and then changed again. These changes were not noticed for several minutes, however, because the same New York Center controller was assigned to both American 11 and United 175. The controller knew American 11 was hijacked; he was focused on searching for it after the aircraft disappeared at 8:46.[123]

At 8:48, while the controller was still trying to locate American 11, a New York Center manager provided the following report on a Command Center teleconference about American 11:

> MANAGER, NEW YORK CENTER: Okay. This is New York Center. We're watching the airplane. I also had conversation with American Airlines, and they've told us that they believe that one of their stewardesses was stabbed and that there are people in the cockpit that have control of the aircraft, and that's all the information they have right now.[124]

The New York Center controller and manager were unaware that American 11 had already crashed.

At 8:51, the controller noticed the transponder change from United 175 and tried to contact the aircraft. There was no response. Beginning at 8:52, the controller made repeated attempts to reach the crew of United 175. Still no response. The controller checked his radio equipment and contacted another controller at 8:53, saying that "we may have a hijack" and that he could not find the aircraft.[125]

Another commercial aircraft in the vicinity then radioed in with "reports over the radio of a commuter plane hitting the World Trade Center." The controller spent the next several minutes handing off the other flights on his scope to other controllers and moving aircraft out of the way of the unidentified aircraft (believed to be United 175) as it moved southwest and then turned northeast toward New York City.[126]

At about 8:55, the controller in charge notified a New York Center manager that she believed United 175 had also been hijacked. The manager tried to notify the regional managers and was told that they were discussing a hijacked aircraft (presumably American 11) and refused to be disturbed. At 8:58, the New York Center controller searching for United 175 told another New York controller "we might have a hijack over here, two of them."[127]

Between 9:01 and 9:02, a manager from New York Center told the Command Center in Herndon:

> MANAGER, NEW YORK CENTER: We have several situations going on here. It's escalating big, big time. We need to get the military involved with us. . . . We're, we're involved with something else, we have other aircraft that may have a similar situation going on here.[128]

The "other aircraft" referred to by New York Center was United 175. Evidence indicates that this conversation was the only notice received by either FAA headquarters or the Herndon Command Center prior to the second crash that there had been a second hijacking.

While the Command Center was told about this "other aircraft" at 9:01, New York Center contacted New York terminal approach control and asked for help in locating United 175.

> TERMINAL: I got somebody who keeps coasting but it looks like he's going into one of the small airports down there.

> CENTER: Hold on a second. I'm trying to bring him up here and get you—There he is right there. Hold on.

> TERMINAL: Got him just out of 9,500–9,000 now.

> CENTER: Do you know who he is?

> TERMINAL: We're just, we just we don't know who he is. We're just picking him up now.

> CENTER (AT 9:02): Alright. Heads up man, it looks like another one coming in.[129]

The controllers observed the plane in a rapid descent; the radar data terminated over Lower Manhattan. At 9:03, United 175 crashed into the South Tower.[130]

Meanwhile, a manager from Boston Center reported that they had deciphered what they had heard in one of the first hijacker transmissions from American 11:

BOSTON CENTER: Hey . . . you still there?

NEW ENGLAND REGION: Yes, I am.

BOSTON CENTER: . . . as far as the tape, Bobby seemed to think the guy said that "we have planes." Now, I don't know if it was because it was the accent, or if there's more than one, but I'm gonna, I'm gonna reconfirm that for you, and I'll get back to you real quick. Okay?

NEW ENGLAND REGION: Appreciate it.

UNIDENTIFIED FEMALE VOICE: They have what?

BOSTON CENTER: Planes, as in plural.

BOSTON CENTER: It sounds like, we're talking to New York, that there's another one aimed at the World Trade Center.

NEW ENGLAND REGION: There's another aircraft?

BOSTON CENTER: A second one just hit the Trade Center.

NEW ENGLAND REGION: Okay. Yeah, we gotta get—we gotta alert the military real quick on this.[131]

Boston Center immediately advised the New England Region that it was going to stop all departures at airports under its control. At 9:05, Boston Center confirmed for both the FAA Command Center and the New England Region that the hijackers aboard American 11 said "we have *planes.*" At the same time, New York Center declared "ATC zero"—meaning that aircraft were not permitted to depart from, arrive at, or travel through New York Center's airspace until further notice.[132]

Within minutes of the second impact, Boston Center instructed its controllers to inform all aircraft in its airspace of the events in New York and to advise aircraft to heighten cockpit security. Boston Center asked the Herndon Command Center to issue a similar cockpit security alert nationwide. We have found no evidence to suggest that the Command Center acted on this request or issued any type of cockpit security alert.[133]

Military Notification and Response.

The first indication that the NORAD air defenders had of the second hijacked aircraft, United 175, came in a phone call from New York Center to NEADS at 9:03. The notice came at about the time the plane was hitting the South Tower.[134]

By 9:08, the mission crew commander at NEADS learned of the second explosion at the World Trade Center and decided against holding the fighters in military airspace away from Manhattan:

MISSION CREW COMMANDER, NEADS: This is what I foresee that we probably need to do. We need to talk to FAA. We need to tell 'em if this stuff is gonna keep on going, we need to take those fighters, put 'em over Manhattan. That's best thing, that's the best play right now. So coordinate with the FAA. Tell 'em if there's more out there, which we don't know, let's get 'em over Manhattan. At least we got some kind of play.[135]

The FAA cleared the airspace. Radar data show that at 9:13, when the Otis fighters were about 115 miles away from the city, the fighters exited their holding pattern and set a course direct for Manhattan. They arrived at 9:25 and established a combat air patrol (CAP) over the city.[136]

Because the Otis fighters had expended a great deal of

fuel in flying first to military airspace and then to New York, the battle commanders were concerned about refueling. NEADS considered scrambling alert fighters from Langley Air Force Base in Virginia to New York, to provide backup. The Langley fighters were placed on battle stations at 9:09.[137] NORAD had no indication that any other plane had been hijacked.

American Airlines Flight 77
FAA Awareness.
American 77 began deviating from its flight plan at 8:54, with a slight turn toward the south. Two minutes later, it disappeared completely from radar at Indianapolis Center, which was controlling the flight.[138]

The controller tracking American 77 told us he noticed the aircraft turning to the southwest, and then saw the data disappear. The controller looked for primary radar returns. He searched along the plane's projected flight path and the airspace to the southwest where it had started to turn. No primary targets appeared. He tried the radios, first calling the aircraft directly, then the airline. Again there was nothing. At this point, the Indianapolis controller had no knowledge of the situation in New York. He did not know that other aircraft had been hijacked. He believed American 77 had experienced serious electrical or mechanical failure, or both, and was gone.[139]

Shortly after 9:00, Indianapolis Center started notifying other agencies that American 77 was missing and had possibly crashed. At 9:08, Indianapolis Center asked Air Force Search and Rescue at Langley Air Force Base to look for a downed aircraft. The center also contacted the West Virginia State Police and asked whether any reports of a downed aircraft had been received. At 9:09, it reported the loss of contact to the FAA regional center, which passed this information to FAA headquarters at 9:24.[140]

By 9:20, Indianapolis Center learned that there were other hijacked aircraft, and began to doubt its initial assumption that American 77 had crashed. A discussion of this con-

cern between the manager at Indianapolis and the Command
Center in Herndon prompted it to notify some FAA field facilities that American 77 was lost. By 9:21, the Command
Center, some FAA field facilities, and American Airlines
had started to search for American 77. They feared it had
been hijacked. At 9:25, the Command Center advised FAA
headquarters of the situation.[141]

The failure to find a primary radar return for American
77 led us to investigate this issue further. Radar reconstruc-
tions performed after 9/11 reveal that FAA radar equipment
tracked the flight from the moment its transponder was
turned off at 8:56. But for 8 minutes and 13 seconds, between 8:56 and 9:05, this primary radar information on
American 77 was not displayed to controllers at Indianapolis Center.[142] The reasons are technical, arising from the
way the software processed radar information, as well as
from poor primary radar coverage where American 77 was
flying.

According to the radar reconstruction, American 77
reemerged as a primary target on Indianapolis Center radar
scopes at 9:05, east of its last known position. The target remained in Indianapolis Center's airspace for another six
minutes, then crossed into the western portion of Washington Center's airspace at 9:10. As Indianapolis Center continued searching for the aircraft, two managers and the
controller responsible for American 77 looked to the west
and southwest along the flight's projected path, not east—
where the aircraft was now heading. Managers did not instruct other controllers at Indianapolis Center to turn on
their primary radar coverage to join in the search for American 77.[143]

In sum, Indianapolis Center never saw Flight 77 turn
around. By the time it reappeared in primary radar coverage,
controllers had either stopped looking for the aircraft because they thought it had crashed or were looking toward the
west. Although the Command Center learned Flight 77 was
missing, neither it nor FAA headquarters issued an all points
bulletin to surrounding centers to search for primary radar

targets. American 77 traveled undetected for 36 minutes on a course heading due east for Washington, D.C.[144]

By 9:25, FAA's Herndon Command Center and FAA headquarters knew two aircraft had crashed into the World Trade Center. They knew American 77 was lost. At least some FAA officials in Boston Center and the New England Region knew that a hijacker on board American 11 had said "we have some planes." Concerns over the safety of other aircraft began to mount. A manager at the Herndon Command Center asked FAA headquarters if they wanted to order a "nationwide ground stop." While this was being discussed by executives at FAA headquarters, the Command Center ordered one at 9:25.[145]

The Command Center kept looking for American 77. At 9:21, it advised the Dulles terminal control facility, and Dulles urged its controllers to look for primary targets. At 9:32, they found one. Several of the Dulles controllers "observed a primary radar target tracking eastbound at a high rate of speed" and notified Reagan National Airport. FAA personnel at both Reagan National and Dulles airports notified the Secret Service. The aircraft's identity or type was unknown.[146]

Reagan National controllers then vectored an unarmed National Guard C-130H cargo aircraft, which had just taken off en route to Minnesota, to identify and follow the suspicious aircraft. The C-130H pilot spotted it, identified it as a Boeing 757, attempted to follow its path, and at 9:38, seconds after impact, reported to the control tower: "looks like that aircraft crashed into the Pentagon sir."[147]

Military Notification and Response.

NORAD heard nothing about the search for American 77. Instead, the NEADS air defenders heard renewed reports about a plane that no longer existed: American 11.

At 9:21, NEADS received a report from the FAA:

FAA: Military, Boston Center. I just had a report that American 11 is still in the air, and it's on its way towards—heading towards Washington.

NEADS: Okay. American 11 is still in the air?

FAA: Yes.

NEADS: On its way towards Washington?

FAA: That was another—it was evidently another aircraft that hit the tower. That's the latest report we have.

NEADS: Okay.

FAA: I'm going to try to confirm an ID for you, but I would assume he's somewhere over, uh, either New Jersey or somewhere further south.

NEADS: Okay. So American 11 isn't the hijack at all then, right?

FAA: No, he is a hijack.

NEADS: He—American 11 is a hijack?

FAA: Yes.

NEADS: And he's heading into Washington?

FAA: Yes. This could be a third aircraft.[148]

The mention of a "third aircraft" was not a reference to American 77. There was confusion at that moment in the FAA. Two planes had struck the World Trade Center, and Boston Center had heard from FAA headquarters in Washington that American 11 was still airborne. We have been unable to identify the source of this mistaken FAA information.

The NEADS technician who took this call from the FAA immediately passed the word to the mission crew commander, who reported to the NEADS battle commander:

Mission Crew Commander, NEADS: Okay, uh, American Airlines is still airborne. Eleven, the first guy, he's heading towards Washington. Okay? I think we need to scramble Langley right now. And I'm gonna take the fighters from Otis, try to chase this guy down if I can find him.[149]

After consulting with NEADS command, the crew commander issued the order at 9:23: "Okay . . . scramble Langley. Head them towards the Washington area. . . . [I]f they're there then we'll run on them. . . . These guys are smart." That order was processed and transmitted to Langley Air Force Base at 9:24. Radar data show the Langley fighters airborne at 9:30. NEADS decided to keep the Otis fighters over New York. The heading of the Langley fighters was adjusted to send them to the Baltimore area. The mission crew commander explained to us that the purpose was to position the Langley fighters between the reported southbound American 11 and the nation's capital.[150]

At the suggestion of the Boston Center's military liaison, NEADS contacted the FAA's Washington Center to ask about American 11. In the course of the conversation, a Washington Center manager informed NEADS: "We're looking—we also lost American 77." The time was 9:34.[151] This was the first notice to the military that American 77 was missing, and it had come by chance. If NEADS had not placed that call, the NEADS air defenders would have received no information whatsoever that the flight was even missing, although the FAA had been searching for it. No one at FAA headquarters ever asked for military assistance with American 77.

At 9:36, the FAA's Boston Center called NEADS and relayed the discovery about an unidentified aircraft closing in on Washington: "Latest report. Aircraft VFR [visual flight rules] six miles southeast of the White House. . . . Six, southwest. Six, southwest of the White House, deviating away." This startling news prompted the mission crew commander at NEADS to take immediate control of the airspace to clear a flight path for the Langley fighters: "Okay, we're going to turn it . . . crank it up. . . . Run them to the White House." He then discovered, to his surprise, that the Langley fighters were not headed north toward the Baltimore area as instructed, but east over the ocean. "I don't care how many windows you break," he said. "Damn it. . . . Okay. Push them back."[152]

The Langley fighters were heading east, not north, for three reasons. First, unlike a normal scramble order, this order did not include a distance to the target or the target's location. Second, a "generic" flight plan—prepared to get the aircraft airborne and out of local airspace quickly—incorrectly led the Langley fighters to believe they were ordered to fly due east (090) for 60 miles. Third, the lead pilot and local FAA controller incorrectly assumed the flight plan instruction to go "090 for 60" superseded the original scramble order.[153]

After the 9:36 call to NEADS about the unidentified aircraft a few miles from the White House, the Langley fighters were ordered to Washington, D.C. Controllers at NEADS located an unknown primary radar track, but "it kind of faded" over Washington. The time was 9:38. The Pentagon had been struck by American 77 at 9:37:46. The Langley fighters were about 150 miles away.[154]

Right after the Pentagon was hit, NEADS learned of another possible hijacked aircraft. It was an aircraft that in fact had not been hijacked at all. After the second World Trade Center crash, Boston Center managers recognized that both aircraft were transcontinental 767 jetliners that had departed Logan Airport. Remembering the "we have some planes" remark, Boston Center guessed that Delta 1989 might also be hijacked. Boston Center called NEADS at 9:41 and identified Delta 1989, a 767 jet that had left Logan Airport for Las Vegas, as a possible hijack. NEADS warned the FAA's Cleveland Center to watch Delta 1989. The Command Center and FAA headquarters watched it too. During the course of the morning, there were multiple erroneous reports of hijacked aircraft. The report of American 11 heading south was the first; Delta 1989 was the second.[155]

NEADS never lost track of Delta 1989, and even ordered fighter aircraft from Ohio and Michigan to intercept it. The flight never turned off its transponder. NEADS soon learned that the aircraft was not hijacked, and tracked Delta 1989 as it reversed course over Toledo, headed east, and landed in Cleveland.[156] But another aircraft was heading toward Washington, an aircraft about which NORAD had heard nothing: United 93.

United Airlines Flight 93
FAA Awareness.

At 9:27, after having been in the air for 45 minutes, United 93 acknowledged a transmission from the Cleveland Center controller. This was the last normal contact the FAA had with the flight.[157]

Less than a minute later, the Cleveland controller and the pilots of aircraft in the vicinity heard "a radio transmission of unintelligible sounds of possible screaming or a struggle from an unknown origin."[158]

The controller responded, seconds later: "Somebody call Cleveland?" This was followed by a second radio transmission, with sounds of screaming. The Cleveland Center controllers began to try to identify the possible source of the transmissions, and noticed that United 93 had descended some 700 feet. The controller attempted again to raise United 93 several times, with no response. At 9:30, the controller began to poll the other flights on his frequency to determine if they had heard the screaming; several said they had.[159]

At 9:32, a third radio transmission came over the frequency: "Keep remaining sitting. We have a bomb on board." The controller understood, but chose to respond: "Calling Cleveland Center, you're unreadable. Say again, slowly." He notified his supervisor, who passed the notice up the chain of command. By 9:34, word of the hijacking had reached FAA headquarters.[160]

FAA headquarters had by this time established an open line of communication with the Command Center at Hern-

don and instructed it to poll all its centers about suspect aircraft. The Command Center executed the request and, a
minute later, Cleveland Center reported that "United 93 may
have a bomb on board." At 9:34, the Command Center relayed the information concerning United 93 to FAA headquarters. At approximately 9:36, Cleveland advised the
Command Center that it was still tracking United 93 and
specifically inquired whether someone had requested the
military to launch fighter aircraft to intercept the aircraft.
Cleveland even told the Command Center it was prepared to
contact a nearby military base to make the request. The
Command Center told Cleveland that FAA personnel well
above them in the chain of command had to make the decision to seek military assistance and were working on the issue.[161]

Between 9:34 and 9:38, the Cleveland controller observed United 93 climbing to 40,700 feet and immediately
moved several aircraft out its way. The controller continued
to try to contact United 93, and asked whether the pilot
could confirm that he had been hijacked.[162] There was no response.

Then, at 9:39, a fourth radio transmission was heard from
United 93:

> ZIAD JARRAH: Uh, this is the captain. Would like you all
> to remain seated. There is a bomb on board and are going
> back to the airport, and to have our demands [unintelligi-
> ble]. Please remain quiet.

The controller responded: "United 93, understand you
have a bomb on board. Go ahead." The flight did not respond.[163]

From 9:34 to 10:08, a Command Center facility manager
provided frequent updates to Acting Deputy Administrator
Monte Belger and other executives at FAA headquarters as
United 93 headed toward Washington, D.C. At 9:41, Cleveland Center lost United 93's transponder signal. The controller located it on primary radar, matched its position with

visual sightings from other aircraft, and tracked the flight as it turned east, then south.[164]

At 9:42, the Command Center learned from news reports that a plane had struck the Pentagon. The Command Center's national operations manager, Ben Sliney, ordered all FAA facilities to instruct all aircraft to land at the nearest airport. This was an unprecedented order. The air traffic control system handled it with great skill, as about 4,500 commercial and general aviation aircraft soon landed without incident.[165]

At 9:46 the Command Center updated FAA headquarters that United 93 was now "twenty-nine minutes out of Washington, D.C."

At 9:49, 13 minutes after Cleveland Center had asked about getting military help, the Command Center suggested that someone at headquarters should decide whether to request military assistance:

> FAA HEADQUARTERS: They're pulling Jeff away to go talk about United 93.
>
> COMMAND CENTER: Uh, do we want to think, uh, about scrambling aircraft?
>
> FAA HEADQUARTERS: Oh, God, I don't know.
>
> COMMAND CENTER: Uh, that's a decision somebody's gonna have to make probably in the next ten minutes.
>
> FAA HEADQUARTERS: Uh, ya know everybody just left the room.[166]

At 9:53, FAA headquarters informed the Command Center that the deputy director for air traffic services was talking to Monte Belger about scrambling aircraft. Then the Command Center informed headquarters that controllers had lost track of United 93 over the Pittsburgh area. Within seconds, the Command Center received a visual report from another aircraft, and informed headquarters that the aircraft was 20 miles northwest of Johnstown. United 93 was spotted by another aircraft, and, at 10:01, the Command Center advised FAA headquarters that one of the aircraft had seen United 93 "waving his wings." The aircraft had witnessed the hijackers' efforts to defeat the passengers' counterattack.[167]

United 93 crashed in Pennsylvania at 10:03:11, 125 miles from Washington, D.C. The precise crash time has been the subject of some dispute. The 10:03:11 impact time is supported by previous National Transportation Safety Board analysis and by evidence from the Commission staff's analysis of radar, the flight data recorder, the cockpit voice recorder, infrared satellite data, and air traffic control transmissions.[168]

Five minutes later, the Command Center forwarded this update to headquarters:

COMMAND CENTER: O.K. Uh, there is now on that United 93.

FAA HEADQUARTERS: Yes.

COMMAND CENTER: There is a report of black smoke in the last position I gave you, fifteen miles south of Johnstown.

FAA HEADQUARTERS: From the airplane or from the ground?

COMMAND CENTER: Uh, they're speculating it's from the aircraft.

FAA HEADQUARTERS: Okay.

COMMAND CENTER: Uh, who, it hit the ground. That's what they're speculating, that's speculation only.[169]

The aircraft that spotted the "black smoke" was the same unarmed Air National Guard cargo plane that had seen American 77 crash into the Pentagon 27 minutes earlier. It had resumed its flight to Minnesota and saw the smoke from the crash of United 93, less than two minutes after the plane went down. At 10:17, the Command Center advised headquarters of its conclusion that United 93 had indeed crashed.[170]

Despite the discussions about military assistance, no one from FAA headquarters requested military assistance regarding United 93. Nor did any manager at FAA headquarters pass any of the information it had about United 93 to the military.

Military Notification and Response.

NEADS first received a call about United 93 from the military liaison at Cleveland Center at 10:07. Unaware that the aircraft had already crashed, Cleveland passed to NEADS the aircraft's last known latitude and longitude. NEADS was never able to locate United 93 on radar because it was already in the ground.[171]

At the same time, the NEADS mission crew commander was dealing with the arrival of the Langley fighters over Washington, D.C., sorting out what their orders were with respect to potential targets. Shortly after 10:10, and having no knowledge either that United 93 had been heading toward Washington or that it had crashed, he explicitly instructed the Langley fighters: "negative—negative clearance to shoot" aircraft over the nation's capital.[172]

The news of a reported bomb on board United 93 spread quickly at NEADS. The air defenders searched for United 93's primary radar return and tried to locate other fighters to scramble. NEADS called Washington Center to report:

NEADS: I also want to give you a heads-up, Washington.

FAA (DC): Go ahead.

NEADS: United nine three, have you got information on that yet?

FAA: Yeah, he's down.

NEADS: He's down?

FAA: Yes.

NEADS: When did he land? 'Cause we have got confirmation—

FAA: He did not land.

NEADS: Oh, he's down? Down?

FAA: Yes. Somewhere up northeast of Camp David.

NEADS: Northeast of Camp David.

FAA: That's the last report. They don't know exactly where.[173]

The time of notification of the crash of United 93 was 10:15.[174] The NEADS air defenders never located the flight or followed it on their radar scopes. The flight had already crashed by the time they learned it was hijacked.

Clarifying the Record

The defense of U.S. airspace on 9/11 was not conducted in accord with preexisting training and protocols. It was improvised by civilians who had never handled a hijacked aircraft that attempted to disappear, and by a military unprepared for the transformation of commercial aircraft into weapons of mass destruction. As it turned out, the NEADS air defenders had nine minutes' notice on the first hijacked plane, no advance notice on the second, no advance notice on the third, and no advance notice on the fourth.

We do not believe that the true picture of that morning reflects discredit on the operational personnel at NEADS or FAA facilities. NEADS commanders and officers actively sought out information, and made the best judgments they could on the basis of what they knew. Individual FAA controllers, facility managers, and Command Center managers thought outside the box in recommending a nationwide alert, in ground-stopping local traffic, and, ultimately, in deciding to land all aircraft and executing that unprecedented order flawlessly.

More than the actual events, inaccurate government accounts of those events made it appear that the military was notified in time to respond to two of the hijackings, raising questions about the adequacy of the response. Those accounts had the effect of deflecting questions about the military's capacity to obtain timely and accurate information from its own sources. In addition, they overstated the FAA's ability to provide the military with timely and useful information that morning.

In public testimony before this Commission in May 2003, NORAD officials stated that at 9:16, NEADS received hijack notification of United 93 from the FAA.[175] This statement was incorrect. There was no hijack to report at 9:16. United 93 was proceeding normally at that time.

In this same public testimony, NORAD officials stated that at 9:24, NEADS received notification of the hijacking of American 77.[176] This statement was also incorrect. The notice NEADS received at 9:24 was that American 11 had not hit the World Trade Center and was heading for Washington, D.C.[177]

In their testimony and in other public accounts, NORAD officials also stated that the Langley fighters were scrambled to respond to the notifications about American 77,[178] United 93, or both. These statements were incorrect as well. The fighters were scrambled because of the report that American 11 was heading south, as is clear not just from taped conversations at NEADS but also from taped conversations at FAA centers; contemporaneous logs compiled at NEADS, Continental Region headquarters, and NORAD; and other records. Yet this response to a phantom aircraft was not recounted in a single public timeline or statement issued by

American Airline Flight 11 (AA 11)
Boston to Los Angeles

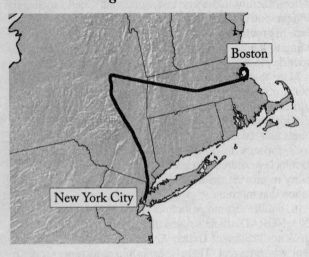

7:59	Takeoff
8:14	Last routine radio communication; likely takeover
8:19	Flight attendant notifies AA of hijacking
8:21	Transponder is turned off
8:23	AA attempts to contact the cockpit
8:25	Boston Center aware of hijacking
8:38	Boston Center notifies NEADS of hijacking
8:46	NEADS scrambles Otis fighter jets in search of AA 11
8:46:40	AA 11 crashes into 1 WTC (North Tower)
8:53	Otis fighter jets airborne
9:16	AA headquarters aware that Flight 11 has crashed into WTC
9:21	Boston Center advises NEADS that AA 11 is airborne heading for Washington
9:24	NEADS scrambles Langley fighter jets in search of AA 11

United Airline Flight 175 (UA 175)
Boston to Los Angeles

8:14	Takeoff
8:42	Last routine radio communication
8:42-8:46	Likely takeover
8:47	Transponder code chages
8:52	Flight attendant notifies UA of hijacking
8:54	UA attempts to contact the cockpit
8:55	New York Center suspects hijacking
9:03:11	Flight 175 crashes into 2 WTC (South Tower)
9:15	New York Center advises NEADS that UA 175 was the second aircraft crashed into WTC
9:20	UA headquarters aware that Flight 175 had crashed into WTC

American Airline Flight 77 (AA 77)
Washington D.C., to Los Angeles

8:20	Takeoff
8:51	Last routine radio communication
8:51-8:54	Likely takeover
8:54	Flight 77 makes unauthorized turn to south
8:56	Transponder is turned off
9:05	AA headquarters aware that Flight 77 is hijacked
9:25	Herndon Command Center orders nationwide ground stop
9:32	Dulles tower observes radar of fast-moving aircraft (later identified as AA 77)
9:34	FAA advises NEADS that AA 77 is missing
9:37:46	AA 77 crashes into the Pentagon
10:30	AA headquarters confirms Flight AA crash into Pentagon

United Airline Flight 93 (UA 93)
Newark to San Francisco

8:42	Takeoff
9:24	Flight 93 receives warning from UA about possible cockpit intrusion
9:27	Last routine radio communication
9:28	Likely takeover
9:34	Herndon Command Center advises FAA headquarters that UA 93 is hijacked
9:36	Flight attendant notifies UA of hijacking; UA attempts to contact the cockpit
9:41	Transponder is turned off
9:57	Passenger revolt begins
10:03:11	Flight 93 crashes in field in Shanksville, PA
10:07	Cleveland Center advises NEADS of UA 93 hijacking
10:15	UA headquarters aware that Flight 93 has crashed in PA; Washington Center advises NEADS that Flight 93 has crashed in PA

the FAA or Department of Defense. The inaccurate accounts
created the impression that the Langley scramble was a logical response to an actual hijacked aircraft.

In fact, not only was the scramble prompted by the mistaken information about American 11, but NEADS never received notice that American 77 was hijacked. It was notified
at 9:34 that American 77 was lost. Then, minutes later,
NEADS was told that an unknown plane was 6 miles southwest of the White House. Only then did the already scrambled airplanes start moving directly toward Washington, D.C.

Thus the military did not have 14 minutes to respond to
American 77, as testimony to the Commission in May 2003
suggested. It had at most one or two minutes to react to the
unidentified plane approaching Washington, and the fighters
were in the wrong place to be able to help. They had been responding to a report about an aircraft that did not exist.

Nor did the military have 47 minutes to respond to United
93, as would be implied by the account that it received notice of the flight's hijacking at 9:16. By the time the military
learned about the flight, it had crashed.

We now turn to the role of national leadership in the
events that morning.

1.3 NATIONAL CRISIS MANAGEMENT

When American 11 struck the World Trade Center at 8:46,
no one in the White House or traveling with the President
knew that it had been hijacked. While that information circulated within the FAA, we found no evidence that the hijacking was reported to any other agency in Washington
before 8:46.[179]

Most federal agencies learned about the crash in New
York from CNN.[180] Within the FAA, the administrator, Jane
Garvey, and her acting deputy, Monte Belger, had not been
told of a confirmed hijacking before they learned from television that a plane had crashed.[181] Others in the agency were
aware of it, as we explained earlier in this chapter.

Inside the National Military Command Center, the deputy director of operations and his assistant began notifying senior Pentagon officials of the incident. At about 9:00, the senior NMCC operations officer reached out to the FAA operations center for information. Although the NMCC was advised of the hijacking of American 11, the scrambling of jets was not discussed.[182]

In Sarasota, Florida, the presidential motorcade was arriving at the Emma E. Booker Elementary School, where President Bush was to read to a class and talk about education. White House Chief of Staff Andrew Card told us he was standing with the President outside the classroom when Senior Advisor to the President Karl Rove first informed them that a small, twin-engine plane had crashed into the World Trade Center. The President's reaction was that the incident must have been caused by pilot error.[183]

At 8:55, before entering the classroom, the President spoke to National Security Advisor Condoleezza Rice, who was at the White House. She recalled first telling the President it was a twin-engine aircraft—and then a commercial aircraft—that had struck the World Trade Center, adding "that's all we know right now, Mr. President."[184]

At the White House, Vice President Dick Cheney had just sat down for a meeting when his assistant told him to turn on his television because a plane had struck the North Tower of the World Trade Center. The Vice President was wondering "how the hell could a plane hit the World Trade Center" when he saw the second aircraft strike the South Tower.[185]

Elsewhere in the White House, a series of 9:00 meetings was about to begin. In the absence of information that the crash was anything other than an accident, the White House staff monitored the news as they went ahead with their regular schedules.[186]

The Agencies Confer

When they learned a second plane had struck the World Trade Center, nearly everyone in the White House told us, they immediately knew it was not an accident. The Secret

Service initiated a number of security enhancements around the White House complex. The officials who issued these orders did not know that there were additional hijacked aircraft, or that one such aircraft was en route to Washington. These measures were precautionary steps taken because of the strikes in New York.[187]

The FAA and White House Teleconferences.

The FAA, the White House, and the Defense Department each initiated a multiagency teleconference before 9:30. Because none of these teleconferences—at least before 10:00—included the right officials from both the FAA and Defense Department, none succeeded in meaningfully coordinating the military and FAA response to the hijackings.

At about 9:20, security personnel at FAA headquarters set up a hijacking teleconference with several agencies, including the Defense Department. The NMCC officer who participated told us that the call was monitored only periodically because the information was sporadic, it was of little value, and there were other important tasks. The FAA manager of the teleconference also remembered that the military participated only briefly before the Pentagon was hit. Both individuals agreed that the teleconference played no role in coordinating a response to the attacks of 9/11. Acting Deputy Administrator Belger was frustrated to learn later in the morning that the military had not been on the call.[188]

At the White House, the video teleconference was conducted from the Situation Room by Richard Clarke, a special assistant to the president long involved in counterterrorism. Logs indicate that it began at 9:25 and included the CIA; the FBI; the departments of State, Justice, and Defense; the FAA; and the White House shelter. The FAA and CIA joined at 9:40. The first topic addressed in the White House video teleconference—at about 9:40—was the physical security of the President, the White House, and federal agencies. Immediately thereafter it was reported that a plane had hit the Pentagon. We found no evidence that video teleconference participants had any prior information that American 77 had been hijacked and was heading directly toward Washington. Indeed, it is not clear to us that the video teleconference was fully under way before 9:37, when the Pentagon was struck.[189]

Garvey, Belger, and other senior officials from FAA headquarters participated in this video teleconference at various times. We do not know who from Defense participated, but we know that in the first hour none of the personnel involved in managing the crisis did. And none of the information conveyed in the White House video teleconference, at least in the first hour, was being passed to the NMCC. As one witness recalled, "[It] was almost like there were parallel decisionmaking processes going on; one was a voice conference orchestrated by the NMCC . . . and then there was the [White House video teleconference]. . . . [I]n my mind they were competing venues for command and control and decisionmaking."[190]

At 10:03, the conference received reports of more missing aircraft, "2 possibly 3 aloft," and learned of a combat air patrol over Washington. There was discussion of the need for rules of engagement. Clarke reported that they were asking the President for authority to shoot down aircraft. Confirmation of that authority came at 10:25, but the commands were already being conveyed in more direct contacts with the Pentagon.[191]

The Pentagon Teleconferences.

Inside the National Military Command Center, the deputy director for operations immediately thought the second strike was a terrorist attack. The job of the NMCC in such an emergency is to gather the relevant parties and establish the chain of command between the National Command Authority—the president and the secretary of defense—and those who need to carry out their orders.[192]

On the morning of September 11, Secretary Rumsfeld was having breakfast at the Pentagon with a group of members of Congress. He then returned to his office for his daily intelligence briefing. The Secretary was informed of the second strike in New York during the briefing; he resumed the briefing while awaiting more information. After the Pentagon was struck, Secretary Rumsfeld went to the parking lot to assist with rescue efforts.[193]

Inside the NMCC, the deputy director for operations called for an all-purpose "significant event" conference. It began at 9:29, with a brief recap: two aircraft had struck the World Trade Center, there was a confirmed hijacking of American 11, and Otis fighters had been scrambled. The FAA was asked to provide an update, but the line was silent because the FAA had not been added to the call. A minute later, the deputy director stated that it had just been confirmed that American 11 was still airborne and heading toward D.C. He directed the transition to an air threat conference call. NORAD confirmed that American 11 was airborne and heading toward Washington, relaying the erroneous FAA information already mentioned. The call then ended, at about 9:34.[194]

It resumed at 9:37 as an air threat conference call,* which lasted more than eight hours. The President, Vice President, Secretary of Defense, Vice Chairman of the Joint Chiefs of Staff, and Deputy National Security Advisor Stephen Hadley all participated in this teleconference at various times, as did military personnel from the White House underground shelter and the President's military aide on Air Force One.[195]

Operators worked feverishly to include the FAA, but they had equipment problems and difficulty finding secure phone numbers. NORAD asked three times before 10:03 to confirm the presence of the FAA in the teleconference. The FAA representative who finally joined the call at 10:17 had no familiarity with or responsibility for hijackings, no access to decisionmakers, and none of the information available to senior FAA officials.[196]

We found no evidence that, at this critical time, NO-

---

*All times given for this conference call are estimates, which we and the Department of Defense believe to be accurate within a ± 3 minute margin of error.

RAD's top commanders, in Florida or Cheyenne Mountain, coordinated with their counterparts at FAA headquarters to improve awareness and organize a common response. Lower-level officials improvised—for example, the FAA's Boston Center bypassed the chain of command and directly contacted NEADS after the first hijacking. But the highest-level Defense Department officials relied on the NMCC's air threat conference, in which the FAA did not participate for the first 48 minutes.[197]

At 9:39, the NMCC's deputy director for operations, a military officer, opened the call from the Pentagon, which had just been hit. He began: "An air attack against North America may be in progress. NORAD, what's the situation?" NORAD said it had conflicting reports. Its latest information was "of a possible hijacked aircraft taking off out of JFK en route to Washington D.C." The NMCC reported a crash into the mall side of the Pentagon and requested that the Secretary of Defense be added to the conference.[198]

At 9:44, NORAD briefed the conference on the possible hijacking of Delta 1989. Two minutes later, staff reported that they were still trying to locate Secretary Rumsfeld and Vice Chairman Myers. The Vice Chairman joined the conference shortly before 10:00; the Secretary, shortly before 10:30. The Chairman was out of the country.[199]

At 9:48, a representative from the White House shelter asked if there were any indications of another hijacked aircraft. The deputy director for operations mentioned the Delta flight and concluded that "that would be the fourth possible hijack." At 9:49, the commander of NORAD directed all air sovereignty aircraft to battle stations, fully armed.[200]

At 9:59, an Air Force lieutenant colonel working in the White House Military Office joined the conference and stated he had just talked to Deputy National Security Advisor Stephen Hadley. The White House requested (1) the implementation of continuity of government measures, (2) fighter escorts for Air Force One, and (3) a fighter combat air patrol over Washington, D.C.[201]

By 10:03, when United 93 crashed in Pennsylvania, there

had been no mention of its hijacking and the FAA had not yet been added to the teleconference.[202]

The President and the Vice President

The President was seated in a classroom when, at 9:05, Andrew Card whispered to him: "A second plane hit the second tower. America is under attack." The President told us his instinct was to project calm, not to have the country see an excited reaction at a moment of crisis. The press was standing behind the children; he saw their phones and pagers start to ring. The President felt he should project strength and calm until he could better understand what was happening.[203]

The President remained in the classroom for another five to seven minutes, while the children continued reading. He then returned to a holding room shortly before 9:15, where he was briefed by staff and saw television coverage. He next spoke to Vice President Cheney, Dr. Rice, New York Governor George Pataki, and FBI Director Robert Mueller. He decided to make a brief statement from the school before leaving for the airport. The Secret Service told us they were anxious to move the President to a safer location, but did not think it imperative for him to run out the door.[204]

Between 9:15 and 9:30, the staff was busy arranging a return to Washington, while the President consulted his senior advisers about his remarks. No one in the traveling party had any information during this time that other aircraft were hijacked or missing. Staff was in contact with the White House Situation Room, but as far as we could determine, no one with the President was in contact with the Pentagon. The focus was on the President's statement to the nation. The only decision made during this time was to return to Washington.[205]

The President's motorcade departed at 9:35, and arrived at the airport between 9:42 and 9:45. During the ride the President learned about the attack on the Pentagon. He boarded the aircraft, asked the Secret Service about the safety of his family, and called the Vice President. According to notes of the call, at about 9:45 the President told the

Vice President: "Sounds like we have a minor war going on here, I heard about the Pentagon. We're at war . . . somebody's going to pay."[206]

About this time, Card, the lead Secret Service agent, the President's military aide, and the pilot were conferring on a possible destination for Air Force One. The Secret Service agent felt strongly that the situation in Washington was too unstable for the President to return there, and Card agreed. The President strongly wanted to return to Washington and only grudgingly agreed to go elsewhere. The issue was still undecided when the President conferred with the Vice President at about the time Air Force One was taking off. The Vice President recalled urging the President not to return to Washington. Air Force One departed at about 9:54 without any fixed destination. The objective was to get up in the air—as fast and as high as possible—and then decide where to go.[207]

At 9:33, the tower supervisor at Reagan National Airport picked up a hotline to the Secret Service and told the Service's operations center that "an aircraft [is] coming at you and not talking with us." This was the first specific report to the Secret Service of a direct threat to the White House. No move was made to evacuate the Vice President at this time. As the officer who took the call explained, "[I was] about to push the alert button when the tower advised that the aircraft was turning south and approaching Reagan National Airport."[208]

American 77 began turning south, away from the White House, at 9:34. It continued heading south for roughly a minute, before turning west and beginning to circle back. This news prompted the Secret Service to order the immediate evacuation of the Vice President just before 9:36. Agents propelled him out of his chair and told him he had to get to the bunker. The Vice President entered the underground tunnel leading to the shelter at 9:37.[209]

Once inside, Vice President Cheney and the agents paused in an area of the tunnel that had a secure phone, a bench, and television. The Vice President asked to speak to

the President, but it took time for the call to be connected.
He learned in the tunnel that the Pentagon had been hit, and
he saw television coverage of smoke coming from the building.[210]

The Secret Service logged Mrs. Cheney's arrival at the
White House at 9:52, and she joined her husband in the tunnel. According to contemporaneous notes, at 9:55 the Vice
President was still on the phone with the President advising
that three planes were missing and one had hit the Pentagon.
We believe this is the same call in which the Vice President
urged the President not to return to Washington. After the
call ended, Mrs. Cheney and the Vice President moved from
the tunnel to the shelter conference room.[211]

United 93 and the Shootdown Order

On the morning of 9/11, the President and Vice President
stayed in contact not by an open line of communication but
through a series of calls. The President told us he was frustrated with the poor communications that morning. He could
not reach key officials, including Secretary Rumsfeld, for a
period of time. The line to the White House shelter conference room—and the Vice President—kept cutting off.[212]

The Vice President remembered placing a call to the
President just after entering the shelter conference room.
There is conflicting evidence about when the Vice President
arrived in the shelter conference room. We have concluded,
from the available evidence, that the Vice President arrived
in the room shortly before 10:00, perhaps at 9:58. The Vice
President recalled being told, just after his arrival, that the
Air Force was trying to establish a combat air patrol over
Washington.[213]

The Vice President stated that he called the President to
discuss the rules of engagement for the CAP. He recalled
feeling that it did no good to establish the CAP unless the pilots had instructions on whether they were authorized to
shoot if the plane would not divert. He said the President
signed off on that concept. The President said he remembered such a conversation, and that it reminded him of when

he had been an interceptor pilot. The President emphasized to us that he had authorized the shootdown of hijacked aircraft.[214]

The Vice President's military aide told us he believed the Vice President spoke to the President just after entering the conference room, but he did not hear what they said. Rice, who entered the room shortly after the Vice President and sat next to him, remembered hearing him inform the President, "Sir, the CAPs are up. Sir, they're going to want to know what to do." Then she recalled hearing him say, "Yes sir." She believed this conversation occurred a few minutes, perhaps five, after they entered the conference room.[215]

We believe this call would have taken place sometime before 10:10 to 10:15. Among the sources that reflect other important events of that morning, there is no documentary evidence for this call, but the relevant sources are incomplete. Others nearby who were taking notes, such as the Vice President's chief of staff, Scooter Libby, who sat next to him, and Mrs. Cheney, did not note a call between the President and Vice President immediately after the Vice President entered the conference room.[216]

At 10:02, the communicators in the shelter began receiving reports from the Secret Service of an inbound aircraft—presumably hijacked—heading toward Washington. That aircraft was United 93. The Secret Service was getting this information directly from the FAA. The FAA may have been tracking the progress of United 93 on a display that showed its projected path to Washington, not its actual radar return. Thus, the Secret Service was relying on projections and was not aware the plane was already down in Pennsylvania.[217]

At some time between 10:10 and 10:15, a military aide told the Vice President and others that the aircraft was 80 miles out. Vice President Cheney was asked for authority to engage the aircraft.[218] His reaction was described by Scooter Libby as quick and decisive, "in about the time it takes a batter to decide to swing." The Vice President authorized fighter aircraft to engage the inbound plane. He told us he based this authorization on his earlier conversation with the President. The military aide returned a few minutes later, probably between 10:12 and 10:18, and said the aircraft was 60 miles out. He again asked for authorization to engage. The Vice President again said yes.[219]

At the conference room table was White House Deputy Chief of Staff Joshua Bolten. Bolten watched the exchanges and, after what he called "a quiet moment," suggested that the Vice President get in touch with the President and confirm the engage order. Bolten told us he wanted to make sure the President was told that the Vice President had executed the order. He said he had not heard any prior discussion on the subject with the President.[220]

The Vice President was logged calling the President at 10:18 for a two-minute conversation that obtained the confirmation. On Air Force One, the President's press secretary was taking notes; Ari Fleischer recorded that at 10:20, the President told him that he had authorized a shootdown of aircraft if necessary.[221]

Minutes went by and word arrived of an aircraft down in Pennsylvania. Those in the shelter wondered if the aircraft had been shot down pursuant to this authorization.[222]

At approximately 10:30, the shelter started receiving reports of another hijacked plane, this time only 5 to 10 miles out. Believing they had only a minute or two, the Vice President again communicated the authorization to "engage" or "take out" the aircraft. At 10:33, Hadley told the air threat conference call: "I need to get word to Dick Myers that our reports are there's an inbound aircraft flying low 5 miles out. The Vice President's guidance was we need to take them out."[223]

Once again, there was no immediate information about the fate of the inbound aircraft. In the apt description of one witness, "It drops below the radar screen and it's just continually hovering in your imagination; you don't know where it is or what happens to it." Eventually, the shelter received word that the alleged hijacker 5 miles away had been a medevac helicopter.[224]

Transmission of the Authorization from the White House to the Pilots

The NMCC learned of United 93's hijacking at about 10:03. At this time the FAA had no contact with the military at the level of national command. The NMCC learned about United 93 from the White House. It, in turn, was informed by the Secret Service's contacts with the FAA.[225]

NORAD had no information either. At 10:07, its representative on the air threat conference call stated that NORAD had "no indication of a hijack heading to DC at this time."[226]

Repeatedly between 10:14 and 10:19, a lieutenant colonel at the White House relayed to the NMCC that the Vice President had confirmed fighters were cleared to engage inbound aircraft if they could verify that the aircraft was hijacked.[227]

The commander of NORAD, General Ralph Eberhart, was en route to the NORAD operations center in Cheyenne Mountain, Colorado, when the shootdown order was communicated on the air threat conference call. He told us that by the time he arrived, the order had already been passed down NORAD's chain of command.[228]

It is not clear how the shootdown order was communicated within NORAD. But we know that at 10:31, General Larry Arnold instructed his staff to broadcast the following over a NORAD instant messaging system: "10:31 Vice president has cleared to us to intercept tracks of interest and shoot them down if they do not respond per [General Arnold]."[229]

In upstate New York, NEADS personnel first learned of the shootdown order from this message:

> FLOOR LEADERSHIP: You need to read this. . . . The Region Commander has declared that we can shoot down aircraft that do not respond to our direction. Copy that?

> CONTROLLERS: Copy that, sir.

FLOOR LEADERSHIP: So if you're trying to divert somebody and he won't divert—

CONTROLLERS: DO [Director of Operations] is saying
no.

FLOOR LEADERSHIP: No? It came over the chat. . . . You
got a conflict on that direction?

CONTROLLERS: Right now no, but—

FLOOR LEADERSHIP: Okay? Okay, you read that from the
Vice President, right? Vice President has cleared. Vice
President has cleared us to intercept traffic and shoot
them down if they do not respond per [General
Arnold].[230]

In interviews with us, NEADS personnel expressed considerable confusion over the nature and effect of the order.
The NEADS commander told us he did not pass along
the order because he was unaware of its ramifications. Both
the mission commander and the senior weapons director indicated they did not pass the order to the fighters circling
Washington and New York because they were unsure how
the pilots would, or should, proceed with this guidance. In
short, while leaders in Washington believed that the fighters
above them had been instructed to "take out" hostile aircraft,
the only orders actually conveyed to the pilots were to "ID
type and tail."[231]
In most cases, the chain of command authorizing the use
of force runs from the president to the secretary of defense
and from the secretary to the combatant commander. The
President apparently spoke to Secretary Rumsfeld for the first
time that morning shortly after 10:00. No one can recall the
content of this conversation, but it was a brief call in which
the subject of shootdown authority was not discussed.[232]
At 10:39, the Vice President updated the Secretary on the
air threat conference:

VICE PRESIDENT: There's been at least three instances here where we've had reports of aircraft approaching Washington—a couple were confirmed hijack. And, pursuant to the President's instructions I gave authorization for them to be taken out. Hello?

SECDEF: Yes, I understand. Who did you give that direction to?

VICE PRESIDENT: It was passed from here through the [operations] center at the White House, from the [shelter].

SECDEF: OK, let me ask the question here. Has that directive been transmitted to the aircraft?

VICE PRESIDENT: Yes, it has.

SECDEF: So we've got a couple of aircraft up there that have those instructions at this present time?

VICE PRESIDENT: That is correct. And it's my understanding they've already taken a couple of aircraft out.

SECDEF: We can't confirm that. We're told that one aircraft is down but we do not have a pilot report that did it.[233]

As this exchange shows, Secretary Rumsfeld was not in the NMCC when the shootdown order was first conveyed. He went from the parking lot to his office (where he spoke to the President), then to the Executive Support Center, where he participated in the White House video teleconference. He moved to the NMCC shortly before 10:30, in order to join Vice Chairman Myers. Secretary Rumsfeld told us he was just gaining situational awareness when he spoke with the Vice President at 10:39. His primary concern was ensuring that the pilots had a clear understanding of their rules of engagement.[234]

The Vice President was mistaken in his belief that shoot-down authorization had been passed to the pilots flying at NORAD's direction. By 10:45 there was, however, another set of fighters circling Washington that had entirely different rules of engagement. These fighters, part of the 113th Wing of the District of Columbia Air National Guard, launched out of Andrews Air Force Base in Maryland in response to information passed to them by the Secret Service. The first of the Andrews fighters was airborne at 10:38.[235]

General David Wherley—the commander of the 113th Wing—reached out to the Secret Service after hearing sec-ondhand reports that it wanted fighters airborne. A Secret Service agent had a phone in each ear, one connected to Wherley and the other to a fellow agent at the White House, relaying instructions that the White House agent said he was getting from the Vice President. The guidance for Wherley was to send up the aircraft, with orders to protect the White House and take out any aircraft that threatened the Capitol. General Wherley translated this in military terms to flying "weapons free"—that is, the decision to shoot rests in the cockpit, or in this case in the cockpit of the lead pilot. He passed these instructions to the pilots that launched at 10:42 and afterward.[236]

Thus, while the fighter pilots under NORAD direction who had scrambled out of Langley never received any type of engagement order, the Andrews pilots were operating weapons free—a permissive rule of engagement. The Presi-dent and the Vice President indicated to us they had not been aware that fighters had been scrambled out of Andrews, at the request of the Secret Service and outside the military chain of command.[237] There is no evidence that NORAD headquarters or military officials in the NMCC knew—dur-ing the morning of September 11—that the Andrews planes were airborne and operating under different rules of engage-ment.

What If?

NORAD officials have maintained consistently that had the passengers not caused United 93 to crash, the military would have prevented it from reaching Washington, D.C. That conclusion is based on a version of events that we now know is incorrect. The Langley fighters were not scrambled in response to United 93; NORAD did not have 47 minutes to intercept the flight; NORAD did not even know the plane was hijacked until after it had crashed. It is appropriate, therefore, to reconsider whether United 93 would have been intercepted.

Had it not crashed in Pennsylvania at 10:03, we estimate that United 93 could not have reached Washington any earlier than 10:13, and probably would have arrived before 10:23. There was only one set of fighters circling Washington during that time frame—the Langley F-16s. They were armed and under NORAD's control. After NEADS learned of the hijacking at 10:07, NORAD would have had from 6 to 16 minutes to locate the flight, receive authorization to shoot it down, and communicate the order to the pilots, who (in the same span) would have had to authenticate the order, intercept the flight, and execute the order.[238]

At that point in time, the Langley pilots did not know the threat they were facing, did not know where United 93 was located, and did not have shootdown authorization.

First, the Langley pilots were never briefed about the reason they were scrambled. As the lead pilot explained, "I reverted to the Russian threat. . . . I'm thinking cruise missile threat from the sea. You know you look down and see the Pentagon burning and I thought the bastards snuck one by us. . . . [Y]ou couldn't see any airplanes, and no one told us anything." The pilots knew their mission was to divert aircraft, but did not know that the threat came from hijacked airliners.[239]

Second, NEADS did not have accurate information on the location of United 93. Presumably FAA would have provided such information, but we do not know how long that would have taken, nor how long it would have taken NEADS to locate the target.

Third, NEADS needed orders to pass to the pilots. At 10:10, the pilots over Washington were emphatically told, "negative clearance to shoot." Shootdown authority was first communicated to NEADS at 10:31. It is possible that NORAD commanders would have ordered a shootdown in the absence of the authorization communicated by the Vice President, but given the gravity of the decision to shoot down a commercial airliner, and NORAD's caution that a mistake not be made, we view this possibility as unlikely.[240]

NORAD officials have maintained that they would have intercepted and shot down United 93. We are not so sure. We are sure that the nation owes a debt to the passengers of United 93. Their actions saved the lives of countless others, and may have saved either the Capitol or the White House from destruction.

The details of what happened on the morning of September 11 are complex, but they play out a simple theme. NORAD and the FAA were unprepared for the type of attacks launched against the United States on September 11, 2001. They struggled, under difficult circumstances, to improvise a homeland defense against an unprecedented challenge they had never before encountered and had never trained to meet.

At 10:02 that morning, an assistant to the mission crew commander at NORAD's Northeast Air Defense Sector in Rome, New York, was working with his colleagues on the floor of the command center. In a brief moment of reflection, he was recorded remarking that "This is a new type of war."[241]

He was, and is, right. But the conflict did not begin on 9/11. It had been publicly declared years earlier, most notably in a declaration faxed early in 1998 to an Arabic-language newspaper in London. Few Americans had noticed it. The fax had been sent from thousands of miles away by the followers of a Saudi exile gathered in one of the most remote and impoverished countries on earth.

CHAPTER TWO

The Foundation of the New Terrorism

2.1 A DECLARATION OF WAR

In February 1998, the 40-year-old Saudi exile Usama Bin Ladin and a fugitive Egyptian physician, Ayman al Zawahiri, arranged from their Afghan headquarters for an Arabic newspaper in London to publish what they termed a fatwa issued in the name of a "World Islamic Front." A fatwa is normally an interpretation of Islamic law by a respected Islamic authority, but neither Bin Ladin, Zawahiri, nor the three others who signed this statement were scholars of Islamic law. Claiming that America had declared war against God and his messenger, they called for the murder of any American, anywhere on earth, as the "individual duty for every Muslim who can do it in any country in which it is possible to do it."[1]

Three months later, when interviewed in Afghanistan by

Note: Islamic names often do not follow the Western practice of the consistent use of surnames. Given the variety of names we mention, we chose to refer to individuals by the last word in the names by which they are known: Nawaf al Hazmi as Hazmi, for instance, omitting the article "al" that would be part of their name in their own societies. We generally make an exception for the more familiar English usage of "Bin" as part of a last name, as in Bin Ladin. Further, there is no universally accepted way to transliterate Arabic words and names into English. We have relied on a mix of common sense, the sound of the name in Arabic, and common usage in source materials, the press, or government documents. When we quote from a source document, we use its translation, e.g., "al Qida" instead of Qaeda.

ABC-TV, Bin Ladin enlarged on these themes.[2] He claimed it was more important for Muslims to kill Americans than to kill other infidels. "It is far better for anyone to kill a single American soldier than to squander his efforts on other activities," he said. Asked whether he approved of terrorism and of attacks on civilians, he replied: "We believe that the worst thieves in the world today and the worst terrorists are the Americans. Nothing could stop you except perhaps retaliation in kind. We do not have to differentiate between military or civilian. As far as we are concerned, they are all targets."

Though novel for its open endorsement of indiscriminate killing, Bin Ladin's 1998 declaration was only the latest in the long series of his public and private calls since 1992 that singled out the United States for attack.

In August 1996, Bin Ladin had issued his own self-styled fatwa calling on Muslims to drive American soldiers out of Saudi Arabia. The long, disjointed document condemned the Saudi monarchy for allowing the presence of an army of infidels in a land with the sites most sacred to Islam, and celebrated recent suicide bombings of American military facilities in the Kingdom. It praised the 1983 suicide bombing in Beirut that killed 241 U.S. Marines, the 1992 bombing in Aden, and especially the 1993 firefight in Somalia after which the United States "left the area carrying disappointment, humiliation, defeat and your dead with you."[3]

Bin Ladin said in his ABC interview that he and his followers had been preparing in Somalia for another long struggle, like that against the Soviets in Afghanistan, but "the United States rushed out of Somalia in shame and disgrace." Citing the Soviet army's withdrawal from Afghanistan as proof that a ragged army of dedicated Muslims could overcome a superpower, he told the interviewer: "We are certain that we shall—with the grace of Allah—prevail over the Americans." He went on to warn that "If the present injustice continues . . . , it will inevitably move the battle to American soil."[4]

Plans to attack the United States were developed with unwavering singlemindedness throughout the 1990s. Bin

Ladin saw himself as called "to follow in the footsteps of the Messenger and to communicate his message to all nations,"[5] and to serve as the rallying point and organizer of a new kind of war to destroy America and bring the world to Islam.

2.2 BIN LADIN'S APPEAL IN THE ISLAMIC WORLD

It is the story of eccentric and violent ideas sprouting in the fertile ground of political and social turmoil. It is the story of an organization poised to seize its historical moment. How did Bin Ladin—with his call for the indiscriminate killing of Americans—win thousands of followers and some degree of approval from millions more?

The history, culture, and body of beliefs from which Bin Ladin has shaped and spread his message are largely unknown to many Americans. Seizing on symbols of Islam's past greatness, he promises to restore pride to people who consider themselves the victims of successive foreign masters. He uses cultural and religious allusions to the holy Qur'an and some of its interpreters. He appeals to people disoriented by cyclonic change as they confront modernity and globalization. His rhetoric selectively draws from multiple sources—Islam, history, and the region's political and economic malaise. He also stresses grievances against the United States widely shared in the Muslim world. He inveighed against the presence of U.S. troops in Saudi Arabia, the home of Islam's holiest sites. He spoke of the suffering of the Iraqi people as a result of sanctions imposed after the Gulf War, and he protested U.S. support of Israel.

Islam
Islam (a word that literally means "surrender to the will of God") arose in Arabia with what Muslims believe are a series of revelations to the Prophet Mohammed from the one and only God, the God of Abraham and of Jesus. These revelations, conveyed by the angel Gabriel, are recorded in the

Qur'an. Muslims believe that these revelations, given to the greatest and last of a chain of prophets stretching from Abraham through Jesus, complete God's message to humanity. The Hadith, which recount Mohammed's sayings and deeds as recorded by his contemporaries, are another fundamental source. A third key element is the Sharia, the code of law derived from the Qur'an and the Hadith.

Islam is divided into two main branches, Sunni and Shia. Soon after the Prophet's death, the question of choosing a new leader, or *caliph*, for the Muslim community, or *Ummah*, arose. Initially, his successors could be drawn from the Prophet's contemporaries, but with time, this was no longer possible. Those who became the Shia held that any leader of the Ummah must be a direct descendant of the Prophet; those who became the Sunni argued that lineal descent was not required if the candidate met other standards of faith and knowledge. After bloody struggles, the Sunni became (and remain) the majority sect. (The Shia are dominant in Iran.) The Caliphate—the institutionalized leadership of the Ummah—thus was a Sunni institution that continued until 1924, first under Arab and eventually under Ottoman Turkish control.

Many Muslims look back at the century after the revelations to the Prophet Mohammed as a golden age. Its memory is strongest among the Arabs. What happened then—the spread of Islam from the Arabian Peninsula throughout the Middle East, North Africa, and even into Europe within less than a century—seemed, and seems, miraculous.[6] Nostalgia for Islam's past glory remains a powerful force.

Islam is both a faith and a code of conduct for all aspects of life. For many Muslims, a good government would be one guided by the moral principles of their faith. This does not necessarily translate into a desire for clerical rule and the abolition of a secular state. It does mean that some Muslims tend to be uncomfortable with distinctions between religion and state, though Muslim rulers throughout history have readily separated the two.

To extremists, however, such divisions, as well as the existence of parliaments and legislation, only prove these rulers to be false Muslims usurping God's authority over all aspects of life. Periodically, the Islamic world has seen surges of what, for want of a better term, is often labeled "fundamentalism."[7] Denouncing waywardness among the faithful, some clerics have appealed for a return to observance of the literal teachings of the Qur'an and Hadith. One scholar from the fourteenth century from whom Bin Ladin selectively quotes, Ibn Taimiyyah, condemned both corrupt rulers and the clerics who failed to criticize them. He urged Muslims to read the Qur'an and the Hadith for themselves, not to depend solely on learned interpreters like himself but to hold one another to account for the quality of their observance.[8]

The extreme Islamist version of history blames the decline from Islam's golden age on the rulers and people who turned away from the true path of their religion, thereby leaving Islam vulnerable to encroaching foreign powers eager to steal their land, wealth, and even their souls.

Bin Ladin's Worldview

Despite his claims to universal leadership, Bin Ladin offers an extreme view of Islamic history designed to appeal mainly to Arabs and Sunnis. He draws on fundamentalists who blame the eventual destruction of the Caliphate on leaders who abandoned the pure path of religious devotion.[9] He repeatedly calls on his followers to embrace martyrdom since "the walls of oppression and humiliation cannot be demolished except in a rain of bullets."[10] For those yearning for a lost sense of order in an older, more tranquil world, he offers his "Caliphate" as an imagined alternative to today's uncertainty. For others, he offers simplistic conspiracies to explain their world.

Bin Ladin also relies heavily on the Egyptian writer Sayyid Qutb. A member of the Muslim Brotherhood[11] executed in 1966 on charges of attempting to overthrow the government, Qutb mixed Islamic scholarship with a very superficial acquaintance with Western history and thought.

Sent by the Egyptian government to study in the United States in the late 1940s, Qutb returned with an enormous loathing of Western society and history. He dismissed Western achievements as entirely material, arguing that Western society possesses "nothing that will satisfy its own conscience and justify its existence."[12]

Three basic themes emerge from Qutb's writings. First, he claimed that the world was beset with barbarism, licentiousness, and unbelief (a condition he called *jahiliyya*, the religious term for the period of ignorance prior to the revelations given to the Prophet Mohammed). Qutb argued that humans can choose only between Islam and jahiliyya. Second, he warned that more people, including Muslims, were attracted to jahiliyya and its material comforts than to his view of Islam; jahiliyya could therefore triumph over Islam. Third, no middle ground exists in what Qutb conceived as a struggle between God and Satan. All Muslims—as he defined them—therefore must take up arms in this fight. Any Muslim who rejects his ideas is just one more nonbeliever worthy of destruction.[13]

Bin Ladin shares Qutb's stark view, permitting him and his followers to rationalize even unprovoked mass murder as righteous defense of an embattled faith. Many Americans have wondered, "Why do 'they' hate us?" Some also ask, "What can we do to stop these attacks?"

Bin Ladin and al Qaeda have given answers to both these questions. To the first, they say that America had attacked Islam; America is responsible for all conflicts involving Muslims. Thus Americans are blamed when Israelis fight with Palestinians, when Russians fight with Chechens, when Indians fight with Kashmiri Muslims, and when the Philippine government fights ethnic Muslims in its southern islands. America is also held responsible for the governments of Muslim countries, derided by al Qaeda as "your agents." Bin Ladin has stated flatly, "Our fight against these governments is not separate from our fight against you."[14] These charges found a ready audience among millions of Arabs and Muslims angry at the United States because of issues ranging from Iraq to Palestine to America's support for their countries' repressive rulers.

Bin Ladin's grievance with the United States may have started in reaction to specific U.S. policies but it quickly became far deeper. To the second question, what America could do, al Qaeda's answer was that America should abandon the Middle East, convert to Islam, and end the immorality and godlessness of its society and culture: "It is saddening to tell you that you are the worst civilization witnessed by the history of mankind." If the United States did not comply, it would be at war with the Islamic nation, a nation that al Qaeda's leaders said "desires death more than you desire life."[15]

History and Political Context

Few fundamentalist movements in the Islamic world gained lasting political power. In the nineteenth and twentieth centuries, fundamentalists helped articulate anticolonial grievances but played little role in the overwhelmingly secular struggles for independence after World War I. Western-educated lawyers, soldiers, and officials led most independence movements, and clerical influence and traditional culture were seen as obstacles to national progress.

After gaining independence from Western powers following World War II, the Arab Middle East followed an arc from initial pride and optimism to today's mix of indifference, cynicism, and despair. In several countries, a dynastic state already existed or was quickly established under a paramount tribal family. Monarchies in countries such as Saudi Arabia, Morocco, and Jordan still survive today. Those in Egypt, Libya, Iraq, and Yemen were eventually overthrown by secular nationalist revolutionaries.

The secular regimes promised a glowing future, often tied to sweeping ideologies (such as those promoted by Egyptian President Gamal Abdel Nasser's Arab Socialism or the Ba'ath Party of Syria and Iraq) that called for a single, secular Arab state. However, what emerged were almost invariably autocratic regimes that were usually unwilling to tolerate any opposition—even in countries, such as Egypt, that had a parliamentary tradition. Over time, their policies—repression, rewards, emigration, and the displacement of popular anger onto scapegoats (generally foreign)—were shaped by the desire to cling to power.

The bankruptcy of secular, autocratic nationalism was evident across the Muslim world by the late 1970s. At the same time, these regimes had closed off nearly all paths for peaceful opposition, forcing their critics to choose silence, exile, or violent opposition. Iran's 1979 revolution swept a Shia theocracy into power. Its success encouraged Sunni fundamentalists elsewhere.

In the 1980s, awash in sudden oil wealth, Saudi Arabia competed with Shia Iran to promote its Sunni fundamentalist interpretation of Islam, Wahhabism. The Saudi government, always conscious of its duties as the custodian of Islam's holiest places, joined with wealthy Arabs from the Kingdom and other states bordering the Persian Gulf in donating money to build mosques and religious schools that could preach and teach their interpretation of Islamic doctrine.

In this competition for legitimacy, secular regimes had no alternative to offer. Instead, in a number of cases their rulers sought to buy off local Islamist movements by ceding control of many social and educational issues. Emboldened rather than satisfied, the Islamists continued to push for power—a trend especially clear in Egypt. Confronted with a violent Islamist movement that killed President Anwar Sadat in 1981, the Egyptian government combined harsh repression of Islamic militants with harassment of moderate Islamic scholars and authors, driving many into exile. In Pakistan, a military regime sought to justify its seizure of power by a pious public stance and an embrace of unprecedented Islamist influence on education and society.

These experiments in political Islam faltered during the 1990s: the Iranian revolution lost momentum, prestige, and public support, and Pakistan's rulers found that most of its population had little enthusiasm for fundamentalist Islam.

Islamist revival movements gained followers across the Muslim world, but failed to secure political power except in Iran and Sudan. In Algeria, where in 1991 Islamists seemed almost certain to win power through the ballot box, the military preempted their victory, triggering a brutal civil war that continues today. Opponents of today's rulers have few, if any, ways to participate in the existing political system. They are thus a ready audience for calls to Muslims to purify their society, reject unwelcome modernization, and adhere strictly to the Sharia.

Social and Economic Malaise

In the 1970s and early 1980s, an unprecedented flood of wealth led the then largely unmodernized oil states to attempt to shortcut decades of development. They funded huge infrastructure projects, vastly expanded education, and created subsidized social welfare programs. These programs established a wide-spread feeling of entitlement without a corresponding sense of social obligations. By the late 1980s, diminishing oil revenues, the economic drain from many unprofitable development projects, and population growth made these entitlement programs unsustainable. The resulting cutbacks created enormous resentment among recipients who had come to see government largesse as their right. This resentment was further stoked by public understanding of how much oil income had gone straight into the pockets of the rulers, their friends, and their helpers.

Unlike the oil states (or Afghanistan, where real economic development has barely begun), the other Arab nations and Pakistan once had seemed headed toward balanced modernization. The established commercial, financial, and industrial sectors in these states, supported by an entrepreneurial spirit and widespread understanding of free enterprise, augured well. But unprofitable heavy industry, state monopolies, and opaque bureaucracies slowly stifled growth. More importantly, these state-centered regimes placed their highest priority on preserving the elite's grip on national wealth. Unwilling to foster dynamic economies that could create jobs attractive to educated young men, the countries became economically stagnant and reliant on the safety valve of worker emigration either to the Arab oil states or to the West. Furthermore, the repression and isolation of women in many Muslim countries have not only seriously limited individual opportunity but also crippled overall economic productivity.[16]

By the 1990s, high birthrates and declining rates of infant mortality had produced a common problem throughout the Muslim world: a large, steadily increasing population of young men without any reasonable expectation of suitable or steady employment—a sure prescription for social turbulence. Many of these young men, such as the enormous number trained only in religious schools, lacked the skills needed by their societies. Far more acquired valuable skills but lived in stagnant economies that could not generate satisfying jobs.

Millions, pursuing secular as well as religious studies, were products of educational systems that generally devoted little if any attention to the rest of the world's thought, history, and culture. The secular education reflected a strong cultural preference for technical fields over the humanities and social sciences. Many of these young men, even if able to study abroad, lacked the perspective and skills needed to understand a different culture.

Frustrated in their search for a decent living, unable to benefit from an education often obtained at the cost of great family sacrifice, and blocked from starting families of their own, some of these young men were easy targets for radicalization.

Bin Ladin's Historical Opportunity

Most Muslims prefer a peaceful and inclusive vision of their faith, not the violent sectarianism of Bin Ladin. Among Arabs, Bin Ladin's followers are commonly nicknamed *takfiri*, or "those who define other Muslims as unbelievers," because of their readiness to demonize and murder those with whom they disagree. Beyond the theology lies the simple human fact that most Muslims, like most other human beings, are repelled by mass murder and barbarism whatever their justification.

"All Americans must recognize that the face of terror is not the true face of Islam," President Bush observed. "Islam is a faith that brings comfort to a billion people around the world. It's a faith that has made brothers and sisters of every race. It's a faith based upon love, not hate."[17] Yet as political, social, and economic problems created flammable societies, Bin Ladin used Islam's most extreme, fundamentalist traditions as his match. All these elements—including religion—combined in an explosive compound.

Other extremists had, and have, followings of their own. But in appealing to societies full of discontent, Bin Ladin remained credible as other leaders and symbols faded. He could stand as a symbol of resistance—above all, resistance to the West and to America. He could present himself and his allies as victorious warriors in the one great successful experience for Islamic militancy in the 1980s: the Afghan jihad against the Soviet occupation.

By 1998, Bin Ladin had a distinctive appeal, as he focused on attacking America. He argued that other extremists, who aimed at local rulers or Israel, did not go far enough. They had not taken on what he called "the head of the snake."[18]

Finally, Bin Ladin had another advantage: a substantial, worldwide organization. By the time he issued his February 1998 declaration of war, Bin Ladin had nurtured that organization for nearly ten years. He could attract, train, and use recruits for ever more ambitious attacks, rallying new adherents with each demonstration that his was the movement of the future.

2.3 THE RISE OF BIN LADIN AND AL QAEDA (1988–1992)

A decade of conflict in Afghanistan, from 1979 to 1989, gave Islamist extremists a rallying point and training field. A Communist government in Afghanistan gained power in 1978 but was unable to establish enduring control. At the end of 1979, the Soviet government sent in military units to ensure that the country would remain securely under Moscow's influence. The response was an Afghan national resistance movement that defeated Soviet forces.[19]

Young Muslims from around the world flocked to Afghanistan to join as volunteers in what was seen as a "holy war"—*jihad*—against an invader. The largest numbers came from the Middle East. Some were Saudis, and among them was Usama Bin Ladin.

Twenty-three when he arrived in Afghanistan in 1980, Bin Ladin was the seventeenth of 57 children of a Saudi construction magnate. Six feet five and thin, Bin Ladin appeared to be ungainly but was in fact quite athletic, skilled as a horseman, runner, climber, and soccer player. He had attended Abdul Aziz University in Saudi Arabia. By some accounts, he had been interested there in religious studies, inspired by tape recordings of fiery sermons by Abdullah Azzam, a Palestinian and a disciple of Qutb. Bin Ladin was conspicuous among the volunteers not because he showed evidence of religious learning but because he had access to some of his family's huge fortune. Though he took part in at least one actual battle, he became known chiefly as a person who generously helped fund the anti-Soviet jihad.[20]

Bin Ladin understood better than most of the volunteers the extent to which the continuation and eventual success of the jihad in Afghanistan depended on an increasingly complex, almost worldwide organization. This organization included a financial support network that came to be known as the "Golden Chain," put together mainly by financiers in Saudi Arabia and the Persian Gulf states. Donations flowed through charities or other nongovernmental organizations (NGOs). Bin Ladin and the "Afghan Arabs" drew largely on funds raised by this network, whose agents roamed world markets to buy arms and supplies for the mujahideen, or "holy warriors."[21]

Mosques, schools, and boardinghouses served as recruiting stations in many parts of the world, including the United States. Some were set up by Islamic extremists or their financial backers. Bin Ladin had an important part in this activity. He and the cleric Azzam had joined in creating a "Bureau of Services" (Mektab al Khidmat, or MAK), which channeled recruits into Afghanistan.[22]

The international environment for Bin Ladin's efforts was ideal. Saudi Arabia and the United States supplied billions of dollars worth of secret assistance to rebel groups in Afghanistan fighting the Soviet occupation. This assistance was funneled through Pakistan: the Pakistani military intelligence service (Inter-Services Intelligence Directorate, or ISID), helped train the rebels and distribute the arms. But Bin Ladin and his comrades had their own sources of support and training, and they received little or no assistance from the United States.[23]

April 1988 brought victory for the Afghan jihad. Moscow declared it would pull its military forces out of Afghanistan within the next nine months. As the Soviets began their withdrawal, the jihad's leaders debated what to do next.

Bin Ladin and Azzam agreed that the organization successfully created for Afghanistan should not be allowed to dissolve. They established what they called a base or foundation (al Qaeda) as a potential general headquarters for future jihad.[24] Though Azzam had been considered number one in the MAK, by August 1988 Bin Ladin was clearly the leader (*emir*) of al Qaeda. This organization's structure included as its operating arms an intelligence component, a military committee, a financial committee, a political committee, and a committee in charge of media affairs and propaganda. It also had an Advisory Council (Shura) made up of Bin Ladin's inner circle.[25]

Bin Ladin's assumption of the helm of al Qaeda was evidence of his growing self-confidence and ambition. He soon made clear his desire for unchallenged control and for preparing the mujahideen to fight anywhere in the world. Azzam, by contrast, favored continuing to fight in Afghanistan until it had a true Islamist government. And, as a Palestinian, he saw Israel as the top priority for the next stage.[26]

Whether the dispute was about power, personal differences, or strategy, it ended on November 24, 1989, when a remotely controlled car bomb killed Azzam and both of his sons. The killers were assumed to be rival Egyptians. The outcome left Bin Ladin indisputably in charge of what remained of the MAK and al Qaeda.[27]

Through writers like Qutb, and the presence of Egyptian Islamist teachers in the Saudi educational system, Islamists already had a strong intellectual influence on Bin Ladin and his al Qaeda colleagues. By the late 1980s, the Egyptian Islamist movement—badly battered in the government crackdown following President Sadat's assassination—was centered in two major organizations: the Islamic Group and the Egyptian Islamic Jihad. A spiritual guide for both, but especially the Islamic Group, was the so-called Blind Sheikh, Omar Abdel Rahman. His preaching had inspired the assassination of Sadat. After being in and out of Egyptian prisons during the 1980s, Abdel Rahman found refuge in the United States. From his headquarters in Jersey City, he distributed messages calling for the murder of unbelievers.[28]

The most important Egyptian in Bin Ladin's circle was a surgeon, Ayman al Zawahiri, who led a strong faction of the Egyptian Islamic Jihad. Many of his followers became important members in the new organization, and his own close ties with Bin Ladin led many to think of him as the deputy head of al Qaeda. He would in fact become Bin Ladin's deputy some years later, when they merged their organizations.[29]

Bin Ladin Moves to Sudan

By the fall of 1989, Bin Ladin had sufficient stature among Islamic extremists that a Sudanese political leader, Hassan al Turabi, urged him to transplant his whole organization to Sudan. Turabi headed the National Islamic Front in a coalition that had recently seized power in Khartoum.[30] Bin Ladin agreed to help Turabi in an ongoing war against African Christian separatists in southern Sudan and also to do some road building. Turabi in return would let Bin Ladin use Sudan as a base for worldwide business operations and for preparations for jihad.[31] While agents of Bin Ladin began to buy property in Sudan in 1990,[32] Bin Ladin himself moved from Afghanistan back to Saudi Arabia.

In August 1990, Iraq invaded Kuwait. Bin Ladin, whose efforts in Afghanistan had earned him celebrity and respect, proposed to the Saudi monarchy that he summon mujahideen for a jihad to retake Kuwait. He was rebuffed, and the Saudis joined the U.S.-led coalition. After the Saudis agreed to allow U.S. armed forces to be based in the Kingdom, Bin Ladin and a number of Islamic clerics began to publicly denounce the arrangement. The Saudi government exiled the clerics and undertook to silence Bin Ladin by, among other things, taking away his passport. With help from a dissident member of the royal family, he managed to get out of the country under the pretext of attending an Islamic gathering in Pakistan in April 1991.[33] By 1994, the Saudi government would freeze his financial assets and revoke his citizenship.[34] He no longer had a country he could call his own.

Bin Ladin moved to Sudan in 1991 and set up a large and complex set of intertwined business and terrorist enterprises. In time, the former would encompass numerous companies and a global network of bank accounts and nongovernmental institutions. Fulfilling his bargain with Turabi, Bin Ladin used his construction company to build a new highway from Khartoum to Port Sudan on the Red Sea coast. Meanwhile, al Qaeda finance officers and top operatives used their positions in Bin Ladin's businesses to acquire weapons, explosives, and technical equipment for terrorist purposes. One founding member, Abu Hajer al Iraqi, used his position as head of a Bin Ladin investment company to carry out procurement trips from western Europe to the Far East. Two others, Wadi al Hage and Mubarak Douri, who had become acquainted in Tucson, Arizona, in the late 1980s, went as far afield as China, Malaysia, the Philippines, and the former Soviet states of Ukraine and Belarus.[35]

Bin Ladin's impressive array of offices covertly provided financial and other support for terrorist activities. The network included a major business enterprise in Cyprus; a "services" branch in Zagreb; an office of the Benevolence International Foundation in Sarajevo, which supported the Bosnian Muslims in their conflict with Serbia and Croatia; and an NGO in Baku, Azerbaijan, that was employed as well by Egyptian Islamic Jihad both as a source and conduit for finances and as a support center for the Muslim rebels in Chechnya. He also made use of the already-established Third World Relief Agency (TWRA) headquartered in Vienna, whose branch office locations included Zagreb and Budapest. (Bin Ladin later set up an NGO in Nairobi as a cover for operatives there.)[36]

Bin Ladin now had a vision of himself as head of an international jihad confederation. In Sudan, he established an "Islamic Army Shura" that was to serve as the coordinating body for the consortium of terrorist groups with which he was forging alliances. It was composed of his own al Qaeda Shura together with leaders or representatives of terrorist organizations that were still independent. In building this Islamic army, he enlisted groups from Saudi Arabia, Egypt, Jordan, Lebanon, Iraq, Oman, Algeria, Libya, Tunisia, Morocco, Somalia, and Eritrea. Al Qaeda also established cooperative but less formal relationships with other extremist groups from these same countries; from the African states of Chad, Mali, Niger, Nigeria, and Uganda; and from the Southeast Asian states of Burma, Thailand, Malaysia, and Indonesia. Bin Ladin maintained connections in the Bosnian conflict as well.[37] The groundwork for a true global terrorist network was being laid.

Bin Ladin also provided equipment and training assistance to the Moro Islamic Liberation Front in the Philippines and also to a newly forming Philippine group that called itself the Abu Sayyaf Brigade, after one of the major Afghan jihadist commanders.[38] Al Qaeda helped Jemaah Islamiya (JI), a nascent organization headed by Indonesian Islamists with cells scattered across Malaysia, Singapore, Indonesia, and the Philippines. It also aided a Pakistani group engaged in insurrectionist attacks in Kashmir. In mid-1991, Bin Ladin dispatched a band of supporters to the northern Afghanistan border to assist the Tajikistan Islamists in the ethnic conflicts that had been boiling there even before the Central Asian departments of the Soviet Union became independent states.[39]

This pattern of expansion through building alliances extended to the United States. A Muslim organization called al Khifa had numerous branch offices, the largest of which was in the Farouq mosque in Brooklyn. In the mid-1980s, it had been set up as one of the first outposts of Azzam and Bin Ladin's MAK.[40] Other cities with branches of al Khifa included Atlanta, Boston, Chicago, Pittsburgh, and Tucson.[41] Al Khifa recruited American Muslims to fight in Afghanistan; some of them would participate in terrorist actions in the United States in the early 1990s and in al Qaeda operations elsewhere, including the 1998 attacks on U.S. embassies in East Africa.

2.4 BUILDING AN ORGANIZATION, DECLARING WAR ON THE UNITED STATES (1992–1996)

Bin Ladin began delivering diatribes against the United States before he left Saudi Arabia. He continued to do so after he arrived in Sudan. In early 1992, the al Qaeda leadership issued a fatwa calling for jihad against the Western "occupation" of Islamic lands. Specifically singling out U.S. forces for attack, the language resembled that which would appear in Bin Ladin's public fatwa in August 1996. In ensuing weeks, Bin Ladin delivered an often-repeated lecture on the need to cut off "the head of the snake."[42]

By this time, Bin Ladin was well-known and a senior figure among Islamist extremists, especially those in Egypt, the Arabian Peninsula, and the Afghanistan-Pakistan border region. Still, he was just one among many diverse terrorist barons. Some of Bin Ladin's close comrades were more peers than subordinates. For example, Usama Asmurai, also known as Wali Khan, worked with Bin Ladin in the early 1980s and helped him in the Philippines and in Tajikistan. The Egyptian spiritual guide based in New Jersey, the Blind Sheikh, whom Bin Ladin admired, was also in the network. Among sympathetic peers in Afghanistan were a few of the warlords still fighting for power and Abu Zubaydah, who helped operate a popular terrorist training camp near the border with Pakistan. There were also rootless but experienced operatives, such as Ramzi Yousef and Khalid Sheikh Mohammed, who—though not necessarily formal members of someone else's organization—were traveling around the world and joining in projects that were supported by or linked to Bin Ladin, the Blind Sheikh, or their associates.[43]

In now analyzing the terrorist programs carried out by members of this network, it would be misleading to apply the label "al Qaeda operations" too often in these early years. Yet it would also be misleading to ignore the significance of these connections. And in this network, Bin Ladin's agenda stood out. While his allied Islamist groups were focused on local battles, such as those in Egypt, Algeria, Bosnia, or Chechnya, Bin Ladin concentrated on attacking the "far enemy"—the United States.

Attacks Known and Suspected

After U.S. troops deployed to Somalia in late 1992, al Qaeda leaders formulated a fatwa demanding their eviction. In December, bombs exploded at two hotels in Aden where U.S.

troops routinely stopped en route to Somalia, killing two, but no Americans. The perpetrators are reported to have belonged to a group from southern Yemen headed by a Yemeni member of Bin Ladin's Islamic Army Shura; some in the group had trained at an al Qaeda camp in Sudan.[44]

Al Qaeda leaders set up a Nairobi cell and used it to send weapons and trainers to the Somali warlords battling U.S. forces, an operation directly supervised by al Qaeda's military leader.[45] Scores of trainers flowed to Somalia over the ensuing months, including most of the senior members and weapons training experts of al Qaeda's military committee. These trainers were later heard boasting that their assistance led to the October 1993 shootdown of two U.S. Black Hawk helicopters by members of a Somali militia group and to the subsequent withdrawal of U.S. forces in early 1994.[46]

In November 1995, a car bomb exploded outside a Saudi-U.S. joint facility in Riyadh for training the Saudi National Guard. Five Americans and two officials from India were killed. The Saudi government arrested four perpetrators, who admitted being inspired by Bin Ladin. They were promptly executed. Though nothing proves that Bin Ladin ordered this attack, U.S. intelligence subsequently learned that al Qaeda leaders had decided a year earlier to attack a U.S. target in Saudi Arabia, and had shipped explosives to the peninsula for this purpose. Some of Bin Ladin's associates later took credit.[47]

In June 1996, an enormous truck bomb detonated in the Khobar Towers residential complex in Dhahran, Saudi Arabia, that housed U.S. Air Force personnel. Nineteen Americans were killed, and 372 were wounded. The operation was carried out principally, perhaps exclusively, by Saudi Hezbollah, an organization that had received support from the government of Iran. While the evidence of Iranian involvement is strong, there are also signs that al Qaeda played some role, as yet unknown.[48]

In this period, other prominent attacks in which Bin Ladin's involvement is at best cloudy are the 1993 bombing of the World Trade Center, a plot that same year to destroy landmarks in New York, and the 1995 Manila air plot to blow up a dozen U.S. airliners over the Pacific. Details on these plots appear in chapter 3.

Another scheme revealed that Bin Ladin sought the capability to kill on a mass scale. His business aides received word that a Sudanese military officer who had been a member of the previous government cabinet was offering to sell weapons-grade uranium. After a number of contacts were made through intermediaries, the officer set the price at $1.5 million, which did not deter Bin Ladin. Al Qaeda representatives asked to inspect the uranium and were shown a cylinder about 3 feet long, and one thought he could pronounce it genuine. Al Qaeda apparently purchased the cylinder, then discovered it to be bogus.[49] But while the effort failed, it shows what Bin Ladin and his associates hoped to do. One of the al Qaeda representatives explained his mission: "it's easy to kill more people with uranium."[50]

Bin Ladin seemed willing to include in the confederation terrorists from almost every corner of the Muslim world. His vision mirrored that of Sudan's Islamist leader, Turabi, who convened a series of meetings under the label Popular Arab and Islamic Conference around the time of Bin Ladin's arrival in that country. Delegations of violent Islamist extremists came from all the groups represented in Bin Ladin's Islamic Army Shura. Representatives also came from organizations such as the Palestine Liberation Organization, Hamas, and Hezbollah.[51]

Turabi sought to persuade Shiites and Sunnis to put aside their divisions and join against the common enemy. In late 1991 or 1992, discussions in Sudan between al Qaeda and Iranian operatives led to an informal agreement to cooperate in providing support—even if only training—for actions carried out primarily against Israel and the United States. Not long afterward, senior al Qaeda operatives and trainers traveled to Iran to receive training in explosives. In the fall of 1993, another such delegation went to the Bekaa Valley in Lebanon for further training in explosives as well as in intelligence and security. Bin Ladin reportedly showed particular interest in learning how to use truck bombs such as the one that had killed 241 U.S. Marines in Lebanon in 1983. The relationship between al Qaeda and Iran demonstrated that Sunni-Shia divisions did not necessarily pose an insurmountable barrier to cooperation in terrorist operations. As will be described in chapter 7, al Qaeda contacts with Iran continued in ensuing years[52]

Bin Ladin was also willing to explore possibilities for cooperation with Iraq, even though Iraq's dictator, Saddam Hussein, had never had an Islamist agenda—save for his opportunistic pose as a defender of the faithful against "Crusaders" during the Gulf War of 1991. Moreover, Bin Ladin had in fact been sponsoring anti-Saddam Islamists in Iraqi Kurdistan, and sought to attract them into his Islamic army.[53]

To protect his own ties with Iraq, Turabi reportedly brokered an agreement that Bin Ladin would stop supporting activities against Saddam. Bin Ladin apparently honored this pledge, at least for a time, although he continued to aid a group of Islamist extremists operating in part of Iraq (Kurdistan) outside of Baghdad's control. In the late 1990s, these extremist groups suffered major defeats by Kurdish forces. In 2001, with Bin Ladin's help they re-formed into an organization called Ansar al Islam. There are indications that by then the Iraqi regime tolerated and may even have helped Ansar al Islam against the common Kurdish enemy.[54]

With the Sudanese regime acting as intermediary, Bin Ladin himself met with a senior Iraqi intelligence officer in Khartoum in late 1994 or early 1995. Bin Ladin is said to have asked for space to establish training camps, as well as assistance in procuring weapons, but there is no evidence that Iraq responded to this request.[55] As described below, the ensuing years saw additional efforts to establish connections.

Sudan Becomes a Doubtful Haven
Not until 1998 did al Qaeda undertake a major terrorist operation of its own, in large part because Bin Ladin lost his

base in Sudan. Ever since the Islamist regime came to power
in Khartoum, the United States and other Western governments had pressed it to stop providing a haven for terrorist
organizations. Other governments in the region, such as
those of Egypt, Syria, Jordan, and even Libya, which were
targets of some of these groups, added their own pressure.
At the same time, the Sudanese regime began to change.
Though Turabi had been its inspirational leader, General
Omar al Bashir, president since 1989, had never been entirely under his thumb. Thus as outside pressures mounted,
Bashir's supporters began to displace those of Turabi.

The attempted assassination in Ethiopia of Egyptian
President Hosni Mubarak in June 1995 appears to have been
a tipping point. The would-be killers, who came from the
Egyptian Islamic Group, had been sheltered in Sudan and
helped by Bin Ladin.[56] When the Sudanese refused to hand
over three individuals identified as involved in the assassination plot, the UN Security Council passed a resolution criticizing their inaction and eventually sanctioned Khartoum in
April 1996.[57]

A clear signal to Bin Ladin that his days in Sudan were
numbered came when the government advised him that it intended to yield to Libya's demands to stop giving sanctuary
to its enemies. Bin Ladin had to tell the Libyans who had
been part of his Islamic army that he could no longer protect
them and that they had to leave the country. Outraged, several Libyan members of al Qaeda and the Islamic Army
Shura renounced all connections with him.[58]

Bin Ladin also began to have serious money problems.
International pressure on Sudan, together with strains in the
world economy, hurt Sudan's currency. Some of Bin Ladin's
companies ran short of funds. As Sudanese authorities became less obliging, normal costs of doing business increased. Saudi pressures on the Bin Ladin family also
probably took some toll. In any case, Bin Ladin found it necessary both to cut back his spending and to control his out-
lays more closely. He appointed a new financial manager,
whom his followers saw as miserly.[59]

Money problems proved costly to Bin Ladin in other ways. Jamal Ahmed al Fadl, a Sudanese-born Arab, had spent time in the United States and had been recruited for the Afghan war through the Farouq mosque in Brooklyn. He had joined al Qaeda and taken the oath of fealty to Bin Ladin, serving as one of his business agents. Then Bin Ladin discovered that Fadl had skimmed about $110,000, and he asked for restitution. Fadl resented receiving a salary of only $500 a month while some of the Egyptians in al Qaeda were given $1,200 a month. He defected and became a star informant for the United States. Also testifying about al Qaeda in a U.S. court was L'Houssaine Kherchtou, who told of breaking with Bin Ladin because of Bin Ladin's professed inability to provide him with money when his wife needed a caesarian section.[60]

In February 1996, Sudanese officials began approaching officials from the United States and other governments, asking what actions of theirs might ease foreign pressure. In secret meetings with Saudi officials, Sudan offered to expel Bin Ladin to Saudi Arabia and asked the Saudis to pardon him. U.S. officials became aware of these secret discussions, certainly by March. Saudi officials apparently wanted Bin Ladin expelled from Sudan. They had already revoked his citizenship, however, and would not tolerate his presence in their country. And Bin Ladin may have no longer felt safe in Sudan, where he had already escaped at least one assassination attempt that he believed to have been the work of the Egyptian or Saudi regimes, or both. In any case, on May 19, 1996, Bin Ladin left Sudan—significantly weakened, despite his ambitions and organizational skills. He returned to Afghanistan.[61]

2.5 AL QAEDA'S RENEWAL IN AFGHANISTAN (1996–1998)

Bin Ladin flew on a leased aircraft from Khartoum to Jalalabad, with a refueling stopover in the United Arab Emirates.[62] He was accompanied by family members and body-guards, as well as by al Qaeda members who had been close associates since his organization's 1988 founding in Afghanistan. Dozens of additional militants arrived on later flights.[63]

Though Bin Ladin's destination was Afghanistan, Pakistan was the nation that held the key to his ability to use Afghanistan as a base from which to revive his ambitious enterprise for war against the United States.

For the first quarter century of its existence as a nation, Pakistan's identity had derived from Islam, but its politics had been decidedly secular. The army was—and remains—the country's strongest and most respected institution, and the army had been and continues to be preoccupied with its rivalry with India, especially over the disputed territory of Kashmir.

From the 1970s onward, religion had become an increasingly powerful force in Pakistani politics. After a coup in 1977, military leaders turned to Islamist groups for support, and fundamentalists became more prominent. South Asia had an indigenous form of Islamic fundamentalism, which had developed in the nineteenth century at a school in the Indian village of Deoband.[64] The influence of the Wahhabi school of Islam had also grown, nurtured by Saudi-funded institutions. Moreover, the fighting in Afghanistan made Pakistan home to an enormous—and generally unwelcome—population of Afghan refugees; and since the badly strained Pakistani education system could not accommodate the refugees, the government increasingly let privately funded religious schools serve as a cost-free alternative. Over time, these schools produced large numbers of half-educated young men with no marketable skills but with deeply held Islamic views.[65]

Pakistan's rulers found these multitudes of ardent young Afghans a source of potential trouble at home but potentially useful abroad. Those who joined the Taliban movement, espousing a ruthless version of Islamic law, perhaps could bring order in chaotic Afghanistan and make it a cooperative ally. They thus might give Pakistan greater security on one of the several borders where Pakistani military officers hoped for what they called "strategic depth."[66]

It is unlikely that Bin Ladin could have returned to Afghanistan had Pakistan disapproved. The Pakistani military intelligence service probably had advance knowledge of his coming, and its officers may have facilitated his travel. During his entire time in Sudan, he had maintained guesthouses and training camps in Pakistan and Afghanistan. These were part of a larger network used by diverse organizations for recruiting and training fighters for Islamic insurgencies in such places as Tajikistan, Kashmir, and Chechnya. Pakistani intelligence officers reportedly introduced Bin Ladin to Taliban leaders in Kandahar, their main base of power, to aid his reassertion of control over camps near Khowst, out of an apparent hope that he would now expand the camps and make them available for training Kashmiri militants.[67]

Yet Bin Ladin was in his weakest position since his early days in the war against the Soviet Union. The Sudanese government had canceled the registration of the main business enterprises he had set up there and then put some of them up for public sale. According to a senior al Qaeda detainee, the government of Sudan seized everything Bin Ladin had possessed there.[68]

He also lost the head of his military committee, Abu Ubaidah al Banshiri, one of the most capable and popular leaders of al Qaeda. While most of the group's key figures had accompanied Bin Ladin to Afghanistan, Banshiri had remained in Kenya to oversee the training and weapons shipments of the cell set up some four years earlier. He died in a ferryboat accident on Lake Victoria just a few days after Bin Ladin arrived in Jalalabad, leaving Bin Ladin with a need to replace him not only in the Shura but also as supervisor of the cells and prospective operations in East Africa.[69] He had to make other adjustments as well, for some al Qaeda members viewed Bin Ladin's return to Afghanistan as occasion to go off in their own directions. Some maintained collaborative relationships with al Qaeda, but many disengaged entirely.[70]

For a time, it may not have been clear to Bin Ladin that the Taliban would be his best bet as an ally. When he arrived in Afghanistan, they controlled much of the country, but key centers, including Kabul, were still held by rival warlords. Bin Ladin went initially to Jalalabad, probably because it was in an area controlled by a provincial council of Islamic leaders who were not major contenders for national power. He found lodgings with Younis Khalis, the head of one of the main mujahideen factions. Bin Ladin apparently kept his options open, maintaining contacts with Gulbuddin Hekmatyar, who, though an Islamic extremist, was also one of the Taliban's most militant opponents. But after September 1996, when first Jalalabad and then Kabul fell to the Taliban, Bin Ladin cemented his ties with them.[71]

That process did not always go smoothly. Bin Ladin, no longer constrained by the Sudanese, clearly thought that he had new freedom to publish his appeals for jihad. At about the time when the Taliban were making their final drive toward Jalalabad and Kabul, Bin Ladin issued his August 1996 fatwa, saying that "We . . . have been prevented from addressing the Muslims," but expressing relief that "by the grace of Allah, a safe base here is now available in the high Hindu Kush mountains in Khurasan." But the Taliban, like the Sudanese, would eventually hear warnings, including from the Saudi monarchy.[72]

Though Bin Ladin had promised Taliban leaders that he would be circumspect, he broke this promise almost immediately, giving an inflammatory interview to CNN in March 1997. The Taliban leader Mullah Omar promptly "invited" Bin Ladin to move to Kandahar, ostensibly in the interests of Bin Ladin's own security but more likely to situate him where he might be easier to control.[73]

There is also evidence that around this time Bin Ladin sent out a number of feelers to the Iraqi regime, offering some cooperation. None are reported to have received a significant response. According to one report, Saddam Hussein's efforts at this time to rebuild relations with the Saudis and other Middle Eastern regimes led him to stay clear of Bin Ladin.[74]

In mid-1998, the situation reversed; it was Iraq that reportedly took the initiative. In March 1998, after Bin Ladin's public fatwa against the United States, two al Qaeda members reportedly went to Iraq to meet with Iraqi intelligence. In July, an Iraqi delegation traveled to Afghanistan to meet first with the Taliban and then with Bin Ladin. Sources reported that one, or perhaps both, of these meetings was apparently arranged through Bin Ladin's Egyptian deputy, Zawahiri, who had ties of his own to the Iraqis. In 1998, Iraq was under intensifying U.S. pressure, which culminated in a series of large air attacks in December.[75]

Similar meetings between Iraqi officials and Bin Ladin or his aides may have occurred in 1999 during a period of some reported strains with the Taliban. According to the reporting, Iraqi officials offered Bin Ladin a safe haven in Iraq. Bin Ladin declined, apparently judging that his circumstances in Afghanistan remained more favorable than the Iraqi alternative. The reports describe friendly contacts and indicate some common themes in both sides' hatred of the United States. But to date we have seen no evidence that these or the earlier contacts ever developed into a collaborative operational relationship. Nor have we seen evidence indicating that Iraq cooperated with al Qaeda in developing or carrying out any attacks against the United States.[76]

Bin Ladin eventually enjoyed a strong financial position in Afghanistan, thanks to Saudi and other financiers associated with the Golden Chain. Through his relationship with Mullah Omar—and the monetary and other benefits that it brought the Taliban—Bin Ladin was able to circumvent restrictions; Mullah Omar would stand by him even when other Taliban leaders raised objections. Bin Ladin appeared to have in Afghanistan a freedom of movement that he had lacked in Sudan. Al Qaeda members could travel freely within the country, enter and exit it without visas or any immigration procedures, purchase and import vehicles and weapons, and enjoy the use of official Afghan Ministry of

Defense license plates. Al Qaeda also used the Afghan state-owned Ariana Airlines to courier money into the country.[77]

The Taliban seemed to open the doors to all who wanted to come to Afghanistan to train in the camps. The alliance with the Taliban provided al Qaeda a sanctuary in which to train and indoctrinate fighters and terrorists, import weapons, forge ties with other jihad groups and leaders, and plot and staff terrorist schemes. While Bin Ladin maintained his own al Qaeda guesthouses and camps for vetting and training recruits, he also provided support to and benefited from the broad infrastructure of such facilities in Afghanistan made available to the global network of Islamist movements. U.S. intelligence estimates put the total number of fighters who underwent instruction in Bin Ladin–supported camps in Afghanistan from 1996 through 9/11 at 10,000 to 20,000.[78]

In addition to training fighters and special operators, this larger network of guesthouses and camps provided a mechanism by which al Qaeda could screen and vet candidates for induction into its own organization. Thousands flowed through the camps, but no more than a few hundred seem to have become al Qaeda members. From the time of its founding, al Qaeda had employed training and indoctrination to identify "worthy" candidates.[79]

Al Qaeda continued meanwhile to collaborate closely with the many Middle Eastern groups—in Egypt, Algeria, Yemen, Lebanon, Morocco, Tunisia, Somalia, and elsewhere—with which it had been linked when Bin Ladin was in Sudan. It also reinforced its London base and its other offices around Europe, the Balkans, and the Caucasus. Bin Ladin bolstered his links to extremists in South and Southeast Asia, including the Malaysian-Indonesian JI and several Pakistani groups engaged in the Kashmir conflict.[80]

The February 1998 fatwa thus seems to have been a kind of public launch of a renewed and stronger al Qaeda, after a year and a half of work. Having rebuilt his fund-raising network, Bin Ladin had again become the rich man of the jihad movement. He had maintained or restored many of his links with terrorists elsewhere in the world. And he had strengthened the internal ties in his own organization.

The inner core of al Qaeda continued to be a hierarchical top-down group with defined positions, tasks, and salaries. Most but not all in this core swore fealty (or *bayat*) to Bin Ladin. Other operatives were committed to Bin Ladin or to his goals and would take assignments for him, but they did not swear bayat and maintained, or tried to maintain, some autonomy. A looser circle of adherents might give money to al Qaeda or train in its camps but remained essentially independent. Nevertheless, they constituted a potential resource for al Qaeda.[81]

Now effectively merged with Zawahiri's Egyptian Islamic Jihad,[82] al Qaeda promised to become the general headquarters for international terrorism, without the need for the Islamic Army Shura. Bin Ladin was prepared to pick up where he had left off in Sudan. He was ready to strike at "the head of the snake."

Al Qaeda's role in organizing terrorist operations had also changed. Before the move to Afghanistan, it had concentrated on providing funds, training, and weapons for actions carried out by members of allied groups. The attacks on the U.S. embassies in East Africa in the summer of 1998 would take a different form—planned, directed, and executed by al Qaeda, under the direct supervision of Bin Ladin and his chief aides.

The Embassy Bombings

As early as December 1993, a team of al Qaeda operatives had begun casing targets in Nairobi for future attacks. It was led by Ali Mohamed, a former Egyptian army officer who had moved to the United States in the mid-1980s, enlisted in the U.S. Army, and became an instructor at Fort Bragg. He had provided guidance and training to extremists at the Farouq mosque in Brooklyn, including some who were subsequently convicted in the February 1993 attack on the

World Trade Center. The casing team also included a computer expert whose write-ups were reviewed by al Qaeda leaders.[83]

The team set up a makeshift laboratory for developing their surveillance photographs in an apartment in Nairobi where the various al Qaeda operatives and leaders based in or traveling to the Kenya cell sometimes met. Banshiri, al Qaeda's military committee chief, continued to be the operational commander of the cell; but because he was constantly on the move, Bin Ladin had dispatched another operative, Khaled al Fawwaz, to serve as the on-site manager. The technical surveillance and communications equipment employed for these casing missions included state-of-the-art video cameras obtained from China and from dealers in Germany. The casing team also reconnoitered targets in Djibouti.[84]

As early as January 1994, Bin Ladin received the surveillance reports, complete with diagrams prepared by the team's computer specialist. He, his top military committee members—Banshiri and his deputy, Abu Hafs al Masri (also known as Mohammed Atef)—and a number of other al Qaeda leaders reviewed the reports. Agreeing that the U.S. embassy in Nairobi was an easy target because a car bomb could be parked close by, they began to form a plan. Al Qaeda had begun developing the tactical expertise for such attacks months earlier, when some of its operatives—top military committee members and several operatives who were involved with the Kenya cell among them—were sent to Hezbollah training camps in Lebanon.[85]

The cell in Kenya experienced a series of disruptions that may in part account for the relatively long delay before the attack was actually carried out. The difficulties Bin Ladin began to encounter in Sudan in 1995, his move to Afghanistan in 1996, and the months spent establishing ties with the Taliban may also have played a role, as did Banshiri's accidental drowning.

In August 1997, the Kenya cell panicked. The London *Daily Telegraph* reported that Madani al Tayyib, formerly head of al Qaeda's finance committee, had turned himself over to the Saudi government. The article said (incorrectly) that the Saudis were sharing Tayyib's information with the U.S. and British authorities.[86] At almost the same time, cell members learned that U.S. and Kenyan agents had searched the Kenya residence of Wadi al Hage, who had become the new on-site manager in Nairobi, and that Hage's telephone was being tapped. Hage was a U.S. citizen who had worked with Bin Ladin in Afghanistan in the 1980s, and in 1992 he went to Sudan to become one of al Qaeda's major financial operatives. When Hage returned to the United States to appear before a grand jury investigating Bin Ladin, the job of cell manager was taken over by Harun Fazul, a Kenyan citizen who had been in Bin Ladin's advance team to Sudan back in 1990. Harun faxed a report on the "security situation" to several sites, warning that "the crew members in East Africa is [sic] in grave danger" in part because "America knows . . . that the followers of [Bin Ladin] . . . carried out the operations to hit Americans in Somalia." The report provided instructions for avoiding further exposure.[87]

On February 23, 1998, Bin Ladin issued his public fatwa. The language had been in negotiation for some time, as part of the merger under way between Bin Ladin's organization and Zawahiri's Egyptian Islamic Jihad. Less than a month after the publication of the fatwa, the teams that were to carry out the embassy attacks were being pulled together in Nairobi and Dar es Salaam. The timing and content of their instructions indicate that the decision to launch the attacks had been made by the time the fatwa was issued.[88]

The next four months were spent setting up the teams in Nairobi and Dar es Salaam. Members of the cells rented residences, and purchased bomb-making materials and transport vehicles. At least one additional explosives expert was brought in to assist in putting the weapons together. In Nairobi, a hotel room was rented to put up some of the operatives. The suicide trucks were purchased shortly before the attack date.[89]

While this was taking place, Bin Ladin continued to push

his public message. On May 7, the deputy head of al Qaeda's military committee, Mohammed Atef, faxed to Bin Ladin's London office a new fatwa issued by a group of sheikhs located in Afghanistan. A week later, it appeared in *Al Quds al Arabi*, the same Arabic-language newspaper in London that had first published Bin Ladin's February fatwa, and it conveyed the same message—the duty of Muslims to carry out holy war against the enemies of Islam and to expel the Americans from the Gulf region. Two weeks after that, Bin Ladin gave a videotaped interview to ABC News with the same slogans, adding that "we do not differentiate between those dressed in military uniforms and civilians; they are all targets in this *fatwa*."[90]

By August 1, members of the cells not directly involved in the attacks had mostly departed from East Africa. The remaining operatives prepared and assembled the bombs, and acquired the delivery vehicles. On August 4, they made one last casing run at the embassy in Nairobi. By the evening of August 6, all but the delivery teams and one or two persons assigned to remove the evidence trail had left East Africa. Back in Afghanistan, Bin Ladin and the al Qaeda leadership had left Kandahar for the countryside, expecting U.S. retaliation. Declarations taking credit for the attacks had already been faxed to the joint al Qaeda–Egyptian Islamic Jihad office in Baku, with instructions to stand by for orders to "instantly" transmit them to *Al Quds al Arabi*. One proclaimed "the formation of the Islamic Army for the Liberation of the Holy Places," and two others—one for each embassy—announced that the attack had been carried out by a "company" of a "battalion" of this "Islamic Army."[91]

On the morning of August 7, the bomb-laden trucks drove into the embassies roughly five minutes apart—about 10:35 A.M. in Nairobi and 10:39 A.M. in Dar es Salaam. Shortly afterward, a phone call was placed from Baku to London. The previously prepared messages were then faxed to London.[92]

The attack on the U.S. embassy in Nairobi destroyed the embassy and killed 12 Americans and 201 others, almost all

Kenyans. About 5,000 people were injured. The attack on the U.S. embassy in Dar es Salaam killed 11 more people, none of them Americans. Interviewed later about the deaths of the Africans, Bin Ladin answered that "when it becomes apparent that it would be impossible to repel these Americans without assaulting them, even if this involved the killing of Muslims, this is permissible under Islam." Asked if he had indeed masterminded these bombings, Bin Ladin said that the World Islamic Front for jihad against "Jews and Crusaders" had issued a "crystal clear" fatwa. If the instigation for jihad against the Jews and the Americans to liberate the holy places "is considered a crime," he said, "let history be a witness that I am a criminal."[93]

CHAPTER THREE

Counterterrorism Evolves

In chapter 2, we described the growth of a new kind of terrorism, and a new terrorist organization—especially from 1988 to 1998, when Usama Bin Ladin declared war and organized the bombing of two U.S. embassies. In this chapter, we trace the parallel evolution of government efforts to counter terrorism by Islamic extremists against the United States.

We mention many personalities in this report. As in any study of the U.S. government, some of the most important characters are institutions. We will introduce various agencies, and how they adapted to a new kind of terrorism.

3.1 FROM THE OLD TERRORISM TO THE NEW: THE FIRST WORLD TRADE CENTER BOMBING

At 18 minutes after noon on February 26, 1993, a huge bomb went off beneath the two towers of the World Trade Center. This was not a suicide attack. The terrorists parked a truck bomb with a timing device on Level B-2 of the underground garage, then departed. The ensuing explosion opened a hole seven stories up. Six people died. More than a thousand were injured. An FBI agent at the scene described the relatively low number of fatalities as a miracle.[1]

President Bill Clinton ordered his National Security Council to coordinate the response. Government agencies swung into action to find the culprits. The Counterterrorist Center located at the CIA combed its files and queried sources around the world. The National Security Agency (NSA), the huge Defense Department signals collection agency, ramped up its communications intercept network and searched its databases for clues.[2] The New York Field Office of the FBI took control of the local investigation and, in the end, set a pattern for future management of terrorist incidents.

Four features of this episode have significance for the story of 9/11.

First, the bombing signaled a new terrorist challenge, one whose rage and malice had no limit. Ramzi Yousef, the Sunni extremist who planted the bomb, said later that he had hoped to kill 250,000 people.[3]

Second, the FBI and the Justice Department did excellent work investigating the bombing. Within days, the FBI identified a truck remnant as part of a Ryder rental van reported stolen in Jersey City the day before the bombing.[4]

Mohammed Salameh, who had rented the truck and reported it stolen, kept calling the rental office to get back his $400 deposit. The FBI arrested him there on March 4, 1993. In short order, the Bureau had several plotters in custody, including Nidal Ayyad, an engineer who had acquired chemicals for the bomb, and Mahmoud Abouhalima, who had helped mix the chemicals.[5]

The FBI identified another conspirator, Ahmad Ajaj, who had been arrested by immigration authorities at John F. Kennedy International Airport in September 1992 and charged with document fraud. His traveling companion was Ramzi Yousef, who had also entered with fraudulent documents but claimed political asylum and was admitted. It quickly became clear that Yousef had been a central player in the attack. He had fled to Pakistan immediately after the bombing and would remain at large for nearly two years.[6]

The arrests of Salameh, Abouhalima, and Ayyad led the

FBI to the Farouq mosque in Brooklyn, where a central figure was Sheikh Omar Abdel Rahman, an extremist Sunni Muslim cleric who had moved to the United States from Egypt in 1990. In speeches and writings, the sightless Rahman, often called the "Blind Sheikh," preached the message of Sayyid Qutb's *Milestones*, characterizing the United States as the oppressor of Muslims worldwide and asserting that it was their religious duty to fight against God's enemies. An FBI informant learned of a plan to bomb major New York landmarks, including the Holland and Lincoln tunnels. Disrupting this "landmarks plot," the FBI in June 1993 arrested Rahman and various confederates.[7]

As a result of the investigations and arrests, the U.S. Attorney for the Southern District of New York prosecuted and convicted multiple individuals, including Ajaj, Salameh, Ayyad, Abouhalima, the Blind Sheikh, and Ramzi Yousef, for crimes related to the World Trade Center bombing and other plots.

An unfortunate consequence of this superb investigative and prosecutorial effort was that it created an impression that the law enforcement system was well-equipped to cope with terrorism. Neither President Clinton, his principal advisers, the Congress, nor the news media felt prompted, until later, to press the question of whether the procedures that put the Blind Sheikh and Ramzi Yousef behind bars would really protect Americans against the new virus of which these individuals were just the first symptoms.[8]

Third, the successful use of the legal system to address the first World Trade Center bombing had the side effect of obscuring the need to examine the character and extent of the new threat facing the United States. The trials did not bring the Bin Ladin network to the attention of the public and policymakers.

The FBI assembled, and the U.S. Attorney's office put forward, some evidence showing that the men in the dock were not the only plotters. Materials taken from Ajaj indicated that the plot or plots were hatched at or near the Khaldan camp, a terrorist training camp on the Afghanistan-Pakistan border.

Ajaj had left Texas in April 1992 to go there to learn how to construct bombs. He had met Ramzi Yousef in Pakistan, where they discussed bombing targets in the United States and assembled a "terrorist kit" that included bomb-making manuals, operations guidance, videotapes advocating terrorist action against the United States, and false identification documents.[9]

Yousef was captured in Pakistan following the discovery by police in the Philippines in January 1995 of the Manila air plot, which envisioned placing bombs on board a dozen trans-Pacific airliners and setting them off simultaneously. Khalid Sheikh Mohammed—Yousef's uncle, then located in Qatar—was a fellow plotter of Yousef's in the Manila air plot and had also wired him some money prior to the Trade Center bombing. The U.S. Attorney obtained an indictment against KSM in January 1996, but an official in the government of Qatar probably warned him about it. Khalid Sheikh Mohammed evaded capture (and stayed at large to play a central part in the 9/11 attacks).[10]

The law enforcement process is concerned with proving the guilt of persons apprehended and charged. Investigators and prosecutors could not present all the evidence of possible involvement of individuals other than those charged, although they continued to pursue such investigations, planning or hoping for later prosecutions. The process was meant, by its nature, to mark for the public the events as finished—case solved, justice done. It was not designed to ask if the events might be harbingers of worse to come. Nor did it allow for aggregating and analyzing facts to see if they could provide clues to terrorist tactics more generally—methods of entry and finance, and mode of operation inside the United States.

Fourth, although the bombing heightened awareness of a new terrorist danger, successful prosecutions contributed to widespread underestimation of the threat. The government's attorneys stressed the seriousness of the crimes, and put forward evidence of Yousef's technical ingenuity. Yet the public image that persisted was not of clever Yousef but of stupid

Salameh going back again and again to reclaim his $400 truck rental deposit.

3.2 ADAPTATION—AND NONADAPTATION—IN THE LAW ENFORCEMENT COMMUNITY

Legal processes were the primary method for responding to these early manifestations of a new type of terrorism. Our overview of U.S. capabilities for dealing with it thus begins with the nation's vast complex of law enforcement agencies.

The Justice Department and the FBI

At the federal level, much law enforcement activity is concentrated in the Department of Justice. For countering terrorism, the dominant agency under Justice is the Federal Bureau of Investigation. The FBI does not have a general grant of authority but instead works under specific statutory authorizations. Most of its work is done in local offices called field offices. There are 56 of them, each covering a specified geographic area, and each quite separate from all others. Prior to 9/11, the special agent in charge was in general free to set his or her office's priorities and assign personnel accordingly.[11]

The office's priorities were driven by two primary concerns. First, performance in the Bureau was generally measured against statistics such as numbers of arrests, indictments, prosecutions, and convictions. Counterterrorism and counterintelligence work, often involving lengthy intelligence investigations that might never have positive or quantifiable results, was not career-enhancing. Most agents who reached management ranks had little counterterrorism experience. Second, priorities were driven at the local level by the field offices, whose concerns centered on traditional crimes such as white-collar offenses and those pertaining to drugs and gangs. Individual field offices made choices to serve local priorities, not national priorities.[12]

The Bureau also operates under an "office of origin" system. To avoid duplication and possible conflicts, the FBI designates a single office to be in charge of an entire investigation. Because the New York Field Office indicted Bin Ladin prior to the East Africa bombings, it became the office of origin for all Bin Ladin cases, including the East Africa bombings and later the attack on the USS *Cole*. Most of the FBI's institutional knowledge on Bin Ladin and al Qaeda resided there. This office worked closely with the U.S. Attorney for the Southern District of New York to identify, arrest, prosecute, and convict many of the perpetrators of the attacks and plots. Field offices other than the specified office of origin were often reluctant to spend much energy on matters over which they had no control and for which they received no credit.[13]

The FBI's domestic intelligence gathering dates from the 1930s. With World War II looming, President Franklin D. Roosevelt ordered FBI Director J. Edgar Hoover to investigate foreign and foreign-inspired subversion—Communist, Nazi, and Japanese. Hoover added investigation of possible espionage, sabotage, or subversion to the duties of field offices. After the war, foreign intelligence duties were assigned to the newly established Central Intelligence Agency. Hoover jealously guarded the FBI's domestic portfolio against all rivals. Hoover felt he was accountable only to the president, and the FBI's domestic intelligence activities kept growing. In the 1960s, the FBI was receiving significant assistance within the United States from the CIA and from Army Intelligence. The legal basis for some of this assistance was dubious.

Decades of encouragement to perform as a domestic intelligence agency abruptly ended in the 1970s. Two years after Hoover's death in 1972, congressional and news media investigations of the Watergate scandals of the Nixon administration expanded into general investigations of foreign and domestic intelligence by the Church and Pike committees.[14] They disclosed domestic intelligence efforts, which included a covert action program that operated from 1956 to

1971 against domestic organizations and, eventually, domestic dissidents. The FBI had spied on a wide range of political figures, especially individuals whom Hoover wanted to discredit (notably the Reverend Martin Luther King, Jr.), and had authorized unlawful wiretaps and surveillance. The shock registered in public opinion polls, where the percentage of Americans declaring a "highly favorable" view of the FBI dropped from 84 percent to 37 percent. The FBI's Domestic Intelligence Division was dissolved.[15]

In 1976, Attorney General Edward Levi adopted domestic security guidelines to regulate intelligence collection in the United States and to deflect calls for even stronger regulation. In 1983, Attorney General William French Smith revised the Levi guidelines to encourage closer investigation of potential terrorism. He also loosened the rules governing authorization for investigations and their duration. Still, his guidelines, like Levi's, took account of the reality that suspicion of "terrorism," like suspicion of "subversion," could lead to making individuals targets for investigation more because of their beliefs than because of their acts. Smith's guidelines also took account of the reality that potential terrorists were often members of extremist religious organizations and that investigation of terrorism could cross the line separating state and church.[16]

In 1986, Congress authorized the FBI to investigate terrorist attacks against Americans that occur outside the United States. Three years later, it added authority for the FBI to make arrests abroad without consent from the host country. Meanwhile, a task force headed by Vice President George H. W. Bush had endorsed a concept already urged by Director of Central Intelligence William Casey—a Counterterrorist Center, where the FBI, the CIA, and other organizations could work together on international terrorism. While it was distinctly a CIA entity, the FBI detailed officials to work at the Center and obtained leads that helped in the capture of persons wanted for trial in the United States.

The strengths that the FBI brought to counterterrorism were nowhere more brilliantly on display than in the case of

Pan American Flight 103, bound from London to New York, which blew up over Lockerbie, Scotland, in December 1988, killing 270 people. Initial evidence pointed to the government of Syria and, later, Iran. The Counterterrorist Center reserved judgment on the perpetrators of the attack. Meanwhile, FBI technicians, working with U.K. security services, gathered and analyzed the widely scattered fragments of the airliner. In 1991, with the help of the Counterterrorist Center, they identified one small fragment as part of a timing device—to the technicians, as distinctive as DNA. It was a Libyan device. Together with other evidence, the FBI put together a case pointing conclusively to the Libyan government. Eventually Libya acknowledged its responsibility.[17] Pan Am 103 became a cautionary tale against rushing to judgment in attributing responsibility for a terrorist act. It also showed again how—given a case to solve—the FBI remained capable of extraordinary investigative success.

FBI Organization and Priorities

In 1993, President Clinton chose Louis Freeh as the Director of the Bureau. Freeh, who would remain Director until June 2001, believed that the FBI's work should be done primarily by the field offices. To emphasize this view he cut headquarters staff and decentralized operations. The special agents in charge gained power, influence, and independence.[18]

Freeh recognized terrorism as a major threat. He increased the number of legal attaché offices abroad, focusing in particular on the Middle East. He also urged agents not to wait for terrorist acts to occur before taking action. In his first budget request to Congress after the 1993 World Trade Center bombing, he stated that "merely solving this type of crime is not enough; it is equally important that the FBI thwart terrorism before such acts can be perpetrated." Within headquarters, he created a Counterterrorism Division that would complement the Counterterrorist Center at the CIA and arranged for exchanges of senior FBI and CIA counterterrorism officials. He pressed for more cooperation between legal attachés and CIA stations abroad.[19]

Freeh's efforts did not, however, translate into a significant shift of resources to counterterrorism. FBI, Justice, and Office of Management and Budget officials said that FBI leadership seemed unwilling to shift resources to terrorism from other areas such as violent crime and drug enforcement; other FBI officials blamed Congress and the OMB for a lack of political will and failure to understand the FBI's counterterrorism resource needs. In addition, Freeh did not impose his views on the field offices. With a few notable exceptions, the field offices did not apply significant resources to terrorism and often reprogrammed funds for other priorities.[20]

In 1998, the FBI issued a five-year strategic plan led by its deputy director, Robert "Bear" Bryant. For the first time, the FBI designated national and economic security, including counterterrorism, as its top priority. Dale Watson, who would later become the head of the new Counterterrorism Division, said that after the East Africa bombings, "the light came on" that cultural change had to occur within the FBI. The plan mandated a stronger intelligence collection effort. It called for a nationwide automated system to facilitate information collection, analysis, and dissemination. It envisioned the creation of a professional intelligence cadre of experienced and trained agents and analysts. If successfully implemented, this would have been a major step toward addressing terrorism systematically, rather than as individual unrelated cases. But the plan did not succeed.[21]

First, the plan did not obtain the necessary human resources. Despite designating "national and economic security" as its top priority in 1998, the FBI did not shift human resources accordingly. Although the FBI's counterterrorism budget tripled during the mid-1990s, FBI counterterrorism spending remained fairly constant between fiscal years 1998 and 2001. In 2000, there were still twice as many agents devoted to drug enforcement as to counterterrorism.[22]

Second, the new division intended to strengthen the FBI's strategic analysis capability faltered. It received insufficient resources and faced resistance from senior managers in the

FBI's operational divisions. The new division was supposed to identify trends in terrorist activity, determine what the FBI did not know, and ultimately drive collection efforts. However, the FBI had little appreciation for the role of analysis. Analysts continued to be used primarily in a tactical fashion—providing support for existing cases. Compounding the problem was the FBI's tradition of hiring analysts from within instead of recruiting individuals with the relevant educational background and expertise.[23]

Moreover, analysts had difficulty getting access to the FBI and intelligence community information they were expected to analyze. The poor state of the FBI's information systems meant that such access depended in large part on an analyst's personal relationships with individuals in the operational units or squads where the information resided. For all of these reasons, prior to 9/11 relatively few strategic analytic reports about counterterrorism had been completed. Indeed, the FBI had never completed an assessment of the overall terrorist threat to the U.S. homeland.[24]

Third, the FBI did not have an effective intelligence collection effort. Collection of intelligence from human sources was limited, and agents were inadequately trained. Only three days of a 16-week agents' course were devoted to counterintelligence and counterterrorism, and most subsequent training was received on the job. The FBI did not have an adequate mechanism for validating source reporting, nor did it have a system for adequately tracking and sharing source reporting, either internally or externally. The FBI did not dedicate sufficient resources to the surveillance and translation needs of counterterrorism agents. It lacked sufficient translators proficient in Arabic and other key languages, resulting in a significant backlog of untranslated intercepts.[25]

Finally, the FBI's information systems were woefully inadequate. The FBI lacked the ability to know what it knew: there was no effective mechanism for capturing or sharing its institutional knowledge. FBI agents did create records of interviews and other investigative efforts, but there were no reports officers to condense the information into meaningful intelligence that could be retrieved and disseminated.[26]

In 1999, the FBI created separate Counterterrorism and Counterintelligence divisions. Dale Watson, the first head of the new Counterterrorism Division, recognized the urgent need to increase the FBI's counterterrorism capability. His plan, called MAXCAP 05, was unveiled in 2000: it set the goal of bringing the Bureau to its "maximum feasible capacity" in counterterrorism by 2005. Field executives told Watson that they did not have the analysts, linguists, or technically trained experts to carry out the strategy. In a report provided to Director Robert Mueller in September 2001, one year after Watson presented his plan to field executives, almost every FBI field office was assessed to be operating below "maximum capacity." The report stated that "the goal to 'prevent terrorism' requires a dramatic shift in emphasis from a reactive capability to highly functioning intelligence capability which provides not only leads and operational support, but clear strategic analysis and direction."[27]

Legal Constraints on the FBI and "the Wall"

The FBI had different tools for law enforcement and intelligence.[28] For criminal matters, it could apply for and use traditional criminal warrants. For intelligence matters involving international terrorism, however, the rules were different. For many years the attorney general could authorize surveillance of foreign powers and agents of foreign powers without any court review, but in 1978 Congress passed the Foreign Intelligence Surveillance Act.[29] This law regulated intelligence collection directed at foreign powers and agents of foreign powers in the United States. In addition to requiring court review of proposed surveillance (and later, physical searches), the 1978 act was interpreted by the courts to require that a search be approved only if its "primary purpose" was to obtain foreign intelligence information. In other words, the authorities of the FISA law could not be used to circumvent traditional criminal warrant requirements. The Justice Department interpreted these rulings as saying that criminal prosecutors could be briefed on FISA information but could not direct or control its collection.[30]

Throughout the 1980s and early 1990s, Justice prosecutors had informal arrangements for obtaining information gathered in the FISA process, the understanding being that they would not improperly exploit that process for their criminal cases. Whether the FBI shared with prosecutors information pertinent to possible criminal investigations was left solely to the judgment of the FBI.[31]

But the prosecution of Aldrich Ames for espionage in 1994 revived concerns about the prosecutors' role in intelligence investigations. The Department of Justice's Office of Intelligence Policy and Review (OIPR) is responsible for reviewing and presenting all FISA applications to the FISA Court. It worried that because of the numerous prior consultations between FBI agents and prosecutors, the judge might rule that the FISA warrants had been misused. If that had happened, Ames might have escaped conviction. Richard Scruggs, the acting head of OIPR, complained to Attorney General Janet Reno about the lack of information-sharing controls. On his own, he began imposing information-sharing procedures for FISA material. The Office of Intelligence Policy and Review became the gatekeeper for the flow of FISA information to criminal prosecutors.[32]

In July 1995, Attorney General Reno issued formal procedures aimed at managing information sharing between Justice Department prosecutors and the FBI. They were developed in a working group led by the Justice Department's Executive Office of National Security, overseen by Deputy Attorney General Jamie Gorelick.[33] These procedures—while requiring the sharing of intelligence information with prosecutors—regulated the manner in which such information could be shared from the intelligence side of the house to the criminal side.

These procedures were almost immediately misunderstood and misapplied. As a result, there was far less information sharing and coordination between the FBI and the Criminal Division in practice than was allowed under the department's procedures. Over time the procedures came to be referred to as "the wall." The term "the wall" is misleading, however, because several factors led to a series of barriers to information sharing that developed.[34]

The Office of Intelligence Policy and Review became the sole gatekeeper for passing information to the Criminal Division. Though Attorney General Reno's procedures did not include such a provision, the Office assumed the role anyway, arguing that its position reflected the concerns of Judge Royce Lamberth, then chief judge of the Foreign Intelligence Surveillance Court. The Office threatened that if it could not regulate the flow of information to criminal prosecutors, it would no longer present the FBI's warrant requests to the FISA Court. The information flow withered.[35]

The 1995 procedures dealt only with sharing between agents and criminal prosecutors, not between two kinds of FBI agents, those working on intelligence matters and those working on criminal matters. But pressure from the Office of Intelligence Policy Review, FBI leadership, and the FISA Court built barriers between agents—even agents serving on the same squads. FBI Deputy Director Bryant reinforced the Office's caution by informing agents that too much information sharing could be a career stopper. Agents in the field began to believe—incorrectly—that no FISA information could be shared with agents working on criminal investigations.[36]

This perception evolved into the still more exaggerated belief that the FBI could not share *any* intelligence information with criminal investigators, even if no FISA procedures had been used. Thus, relevant information from the National Security Agency and the CIA often failed to make its way to criminal investigators. Separate reviews in 1999, 2000, and 2001 concluded independently that information sharing was not occurring, and that the intent of the 1995 procedures was ignored routinely.[37] We will describe some of the unfortunate consequences of these accumulated institutional beliefs and practices in chapter 8.

There were other legal limitations. Both prosecutors and FBI agents argued that they were barred by court rules from sharing grand jury information, even though the prohibition applied only to that small fraction that had been presented to a grand jury, and even that prohibition had exceptions. But as interpreted by FBI field offices, this prohibition could conceivably apply to much of the information unearthed in an investigation. There were also restrictions, arising from executive order, on the commingling of domestic information with foreign intelligence. Finally the NSA began putting caveats on its Bin Ladin–related reports that required prior approval before sharing their contents with criminal investigators and prosecutors. These developments further blocked the arteries of information sharing.[38]

Other Law Enforcement Agencies

The Justice Department is much more than the FBI. It also has a U.S. Marshals Service, almost 4,000 strong on 9/11 and especially expert in tracking fugitives, with much local police knowledge. The department's Drug Enforcement Administration had, as of 2001, more than 4,500 agents.[39] There were a number of occasions when DEA agents were able to introduce sources to the FBI or CIA for counterterrorism use.

The Immigration and Naturalization Service (INS), with its 9,000 Border Patrol agents, 4,500 inspectors, and 2,000 immigration special agents, had perhaps the greatest potential to develop an expanded role in counterterrorism. However, the INS was focused on the formidable challenges posed by illegal entry over the southwest border, criminal aliens, and a growing backlog in the applications for naturalizing immigrants. The White House, the Justice Department, and above all the Congress reinforced these concerns. In addition, when Doris Meissner became INS Commissioner in 1993, she found an agency seriously hampered by outdated technology and insufficient human resources. Border Patrol agents were still using manual typewriters; inspectors at ports of entry were using a paper watchlist; the asylum and other benefits systems did not effectively deter fraudulent applicants.[40]

Commissioner Meissner responded in 1993 to the World Trade Center bombing by providing seed money to the State Department's Consular Affairs Bureau to automate its terrorist watchlist, used by consular officers and border inspectors. The INS assigned an individual in a new "lookout" unit to work with the State Department in watchlisting suspected terrorists and with the intelligence community and the FBI in determining how to deal with them when they appeared at ports of entry. By 1998, 97 suspected terrorists had been denied admission at U.S. ports of entry because of the watchlist.[41]

How to conduct deportation cases against aliens who were suspected terrorists caused significant debate. The INS had immigration law expertise and authority to bring the cases, but the FBI possessed the classified information sometimes needed as evidence, and information-sharing conflicts resulted. New laws in 1996 authorized the use of classified evidence in removal hearings, but the INS removed only a handful of the aliens with links to terrorist activity (none identified as associated with al Qaeda) using classified evidence.[42]

Midlevel INS employees proposed comprehensive counterterrorism proposals to management in 1986, 1995, and 1997. No action was taken on them. In 1997, a National Security Unit was set up to handle alerts, track potential terrorist cases for possible immigration enforcement action, and work with the rest of the Justice Department. It focused on the FBI's priorities of Hezbollah and Hamas, and began to examine how immigration laws could be brought to bear on terrorism. For instance, it sought unsuccessfully to require that CIA security checks be completed before naturalization applications were approved.[43] Policy questions, such as whether resident alien status should be revoked upon the person's conviction of a terrorist crime, were not addressed.

Congress, with the support of the Clinton administration, doubled the number of Border Patrol agents required along the border with Mexico to one agent every quarter mile by 1999. It rejected efforts to bring additional resources to bear in the north. The border with Canada had one agent for every 13.25 miles. Despite examples of terrorists entering from Canada, awareness of terrorist activity in Canada and its more lenient immigration laws, and an inspector general's report recommending that the Border Patrol develop a northern border strategy, the only positive step was that the number of Border Patrol agents was not cut any further.[44]

Inspectors at the ports of entry were not asked to focus on terrorists. Inspectors told us they were not even aware that when they checked the names of incoming passengers against the automated watchlist, they were checking in part for terrorists. In general, border inspectors also did not have the information they needed to make fact-based determinations of admissibility. The INS initiated but failed to bring to completion two efforts that would have provided inspectors with information relevant to counterterrorism—a proposed system to track foreign student visa compliance and a program to establish a way of tracking travelers' entry to and exit from the United States.[45]

In 1996, a new law enabled the INS to enter into agreements with state and local law enforcement agencies through which the INS provided training and the local agencies exercised immigration enforcement authority. Terrorist watchlists were not available to them. Mayors in cities with large immigrant populations sometimes imposed limits on city employee cooperation with federal immigration agents. A large population lives outside the legal framework. Fraudulent documents could be easily obtained. Congress kept the number of INS agents static in the face of the overwhelming problem.[46]

The chief vehicle for INS and for state and local participation in law enforcement was the Joint Terrorism Task Force (JTTF), first tried out in New York City in 1980 in response to a spate of incidents involving domestic terrorist organizations. This task force was managed by the New York Field Office of the FBI, and its existence provided an opportunity to exchange information and, as happened after the first World Trade Center bombing, to enlist local officers, as well as other agency representatives, as partners in the FBI investigation. The FBI expanded the number of JTTFs throughout the 1990s, and by 9/11 there were 34. While useful, the JTTFs had limitations. They set priorities in accordance with regional and field office concerns, and most were not fully staffed. Many state and local entities believed they had little to gain from having a full-time representative on a JTTF.[47]

Other federal law enforcement resources, also not seriously enlisted for counterterrorism, were to be found in the Treasury Department.

Treasury housed the Secret Service, the Customs Service, and the Bureau of Alcohol, Tobacco, and Firearms. Given the Secret Service's mission to protect the president and other high officials, its agents did become involved with those of the FBI whenever terrorist assassination plots were rumored.

The Customs Service deployed agents at all points of entry into the United States. Its agents worked alongside INS agents, and the two groups sometimes cooperated. In the winter of 1999–2000, as will be detailed in chapter 6, questioning by an especially alert Customs inspector led to the arrest of an al Qaeda terrorist whose apparent mission was to bomb Los Angeles International Airport.

The Bureau of Alcohol, Tobacco, and Firearms was used on occasion by the FBI as a resource. The ATF's laboratories and analysis were critical to the investigation of the February 1993 bombing of the World Trade Center and the April 1995 bombing of the Alfred P. Murrah Federal Building in Oklahoma City.[48]

Before 9/11, with the exception of one portion of the FBI, very little of the sprawling U.S. law enforcement community was engaged in countering terrorism. Moreover, law enforcement could be effective only after specific individuals were identified, a plot had formed, or an attack had already occurred. Responsible individuals had to be located, apprehended, and transported back to a U.S. court for prosecution. As FBI agents emphasized to us, the FBI and the Justice Department do not have cruise missiles. They declare war by indicting someone. They took on the lead role in addressing terrorism because they were asked to do so.[49]

3.3 . . . AND IN THE FEDERAL AVIATION ADMINISTRATION

The Federal Aviation Administration (FAA) within the Department of Transportation had been vested by Congress with the sometimes conflicting mandate of regulating the safety and security of U.S. civil aviation while also promoting the civil aviation industry. The FAA had a security mission to protect the users of commercial air transportation against terrorism and other criminal acts. In the years before 9/11, the FAA perceived sabotage as a greater threat to aviation than hijacking. First, no domestic hijacking had occurred in a decade. Second, the commercial aviation system was perceived as more vulnerable to explosives than to weapons such as firearms. Finally, explosives were perceived as deadlier than hijacking and therefore of greater consequence. In 1996, a presidential commission on aviation safety and security chaired by Vice President Al Gore reinforced the prevailing concern about sabotage and explosives on aircraft. The Gore Commission also flagged, as a new danger, the possibility of attack by surface-to-air missiles. Its 1997 final report did not discuss the possibility of suicide hijackings.[50]

The FAA set and enforced aviation security rules, which airlines and airports were required to implement. The rules were supposed to produce a "layered" system of defense. This meant that the failure of any one layer of security would not be fatal, because additional layers would provide backup security. But each layer relevant to hijackings—intelligence, passenger prescreening, checkpoint screening, and onboard security—was seriously flawed prior to 9/11. Taken together, they did not stop any of the 9/11 hijackers from getting on board four different aircraft at three different airports.[51]

The FAA's policy was to use intelligence to identify both specific plots and general threats to civil aviation security, so that the agency could develop and deploy appropriate countermeasures. The FAA's 40-person intelligence unit was supposed to receive a broad range of intelligence data from the FBI, CIA, and other agencies so that it could make assessments about the threat to aviation. But the large volume of data contained little pertaining to the presence and activities of terrorists in the United States. For example, information on the FBI's effort in 1998 to assess the potential use of flight training by terrorists and the Phoenix electronic communication of 2001 warning of radical Middle Easterners attending flight school were not passed to FAA headquarters. Several top FAA intelligence officials called the domestic threat picture a serious blind spot.[52]

Moreover, the FAA's intelligence unit did not receive much attention from the agency's leadership. Neither Administrator Jane Garvey nor her deputy routinely reviewed daily intelligence, and what they did see was screened for them. She was unaware of a great amount of hijacking threat information from her own intelligence unit, which, in turn, was not deeply involved in the agency's policymaking process. Historically, decisive security action took place only after a disaster had occurred or a specific plot had been discovered.[53]

The next aviation security layer was passenger prescreening. The FAA directed air carriers not to fly individuals known to pose a "direct" threat to civil aviation. But as of 9/11, the FAA's "no-fly" list contained the names of just 12 terrorist suspects (including 9/11 mastermind Khalid Sheikh Mohammed), even though government watchlists contained the names of many thousands of known and suspected terrorists. This astonishing mismatch existed despite the Gore

Commission's having called on the FBI and CIA four years earlier to provide terrorist watchlists to improve prescreening. The longtime chief of the FAA's civil aviation security division testified that he was not even aware of the State Department's TIPOFF list of known and suspected terrorists (some 60,000 before 9/11) until he heard it mentioned during the Commission's January 26, 2004, public hearing. The FAA had access to some TIPOFF data, but apparently found it too difficult to use.[54]

The second part of prescreening called on the air carriers to implement an FAA-approved computerized algorithm (known as CAPPS, for Computer Assisted Passenger Prescreening System) designed to identify passengers whose profile suggested they might pose more than a minimal risk to aircraft. Although the algorithm included hijacker profile data, at that time only passengers checking bags were eligible to be selected by CAPPS for additional scrutiny. Selection entailed only having one's checked baggage screened for explosives or held off the airplane until one had boarded. Primarily because of concern regarding potential discrimination and the impact on passenger throughput, "selectees" were no longer required to undergo extraordinary screening of their carry-on baggage as had been the case before the system was computerized in 1997.[55] This policy change also reflected the perception that nonsuicide sabotage was the primary threat to civil aviation.

Checkpoint screening was considered the most important and obvious layer of security. Walk-through metal detectors and X-ray machines operated by trained screeners were employed to stop prohibited items. Numerous government reports indicated that checkpoints performed poorly, often failing to detect even obvious FAA test items. Many deadly and dangerous items did not set off metal detectors, or were hard to distinguish in an X-ray machine from innocent everyday items.[56]

While FAA rules did not expressly prohibit knives with blades under 4 inches long, the airlines' checkpoint operations guide (which was developed in cooperation with the

FAA), explicitly permitted them. The FAA's basis for this policy was (1) the agency did not consider such items to be menacing, (2) most local laws did not prohibit individuals from carrying such knives, and (3) such knives would have been difficult to detect unless the sensitivity of metal detectors had been greatly increased. A proposal to ban knives altogether in 1993 had been rejected because small cutting implements were difficult to detect and the number of innocent "alarms" would have increased significantly, exacerbating congestion problems at checkpoints.[57]

Several years prior to 9/11, an FAA requirement for screeners to conduct "continuous" and "random" hand searches of carry-on luggage at checkpoints had been replaced by explosive trace detection or had simply become ignored by the air carriers. Therefore, secondary screening of individuals and their carry-on bags to identify weapons (other than bombs) was nonexistent, except for passengers who triggered the metal detectors. Even when small knives were detected by secondary screening, they were usually returned to the traveler. Reportedly, the 9/11 hijackers were instructed to use items that would be undetectable by airport checkpoints.[58]

In the pre-9/11 security system, the air carriers played a major role. As the Inspector General of the Department of Transportation told us, there were great pressures from the air carriers to control security costs and to "limit the impact of security requirements on aviation operations, so that the industry could concentrate on its primary mission of moving passengers and aircraft. . . . [T]hose counterpressures in turn manifested themselves as significant weaknesses in security." A longtime FAA security official described the air carriers' approach to security regulation as "decry, deny and delay" and told us that while "the air carriers had seen the enlightened hand of self-interest with respect to safety, they hadn't seen it in the security arena."[59]

The final layer, security on board commercial aircraft, was not designed to counter suicide hijackings. The FAA-approved "Common Strategy" had been elaborated over decades of experience with scores of hijackings, beginning in the 1960s. It taught flight crews that the best way to deal with hijackers was to accommodate their demands, get the plane to land safely, and then let law enforcement or the military handle the situation. According to the FAA, the record had shown that the longer a hijacking persisted, the more likely it was to end peacefully. The strategy operated on the fundamental assumption that hijackers issue negotiable demands (most often for asylum or the release of prisoners) and that, as one FAA official put it, "suicide wasn't in the game plan" of hijackers. FAA training material provided no guidance for flight crews should violence occur.[60]

This prevailing Common Strategy of cooperation and nonconfrontation meant that even a hardened cockpit door would have made little difference in a hijacking. As the chairman of the Security Committee of the Air Line Pilots Association observed when proposals were made in early 2001 to install reinforced cockpit doors in commercial aircraft, "Even if you make a vault out of the door, if they have a noose around my flight attendant's neck, I'm going to open the door." Prior to 9/11, FAA regulations mandated that cockpit doors permit ready access into and out of the cockpit in the event of an emergency. Even so, rules implemented in the 1960s required air crews to keep the cockpit door closed and locked in flight. This requirement was not always observed or vigorously enforced.[61]

As for law enforcement, there were only 33 armed and trained federal air marshals as of 9/11. They were not deployed on U.S. domestic flights, except when in transit to provide security on international departures. This policy reflected the FAA's view that domestic hijacking was in check—a view held confidently as no terrorist had hijacked a U.S. commercial aircraft anywhere in the world since 1986.[62]

In the absence of any recent aviation security incident and without "specific and credible" evidence of a plot directed at civil aviation, the FAA's leadership focused elsewhere, including on operational concerns and the ever-present issue of safety. FAA Administrator Garvey recalled that "every day in 2001 was like the day before Thanksgiving." Heeding calls for improved air service, Congress concentrated its efforts on a "passenger bill of rights," to improve capacity, efficiency, and customer satisfaction in the aviation system. There was no focus on terrorism.[63]

3.4 . . . AND IN THE INTELLIGENCE COMMUNITY

The National Security Act of 1947 created the position of Director of Central Intelligence (DCI). Independent from the departments of Defense, State, Justice, and other policy departments, the DCI heads the U.S. intelligence community and provides intelligence to federal entities.

The sole element of the intelligence community independent from a cabinet agency is the CIA. As an independent agency, it collects, analyzes, and disseminates intelligence from all sources. The CIA's number one customer is the president of the United States, who also has the authority to direct it to conduct covert operations.[64] Although covert actions represent a very small fraction of the Agency's entire budget, these operations have at times been controversial and over time have dominated the public's perception of the CIA.

The DCI is confirmed by the Senate but is not technically a member of the president's cabinet. The director's power under federal law over the loose, confederated "intelligence community" is limited.[65] He or she states the community's priorities and coordinates development of intelligence agency budget requests for submission to Congress.

This responsibility gives many the false impression that the DCI has line authority over the heads of these agencies and has the power to shift resources within these budgets as the need arises. Neither is true. In fact, the DCI's real authority has been directly proportional to his personal closeness to the president, which has waxed and waned over the years, and to others in government, especially the secretary of defense.

Intelligence agencies under the Department of Defense account for approximately 80 percent of all U.S. spending for intelligence, including some that supports a national customer base and some that supports specific Defense Department or military service needs.[66] As they are housed in the Defense Department, these agencies are keenly attentive to the military's strategic and tactical requirements.

One of the intelligence agencies in Defense with a national customer base is the National Security Agency, which intercepts and analyzes foreign communications and breaks codes. The NSA also creates codes and ciphers to protect government information. Another is the recently renamed National Geospatial-Intelligence Agency (NGA), which provides and analyzes imagery and produces a wide array of products, including maps, navigation tools, and surveillance intelligence. A third such agency in Defense is the National Reconnaissance Office. It develops, procures, launches, and maintains in orbit information-gathering satellites that serve other government agencies.

The Defense Intelligence Agency supports the secretary of defense, Joint Chiefs of Staff, and military field commanders. It does some collection through human sources as well as some technical intelligence collection. The Army, Navy, Air Force, and Marine Corps have their own intelligence components that collect information, help them decide what weapons to acquire, and serve the tactical intelligence needs of their respective services.

In addition to those from the Department of Defense, other elements in the intelligence community include the national security parts of the FBI; the Bureau of Intelligence and Research in the State Department; the intelligence component of the Treasury Department; the Energy Department's Office of Intelligence and Counterintelligence, the former of which, through leveraging the expertise of the national laboratory system, has special competence in nuclear weapons; the Office of Intelligence of the Coast Guard; and, today, the Directorate of Intelligence Analysis and Infrastructure Protection in the Department of Homeland Security.

The National Security Agency

The National Security Agency's intercepts of terrorist communications often set off alarms elsewhere in the government. Often, too, its intercepts are conclusive elements in the analyst's jigsaw puzzle. NSA engineers build technical systems to break ciphers and to make sense of today's complex signals environment. Its analysts listen to conversations between foreigners not meant for them. They also perform "traffic analysis"—studying technical communications systems and codes as well as foreign organizational structures, including those of terrorist organizations.

Cold War adversaries used very hierarchical, familiar, and predictable military command and control methods. With globalization and the telecommunications revolution, and with loosely affiliated but networked adversaries using commercial devices and encryption, the technical impediments to signals collection grew at a geometric rate. At the same time, the end of the Cold War and the resultant cuts in national security funding forced intelligence agencies to cut systems and seek economies of scale. Modern adversaries are skilled users of communications technologies. The NSA's challenges, and its opportunities, increased exponentially in "volume, variety, and velocity."[67]

The law requires the NSA to not deliberately collect data on U.S. citizens or on persons in the United States without a warrant based on foreign intelligence requirements. Also, the NSA was supposed to let the FBI know of any indication of crime, espionage, or "terrorist enterprise" so that the FBI could obtain the appropriate warrant. Later in this story, we will learn that while the NSA had the technical capability to report on communications with suspected terrorist facilities in the Middle East, the NSA did not seek FISA Court warrants to collect communications between individuals in the

United States and foreign countries, because it believed that this was an FBI role. It also did not want to be viewed as targeting persons in the United States and possibly violating laws that governed NSA's collection of foreign intelligence.[68]

An almost obsessive protection of sources and methods by the NSA, and its focus on foreign intelligence, and its avoidance of anything domestic would, as will be seen, be important elements in the story of 9/11.

Technology as an Intelligence Asset and Liability

The application of newly developed scientific technology to the mission of U.S. war fighters and national security decisionmakers is one of the great success stories of the twentieth century. It did not happen by accident. Recent wars have been waged and won decisively by brave men and women using advanced technology that was developed, authorized, and paid for by conscientious and diligent executive and legislative branch leaders many years earlier.

The challenge of technology, however, is a daunting one. It is expensive, sometimes fails, and often can create problems as well as solve them. Some of the advanced technologies that gave us insight into the closed-off territories of the Soviet Union during the Cold War are of limited use in identifying and tracking individual terrorists.

Terrorists, in turn, have benefited from this same rapid development of communication technologies. They simply could buy off the shelf and harvest the products of a $3 trillion a year telecommunications industry. They could acquire without great expense communication devices that were varied, global, instantaneous, complex, and encrypted.

The emergence of the World Wide Web has given terrorists a much easier means of acquiring information and exercising command and control over their operations. The operational leader of the 9/11 conspiracy, Mohamed Atta, went online from Hamburg, Germany, to research U.S. flight schools. Targets of intelligence collection have become more sophisticated. These changes have made surveillance and threat warning more difficult.

Despite the problems that technology creates, Americans' love affair with it leads them to also regard it as the solution. But technology produces its best results when an organization has the doctrine, structure, and incentives to exploit it. For example, even the best information technology will not improve information sharing so long as the intelligence agencies' personnel and security systems reward protecting information rather than disseminating it.

The CIA

The CIA is a descendant of the Office of Strategic Services (OSS), which President Roosevelt created early in World War II after having first thought the FBI might take that role. The father of the OSS was William J. "Wild Bill" Donovan, a Wall Street lawyer. He recruited into the OSS others like himself—well traveled, well connected, well-to-do professional men and women.[69]

An innovation of Donovan's, whose legacy remains part of U.S. intelligence today, was the establishment of a Research and Analysis Branch. There large numbers of scholars from U.S. universities pored over accounts from spies, communications intercepted by the armed forces, transcripts of radio broadcasts, and publications of all types, and prepared reports on economic, political, and social conditions in foreign theaters of operation.

At the end of World War II, to Donovan's disappointment, President Harry Truman dissolved the Office of Strategic Services. Four months later, the President directed that "all Federal foreign intelligence activities be planned, developed and coordinated so as to assure the most effective accomplishment of the intelligence mission related to the national security," under a National Intelligence Authority consisting of the secretaries of State, War, and the Navy, and a personal representative of the president. This body was to be assisted by a Central Intelligence Group, made up of persons detailed from the departments of each of the members and headed by a Director of Central Intelligence.[70]

Subsequently, President Truman agreed to the National Security Act of 1947, which, among other things, established the Central Intelligence Agency, under the Director of Central Intelligence. Lobbying by the FBI, combined with fears of creating a U.S. Gestapo,[71] led to the FBI's being assigned responsibility for internal security functions and counterespionage. The CIA was specifically accorded "no police, subpoena, or law enforcement powers or internal security functions."[72] This structure built in tensions between the CIA and the Defense Department's intelligence agencies, and between the CIA and the FBI.

Clandestine and Covert Action.

With this history, the CIA brought to the era of 9/11 many attributes of an elite organization, viewing itself as serving on the nation's front lines to engage America's enemies. Officers in its Clandestine Service, under what became the Directorate of Operations, fanned out into stations abroad. Each chief of station was a very important person in the organization, given the additional title of the DCI's representative in that country. He (occasionally she) was governed by an operating directive that listed operational priorities issued by the relevant regional division of the Directorate, constrained by centrally determined allocations of resources.

Because the conduct of espionage was a high-risk activity, decisions on the clandestine targeting, recruitment, handling, and termination of secret sources and the dissemination of collected information required Washington's approval and action. But in this decentralized system, analogous in some ways to the culture of the FBI field offices in the United States, everyone in the Directorate of Operations presumed that it was the job of headquarters to support the field, rather than manage field activities.

In the 1960s, the CIA suffered exposure of its botched effort to land Cuban exiles at the Bay of Pigs. The Vietnam War brought on more criticism. A prominent feature of the

Watergate era was investigations of the CIA by committees headed by Frank Church in the Senate and Otis Pike in the House. They published evidence that the CIA had secretly planned to assassinate Fidel Castro and other foreign leaders. The President had not taken plain responsibility for these judgments. CIA officials had taken most of the blame, saying they had done so in order to preserve the President's "plausible deniability."[73]

After the Watergate era, Congress established oversight committees to ensure that the CIA did not undertake covert action contrary to basic American law. Case officers in the CIA's Clandestine Service interpreted legislation, such as the Hughes-Ryan Amendment requiring that the president approve and report to Congress any covert action, as sending a message to them that covert action often leads to trouble and can severely damage one's career. Controversies surrounding Central American covert action programs in the mid-1980s led to the indictment of several senior officers of the Clandestine Service. During the 1990s, tension sometimes arose, as it did in the effort against al Qaeda, between policymakers who wanted the CIA to undertake more aggressive covert action and wary CIA leaders who counseled prudence and making sure that the legal basis and presidential authorization for their actions were undeniably clear.

The Clandestine Service felt the impact of the post–Cold War peace dividend, with cuts beginning in 1992. As the number of officers declined and overseas facilities were closed, the DCI and his managers responded to developing crises in the Balkans or in Africa by "surging," or taking officers from across the service to use on the immediate problem. In many cases the surge officers had little familiarity with the new issues. Inevitably, some parts of the world and some collection targets were not fully covered, or not covered at all. This strategy also placed great emphasis on close relations with foreign liaison services, whose help was needed to gain information that the United States itself did not have the capacity to collect.

The nadir for the Clandestine Service was in 1995, when

only 25 trainees became new officers.[74] In 1998, the DCI was able to persuade the administration and the Congress to endorse a long-range rebuilding program. It takes five to seven years of training, language study, and experience to bring a recruit up to full performance.[75]

Analysis.

The CIA's Directorate of Intelligence retained some of its original character of a university gone to war. Its men and women tended to judge one another by the quantity and quality of their publications (in this case, classified publications). Apart from their own peers, they looked for approval and guidance to policymakers. During the 1990s and today, particular value is attached to having a contribution included in one of the classified daily "newspapers"—the Senior Executive Intelligence Brief—or, better still, selected for inclusion in the President's Daily Brief.[76]

The CIA had been created to wage the Cold War. Its steady focus on one or two primary adversaries, decade after decade, had at least one positive effect: it created an environment in which managers and analysts could safely invest time and resources in basic research, detailed and reflective. Payoffs might not be immediate. But when they wrote their estimates, even in brief papers, they could draw on a deep base of knowledge.

When the Cold War ended, those investments could not easily be reallocated to new enemies. The cultural effects ran even deeper. In a more fluid international environment with uncertain, changing goals and interests, intelligence managers no longer felt they could afford such a patient, strategic approach to long-term accumulation of intellectual capital. A university culture with its versions of books and articles was giving way to the culture of the newsroom.

During the 1990s, the rise of round-the-clock news shows and the Internet reinforced pressure on analysts to pass along fresh reports to policymakers at an ever-faster pace, trying to add context or supplement what their customers were receiving from the media. Weaknesses in all-source and strategic analysis were highlighted by a panel, chaired by Admiral David Jeremiah, that critiqued the intelligence community's failure to foresee the nuclear weapons tests by India and Pakistan in 1998, as well as by a 1999 panel, chaired by Donald Rumsfeld, that discussed the community's limited ability to assess the ballistic missile threat to the United States. Both reports called attention to the dispersal of effort on too many priorities, the declining attention to the craft of strategic analysis, and security rules that prevented adequate sharing of information. Another Cold War craft had been an elaborate set of methods for warning against surprise attack, but that too had faded in analyzing new dangers like terrorism.[77]

Security.

Another set of experiences that would affect the capacity of the CIA to cope with the new terrorism traced back to the early Cold War, when the Agency developed a concern, bordering on paranoia, about penetration by the Soviet KGB. James Jesus Angleton, who headed counterintelligence in the CIA until the early 1970s, became obsessed with the belief that the Agency harbored one or more Soviet "moles." Although the pendulum swung back after Angleton's forced retirement, it did not go very far. Instances of actual Soviet penetration kept apprehensions high.[78] Then, in the early 1990s, came the Aldrich Ames espionage case, which intensely embarrassed the CIA. Though obviously unreliable, Ames had been protected and promoted by fellow officers while he paid his bills by selling to the Soviet Union the names of U.S. operatives and agents, a number of whom died as a result.

The concern about security vastly complicated information sharing. Information was compartmented in order to protect it against exposure to skilled and technologically sophisticated adversaries. There were therefore numerous restrictions on handling information and a deep suspicion about sending information over newfangled electronic systems, like email, to other agencies of the U.S. government.[79]

Security concerns also increased the difficulty of recruiting officers qualified for counterterrorism. Very few American colleges or universities offered programs in Middle Eastern languages or Islamic studies. The total number of undergraduate degrees granted in Arabic in all U.S. colleges and universities in 2002 was six.[80] Many who had traveled much outside the United States could expect a very long wait for initial clearance. Anyone who was foreign-born or had numerous relatives abroad was well-advised not even to apply. With budgets for the CIA shrinking after the end of the Cold War, it was not surprising that, with some notable exceptions, new hires in the Clandestine Service tended to have qualifications similar to those of serving officers: that is, they were suited for traditional agent recruitment or for exploiting liaison relationships with foreign services but were not equipped to seek or use assets inside the terrorist network.

Early Counterterrorism Efforts

In the 1970s and 1980s, terrorism had been tied to regional conflicts, mainly in the Middle East. The majority of terrorist groups either were sponsored by governments or, like the Palestine Liberation Organization, were militants trying to create governments.

In the mid-1980s, on the basis of a report from a task force headed by Vice President George Bush and after terrorist attacks at airports in Rome and Athens, the DCI created a Counterterrorist Center to unify activities across the Directorate of Operations and the Directorate of Intelligence. The Counterterrorist Center had representation from the FBI and other agencies. In the formal table of organization it reported to the DCI, but in fact most of the Center's chiefs belonged to the Clandestine Service and usually looked for guidance to the head of the Directorate of Operations.[81]

The Center stimulated and coordinated collection of information by CIA stations, compiled the results, and passed selected reports to appropriate stations, the Directorate of

Intelligence analysts, other parts of the intelligence community, or to policymakers. The Center protected its bureaucratic turf. The Director of Central Intelligence had once had a national intelligence officer for terrorism to coordinate analysis; that office was abolished in the late 1980s and its duties absorbed in part by the Counterterrorist Center. Though analysts assigned to the Center produced a large number of papers, the focus was support to operations. A CIA inspector general's report in 1994 criticized the Center's capacity to provide warning of terrorist attacks.[82]

Subsequent chapters will raise the issue of whether, despite tremendous talent, energy, and dedication, the intelligence community failed to do enough in coping with the challenge from Bin Ladin and al Qaeda. Confronted with such questions, managers in the intelligence community often responded that they had meager resources with which to work.[83]

Cuts in national security expenditures at the end of the Cold War led to budget cuts in the national foreign intelligence program from fiscal year 1990 to 1996 and essentially flat budgets from fiscal years 1996 to 2000 (except for the so-called Gingrich supplemental to the FY1999 budget and two later, smaller supplementals). These cuts compounded the difficulties of the intelligence agencies. Policymakers were asking them to move into the digitized future to fight against computer-to-computer communications and modern communication systems, while maintaining capability against older systems, such as high-frequency radios and ultra-high- and very-high-frequency (line of sight) systems that work like old-style television antennas. Also, demand for imagery increased dramatically following the success of the 1991 Gulf War. Both these developments, in turn, placed a premium on planning the next generation of satellite systems, the cost of which put great pressure on the rest of the intelligence budget. As a result, intelligence agencies experienced staff reductions, affecting both operators and analysts.[84]

Yet at least for the CIA, part of the burden in tackling terrorism arose from the background we have described: an organization capable of attracting extraordinarily motivated people but institutionally averse to risk, with its capacity for covert action atrophied, predisposed to restrict the distribution of information, having difficulty assimilating new types of personnel, and accustomed to presenting descriptive reportage of the latest intelligence. The CIA, to put it another way, needed significant change in order to get maximum effect in counterterrorism. President Clinton appointed George Tenet as DCI in 1997, and by all accounts terrorism was a priority for him. But Tenet's own assessment, when questioned by the Commission, was that in 2004, the CIA's clandestine service was still at least five years away from being fully ready to play its counterterrorism role.[85] And while Tenet was clearly the leader of the CIA, the intelligence community's confederated structure left open the question of who really was in charge of the entire U.S. intelligence effort.

3.5 . . . AND IN THE STATE DEPARTMENT AND THE DEFENSE DEPARTMENT

The State Department

The Commission asked Deputy Secretary of State Richard Armitage in 2004 why the State Department had so long pursued what seemed, and ultimately proved, to be a hopeless effort to persuade the Taliban regime in Afghanistan to deport Bin Ladin. Armitage replied: "We do what the State Department does, we don't go out and fly bombers, we don't do things like that[;] . . . we do *our* part in these things."[86]

Fifty years earlier, the person in Armitage's position would not have spoken of the Department of State as having such a limited role. Until the late 1950s, the department dominated the processes of advising the president and Congress on U.S. relations with the rest of the world. The National Security Council was created in 1947 largely as a result of lobbying from the Pentagon for a forum where the military could object if they thought the State Department was setting national objectives that the United States did not have the wherewithal to pursue.

The State Department retained primacy until the 1960s, when the Kennedy and Johnson administrations turned instead to Robert McNamara's Defense Department, where a mini-state department was created to analyze foreign policy issues. President Richard Nixon then concentrated policy planning and policy coordination in a powerful National Security Council staff, overseen by Henry Kissinger.

In later years, individual secretaries of state were important figures, but the department's role continued to erode. State came into the 1990s overmatched by the resources of other departments and with little support for its budget either in the Congress or in the president's Office of Management and Budget.

Like the FBI and the CIA's Directorate of Operations, the State Department had a tradition of emphasizing service in the field over service in Washington. Even ambassadors, however, often found host governments not only making connections with the U.S. government through their own missions in Washington, but working through the CIA station or a Defense attaché. Increasingly, the embassies themselves were overshadowed by powerful regional commanders in chief reporting to the Pentagon.[87]

Counterterrorism

In the 1960s and 1970s, the State Department managed counterterrorism policy. It was the official channel for communication with the governments presumed to be behind the terrorists. Moreover, since terrorist incidents of this period usually ended in negotiations, an ambassador or other embassy official was the logical person to represent U.S. interests.

Keeping U.S. diplomatic efforts against terrorism coherent was a recurring challenge. In 1976, at the direction of Congress, the department elevated its coordinator for combating terrorism to the rank equivalent to an assistant secretary of state. As an "ambassador at large," this official sought to increase the visibility of counterterrorism matters within the department and to help integrate U.S. policy implementation among government agencies. The prolonged crisis of 1979–1981, when 53 Americans were held hostage at the U.S. embassy in Tehran, ended the State Department leadership in counterterrorism. President Carter's assertive national security advisor, Zbigniew Brzezinski, took charge, and the coordination function remained thereafter in the White House.

President Reagan's second secretary of state, George Shultz, advocated active U.S. efforts to combat terrorism, often recommending the use of military force. Secretary of Defense Caspar Weinberger opposed Shultz, who made little headway against Weinberger, or even within his own department. Though Shultz elevated the status and visibility of counterterrorism coordination by appointing as coordinator first L. Paul Bremer and then Robert Oakley, both senior career ambassadors of high standing in the Foreign Service, the department continued to be dominated by regional bureaus for which terrorism was not a first-order concern.

Secretaries of state after Shultz took less personal interest in the problem. Only congressional opposition prevented President Clinton's first secretary of state, Warren Christopher, from merging terrorism into a new bureau that would have also dealt with narcotics and crime. The coordinator under Secretary Madeleine Albright told the Commission that his job was seen as a minor one within the department.[88] Although the description of his status has been disputed, and Secretary Albright strongly supported the August 1998 strikes against Bin Ladin, the role played by the Department of State in counterterrorism was often cautionary before 9/11. This was a reflection of the reality that counterterrorism priorities nested within broader foreign policy aims of the U.S. government.

State Department consular officers around the world, it should not be forgotten, were constantly challenged by the problem of terrorism, for they handled visas for travel to the United States. After it was discovered that Abdel Rahman, the Blind Sheikh, had come and gone almost at will, State initiated significant reforms to its watchlist and visa-processing policies. In 1993, Congress passed legislation allowing State to retain visa-processing fees for border security; those fees were then used by the department to fully automate the terrorist watchlist. By the late 1990s, State had created a worldwide, real-time electronic database of visa, law enforcement, and watchlist information, the core of the post-9/11 border screening systems. Still, as will be seen later, the system had many holes.[89]

The Department of Defense

The Department of Defense is the behemoth among federal agencies. With an annual budget larger than the gross domestic product of Russia, it is an empire. The Defense Department is part civilian, part military. The civilian secretary of defense has ultimate control, under the president. Among the uniformed military, the top official is the chairman of the Joint Chiefs of Staff, who is supported by a Joint Staff divided into standard military staff compartments—J-2 (intelligence), J-3 (operations), and so on.

Because of the necessary and demanding focus on the differing mission of each service, and their long and proud traditions, the Army, Navy, Air Force, and Marine Corps have often fought ferociously over roles and missions in war fighting and over budgets and posts of leadership. Two developments diminished this competition.

The first was the passage by Congress in 1986 of the Goldwater-Nichols Act, which, among other things, mandated that promotion to high rank required some period of duty with a different service or with a joint (i.e., multiservice) command. This had strong and immediate effects, loosening the loyalties of senior officers to their separate services and causing them to think more broadly about the military establishment as a whole.[90] However, it also may have lessened the diversity of military advice and options presented to the president. The Goldwater-Nichols example is seen by some as having lessons applicable to lessening competition and increasing cooperation in other parts of the federal bureaucracy, particularly the law enforcement and intelligence communities.

The second, related development was a significant transfer of planning and command responsibilities from the service chiefs and their staffs to the joint and unified commands outside of Washington, especially those for Strategic Forces and for four regions: Europe, the Pacific, the Center, and the South. Posts in these commands became prized assignments for ambitious officers, and the voices of their five commanders in chief became as influential as those of the service chiefs.

Counterterrorism

The Pentagon first became concerned about terrorism as a result of hostage taking in the 1970s. In June 1976, Palestinian terrorists seized an Air France plane and landed it at Entebbe in Uganda, holding 105 Israelis and other Jews as hostages. A special Israeli commando force stormed the plane, killed all the terrorists, and rescued all but one of the hostages. In October 1977, a West German special force dealt similarly with a Lufthansa plane sitting on a tarmac in Mogadishu: every terrorist was killed, and every hostage brought back safely. The White House, members of Congress, and the news media asked the Pentagon whether the United States was prepared for similar action. The answer was no. The Army immediately set about creating the Delta Force, one of whose missions was hostage rescue.

The first test for the new force did not go well. It came in April 1980 during the Iranian hostage crisis, when Navy helicopters with Marine pilots flew to a site known as Desert One, some 200 miles southeast of Tehran, to rendezvous with Air Force planes carrying Delta Force commandos and fresh fuel. Mild sandstorms disabled three of the helicopters, and the commander ordered the mission aborted. But foul-ups on the ground resulted in the loss of eight aircraft, five airmen, and three marines. Remembered as "Desert One," this failure remained vivid for members of the armed forces. It also contributed to the later Goldwater-Nichols reforms.

In 1983 came Hezbollah's massacre of the Marines in Beirut. President Reagan quickly withdrew U.S. forces from Lebanon—a reversal later routinely cited by jihadists as evidence of U.S. weakness. A detailed investigation produced a list of new procedures that would become customary for forces deployed abroad. They involved a number of defensive measures, including caution not only about strange cars and trucks but also about unknown aircraft overhead. "Force protection" became a significant claim on the time and resources of the Department of Defense.

A decade later, the military establishment had another experience that evoked both Desert One and the withdrawal from Beirut. The first President Bush had authorized the use of U.S. military forces to ensure humanitarian relief in wartorn Somalia. Tribal factions interfered with the supply missions. By the autumn of 1993, U.S. commanders concluded that the main source of trouble was a warlord, Mohammed Farrah Aidid. An Army special force launched a raid on Mogadishu to capture him. In the course of a long night, two Black Hawk helicopters were shot down, 73 Americans were wounded, 18 were killed, and the world's television screens showed images of an American corpse dragged through the streets by exultant Somalis. Under pressure from Congress, President Clinton soon ordered the withdrawal of U.S. forces. "Black Hawk down" joined "Desert One" as a symbol among Americans in uniform, code phrases used to evoke the risks of daring exploits without maximum preparation, overwhelming force, and a well-defined mission.

In 1995–1996, the Defense Department began to invest effort in planning how to handle the possibility of a domestic terrorist incident involving weapons of mass destruction (WMD). The idea of a domestic command for homeland defense began to be discussed in 1997, and in 1999 the Joint

Chiefs developed a concept for the establishment of a domestic Unified Command. Congress killed the idea. Instead, the Department established the Joint Forces Command, located at Norfolk, Virginia, making it responsible for military response to domestic emergencies, both natural and man-made.[91]

Pursuant to the Nunn-Lugar-Domenici Domestic Preparedness Program, the Defense Department began in 1997 to train first responders in 120 of the nation's largest cities. As a key part of its efforts, Defense created National Guard WMD Civil Support Teams to respond in the event of a WMD terrorist incident. A total of 32 such National Guard teams were authorized by fiscal year 2001. Under the command of state governors, they provided support to civilian agencies to assess the nature of the attack, offer medical and technical advice, and coordinate state and local responses.[92]

The Department of Defense, like the Department of State, had a coordinator who represented the department on the interagency committee concerned with counterterrorism. By the end of President Clinton's first term, this official had become the assistant secretary of defense for special operations and low-intensity conflict.[93]

The experience of the 1980s had suggested to the military establishment that if it were to have a role in counterterrorism, it would be a traditional military role—to act against state sponsors of terrorism. And the military had what seemed an excellent example of how to do it. In 1986, a bomb went off at a disco in Berlin, killing two American soldiers. Intelligence clearly linked the bombing to Libya's Colonel Muammar Qadhafi. President Reagan ordered air strikes against Libya. The operation was not cost free: the United States lost two planes. Evidence accumulated later, including the 1988 bombing of Pan Am 103, clearly showed that the operation did not curb Qadhafi's interest in terrorism. However, it was seen at the time as a success. The lesson then taken from Libya was that terrorism could be stopped by the use of U.S. air power that inflicted pain on the authors or sponsors of terrorist acts.

This lesson was applied, using Tomahawk missiles, early in the Clinton administration. George H. W. Bush was scheduled to visit Kuwait to be honored for his rescue of that country in the Gulf War of 1991. Kuwaiti security services warned Washington that Iraqi agents were planning to assassinate the former president. President Clinton not only ordered precautions to protect Bush but asked about options for a reprisal against Iraq. The Pentagon proposed 12 targets for Tomahawk missiles. Debate in the White House and at the CIA about possible collateral damage pared the list down to three, then to one—Iraqi intelligence headquarters in central Baghdad. The attack was made at night, to minimize civilian casualties. Twenty-three missiles were fired. Other than one civilian casualty, the operation seemed completely successful: the intelligence headquarters was demolished. No further intelligence came in about terrorist acts planned by Iraq.[94]

The 1986 attack in Libya and the 1993 attack on Iraq symbolized for the military establishment effective use of military power for counterterrorism—limited retaliation with air power, aimed at deterrence. What remained was the hard question of how deterrence could be effective when the adversary was a loose transnational network.

3.6 . . . AND IN THE WHITE HOUSE

Because coping with terrorism was not (and is not) the sole province of any component of the U.S. government, some coordinating mechanism is necessary. When terrorism was not a prominent issue, the State Department could perform this role. When the Iranian hostage crisis developed, this procedure went by the board: National Security Advisor Zbigniew Brzezinski took charge of crisis management.

The Reagan administration continued and formalized the practice of having presidential staff coordinate counterterrorism. After the killing of the marines in Beirut, President Reagan signed National Security Directive 138, calling for a "shift . . . from passive to active defense measures" and re-programming or adding new resources to effect the shift. It directed the State Department "to intensify efforts to achieve cooperation of other governments" and the CIA to "intensify use of liaison and other intelligence capabilities and also to develop plans and capability to preempt groups and individuals planning strikes against U.S. interests."[95]

Speaking to the American Bar Association in July 1985, the President characterized terrorism as "an act of war" and declared: "There can be no place on earth left where it is safe for these monsters to rest, to train, or practice their cruel and deadly skills. We must act together, or unilaterally, if necessary to ensure that terrorists have no sanctuary—any-where."[96] The air strikes against Libya were one manifesta-tion of this strategy.

Through most of President Reagan's second term, the co-ordination of counterterrorism was overseen by a high-level interagency committee chaired by the deputy national secu-rity adviser. But the Reagan administration closed with a major scandal that cast a cloud over the notion that the White House should guide counterterrorism.

President Reagan was concerned because Hezbollah was taking Americans hostage and periodically killing them. He was also constrained by a bill he signed into law that made it illegal to ship military aid to anticommunist Contra guerril-las in Nicaragua, whom he strongly supported. His national security adviser, Robert McFarlane, and McFarlane's deputy, Admiral John Poindexter, thought the hostage prob-lem might be solved and the U.S. position in the Middle East improved if the United States quietly negotiated with Iran about exchanging hostages for modest quantities of arms. Shultz and Weinberger, united for once, opposed McFarlane and Poindexter.

A staffer for McFarlane and Poindexter, Marine Lieu-tenant Colonel Oliver North, developed a scheme to trade U.S. arms for hostages and divert the proceeds to the Con-tras to get around U.S. law. He may have had encourage-ment from Director of Central Intelligence William Casey.[97]

When the facts were revealed in 1986 and 1987, it appeared to be the 1970s all over again: a massive abuse of covert action. Now, instead of stories about poisoned cigars and Mafia hit men, Americans heard testimony about a secret visit to Tehran by McFarlane, using an assumed name and bearing a chocolate cake decorated with icing depicting a key. An investigation by a special counsel resulted in the indictment of McFarlane, Poindexter, North, and ten others, including several high-ranking officers from the CIA's Clandestine Service. The investigations spotlighted the importance of accountability and official responsibility for faithful execution of laws. For the story of 9/11, the significance of the Iran-Contra affair was that it made parts of the bureaucracy reflexively skeptical about any operating directive from the White House.[98]

As the national security advisor's function expanded, the procedures and structure of the advisor's staff, conventionally called the National Security Council staff, became more formal. The advisor developed recommendations for presidential directives, differently labeled by each president. For President Clinton, they were to be Presidential Decision Directives; for President George W. Bush, National Security Policy Directives. These documents and many others requiring approval by the president worked their way through interagency committees usually composed of departmental representatives at the assistant secretary level or just below it. The NSC staff had senior directors who would sit on these interagency committees, often as chair, to facilitate agreement and to represent the wider interests of the national security advisor.

When President Clinton took office, he decided right away to coordinate counterterrorism from the White House. On January 25, 1993, Mir Amal Kansi, an Islamic extremist from Pakistan, shot and killed two CIA employees at the main highway entrance to CIA headquarters in Virginia. (Kansi drove away and was captured abroad much later.) Only a month afterward came the World Trade Center bombing and, a few weeks after that, the Iraqi plot against former President Bush.

President Clinton's first national security advisor, Anthony Lake, had retained from the Bush administration the staffer who dealt with crime, narcotics, and terrorism (a portfolio often known as "drugs and thugs"), the veteran civil servant Richard Clarke. President Clinton and Lake turned to Clarke to do the staff work for them in coordinating counterterrorism. Before long, he would chair a midlevel interagency committee eventually titled the Counterterrorism Security Group (CSG). We will later tell of Clarke's evolution as adviser on and, in time, manager of the U.S. counterterrorist effort.

When explaining the missile strike against Iraq provoked by the plot to kill President Bush, President Clinton stated: "From the first days of our Revolution, America's security has depended on the clarity of the message: Don't tread on us. A firm and commensurate response was essential to protect our sovereignty, to send a message to those who engage in state-sponsored terrorism, to deter further violence against our people, and to affirm the expectation of civilized behavior among nations."[99]

In his State of the Union message in January 1995, President Clinton promised "comprehensive legislation to strengthen our hand in combating terrorists, whether they strike at home or abroad." In February, he sent Congress proposals to extend federal criminal jurisdiction, to make it easier to deport terrorists, and to act against terrorist fundraising. In early May, he submitted a bundle of strong amendments. The interval had seen the news from Tokyo in March that a doomsday cult, Aum Shinrikyo, had released sarin nerve gas in a subway, killing 12 and injuring thousands. The sect had extensive properties and laboratories in Japan and offices worldwide, including one in New York. Neither the FBI nor the CIA had ever heard of it. In April had come the bombing of the Murrah federal building in Oklahoma City; immediate suspicions that it had been the work of Islamists turned out to be wrong, and the bombers proved to be American antigovernment extremists named Timothy McVeigh and Terry Nichols. President Clinton proposed to amend his earlier proposals by increasing wiretap and electronic surveillance authority for the FBI, requiring that explosives carry traceable taggants, and providing substantial new money not only for the FBI and CIA but also for local police.[100]

President Clinton issued a classified directive in June 1995, Presidential Decision Directive 39, which said that the United States should "deter, defeat and respond vigorously to all terrorist attacks on our territory and against our citizens." The directive called terrorism both a matter of national security and a crime, and it assigned responsibilities to various agencies. Alarmed by the incident in Tokyo, President Clinton made it the very highest priority for his own staff and for all agencies to prepare to detect and respond to terrorism that involved chemical, biological, or nuclear weapons.[101]

During 1995 and 1996, President Clinton devoted considerable time to seeking cooperation from other nations in denying sanctuary to terrorists. He proposed significantly larger budgets for the FBI, with much of the increase designated for counterterrorism. For the CIA, he essentially stopped cutting allocations and supported requests for supplemental funds for counterterrorism.[102]

When announcing his new national security team after being reelected in 1996, President Clinton mentioned terrorism first in a list of several challenges facing the country.[103] In 1998, after Bin Ladin's fatwa and other alarms, President Clinton accepted a proposal from his national security advisor, Samuel "Sandy" Berger, and gave Clarke a new position as national coordinator for security, infrastructure protection, and counterterrorism. He issued two Presidential Decision Directives, numbers 62 and 63, that built on the assignments to agencies that had been made in Presidential Decision Directive 39; laid out ten program areas for counterterrorism; and enhanced, at least on paper, Clarke's authority to police these assignments. Because of concerns especially on the part of Attorney General Reno, this new authority was defined in precise and limiting language. Clarke was only to "provide advice" regarding budgets and to "coordinate the development of interagency agreed guidelines" for action.[104]

Clarke also was awarded a seat on the cabinet-level Principals Committee when it met on his issues—a highly unusual step for a White House staffer. His interagency body, the CSG, ordinarily reported to the Deputies Committee of subcabinet officials, unless Berger asked them to report directly to the principals. The complementary directive, number 63, defined the elements of the nation's critical infrastructure and considered ways to protect it. Taken together, the two directives basically left the Justice Department and the FBI in charge at home and left terrorism abroad to the CIA, the State Department, and other agencies, under Clarke's and Berger's coordinating hands.

Explaining the new arrangement and his concerns in another commencement speech, this time at the Naval Academy, in May 1998, the President said:

> First, we will use our new integrated approach to intensify the fight against all forms of terrorism: to capture terrorists, no matter where they hide; to work with other nations to eliminate terrorist sanctuaries overseas; to respond rapidly and effectively to protect Americans from terrorism at home and abroad. Second, we will launch a comprehensive plan to detect, deter, and defend against attacks on our critical infrastructures, our power systems, water supplies, police, fire, and medical services, air traffic control, financial services, telephone systems, and computer network. . . . Third, we will undertake a concerted effort to prevent the spread and use of biological weapons and to protect our people in the event these terrible weapons are ever unleashed by a rogue state, a terrorist group, or an international criminal organization. . . . Finally, we must do more to protect our civilian population from biological weapons.[105]

Clearly, the President's concern about terrorism had steadily risen. That heightened worry would become even more obvious early in 1999, when he addressed the National Academy of Sciences and presented his most somber account yet of what could happen if the United States were hit, unprepared, by terrorists wielding either weapons of mass destruction or potent cyberweapons.

3.7 . . . AND IN THE CONGRESS

Since the beginning of the Republic, few debates have been as hotly contested as the one over executive versus legislative powers. At the Constitutional Convention, the founders sought to create a strong executive but check its powers. They left those powers sufficiently ambiguous so that room was left for Congress and the president to struggle over the direction of the nation's security and foreign policies.

The most serious question has centered on whether or not the president needs congressional authorization to wage war. The current status of that debate seems to have settled into a recognition that a president can deploy military forces for small and limited operations, but needs at least congressional support if not explicit authorization for large and more open-ended military operations.

This calculus becomes important in this story as both President Clinton and President Bush chose not to seek a declaration of war on Bin Ladin after he had declared and begun to wage war on us, a declaration that they did not acknowledge publicly. Not until after 9/11 was a congressional authorization sought.

The most substantial change in national security oversight in Congress took place following World War II. The Congressional Reorganization Act of 1946 created the modern Armed Services committees that have become so powerful today. One especially noteworthy innovation was the creation of the Joint House-Senate Atomic Energy Committee, which is credited by many with the development of our nuclear deterrent capability and was also criticized for wielding too much power relative to the executive branch.

Ironically, this committee was eliminated in the 1970s as Congress was undertaking the next most important reform of oversight in response to the Church and Pike investigations into abuses of power. In 1977, the House and Senate created select committees to exercise oversight of the executive branch's conduct of intelligence operations.

The Intelligence Committees

The House and Senate select committees on intelligence share some important characteristics. They have limited authorities. They do not have exclusive authority over intelligence agencies. Appropriations are ultimately determined by the Appropriations committees. The Armed Services committees exercise jurisdiction over the intelligence agencies within the Department of Defense (and, in the case of the Senate, over the Central Intelligence Agency). One consequence is that the rise and fall of intelligence budgets are tied directly to trends in defense spending.

The president is required by law to ensure the congressional Intelligence committees are kept fully and currently informed of the intelligence activities of the United States. The committees allow the CIA to some extent to withhold information in order to protect sources, methods, and operations. The CIA must bring presidentially authorized covert action Findings and Memoranda of Notification to the Intelligence committees, and it must detail its failures. The committees conduct their most important work in closed hearings or briefings in which security over classified material can be maintained.

Members of the Intelligence committees serve for a limited time, a restriction imposed by each chamber. Many members believe these limits prevent committee members from developing the necessary expertise to conduct effective oversight.

Secrecy, while necessary, can also harm oversight. The overall budget of the intelligence community is classified, as are most of its activities. Thus, the Intelligence committees cannot take advantage of democracy's best oversight mechanism: public disclosure. This makes them significantly different from other congressional oversight committees, which are often spurred into action by the work of investigative journalists and watchdog organizations.

Adjusting to the Post-Cold War Era

The unexpected and rapid end of the Cold War in 1991 created trauma in the foreign policy and national security community both in and out of government. While some criticized the intelligence community for failing to forecast the collapse of the Soviet Union (and used this argument to propose drastic cuts in intelligence agencies), most recognized that the good news of being relieved of the substantial burden of maintaining a security structure to meet the Soviet challenge was accompanied by the bad news of increased insecurity. In many directions, the community faced threats and intelligence challenges that it was largely unprepared to meet.

So did the intelligence oversight committees. New digitized technologies, and the demand for imagery and continued capability against older systems, meant the need to spend more on satellite systems at the expense of human efforts. In addition, denial and deception became more effective as targets learned from public sources what our intelligence agencies were doing. There were comprehensive reform proposals of the intelligence community, such as those offered by Senators Boren and McCurdy. That said, Congress still took too little action to address institutional weaknesses.[106]

With the Cold War over, and the intelligence community roiled by the Ames spy scandal, a presidential commission chaired first by former secretary of defense Les Aspin and later by former secretary of defense Harold Brown examined the intelligence community's future. After it issued recommendations addressing the DCI's lack of personnel and budget authority over the intelligence community, the Intelligence committees in 1996 introduced implementing legislation to remedy these problems.

The Department of Defense and its congressional authorizing committees rose in opposition to the proposed changes. The President and DCI did not actively support these changes. Relatively small changes made in 1996 gave the DCI consultative authority and created a new deputy for management and assistant DCIs for collection and analysis. These reforms occurred only after the Senate Select Committee on Intelligence took the unprecedented step of threatening to bring down the defense authorization bill. Indeed, rather than increasing the DCI's authorities over national intelligence, the 1990s witnessed movement in the opposite direction through, for example, the transfer of the CIA's imaging analysis capability to the new imagery and mapping agency created within the Department of Defense.

Congress Adjusts

Congress as a whole, like the executive branch, adjusted slowly to the rise of transnational terrorism as a threat to national security. In particular, the growing threat and capabilities of Bin Ladin were not understood in Congress. As the most representative branch of the federal government, Congress closely tracks trends in what public opinion and the electorate identify as key issues. In the years before September 11, terrorism seldom registered as important. To the extent that terrorism did break through and engage the attention of the Congress as a whole, it would briefly command attention after a specific incident, and then return to a lower rung on the public policy agenda.

Several points about Congress are worth noting. First, Congress always has a strong orientation toward domestic affairs. It usually takes on foreign policy and national security issues after threats are identified and articulated by the administration. In the absence of such a detailed—and repeated—articulation, national security tends not to rise very high on the list of congressional priorities. Presidents are selective in their use of political capital for international issues. In the decade before 9/11, presidential discussion of and congressional and public attention to foreign affairs and national security were dominated by other issues—among them, Haiti, Bosnia, Russia, China, Somalia, Kosovo, NATO enlargement, the Middle East peace process, missile defense, and globalization. Terrorism infrequently took center stage; and when it did, the context was often terrorists' tactics—a chemical, biological, nuclear, or computer threat—not terrorist organizations.[107]

Second, Congress tends to follow the overall lead of the president on budget issues with respect to national security matters. There are often sharp arguments about individual programs and internal priorities, but by and large the overall funding authorized and appropriated by the Congress comes out close to the president's request. This tendency was certainly illustrated by the downward trends in spending on defense, intelligence, and foreign affairs in the first part of the 1990s. The White House, to be sure, read the political signals coming from Capitol Hill, but the Congress largely acceded to the executive branch's funding requests. In the second half of the decade, Congress appropriated some 98 percent of what the administration requested for intelligence programs. Apart from the Gingrich supplemental of $1.5 billion for overall intelligence programs in fiscal year 1999, the key decisions on overall allocation of resources for national security issues in the decade before 9/11—including counterterrorism funding—were made in the president's Office of Management and Budget.[108]

Third, Congress did not reorganize itself after the end of the Cold War to address new threats. Recommendations by the Joint Committee on the Organization of Congress were implemented, in part, in the House of Representatives after the 1994 elections, but there was no reorganization of national security functions. The Senate undertook no appreciable changes. Traditional issues—foreign policy, defense, intelligence—continued to be handled by committees whose structure remained largely unaltered, while issues such as transnational terrorism fell between the cracks. Terrorism came under the jurisdiction of at least 14 different committees in the House alone, and budget and oversight functions in the House and Senate concerning terrorism were also splintered badly among committees. Little effort was made to consider an integrated policy toward terrorism, which might range from identifying the threat to addressing vulnerabilities in critical infrastructure; and the piecemeal approach in the Congress contributed to the problems of the executive branch in formulating such a policy.[109]

Fourth, the oversight function of Congress has diminished over time. In recent years, traditional review of the administration of programs and the implementation of laws has been replaced by "a focus on personal investigations, possible scandals, and issues designed to generate media attention." The unglamorous but essential work of oversight has been neglected, and few members past or present believe it is performed well. DCI Tenet told us: "We ran from threat to threat to threat. . . . [T]here was not a system in place to say, 'You got to go back and do this and this and this.'" Not just the DCI but the entire executive branch needed help from Congress in addressing the questions of counterterrorism strategy and policy, looking past day-to-day concerns. Members of Congress, however, also found their time spent on such everyday matters, or in looking back to investigate mistakes, and often missed the big questions—as did the executive branch. Staff tended as well to focus on parochial considerations, seeking to add or cut funding for individual (often small) programs, instead of emphasizing comprehensive oversight projects.[110]

Fifth, on certain issues, other priorities pointed Congress in a direction that was unhelpful in meeting the threats that were emerging in the months leading up to 9/11. Committees with oversight responsibility for aviation focused overwhelmingly on airport congestion and the economic health of the airlines, not aviation security. Committees with responsibility for the INS focused on the Southwest border, not on terrorists. Justice Department officials told us that committees with responsibility for the FBI tightly restricted appropriations for improvements in information technology, in part because of concerns about the FBI's ability to manage such projects. Committees responsible for South Asia spent the decade of the 1990s imposing sanctions on Pakistan, leaving presidents with little leverage to alter Pakistan's policies before 9/11. Committees with responsibility for the Defense Department paid little heed to developing military responses to terrorism and stymied intelligence reform. All committees found themselves swamped in the minutiae of the budget process, with little time for consideration of longer-term questions, or what many members past and present told us was the proper conduct of oversight.[111]

Each of these trends contributed to what can only be described as Congress's slowness and inadequacy in treating the issue of terrorism in the years before 9/11. The legislative branch adjusted little and did not restructure itself to address changing threats.[112] Its attention to terrorism was episodic and splintered across several committees. Congress gave little guidance to executive branch agencies, did not reform them in any significant way, and did not systematically perform oversight to identify, address, and attempt to resolve the many problems in national security and domestic agencies that became apparent in the aftermath of 9/11.

Although individual representatives and senators took significant steps, the overall level of attention in the Congress to the terrorist threat was low. We examined the number of hearings on terrorism from January 1998 to September 2001. The Senate Armed Services Committee held nine—four related to the attack on the USS *Cole*. The House Armed Services Committee also held nine, six of them by a special oversight panel on terrorism. The Senate Foreign Relations Committee and its House counterpart both held four. The Senate Select Committee on Intelligence, in addition to its annual worldwide threat hearing, held eight; its House counterpart held perhaps two exclusively devoted to counterterrorism, plus the briefings by its terrorist working group. The Senate and House intelligence panels did not raise public and congressional attention on Bin Ladin and al Qaeda prior to the joint inquiry into the attacks of September 11, perhaps in part because of the classified nature of their work. Yet in the context of committees that each hold scores of hearings every year on issues in their jurisdiction, this list is not impressive. Terrorism was a second- or third-order priority within the committees of Congress responsible for national security.[113]

In fact, Congress had a distinct tendency to push questions of emerging national security threats off its own plate, leaving them for others to consider. Congress asked outside commissions to do the work that arguably was at the heart of its own oversight responsibilities.[114] Beginning in 1999, the reports of these commissions made scores of recommendations to address terrorism and homeland security but drew little attention from Congress. Most of their impact came after 9/11.

CHAPTER FOUR

Responses to Al Qaeda's Initial Assaults

4.1 BEFORE THE BOMBINGS IN KENYA AND TANZANIA

Although the 1995 National Intelligence Estimate had warned of a new type of terrorism, many officials continued to think of terrorists as agents of states (Saudi Hezbollah acting for Iran against Khobar Towers) or as domestic criminals (Timothy McVeigh in Oklahoma City). As we pointed out in chapter 3, the White House is not a natural locus for program management. Hence, government efforts to cope with terrorism were essentially the work of individual agencies.

President Bill Clinton's counterterrorism Presidential Decision Directives in 1995 (no. 39) and May 1998 (no. 62) reiterated that terrorism was a national security problem, not just a law enforcement issue. They reinforced the authority of the National Security Council (NSC) to coordinate domestic as well as foreign counterterrorism efforts, through Richard Clarke and his interagency Counterterrorism Security Group (CSG). Spotlighting new concerns about unconventional attacks, these directives assigned tasks to lead agencies but did not differentiate types of terrorist threats. Thus, while Clarke might prod or push agencies to act, what actually happened was usually decided at the State Department, the Pentagon, the CIA, or the Justice Department. The efforts of these agencies were sometimes energetic and sometimes effective. Terrorist plots were disrupted and individual terrorists were captured. But the United States did not, before 9/11, adopt as a clear strategic objective the elimination of al Qaeda.

Early Efforts against Bin Ladin

Until 1996, hardly anyone in the U.S. government understood that Usama Bin Ladin was an inspirer and organizer of the new terrorism. In 1993, the CIA noted that he had paid for the training of some Egyptian terrorists in Sudan. The State Department detected his money in aid to the Yemeni terrorists who set a bomb in an attempt to kill U.S. troops in Aden in 1992. State Department sources even saw suspicious links with Omar Abdel Rahman, the "Blind Sheikh" in the New York area, commenting that Bin Ladin seemed "committed to financing 'Jihads' against 'anti Islamic' regimes worldwide." After the department designated Sudan a state sponsor of terrorism in 1993, it put Bin Ladin on its TIPOFF watchlist, a move that might have prevented his getting a visa had he tried to enter the United States. As late as 1997, however, even the CIA's Counterterrorist Center continued to describe him as an "extremist financier."[1]

In 1996, the CIA set up a special unit of a dozen officers to analyze intelligence on and plan operations against Bin Ladin. David Cohen, the head of the CIA's Directorate of Operations, wanted to test the idea of having a "virtual station"—a station based at headquarters but collecting and operating against a subject much as stations in the field focus on a country. Taking his cue from National Security Advisor Anthony Lake, who expressed special interest in terrorist finance, Cohen formed his virtual station as a terrorist financial links unit. He had trouble getting any Directorate of Operations officer to run it; he finally recruited a former analyst who was then running the Islamic Extremist Branch of the Counterterrorist Center. This officer, who was especially knowledgeable about Afghanistan, had noticed a recent stream of reports about Bin Ladin and something called al Qaeda, and suggested to Cohen that the station focus on this one individual. Cohen agreed. Thus was born the Bin Ladin unit.[2]

In May 1996, Bin Ladin left Sudan for Afghanistan. A few months later, as the Bin Ladin unit was gearing up, Jamal Ahmed al Fadl walked into a U.S. embassy in Africa, established his bona fides as a former senior employee of Bin Ladin, and provided a major breakthrough of intelligence on the creation, character, direction, and intentions of al Qaeda. Corroborating evidence came from another walk-in source at a different U.S. embassy. More confirmation was supplied later that year by intelligence and other sources, including material gathered by FBI agents and Kenyan police from an al Qaeda cell in Nairobi.[3]

By 1997, officers in the Bin Ladin unit recognized that Bin Ladin was more than just a financier. They learned that al Qaeda had a military committee that was planning operations against U.S. interests worldwide and was actively trying to obtain nuclear material. Analysts assigned to the station looked at the information it had gathered and "found connections everywhere," including links to the attacks on U.S. troops in Aden and Somalia in 1992 and 1993 and to the Manila air plot in the Philippines in 1994–1995.[4]

The Bin Ladin station was already working on plans for offensive operations against Bin Ladin. These plans were directed at both physical assets and sources of finance. In the end, plans to identify and attack Bin Ladin's money sources did not go forward.[5]

In late 1995, when Bin Ladin was still in Sudan, the State Department and the CIA learned that Sudanese officials were discussing with the Saudi government the possibility of expelling Bin Ladin. U.S. Ambassador Timothy Carney encouraged the Sudanese to pursue this course. The Saudis, however, did not want Bin Ladin, giving as their reason their revocation of his citizenship.[6]

Sudan's minister of defense, Fatih Erwa, has claimed that Sudan offered to hand Bin Ladin over to the United States. The Commission has found no credible evidence that this was so. Ambassador Carney had instructions only to push the Sudanese to expel Bin Ladin. Ambassador Carney had no legal basis to ask for more from the Sudanese since, at the time, there was no indictment outstanding.[7]

The chief of the Bin Ladin station, whom we will call "Mike," saw Bin Ladin's move to Afghanistan as a stroke of luck. Though the CIA had virtually abandoned Afghanistan after the Soviet withdrawal, case officers had reestablished old contacts while tracking down Mir Amal Kansi, the Pakistani gunman who had murdered two CIA employees in January 1993. These contacts contributed to intelligence about Bin Ladin's local movements, business activities, and security and living arrangements, and helped provide evidence that he was spending large amounts of money to help the Taliban. The chief of the Counterterrorist Center, whom we will call "Jeff," told Director George Tenet that the CIA's intelligence assets were "near to providing real-time information about Bin Ladin's activities and travels in Afghanistan." One of the contacts was a group associated with particular tribes among Afghanistan's ethnic Pashtun community.[8]

By the fall of 1997, the Bin Ladin unit had roughed out a plan for these Afghan tribals to capture Bin Ladin and hand him over for trial either in the United States or in an Arab country. In early 1998, the cabinet-level Principals Committee apparently gave the concept its blessing.[9]

On their own separate track, getting information but not direction from the CIA, the FBI's New York Field Office and the U.S. Attorney for the Southern District of New York were preparing to ask a grand jury to indict Bin Ladin. The Counterterrorist Center knew that this was happening.[10] The eventual charge, conspiring to attack U.S. defense installations, was finally issued from the grand jury in June 1998— as a sealed indictment. The indictment was publicly disclosed in November of that year.

When Bin Ladin moved to Afghanistan in May 1996, he became a subject of interest to the State Department's South Asia bureau. At the time, as one diplomat told us, South Asia was seen in the department and the government generally as a low priority. In 1997, as Madeleine Albright was beginning her tenure as secretary of state, an NSC policy review concluded that the United States should pay more attention not just to India but also to Pakistan and Afghanistan.[11] With regard to Afghanistan, another diplomat said, the United States at the time had "no policy."[12]

In the State Department, concerns about India-Pakistan tensions often crowded out attention to Afghanistan or Bin Ladin. Aware of instability and growing Islamic extremism in Pakistan, State Department officials worried most about an arms race and possible war between Pakistan and India. After May 1998, when both countries surprised the United States by testing nuclear weapons, these dangers became daily first-order concerns of the State Department.[13]

In Afghanistan, the State Department tried to end the civil war that had continued since the Soviets' withdrawal. The South Asia bureau believed it might have a carrot for Afghanistan's warring factions in a project by the Union Oil Company of California (UNOCAL) to build a pipeline across the country. While there was probably never much chance of the pipeline actually being built, the Afghan desk hoped that the prospect of shared pipeline profits might lure faction leaders to a conference table. U.S. diplomats did not favor the Taliban over the rival factions. Despite growing concerns, U.S. diplomats were willing at the time, as one official said, to "give the Taliban a chance."[14]

Though Secretary Albright made no secret of thinking the Taliban "despicable," the U.S. ambassador to the United Nations, Bill Richardson, led a delegation to South Asia—including Afghanistan—in April 1998. No U.S. official of such rank had been to Kabul in decades. Ambassador Richardson went primarily to urge negotiations to end the civil war. In view of Bin Ladin's recent public call for all Muslims to kill Americans, Richardson asked the Taliban to expel Bin Ladin. They answered that they did not know his whereabouts. In any case, the Taliban said, Bin Ladin was not a threat to the United States.[15]

In sum, in late 1997 and the spring of 1998, the lead U.S.

agencies each pursued their own efforts against Bin Ladin. The CIA's Counterterrorist Center was developing a plan to capture and remove him from Afghanistan. Parts of the Justice Department were moving toward indicting Bin Ladin, making possible a criminal trial in a New York court. Meanwhile, the State Department was focused more on lessening Indo-Pakistani nuclear tensions, ending the Afghan civil war, and ameliorating the Taliban's human rights abuses than on driving out Bin Ladin. Another key actor, Marine General Anthony Zinni, the commander in chief of the U.S. Central Command, shared the State Department's view.[16]

The CIA Develops a Capture Plan

Initially, the DCI's Counterterrorist Center and its Bin Ladin unit considered a plan to ambush Bin Ladin when he traveled between Kandahar, the Taliban capital where he sometimes stayed the night, and his primary residence at the time, Tarnak Farms. After the Afghan tribals reported that they had tried such an ambush and failed, the Center gave up on it, despite suspicions that the tribals' story might be fiction. Thereafter, the capture plan focused on a nighttime raid on Tarnak Farms.[17]

A compound of about 80 concrete or mud-brick buildings surrounded by a 10-foot wall, Tarnak Farms was located in an isolated desert area on the outskirts of the Kandahar airport. CIA officers were able to map the entire site, identifying the houses that belonged to Bin Ladin's wives and the one where Bin Ladin himself was most likely to sleep. Working with the tribals, they drew up plans for the raid. They ran two complete rehearsals in the United States during the fall of 1997.[18]

By early 1998, planners at the Counterterrorist Center were ready to come back to the White House to seek formal approval. Tenet apparently walked National Security Advisor Sandy Berger through the basic plan on February 13. One group of tribals would subdue the guards, enter Tarnak Farms stealthily, grab Bin Ladin, take him to a desert site outside Kandahar, and turn him over to a second group. This second group of tribals would take him to a desert landing zone already tested in the 1997 Kansi capture. From there, a CIA plane would take him to New York, an Arab capital, or wherever he was to be arraigned. Briefing papers prepared by the Counterterrorist Center acknowledged that hitches might develop. People might be killed, and Bin Ladin's supporters might retaliate, perhaps taking U.S. citizens in Kandahar hostage. But the briefing papers also noted that there was risk in not acting. "Sooner or later," they said, "Bin Ladin will attack U.S. interests, perhaps using WMD [weapons of mass destruction]."[19]

Clarke's Counterterrorism Security Group reviewed the capture plan for Berger. Noting that the plan was in a "very early stage of development," the NSC staff then told the CIA planners to go ahead and, among other things, start drafting any legal documents that might be required to authorize the covert action. The CSG apparently stressed that the raid should target Bin Ladin himself, not the whole compound.[20]

The CIA planners conducted their third complete rehearsal in March, and they again briefed the CSG. Clarke wrote Berger on March 7 that he saw the operation as "somewhat embryonic" and the CIA as "months away from doing anything."[21]

"Mike" thought the capture plan was "the perfect operation." It required minimum infrastructure. The plan had now been modified so that the tribals would keep Bin Ladin in a hiding place for up to a month before turning him over to the United States—thereby increasing the chances of keeping the U.S. hand out of sight. "Mike" trusted the information from the Afghan network; it had been corroborated by other means, he told us. The lead CIA officer in the field, Gary Schroen, also had confidence in the tribals. In a May 6 cable to CIA headquarters, he pronounced their planning "almost as professional and detailed . . . as would be done by any U.S. military special operations element." He and the other officers who had worked through the plan with the tribals judged it "about as good as it can be." (By that, Schroen explained, he meant that the chance of capturing or killing Bin

Ladin was about 40 percent.) Although the tribals thought they could pull off the raid, if the operation were approved by headquarters and the policymakers, Schroen wrote there was going to be a point when "we step back and keep our fingers crossed that the [tribals] prove as good (and as lucky) as they think they will be."[22]

Military officers reviewed the capture plan and, according to "Mike," "found no showstoppers." The commander of Delta Force felt "uncomfortable" with having the tribals hold Bin Ladin captive for so long, and the commander of Joint Special Operations Forces, Lieutenant General Michael Canavan, was worried about the safety of the tribals inside Tarnak Farms. General Canavan said he had actually thought the operation too complicated for the CIA—"out of their league"—and an effort to get results "on the cheap." But a senior Joint Staff officer described the plan as "generally, not too much different than we might have come up with ourselves." No one in the Pentagon, so far as we know, advised the CIA or the White House not to proceed.[23]

In Washington, Berger expressed doubt about the dependability of the tribals. In his meeting with Tenet, Berger focused most, however, on the question of what was to be done with Bin Ladin if he were actually captured. He worried that the hard evidence against Bin Ladin was still skimpy and that there was a danger of snatching him and bringing him to the United States only to see him acquitted.[24]

On May 18, CIA's managers reviewed a draft Memorandum of Notification (MON), a legal document authorizing the capture operation. A 1986 presidential finding had authorized worldwide covert action against terrorism and probably provided adequate authority. But mindful of the old "rogue elephant" charge, senior CIA managers may have wanted something on paper to show that they were not acting on their own.

Discussion of this memorandum brought to the surface an unease about paramilitary covert action that had become ingrained, at least among some CIA senior managers. James Pavitt, the assistant head of the Directorate of Operations, expressed concern that people might get killed; it appears he thought the operation had at least a slight flavor of a plan for an assassination. Moreover, he calculated that it would cost several million dollars. He was not prepared to take that money "out of hide," and he did not want to go to all the necessary congressional committees to get special money. Despite Pavitt's misgivings, the CIA leadership cleared the draft memorandum and sent it on to the National Security Council.[25]

Counterterrorist Center officers briefed Attorney General Janet Reno and FBI Director Louis Freeh, telling them that the operation had about a 30 percent chance of success. The Center's chief, "Jeff," joined John O'Neill, the head of the FBI's New York Field Office, in briefing Mary Jo White, the U.S. Attorney for the Southern District of New York, and her staff. Though "Jeff" also used the 30 percent success figure, he warned that someone would surely be killed in the operation. White's impression from the New York briefing was that the chances of capturing Bin Ladin alive were nil.[26]

From May 20 to 24, the CIA ran a final, graded rehearsal of the operation, spread over three time zones, even bringing in personnel from the region. The FBI also participated. The rehearsal went well. The Counterterrorist Center planned to brief cabinet-level principals and their deputies the following week, giving June 23 as the date for the raid, with Bin Ladin to be brought out of Afghanistan no later than July 23.[27]

On May 20, Director Tenet discussed the high risk of the operation with Berger and his deputies, warning that people might be killed, including Bin Ladin. Success was to be defined as the exfiltration of Bin Ladin out of Afghanistan.[28] A meeting of principals was scheduled for May 29 to decide whether the operation should go ahead.

The principals did not meet. On May 29, "Jeff" informed "Mike" that he had just met with Tenet, Pavitt, and the chief of the Directorate's Near Eastern Division. The decision was made not to go ahead with the operation. "Mike" cabled the field that he had been directed to "stand down on the operation for the time being." He had been told, he wrote, that cabinet-level officials thought the risk of civilian casualties—"collateral damage"—was too high. They were concerned about the tribals' safety, and had worried that "the purpose and nature of the operation would be subject to unavoidable misinterpretation and misrepresentation—and probably recriminations—in the event that Bin Ladin, despite our best intentions and efforts, did not survive."[29]

Impressions vary as to who actually decided not to proceed with the operation. Clarke told us that the CSG saw the plan as flawed. He was said to have described it to a colleague on the NSC staff as "half-assed" and predicted that the principals would not approve it. "Jeff" thought the decision had been made at the cabinet level. Pavitt thought that it was Berger's doing, though perhaps on Tenet's advice. Tenet told us that given the recommendation of his chief operations officers, he alone had decided to "turn off" the operation. He had simply informed Berger, who had not pushed back. Berger's recollection was similar. He said the plan was never presented to the White House for a decision.[30]

The CIA's senior management clearly did not think the plan would work. Tenet's deputy director of operations wrote to Berger a few weeks later that the CIA assessed the tribals' ability to capture Bin Ladin and deliver him to U.S. officials as low. But working-level CIA officers were disappointed. Before it was canceled, Schroen described it as the "best plan we are going to come up with to capture [Bin Ladin] while he is in Afghanistan and bring him to justice."[31] No capture plan before 9/11 ever again attained the same level of detail and preparation. The tribals' reported readiness to act diminished. And Bin Ladin's security precautions and defenses became more elaborate and formidable.

At this time, 9/11 was more than three years away. It was the duty of Tenet and the CIA leadership to balance the risks of inaction against jeopardizing the lives of their operatives and agents. And they had reason to worry about failure: millions of dollars down the drain; a shoot-out that could be seen as an assassination; and, if there were repercussions in

Pakistan, perhaps a coup. The decisions of the U.S. government in May 1998 were made, as Berger has put it, from the vantage point of the driver looking through a muddy windshield moving forward, not through a clean rearview mirror.[32]

Looking for Other Options

The Counterterrorist Center continued to track Bin Ladin and to contemplate covert action. The most hopeful possibility seemed now to lie in diplomacy—but not diplomacy managed by the Department of State, which focused primarily on India-Pakistan nuclear tensions during the summer of 1998. The CIA learned in the spring of 1998 that the Saudi government had quietly disrupted Bin Ladin cells in its country that were planning to attack U.S. forces with shoulder-fired missiles. They had arrested scores of individuals, with no publicity. When thanking the Saudis, Director Tenet took advantage of the opening to ask them to help against Bin Ladin. The response was encouraging enough that President Clinton made Tenet his informal personal representative to work with the Saudis on terrorism, and Tenet visited Riyadh in May and again in early June.[33]

Saudi Crown Prince Abdullah, who had taken charge from the ailing King Fahd, promised Tenet an all-out secret effort to persuade the Taliban to expel Bin Ladin so that he could be sent to the United States or to another country for trial. The Kingdom's emissary would be its intelligence chief, Prince Turki bin Faisal. Vice President Al Gore later added his thanks to those of Tenet, both making clear that they spoke with President Clinton's blessing. Tenet reported that it was imperative to get an indictment against Bin Ladin. The New York grand jury issued its sealed indictment a few days later, on June 10. Tenet also recommended that no action be taken on other U.S. options, such as the covert action plan.[34]

Prince Turki followed up in meetings during the summer with Mullah Omar and other Taliban leaders. Apparently employing a mixture of possible incentives and threats,

Turki received a commitment that Bin Ladin would be expelled, but Mullah Omar did not make good on this promise.[35]

On August 5, Clarke chaired a CSG meeting on Bin Ladin. In the discussion of what might be done, the note taker wrote, "there was a dearth of bright ideas around the table, despite a consensus that the [government] ought to pursue every avenue it can to address the problem."[36]

4.2 CRISIS: AUGUST 1998

On August 7, 1998, National Security Advisor Berger woke President Clinton with a phone call at 5:35 A.M. to tell him of the almost simultaneous bombings of the U.S. embassies in Nairobi, Kenya, and Dar es Salaam, Tanzania. Suspicion quickly focused on Bin Ladin. Unusually good intelligence, chiefly from the yearlong monitoring of al Qaeda's cell in Nairobi, soon firmly fixed responsibility on him and his associates.[37]

Debate about what to do settled very soon on one option: Tomahawk cruise missiles. Months earlier, after cancellation of the covert capture operation, Clarke had prodded the Pentagon to explore possibilities for military action. On June 2, General Hugh Shelton, the chairman of the Joint Chiefs of Staff, had directed General Zinni at Central Command to develop a plan, which he had submitted during the first week of July. Zinni's planners surely considered the two previous times the United States had used force to respond to terrorism, the 1986 strike on Libya and the 1993 strike against Iraq. They proposed firing Tomahawks against eight terrorist camps in Afghanistan, including Bin Ladin's compound at Tarnak Farms.[38] After the embassy attacks, the Pentagon offered this plan to the White House.

The day after the embassy bombings, Tenet brought to a principals meeting intelligence that terrorist leaders were expected to gather at a camp near Khowst, Afghanistan, to plan future attacks. According to Berger, Tenet said that several hundred would attend, including Bin Ladin. The CIA described the area as effectively a military cantonment, away from civilian population centers and overwhelmingly populated by jihadists. Clarke remembered sitting next to Tenet in a White House meeting, asking Tenet "You thinking what I'm thinking?" and his nodding "yes."[39] The principals quickly reached a consensus on attacking the gathering. The strike's purpose was to kill Bin Ladin and his chief lieutenants.[40]

Berger put in place a tightly compartmented process designed to keep all planning secret. On August 11, General Zinni received orders to prepare detailed plans for strikes against the sites in Afghanistan. The Pentagon briefed President Clinton about these plans on August 12 and 14. Though the principals hoped that the missiles would hit Bin Ladin, NSC staff recommended the strike whether or not there was firm evidence that the commanders were at the facilities.[41]

Considerable debate went to the question of whether to strike targets outside of Afghanistan, including two facilities in Sudan. One was a tannery believed to belong to Bin Ladin. The other was al Shifa, a Khartoum pharmaceutical plant, which intelligence reports said was manufacturing a precursor ingredient for nerve gas with Bin Ladin's financial support. The argument for hitting the tannery was that it could hurt Bin Ladin financially. The argument for hitting al Shifa was that it would lessen the chance of Bin Ladin's having nerve gas for a later attack.[42]

Ever since March 1995, American officials had had in the backs of their minds Aum Shinrikyo's release of sarin nerve gas in the Tokyo subway. President Clinton himself had expressed great concern about chemical and biological terrorism in the United States. Bin Ladin had reportedly been heard to speak of wanting a "Hiroshima" and at least 10,000 casualties. The CIA reported that a soil sample from the vicinity of the al Shifa plant had tested positive for EMPTA, a precursor chemical for VX, a nerve gas whose lone use was for mass killing. Two days before the embassy bombings, Clarke's staff wrote that Bin Ladin "has invested in and almost certainly has access to VX produced at a plant in Sudan."[43] Senior State Department officials believed that they had received a similar verdict independently, though they and Clarke's staff were probably relying on the same report. Mary McCarthy, the NSC senior director responsible for intelligence programs, initially cautioned Berger that the "bottom line" was that "we will need much better intelligence on this facility before we seriously consider any options." She added that the link between Bin Ladin and al Shifa was "rather uncertain at this point." Berger has told us that he thought about what might happen if the decision went against hitting al Shifa, and nerve gas was used in a New York subway two weeks later.[44]

By the early hours of the morning of August 20, President Clinton and all his principal advisers had agreed to strike Bin Ladin camps in Afghanistan near Khowst, as well as hitting al Shifa. The President took the Sudanese tannery off the target list because he saw little point in killing uninvolved people without doing significant harm to Bin Ladin. The principal with the most qualms regarding al Shifa was Attorney General Reno. She expressed concern about attacking two Muslim countries at the same time. Looking back, she said that she felt the "premise kept shifting."[45]

Later on August 20, Navy vessels in the Arabian Sea fired their cruise missiles. Though most of them hit their intended targets, neither Bin Ladin nor any other terrorist leader was killed. Berger told us that an after-action review by Director Tenet concluded that the strikes had killed 20–30 people in the camps but probably missed Bin Ladin by a few hours. Since the missiles headed for Afghanistan had had to cross Pakistan, the Vice Chairman of the Joint Chiefs was sent to meet with Pakistan's army chief of staff to assure him the missiles were not coming from India. Officials in Washington speculated that one or another Pakistani official might have sent a warning to the Taliban or Bin Ladin.[46]

The air strikes marked the climax of an intense 48-hour period in which Berger notified congressional leaders, the principals called their foreign counterparts, and President

Clinton flew back from his vacation on Martha's Vineyard to address the nation from the Oval Office. The President spoke to the congressional leadership from Air Force One, and he called British Prime Minister Tony Blair, Pakistani Prime Minister Nawaz Sharif, and Egyptian President Hosni Mubarak from the White House.[47] House Speaker Newt Gingrich and Senate Majority Leader Trent Lott initially supported the President. The next month, Gingrich's office dismissed the cruise missile attacks as "pinpricks."[48]

At the time, President Clinton was embroiled in the Lewinsky scandal, which continued to consume public attention for the rest of that year and the first months of 1999. As it happened, a popular 1997 movie, *Wag the Dog*, features a president who fakes a war to distract public attention from a domestic scandal. Some Republicans in Congress raised questions about the timing of the strikes. Berger was particularly rankled by an editorial in the *Economist* that said that only the future would tell whether the U.S. missile strikes had "created 10,000 new fanatics where there would have been none."[49]

Much public commentary turned immediately to scalding criticism that the action was too aggressive. The Sudanese denied that al Shifa produced nerve gas, and they allowed journalists to visit what was left of a seemingly harmless facility. President Clinton, Vice President Gore, Berger, Tenet, and Clarke insisted to us that their judgment was right, pointing to the soil sample evidence. No independent evidence has emerged to corroborate the CIA's assessment.[50]

Everyone involved in the decision had, of course, been aware of President Clinton's problems. He told them to ignore them. Berger recalled the President saying to him "that they were going to get crap either way, so they should do the right thing."[51] All his aides testified to us that they based their advice solely on national security considerations. We have found no reason to question their statements.

The failure of the strikes, the "wag the dog" slur, the intense partisanship of the period, and the nature of the al Shifa evidence likely had a cumulative effect on future decisions about the use of force against Bin Ladin. Berger told us that he did not feel any sense of constraint.[52]

The period after the August 1998 embassy bombings was critical in shaping U.S. policy toward Bin Ladin. Although more Americans had been killed in the 1996 Khobar Towers attack, and many more in Beirut in 1983, the overall loss of life rivaled the worst attacks in memory. More ominous, perhaps, was the demonstration of an operational capability to coordinate two nearly simultaneous attacks on U.S. embassies in different countries.

Despite the availability of information that al Qaeda was a global network, in 1998 policymakers knew little about the organization. The reams of new information that the CIA's Bin Ladin unit had been developing since 1996 had not been pulled together and synthesized for the rest of the government. Indeed, analysts in the unit felt that they were viewed as alarmists even within the CIA. A National Intelligence Estimate on terrorism in 1997 had only briefly mentioned Bin Ladin, and no subsequent national estimate would authoritatively evaluate the terrorism danger until after 9/11. Policymakers knew there was a dangerous individual, Usama Bin Ladin, whom they had been trying to capture and bring to trial. Documents at the time referred to Bin Ladin "and his associates" or Bin Ladin and his "network." They did not emphasize the existence of a structured worldwide organization gearing up to train thousands of potential terrorists.[53]

In the critical days and weeks after the August 1998 attacks, senior policymakers in the Clinton administration had to reevaluate the threat posed by Bin Ladin. Was this just a new and especially venomous version of the ordinary terrorist threat America had lived with for decades, or was it radically new, posing a danger beyond any yet experienced?

Even after the embassy attacks, Bin Ladin had been responsible for the deaths of fewer than 50 Americans, most of them overseas. An NSC staffer working for Richard Clarke told us the threat was seen as one that could cause hundreds of casualties, not thousands.[54] Even officials who acknowledge a vital threat intellectually may not be ready to act on such beliefs at great cost or at high risk.

Therefore, the government experts who believed that Bin Ladin and his network posed such a novel danger needed a way to win broad support for their views, or at least spotlight the areas of dispute. The Presidential Daily Brief and the similar, more widely circulated daily reports for high officials—consisting mainly of brief reports of intelligence "news" without much analysis or context—did not provide such a vehicle. The national intelligence estimate has often played this role, and is sometimes controversial for this very reason. It played no role in judging the threat posed by al Qaeda, either in 1998 or later.

In the late summer and fall of 1998, the U.S. government also was worrying about the deployment of military power in two other ongoing conflicts. After years of war in the Balkans, the United States had finally committed itself to significant military intervention in 1995–1996. Already maintaining a NATO-led peacekeeping force in Bosnia, U.S. officials were beginning to consider major combat operations against Serbia to protect Muslim civilians in Kosovo from ethnic cleansing. Air strikes were threatened in October 1998; a full-scale NATO bombing campaign against Serbia was launched in March 1999.[55]

In addition, the Clinton administration was facing the possibility of major combat operations against Iraq. Since 1996, the UN inspections regime had been increasingly obstructed by Saddam Hussein. The United States was threatening to attack unless unfettered inspections could resume. The Clinton administration eventually launched a large-scale set of air strikes against Iraq, Operation Desert Fox, in December 1998. These military commitments became the context in which the Clinton administration had to consider opening another front of military engagement against a new terrorist threat based in Afghanistan.

A Follow-On Campaign?

Clarke hoped the August 1998 missile strikes would mark the beginning of a sustained campaign against Bin Ladin. Clarke was, as he later admitted, "obsessed" with Bin Ladin, and the embassy bombings gave him new scope for pursuing his obsession. Terrorism had moved high up among the President's concerns, and Clarke's position had elevated accordingly. The CSG, unlike most standing interagency committees, did not have to report through the Deputies Committee. Although such a reporting relationship had been prescribed in the May 1998 presidential directive (after expressions of concern by Attorney General Reno, among others), that directive contained an exception that permitted the CSG to report directly to the principals if Berger so elected. In practice, the CSG often reported not even to the full Principals Committee but instead to the so-called Small Group formed by Berger, consisting only of those principals cleared to know about the most sensitive issues connected with counterterrorism activities concerning Bin Ladin or the Khobar Towers investigation.[56]

For this inner cabinet, Clarke drew up what he called "Political-Military Plan Delenda." The Latin *delenda*, meaning that something "must be destroyed," evoked the famous Roman vow to destroy its rival, Carthage. The overall goal of Clarke's paper was to "immediately eliminate any significant threat to Americans" from the "Bin Ladin network."[57] The paper called for diplomacy to deny Bin Ladin sanctuary; covert action to disrupt terrorist activities, but above all to capture Bin Ladin and his deputies and bring them to trial; efforts to dry up Bin Ladin's money supply; and preparation for follow-on military action. The status of the document was and remained uncertain. It was never formally adopted by the principals, and participants in the Small Group now have little or no recollection of it. It did, however, guide Clarke's efforts.

The military component of Clarke's plan was its most fully articulated element. He envisioned an ongoing campaign of strikes against Bin Ladin's bases in Afghanistan or elsewhere, whenever target information was ripe. Acknowledging that individual targets might not have much value, he cautioned Berger not to expect ever again to have an assembly of terrorist leaders in his sights. But he argued that rolling attacks might persuade the Taliban to hand over Bin Ladin and, in any case, would show that the action in August was not a "one-off" event. It would show that the United States was committed to a relentless effort to take down Bin Ladin's network.[58]

Members of the Small Group found themselves unpersuaded of the merits of rolling attacks. Defense Secretary William Cohen told us Bin Ladin's training camps were primitive, built with "rope ladders"; General Shelton called them "jungle gym" camps. Neither thought them worthwhile targets for very expensive missiles. President Clinton and Berger also worried about the *Economist*'s point—that attacks that missed Bin Ladin could enhance his stature and win him new recruits. After the United States launched air attacks against Iraq at the end of 1998 and against Serbia in 1999, in each case provoking world-wide criticism, Deputy National Security Advisor James Steinberg added the argument that attacks in Afghanistan offered "little benefit, lots of blowback against [a] bomb-happy U.S."[59]

During the last week of August 1998, officials began considering possible follow-on strikes. According to Clarke, President Clinton was inclined to launch further strikes sooner rather than later. On August 27, Under Secretary of Defense for Policy Walter Slocombe advised Secretary Cohen that the available targets were not promising. The experience of the previous week, he wrote, "has only confirmed the importance of defining a clearly articulated rationale for military action" that was effective as well as justified. But Slocombe worried that simply striking some of these available targets did not add up to an effective strategy.[60]

Defense officials at a lower level, in the Office of the Assistant Secretary for Special Operations and Low-Intensity Conflict, tried to meet Slocombe's objections. They developed a plan that, unlike Clarke's, called not for particular strikes but instead for a broad change in national strategy and in the institutional approach of the Department of Defense, implying a possible need for large-scale operations across the whole spectrum of U.S. military capabilities. It urged the department to become a lead agency in driving a national counterterrorism strategy forward, to "champion a national effort to take up the gauntlet that international terrorists have thrown at our feet." The authors expressed concern that "we have not fundamentally altered our philosophy or our approach" even though the terrorist threat had grown. They outlined an eight-part strategy "to be more proactive and aggressive." The future, they warned, might bring "horrific attacks," in which case "we will have no choice nor, unfortunately, will we have a plan." The assistant secretary, Allen Holmes, took the paper to Slocombe's chief deputy, Jan Lodal, but it went no further. Its lead author recalls being told by Holmes that Lodal thought it was too aggressive. Holmes cannot recall what was said, and Lodal cannot remember the episode or the paper at all.[61]

4.3 DIPLOMACY

After the August missile strikes, diplomatic options to press the Taliban seemed no more promising than military options. The United States had issued a formal warning to the Taliban, and also to Sudan, that they would be held directly responsible for any attacks on Americans, wherever they occurred, carried out by the Bin Ladin network as long as they continued to provide sanctuary to it.[62]

For a brief moment, it had seemed as if the August strikes might have shocked the Taliban into thinking of giving up Bin Ladin. On August 22, the reclusive Mullah Omar told a working-level State Department official that the strikes were counterproductive but added that he would be open to a dialogue with the United States on Bin Ladin's presence in Afghanistan.[63] Meeting in Islamabad with William Milam, the U.S. ambassador to Pakistan, Taliban delegates said it was against their culture to expel someone seeking sanctuary but asked what would happen to Bin Ladin should he be sent to Saudi Arabia.[64]

Yet in September 1998, when the Saudi emissary, Prince Turki, asked Mullah Omar whether he would keep his earlier promise to expel Bin Ladin, the Taliban leader said no. Both sides shouted at each other, with Mullah Omar denouncing the Saudi government. Riyadh then suspended its diplomatic relations with the Taliban regime. (Saudi Arabia, Pakistan, and the United Arab Emirates were the only countries that recognized the Taliban as the legitimate government of Afghanistan.) Crown Prince Abdullah told President Clinton and Vice President Gore about this when he visited Washington in late September. His account confirmed reports that the U.S. government had received independently.[65]

Other efforts with the Saudi government centered on improving intelligence sharing and permitting U.S. agents to interrogate prisoners in Saudi custody. The history of such cooperation in 1997 and 1998 had been strained.[66] Several officials told us, in particular, that the United States could not get direct access to an important al Qaeda financial official, Madani al Tayyib, who had been detained by the Saudi government in 1997.[67] Though U.S. officials repeatedly raised the issue, the Saudis provided limited information. In his September 1998 meeting with Crown Prince Abdullah, Vice President Gore, while thanking the Saudi government for their responsiveness, renewed the request for direct U.S. access to Tayyib.[68] The United States never obtained this access.

An NSC staff-led working group on terrorist finances asked the CIA in November 1998 to push again for access to Tayyib and to see "if it is possible to elaborate further on the ties between Usama bin Ladin and prominent individuals in Saudi Arabia, including especially the Bin Ladin family."[69] One result was two NSC-led interagency trips to Persian Gulf states in 1999 and 2000. During these trips the NSC,

Treasury, and intelligence representatives spoke with Saudi officials, and later interviewed members of the Bin Ladin family, about Usama's inheritance. The Saudis and the Bin Ladin family eventually helped in this particular effort and U.S. officials ultimately learned that Bin Ladin was not financing al Qaeda out of a personal inheritance.[70] But Clarke was frustrated about how little the Agency knew, complaining to Berger that four years after "we first asked CIA to track down [Bin Ladin]'s finances" and two years after the creation of the CIA's Bin Ladin unit, the Agency said it could only guess at how much aid Bin Ladin gave to terrorist groups, what were the main sources of his budget, or how he moved his money.[71]

The other diplomatic route to get at Bin Ladin in Afghanistan ran through Islamabad. In the summer before the embassy bombings, the State Department had been heavily focused on rising tensions between India and Pakistan and did not aggressively challenge Pakistan on Afghanistan and Bin Ladin. But State Department counterterrorism officials wanted a stronger position; the department's acting counterterrorism coordinator advised Secretary Albright to designate Pakistan as a state sponsor of terrorism, noting that despite high-level Pakistani assurances, the country's military intelligence service continued "activities in support of international terrorism" by supporting attacks on civilian targets in Kashmir. This recommendation was opposed by the State Department's South Asia bureau, which was concerned that it would damage already sensitive relations with Pakistan in the wake of the May 1998 nuclear tests by both Pakistan and India. Secretary Albright rejected the recommendation on August 5, 1998, just two days before the embassy bombings.[72] She told us that, in general, putting the Pakistanis on the terrorist list would eliminate any influence the United States had over them.[73] In October, an NSC counterterrorism official noted that Pakistan's pro-Taliban military intelligence service had been training Kashmiri jihadists in one of the camps hit by U.S. missiles, leading to the death of Pakistanis.[74]

After flying to Nairobi and bringing home the coffins of the American dead, Secretary Albright increased the department's focus on counterterrorism. According to Ambassador Milam, the bombings were a "wake-up call," and he soon found himself spending 45 to 50 percent of his time working the Taliban-Bin Ladin portfolio.[75] But Pakistan's military intelligence service, known as the ISID (Inter-Services Intelligence Directorate), was the Taliban's primary patron, which made progress difficult.

Additional pressure on the Pakistanis—beyond demands to press the Taliban on Bin Ladin—seemed unattractive to most officials of the State Department. Congressional sanctions punishing Pakistan for possessing nuclear arms prevented the administration from offering incentives to Islamabad.[76] In the words of Deputy Secretary of State Strobe Talbott, Washington's Pakistan policy was "stickheavy." Talbott felt that the only remaining sticks were additional sanctions that would have bankrupted the Pakistanis, a dangerous move that could have brought "total chaos" to a nuclear-armed country with a significant number of Islamic radicals.[77]

The Saudi government, which had a long and close relationship with Pakistan and provided it oil on generous terms, was already pressing Sharif with regard to the Taliban and Bin Ladin. A senior State Department official concluded that Saudi Crown Prince Abdullah put "a tremendous amount of heat" on the Pakistani prime minister during the prince's October 1998 visit to Pakistan.[78]

The State Department urged President Clinton to engage the Pakistanis. Accepting this advice, President Clinton invited Sharif to Washington, where they talked mostly about India but also discussed Bin Ladin. After Sharif went home, the President called him and raised the Bin Ladin subject again. This effort elicited from Sharif a promise to talk with the Taliban.[79]

Mullah Omar's position showed no sign of softening. One intelligence report passed to Berger by the NSC staff quoted Bin Ladin as saying that Mullah Omar had given him a completely free hand to act in any country, though asking that he not claim responsibility for attacks in Pakistan or Saudi Arabia. Bin Ladin was described as grabbing his beard and saying emotionally, "By Allah, by God, the Americans will still be amazed. The so-called United States will suffer the same fate as the Russians. Their state will collapse, too."[80]

Debate in the State Department intensified after December 1998, when Michael Sheehan became counterterrorism coordinator. A onetime special forces officer, he had worked with Albright when she was ambassador to the United Nations and had served on the NSC staff with Clarke. He shared Clarke's obsession with terrorism, and had little hesitation about locking horns with the regional bureaus. Through every available channel, he repeated the earlier warning to the Taliban of the possible dire consequences—including military strikes—if Bin Ladin remained their guest and conducted additional attacks. Within the department, he argued for designating the Taliban regime a state sponsor of terrorism. This was technically difficult to do, for calling it a state would be tantamount to diplomatic recognition, which the United States had thus far withheld. But Sheehan urged the use of any available weapon against the Taliban. He told us that he thought he was regarded in the department as "a one-note Johnny nutcase."[81]

In early 1999, the State Department's counterterrorism office proposed a comprehensive diplomatic strategy for all states involved in the Afghanistan problem, including Pakistan. It specified both carrots and hard-hitting sticks—among them, certifying Pakistan as uncooperative on terrorism. Albright said the original carrots and sticks listed in a decision paper for principals may not have been used as "described on paper" but added that they were used in other ways or in varying degrees. But the paper's author, Ambassador Sheehan, was frustrated and complained to us that the original plan "had been watered down to the point that nothing was then done with it."[82]

The cautiousness of the South Asia bureau was reinforced

when, in May 1999, Pakistani troops were discovered to have infiltrated into an especially mountainous area of Kashmir. A limited war began between India and Pakistan, euphemistically called the "Kargil crisis," as India tried to drive the Pakistani forces out. Patience with Pakistan was wearing thin, inside both the State Department and the NSC. Bruce Riedel, the NSC staff member responsible for Pakistan, wrote Berger that Islamabad was "behaving as a rogue state in two areas—backing Taliban/UBL terror and provoking war with India."[83]

Discussion within the Clinton administration on Afghanistan then concentrated on two main alternatives. The first, championed by Riedel and Assistant Secretary of State Karl Inderfurth, was to undertake a major diplomatic effort to end the Afghan civil war and install a national unity government. The second, favored by Sheehan, Clarke, and the CIA, called for labeling the Taliban a terrorist group and ultimately funneling secret aid to its chief foe, the Northern Alliance. This dispute would go back and forth throughout 1999 and ultimately become entangled with debate about enlisting the Northern Alliance as an ally for covert action.[84]

Another diplomatic option may have been available: nurturing Afghan exile groups as a possible moderate governing alternative to the Taliban. In late 1999, Washington provided some support for talks among the leaders of exile Afghan groups, including the ousted Rome-based King Zahir Shah and Hamid Karzai, about bolstering anti-Taliban forces inside Afghanistan and linking the Northern Alliance with Pashtun groups. One U.S. diplomat later told us that the exile groups were not ready to move forward and that coordinating fractious groups residing in Bonn, Rome, and Cyprus proved extremely difficult.[85]

Frustrated by the Taliban's resistance, two senior State Department officials suggested asking the Saudis to offer the Taliban $250 million for Bin Ladin. Clarke opposed having the United States facilitate a "huge grant to a regime as heinous as the Taliban" and suggested that the idea might not seem attractive to either Secretary Albright or First Lady

Hillary Rodham Clinton—both critics of the Taliban's record on women's rights.[86] The proposal seems to have quietly died.

Within the State Department, some officials delayed Sheehan and Clarke's push either to designate Taliban-controlled Afghanistan as a state sponsor of terrorism or to designate the regime as a foreign terrorist organization (thereby avoiding the issue of whether to recognize the Taliban as Afghanistan's government). Sheehan and Clarke prevailed in July 1999, when President Clinton issued an executive order effectively declaring the Taliban regime a state sponsor of terrorism.[87] In October, a UN Security Council Resolution championed by the United States added economic and travel sanctions.[88]

With UN sanctions set to come into effect in November, Clarke wrote Berger that "the Taliban appear to be up to something."[89] Mullah Omar had shuffled his "cabinet" and hinted at Bin Ladin's possible departure. Clarke's staff thought his most likely destination would be Somalia; Chechnya seemed less appealing with Russia on the offensive. Clarke commented that Iraq and Libya had previously discussed hosting Bin Ladin, though he and his staff had their doubts that Bin Ladin would trust secular Arab dictators such as Saddam Hussein or Muammar Qadhafi. Clarke also raised the "remote possibility" of Yemen, which offered vast uncontrolled spaces. In November, the CSG discussed whether the sanctions had rattled the Taliban, who seemed "to be looking for a face-saving way out of the Bin Ladin issue."[90]

In fact none of the outside pressure had any visible effect on Mullah Omar, who was unconcerned about commerce with the outside world. Omar had virtually no diplomatic contact with the West, since he refused to meet with non-Muslims. The United States learned that at the end of 1999, the Taliban Council of Ministers unanimously reaffirmed that their regime would stick by Bin Ladin. Relations between Bin Ladin and the Taliban leadership were sometimes tense, but the foundation was deep and personal.[91] Indeed,

Mullah Omar had executed at least one subordinate who opposed his pro-Bin Ladin policy.[92]

The United States would try tougher sanctions in 2000. Working with Russia (a country involved in an ongoing campaign against Chechen separatists, some of whom received support from Bin Ladin), the United States persuaded the United Nations to adopt Security Council Resolution 1333, which included an embargo on arms shipments to the Taliban, in December 2000.[93] The aim of the resolution was to hit the Taliban where it was most sensitive—on the battlefield against the Northern Alliance—and criminalize giving them arms and providing military "advisers," which Pakistan had been doing.[94] Yet the passage of the resolution had no visible effect on Omar, nor did it halt the flow of Pakistani military assistance to the Taliban.[95]

U.S. authorities had continued to try to get cooperation from Pakistan in pressing the Taliban to stop sheltering Bin Ladin. President Clinton contacted Sharif again in June 1999, partly to discuss the crisis with India but also to urge Sharif, "in the strongest way I can," to persuade the Taliban to expel Bin Ladin.[96] The President suggested that Pakistan use its control over oil supplies to the Taliban and over Afghan imports through Karachi. Sharif suggested instead that Pakistani forces might try to capture Bin Ladin themselves. Though no one in Washington thought this was likely to happen, President Clinton gave the idea his blessing.[97]

The President met with Sharif in Washington in early July. Though the meeting's main purpose was to seal the Pakistani prime minister's decision to withdraw from the Kargil confrontation in Kashmir, President Clinton complained about Pakistan's failure to take effective action with respect to the Taliban and Bin Ladin. Sharif came back to his earlier proposal and won approval for U.S. assistance in training a Pakistani special forces team for an operation against Bin Ladin. Then, in October 1999, Sharif was deposed by General Pervez Musharraf, and the plan was terminated.[98]

At first, the Clinton administration hoped that Mushar-

raf's coup might create an opening for action on Bin Ladin.
A career military officer, Musharraf was thought to have the
political strength to confront and influence the Pakistani
military intelligence service, which supported the Taliban.
Berger speculated that the new government might use Bin
Ladin to buy concessions from Washington, but neither side
ever developed such an initiative.[99]

By late 1999, more than a year after the embassy bombings, diplomacy with Pakistan, like the efforts with the Taliban, had, according to Under Secretary of State Thomas
Pickering, "borne little fruit."[100]

4.4 COVERT ACTION

As part of the response to the embassy bombings, President
Clinton signed a Memorandum of Notification authorizing
the CIA to let its tribal assets use force to capture Bin Ladin
and his associates. CIA officers told the tribals that the plan
to capture Bin Ladin, which had been "turned off" three
months earlier, was back on. The memorandum also authorized the CIA to attack Bin Ladin in other ways. Also, an executive order froze financial holdings that could be linked to
Bin Ladin.[101]

The counterterrorism staff at CIA thought it was gaining
a better understanding of Bin Ladin and his network. In
preparation for briefing the Senate Select Committee on Intelligence on September 2, Tenet was told that the intelligence community knew more about Bin Ladin's network
"than about any other top tier terrorist organization."[102]

The CIA was using this knowledge to disrupt a number
of Bin Ladin–associated cells. Working with Albanian authorities, CIA operatives had raided an al Qaeda forgery operation and another terrorist cell in Tirana. These operations
may have disrupted a planned attack on the U.S. embassy in
Tirana, and did lead to the rendition of a number of al
Qaeda–related terrorist operatives. After the embassy bombings, there were arrests in Azerbaijan, Italy, and Britain.

Several terrorists were sent to an Arab country. The CIA described working with FBI operatives to prevent a planned attack on the U.S. embassy in Uganda, and a number of suspects were arrested. On September 16, Abu Hajer, one of Bin Ladin's deputies in Sudan and the head of his computer operations and weapons procurement, was arrested in Germany. He was the most important Bin Ladin lieutenant captured thus far. Clarke commented to Berger with satisfaction that August and September had brought the "greatest number of terrorist arrests in a short period of time that we have ever arranged/facilitated."[103]

Given the President's August Memorandum of Notification, the CIA had already been working on new plans for using the Afghan tribals to capture Bin Ladin. During September and October, the tribals claimed to have tried at least four times to ambush Bin Ladin. Senior CIA officials doubted whether any of these ambush attempts had actually occurred. But the tribals did seem to have success in reporting where Bin Ladin was.[104]

This information was more useful than it had been in the past; since the August missile strikes, Bin Ladin had taken to moving his sleeping place frequently and unpredictably and had added new bodyguards. Worst of all, al Qaeda's senior leadership had stopped using a particular means of communication almost immediately after a leak to the *Washington Times*.[105] This made it much more difficult for the National Security Agency to intercept his conversations. But since the tribals seemed to know where Bin Ladin was or would be, an alternative to capturing Bin Ladin would be to mark his location and call in another round of missile strikes.

On November 3, the Small Group met to discuss these problems, among other topics. Preparing Director Tenet for a Small Group meeting in mid-November, the Counterterrorist Center stressed, "At this point we cannot predict when or if a capture operation will be executed by our assets."[106]

U.S. counterterrorism officials also worried about possible domestic attacks. Several intelligence reports, some of dubious sourcing, mentioned Washington as a possible target. On October 26, Clarke's CSG took the unusual step of holding a meeting dedicated to trying "to evaluate the threat of a terrorist attack in the United States by the Usama bin Ladin network."[107] The CSG members were "urged to be as creative as possible in their thinking" about preventing a Bin Ladin attack on U.S. territory. Participants noted that while the FBI had been given additional resources for such efforts, both it and the CIA were having problems exploiting leads by tracing U.S. telephone numbers and translating documents obtained in cell disruptions abroad. The Justice Department reported that the current guidelines from the Attorney General gave sufficient legal authority for domestic investigation and surveillance.[108]

Though intelligence gave no clear indication of what might be afoot, some intelligence reports mentioned chemical weapons, pointing toward work at a camp in southern Afghanistan called Derunta. On November 4, 1998, the U.S. Attorney's Office for the Southern District of New York unsealed its indictment of Bin Ladin, charging him with conspiracy to attack U.S. defense installations. The indictment also charged that al Qaeda had allied itself with Sudan, Iran, and Hezbollah. The original sealed indictment had added that al Qaeda had "reached an understanding with the government of Iraq that al Qaeda would not work against that government and that on particular projects, specifically including weapons development, al Qaeda would work cooperatively with the Government of Iraq."[109] This passage led Clarke, who for years had read intelligence reports on Iraqi-Sudanese cooperation on chemical weapons, to speculate to Berger that a large Iraqi presence at chemical facilities in Khartoum was "probably a direct result of the Iraq–Al Qida agreement." Clarke added that VX precursor traces found near al Shifa were the "exact formula used by Iraq."[110] This language about al Qaeda's "understanding" with Iraq had been dropped, however, when a superseding indictment was filed in November 1998.[111]

On Friday, December 4, 1998, the CIA included an article in the Presidential Daily Brief describing intelligence,

The following is the text of an item from the Presidential Daily Brief received by President William J. Clinton on December 4, 1998. Redacted material is indicated in brackets.

SUBJECT: Bin Ladin Preparing to Hijack US Aircraft and Other Attacks

1. Reporting [—] suggests Bin Ladin and his allies are preparing for attacks in the US, including an aircraft hijacking to obtain the release of Shaykh 'Umar 'Abd al-Rahman, Ramzi Yousef, and Muhammad Sadiq 'Awda. One source quoted a senior member of the Gama'at al-Islamiyya (IG) saying that, as of late October, the IG had completed planning for an operation in the US on behalf of Bin Ladin, but that the operation was on hold. A senior Bin Ladin operative from Saudi Arabia was to visit IG counterparts in the US soon thereafter to discuss options—perhaps including an aircraft hijacking.

- IG leader Islambuli in late September was planning to hijack a US airliner during the "next couple of weeks" to free 'Abd al-Rahman and the other prisoners, according to what may be a different source.
- The same source late last month said that Bin Ladin might implement plans to hijack US aircraft before the beginning of Ramadan on 20 December and that two members of the operational team had evaded security checks during a recent trial run at an unidentified New York airport. [—]

2. Some members of the Bin Ladin network have received hijack training, according to various sources, but no group directly tied to Bin Ladin's al-Qa'ida organization has ever carried out an aircraft hijacking. Bin Ladin could be weighing other types of operations against US

aircraft. According to [—] the IG in October obtained
SA-7 missiles and intended to move them from Yemen
into Saudi Arabia to shoot down an Egyptian plane or, if
unsuccessful, a US military or civilian aircraft.

- A [—] in October told us that unspecified "extremist
  elements" in Yemen had acquired SA-7s. [—]

3. [—] indicate the Bin Ladin organization or its allies
are moving closer to implementing anti-US attacks at unspecified locations, but we do not know whether they are
related to attacks on aircraft. A Bin Ladin associate in
Sudan late last month told a colleague in Kandahar that
he had shipped a group of containers to Afghanistan. Bin
Ladin associates also talked about the movement of containers to Afghanistan before the East Africa bombings.

- In other [—] Bin Ladin associates last month discussed picking up a package in Malaysia. One told
  his colleague in Malaysia that "they" were in the
  "ninth month [of pregnancy]."
- An alleged Bin Ladin supporter in Yemen late last
  month remarked to his mother that he planned to
  work in "commerce" from abroad and said his impending "marriage," which would take place soon,
  would be a "surprise." "Commerce" and "marriage"
  often are codewords for terrorist attacks. [—]

received from a friendly government, about a threatened hijacking in the United States. This article was declassified at
our request.

The same day, Clarke convened a meeting of his CSG to
discuss both the hijacking concern and the antiaircraft missile threat. To address the hijacking warning, the group
agreed that New York airports should go to maximum secu-

rity starting that weekend. They agreed to boost security at other East coast airports. The CIA agreed to distribute versions of the report to the FBI and FAA to pass to the New York Police Department and the airlines. The FAA issued a security directive on December 8, with specific requirements for more intensive air carrier screening of passengers and more oversight of the screening process, at all three New York City area airports.[112]

The intelligence community could learn little about the source of the information. Later in December and again in early January 1999, more information arrived from the same source, reporting that the planned hijacking had been stalled because two of the operatives, who were sketchily described, had been arrested near Washington, D.C. or New York. After investigation, the FBI could find no information to support the hijack threat; nor could it verify any arrests like those described in the report. The FAA alert at the New York area airports ended on January 31, 1999.[113]

On December 17, the day after the United States and Britain began their Desert Fox bombing campaign against Iraq, the Small Group convened to discuss intelligence suggesting imminent Bin Ladin attacks on the U.S. embassies in Qatar and Ethiopia. The next day, Director Tenet sent a memo to the President, the cabinet, and senior officials throughout the government describing reports that Bin Ladin planned to attack U.S. targets very soon, possibly over the next few days, before Ramadan celebrations began. Tenet said he was "greatly concerned."[114]

With alarms sounding, members of the Small Group considered ideas about how to respond to or prevent such attacks. Generals Shelton and Zinni came up with military options. Special Operations Forces were later told that they might be ordered to attempt very high-risk in-and-out raids either in Khartoum, to capture a senior Bin Ladin operative known as Abu Hafs the Mauritanian—who appeared to be engineering some of the plots—or in Kandahar, to capture Bin Ladin himself. Shelton told us that such operations are not risk free, invoking the memory of the 1993 "Black Hawk down" fiasco in Mogadishu.[115]

The CIA reported on December 18 that Bin Ladin might be traveling to Kandahar and could be targeted there with cruise missiles. Vessels with Tomahawk cruise missiles were on station in the Arabian Sea, and could fire within a few hours of receiving target data.[116]

On December 20, intelligence indicated Bin Ladin would be spending the night at the Haji Habash house, part of the governor's residence in Kandahar. The chief of the Bin Ladin unit, "Mike," told us that he promptly briefed Tenet and his deputy, John Gordon. From the field, the CIA's Gary Schroen advised: "Hit him tonight—we may not get another chance." An urgent teleconference of principals was arranged.[117]

The principals considered a cruise missile strike to try to kill Bin Ladin. One issue they discussed was the potential collateral damage—the number of innocent bystanders who would be killed or wounded. General Zinni predicted a number well over 200 and was concerned about damage to a nearby mosque. The senior intelligence officer on the Joint Staff apparently made a different calculation, estimating half as much collateral damage and not predicting damage to the mosque. By the end of the meeting, the principals decided against recommending to the President that he order a strike. A few weeks later, in January 1999, Clarke wrote that the principals had thought the intelligence only half reliable and had worried about killing or injuring perhaps 300 people. Tenet said he remembered doubts about the reliability of the source and concern about hitting the nearby mosque. "Mike" remembered Tenet telling him that the military was concerned that a few hours had passed since the last sighting of Bin Ladin and that this persuaded everyone that the chance of failure was too great.[118]

Some lower-level officials were angry. "Mike" reported to Schroen that he had been unable to sleep after this decision. "I'm sure we'll regret not acting last night," he wrote, criticizing the principals for "worrying that some stray shrapnel might hit the Habash mosque and 'offend' Muslims." He commented that they had not shown comparable sensitivity when deciding to bomb Muslims in Iraq. The principals, he said, were "obsessed" with trying to get others—Saudis, Pakistanis, Afghan tribals—to "do what we won't do." Schroen was disappointed too. "We should have done it last night," he wrote. "We may well come to regret the decision not to go ahead."[119] The Joint Staff's deputy director for operations agreed, even though he told us that later intelligence appeared to show that Bin Ladin had left his quarters before the strike would have occurred. Missing Bin Ladin, he said, "would have caused us a hell of a problem, but it was a shot we should have taken, and we would have had to pay the price."[120]

The principals began considering other, more aggressive covert alternatives using the tribals. CIA officers suggested that the tribals would prefer to try a raid rather than a roadside ambush because they would have better control, it would be less dangerous, and it played more to their skills and experience. But everyone knew that if the tribals were to conduct such a raid, guns would be blazing. The current Memorandum of Notification instructed the CIA to capture Bin Ladin and to use lethal force only in self-defense. Work now began on a new memorandum that would give the tribals more latitude. The intention was to say that they could use lethal force if the attempted capture seemed impossible to complete successfully.[121]

Early drafts of this highly sensitive document emphasized that it authorized only a capture operation. The tribals were to be paid only if they captured Bin Ladin, not if they killed him. Officials throughout the government approved this draft. But on December 21, the day after principals decided not to launch the cruise missile strike against Kandahar, the CIA's leaders urged strengthening the language to allow the tribals to be paid whether Bin Ladin was captured *or* killed. Berger and Tenet then worked together to take this line of thought even further.[122]

They finally agreed, as Berger reported to President Clinton, that an extraordinary step was necessary. The new memorandum would allow the killing of Bin Ladin if the CIA and the tribals judged that capture was not feasible (a judgment it already seemed clear they had reached). The Justice Department lawyer who worked on the draft told us that what was envisioned was a group of tribals assaulting a location, leading to a shoot-out. Bin Ladin and others would be captured if possible, but probably would be killed. The administration's position was that under the law of armed conflict, killing a person who posed an imminent threat to the United States would be an act of self-defense, not an assassination. On Christmas Eve 1998, Berger sent a final draft to President Clinton, with an explanatory memo. The President approved the document.[123]

Because the White House considered this operation highly sensitive, only a tiny number of people knew about this Memorandum of Notification. Berger arranged for the NSC's legal adviser to inform Albright, Cohen, Shelton, and Reno. None was allowed to keep a copy. Congressional leaders were briefed, as required by law. Attorney General Reno had sent a letter to the President expressing her concern: she warned of possible retaliation, including the targeting of U.S. officials. She did not pose any legal objection. A copy of the final document, along with the carefully crafted instructions that were to be sent to the tribals, was given to Tenet.[124]

A message from Tenet to CIA field agents directed them to communicate to the tribals the instructions authorized by the President: the United States preferred that Bin Ladin and his lieutenants be captured, but if a successful capture operation was not feasible, the tribals were permitted to kill them. The instructions added that the tribals must avoid killing others unnecessarily and must not kill or abuse Bin Ladin or his lieutenants if they surrendered. Finally, the tribals would not be paid if this set of requirements was not met.[125]

The field officer passed these instructions to the tribals

word for word. But he prefaced the directions with a message: "From the American President down to the average man in the street, we want him [Bin Ladin] stopped." If the tribals captured Bin Ladin, the officer assured them that he would receive a fair trial under U.S., law and be treated humanely. The CIA officer reported that the tribals said they "fully understand the contents, implications and the spirit of the message" and that that their response was, "We will try our best to capture Bin Ladin alive and will have no intention of killing or harming him on purpose." The tribals explained that they wanted to prove that their standards of behavior were more civilized than those of Bin Ladin and his band of terrorists. In an additional note addressed to Schroen, the tribals noted that if they were to adopt Bin Ladin's ethics, "we would have finished the job long before," but they had been limited by their abilities and "by our beliefs and laws we have to respect."[126]

Schroen and "Mike" were impressed by the tribals' reaction. Schroen cabled that the tribals were not in it for the money but as an investment in the future of Afghanistan. "Mike" agreed that the tribals' reluctance to kill was not a "showstopper." "From our view," he wrote, "that seems in character and fair enough."[127]

Policymakers in the Clinton administration, including the President and his national security advisor, told us that the President's intent regarding covert action against Bin Ladin was clear: he wanted him dead. This intent was never well communicated or understood within the CIA. Tenet told the Commission that except in one specific case (discussed later), the CIA was authorized to kill Bin Ladin only in the context of a capture operation. CIA senior managers, operators, and lawyers confirmed this understanding. "We always talked about how much easier it would have been to kill him," a former chief of the Bin Ladin unit said.[128]

In February 1999, another draft Memorandum of Notification went to President Clinton. It asked him to allow the CIA to give exactly the same guidance to the Northern Alliance as had just been given to the tribals: they could kill

Bin Ladin if a successful capture operation was not feasible. On this occasion, however, President Clinton crossed out key language he had approved in December and inserted more ambiguous language. No one we interviewed could shed light on why the President did this. President Clinton told the Commission that he had no recollection of why he rewrote the language.[129]

Later in 1999, when legal authority was needed for enlisting still other collaborators and for covering a wider set of contingencies, the lawyers returned to the language used in August 1998, which authorized force only in the context of a capture operation. Given the closely held character of the document approved in December 1998, and the subsequent return to the earlier language, it is possible to understand how the former White House officials and the CIA officials might disagree as to whether the CIA was ever authorized by the President to kill Bin Ladin.[130]

The dispute turned out to be somewhat academic, as the limits of available legal authority were not tested. Clarke commented to Berger that "despite 'expanded' authority for CIA's sources to engage in direct action, they have shown no inclination to do so." He added that it was his impression that the CIA thought the tribals unlikely to act against Bin Ladin and hence relying on them was "unrealistic."[131] Events seemed to bear him out, since the tribals did not stage an attack on Bin Ladin or his associates during 1999.

The tribals remained active collectors of intelligence, however, providing good but not predictive information about Bin Ladin's whereabouts. The CIA also tried to improve its intelligence reporting on Bin Ladin by what Tenet's assistant director for collection, the indefatigable Charles Allen, called an "all-out, all-agency, seven-days-a-week" effort.[132] The effort might have had an effect. On January 12, 1999, Clarke wrote Berger that the CIA's confidence in the tribals' reporting had increased. It was now higher than it had been on December 20.[133]

In February 1999, Allen proposed flying a U-2 mission over Afghanistan to build a baseline of intelligence outside the areas where the tribals had coverage. Clarke was nervous about such a mission because he continued to fear that Bin Ladin might leave for someplace less accessible. He wrote Deputy National Security Advisor Donald Kerrick that one reliable source reported Bin Ladin's having met with Iraqi officials, who "may have offered him asylum." Other intelligence sources said that some Taliban leaders, though not Mullah Omar, had urged Bin Ladin to go to Iraq. If Bin Ladin actually moved to Iraq, wrote Clarke, his network would be at Saddam Hussein's service, and it would be "virtually impossible" to find him. Better to get Bin Ladin in Afghanistan, Clarke declared.[134] Berger suggested sending one U-2 flight, but Clarke opposed even this. It would require Pakistani approval, he wrote; and "Pak[istan's] intel[ligence service] is in bed with" Bin Ladin and would warn him that the United States was getting ready for a bombing campaign: "Armed with that knowledge, old wily Usama will likely boogie to Baghdad."[135] Though told also by Bruce Riedel of the NSC staff that Saddam Hussein wanted Bin Ladin in Baghdad, Berger conditionally authorized a single U-2 flight. Allen meanwhile had found other ways of getting the information he wanted. So the U-2 flight never occurred.[136]

4.5 SEARCHING FOR FRESH OPTIONS

"Boots on the Ground?"

Starting on the day the August 1998 strikes were launched, General Shelton had issued a planning order to prepare follow-on strikes and think beyond just using cruise missiles.[137] The initial strikes had been called Operation Infinite Reach. The follow-on plans were given the code name Operation Infinite Resolve.

At the time, any actual military action in Afghanistan would have been carried out by General Zinni's Central Command. This command was therefore the locus for most military planning. Zinni was even less enthusiastic than Cohen and Shelton about follow-on cruise missile strikes. He knew that the Tomahawks did not always hit their targets. After the August 20 strikes, President Clinton had had to call Pakistani Prime Minister Sharif to apologize for a wayward missile that had killed several people in a Pakistani village. Sharif had been understanding, while commenting on American "overkill."[138]

Zinni feared that Bin Ladin would in the future locate himself in cities, where U.S. missiles could kill thousands of Afghans. He worried also lest Pakistani authorities not get adequate warning, think the missiles came from India, and do something that everyone would later regret. Discussing potential repercussions in the region of his military responsibility, Zinni said, "It was easy to take the shot from Washington and walk away from it. We had to live there."[139]

Zinni's distinct preference would have been to build up counterterrorism capabilities in neighboring countries such as Uzbekistan. But he told us that he could not drum up much interest in or money for such a purpose from Washington, partly, he thought, because these countries had dictatorial governments.[140]

After the decision—in which fear of collateral damage was an important factor—not to use cruise missiles against Kandahar in December 1998, Shelton and officers in the Pentagon developed plans for using an AC-130 gunship instead of cruise missile strikes. Designed specifically for the special forces, the version of the AC-130 known as "Spooky" can fly in fast or from high altitude, undetected by radar; guided to its zone by extraordinarily complex electronics, it is capable of rapidly firing precision-guided 25, 40, and 105 mm projectiles. Because this system could target more precisely than a salvo of cruise missiles, it had a much lower risk of causing collateral damage. After giving Clarke a briefing and being encouraged to proceed, Shelton formally directed Zinni and General Peter Schoomaker, who headed the Special Operations Command, to develop plans for an AC-130 mission against Bin Ladin's headquarters and infrastructure in Afghanistan. The Joint Staff prepared a decision paper for deployment of the Special Operations aircraft.[141]

Though Berger and Clarke continued to indicate interest in this option, the AC-130s were never deployed. Clarke wrote at the time that Zinni opposed their use, and John Maher, the Joint Staff's deputy director of operations, agreed that this was Zinni's position. Zinni himself does not recall blocking the option. He told us that he understood the Special Operations Command had never thought the intelligence good enough to justify actually moving AC-130s into position. Schoomaker says, on the contrary, that he thought the AC-130 option feasible.[142]

The most likely explanation for the two generals' differing recollections is that both of them thought serious preparation for any such operations would require a long-term redeployment of Special Operations forces to the Middle East or South Asia. The AC-130s would need bases because the aircraft's unrefueled range was only a little over 2,000 miles. They needed search-and-rescue backup, which would have still less range. Thus an AC-130 deployment had to be embedded in a wider political and military concept involving Pakistan or other neighboring countries to address issues relating to basing and overflight. No one ever put such an initiative on the table. Zinni therefore cautioned about simply ordering up AC-130 deployments for a quick strike; Schoomaker planned for what he saw as a practical strike option; and the underlying issues were not fully engaged. The Joint Staff decision paper was never turned into an interagency policy paper.

The same was true for the option of using ground units from the Special Operations Command. Within the command, some officers—such as Schoomaker—wanted the mission of "putting boots on the ground" to get at Bin Ladin and al Qaeda. At the time, Special Operations was designated as a "supporting command," not a "supported command": that is, it supported a theater commander and did not prepare its own plans for dealing with al Qaeda. Schoomaker proposed to Shelton and Cohen that Special

Operations become a supported command, but the proposal was not adopted. Had it been accepted, he says, he would have taken on the al Qaeda mission instead of deferring to Zinni. Lieutenant General William Boykin, the current deputy under secretary of defense for intelligence and a founding member of Delta Force, told us that "opportunities were missed because of an unwillingness to take risks and a lack of vision and understanding."[143]

President Clinton relied on the advice of General Shelton, who informed him that without intelligence on Bin Ladin's location, a commando raid's chance of failure was high. Shelton told President Clinton he would go forward with "boots on the ground" if the President ordered him to do so; however, he had to ensure that the President was completely aware of the large logistical problems inherent in a military operation.[144]

The Special Operations plans were apparently conceived as another quick strike option—an option to insert forces after the United States received actionable intelligence. President Clinton told the Commission that "if we had had really good intelligence about . . . where [Usama Bin Ladin] was, I would have done it." Zinni and Schoomaker did make preparations for possible very high risk in-and-out operations to capture or kill terrorists. Cohen told the Commission that the notion of putting military personnel on the ground without some reasonable certitude that Bin Ladin was in a particular location would have resulted in the mission's failure and the loss of life in a fruitless effort.[145] None of these officials was aware of the ambitious plan developed months earlier by lower-level Defense officials.

In our interviews, some military officers repeatedly invoked the analogy of Desert One and the failed 1980 hostage rescue mission in Iran.[146] They were dubious about a quick strike approach to using Special Operations Forces, which they thought complicated and risky. Such efforts would have required bases in the region, but all the options were unappealing. Pro-Taliban elements of Pakistan's military might warn Bin Ladin or his associates of pending operations. With nearby basing options limited, an alternative was to fly from ships in the Arabian Sea or from land bases in the Persian Gulf, as was done after 9/11. Such operations would then have to be supported from long distances, overflying the airspace of nations that might not have been supportive or aware of U.S. efforts.[147]

However, if these hurdles were addressed, and if the military could then operate regularly in the region for a long period, perhaps clandestinely, it might attempt to gather intelligence and wait for an opportunity. One Special Operations commander said his view of actionable intelligence was that if you "give me the action, I will give you the intelligence."[148] But this course would still be risky, in light both of the difficulties already mentioned and of the danger that U.S. operations might fail disastrously. We have found no evidence that such a long-term political-military approach for using Special Operations Forces in the region was proposed to or analyzed by the Small Group, even though such capability had been honed for at least a decade within the Defense Department.

Therefore the debate looked to some like bold proposals from civilians meeting hypercaution from the military. Clarke saw it this way. Of the military, he said to us, "They were very, very, very reluctant."[149] But from another perspective, poorly informed proposals for bold action were pitted against experienced professional judgment. That was how Secretary of Defense Cohen viewed it. He said to us: "I would have to place my judgment call in terms of, do I believe that the chairman of the Joint Chiefs, former commander of Special Forces command, is in a better position to make a judgment on the feasibility of this than, perhaps, Mr. Clarke?"[150]

Beyond a large-scale political-military commitment to build up a covert or clandestine capability using American personnel on the ground, either military or CIA, there was a still larger option that could have been considered—invading Afghanistan itself. Every official we questioned about the possibility of an invasion of Afghanistan said that it was almost unthinkable, absent a provocation such as 9/11, because of poor prospects for cooperation from Pakistan and other nations and because they believed the public would not support it. Cruise missiles were and would remain the only military option on the table.

The Desert Camp, February 1999

Early in 1999, the CIA received reporting that Bin Ladin was spending much of his time at one of several camps in the Afghan desert south of Kandahar. At the beginning of February, Bin Ladin was reportedly located in the vicinity of the Sheikh Ali camp, a desert hunting camp being used by visitors from a Gulf state. Public sources have stated that these visitors were from the United Arab Emirates.[151]

Reporting from the CIA's assets provided a detailed description of the hunting camp, including its size, location, resources, and security, as well as of Bin Ladin's smaller, adjacent camp.[152] Because this was not in an urban area, missiles launched against it would have less risk of causing collateral damage. On February 8, the military began to ready itself for a possible strike.[153] The next day, national technical intelligence confirmed the location and description of the larger camp and showed the nearby presence of an official aircraft of the United Arab Emirates. But the location of Bin Ladin's quarters could not be pinned down so precisely.[154] The CIA did its best to answer a host of questions about the larger camp and its residents and about Bin Ladin's daily schedule and routines to support military contingency planning. According to reporting from the tribals, Bin Ladin regularly went from his adjacent camp to the larger camp where he visited the Emiratis; the tribals expected him to be at the hunting camp for such a visit at least until midmorning on February 11.[155] Clarke wrote to Berger's deputy on February 10 that the military was then doing targeting work to hit the main camp with cruise missiles and should be in position to strike the following morning.[156] Speaker of the House Dennis Hastert appears to have been briefed on the situation.[157]

No strike was launched. By February 12 Bin Ladin had apparently moved on, and the immediate strike plans became moot.[158] According to CIA and Defense officials, policymakers were concerned about the danger that a strike would kill an Emirati prince or other senior officials who might be with Bin Ladin or close by. Clarke told us the strike was called off after consultations with Director Tenet because the intelligence was dubious, and it seemed to Clarke as if the CIA was presenting an option to attack America's best counterterrorism ally in the Gulf. The lead CIA official in the field, Gary Schroen, felt that the intelligence reporting in this case was very reliable; the Bin Ladin unit chief, "Mike," agreed. Schroen believes today that this was a lost opportunity to kill Bin Ladin before 9/11.[159]

Even after Bin Ladin's departure from the area, CIA officers hoped he might return, seeing the camp as a magnet that could draw him for as long as it was still set up. The military maintained readiness for another strike opportunity.[160] On March 7, 1999, Clarke called a UAE official to express his concerns about possible associations between Emirati officials and Bin Ladin. Clarke later wrote in a memorandum of this conversation that the call had been approved at an interagency meeting and cleared with the CIA.[161] When the former Bin Ladin unit chief found out about Clarke's call, he questioned CIA officials, who denied having given such a clearance.[162] Imagery confirmed that less than a week after Clarke's phone call the camp was hurriedly dismantled, and the site was deserted.[163] CIA officers, including Deputy Director for Operations Pavitt, were irate. "Mike" thought the dismantling of the camp erased a possible site for targeting Bin Ladin.[164]

The United Arab Emirates was becoming both a valued counterterrorism ally of the United States and a persistent counterterrorism problem. From 1999 through early 2001, the United States, and President Clinton personally, pressed the UAE, one of the Taliban's only travel and financial outlets to the outside world, to break off its ties and enforce sanctions, especially those relating to flights to and from

Afghanistan.[165] These efforts achieved little before 9/11.

In July 1999, UAE Minister of State for Foreign Affairs Hamdan bin Zayid threatened to break relations with the Taliban over Bin Ladin.[166] The Taliban did not take him seriously, however. Bin Zayid later told an American diplomat that the UAE valued its relations with the Taliban because the Afghan radicals offered a counterbalance to "Iranian dangers" in the region, but he also noted that the UAE did not want to upset the United States.[167]

Looking for New Partners

Although not all CIA officers had lost faith in the tribals' capabilities—many judged them to be good reporters—few believed they would carry out an ambush of Bin Ladin. The chief of the Counterterrorist Center compared relying on the tribals to playing the lottery.[168] He and his associates, supported by Clarke, pressed for developing a partnership with the Northern Alliance, even though doing so might bring the United States squarely behind one side in Afghanistan's long-running civil war.

The Northern Alliance was dominated by Tajiks and drew its strength mainly from the northern and eastern parts of Afghanistan. In contrast, Taliban members came principally from Afghanistan's most numerous ethnic group, the Pashtuns, who are concentrated in the southern part of the country, extending into the North-West Frontier and Baluchistan provinces of Pakistan.[169]

Because of the Taliban's behavior and its association with Pakistan, the Northern Alliance had been able at various times to obtain assistance from Russia, Iran, and India. The alliance's leader was Afghanistan's most renowned military commander, Ahmed Shah Massoud. Reflective and charismatic, he had been one of the true heroes of the war against the Soviets. But his bands had been charged with more than one massacre, and the Northern Alliance was widely thought to finance itself in part through trade in heroin. Nor had Massoud shown much aptitude for governing except as a ruthless warlord. Nevertheless, Tenet told us Massoud seemed the most interesting possible new ally against Bin Ladin.[170]

In February 1999, Tenet sought President Clinton's authorization to enlist Massoud and his forces as partners. In response to this request, the President signed the Memorandum of Notification whose language he personally altered. Tenet says he saw no significance in the President's changes. So far as he was concerned, it was the language of August 1998, expressing a preference for capture but accepting the possibility that Bin Ladin could not be brought out alive. "We were plowing the same ground," Tenet said.[171]

CIA officers described Massoud's reaction when he heard that the United States wanted him to capture and not kill Bin Ladin. One characterized Massoud's body language as "a wince." Schroen recalled Massoud's response as "You guys are crazy—you haven't changed a bit." In Schroen's opinion, the capture proviso inhibited Massoud and his forces from going after Bin Ladin but did not completely stop them.[172] The idea, however, was a long shot. Bin Ladin's usual base of activity was near Kandahar, far from the front lines of Taliban operations against the Northern Alliance.

Kandahar, May 1999

It was in Kandahar that perhaps the last, and most likely the best, opportunity arose for targeting Bin Ladin with cruise missiles before 9/11. In May 1999, CIA assets in Afghanistan reported on Bin Ladin's location in and around Kandahar over the course of five days and nights. The reporting was very detailed and came from several sources. If this intelligence was not "actionable," working-level officials said at the time and today, it was hard for them to imagine how any intelligence on Bin Ladin in Afghanistan would meet the standard. Communications were good, and the cruise missiles were ready. "This was in our strike zone," a senior military officer said. "It was a fat pitch, a home run." He expected the missiles to fly. When the decision came back that they should stand down, not shoot, the officer said, "we all just slumped." He told us he knew of no one at the Pentagon or the CIA who thought it was a bad gamble. Bin Ladin "should have been a dead man" that night, he said.[173]

Working-level CIA officials agreed. While there was a conflicting intelligence report about Bin Ladin's where-abouts, the experts discounted it. At the time, CIA working-level officials were told by their managers that the strikes were not ordered because the military doubted the intelligence and worried about collateral damage. Replying to a frustrated colleague in the field, the Bin Ladin unit chief wrote: "having a chance to get [Bin Ladin] three times in 36 hours and foregoing the chance each time has made me a bit angry. . . . [T]he DCI finds himself alone at the table, with the other princip[als] basically saying 'we'll go along with your decision Mr. Director,' and implicitly saying that the Agency will hang alone if the attack doesn't get Bin Ladin."[174] But the military officer quoted earlier recalled that the Pentagon had been willing to act. He told us that Clarke informed him and others that Tenet assessed the chance of the intelligence being accurate as 50–50. This officer believed that Tenet's assessment was the key to the decision.[175]

Tenet told us he does not remember any details about this episode, except that the intelligence came from a single un-corroborated source and that there was a risk of collateral damage. The story is further complicated by Tenet's absence from the critical principals meeting on this strike (he was ap-parently out of town); his deputy, John Gordon, was repre-senting the CIA. Gordon recalled having presented the intelligence in a positive light, with appropriate caveats, but stating that this intelligence was about as good as it could get.[176]

Berger remembered only that in all such cases, the call had been Tenet's. Berger felt sure that Tenet was eager to get Bin Ladin. In his view, Tenet did his job responsibly. "George would call and say, 'We just don't have it,' " Berger said.[177]

The decision not to strike in May 1999 may now seem hard to understand. In fairness, we note two points: First, in

December 1998, the principals' wariness about ordering a strike appears to have been vindicated: Bin Ladin left his room unexpectedly, and if a strike had been ordered he would not have been hit. Second, the administration, and the CIA in particular, was in the midst of intense scrutiny and criticism in May 1999 because faulty intelligence had just led the United States to mistakenly bomb the Chinese embassy in Belgrade during the NATO war against Serbia. This episode may have made officials more cautious than might otherwise have been the case.[178]

From May 1999 until September 2001, policymakers did not again actively consider a missile strike against Bin Ladin.[179] The principals did give some further consideration in 1999 to more general strikes, reviving Clarke's "Delenda" notion of hitting camps and infrastructure to disrupt al Qaeda's organization. In the first months of 1999, the Joint Staff had developed broader target lists to undertake a "focused campaign" against the infrastructure of Bin Ladin's network and to hit Taliban government sites as well. General Shelton told us that the Taliban targets were "easier" to hit and more substantial.[180]

Part of the context for considering broader strikes in the summer of 1999 was renewed worry about Bin Ladin's ambitions to acquire weapons of mass destruction. In May and June, the U.S. government received a flurry of ominous reports, including more information about chemical weapons training or development at the Derunta camp and possible attempts to amass nuclear material at Herat.[181]

By late June, U.S. and other intelligence services had concluded that al Qaeda was in pre-attack mode, perhaps again involving Abu Hafs the Mauritanian. On June 25, at Clarke's request, Berger convened the Small Group in his office to discuss the alert, Bin Ladin's WMD programs, and his location. "Should we pre-empt by attacking UBL facilities?" Clarke urged Berger to ask his colleagues.[182]

In his handwritten notes on the meeting paper, Berger jotted down the presence of 7 to 11 families in the Tarnak Farms facility, which could mean 60–65 casualties. Berger noted the possible "slight impact" on Bin Ladin and added, "if he responds, we're blamed."[183] The NSC staff raised the option of waiting until after a terrorist attack, and then retaliating, including possible strikes on the Taliban. But Clarke observed that Bin Ladin would probably empty his camps after an attack.[184]

The military route seemed to have reached a dead end. In December 1999, Clarke urged Berger to ask the principals to ask themselves: "Why have there been no real options lately for direct US military action?"[185] There are no notes recording whether the question was discussed or, if it was, how it was answered.

Reports of possible attacks by Bin Ladin kept coming in throughout 1999. They included a threat to blow up the FBI building in Washington, D.C. In September, the CSG reviewed a possible threat to a flight out of Los Angeles or New York.[186] These warnings came amid dozens of others that flooded in.

With military and diplomatic options practically exhausted by the summer of 1999, the U.S. government seemed to be back where it had been in the summer of 1998—relying on the CIA to find some other option. That picture also seemed discouraging. Several disruptions and renditions aimed against the broader al Qaeda network had succeeded.[187] But covert action efforts in Afghanistan had not been fruitful.

In mid-1999, new leaders arrived at the Counterterrorist Center and the Bin Ladin unit. The new director of CTC, replacing "Jeff," was Cofer Black. The new head of the section that included the Bin Ladin unit was "Richard." Black, "Richard," and their colleagues began working on a new operational strategy for attacking al Qaeda; their starting point was to get better intelligence, relying more on the CIA's own sources and less on the tribals.[188]

In July 1999, President Clinton authorized the CIA to work with several governments to capture Bin Ladin, and extended the scope of efforts to Bin Ladin's principal lieutenants. The President reportedly also authorized a covert action under carefully limited circumstances which, if successful, would have resulted in Bin Ladin's death.[189] Attorney General Reno again expressed concerns on policy grounds. She was worried about the danger of retaliation. The CIA also developed the short-lived effort to work with a Pakistani team that we discussed earlier, and an initiative to work with Uzbekistan. The Uzbeks needed basic equipment and training. No action could be expected before March 2000, at the earliest.[190]

In fall 1999, DCI Tenet unveiled the CIA's new Bin Ladin strategy. It was called, simply, "the Plan." The Plan proposed continuing disruption and rendition operations worldwide. It announced a program for hiring and training better officers with counterterrorism skills, recruiting more assets, and trying to penetrate al Qaeda's ranks. The Plan aimed to close gaps in technical intelligence collection (signal and imagery) as well. In addition, the CIA would increase contacts with the Northern Alliance rebels fighting the Taliban.[191]

With a new operational strategy, the CIA evaluated its capture options. None scored high marks. The CIA had no confidence in the Pakistani effort. In the event that Bin Ladin traveled to the Kandahar region in southern Afghanistan, the tribal network there was unlikely to attack a heavily guarded Bin Ladin; the Counterterrorist Center rated the chance of success at less than 10 percent. To the northwest, the Uzbeks might be ready for a cross-border sortie in six months; their chance of success was also rated at less than 10 percent.[192]

In the northeast were Massoud's Northern Alliance forces—perhaps the CIA's best option. In late October, a group of officers from the Counterterrorist Center flew into the Panjshir Valley to meet up with Massoud, a hazardous journey in rickety helicopters that would be repeated several times in the future. Massoud appeared committed to helping the United States collect intelligence on Bin Ladin's activities and whereabouts and agreed to try to capture him if the opportunity arose. The Bin Ladin unit was satisfied that its reporting on Bin Ladin would now have a second source.

But it also knew that Massoud would act against Bin Ladin only if his own interests and those of the United States intersected. By early December, the CIA rated this possibility at less than 15 percent.[193]

Finally, the CIA considered the possibility of putting U.S. personnel on the ground in Afghanistan. The CIA had been discussing this option with Special Operations Command and found enthusiasm on the working level but reluctance at higher levels. CIA saw a 95 percent chance of Special Operations Command forces capturing Bin Ladin if deployed—but less than a 5 percent chance of such a deployment. Sending CIA officers into Afghanistan was to be considered "if the *gain* clearly outweighs the *risk*"—but at this time no such gains presented themselves to warrant the risk.[194]

As mentioned earlier, such a protracted deployment of U.S. Special Operations Forces into Afghanistan, perhaps as part of a team joined to a deployment of the CIA's own officers, would have required a major policy initiative (probably combined with efforts to secure the support of at least one or two neighboring countries) to make a long-term commitment, establish a durable presence on the ground, and be prepared to accept the associated risks and costs. Such a military plan was never developed for interagency consideration before 9/11. As 1999 came to a close, the CIA had a new strategic plan in place for capturing Bin Ladin, but no option was rated as having more than a 15 percent chance of achieving that objective.

CHAPTER FIVE

Al Qaeda Aims at the American Homeland

5.1 TERRORIST ENTREPRENEURS

By early 1999, al Qaeda was already a potent adversary of the United States. Bin Ladin and his chief of operations, Abu Hafs al Masri, also known as Mohammed Atef, occupied undisputed leadership positions atop al Qaeda's organizational structure. Within this structure, al Qaeda's worldwide terrorist operations relied heavily on the ideas and work of enterprising and strong-willed field commanders who enjoyed considerable autonomy. To understand how the organization actually worked and to introduce the origins of the 9/11 plot, we briefly examine three of these subordinate commanders: Khalid Sheikh Mohammed (KSM), Riduan Isamuddin (better known as Hambali), and Abd al Rahim al Nashiri. We will devote the most attention to Khalid Sheikh Mohammed, the chief manager of the "planes operation."

Khalid Sheikh Mohammed

No one exemplifies the model of the terrorist entrepreneur more clearly than Khalid Sheikh Mohammed, the principal architect of the 9/11 attacks. KSM followed a rather tortuous path to his eventual membership in al Qaeda.[1] Highly educated and equally comfortable in a government office or a terrorist safehouse, KSM applied his imagination, technical aptitude, and managerial skills to hatching and planning an extraordinary array of terrorist schemes. These ideas included conventional car bombing, political assassination, aircraft bombing, hijacking, reservoir poisoning, and, ultimately, the use of aircraft as missiles guided by suicide operatives.

Like his nephew Ramzi Yousef (three years KSM's junior), KSM grew up in Kuwait but traces his ethnic lineage to the Baluchistan region straddling Iran and Pakistan. Raised in a religious family, KSM claims to have joined the Muslim Brotherhood at age 16 and to have become enamored of violent jihad at youth camps in the desert. In 1983, following his graduation from secondary school, KSM left Kuwait to enroll at Chowan College, a small Baptist school in Murfreesboro, North Carolina. After a semester at Chowan, KSM transferred to North Carolina Agricultural and Technical State University in Greensboro, which he attended with Yousef's brother, another future al Qaeda member. KSM earned a degree in mechanical engineering in December 1986.[3]

Although he apparently did not attract attention for extreme Islamist beliefs or activities while in the United States, KSM plunged into the anti-Soviet Afghan jihad soon after graduating from college. Visiting Pakistan for the first time in early 1987, he traveled to Peshawar, where his brother Zahid introduced him to the famous Afghan *mujahid* Abdul Rasul Sayyaf, head of the Hizbul-Ittihad El-Islami (Islamic Union Party). Sayyaf became KSM's mentor and provided KSM with military training at Sayyaf's Sada camp. KSM claims he then fought the Soviets and remained at the front for three months before being summoned to perform administrative duties for Abdullah Azzam. KSM next took a job working for an electronics firm that catered to the communications needs of Afghan groups, where he learned about drills used to excavate caves in Afghanistan.[4]

Between 1988 and 1992, KSM helped run a nongovernmental organization (NGO) in Peshawar and Jalalabad; sponsored by Sayyaf, it was designed to aid young Afghan mujahideen. In 1992, KSM spent some time fighting alongside the mujahideen in Bosnia and supporting that effort

Detainee Interrogation Reports

Chapters 5 and 7 rely heavily on information obtained from captured al Qaeda members. A number of these "detainees" have firsthand knowledge of the 9/11 plot.

Assessing the truth of statements by these witnesses—sworn enemies of the United States—is challenging. Our access to them has been limited to the review of intelligence reports based on communications received from the locations where the actual interrogations take place. We submitted questions for use in the interrogations, but had no control over whether, when, or how questions of particular interest would be asked. Nor were we allowed to talk to the interrogators so that we could better judge the credibility of the detainees and clarify ambiguities in the reporting. We were told that our requests might disrupt the sensitive interrogation process.

We have nonetheless decided to include information from captured 9/11 conspirators and al Qaeda members in our report. We have evaluated their statements carefully and have attempted to corroborate them with documents and statements of others. In this report, we indicate where such statements provide the foundation for our narrative. We have been authorized to identify by name only ten detainees whose custody has been confirmed officially by the U.S. government.[2]

with financial donations. After returning briefly to Pakistan, he moved his family to Qatar at the suggestion of the former minister of Islamic affairs of Qatar, Sheikh Abdallah bin Khalid bin Hamad al Thani. KSM took a position in Qatar as project engineer with the Qatari Ministry of Electricity and Water. Although he engaged in extensive international travel during his tenure at the ministry—much of it in furtherance of terrorist activity—KSM would hold his position there until early 1996, when he fled to Pakistan to avoid capture by U.S. authorities.[5]

KSM first came to the attention of U.S. law enforcement as a result of his cameo role in the first World Trade Center bombing. According to KSM, he learned of Ramzi Yousef's intention to launch an attack inside the United States in 1991 or 1992, when Yousef was receiving explosives training in Afghanistan. During the fall of 1992, while Yousef was building the bomb he would use in that attack, KSM and Yousef had numerous telephone conversations during which Yousef discussed his progress and sought additional funding. On November 3, 1992, KSM wired $660 from Qatar to the bank account of Yousef's co-conspirator, Mohammed Salameh. KSM does not appear to have contributed any more substantially to this operation.[6]

Yousef's instant notoriety as the mastermind of the 1993 World Trade Center bombing inspired KSM to become involved in planning attacks against the United States. By his own account, KSM's animus toward the United States stemmed not from his experiences there as a student, but rather from his violent disagreement with U.S. foreign policy favoring Israel. In 1994, KSM accompanied Yousef to the Philippines, and the two of them began planning what is now known as the Manila air or "Bojinka" plot—the intended bombing of 12 U.S. commercial jumbo jets over the Pacific during a two-day span. This marked the first time KSM took part in the actual planning of a terrorist operation. While sharing an apartment in Manila during the summer of 1994, he and Yousef acquired chemicals and other materials necessary to construct bombs and timers. They also cased target flights to Hong Kong and Seoul that would have onward legs to the United States. During this same period, KSM and Yousef also developed plans to assassinate President Clinton during his November 1994 trip to Manila, and to bomb U.S.-bound cargo carriers by smuggling jackets containing nitrocellulose on board.[7]

KSM left the Philippines in September 1994 and met up with Yousef in Karachi following their casing flights. There they enlisted Wali Khan Amin Shah, also known as Usama Asmurai, in the Manila air plot. During the fall of 1994, Yousef returned to Manila and successfully tested the digital watch timer he had invented, bombing a movie theater and a Philippine Airlines flight en route to Tokyo. The plot unraveled after the Philippine authorities discovered Yousef's bomb-making operation in Manila; but by that time, KSM was safely back at his government job in Qatar. Yousef attempted to follow through on the cargo carriers plan, but he was arrested in Islamabad by Pakistani authorities on February 7, 1995, after an accomplice turned him in.[8]

KSM continued to travel among the worldwide jihadist community after Yousef's arrest, visiting the Sudan, Yemen, Malaysia, and Brazil in 1995. No clear evidence connects him to terrorist activities in those locations. While in Sudan, he reportedly failed in his attempt to meet with Bin Ladin. But KSM did see Atef, who gave him a contact in Brazil. In January 1996, well aware that U.S. authorities were chasing him, he left Qatar for good and fled to Afghanistan, where he renewed his relationship with Rasul Sayyaf.[9]

Just as KSM was reestablishing himself in Afghanistan in mid-1996, Bin Ladin and his colleagues were also completing their migration from Sudan. Through Atef, KSM arranged a meeting with Bin Ladin in Tora Bora, a mountainous redoubt from the Afghan war days. At the meeting, KSM presented the al Qaeda leader with a menu of ideas for terrorist operations. According to KSM, this meeting was the first time he had seen Bin Ladin since 1989. Although they had fought together in 1987, Bin Ladin and KSM did not yet enjoy an especially close working relationship. Indeed, KSM has acknowledged that Bin Ladin likely agreed to meet with him because of the renown of his nephew, Yousef.[10]

At the meeting, KSM briefed Bin Ladin and Atef on the first World Trade Center bombing, the Manila air plot, the cargo carriers plan, and other activities pursued by KSM and his colleagues in the Philippines. KSM also presented a pro-

posal for an operation that would involve training pilots who
would crash planes into buildings in the United States. This
proposal eventually would become the 9/11 operation.[11]

KSM knew that the successful staging of such an attack
would require personnel, money, and logistical support that
only an extensive and well-funded organization like al
Qaeda could provide. He thought the operation might appeal
to Bin Ladin, who had a long record of denouncing the
United States.[12]

From KSM's perspective, Bin Ladin was in the process
of consolidating his new position in Afghanistan while hearing out others' ideas, and had not yet settled on an agenda for
future anti-U.S. operations. At the meeting, Bin Ladin listened to KSM's ideas without much comment, but did ask
KSM formally to join al Qaeda and move his family to
Afghanistan.[13]

KSM declined. He preferred to remain independent and
retain the option of working with other mujahideen groups
still operating in Afghanistan, including the group led by his
old mentor, Sayyaf. Sayyaf was close to Ahmed Shah Massoud, the leader of the Northern Alliance. Therefore working with him might be a problem for KSM because Bin
Ladin was building ties to the rival Taliban.

After meeting with Bin Ladin, KSM says he journeyed
onward to India, Indonesia, and Malaysia, where he met
with Jemaah Islamiah's Hambali. Hambali was an Indonesian veteran of the Afghan war looking to expand the jihad
into Southeast Asia. In Iran, KSM rejoined his family and
arranged to move them to Karachi; he claims to have relocated by January 1997.[14]

After settling his family in Karachi, KSM tried to join the
mujahid leader Ibn al Khattab in Chechnya. Unable to travel
through Azerbaijan, KSM returned to Karachi and then to
Afghanistan to renew contacts with Bin Ladin and his colleagues. Though KSM may not have been a member of al
Qaeda at this time, he admits traveling frequently between
Pakistan and Afghanistan in 1997 and the first half of 1998,

visiting Bin Ladin and cultivating relationships with his lieutenants, Atef and Sayf al Adl, by assisting them with computer and media projects.[15]

According to KSM, the 1998 bombings of the U.S. embassies in Nairobi and Dar es Salaam marked a watershed in the evolution of the 9/11 plot. KSM claims these bombings convinced him that Bin Ladin was truly committed to attacking the United States. He continued to make himself useful, collecting news articles and helping other al Qaeda members with their outdated computer equipment. Bin Ladin, apparently at Atef's urging, finally decided to give KSM the green light for the 9/11 operation sometime in late 1998 or early 1999.[16]

KSM then accepted Bin Ladin's standing invitation to move to Kandahar and work directly with al Qaeda. In addition to supervising the planning and preparations for the 9/11 operation, KSM worked with and eventually led al Qaeda's media committee. But KSM states he refused to swear a formal oath of allegiance to Bin Ladin, thereby retaining a last vestige of his cherished autonomy.[17]

At this point, late 1998 to early 1999, planning for the 9/11 operation began in earnest. Yet while the 9/11 project occupied the bulk of KSM's attention, he continued to consider other possibilities for terrorist attacks. For example, he sent al Qaeda operative Issa al Britani to Kuala Lumpur, Malaysia, to learn about the jihad in Southeast Asia from Hambali. Thereafter, KSM claims, at Bin Ladin's direction in early 2001, he sent Britani to the United States to case potential economic and "Jewish" targets in New York City. Furthermore, during the summer of 2001, KSM approached Bin Ladin with the idea of recruiting a Saudi Arabian air force pilot to commandeer a Saudi fighter jet and attack the Israeli city of Eilat. Bin Ladin reportedly liked this proposal, but he instructed KSM to concentrate on the 9/11 operation first. Similarly, KSM's proposals to Atef around this same time for attacks in Thailand, Singapore, Indonesia, and the Maldives were never executed, although Hambali's Jemaah Islamiah operatives did some casing of possible targets.[18]

KSM appears to have been popular among the al Qaeda rank and file. He was reportedly regarded as an effective leader, especially after the 9/11 attacks. Co-workers describe him as an intelligent, efficient, and even-tempered manager who approached his projects with a single-minded dedication that he expected his colleagues to share. Al Qaeda associate Abu Zubaydah has expressed more qualified admiration for KSM's innate creativity, emphasizing instead his ability to incorporate the improvements suggested by others. Nashiri has been similarly measured, observing that although KSM floated many general ideas for attacks, he rarely conceived a specific operation himself.[19] Perhaps these estimates reflect a touch of jealousy; in any case, KSM was plainly a capable coordinator, having had years to hone his skills and build relationships.

Hambali

Al Qaeda's success in fostering terrorism in Southeast Asia stems largely from its close relationship with Jemaah Islamiah (JI). In that relationship, Hambali became the key coordinator. Born and educated in Indonesia, Hambali moved to Malaysia in the early 1980s to find work. There he claims to have become a follower of the Islamist extremist teachings of various clerics, including one named Abdullah Sungkar. Sungkar first inspired Hambali to share the vision of establishing a radical Islamist regime in Southeast Asia, then furthered Hambali's instruction in jihad by sending him to Afghanistan in 1986. After undergoing training at Rasul Sayyaf's Sada camp (where KSM would later train), Hambali fought against the Soviets; he eventually returned to Malaysia after 18 months in Afghanistan. By 1998, Hambali would assume responsibility for the Malaysia/Singapore region within Sungkar's newly formed terrorist organization, the JI.[20]

Also by 1998, Sungkar and JI spiritual leader Abu Bakar Bashir had accepted Bin Ladin's offer to ally JI with al Qaeda in waging war against Christians and Jews.[21] Hambali met with KSM in Karachi to arrange for JI members to receive training in Afghanistan at al Qaeda's camps. In addition to his close working relationship with KSM, Hambali soon began dealing with Atef as well. Al Qaeda began funding JI's increasingly ambitious terrorist plans, which Atef and KSM sought to expand. Under this arrangement, JI would perform the necessary casing activities and locate bomb-making materials and other supplies. Al Qaeda would underwrite operations, provide bomb-making expertise, and deliver suicide operatives.[22]

The al Qaeda–JI partnership yielded a number of proposals that would marry al Qaeda's financial and technical strengths with JI's access to materials and local operatives. Here, Hambali played the critical role of coordinator, as he distributed al Qaeda funds earmarked for the joint operations. In one especially notable example, Atef turned to Hambali when al Qaeda needed a scientist to take over its biological weapons program. Hambali obliged by introducing a U.S.-educated JI member, Yazid Sufaat, to Ayman al Zawahiri in Kandahar. In 2001, Sufaat would spend several months attempting to cultivate anthrax for al Qaeda in a laboratory he helped set up near the Kandahar airport.[23]

Hambali did not originally orient JI's operations toward attacking the United States, but his involvement with al Qaeda appears to have inspired him to pursue American targets. KSM, in his post-capture interrogations, has taken credit for this shift, claiming to have urged the JI operations chief to concentrate on attacks designed to hurt the U.S. economy.[24] Hambali's newfound interest in striking against the United States manifested itself in a spate of terrorist plans. Fortunately, none came to fruition.

In addition to staging actual terrorist attacks in partnership with al Qaeda, Hambali and JI assisted al Qaeda operatives passing through Kuala Lumpur. One important occasion was in December 1999–January 2000. Hambali accommodated KSM's requests to help several veterans whom KSM had just finished training in Karachi. They included Tawfiq bin Attash, also known as Khallad, who later would help bomb the USS *Cole*, and future 9/11 hijackers Nawaf al

Hazmi and Khalid al Mihdhar. Hambali arranged lodging
for them and helped them purchase airline tickets for their
onward travel. Later that year, Hambali and his crew would
provide accommodations and other assistance (including information on flight schools and help in acquiring ammonium nitrate) for Zacarias Moussaoui, an al Qaeda operative
sent to Malaysia by Atef and KSM.[25]

Hambali used Bin Ladin's Afghan facilities as a training
ground for JI recruits. Though he had a close relationship
with Atef and KSM, he maintained JI's institutional independence from al Qaeda. Hambali insists that he did not discuss operations with Bin Ladin or swear allegiance to him,
having already given such a pledge of loyalty to Bashir,
Sungkar's successor as JI leader. Thus, like any powerful bu-
reaucrat defending his domain, Hambali objected when al
Qaeda leadership tried to assign JI members to terrorist projects without notifying him.[26]

Abd al Rahim al Nashiri

KSM and Hambali both decided to join forces with al Qaeda
because their terrorist aspirations required the money and
manpower that only a robust organization like al Qaeda
could supply. On the other hand, Abd al Rahim al Nashiri—
the mastermind of the *Cole* bombing and the eventual head
of al Qaeda operations in the Arabian Peninsula—appears to
have originally been recruited to his career as a terrorist by
Bin Ladin himself.

Having already participated in the Afghan jihad, Nashiri
accompanied a group of some 30 mujahideen in pursuit of
jihad in Tajikistan in 1996. When serious fighting failed to
materialize, the group traveled to Jalalabad and encountered
Bin Ladin, who had recently returned from Sudan. Bin
Ladin addressed them at length, urging the group to join him
in a "jihad against the Americans." Although all were urged
to swear loyalty to Bin Ladin, many, including Nashiri,
found the notion distasteful and refused. After several days
of indoctrination that included a barrage of news clippings
and television documentaries, Nashiri left Afghanistan, first

returning to his native Saudi Arabia and then visiting his home in Yemen. There, he says, the idea for his first terrorist operation took shape as he noticed many U.S. and other foreign ships plying the waters along the southwest coast of Yemen.[27]

Nashiri returned to Afghanistan, probably in 1997, primarily to check on relatives fighting there and also to learn about the Taliban. He again encountered Bin Ladin, still recruiting for "the coming battle with the United States." Nashiri pursued a more conventional military jihad, joining the Taliban forces in their fight against Ahmed Massoud's Northern Alliance and shuttling back and forth between the front and Kandahar, where he would see Bin Ladin and meet with other mujahideen. During this period, Nashiri also led a plot to smuggle four Russian-made antitank missiles into Saudi Arabia from Yemen in early 1998 and helped an embassy bombing operative obtain a Yemeni passport.[28]

At some point, Nashiri joined al Qaeda. His cousin, Jihad Mohammad Ali al Makki, also known as Azzam, was a suicide bomber for the Nairobi attack. Nashiri traveled between Yemen and Afghanistan. In late 1998, Nashiri proposed mounting an attack against a U.S. vessel. Bin Ladin approved. He directed Nashiri to start the planning and send operatives to Yemen, and he later provided money.[29]

Nashiri reported directly to Bin Ladin, the only other person who, according to Nashiri, knew all the details of the operation. When Nashiri had difficulty finding U.S. naval vessels to attack along the western coast of Yemen, Bin Ladin reportedly instructed him to case the Port of Aden, on the southern coast, instead.[30] The eventual result was an attempted attack on the USS *The Sullivans* in January 2000 and the successful attack, in October 2000, on the USS *Cole*.

Nashiri's success brought him instant status within al Qaeda. He later was recognized as the chief of al Qaeda operations in and around the Arabian Peninsula. While Nashiri continued to consult Bin Ladin on the planning of subsequent terrorist projects, he retained discretion in selecting operatives and devising attacks. In the two years between the *Cole* bombing and Nashiri's capture, he would supervise several more proposed operations for al Qaeda. The October 6, 2002, bombing of the French tanker *Limburg* in the Gulf of Aden also was Nashiri's handiwork. Although Bin Ladin urged Nashiri to continue plotting strikes against U.S. interests in the Persian Gulf, Nashiri maintains that he actually delayed one of these projects because of security concerns.[31] Those concerns, it seems, were well placed, as Nashiri's November 2002 capture in the United Arab Emirates finally ended his career as a terrorist.

5.2 THE "PLANES OPERATION"

According to KSM, he started to think about attacking the United States after Yousef returned to Pakistan following the 1993 World Trade Center bombing. Like Yousef, KSM reasoned he could best influence U.S. policy by targeting the country's economy. KSM and Yousef reportedly brainstormed together about what drove the U.S. economy. New York, which KSM considered the economic capital of the United States, therefore became the primary target. For similar reasons, California also became a target for KSM.[32]

KSM claims that the earlier bombing of the World Trade Center taught him that bombs and explosives could be problematic, and that he needed to graduate to a more novel form of attack. He maintains that he and Yousef began thinking about using aircraft as weapons while working on the Manila air/Bojinka plot, and speculated about striking the World Trade Center and CIA headquarters as early as 1995.[33]

Certainly KSM was not alone in contemplating new kinds of terrorist operations. A study reportedly conducted by Atef, while he and Bin Ladin were still in Sudan, concluded that traditional terrorist hijacking operations did not fit the needs of al Qaeda, because such hijackings were used to negotiate the release of prisoners rather than to inflict mass casualties. The study is said to have considered the feasibility of hijacking planes and blowing them up in flight, paralleling the Bojinka concept. Such a study, if it actually existed, yields significant insight into the thinking of al Qaeda's leaders: (1) they rejected hijackings aimed at gaining the release of imprisoned comrades as too complex, because al Qaeda had no friendly countries in which to land a plane and then negotiate; (2) they considered the bombing of commercial flights in midair—as carried out against Pan Am Flight 103 over Lockerbie, Scotland—a promising means to inflict massive casualties; and (3) they did not yet consider using hijacked aircraft as weapons against other targets.[34]

KSM has insisted to his interrogators that he always contemplated hijacking and crashing large commercial aircraft. Indeed, KSM describes a grandiose original plan: a total of ten aircraft to be hijacked, nine of which would crash into targets on both coasts—they included those eventually hit on September 11 plus CIA and FBI headquarters, nuclear power plants, and the tallest buildings in California and the state of Washington. KSM himself was to land the tenth plane at a U.S. airport and, after killing all adult male passengers on board and alerting the media, deliver a speech excoriating U.S. support for Israel, the Philippines, and repressive governments in the Arab world. Beyond KSM's rationalizations about targeting the U.S. economy, this vision gives a better glimpse of his true ambitions. This is theater, a spectacle of destruction with KSM as the self-cast star—the superterrorist.[35]

KSM concedes that this proposal received a lukewarm response from al Qaeda leaders skeptical of its scale and complexity. Although Bin Ladin listened to KSM's proposal, he was not convinced that it was practical. As mentioned earlier, Bin Ladin was receiving numerous ideas for potential operations—KSM's proposal to attack U.S. targets with commercial airplanes was only one of many.[36]

KSM presents himself as an entrepreneur seeking ven-

ture capital and people. He simply wanted al Qaeda to supply the money and operatives needed for the attack while retaining his independence. It is easy to question such a
statement. Money is one thing; supplying a cadre of trained
operatives willing to die is much more. Thus, although KSM
contends he would have been just as likely to consider working with any comparable terrorist organization, he gives no
indication of what other groups he thought could supply
such exceptional commodities.[37]

KSM acknowledges formally joining al Qaeda, in late
1998 or 1999, and states that soon afterward, Bin Ladin also
made the decision to support his proposal to attack the
United States using commercial airplanes as weapons.
Though KSM speculates about how Bin Ladin came to share
his preoccupation with attacking America, Bin Ladin in fact
had long been an opponent of the United States. KSM thinks
that Atef may have persuaded Bin Ladin to approve this specific proposal. Atef's role in the entire operation is unques-
tionably very significant but tends to fade into the
background, in part because Atef himself is not available to
describe it. He was killed in November 2001 by an American air strike in Afghanistan.[38]

Bin Ladin summoned KSM to Kandahar in March or
April 1999 to tell him that al Qaeda would support his proposal. The plot was now referred to within al Qaeda as the
"planes operation."[39]

The Plan Evolves

Bin Ladin reportedly discussed the planes operation with
KSM and Atef in a series of meetings in the spring of 1999
at the al Matar complex near Kandahar. KSM's original concept of using one of the hijacked planes to make a media
statement was scrapped, but Bin Ladin considered the basic
idea feasible. Bin Ladin, Atef, and KSM developed an initial
list of targets. These included the White House, the U.S.
Capitol, the Pentagon, and the World Trade Center. According to KSM, Bin Ladin wanted to destroy the White House

and the Pentagon, KSM wanted to strike the World Trade Center, and all of them wanted to hit the Capitol. No one else was involved in the initial selection of targets.[40]

Bin Ladin also soon selected four individuals to serve as suicide operatives: Khalid al Mihdhar, Nawaf al Hazmi, Khallad, and Abu Bara al Yemeni. During the al Matar meetings, Bin Ladin told KSM that Mihdhar and Hazmi were so eager to participate in an operation against the United States that they had already obtained U.S. visas. KSM states that they had done so on their own after the suicide of their friend Azzam (Nashiri's cousin) in carrying out the Nairobi bombing. KSM had not met them. His only guidance from Bin Ladin was that the two should eventually go to the United States for pilot training.[41]

Hazmi and Mihdhar were Saudi nationals, born in Mecca. Like the others in this initial group of selectees, they were already experienced mujahideen. They had traveled together to fight in Bosnia in a group that journeyed to the Balkans in 1995. By the time Hazmi and Mihdhar were assigned to the planes operation in early 1999, they had visited Afghanistan on several occasions.[42]

Khallad was another veteran mujahid, like much of his family. His father had been expelled from Yemen because of his extremist views. Khallad had grown up in Saudi Arabia, where his father knew Bin Ladin, Abdullah Azzam, and Omar Abdel Rahman (the "Blind Sheikh"). Khallad departed for Afghanistan in 1994 at the age of 15. Three years later, he lost his lower right leg in a battle with the Northern Alliance, a battle in which one of his brothers died. After this experience, he pledged allegiance to Bin Ladin—whom he had first met as a child in Jeddah—and volunteered to become a suicide operative.[43]

When Khallad applied for a U.S. visa, however, his application was denied. Earlier in 1999, Bin Ladin had sent Khallad to Yemen to help Nashiri obtain explosives for the planned ship-bombing and to obtain a visa to visit the United States, so that he could participate in an operation there. Khallad applied under another name, using the cover story that he would be visiting a medical clinic to obtain a new prosthesis for his leg. Another al Qaeda operative gave Khallad the name of a person living in the United States whom Khallad could use as a point of contact on a visa application. Khallad contacted this individual to help him get an appointment at a U.S. clinic. While Khallad was waiting for the letter from the clinic confirming the appointment, however, he was arrested by Yemeni authorities. The arrest resulted from mistaken identity: Khallad was driving the car of another conspirator in the ship-bombing plot who was wanted by the Yemeni authorities.[44]

Khallad was released sometime during the summer of 1999, after his father and Bin Ladin intervened on his behalf. Khallad learned later that the al Qaeda leader, apparently concerned that Khallad might reveal Nashiri's operation while under interrogation, had contacted a Yemeni official to demand Khallad's release, suggesting that Bin Ladin would not confront the Yemenis if they did not confront him. This account has been corroborated by others. Giving up on acquiring a U.S. visa and concerned that the United States might learn of his ties to al Qaeda, Khallad returned to Afghanistan.[45]

Travel issues thus played a part in al Qaeda's operational planning from the very start. During the spring and summer of 1999, KSM realized that Khallad and Abu Bara, both of whom were Yemenis, would not be able to obtain U.S. visas as easily as Saudi operatives like Mihdhar and Hazmi. Although Khallad had been unable to acquire a U.S. visa, KSM still wanted him and Abu Bara, as well as another Yemeni operative from Bin Ladin's security detail, to participate in the planes operation. Yet because individuals with Saudi passports could travel much more easily than Yemeni, particularly to the United States, there were fewer martyrdom opportunities for Yemenis. To overcome this problem, KSM decided to split the planes operation into two components.[46]

The first part of the planes operation—crashing hijacked aircraft into U.S. targets—would remain as planned, with

Mihdhar and Hazmi playing key roles. The second part, however, would now embrace the idea of using suicide operatives to blow up planes, a refinement of KSM's old Manila air plot. The operatives would hijack U.S.-flagged commercial planes flying Pacific routes across East Asia and destroy them in midair, possibly with shoe bombs, instead of flying them into targets. (An alternate scenario apparently involved flying planes into U.S. targets in Japan, Singapore, or Korea.) This part of the operation has been confirmed by Khallad, who said that they contemplated hijacking several planes, probably originating in Thailand, South Korea, Hong Kong, or Malaysia, and using Yemenis who would not need pilot training because they would simply down the planes. All the planes hijacked in the United States and East Asia were to be crashed or exploded at about the same time to maximize the attack's psychological impact.[47]

Training and Deployment to Kuala Lumpur

In the fall of 1999, the four operatives selected by Bin Ladin for the planes operation were chosen to attend an elite training course at al Qaeda's Mes Aynak camp in Afghanistan. Bin Ladin personally selected the veteran fighters who received this training, and several of them were destined for important operations. One example is Ibrahim al Thawar, or Nibras, who would participate in the October 12, 2000, suicide attack on the USS *Cole*. According to KSM, this training was not given specifically in preparation for the planes operation or any other particular al Qaeda venture. Although KSM claims not to have been involved with the training or to have met with the future 9/11 hijackers at Mes Aynak, he says he did visit the camp while traveling from Kandahar to Kabul with Bin Ladin and others.[48]

The Mes Aynak training camp was located in an abandoned Russian copper mine near Kabul. The camp opened in 1999, after the United States had destroyed the training camp near Khowst with cruise missiles in August 1998, and before the Taliban granted al Qaeda permission to open the al Faruq camp in Kandahar. Thus, for a brief period in 1999,

Mes Aynak was the only al Qaeda camp operating in Afghanistan. It offered a full range of instruction, including an advanced commando course taught by senior al Qaeda member Sayf al Adl. Bin Ladin paid particular attention to the 1999 training session. When Salah al Din, the trainer for the session, complained about the number of trainees and said that no more than 20 could be handled at once, Bin Ladin insisted that everyone he had selected receive the training.[49]

The special training session at Mes Aynak was rigorous and spared no expense. The course focused on physical fitness, firearms, close quarters combat, shooting from a motorcycle, and night operations. Although the subjects taught differed little from those offered at other camps, the course placed extraordinary physical and mental demands on its participants, who received the best food and other amenities to enhance their strength and morale.[50]

Upon completing the advanced training at Mes Aynak, Hazmi, Khallad, and Abu Bara went to Karachi, Pakistan. There KSM instructed them on Western culture and travel. Much of his activity in mid-1999 had revolved around the collection of training and informational materials for the participants in the planes operation. For instance, he collected Western aviation magazines; telephone directories for American cities such as San Diego and Long Beach, California; brochures for schools; and airline timetables, and he conducted Internet searches on U.S. flight schools. He also purchased flight simulator software and a few movies depicting hijackings. To house his students, KSM rented a safehouse in Karachi with money provided by Bin Ladin.[51]

In early December 1999, Khallad and Abu Bara arrived in Karachi. Hazmi joined them there a few days later. On his way to Karachi, Hazmi spent a night in Quetta at a safehouse where, according to KSM, an Egyptian named Mohamed Atta simultaneously stayed on his way to Afghanistan for jihad training.[52]

Mihdhar did not attend the training in Karachi with the others. KSM says that he never met with Mihdhar in 1999 but assumed that Bin Ladin and Atef had briefed Mihdhar on the planes operation and had excused him from the Karachi training.[53]

The course in Karachi apparently lasted about one or two weeks. According to KSM, he taught the three operatives basic English words and phrases. He showed them how to read phone books, interpret airline timetables, use the Internet, use code words in communications, make travel reservations, and rent an apartment. Khallad adds that the training involved using flight simulator computer games, viewing movies that featured hijackings, and reading flight schedules to determine which flights would be in the air at the same time in different parts of the world. They used the game software to increase their familiarity with aircraft models and functions, and to highlight gaps in cabin security. While in Karachi, they also discussed how to case flights in Southeast Asia. KSM told them to watch the cabin doors at takeoff and landing, to observe whether the captain went to the lavatory during the flight, and to note whether the flight attendants brought food into the cockpit. KSM, Khallad, and Hazmi also visited travel agencies to learn the visa requirements for Asian countries.[54]

The four trainees traveled to Kuala Lumpur: Khallad, Abu Bara, and Hazmi came from Karachi; Mihdhar traveled from Yemen. As discussed in chapter 6, U.S. intelligence would analyze communications associated with Mihdhar, whom they identified during this travel, and Hazmi, whom they could have identified but did not.[55]

According to KSM, the four operatives were aware that they had volunteered for a suicide operation, either in the United States or in Asia. With different roles, they had different tasks. Hazmi and Mihdhar were sent to Kuala Lumpur before proceeding to their final destination—the United States. According to KSM, they were to use Yemeni documents to fly to Malaysia, then proceed to the United States using their Saudi passports to conceal their prior travels to and from Pakistan. KSM had doctored Hazmi's Saudi passport so it would appear as if Hazmi had traveled to Kuala Lumpur from Saudi Arabia via Dubai. Khallad and Abu

Bara went to Kuala Lumpur to study airport security and conduct casing flights. According to Khallad, he and Abu Bara departed for Malaysia in mid-December 1999. Hazmi joined them about ten days later after briefly returning to Afghanistan to attend to some passport issues.[56]

Khallad had originally scheduled his trip in order to receive a new prosthesis at a Kuala Lumpur clinic called Endolite, and Bin Ladin suggested that he use the opportunity to case flights as well. According to Khallad, Malaysia was an ideal destination because its government did not require citizens of Saudi Arabia or other Gulf states to have a visa. Malaysian security was reputed to be lax when it came to Islamist jihadists. Also, other mujahideen wounded in combat had reportedly received treatment at the Endolite clinic and successfully concealed the origins of their injuries. Khallad said he got the money for the prosthesis from his father, Bin Ladin, and another al Qaeda colleague.[57]

According to Khallad, when he and Abu Bara arrived in Kuala Lumpur they contacted Hambali to let him know where they were staying, since he was to be kept informed of al Qaeda activities in Southeast Asia. Hambali picked up Khallad and Abu Bara and brought them to his home, enlisting the help of a colleague who spoke better Arabic. Hambali then took them to the clinic.[58]

On December 31, Khallad flew from Kuala Lumpur to Bangkok; the next day, he flew to Hong Kong aboard a U.S. airliner. He flew in first class, which he realized was a mistake because this seating assignment on that flight did not afford him a view of the cockpit. He claims to have done what he could to case the flight, testing security by carrying a box cutter in his toiletries kit onto the flight to Hong Kong. Khallad returned to Bangkok the following day. At the airport, the security officials searched his carry-on bag and even opened the toiletries kit, but just glanced at the contents and let him pass. On this flight, Khallad waited until most of the first-class passengers were dozing, then got up and removed the kit from his carry-on. None of the flight attendants took notice.[59]

After completing his casing mission, Khallad returned to Kuala Lumpur. Hazmi arrived in Kuala Lumpur soon thereafter and may even have stayed briefly with Khallad and Abu Bara at Endolite. Mihdhar arrived on January 5, probably one day after Hazmi. All four operatives stayed at the apartment of Yazid Sufaat, the Malaysian JI member who made his home available at Hambali's request. According to Khallad, he and Hazmi spoke about the possibility of hijacking planes and crashing them or holding passengers as hostages, but only speculatively. Khallad admits being aware at the time that Hazmi and Mihdhar were involved in an operation involving planes in the United States but denies knowing details of the plan.[60]

While in Kuala Lumpur, Khallad wanted to go to Singapore to meet Nibras and Fahd al Quso, two of the operatives in Nashiri's ship-bombing operation. An attempt to execute that plan by attacking the USS *The Sullivans* had failed just a few days earlier. Nibras and Quso were bringing Khallad money from Yemen, but were stopped in Bangkok because they lacked visas to continue on to Singapore. Also unable to enter Singapore, Khallad moved the meeting to Bangkok. Hazmi and Mihdhar decided to go there as well, reportedly because they thought it would enhance their cover as tourists to have passport stamps from a popular tourist destination such as Thailand. With Hambali's help, the three obtained tickets for a flight to Bangkok and left Kuala Lumpur together. Abu Bara did not have a visa permitting him to return to Pakistan, so he traveled to Yemen instead.[61]

In Bangkok, Khallad took Hazmi and Mihdhar to one hotel, then went to another hotel for his meeting on the maritime attack plan. Hazmi and Mihdhar soon moved to that same hotel, but Khallad insists that the two sets of operatives never met with each other or anyone else. After conferring with the ship-bombing operatives, Khallad returned to Karachi and then to Kandahar, where he reported on his casing mission to Bin Ladin.[62]

Bin Ladin canceled the East Asia part of the planes operation in the spring of 2000. He evidently decided it would be too difficult to coordinate this attack with the operation in the United States. As for Hazmi and Mihdhar, they had left Bangkok a few days before Khallad and arrived in Los Angeles on January 15, 2000.[63]

Meanwhile, the next group of al Qaeda operatives destined for the planes operation had just surfaced in Afghanistan. As Hazmi and Mihdhar were deploying from Asia to the United States, al Qaeda's leadership was recruiting and training four Western-educated men who had recently arrived in Kandahar. Though they hailed from four different countries—Egypt, the United Arab Emirates, Lebanon, and Yemen—they had formed a close-knit group as students in Hamburg, Germany. The new recruits had come to Afghanistan aspiring to wage jihad in Chechnya. But al Qaeda quickly recognized their potential and enlisted them in its anti-U.S. jihad.

5.3 THE HAMBURG CONTINGENT

Although Bin Ladin, Atef, and KSM initially contemplated using established al Qaeda members to execute the planes operation, the late 1999 arrival in Kandahar of four aspiring jihadists from Germany suddenly presented a more attractive alternative. The Hamburg group shared the anti-U.S. fervor of the other candidates for the operation, but added the enormous advantages of fluency in English and familiarity with life in the West, based on years that each member of the group had spent living in Germany. Not surprisingly, Mohamed Atta, Ramzi Binalshibh, Marwan al Shehhi, and Ziad Jarrah would all become key players in the 9/11 conspiracy.

Mohamed Atta

Mohamed Atta was born on September 1, 1968, in Kafr el Sheikh, Egypt, to a middle-class family headed by his father, an attorney. After graduating from Cairo University with a degree in architectural engineering in 1990, Atta worked as

an urban planner in Cairo for a couple of years. In the fall of
1991, he asked a German family he had met in Cairo to help
him continue his education in Germany. They suggested he
come to Hamburg and invited him to live with them there, at
least initially. After completing a course in German, Atta
traveled to Germany for the first time in July 1992. He
resided briefly in Stuttgart and then, in the fall of 1992,
moved to Hamburg to live with his host family. After en-
rolling at the University of Hamburg, he promptly transferred into the city engineering and planning course at the
Technical University of Hamburg-Harburg, where he would
remain registered as a student until the fall of 1999. He appears to have applied himself fairly seriously to his studies
(at least in comparison to his jihadist friends) and actually
received his degree shortly before traveling to Afghanistan.
In school, Atta came across as very intelligent and reasonably pleasant, with an excellent command of the German
language.[64]

When Atta arrived in Germany, he appeared religious, but
not fanatically so. This would change, especially as his tendency to assert leadership became increasingly pronounced.
According to Binalshibh, as early as 1995 Atta sought to organize a Muslim student association in Hamburg. In the fall
of 1997, he joined a working group at the Quds mosque in
Hamburg, a group designed to bridge the gap between Muslims and Christians. Atta proved a poor bridge, however, because of his abrasive and increasingly dogmatic personality.
But among those who shared his beliefs, Atta stood out as a
decisionmaker. Atta's friends during this period remember
him as charismatic, intelligent, and persuasive, albeit intol-
erant of dissent.[65]

In his interactions with other students, Atta voiced viru-
lently anti-Semitic and anti-American opinions, ranging
from condemnations of what he described as a global Jewish
movement centered in New York City that supposedly controlled the financial world and the media, to polemics
against governments of the Arab world. To him, Saddam

Hussein was an American stooge set up to give Washington an excuse to intervene in the Middle East. Within his circle, Atta advocated violent jihad. He reportedly asked one individual close to the group if he was "ready to fight for [his] belief" and dismissed him as too weak for jihad when the person declined. On a visit home to Egypt in 1998, Atta met one of his college friends. According to this friend, Atta had changed a great deal, had grown a beard, and had "obviously adopted fundamentalism" by that time.[66]

Ramzi Binalshibh

Ramzi Binalshibh was born on May 1, 1972, in Ghayl Bawazir, Yemen. There does not seem to be anything remarkable about his family or early background. A friend who knew Binalshibh in Yemen remembers him as "religious, but not too religious." From 1987 to 1995, Binalshibh worked as a clerk for the International Bank of Yemen. He first attempted to leave Yemen in 1995, when he applied for a U.S. visa. After his application was rejected, he went to Germany and applied for asylum under the name Ramzi Omar, claiming to be a Sudanese citizen seeking asylum. While his asylum petition was pending, Binalshibh lived in Hamburg and associated with individuals from several mosques there. In 1997, after his asylum application was denied, Binalshibh went home to Yemen but returned to Germany shortly thereafter under his true name, this time registering as a student in Hamburg. Binalshibh continually had academic problems, failing tests and cutting classes; he was expelled from one school in September 1998.[67]

According to Binalshibh, he and Atta first met at a mosque in Hamburg in 1995. The two men became close friends and became identified with their shared extremist outlook. Like Atta, by the late 1990s Binalshibh was decrying what he perceived to be a "Jewish world conspiracy." He proclaimed that the highest duty of every Muslim was to pursue jihad, and that the highest honor was to die during the jihad. Despite his rhetoric, however, Binalshibh presented a more amiable figure than the austere Atta, and was known within the community as being sociable, extroverted, polite, and adventuresome.[68]

In 1998, Binalshibh and Atta began sharing an apartment in the Harburg section of Hamburg, together with a young student from the United Arab Emirates named Marwan al Shehhi.[69]

Marwan al Shehhi

Marwan al Shehhi was born on May 9, 1978, in Ras al Khaimah, the United Arab Emirates. His father, who died in 1997, was a prayer leader at the local mosque. After graduating from high school in 1995, Shehhi joined the Emirati military and received half a year of basic training before gaining admission to a military scholarship program that would fund his continued study in Germany.[70]

Shehhi first entered Germany in April 1996. After sharing an apartment in Bonn for two months with three other scholarship students, Shehhi moved in with a German family, with whom he resided for several months before moving into his own apartment. During this period, he came across as very religious, praying five times a day. Friends also remember him as convivial and "a regular guy," wearing Western clothes and occasionally renting cars for trips to Berlin, France, and the Netherlands.[71]

As a student, Shehhi was less than a success. Upon completing a course in German, he enrolled at the University of Bonn in a program for technical, mathematical, and scientific studies. In June 1997, he requested a leave from his studies, citing the need to attend to unspecified "problems" in his home country. Although the university denied his request, Shehhi left anyway, and consequently was compelled to repeat the first semester of his studies. In addition to having academic difficulties at this time, Shehhi appeared to become more extreme in the practice of his faith; for example, he specifically avoided restaurants that cooked with or served alcohol. In late 1997, he applied for permission to complete his course work in Hamburg, a request apparently motivated by his desire to join Atta and Binalshibh. Just how and when the three of them first met remains unclear, although they seemed to know each other already when Shehhi relocated to Hamburg in early 1998. Atta and Binalshibh moved into his apartment in April.[72]

The transfer to Hamburg did not help Shehhi's academic progress; he was directed by the scholarship program administrators at the Emirati embassy to repeat his second semester starting in August 1998, but back in Bonn. Shehhi initially flouted this directive, however, and did not reenroll at the University of Bonn until the following January, barely passing his course there. By the end of July 1999, he had returned to Hamburg, applying to study shipbuilding at the Technical University and, more significantly, residing once again with Atta and Binalshibh, in an apartment at 54 Marienstrasse.[73]

After Shehhi moved in with Atta and Binalshibh, his evolution toward Islamic fundamentalism became more pronounced. A fellow Emirati student who came to Hamburg to visit Shehhi noticed he no longer lived as comfortably as before. Shehhi now occupied an old apartment with a roommate, had no television, and wore inexpensive clothes. When asked why he was living so frugally, Shehhi responded that he was living the way the Prophet had lived.[74] Similarly, when someone asked why he and Atta never laughed, Shehhi retorted, "How can you laugh when people are dying in Palestine?"[75]

Ziad Jarrah

Born on May 11, 1975, in Mazraa, Lebanon, Ziad Jarrah came from an affluent family and attended private, Christian schools. Like Atta, Binalshibh, and Shehhi, Jarrah aspired to pursue higher education in Germany. In April 1996, he and a cousin enrolled at a junior college in Greifswald, in northeastern Germany. There Jarrah met and became intimate with Aysel Senguen, the daughter of Turkish immigrants, who was preparing to study dentistry.[76]

Even with the benefit of hindsight, Jarrah hardly seems a

likely candidate for becoming an Islamic extremist. Far from displaying radical beliefs when he first moved to Germany, he arrived with a reputation for knowing where to find the best discos and beaches in Beirut, and in Greifswald was known to enjoy student parties and drinking beer. Although he continued to share an apartment in Greifswald with his cousin, Jarrah was mostly at Senguen's apartment. Witnesses interviewed by German authorities after 9/11, however, recall that Jarrah started showing signs of radicalization as early as the end of 1996. After returning from a trip home to Lebanon, Jarrah started living more strictly according to the Koran. He read brochures in Arabic about jihad, held forth to friends on the subject of holy war, and professed disaffection with his previous life and a desire not to leave the world "in a natural way."[77]

In September 1997, Jarrah abruptly switched his intended course of study from dentistry to aircraft engineering—at the Technical University of Hamburg-Harburg. His motivation for this decision remains unclear. The rationale he expressed to Senguen—that he had been interested in aviation since playing with toy airplanes as a child—rings somewhat hollow. In any event, Jarrah appears already to have had Hamburg contacts by this time, some of whom may have played a role in steering him toward Islamic extremism.[78]

Following his move to Hamburg that fall, he began visiting Senguen in Greifswald on weekends, until she moved to the German city of Bochum one year later to enroll in dental school. Around the same time, he began speaking increasingly about religion, and his visits to Senguen became less and less frequent. He began criticizing her for not being religious enough and for dressing too provocatively. He grew a full beard and started praying regularly. He refused to introduce her to his Hamburg friends because, he told her, they were religious Muslims and her refusal to become more observant embarrassed him. At some point in 1999, Jarrah told Senguen that he was planning to wage a jihad because there was no greater honor than to die for Allah. Although Jarrah's transformation generated numerous quarrels, their breakups invariably were followed by reconciliation.[79]

Forming a Cell

In Hamburg, Jarrah had a succession of living accommodations, but he apparently never resided with his future co-conspirators. It is not clear how and when he became part of Atta's circle. He became particularly friendly with Binal-shibh after meeting him at the Quds mosque in Hamburg, which Jarrah began attending regularly in late 1997. The worshippers at this mosque featured an outspoken, flamboyant Islamist named Mohammed Haydar Zammar. A well-known figure in the Muslim community (and to German and U.S. intelligence agencies by the late 1990s), Zammar had fought in Afghanistan and relished any opportunity to extol the virtues of violent jihad. Indeed, a witness has reported hearing Zammar press Binalshibh to fulfill his duty to wage jihad. Moreover, after 9/11, Zammar reportedly took credit for influencing not just Binalshibh but the rest of the Hamburg group. In 1998, Zammar encouraged them to participate in jihad and even convinced them to go to Afghanistan.[80]

Owing to Zammar's persuasion or some other source of inspiration, Atta, Binalshibh, Shehhi, and Jarrah eventually prepared themselves to translate their extremist beliefs into action. By late 1999, they were ready to abandon their student lives in Germany in favor of violent jihad. This final stage in their evolution toward embracing Islamist extremism did not entirely escape the notice of the people around them. The foursome became core members of a group of radical Muslims, often hosting sessions at their Marien-strasse apartment that involved extremely anti-American discussions. Meeting three to four times a week, the group became something of a "sect" whose members, according to one participant in the meetings, tended to deal only with each other.[81] Atta's rent checks for the apartment provide evidence of the importance that the apartment assumed as a center for the group, as he would write on them the notation "Dar el Ansar," or "house of the followers."[82]

In addition to Atta, Binalshibh, Shehhi, and Jarrah, the group included other extremists, some of whom also would attend al Qaeda training camps and, in some instances, would help the 9/11 hijackers as they executed the plot:

- Said Bahaji, son of a Moroccan immigrant, was the only German citizen in the group. Educated in Morocco, Bahaji returned to Germany to study electrical engineering at the Technical University of Hamburg-Harburg. He spent five months in the German army before obtaining a medical discharge, and lived with Atta and Binalshibh at 54 Marienstrasse for eight months between November 1998 and July 1999. Described as an insecure follower with no personality and with limited knowledge of Islam, Bahaji nonetheless professed his readiness to engage in violence. Atta and Binalshibh used Bahaji's computer for Internet research, as evidenced by documents and diskettes seized by German authorities after 9/11.[83]
- Zakariya Essabar, a Moroccan citizen, moved to Germany in February 1997 and to Hamburg in 1998, where he studied medical technology. Soon after moving to Hamburg, Essabar met Binalshibh and the others through a Turkish mosque. Essabar turned extremist fairly suddenly, probably in 1999, and reportedly pressured one acquaintance with physical force to become more religious, grow a beard, and compel his wife to convert to Islam. Essabar's parents were said to have made repeated but unsuccessful efforts to sway him from this lifestyle. Shortly before the 9/11 attacks, he would travel to Afghanistan to communicate the date for the attacks to the al Qaeda leadership.[84]
- Mounir el Motassadeq, another Moroccan, came to Germany in 1993, moving to Hamburg two years later to study electrical engineering at the Technical University. A witness has recalled Motassadeq saying that he would kill his entire family if his religious beliefs demanded it. One of Motassadeq's roommates recalls him

referring to Hitler as a "good man" and organizing film sessions that included speeches by Bin Ladin. Motassadeq would help conceal the Hamburg group's trip to Afghanistan in late 1999.[85]

• Abdelghani Mzoudi, also a Moroccan, arrived in Germany in the summer of 1993, after completing university courses in physics and chemistry. Mzoudi studied in Dortmund, Bochum, and Muenster before moving to Hamburg in 1995. Mzoudi described himself as a weak Muslim when he was home in Morocco, but much more devout when he was back in Hamburg. In April 1996, Mzoudi and Motassadeq witnessed the execution of Atta's will.[86]

During the course of 1999, Atta and his group became ever more extreme and secretive, speaking only in Arabic to conceal the content of their conversations.[87] When the four core members of the Hamburg cell left Germany to journey to Afghanistan late that year, it seems unlikely that they already knew about the planes operation; no evidence connects them to al Qaeda before that time. Witnesses have attested, however, that their pronouncements reflected ample predisposition toward taking some action against the United States.[88] In short, they fit the bill for Bin Ladin, Atef, and KSM.

Going to Afghanistan

The available evidence indicates that in 1999, Atta, Binalshibh, Shehhi, and Jarrah decided to fight in Chechnya against the Russians. According to Binalshibh, a chance meeting on a train in Germany caused the group to travel to Afghanistan instead. An individual named Khalid al Masri approached Binalshibh and Shehhi (because they were Arabs with beards, Binalshibh thinks) and struck up a conversation about jihad in Chechnya. When they later called Masri and expressed interest in going to Chechnya, he told them to contact Abu Musab in Duisburg, Germany. Abu Musab turned out to be Mohamedou Ould Slahi, a signifi-

cant al Qaeda operative who, even then, was well known to
U.S. and German intelligence, though neither government
apparently knew he was operating in Germany in late 1999.
When telephoned by Binalshibh and Shehhi, Slahi report-
edly invited these promising recruits to come see him in
Duisburg.[89]

Binalshibh, Shehhi, and Jarrah made the trip. When they
arrived, Slahi explained that it was difficult to get to Chechnya at that time because many travelers were being detained
in Georgia. He recommended they go to Afghanistan instead, where they could train for jihad before traveling onward to Chechnya. Slahi instructed them to obtain Pakistani
visas and then return to him for further directions on how to
reach Afghanistan. Although Atta did not attend the meeting,
he joined in the plan with the other three. After obtaining the
necessary visas, they received Slahi's final instructions on
how to travel to Karachi and then Quetta, where they were to
contact someone named Umar al Masri at the Taliban office.[90]

Following Slahi's advice, Atta and Jarrah left Hamburg
during the last week of November 1999, bound for Karachi.
Shehhi left for Afghanistan around the same time; Binalshibh, about two weeks later. Binalshibh remembers that
when he arrived at the Taliban office in Quetta, there was no
one named Umar al Masri. The name, apparently, was simply a code; a group of Afghans from the office promptly es-
corted him to Kandahar. There Binalshibh rejoined Atta and
Jarrah, who said they already had pledged loyalty to Bin
Ladin and urged him to do the same. They also informed
him that Shehhi had pledged as well and had already left for
the United Arab Emirates to prepare for the mission. Binalshibh soon met privately with Bin Ladin, accepted the al
Qaeda leader's invitation to work under him, and added his
own pledge to those of his Hamburg colleagues. By this
time, Binalshibh claims, he assumed he was volunteering for
a martyrdom operation.[91]

Atta, Jarrah, and Binalshibh then met with Atef, who told
them they were about to undertake a highly secret mission.

As Binalshibh tells it, Atef instructed the three to return to Germany and enroll in flight training. Atta—whom Bin Ladin chose to lead the group—met with Bin Ladin several times to receive additional instructions, including a preliminary list of approved targets: the World Trade Center, the Pentagon, and the U.S. Capitol.[92] The new recruits also learned that an individual named Rabia al Makki (Nawaf al Hazmi) would be part of the operation.[93]

In retrospect, the speed with which Atta, Shehhi, Jarrah, and Binalshibh became core members of the 9/11 plot— with Atta designated its operational leader—is remarkable. They had not yet met with KSM when all this occurred. It is clear, then, that Bin Ladin and Atef were very much in charge of the operation. That these candidates were selected so quickly—before comprehensive testing in the training camps or in operations—demonstrates that Bin Ladin and Atef probably already understood the deficiencies of their initial team, Hazmi and Mihdhar. The new recruits from Germany possessed an ideal combination of technical skill and knowledge that the original 9/11 operatives, veteran fighters though they were, lacked. Bin Ladin and Atef wasted no time in assigning the Hamburg group to the most ambitious operation yet planned by al Qaeda.

Bin Ladin and Atef also plainly judged that Atta was best suited to be the tactical commander of the operation. Such a quick and critical judgment invites speculation about whether they had already taken Atta's measure at some earlier meeting. To be sure, some gaps do appear in the record of Atta's known whereabouts during the preceding years. One such gap is February–March 1998, a period for which there is no evidence of his presence in Germany and when he conceivably could have been in Afghanistan.[94] Yet to date, neither KSM, Binalshibh, nor any other al Qaeda figure interrogated about the 9/11 plot has claimed that Atta or any other member of the Hamburg group traveled to Afghanistan before the trip in late 1999.

While the four core Hamburg cell members were in Afghanistan, their associates back in Hamburg handled their affairs so that their trip could be kept secret. Motassadeq appears to have done the most. He terminated Shehhi's apartment lease, telling the landlord that Shehhi had returned to the UAE for family reasons, and used a power of attorney to pay bills from Shehhi's bank account.[95] Motassadeq also assisted Jarrah, offering to look after Aysel Senguen in Jarrah's absence. Said Bahaji attended to similar routine matters for Atta and Binalshibh, thereby helping them remain abroad without drawing attention to their absence.[96]

Preparing for the Operation

In early 2000, Atta, Jarrah, and Binalshibh returned to Hamburg. Jarrah arrived first, on January 31, 2000.[97] According to Binalshibh, he and Atta left Kandahar together and proceeded first to Karachi, where they met KSM and were instructed by him on security and on living in the United States. Shehhi apparently had already met with KSM before returning to the UAE. Atta returned to Hamburg in late February, and Binalshibh arrived shortly thereafter. Shehhi's travels took him to the UAE (where he acquired a new passport and a U.S. visa), Saudi Arabia, Bahrain, and one or more other destinations. Shehhi also returned to Germany, possibly sometime in March.[98]

After leaving Afghanistan, the hijackers made clear efforts to avoid appearing radical. Once back in Hamburg, they distanced themselves from conspicuous extremists like Zammar, whom they knew attracted unwanted attention from the authorities.[99] They also changed their appearance and behavior. Atta wore Western clothing, shaved his beard, and no longer attended extremist mosques. Jarrah also no longer wore a full beard and, according to Senguen, acted much more the way he had when she first met him. And when Shehhi, while still in the UAE in January 2000, held a belated wedding celebration (he actually had been married in 1999), a friend of his was surprised to see that he had shaved off his beard and was acting like his old self again.[100]

But Jarrah's apparent efforts to appear less radical did not completely conceal his transformation from his Lebanese family, which grew increasingly concerned about his fanaticism. Soon after Jarrah returned to Germany, his father asked Jarrah's cousin—a close companion from boyhood—to intercede. The cousin's ensuing effort to persuade Jarrah to depart from "the path he was taking" proved unavailing.[101] Yet Jarrah clearly differed from the other hijackers in that he maintained much closer contact with his family and continued his intimate relationship with Senguen. These ties may well have caused him to harbor some doubts about going through with the plot, even as late as the summer of 2001, as discussed in chapter 7.

After leaving Afghanistan, the four began researching flight schools and aviation training. In early January 2000, Ali Abdul Aziz Ali—a nephew of KSM living in the UAE who would become an important facilitator in the plot—used Shehhi's credit card to order a Boeing 747-400 flight simulator program and a Boeing 767 flight deck video, together with attendant literature; Ali had all these items shipped to his employer's address. Jarrah soon decided that the schools in Germany were not acceptable and that he would have to learn to fly in the United States. Binalshibh also researched flight schools in Europe, and in the Netherlands he met a flight school director who recommended flight schools in the United States because they were less expensive and required shorter training periods.[102]

In March 2000, Atta emailed 31 different U.S. flight schools on behalf of a small group of men from various Arab countries studying in Germany who, while lacking prior training, were interested in learning to fly in the United States. Atta requested information about the cost of the training, potential financing, and accommodations.[103]

Before seeking visas to enter the United States, Atta, Shehhi, and Jarrah obtained new passports, each claiming that his old passport had been lost. Presumably they were concerned that the Pakistani visas in their old passports would raise suspicions about possible travel to Afghanistan. Shehhi obtained his visa on January 18, 2000; Atta, on May 18; and Jarrah, on May 25.[104] Binalshibh's visa request was rejected,

however, as were his three subsequent applications.[105] Binalshibh proved unable to obtain a visa, a victim of the general-
ized suspicion that visa applicants from Yemen—especially
young men applying in another country (Binalshibh first applied in Berlin)—might join the ranks of undocumented
aliens seeking work in the United States. Before 9/11, security concerns were not a major factor in visa issuance unless
the applicant already was on a terrorist watchlist, and none
of these four men was. Concerns that Binalshibh intended to
immigrate to the United States doomed his chances to participate firsthand in the 9/11 attacks. Although Binalshibh
had to remain behind, he would provide critical assistance
from abroad to his co-conspirators.

Once again, the need for travel documents dictated al
Qaeda's plans.

Travel

It should by now be apparent how significant travel was in
the planning undertaken by a terrorist organization as far-
flung as al Qaeda. The story of the plot includes references
to dozens of international trips. Operations required travel,
as did basic communications and the movement of money.
Where electronic communications were regarded as insecure, al Qaeda relied even more heavily on couriers.

KSM and Abu Zubaydah each played key roles in facili-
tating travel for al Qaeda operatives. In addition, al Qaeda
had an office of passports and host country issues under its
security committee. The office was located at the Kandahar
airport and was managed by Atef. The committee altered papers, including passports, visas, and identification cards.[106]

Moreover, certain al Qaeda members were charged with
organizing passport collection schemes to keep the pipeline
of fraudulent documents flowing. To this end, al Qaeda required jihadists to turn in their passports before going to the
front lines in Afghanistan. If they were killed, their passports
were recycled for use.[107] The operational mission training
course taught operatives how to forge documents. Certain
passport alteration methods, which included substituting

photos and erasing and adding travel cachets, were also taught. Manuals demonstrating the technique for "cleaning" visas were reportedly circulated among operatives. Mohamed Atta and Zakariya Essabar were reported to have been trained in passport alteration.[108]

The purpose of all this training was twofold: to develop an institutional capacity for document forgery and to enable operatives to make necessary adjustments in the field. It was well-known, for example, that if a Saudi traveled to Afghanistan via Pakistan, then on his return to Saudi Arabia his passport, bearing a Pakistani stamp, would be confiscated. So operatives either erased the Pakistani visas from their passports or traveled through Iran, which did not stamp visas directly into passports.[109]

5.4 A MONEY TRAIL?

Bin Ladin and his aides did not need a very large sum to finance their planned attack on America. The 9/11 plotters eventually spent somewhere between $400,000 and $500,000 to plan and conduct their attack. Consistent with the importance of the project, al Qaeda funded the plotters. KSM provided his operatives with nearly all the money they needed to travel to the United States, train, and live. The plotters' tradecraft was not especially sophisticated, but it was good enough. They moved, stored, and spent their money in ordinary ways, easily defeating the detection mechanisms in place at the time.[110] The origin of the funds remains unknown, although we have a general idea of how al Qaeda financed itself during the period leading up to 9/11.

General Financing

As we explained in chapter 2, Bin Ladin did not fund al Qaeda through a personal fortune and a network of businesses in Sudan. Instead, al Qaeda relied primarily on a fund-raising network developed over time. The CIA now estimates that it cost al Qaeda about $30 million per year to sustain its activities before 9/11 and that this money was raised almost entirely through donations.[111]

For many years, the United States thought Bin Ladin financed al Qaeda's expenses through a vast personal inheritance. Bin Ladin purportedly inherited approximately $300 million when his father died, and was rumored to have had access to these funds to wage jihad while in Sudan and Afghanistan and to secure his leadership position in al Qaeda. In early 2000, the U.S. government discovered a different reality: roughly from 1970 through 1994, Bin Ladin received about $1 million per year—a significant sum, to be sure, but not a $300 million fortune that could be used to fund jihad.[112] Then, as part of a Saudi government crackdown early in the 1990s, the Bin Ladin family was forced to find a buyer for Usama's share of the family company in 1994. The Saudi government subsequently froze the proceeds of the sale. This action had the effect of divesting Bin Ladin of what otherwise might indeed have been a large fortune.[113]

Nor were Bin Ladin's assets in Sudan a source of money for al Qaeda. When Bin Ladin lived in Sudan from 1991 to 1996, he owned a number of businesses and other assets. These could not have provided significant income, as most were small or not economically viable. When Bin Ladin left in 1996, it appears that the Sudanese government expropriated all his assets: he left Sudan with practically nothing. When Bin Ladin arrived in Afghanistan, he relied on the Taliban until he was able to reinvigorate his fund-raising efforts by drawing on ties to wealthy Saudi individuals that he had established during the Afghan war in the 1980s.[114]

Al Qaeda appears to have relied on a core group of financial facilitators who raised money from a variety of donors and other fund-raisers, primarily in the Gulf countries and particularly in Saudi Arabia.[115] Some individual donors surely knew, and others did not, the ultimate destination of their donations. Al Qaeda and its friends took advantage of Islam's strong calls for charitable giving, *zakat*. These financial facilitators also appeared to rely heavily on certain imams at mosques who were willing to divert zakat donations to al Qaeda's cause.[116]

Al Qaeda also collected money from employees of corrupt charities.[117] It took two approaches to using charities for fund-raising. One was to rely on al Qaeda sympathizers in specific foreign branch offices of large, international charities—particularly those with lax external oversight and ineffective internal controls, such as the Saudi-based al Haramain Islamic Foundation.[118] Smaller charities in various parts of the globe were funded by these large Gulf charities and had employees who would siphon the money to al Qaeda.[119]

In addition, entire charities, such as the al Wafa organization, may have wittingly participated in funneling money to al Qaeda. In those cases, al Qaeda operatives controlled the entire organization, including access to bank accounts.[120] Charities were a source of money and also provided significant cover, which enabled operatives to travel undetected under the guise of working for a humanitarian organization.

It does not appear that any government other than the Taliban financially supported al Qaeda before 9/11, although some governments may have contained al Qaeda sympathizers who turned a blind eye to al Qaeda's fund-raising activities.[121] Saudi Arabia has long been considered the primary source of al Qaeda funding, but we have found no evidence that the Saudi government as an institution or senior Saudi officials individually funded the organization. (This conclusion does not exclude the likelihood that charities with significant Saudi government sponsorship diverted funds to al Qaeda.)[122]

Still, al Qaeda found fertile fund-raising ground in Saudi Arabia, where extreme religious views are common and charitable giving was both essential to the culture and subject to very limited oversight.[123] Al Qaeda also sought money from wealthy donors in other Gulf states.

Al Qaeda frequently moved the money it raised by *hawala*, an informal and ancient trust-based system for transferring funds.[124] In some ways, al Qaeda had no choice after its move to Afghanistan in 1996: first, the banking system there was antiquated and undependable; and second, formal banking was risky due to the scrutiny that al Qaeda received after the August 1998 East Africa embassy bombings, including UN resolutions against it and the Taliban.[125] Bin Ladin relied on the established hawala networks operating in Pakistan, in Dubai, and throughout the Middle East to transfer funds efficiently. Hawaladars associated with al Qaeda may have used banks to move and store money, as did various al Qaeda fund-raisers and operatives outside of Afghanistan, but there is little evidence that Bin Ladin or core al Qaeda members used banks while in Afghanistan.[126]

Before 9/11, al Qaeda spent funds as quickly as it received them. Actual terrorist operations represented a relatively small part of al Qaeda's estimated $30 million annual operating budget. Al Qaeda funded salaries for jihadists, training camps, airfields, vehicles, arms, and the development of training manuals. Bin Ladin provided approximately $10–$20 million per year to the Taliban in return for safe haven. Bin Ladin also may have used money to create alliances with other terrorist organizations, although it is unlikely that al Qaeda was funding an overall jihad program. Rather, Bin Ladin selectively provided startup funds to new groups or money for specific terrorist operations.[127]

Al Qaeda has been alleged to have used a variety of illegitimate means, particularly drug trafficking and conflict diamonds, to finance itself. While the drug trade was a source of income for the Taliban, it did not serve the same purpose for al Qaeda, and there is no reliable evidence that Bin Ladin was involved in or made his money through drug trafficking.[128] Similarly, we have seen no persuasive evidence that al Qaeda funded itself by trading in African conflict diamonds.[129] There also have been claims that al Qaeda financed itself through manipulation of the stock market based on its advance knowledge of the 9/11 attacks. Exhaustive investigations by the Securities and Exchange Commission, FBI, and other agencies have uncovered no evidence that anyone with advance knowledge of the attacks profited through securities transactions.[130]

To date, the U.S. government has not been able to determine the origin of the money used for the 9/11 attacks. Ultimately the question is of little practical significance. Al Qaeda had many avenues of funding. If a particular funding source had dried up, al Qaeda could have easily tapped a different source or diverted funds from another project to fund an operation that cost $400,000–$500,000 over nearly two years.

The Funding of the 9/11 Plot

As noted above, the 9/11 plotters spent somewhere between $400,000 and $500,000 to plan and conduct their attack. The available evidence indicates that the 19 operatives were funded by al Qaeda, either through wire transfers or cash provided by KSM, which they carried into the United States or deposited in foreign accounts and accessed from this country. Our investigation has uncovered no credible evidence that any person in the United States gave the hijackers substantial financial assistance. Similarly, we have seen no evidence that any foreign government—or foreign government official—supplied any funding.[131]

We have found no evidence that the Hamburg cell members (Atta, Shehhi, Jarrah, and Binalshibh) received funds from al Qaeda before late 1999. It appears they supported themselves. KSM, Binalshibh, and another plot facilitator, Mustafa al Hawsawi, each received money, in some cases perhaps as much as $10,000, to perform their roles in the plot.[132]

After the Hamburg recruits joined the 9/11 conspiracy, al Qaeda began giving them money. Our knowledge of the funding during this period, before the operatives entered the United States, remains murky. According to KSM, the Hamburg cell members each received $5,000 to pay for their return to Germany from Afghanistan after they had been selected to join the plot, and they received additional funds for travel from Germany to the United States. Financial transactions of the plotters are discussed in more detail in chapter 7.

Requirements for a Successful Attack

As some of the core operatives prepared to leave for the United States, al Qaeda's leaders could have reflected on what they needed to be able to do in order to organize and conduct a complex international terrorist operation to inflict catastrophic harm. We believe such a list of requirements would have included

- leaders able to evaluate, approve, and supervise the planning and direction of the operation;
- communications sufficient to enable planning and direction of the operatives and those who would be helping them;
- a personnel system that could recruit candidates, vet them, indoctrinate them, and give them necessary training;
- an intelligence effort to gather required information and form assessments of enemy strengths and weaknesses;
- the ability to move people; and
- the ability to raise and move the necessary money.

The information we have presented about the development of the planes operation shows how, by the spring and summer of 2000, al Qaeda was able to meet these requirements.

By late May 2000, two operatives assigned to the planes operation were already in the United States. Three of the four Hamburg cell members would soon arrive.

CHAPTER SIX

From Threat to Threat

In chapter 3 and 4 we described how the U.S. government adjusted its existing agencies and capacities to address the emerging threat from Usama Bin Ladin and his associates. After the August 1998 bombings of the American embassies in Kenya and Tanzania, President Bill Clinton and his chief aides explored ways of getting Bin Ladin expelled from Afghanistan or possibly capturing or even killing him. Although disruption efforts around the world had achieved some successes, the core of Bin Ladin's organization remained intact.

President Clinton was deeply concerned about Bin Ladin. He and his national security advisor, Samuel "Sandy" Berger, ensured they had a special daily pipeline of reports feeding them the latest updates on Bin Ladin's reported location.[1] In public, President Clinton spoke repeatedly about the threat of terrorism, referring to terrorist training camps but saying little about Bin Ladin and nothing about al Qaeda. He explained to us that this was deliberate—intended to avoid enhancing Bin Ladin's stature by giving him unnecessary publicity. His speeches focused especially on the danger of nonstate actors and of chemical and biological weapons.[2]

As the millennium approached, the most publicized worries were not about terrorism but about computer breakdowns—the Y2K scare. Some government officials were

concerned that terrorists would take advantage of such
breakdowns.[3]

6.1 THE MILLENNIUM CRISIS

"Bodies Will Pile Up in Sacks"

On November 30, 1999, Jordanian intelligence intercepted a
telephone call between Abu Zubaydah, a longtime ally of
Bin Ladin, and Khadr Abu Hoshar, a Palestinian extremist.
Abu Zubaydah said, "The time for training is over." Suspecting that this was a signal for Abu Hoshar to commence a terrorist operation, Jordanian police arrested Abu Hoshar and
15 others and informed Washington.[4]

One of the 16, Raed Hijazi, had been born in California
to Palestinian parents; after spending his childhood in the
Middle East, he had returned to northern California, taken
refuge in extremist Islamist beliefs, and then made his way
to Abu Zubaydah's Khaldan camp in Afghanistan, where he
learned the fundamentals of guerrilla warfare. He and his
younger brother had been recruited by Abu Hoshar into a
loosely knit plot to attack Jewish and American targets in
Jordan.[5]

After late 1996, when Abu Hoshar was arrested and
jailed, Hijazi moved back to the United States, worked as a
cabdriver in Boston, and sent money back to his fellow plotters. After Abu Hoshar's release, Hijazi shuttled between
Boston and Jordan gathering money and supplies. With Abu
Hoshar, he recruited in Turkey and Syria as well as Jordan;
with Abu Zubaydah's assistance, Abu Hoshar sent these recruits to Afghanistan for training.[6]

In late 1998, Hijazi and Abu Hoshar had settled on a plan.
They would first attack four targets: the SAS Radisson Hotel
in downtown Amman, the border crossings from Jordan into
Israel, and two Christian holy sites, at a time when all these
locations were likely to be thronged with American and
other tourists. Next, they would target a local airport and
other religious and cultural sites. Hijazi and Abu Hoshar

cased the intended targets and sent reports to Abu Zubaydah, who approved their plan. Finally, back in Amman from Boston, Hijazi gradually accumulated bomb-making materials, including sulfuric acid and 5,200 pounds of nitric acid, which were then stored in an enormous subbasement dug by the plotters over a period of two months underneath a rented house.[7]

In early 1999, Hijazi and Abu Hoshar contacted Khalil Deek, an American citizen and an associate of Abu Zubaydah who lived in Peshawar, Pakistan, and who, with Afghanistan-based extremists, had created an electronic version of a terrorist manual, the *Encyclopedia of Jihad*. They obtained a CD-ROM of this encyclopedia from Deek.[8] In June, with help from Deek, Abu Hoshar arranged with Abu Zubaydah for Hijazi and three others to go to Afghanistan for added training in handling explosives. In late November 1999, Hijazi reportedly swore before Abu Zubaydah the *bayat* to Bin Ladin, committing himself to do anything Bin Ladin ordered. He then departed for Jordan and was at a waypoint in Syria when Abu Zubaydah sent Abu Hoshar the message that prompted Jordanian authorities to roll up the whole cell.[9]

After the arrests of Abu Hoshar and 15 others, the Jordanians tracked Deek to Peshawar, persuaded Pakistan to extradite him, and added him to their catch. Searches in Amman found the rented house and, among other things, 71 drums of acids, several forged Saudi passports, detonators, and Deek's *Encyclopedia*. Six of the accomplices were sentenced to death. In custody, Hijazi's younger brother said that the group's motto had been "The season is coming, and bodies will pile up in sacks."[10]

Diplomacy and Disruption

On December 4, as news came in about the discoveries in Jordan, National Security Council (NSC) Counterterrorism Coordinator Richard Clarke wrote Berger, "If George's [Tenet's] story about a planned series of UBL attacks at the Millennium is true, we will need to make some decisions

NOW." He told us he held several conversations with President Clinton during the crisis. He suggested threatening reprisals against the Taliban in Afghanistan in the event of any attacks on U.S. interests, anywhere, by Bin Ladin. He further proposed to Berger that a strike be made during the last week of 1999 against al Qaeda camps in Afghanistan—a proposal not adopted.[11]

Warned by the CIA that the disrupted Jordanian plot was probably part of a larger series of attacks intended for the millennium, some possibly involving chemical weapons, the Principals Committee met on the night of December 8 and decided to task Clarke's Counterterrorism Security Group (CSG) to develop plans to deter and disrupt al Qaeda plots.[12]

Michael Sheehan, the State Department member of the CSG, communicated warnings to the Taliban that they would be held responsible for future al Qaeda attacks. "Mike was not diplomatic," Clarke reported to Berger. With virtually no evidence of a Taliban response, a new approach was made to Pakistan.[13] General Anthony Zinni, the commander of Central Command (CENTCOM), was designated as the President's special envoy and sent to ask General Musharraf to "take whatever action you deem necessary to resolve the Bin Ladin problem at the earliest possible time." But Zinni came back empty-handed. As Ambassador William Milam reported from Islamabad, Musharraf was "unwilling to take the political heat at home."[14]

The CIA worked hard with foreign security services to detain or at least keep an eye on suspected Bin Ladin associates. Tenet spoke to 20 of his foreign counterparts. Disruption and arrest operations were mounted against terrorists in eight countries.[15] In mid-December, President Clinton signed a Memorandum of Notification (MON) giving the CIA broader authority to use foreign proxies to detain Bin Ladin lieutenants, without having to transfer them to U.S. custody. The authority was to capture, not kill, though lethal force might be used if necessary.[16] Tenet would later send a message to all CIA personnel overseas, saying, "The threat could not be more real. . . . Do whatever is necessary to disrupt UBL's plans. . . . The American people are counting on you and me to take every appropriate step to protect them during this period." The State Department issued a world-wide threat advisory to its posts overseas.[17]

Then, on December 14, an Algerian jihadist was caught bringing a load of explosives into the United States.

Ressam's Arrest

Ahmed Ressam, 23, had illegally immigrated to Canada in 1994. Using a falsified passport and a bogus story about per-secution in Algeria, Ressam entered Montreal and claimed political asylum. For the next few years he supported himself with petty crime. Recruited by an alumnus of Abu Zubaydah's Khaldan camp, Ressam trained in Afghanistan in 1998, learning, among other things, how to place cyanide near the air intake of a building to achieve maximum lethal-ity at minimum personal risk. Having joined other Algerians in planning a possible attack on a U.S. airport or consulate, Ressam left Afghanistan in early 1999 carrying precursor chemicals for explosives disguised in toiletry bottles, a note-book containing bomb assembly instructions, and $12,000. Back in Canada, he went about procuring weapons, chemi-cals, and false papers.[18]

In early summer 1999, having learned that not all of his colleagues could get the travel documents to enter Canada, Ressam decided to carry out the plan alone. By the end of the summer he had chosen three Los Angeles–area airports as potential targets, ultimately fixing on Los Angeles Inter-national (LAX) as the largest and easiest to operate in sur-reptitiously. He bought or stole chemicals and equipment for his bomb, obtaining advice from three Algerian friends, all of whom were wanted by authorities in France for their roles in past terrorist attacks there. Ressam also acquired new confederates. He promised to help a New York–based part-ner, Abdelghani Meskini, get training in Afghanistan if Me-skini would help him maneuver in the United States.[19]

In December 1999, Ressam began his final preparations. He called an Afghanistan-based facilitator to inquire into whether Bin Ladin wanted to take credit for the attack, but he did not get a reply. He spent a week in Vancouver preparing the explosive components with a close friend. The chemicals were so caustic that the men kept their windows open, despite the freezing temperatures outside, and sucked on cough drops to soothe their irritated throats.[20] While in Vancouver, Ressam also rented a Chrysler sedan for his travel into the United States, and packed the explosives in the trunk's spare tire well.[21]

On December 14, 1999, Ressam drove his rental car onto the ferry from Victoria, Canada, to Port Angeles, Washington. Ressam planned to drive to Seattle and meet Meskini, with whom he would travel to Los Angeles and case LAX. They planned to detonate the bomb on or around January 1, 2000. At the Immigration and Naturalization Service (INS) preinspection station in Victoria, Ressam presented officials with his genuine but fraudulently obtained Canadian passport, from which he had torn the Afghanistan entry and exit stamps. The INS agent on duty ran the passport through a variety of databases but, since it was not in Ressam's name, he did not pick up the pending Canadian arrest warrants. After a cursory examination of Ressam's car, the INS agents allowed Ressam to board the ferry.[26]

Late in the afternoon of December 14, Ressam arrived in Port Angeles. He waited for all the other cars to depart the ferry, assuming (incorrectly) that the last car off would draw less scrutiny. Customs officers assigned to the port, noticing Ressam's nervousness, referred him to secondary inspection. When asked for additional identification, Ressam handed the Customs agent a Price Costco membership card in the same false name as his passport. As that agent began an initial pat-down, Ressam panicked and tried to run away.[27]

Inspectors examining Ressam's rental car found the explosives concealed in the spare tire well, but at first they assumed the white powder and viscous liquid were drug-related—until an inspector pried apart and identified one of the four timing devices concealed within black boxes.

A Case Study in Terrorist Travel

Following a familiar terrorist pattern, Ressam and his associates used fraudulent passports and immigration fraud to travel. In Ressam's case, this involved flying from France to Montreal using a photo-substituted French passport under a false name. Under questioning, Ressam admitted the passport was fraudulent and claimed political asylum. He was released pending a hearing, which he failed to attend. His political asylum claim was denied. He was arrested again, released again, and given another hearing date. Again, he did not show. He was arrested four times for thievery, usually from tourists, but was neither jailed nor deported. He also supported himself by selling stolen documents to a friend who was a document broker for Islamist terrorists.[22]

Ressam eventually obtained a genuine Canadian passport through a document vendor who stole a blank baptismal certificate from a Catholic church. With this document he was able to obtain a Canadian passport under the name of Benni Antoine Noris. This enabled him to travel to Pakistan, and from there to Afghanistan for his training, and then return to Canada. Impressed, Abu Zubaydah asked Ressam to get more genuine Canadian passports and to send them to him for other terrorists to use.[23]

Another conspirator, Abdelghani Meskini, used a stolen identity to travel to Seattle on December 11, 1999, at the request of Mokhtar Haouari, another conspirator. Haouari provided fraudulent passports and visas to assist Ressam and Meskini's planned getaway from the United States to Algeria, Pakistan, and Afghanistan.[24] One of Meskini's associates, Abdel Hakim Tizegha, also filed a claim for political asylum. He was released pending a hearing, which was adjourned and rescheduled five times. His claim was finally denied two years after his initial filing. His attorney appealed the decision, and Tizegha was allowed to remain in the country pending the appeal. Nine months later, his attorney notified the court that he could not locate his client. A warrant of deportation was issued.[25]

Ressam was placed under arrest. Investigators guessed his target was in Seattle. They did not learn about the Los Angeles airport planning until they reexamined evidence seized in Montreal in 2000; they obtained further details when Ressam began cooperating in May 2001.[28]

Emergency Cooperation

After the disruption of the plot in Amman, it had not escaped notice in Washington that Hijazi had lived in California and driven a cab in Boston and that Deek was a naturalized U.S. citizen who, as Berger reminded President Clinton, had been in touch with extremists in the United States as well as abroad.[29] Before Ressam's arrest, Berger saw no need to raise a public alarm at home—although the FBI put all field offices on alert.[30]

Now, following Ressam's arrest, the FBI asked for an unprecedented number of special wiretaps. Both Berger and Tenet told us that their impression was that more Foreign Intelligence Surveillance Act (FISA) wiretap requests were processed during the millennium alert than ever before.[31]

The next day, writing about Ressam's arrest and links to a cell in Montreal, Berger informed the President that the FBI would advise police in the United States to step up activities but would still try to avoid undue public alarm by stressing that the government had no specific information about planned attacks.[32]

At a December 22 meeting of the Small Group of principals, FBI Director Louis Freeh briefed officials from the NSC staff, CIA, and Justice on wiretaps and investigations inside the United States, including a Brooklyn entity tied to the Ressam arrest, a seemingly unreliable foreign report of possible attacks on seven U.S. cities, two Algerians detained on the Canadian border, and searches in Montreal related to a jihadist cell. The Justice Department released a statement on the alert the same day.[33]

Clarke's staff warned, *"Foreign terrorist sleeper cells are present in the US and attacks in the US are likely."*[34] Clarke asked Berger to try to make sure that the domestic agencies remained alert. "Is there a threat to civilian aircraft?" he wrote. Clarke also asked the principals in late December to discuss a foreign security service report about a Bin Ladin plan to put bombs on transatlantic flights.[35]

The CSG met daily. Berger said that the principals met constantly.[36] Later, when asked what made her decide to ask Ressam to step out of his vehicle, Diana Dean, a Customs inspector who referred Ressam to secondary inspection, testified that it was her "training and experience."[37] It appears that the heightened sense of alert at the national level played no role in Ressam's detention.

There was a mounting sense of public alarm. The earlier Jordanian arrests had been covered in the press, and Ressam's arrest was featured on network evening news broadcasts throughout the Christmas season.[38]

The FBI was more communicative during the millennium crisis than it had ever been. The senior FBI official for counterterrorism, Dale Watson, was a regular member of the CSG, and Clarke had good relations both with him and with some of the FBI agents handling al Qaeda–related investigations, including John O'Neill in New York. As a rule, however, neither Watson nor these agents brought much information to the group. The FBI simply did not produce the kind of intelligence reports that other agencies routinely wrote and disseminated. As law enforcement officers, Bureau agents tended to write up only witness interviews. Written case analysis usually occurred only in memoranda to supervisors requesting authority to initiate or expand an investigation.[39]

But during the millennium alert, with its direct links into the United States from Hijazi, Deek, and Ressam, FBI officials were briefing in person about ongoing investigations, not relying on the dissemination of written reports. Berger told us that it was hard for FBI officials to hold back information in front of a cabinet-rank group. After the alert, according to Berger and members of the NSC staff, the FBI returned to its normal practice of withholding written reports and saying little about investigations or witness interviews, taking the position that any information related to pending investigations might be presented to a grand jury and hence could not be disclosed under then-prevailing federal law.[40]

The terrorist plots that were broken up at the end of 1999 display the variety of operations that might be attributed, however indirectly, to al Qaeda. The Jordanian cell was a loose affiliate; we now know that it sought approval and training from Afghanistan, and at least one key member swore loyalty to Bin Ladin. But the cell's plans and preparations were autonomous. Ressam's ties to al Qaeda were even looser. Though he had been recruited, trained, and prepared in a network affiliated with the organization and its allies, Ressam's own plans were, nonetheless, essentially independent.

Al Qaeda, and Bin Ladin himself, did have at least one operation of their very own in mind for the millennium period. In chapter 5 we introduced an al Qaeda operative named Nashiri. Working with Bin Ladin, he was developing a plan to attack a ship near Yemen. On January 3, an attempt was made to attack a U.S. warship in Aden, the USS *The Sullivans*. The attempt failed when the small boat, overloaded with explosives, sank. The operatives salvaged their equipment without the attempt becoming known, and they put off their plans for another day.

Al Qaeda's "planes operation" was also coming along. In January 2000, the United States caught a glimpse of its preparations.

A Lost Trail in Southeast Asia

In late 1999, the National Security Agency (NSA) analyzed communications associated with a suspected terrorist facility in the Middle East, indicating that several members of "an operational cadre" were planning to travel to Kuala Lumpur in early January 2000. Initially, only the first names of three were known—"Nawaf," "Salem," and "Khalid." NSA analysts surmised correctly that Salem was Nawaf's younger brother. Seeing links not only with al Qaeda but specifically with the 1998 embassy bombings, a CIA desk officer guessed that "something more nefarious [was] afoot."[41]

In chapter 5, we discussed the dispatch of two operatives to the United States for their part in the planes operation—Nawaf al Hazmi and Khalid al Mihdhar. Two more, Khallad and Abu Bara, went to Southeast Asia to case flights for the part of the operation that was supposed to unfold there.[42] All made their way to Southeast Asia from Afghanistan and Pakistan, except for Mihdhar, who traveled from Yemen.[43]

Though Nawaf's trail was temporarily lost, the CIA soon identified "Khalid" as Khalid al Mihdhar.[44] He was located leaving Yemen and tracked until he arrived in Kuala Lumpur on January 5, 2000.[45] Other Arabs, unidentified at the time, were watched as they gathered with him in the Malaysian capital.[46]

On January 8, the surveillance teams reported that three of the Arabs had suddenly left Kuala Lumpur on a short flight to Bangkok.[47] They identified one as Mihdhar. They later learned that one of his companions was named Alhazmi, although it was not yet known that he was "Nawaf." The only identifier available for the third person was part of a name—Salahsae.[48] In Bangkok, CIA officers received the information too late to track the three men as they came in, and the travelers disappeared into the streets of Bangkok.[49]

The Counterterrorist Center (CTC) had briefed the CIA leadership on the gathering in Kuala Lumpur, and the information had been passed on to Berger and the NSC staff and to Director Freeh and others at the FBI (though the FBI noted that the CIA had the lead and would let the FBI know if a domestic angle arose). The head of the Bin Ladin unit kept providing updates, unaware at first even that the Arabs had left Kuala Lumpur, let alone that their trail had been lost in Bangkok.[50] When this bad news arrived, the names were put on a Thai watchlist so that Thai authorities could inform the United States if any of them departed from Thailand.[51]

Several weeks later, CIA officers in Kuala Lumpur prodded colleagues in Bangkok for additional information regarding the three travelers.[52] In early March 2000, Bangkok reported that Nawaf al Hazmi, now identified for the first time with his full name, had departed on January 15 on a United Airlines flight to Los Angeles. As for Khalid al Mihdhar, there was no report of his departure even though he had accompanied Hazmi on the United flight to Los Angeles.[53] No one outside of the Counterterrorist Center was told any of this. The CIA did not try to register Mihdhar or Hazmi with the State Department's TIPOFF watchlist—either in January, when word arrived of Mihdhar's visa, or in March, when word came that Hazmi, too, had had a U.S. visa and a ticket to Los Angeles.[54]

None of this information—about Mihdhar's U.S. visa or Hazmi's travel to the United States—went to the FBI, and nothing more was done to track any of the three until January 2001, when the investigation of another bombing, that of the USS *Cole*, reignited interest in Khallad. We will return to that story in chapter 8.

6.2 POST-CRISIS REFLECTION: AGENDA FOR 2000

After the millennium alert, elements of the U.S. government reviewed their performance. The CIA's leadership was told that while a number of plots had been disrupted, the millennium might be only the "kick-off" for a period of extended attacks.[55] Clarke wrote Berger on January 11, 2000, that the CIA, the FBI, Justice, and the NSC staff had come to two main conclusions. First, U.S. disruption efforts thus far had "not put too much of a dent" in Bin Ladin's network. If the United States wanted to "roll back" the threat, disruption would have to proceed at "a markedly different tempo." Second, "sleeper cells" and "a variety of terrorist groups" had turned up at home.[56] As one of Clarke's staff noted, only a "chance discovery" by U.S. Customs had prevented a possible attack.[57] Berger gave his approval for the NSC staff to commence an "after-action review," anticipating new budget

requests. He also asked DCI Tenet to review the CIA's counterterrorism strategy and come up with a plan for "where we
go from here."[58]

The NSC staff advised Berger that the United States had
only been "nibbling at the edges" of Bin Ladin's network
and that more terror attacks were a question not of "if" but
rather of "when" and "where."[59] The Principals Committee
met on March 10, 2000, to review possible new moves. The
principals ended up agreeing that the government should
take three major steps. First, more money should go to the
CIA to accelerate its efforts to "seriously attrit" al Qaeda.
Second, there should be a crackdown on foreign terrorist organizations in the United States. Third, immigration law enforcement should be strengthened, and the INS should
tighten controls on the Canadian border (including stepping
up U.S.-Canada cooperation). The principals endorsed the
proposed programs; some, like expanding the number of
Joint Terrorism Task Forces, moved forward, and others, like
creating a centralized translation unit for domestic intelligence intercepts in Arabic and other languages, did not.[60]

Pressing Pakistan

While this process moved along, diplomacy continued its
rounds. Direct pressure on the Taliban had proved unsuccessful. As one NSC staff note put it, "Under the Taliban,
Afghanistan is not so much a state sponsor of terrorism as it
is a state sponsored by terrorists."[61] In early 2000, the United
States began a high-level effort to persuade Pakistan to use
its influence over the Taliban.

In January 2000, Assistant Secretary of State Karl Inderfurth and the State Department's counterterrorism coordinator, Michael Sheehan, met with General Musharraf in
Islamabad, dangling before him the possibility of a presidential visit in March as a reward for Pakistani cooperation.
Such a visit was coveted by Musharraf, partly as a sign of
his government's legitimacy. He told the two envoys that he
would meet with Mullah Omar and press him on Bin Ladin.
They left, however, reporting to Washington that Pakistan

was unlikely in fact to do anything, "given what it sees as the benefits of Taliban control of Afghanistan."[62]

President Clinton was scheduled to travel to India. The State Department felt that he should not visit India without also visiting Pakistan. The Secret Service and the CIA, however, warned in the strongest terms that visiting Pakistan would risk the President's life. Counterterrorism officials also argued that Pakistan had not done enough to merit a presidential visit. But President Clinton insisted on including Pakistan in the itinerary for his trip to South Asia.[63] His one-day stopover on March 25, 2000, was the first time a U.S. president had been there since 1969. At his meeting with Musharraf and others, President Clinton concentrated on tensions between Pakistan and India and the dangers of nuclear proliferation, but also discussed Bin Ladin. President Clinton told us that when he pulled Musharraf aside for a brief, one-on-one meeting, he pleaded with the general for help regarding Bin Ladin. "I offered him the moon when I went to see him, in terms of better relations with the United States, if he'd help us get Bin Ladin and deal with another issue or two."[64]

The U.S. effort continued. Early in May, President Clinton urged Musharraf to carry through on his promise to visit Afghanistan and press Mullah Omar to expel Bin Ladin.[65] At the end of the month, Under Secretary of State Thomas Pickering followed up with a trip to the region.[66] In June, DCI Tenet traveled to Pakistan with the same general message.[67] By September, the United States was becoming openly critical of Pakistan for supporting a Taliban military offensive aimed at completing the conquest of Afghanistan.[68]

In December, taking a step proposed by the State Department some months earlier, the United States led a campaign for new UN sanctions, which resulted in UN Security Council Resolution 1333, again calling for Bin Ladin's expulsion and forbidding any country to provide the Taliban with arms or military assistance.[69] This, too, had little if any effect. The Taliban did not expel Bin Ladin. Pakistani arms continued to flow across the border.

Secretary of State Madeleine Albright told us, "We did not have a strong hand to play with the Pakistanis. Because of the sanctions required by U.S. law, we had few carrots to offer."[70] Congress had blocked most economic and military aid to Pakistan because of that country's nuclear arms program and Musharraf's coup. Sheehan was critical of Musharraf, telling us that the Pakistani leader "blew a chance to remake Pakistan."[71]

Building New Capabilities: The CIA

The after-action review had treated the CIA as the lead agency for any offensive against al Qaeda, and the principals, at their March 10 meeting, had endorsed strengthening the CIA's capability for that role. To the CTC, that meant proceeding with "the Plan," which it had put forward half a year earlier—hiring and training more case officers and building up the capabilities of foreign security services that provided intelligence via liaison. On occasion, as in Jordan in December 1999, these liaison services took direct action against al Qaeda cells.[72]

In the CTC and higher up, the CIA's managers believed that they desperately needed funds just to continue their current counterterrorism effort, for they reckoned that the millennium alert had already used up all of the Center's funds for the current fiscal year; the Bin Ladin unit had spent 140 percent of its allocation. Tenet told us he met with Berger to discuss funding for counterterrorism just two days after the principals' meeting.[73]

While Clarke strongly favored giving the CIA more money for counterterrorism, he differed sharply with the CIA's managers about where it should come from. They insisted that the CIA had been shortchanged ever since the end of the Cold War. Their ability to perform any mission, counterterrorism included, they argued, depended on preserving what they had, restoring what they had lost since the beginning of the 1990s, and building from there—with across-the-board recruitment and training of new case officers, and the reopening of closed stations. To finance the counterterrorism effort, Tenet had gone to congressional leaders after the 1998 embassy bombings and persuaded them to give the CIA a special supplemental appropriation. Now, in the aftermath of the millennium alert, Tenet wanted a boost in overall funds for the CIA *and* another supplemental appropriation specifically for counterterrorism.[74]

To Clarke, this seemed evidence that the CIA's leadership did not give sufficient priority to the battle against Bin Ladin and al Qaeda. He told us that James Pavitt, the head of the CIA's Directorate of Operations, "said if there's going to be money spent on going after Bin Ladin, it should be given to him. . . . My view was that he had had a lot of money to do it and a long time to do it, and I didn't want to put more good money after bad."[75] The CIA had a very different attitude: Pavitt told us that while the CIA's Bin Ladin unit did "extraordinary and commendable work," his chief of station in London "was just as much part of the al Qaeda struggle as an officer sitting in [the Bin Ladin unit]."[76]

The dispute had large managerial implications, for Clarke had found allies in the Office of Management and Budget (OMB). They had supplied him with the figures he used to argue that CIA spending on counterterrorism from its baseline budget had shown almost no increase.[77]

Berger met twice with Tenet in April to try to resolve the dispute. The Deputies Committee met later in the month to review fiscal year 2000 and 2001 budget priorities and offsets for the CIA and other agencies. In the end, Tenet obtained a modest supplemental appropriation, which funded counterterrorism without requiring much reprogramming of baseline funds. But the CIA still believed that it remained underfunded for counterterrorism.[78]

Terrorist Financing

The second major point on which the principals had agreed on March 10 was the need to crack down on terrorist organizations and curtail their fund-raising.

The embassy bombings of 1998 had focused attention on al Qaeda's finances. One result had been the creation of an

NSC-led interagency committee on terrorist financing. On its recommendation, the President had designated Bin Ladin and al Qaeda as subject to sanctions under the International Emergency Economic Powers Act. This gave the Treasury Department's Office of Foreign Assets Control (OFAC) the ability to search for and freeze any Bin Ladin or al Qaeda assets that reached the U.S. financial system. But since OFAC had little information to go on, few funds were frozen.[79]

In July 1999, the President applied the same designation to the Taliban for harboring Bin Ladin. Here, OFAC had more success. It blocked more than $34 million in Taliban assets held in U.S. banks. Another $215 million in gold and $2 million in demand deposits, all belonging to the Afghan central bank and held by the Federal Reserve Bank of New York, were also frozen.[80] After October 1999, when the State Department formally designated al Qaeda a "foreign terrorist organization," it became the duty of U.S. banks to block its transactions and seize its funds.[81] Neither this designation nor UN sanctions had much additional practical effect; the sanctions were easily circumvented, and there were no multilateral mechanisms to ensure that other countries' financial systems were not used as conduits for terrorist funding.[82]

Attacking the funds of an institution, even the Taliban, was easier than finding and seizing the funds of a clandestine worldwide organization like al Qaeda. Although the CIA's Bin Ladin unit had originally been inspired by the idea of studying terrorist financial links, few personnel assigned to it had any experience in financial investigations. Any terrorist-financing intelligence appeared to have been collected collaterally, as a consequence of gathering other intelligence. This attitude may have stemmed in large part from the chief of this unit, who did not believe that simply following the money from point A to point B revealed much about the terrorists' plans and intentions. As a result, the CIA placed little emphasis on terrorist financing.[83]

Nevertheless, the CIA obtained a general understanding of how al Qaeda raised money. It knew relatively early, for example, about the loose affiliation of financial institutions, businesses, and wealthy individuals who supported extremist Islamic activities.[84] Much of the early reporting on al Qaeda's financial situation and its structure came from Jamal Ahmed al Fadl, whom we have mentioned earlier in the report.[85] After the 1998 embassy bombings, the U.S. government tried to develop a clearer picture of Bin Ladin's finances. A U.S. interagency group traveled to Saudi Arabia twice, in 1999 and 2000, to get information from the Saudis about their understanding of those finances. The group eventually concluded that the oft-repeated assertion that Bin Ladin was funding al Qaeda from his personal fortune was in fact not true.

The officials developed a new theory: al Qaeda was getting its money elsewhere, and the United States needed to focus on other sources of funding, such as charities, wealthy donors, and financial facilitators. Ultimately, although the intelligence community devoted more resources to the issue and produced somewhat more intelligence,[86] it remained difficult to distinguish al Qaeda's financial transactions among the vast sums moving in the international financial system. The CIA was not able to find or disrupt al Qaeda's money flows.[87]

The NSC staff thought that one possible solution to these weaknesses in the intelligence community was to create an all-source terrorist-financing intelligence analysis center. Clarke pushed for the funding of such a center at Treasury, but neither Treasury nor the CIA was willing to commit the resources.[88]

Within the United States, various FBI field offices gathered intelligence on organizations suspected of raising funds for al Qaeda or other terrorist groups. By 9/11, FBI agents understood that there were extremist organizations operating within the United States supporting a global jihadist movement and with substantial connections to al Qaeda. The FBI operated a web of informants, conducted electronic surveillance, and had opened significant investigations in a number of field offices, including New York, Chicago, Detroit, San

Diego, and Minneapolis. On a national level, however, the FBI never used the information to gain a systematic or strategic understanding of the nature and extent of al Qaeda fundraising.[89]

Treasury regulators, as well as U.S. financial institutions, were generally focused on finding and deterring or disrupting the vast flows of U.S. currency generated by drug trafficking and high-level international fraud. Large-scale scandals, such as the use of the Bank of New York by Russian money launderers to move millions of dollars out of Russia, captured the attention of the Department of the Treasury and of Congress.[90] Before 9/11, Treasury did not consider terrorist financing important enough to mention in its national strategy for money laundering.[91]

Border Security

The third point on which the principals had agreed on March 10 was the need for attention to America's porous borders and the weak enforcement of immigration laws. Drawing on ideas from government officials, Clarke's working group developed a menu of proposals to bolster border security. Some reworked or reiterated previous presidential directives.[92] They included

- creating an interagency center to target illegal entry and human traffickers;
- imposing tighter controls on student visas;[93]
- taking legal action to prevent terrorists from coming into the United States and to remove those already here, detaining them while awaiting removal proceedings;[94]
- further increasing the number of immigration agents to FBI Joint Terrorism Task Forces to help investigate immigration charges against individuals suspected of terrorism;[95]
- activating a special court to enable the use of classified evidence in immigration-related national security cases;[96] and

- both implementing new security measures for U.S. passports and working with the United Nations and foreign governments to raise global security standards for travel documents.[97]

Clarke's working group compiled new proposals as well, such as

- undertaking a Joint Perimeter Defense program with Canada to establish cooperative intelligence and law enforcement programs, leading to joint operations based on shared visa and immigration data and joint border patrols;
- staffing land border crossings 24/7 and equipping them with video cameras, physical barriers, and means to detect weapons of mass destruction (WMD); and
- addressing the problem of migrants—possibly including terrorists—who destroy their travel documents so they cannot be returned to their countries of origin.[98]

These proposals were praiseworthy in principle. In practice, however, they required action by weak, chronically underfunded executive agencies and powerful congressional committees, which were more responsive to well-organized interest groups than to executive branch interagency committees. The changes sought by the principals in March 2000 were only beginning to occur before 9/11.

"Afghan Eyes"

In early March 2000, when President Clinton received an update on U.S. covert action efforts against Bin Ladin, he wrote in the memo's margin that the United States could surely do better. Military officers in the Joint Staff told us that they shared this sense of frustration. Clarke used the President's comment to push the CSG to brainstorm new ideas, including aid to the Northern Alliance.[99]

Back in December 1999, Northern Alliance leader Ahmed Shah Massoud had offered to stage a rocket attack against Bin Ladin's Derunta training complex. Officers at the CIA had worried that giving him a green light might cross the line into violation of the assassination ban. Hence, Massoud was told not to take any such action without explicit U.S. authorization.[100] In the spring of 2000, after the CIA had sent out officers to explore possible closer relationships with both the Uzbeks and the Northern Alliance, discussions took place in Washington between U.S. officials and delegates sent by Massoud.[101]

The Americans agreed that Massoud should get some modest technical help so he could work on U.S. priorities— collecting intelligence on and possibly acting against al Qaeda. But Massoud wanted the United States both to become his ally in trying to overthrow the Taliban and to recognize that they were fighting common enemies. Clarke and Cofer Black, the head of the Counterterrorist Center, wanted to take this next step. Proposals to help the Northern Alliance had been debated in the U.S. government since 1999 and, as we mentioned in chapter 4, the U.S. government as a whole had been wary of endorsing them, largely because of the Northern Alliance's checkered history, its limited base of popular support in Afghanistan, and Pakistan's objections.[102]

CIA officials also began pressing proposals to use their ties with the Northern Alliance to get American agents on the ground in Afghanistan for an extended period, setting up their own base for covert intelligence collection and activity in the Panjshir Valley and lessening reliance on foreign proxies. "There's no substitute for face-to-face," one officer told us.[103] But the CIA's institutional capacity for such direct action was weak, especially if it was not working jointly with the U.S. military. The idea was turned down as too risky.[104]

In the meantime, the CIA continued to work with its tribal assets in southern Afghanistan. In early August, the tribals reported an attempt to ambush Bin Ladin's convoy as he traveled on the road between Kabul and Kandahar city— their first such reported interdiction attempt in more than a

year and a half. But it was not a success. According to the
tribals' own account, when they approached one of the vehicles, they quickly determined that women and children were
inside and called off the ambush. Conveying this information to the NSC staff, the CIA noted that they had no independent corroboration for this incident, but that the tribals
had acted within the terms of the CIA's authorities in
Afghanistan.[105]

In 2000, plans continued to be developed for potential
military operations in Afghanistan. Navy vessels that could
launch missiles into Afghanistan were still on call in the
north Arabian Sea.[106] In the summer, the military refined its
list of strikes and Special Operations possibilities to a set of
13 options within the Operation Infinite Resolve plan.[107] Yet
planning efforts continued to be limited by the same operational and policy concerns encountered in 1998 and 1999.
Although the intelligence community sometimes knew
where Bin Ladin was, it had been unable to provide intelligence considered sufficiently reliable to launch a strike.
Above all, the United States did not have American eyes on
the target. As one military officer put it, we had our hand on
the door, but we couldn't open the door and walk in.[108]

At some point during this period, President Clinton expressed his frustration with the lack of military options to
take out Bin Ladin and the al Qaeda leadership, remarking
to General Hugh Shelton, "You know, it would scare the shit
out of al-Qaeda if suddenly a bunch of black ninjas rap-
pelled out of helicopters into the middle of their camp."[109]
Although Shelton told the Commission he did not remember
the statement, President Clinton recalled this remark as "one
of the many things I said." The President added, however,
that he realized nothing would be accomplished if he lashed
out in anger. Secretary of Defense William Cohen thought
that the President might have been making a hypothetical
statement. Regardless, he said, the question remained how to
get the "ninjas" into and out of the theater of operations.[110]
As discussed in chapter 4, plans of this kind were never carried out before 9/11.

In late 1999 or early 2000, the Joint Staff's director of operations, Vice Admiral Scott Fry, directed his chief information operations officer, Brigadier General Scott Gration, to develop innovative ways to get better intelligence on Bin Ladin's whereabouts. Gration and his team worked on a number of different ideas aimed at getting reliable American eyes on Bin Ladin in a way that would reduce the lag time between sighting and striking.[111]

One option was to use a small, unmanned U.S. Air Force drone called the Predator, which could survey the territory below and send back video footage. Another option—eventually dismissed as impractical—was to place a powerful long-range telescope on a mountain within range of one of Bin Ladin's training camps. Both proposals were discussed with General Shelton, the chairman of the Joint Chiefs of Staff, and then briefed to Clarke's office at the White House as the CSG was searching for new ideas. In the spring of 2000, Clarke brought in the CIA's assistant director for collection, Charles Allen, to work together with Fry on a joint CIA-Pentagon effort that Clarke dubbed "Afghan Eyes."[112] After much argument between the CIA and the Defense Department about who should pay for the program, the White House eventually imposed a cost-sharing agreement. The CIA agreed to pay for Predator operations as a 60-day "proof of concept" trial run.[113]

The Small Group backed Afghan Eyes at the end of June 2000. By mid-July, testing was completed and the equipment was ready, but legal issues were still being ironed out.[114] By August 11, the principals had agreed to deploy the Predator.[115] The NSC staff considered how to use the information the drones would be relaying from Afghanistan. Clarke's deputy, Roger Cressey, wrote to Berger that emergency CSG and Principals Committee meetings might be needed to act on video coming in from the Predator if it proved able to lock in Bin Ladin's location. In the memo's margin, Berger wrote that before considering action, "I will want *more* than verified location: we will need, at least, data on *pattern* of movements to provide some assurance he will remain in place." President Clinton was kept up to date.[116]

On September 7, the Predator flew for the first time over Afghanistan. When Clarke saw video taken during the trial flight, he described the imagery to Berger as "truly astonishing," and he argued immediately for more flights seeking to find Bin Ladin and target him for cruise missile or air attack. Even if Bin Ladin were not found, Clarke said, Predator missions might identify additional worthwhile targets, such as other al Qaeda leaders or stocks of chemical or biological weapons.[117]

Clarke was not alone in his enthusiasm. He had backing from Cofer Black and Charles Allen at the CIA. Ten out of 15 trial missions of the Predator over Afghanistan were rated successful. On the first flight, a Predator saw a security detail around a tall man in a white robe at Bin Ladin's Tarnak Farms compound outside Kandahar. After a second sighting of the "man in white" at the compound on September 28, intelligence community analysts determined that he was probably Bin Ladin.[118]

During at least one trial mission, the Taliban spotted the Predator and scrambled MiG fighters to try, without success, to intercept it. Berger worried that a Predator might be shot down, and warned Clarke that a shootdown would be a "bonanza" for Bin Ladin and the Taliban.[119]

Still, Clarke was optimistic about Predator—as well as progress with disruptions of al Qaeda cells elsewhere. Berger was more cautious, praising the NSC staff's performance but observing that this was no time for complacency. "Unfortunately," he wrote, "the light at the end of the tunnel is another tunnel."[120]

6.3 THE ATTACK ON THE USS *COLE*

Early in chapter 5 we introduced, along with Khalid Sheikh Mohammed, two other men who became operational coordinators for al Qaeda: Khallad and Nashiri. As we explained, both were involved during 1998 and 1999 in preparing to attack a ship off the coast of Yemen with a boatload of explosives. They had originally targeted a commercial vessel, specifically an oil tanker, but Bin Ladin urged them to look for a U.S. warship instead. In January 2000, their team had attempted to attack a warship in the port of Aden, but the attempt failed when the suicide boat sank. More than nine months later, on October 12, 2000, al Qaeda operatives in a small boat laden with explosives attacked a U.S. Navy destroyer, the USS *Cole*. The blast ripped a hole in the side of the *Cole*, killing 17 members of the ship's crew and wounding at least 40.[121]

The plot, we now know, was a full-fledged al Qaeda operation, supervised directly by Bin Ladin. He chose the target and location of the attack, selected the suicide operatives, and provided the money needed to purchase explosives and equipment. Nashiri was the field commander and managed the operation in Yemen. Khallad helped in Yemen until he was arrested in a case of mistaken identity and freed with Bin Ladin's help, as we also mentioned earlier. Local al Qaeda coordinators included Jamal al Badawi and Fahd al Quso, who was supposed to film the attack from a nearby apartment. The two suicide operatives chosen were Hassan al Khamri and Ibrahim al Thawar, also known as Nibras. Nibras and Quso delivered money to Khallad in Bangkok during Khallad's January 2000 trip to Kuala Lumpur and Bangkok.[122]

In September 2000, Bin Ladin reportedly told Nashiri that he wanted to replace Khamri and Nibras. Nashiri was angry and disagreed, telling others he would go to Afghanistan and explain to Bin Ladin that the new operatives were already trained and ready to conduct the attack. Prior to departing, Nashiri gave Nibras and Khamri instructions to execute the attack on the next U.S. warship that entered the port of Aden.[123]

While Nashiri was in Afghanistan, Nibras and Khamri saw their chance. They piloted the explosives-laden boat alongside the USS *Cole*, made friendly gestures to crew members, and detonated the bomb. Quso did not arrive at the apartment in time to film the attack.[124]

Back in Afghanistan, Bin Ladin anticipated U.S. military retaliation. He ordered the evacuation of al Qaeda's Kandahar airport compound and fled—first to the desert area near Kabul, then to Khowst and Jalalabad, and eventually back to Kandahar. In Kandahar, he rotated between five to six residences, spending one night at each residence. In addition, he sent his senior advisor, Mohammed Atef, to a different part of Kandahar and his deputy, Ayman al Zawahiri, to Kabul so that all three could not be killed in one attack.[125]

There was no American strike. In February 2001, a source reported that an individual whom he identified as the big instructor (probably a reference to Bin Ladin) complained frequently that the United States had not yet attacked. According to the source, Bin Ladin wanted the United States to attack, and if it did not he would launch something bigger.[126]

The attack on the USS *Cole* galvanized al Qaeda's recruitment efforts. Following the attack, Bin Ladin instructed the media committee, then headed by Khalid Sheikh Mohammed, to produce a propaganda video that included a reenactment of the attack along with images of the al Qaeda training camps and training methods; it also highlighted Muslim suffering in Palestine, Kashmir, Indonesia, and Chechnya. Al Qaeda's image was very important to Bin Ladin, and the video was widely disseminated. Portions were aired on Al Jazeera, CNN, and other television outlets. It was also disseminated among many young men in Saudi Arabia and Yemen, and caused many extremists to travel to Afghanistan for training and jihad. Al Qaeda members considered the video an effective tool in their struggle for preeminence among other Islamist and jihadist movements.[127]

Investigating the Attack
Teams from the FBI, the Naval Criminal Investigative Service, and the CIA were immediately sent to Yemen to investigate the attack. With difficulty, Barbara Bodine, the U.S. ambassador to Yemen, tried to persuade the Yemeni government to accept these visitors and allow them to carry arms,

though the Yemenis balked at letting Americans openly carry long guns (rifles, shotguns, automatic weapons). Meanwhile, Bodine and the leader of the FBI team, John O'Neill, clashed repeatedly—to the point that after O'Neill had been rotated out of Yemen but wanted to return, Bodine refused the request. Despite the initial tension, the Yemeni and American investigations proceeded. Within a few weeks, the outline of the story began to emerge.[128]

On the day of the *Cole* attack, a list of suspects was assembled that included al Qaeda's affiliate Egyptian Islamic Jihad. U.S. counterterrorism officials told us they immediately assumed that al Qaeda was responsible. But as Deputy DCI John McLaughlin explained to us, it was not enough for the attack to smell, look, and taste like an al Qaeda operation. To make a case, the CIA needed not just a guess but a link to someone known to be an al Qaeda operative.[129]

Within the first weeks after the attack, the Yemenis found and arrested both Badawi and Quso, but did not let the FBI team participate in the interrogations. The CIA described initial Yemeni support after the *Cole* as "slow and inadequate." President Clinton, Secretary Albright, and DCI Tenet all intervened to help. Because the information was secondhand, the U.S. team could not make its own assessment of its reliability.[130]

On November 11, the Yemenis provided the FBI with new information from the interrogations of Badawi and Quso, including descriptions of individuals from whom the detainees had received operational direction. One of them was Khallad, who was described as having lost his leg. The detainees said that Khallad helped direct the *Cole* operation from Afghanistan or Pakistan. The Yemenis (correctly) judged that the man described as Khallad was Tawfiq bin Attash.[131]

An FBI special agent recognized the name Khallad and connected this news with information from an important al Qaeda source who had been meeting regularly with CIA and FBI officers. The source had called Khallad Bin Ladin's "run boy," and described him as having lost one leg in an explosives accident at a training camp a few years earlier. To confirm the identification, the FBI agent asked the Yemenis for their photo of Khallad. The Yemenis provided the photo on November 22, reaffirming their view that Khallad had been an intermediary between the plotters and Bin Ladin. (In a meeting with U.S. officials a few weeks later, on December 16, the source identified Khallad from the Yemeni photograph.)[132]

U.S. intelligence agencies had already connected Khallad to al Qaeda terrorist operations, including the 1998 embassy bombings. By this time the Yemenis also had identified Nashiri, whose links to al Qaeda and the 1998 embassy bombings were even more well-known.[133]

In other words, the Yemenis provided strong evidence connecting the *Cole* attack to al Qaeda during the second half of November, identifying individual operatives whom the United States knew were part of al Qaeda. During December the United States was able to corroborate this evidence. But the United States did not have evidence about Bin Ladin's personal involvement in the attacks until Nashiri and Khallad were captured in 2002 and 2003.

Considering a Response

The *Cole* attack prompted renewed consideration of what could be done about al Qaeda. According to Clarke, Berger upbraided DCI Tenet so sharply after the *Cole* attack—repeatedly demanding to know why the United States had to put up with such attacks—that Tenet walked out of a meeting of the principals.[134]

The CIA got some additional covert action authorities, adding several other individuals to the coverage of the July 1999 Memorandum of Notification that allowed the United States to develop capture operations against al Qaeda leaders in a variety of places and circumstances. Tenet developed additional options, such as strengthening relationships with the Northern Alliance and the Uzbeks and slowing recent al Qaeda–related activities in Lebanon.[135]

On the diplomatic track, Berger agreed on October 30,

2000, to let the State Department make another approach to Taliban Deputy Foreign Minister Abdul Jalil about expelling Bin Ladin. The national security advisor ordered that the U.S. message "be stern and foreboding." This warning was similar to those issued in 1998 and 1999. Meanwhile, the administration was working with Russia on new UN sanctions against Mullah Omar's regime.[136]

President Clinton told us that before he could launch further attacks on al Qaeda in Afghanistan, or deliver an ultimatum to the Taliban threatening strikes if they did not immediately expel Bin Ladin, the CIA or the FBI had to be sure enough that they would "be willing to stand up in public and say, we believe that he [Bin Ladin] did this." He said he was very frustrated that he could not get a definitive enough answer to do something about the *Cole* attack.[137] Similarly, Berger recalled that to go to war, a president needs to be able to say that his senior intelligence and law enforcement officers have concluded who is responsible. He recalled that the intelligence agencies had strong suspicions, but had reached "no conclusion by the time we left office that it was al Qaeda."[138]

Our only sources for what intelligence officials thought at the time are what they said in informal briefings. Soon after the *Cole* attack and for the remainder of the Clinton administration, analysts stopped distributing written reports about who was responsible. The topic was obviously sensitive, and both Ambassador Bodine in Yemen and CIA analysts in Washington presumed that the government did not want reports circulating around the agencies that might become public, impeding law enforcement actions or backing the President into a corner.[139]

Instead the White House and other principals relied on informal updates as more evidence came in. Though Clarke worried that the CIA might be equivocating in assigning responsibility to al Qaeda, he wrote Berger on November 7 that the analysts had described their case by saying that "it has web feet, flies, and quacks." On November 10, CIA analysts briefed the Small Group of principals on their preliminary findings that the attack was carried out by a cell of Yemeni residents with some ties to the transnational mujahideen network. According to the briefing, these residents likely had some support from al Qaeda. But the information on outside sponsorship, support, and direction of the operation was inconclusive. The next day, Berger and Clarke told President Clinton that while the investigation was continuing, it was becoming increasingly clear that al Qaeda had planned and directed the bombing.[140]

In mid-November, as the evidence of al Qaeda involvement mounted, Berger asked General Shelton to reevaluate military plans to act quickly against Bin Ladin. General Shelton tasked General Tommy Franks, the new commander of CENTCOM, to look again at the options. Shelton wanted to demonstrate that the military was imaginative and knowledgeable enough to move on an array of options, and to show the complexity of the operations. He briefed Berger on the "Infinite Resolve" strike options developed since 1998, which the Joint Staff and CENTCOM had refined during the summer into a list of 13 possibilities or combinations. CENTCOM added a new "phased campaign" concept for wider-ranging strikes, including attacks against the Taliban. For the first time, these strikes envisioned an air campaign against Afghanistan of indefinite duration. Military planners did not include contingency planning for an invasion of Afghanistan. The concept was briefed to Deputy National Security Advisor Donald Kerrick on December 20, and to other officials.[141]

On November 25, Berger and Clarke wrote President Clinton that although the FBI and CIA investigations had not reached a formal conclusion, they believed the investigations would soon conclude that the attack had been carried out by a large cell whose senior members belonged to al Qaeda. Most of those involved had trained in Bin Ladin–operated camps in Afghanistan, Berger continued. So far, Bin Ladin had not been tied personally to the attack and nobody had heard him directly order it, but two intelligence reports suggested that he was involved. When discussing possible responses, though, Berger referred to the premise—al Qaeda responsibility—as an "unproven assumption."[142]

In the same November 25 memo, Berger informed President Clinton about a closely held idea: a last-chance ultimatum for the Taliban. Clarke was developing the idea with specific demands: immediate extradition of Bin Ladin and his lieutenants to a legitimate government for trial, observable closure of all terrorist facilities in Afghanistan, and expulsion of all terrorists from Afghanistan within 90 days. Noncompliance would mean U.S. "force directed at the Taliban itself" and U.S. efforts to ensure that the Taliban would never defeat the Northern Alliance. No such ultimatum was issued.[143]

Nearly a month later, on December 21, the CIA made another presentation to the Small Group of principals on the investigative team's findings. The CIA's briefing slides said that their "preliminary judgment" was that Bin Ladin's al Qaeda group "supported the attack" on the *Cole*, based on strong circumstantial evidence tying key perpetrators of the attack to al Qaeda. The CIA listed the key suspects, including Nashiri. In addition, the CIA detailed the timeline of the operation, from the mid-1999 preparations, to the failed attack on the USS *The Sullivans* on January 3, 2000, through a meeting held by the operatives the day before the attack.[144]

The slides said that so far the CIA had "no definitive answer on [the] crucial question of outside direction of the attack—how and by whom." The CIA noted that the Yemenis claimed that Khallad helped direct the operation from Afghanistan or Pakistan, possibly as Bin Ladin's intermediary, but that it had not seen the Yemeni evidence. However, the CIA knew from both human sources and signals intelligence that Khallad was tied to al Qaeda. The prepared briefing concluded that while some reporting about al Qaeda's role might have merit, those reports offered few specifics. Intelligence gave some ambiguous indicators of al Qaeda direction of the attack.[145]

This, President Clinton and Berger told us, was not the conclusion they needed in order to go to war or deliver an ultimatum to the Taliban threatening war. The election and change of power was not the issue, President Clinton added. There was enough time. If the agencies had given him a definitive answer, he said, he would have sought a UN Security Council ultimatum and given the Taliban one, two, or three days before taking further action against both al Qaeda and the Taliban. But he did not think it would be responsible for a president to launch an invasion of another country just based on a "preliminary judgment."[146]

Other advisers have echoed this concern. Some of Secretary Albright's advisers warned her at the time to be sure the evidence conclusively linked Bin Ladin to the *Cole* before considering any response, especially a military one, because such action might inflame the Islamic world and increase support for the Taliban. Defense Secretary Cohen told us it would not have been prudent to risk killing civilians based only on an assumption that al Qaeda was responsible. General Shelton added that there was an outstanding question as to who was responsible and what the targets were.[147]

Clarke recalled that while the Pentagon and the State Department had reservations about retaliation, the issue never came to a head because the FBI and the CIA never reached a firm conclusion. He thought they were "holding back." He said he did not know why, but his impression was that Tenet and Reno possibly thought the White House "didn't really want to know," since the principals' discussions by November suggested that there was not much White House interest in conducting further military operations against Afghanistan in the administration's last weeks. He thought that, instead, President Clinton, Berger, and Secretary Albright were concentrating on a last-minute push for a peace agreement between the Palestinians and the Israelis.[148]

Some of Clarke's fellow counterterrorism officials, such as the State Department's Sheehan and the FBI's Watson, shared his disappointment that no military response occurred at the time. Clarke recently recalled that an angry Sheehan asked rhetorically of Defense officials: "Does al Qaeda have to attack the Pentagon to get their attention?"[149]

On the question of evidence, Tenet told us he was surprised to hear that the White House was awaiting a conclusion from him on responsibility for the *Cole* attack before taking action against al Qaeda. He did not recall Berger or anyone else telling him that they were waiting for the magic words from the CIA and the FBI. Nor did he remember having any discussions with Berger or the President about retaliation. Tenet told us he believed that it was up to him to present the case. Then it was up to the principals to decide if the case was good enough to justify using force. He believed he laid out what was knowable relatively early in the investigation, and that this evidence never really changed until after 9/11.[150]

A CIA official told us that the CIA's analysts chose the term "preliminary judgment" because of their notion of how an intelligence standard of proof differed from a legal standard. Because the attack was the subject of a criminal investigation, they told us, the term *preliminary* was used to avoid locking the government in with statements that might later be obtained by defense lawyers in a future court case. At the time, Clarke was aware of the problem of distinguishing between an intelligence case and a law enforcement case. Asking U.S. law enforcement officials to concur with an intelligence-based case before their investigation had been concluded "could give rise to charges that the administration had acted before final culpability had been determined."[151]

There was no interagency consideration of just what military action might have looked like in practice—either the Pentagon's new "phased campaign" concept or a prolonged air campaign in Afghanistan. Defense officials, such as Under Secretary Walter Slocombe and Vice Admiral Fry, told us the military response options were still limited. Bin Ladin continued to be elusive. They felt, just as they had for the past two years, that hitting inexpensive and rudimentary training camps with costly missiles would not do much good and might even help al Qaeda if the strikes failed to kill Bin Ladin.[152]

In late 2000, the CIA and the NSC staff began thinking about the counterterrorism policy agenda they would present to the new administration. The Counterterrorist Center put down its best ideas for the future, assuming it was free of any prior policy or financial constraints. The paper was therefore informally referred to as the "Blue Sky" memo; it was sent to Clarke on December 29. The memo proposed

- A major effort to support the Northern Alliance through intelligence sharing and increased funding so that it could stave off the Taliban army and tie down al Qaeda fighters. This effort was not intended to remove the Taliban from power, a goal that was judged impractical and too expensive for the CIA alone to attain.
- Increased support to the Uzbeks to strengthen their ability to fight terrorism and assist the United States in doing so.
- Assistance to anti-Taliban groups and proxies who might be encouraged to passively resist the Taliban.

The CIA memo noted that there was "no single 'silver bullet' available to deal with the growing problems in Afghanistan." A multifaceted strategy would be needed to produce change.[153]

No action was taken on these ideas in the few remaining weeks of the Clinton administration. Berger did not recall seeing or being briefed on the Blue Sky memo. Nor was the memo discussed during the transition with incoming top Bush administration officials. Tenet and his deputy told us they pressed these ideas as options after the new team took office.[154]

As the Clinton administration drew to a close, Clarke and his staff developed a policy paper of their own, the first such comprehensive effort since the Delenda plan of 1998. The resulting paper, entitled "Strategy for Eliminating the Threat from the Jihadist Networks of al Qida: Status and Prospects," reviewed the threat and the record to date, incorporated the CIA's new ideas from the Blue Sky memo, and posed several near-term policy options.

Clarke and his staff proposed a goal to "roll back" al

Qaeda over a period of three to five years. Over time, the policy should try to weaken and eliminate the network's infrastructure in order to reduce it to a "rump group" like other formerly feared but now largely defunct terrorist organizations of the 1980s. "Continued anti-al Qida operations at the current level will prevent some attacks," Clarke's office wrote, "but will not seriously attrit their ability to plan and conduct attacks." The paper backed covert aid to the Northern Alliance, covert aid to Uzbekistan, and renewed Predator flights in March 2001. A sentence called for military action to destroy al Qaeda command-and-control targets and infrastructure and Taliban military and command assets. The paper also expressed concern about the presence of al Qaeda operatives in the United States.[155]

6.4 CHANGE AND CONTINUITY

On November 7, 2000, American voters went to the polls in what turned out to be one of the closest presidential contests in U.S. history—an election campaign during which there was a notable absence of serious discussion of the al Qaeda threat or terrorism. Election night became a 36-day legal fight. Until the Supreme Court's 5–4 ruling on December 12 and Vice President Al Gore's concession, no one knew whether Gore or his Republican opponent, Texas Governor George W. Bush, would become president in 2001.

The dispute over the election and the 36-day delay cut in half the normal transition period. Given that a presidential election in the United States brings wholesale change in personnel, this loss of time hampered the new administration in identifying, recruiting, clearing, and obtaining Senate confirmation of key appointees.

From the Old to the New

The principal figures on Bush's White House staff would be National Security Advisor Condoleezza Rice, who had been a member of the NSC staff in the administration of George

H. W. Bush; Rice's deputy, Stephen Hadley, who had been an assistant secretary of defense under the first Bush; and Chief of Staff Andrew Card, who had served that same administration as deputy chief of staff, then secretary of transportation. For secretary of state, Bush chose General Colin Powell, who had been national security advisor for President Ronald Reagan and then chairman of the Joint Chiefs of Staff. For secretary of defense he selected Donald Rumsfeld, a former member of Congress, White House chief of staff, and, under President Gerald Ford, already once secretary of defense. Bush decided fairly soon to keep Tenet as Director of Central Intelligence. Louis Freeh, who had statutory ten-year tenure, would remain director of the FBI until his voluntary retirement in the summer of 2001.

Bush and his principal advisers had all received briefings on terrorism, including Bin Ladin. In early September 2000, Acting Deputy Director of Central Intelligence John McLaughlin led a team to Bush's ranch in Crawford, Texas, and gave him a wide-ranging, four-hour review of sensitive information. Ben Bonk, deputy chief of the CIA's Counterterrorist Center, used one of the four hours to deal with terrorism. To highlight the danger of terrorists obtaining chemical, biological, radiological, or nuclear weapons, Bonk brought along a mock-up suitcase to evoke the way the Aum Shinrikyo doomsday cult had spread deadly sarin nerve agent on the Tokyo subway in 1995. Bonk told Bush that Americans would die from terrorism during the next four years.[156] During the long contest after election day, the CIA set up an office in Crawford to pass intelligence to Bush and some of his key advisers.[157] Tenet, accompanied by his deputy director for operations, James Pavitt, briefed President-elect Bush at Blair House during the transition. President Bush told us he asked Tenet whether the CIA could kill Bin Ladin, and Tenet replied that killing Bin Ladin would have an effect but would not end the threat. President Bush told us Tenet said to him that the CIA had all the authority it needed.[158]

In December, Bush met with Clinton for a two-hour, one-on-one discussion of national security and foreign policy challenges. Clinton recalled saying to Bush, "I think you will find that by far your biggest threat is Bin Ladin and the al Qaeda." Clinton told us that he also said, "One of the great regrets of my presidency is that I didn't get him [Bin Ladin] for you, because I tried to."[159] Bush told the Commission that he felt sure President Clinton had mentioned terrorism, but did not remember much being said about al Qaeda. Bush recalled that Clinton had emphasized other issues such as North Korea and the Israeli-Palestinian peace process.[160]

In early January, Clarke briefed Rice on terrorism. He gave similar presentations—describing al Qaeda as both an adaptable global network of jihadist organizations and a lethal core terrorist organization—to Vice President–elect Cheney, Hadley, and Secretary of State–designate Powell. One line in the briefing slides said that al Qaeda had sleeper cells in more than 40 countries, including the United States.[161] Berger told us that he made a point of dropping in on Clarke's briefing of Rice to emphasize the importance of the issue. Later the same day, Berger met with Rice. He says that he told her the Bush administration would spend more time on terrorism in general and al Qaeda in particular than on anything else. Rice's recollection was that Berger told her she would be surprised at how much more time she was going to spend on terrorism than she expected, but that the bulk of their conversation dealt with the faltering Middle East peace process and North Korea. Clarke said that the new team, having been out of government for eight years, had a steep learning curve to understand al Qaeda and the new transnational terrorist threat.[162]

Organizing a New Administration

During the short transition, Rice and Hadley concentrated on staffing and organizing the NSC.[163] Their policy priorities differed from those of the Clinton administration. Those priorities included China, missile defense, the collapse of the Middle East peace process, and the Persian Gulf.[164] Generally aware that terrorism had changed since the first Bush

administration, they paid particular attention to the question
of how counterterrorism policy should be coordinated. Rice
had asked University of Virginia history professor Philip Zelikow to advise her on the transition.[165] Hadley and Zelikow
asked Clarke and his deputy, Roger Cressey, for a special
briefing on the terrorist threat and how Clarke's Transnational Threats Directorate and Counterterrorism Security
Group functioned.[166]

In the NSC during the first Bush administration, many
tough issues were addressed at the level of the Deputies
Committee. Issues did not go to the principals unless the
deputies had been unable to resolve them. Presidential Decision Directive 62 of the Clinton administration had said
specifically that Clarke's Counterterrorism Security Group
should report through the Deputies Committee or, at
Berger's discretion, directly to the principals. Berger had in
practice allowed Clarke's group to function as a parallel
deputies committee, reporting directly to those members of
the Principals Committee who sat on the special Small
Group. There, Clarke himself sat as a de facto principal.

Rice decided to change the special structure that had been
built to coordinate counterterrorism policy. It was important
to sound policymaking, she felt, that Clarke's interagency
committee—like all others—report to the principals through
the deputies.[167]

Rice made an initial decision to hold over both Clarke
and his entire counterterrorism staff, a decision that she
called rare for a new administration. She decided also that
Clarke should retain the title of national counterterrorism
coordinator, although he would no longer be a de facto
member of the Principals Committee on his issues. The decision to keep Clarke, Rice said, was "not uncontroversial,"
since he was known as someone who "broke china," but she
and Hadley wanted an experienced crisis manager. No one
else from Berger's staff had Clarke's detailed knowledge of
the levers of government.[168]

Clarke was disappointed at what he perceived as a demo-
tion. He also worried that reporting through the Deputies

Committee would slow decisionmaking on counterterrorism.[169]

The result, amid all the changes accompanying the transition, was significant continuity in counterterrorism policy. Clarke and his Counterterrorism Security Group would continue to manage coordination. Tenet remained Director of Central Intelligence and kept the same chief subordinates, including Black and his staff at the Counterterrorist Center. Shelton remained chairman of the Joint Chiefs, with the Joint Staff largely the same. At the FBI, Director Freeh and Assistant Director for Counterterrorism Dale Watson remained. Working-level counterterrorism officials at the State Department and the Pentagon stayed on, as is typically the case. The changes were at the cabinet and subcabinet level and in the CSG's reporting arrangements. At the subcabinet level, there were significant delays in the confirmation of key officials, particularly at the Defense Department.

The procedures of the Bush administration were to be at once more formal and less formal than its predecessor's. President Clinton, a voracious reader, received his daily intelligence briefings in writing. He often scrawled questions and comments in the margins, eliciting written responses. The new president, by contrast, reinstated the practice of face-to-face briefings from the DCI. President Bush and Tenet met in the Oval Office at 8:00 A.M., with Vice President Cheney, Rice, and Card usually also present. The President and the DCI both told us that these daily sessions provided a useful opportunity for exchanges on intelligence issues.[170]

The President talked with Rice every day, and she in turn talked by phone at least daily with Powell and Rumsfeld. As a result, the President often felt less need for formal meetings. If, however, he decided that an event or an issue called for action, Rice would typically call on Hadley to have the Deputies Committee develop and review options. The President said that this process often tried his patience but that he understood the necessity for coordination.[171]

Early Decisions

Within the first few days after Bush's inauguration, Clarke approached Rice in an effort to get her—and the new President—to give terrorism very high priority and to act on the agenda that he had pushed during the last few months of the previous administration. After Rice requested that all senior staff identify desirable major policy reviews or initiatives, Clarke submitted an elaborate memorandum on January 25, 2001. He attached to it his 1998 Delenda Plan and the December 2000 strategy paper. "We *urgently* need . . . a Principals level review on the *al Qida* network," Clarke wrote.[172]

He wanted the Principals Committee to decide whether al Qaeda was "a first order threat" or a more modest worry being overblown by "chicken little" alarmists. Alluding to the transition briefing that he had prepared for Rice, Clarke wrote that al Qaeda "is not some narrow, little terrorist issue that needs to be included in broader regional policy." Two key decisions that had been deferred, he noted, concerned covert aid to keep the Northern Alliance alive when fighting began again in Afghanistan in the spring, and covert aid to the Uzbeks. Clarke also suggested that decisions should be made soon on messages to the Taliban and Pakistan over the al Qaeda sanctuary in Afghanistan, on possible new money for CIA operations, and on "when and how . . . to respond to the attack on the USS Cole."[173]

The national security advisor did not respond directly to Clarke's memorandum. No Principals Committee meeting on al Qaeda was held until September 4, 2001 (although the Principals Committee met frequently on other subjects, such as the Middle East peace process, Russia, and the Persian Gulf).[174] But Rice and Hadley began to address the issues Clarke had listed. What to do or say about the *Cole* had been an obvious question since inauguration day. When the attack occurred, 25 days before the election, candidate Bush had said to CNN, "I hope that we can gather enough intelligence to figure out who did the act and take the necessary action. There must be a consequence."[175] Since the Clinton administration had not responded militarily, what was the Bush administration to do?

On January 25, Tenet briefed the President on the *Cole* investigation. The written briefing repeated for top officials of the new administration what the CIA had told the Clinton White House in November. This included the "preliminary judgment" that al Qaeda was responsible, with the caveat that no evidence had yet been found that Bin Ladin himself ordered the attack. Tenet told us he had no recollection of a conversation with the President about this briefing.[176]

In his January 25 memo, Clarke had advised Rice that the government should respond to the *Cole* attack, but "should take advantage of the policy that 'we will respond at a time, place and manner of our own choosing' and not be forced into knee-jerk responses."[177] Before Vice President Cheney visited the CIA in mid-February, Clarke sent him a memo—outside the usual White House document-management system—suggesting that he ask CIA officials "what additional information is needed before CIA can definitively conclude that al-Qida was responsible" for the *Cole*.[178] In March 2001, the CIA's briefing slides for Rice were still describing the CIA's "preliminary judgment" that a "strong circumstantial case" could be made against al Qaeda but noting that the CIA continued to lack "conclusive information on external command and control" of the attack.[179] Clarke and his aides continued to provide Rice and Hadley with evidence reinforcing the case against al Qaeda and urging action.[180]

The President explained to us that he had been concerned lest an ineffectual air strike just serve to give Bin Ladin a propaganda advantage. He said he had not been told about Clinton administration warnings to the Taliban. The President told us that he had concluded that the United States must use ground forces for a job like this.[181]

Rice told us that there was never a formal, recorded decision not to retaliate specifically for the *Cole* attack. Exchanges with the President, between the President and Tenet, and between herself and Powell and Rumsfeld had produced a consensus that "tit-for-tat" responses were likely to be counterproductive. This had been the case, she thought, with the cruise missile strikes of August 1998. The new team at the Pentagon did not push for action. On the contrary, Rumsfeld thought that too much time had passed and his deputy, Paul Wolfowitz, thought that the *Cole* attack was "stale." Hadley said that in the end, the administration's real response to the *Cole* would be a new, more aggressive strategy against al Qaeda.[182]

The administration decided to propose to Congress a substantial increase in counterterrorism funding for national security agencies, including the CIA and the FBI. This included a 27 percent increase in counterterrorism funding for the CIA.[183]

Starting a Review

In early March, the administration postponed action on proposals for increasing aid to the Northern Alliance and the Uzbeks. Rice noted at the time that a more wide-ranging examination of policy toward Afghanistan was needed first. She wanted the review very soon.[184]

Rice and others recalled the President saying, "I'm tired of swatting at flies."[185] The President reportedly also said, "I'm tired of playing defense. I want to play offense. I want to take the fight to the terrorists."[186] President Bush explained to us that he had become impatient. He apparently had heard proposals for rolling back al Qaeda but felt that catching terrorists one by one or even cell by cell was not an approach likely to succeed in the long run. At the same time, he said, he understood that policy had to be developed slowly so that diplomacy and financial and military measures could mesh with one another.[187]

Hadley convened an informal Deputies Committee meeting on March 7, when some of the deputies had not yet been confirmed. For the first time, Clarke's various proposals— for aid to the Northern Alliance and the Uzbeks and for Predator missions—went before the group that, in the Bush NSC, would do most of the policy work. Though they made no decisions on these specific proposals, Hadley apparently concluded that there should be a presidential national security policy directive (NSPD) on terrorism.[188]

Clarke would later express irritation about the deputies' insistence that a strategy for coping with al Qaeda be framed within the context of a regional policy. He doubted that the benefits would compensate for the time lost. The administration had in fact proceeded with Principals Committee meetings on topics including Iraq and Sudan without prior contextual review, and Clarke favored moving ahead similarly with a narrow counterterrorism agenda.[189] But the President's senior advisers saw the al Qaeda problem as part of a puzzle that could not be assembled without filling in the pieces for Afghanistan and Pakistan. Rice deferred a Principals Committee meeting on al Qaeda until the deputies had developed a new policy for their consideration.

The full Deputies Committee discussed al Qaeda on April 30. CIA briefing slides described al Qaeda as the "most dangerous group we face," citing its "leadership, experience, resources, safe haven in Afghanistan, [and] focus on attacking U.S." The slides warned, "There will be more attacks."[190]

At the meeting, the deputies endorsed covert aid to Uzbekistan. Regarding the Northern Alliance, they "agreed to make no major commitment at this time." Washington would first consider options for aiding other anti-Taliban groups.[191] Meanwhile, the administration would "initiate a comprehensive review of U.S. policy on Pakistan" and explore policy options on Afghanistan, "including the option of supporting regime change."[192] Working-level officials were also to consider new steps on terrorist financing and America's perennially troubled public diplomacy efforts in the Muslim world, where NSC staff warned that "we have by and large ceded the court of public opinion" to al Qaeda.

While Clarke remained concerned about the pace of the policy review, he now saw a greater possibility of persuading the deputies to recognize the changed nature of terrorism.[193] The process of fleshing out that strategy was under way.

6.5 THE NEW ADMINISTRATION'S APPROACH

The Bush administration in its first months faced many problems other than terrorism. They included the collapse of the Middle East peace process and, in April, a crisis over a U.S. "spy plane" brought down in Chinese territory. The new administration also focused heavily on Russia, a new nuclear strategy that allowed missile defenses, Europe, Mexico, and the Persian Gulf.

In the spring, reporting on terrorism surged dramatically. In chapter 8, we will explore this reporting and the ways agencies responded. These increasingly alarming reports, briefed to the President and top officials, became part of the context in which the new administration weighed its options for policy on al Qaeda.

Except for a few reports that the CSG considered and apparently judged to be unreliable, none of these pointed specifically to possible al Qaeda action inside the United States—although the CSG continued to be concerned about the domestic threat. The mosaic of threat intelligence came from the Counterterrorist Center, which collected only abroad. Its reports were not supplemented by reports from the FBI. Clarke had expressed concern about an al Qaeda presence in the United States, and he worried about an attack on the White House by "Hizbollah, Hamas, al Qida and other terrorist organizations."[194]

In May, President Bush announced that Vice President Cheney would himself lead an effort looking at preparations for managing a possible attack by weapons of mass destruction and at more general problems of national preparedness. The next few months were mainly spent organizing the effort and bringing an admiral from the Sixth Fleet back to Washington to manage it. The Vice President's task force was just getting under way when the 9/11 attack occurred.[19]

On May 29, at Tenet's request, Rice and Tenet converted their usual weekly meeting into a broader discussion on a

Qaeda; participants included Clarke, CTC chief Cofer Black, and "Richard," a group chief with authority over the Bin Ladin unit. Rice asked about "taking the offensive" and whether any approach could be made to influence Bin Ladin or the Taliban. Clarke and Black replied that the CIA's ongoing disruption activities *were* "taking the offensive" and that Bin Ladin could not be deterred. A wide-ranging discussion then ensued about "breaking the back" of Bin Ladin's organization.[196]

Tenet emphasized the ambitious plans for covert action that the CIA had developed in December 2000. In discussing the draft authorities for this program in March, CIA officials had pointed out that the spending level envisioned for these plans was larger than the CIA's entire current budget for counterterrorism covert action. It would be a multi-year program, requiring such levels of spending for about five years.[197]

The CIA official, "Richard," told us that Rice "got it." He said she agreed with his conclusions about what needed to be done, although he complained to us that the policy process did not follow through quickly enough.[198] Clarke and Black were asked to develop a range of options for attacking Bin Ladin's organization, from the least to most ambitious.[199]

Rice and Hadley asked Clarke and his staff to draw up the new presidential directive. On June 7, Hadley circulated the first draft, describing it as "an admittedly ambitious" program for confronting al Qaeda.[200] The draft NSPD's goal was to "eliminate the al Qida network of terrorist groups as a threat to the United States and to friendly governments." It called for a multi-year effort involving diplomacy, covert action, economic measures, law enforcement, public diplomacy, and if necessary military efforts. The State Department was to work with other governments to end all al Qaeda sanctuaries, and also to work with the Treasury Department to disrupt terrorist financing. The CIA was to develop an expanded covert action program including significant additional funding and aid to anti-Taliban groups. The draft also tasked

OMB with ensuring that sufficient funds to support this program were found in U.S. budgets from fiscal years 2002 to 2006.[201]

Rice viewed this draft directive as the embodiment of a comprehensive new strategy employing all instruments of national power to eliminate the al Qaeda threat. Clarke, however, regarded the new draft as essentially similar to the proposal he had developed in December 2000 and put forward to the new administration in January 2001.[202] In May or June, Clarke asked to be moved from his counterterrorism portfolio to a new set of responsibilities for cybersecurity. He told us that he was frustrated with his role and with an administration that he considered not "serious about al Qaeda."[203] If Clarke was frustrated, he never expressed it to her, Rice told us.[204]

Diplomacy in Blind Alleys
Afghanistan.
The new administration had already begun exploring possible diplomatic options, retracing many of the paths traveled by its predecessors. U.S. envoys again pressed the Taliban to turn Bin Ladin "over to a country where he could face justice" and repeated, yet again, the warning that the Taliban would be held responsible for any al Qaeda attacks on U.S. interests.[205] The Taliban's representatives repeated their old arguments. Deputy Secretary of State Richard Armitage told us that while U.S. diplomats were becoming more active on Afghanistan through the spring and summer of 2001, "it would be wrong for anyone to characterize this as a dramatic shift from the previous administration."[206]

In deputies meetings at the end of June, Tenet was tasked to assess the prospects for Taliban cooperation with the United States on al Qaeda. The NSC staff was tasked to flesh out options for dealing with the Taliban. Revisiting these issues tried the patience of some of the officials who felt they had already been down these roads and who found the NSC's procedures slow. "We weren't going fast enough,"

Armitage told us. Clarke kept arguing that moves against the Taliban and al Qaeda should not have to wait months for a larger review of U.S. policy in South Asia. "For the government," Hadley said to us, "we moved it along as fast as we could move it along."[207]

As all hope in moving the Taliban faded, debate revived about giving covert assistance to the regime's opponents. Clarke and the CIA's Cofer Black renewed the push to aid the Northern Alliance. Clarke suggested starting with modest aid, just enough to keep the Northern Alliance in the fight and tie down al Qaeda terrorists, without aiming to overthrow the Taliban.[208]

Rice, Hadley, and the NSC staff member for Afghanistan, Zalmay Khalilzad, told us they opposed giving aid to the Northern Alliance alone. They argued that the program needed to have a big part for Pashtun opponents of the Taliban. They also thought the program should be conducted on a larger scale than had been suggested. Clarke concurred with the idea of a larger program, but he warned that delay risked the Northern Alliance's final defeat at the hands of the Taliban.[209]

During the spring, the CIA, at the NSC's request, had developed draft legal authorities—a presidential finding—to undertake a large-scale program of covert assistance to the Taliban's foes. The draft authorities expressly stated that the goal of the assistance was *not* to overthrow the Taliban. But even this program would be very costly. This was the context for earlier conversations, when in March Tenet stressed the need to consider the impact of such a large program on the political situation in the region and in May Tenet talked to Rice about the need for a multiyear financial commitment.[210]

By July, the deputies were moving toward agreement that some last effort should be made to convince the Taliban to shift position and then, if that failed, the administration would move on the significantly enlarged covert action program. As the draft presidential directive was circulated in July, the State Department sent the deputies a lengthy historical review of U.S. efforts to engage the Taliban about Bin Ladin from 1996 on. "These talks have been fruitless," the State Department concluded.[211]

Arguments in the summer brought to the surface the more fundamental issue of whether the U.S. covert action program should seek to overthrow the regime, intervening decisively in the civil war in order to change Afghanistan's government. By the end of a deputies meeting on September 10, officials formally agreed on a three-phase strategy. First an envoy would give the Taliban a last chance. If this failed, continuing diplomatic pressure would be combined with the planned covert action program encouraging anti-Taliban Afghans of all major ethnic groups to stalemate the Taliban in the civil war and attack al Qaeda bases, while the United States developed an international coalition to undermine the regime. In phase three, if the Taliban's policy still did not change, the deputies agreed that the United States would try covert action to topple the Taliban's leadership from within.[212]

The deputies agreed to revise the al Qaeda presidential directive, then being finalized for presidential approval, in order to add this strategy to it. Armitage explained to us that after months of continuing the previous administration's policy, he and Powell were bringing the State Department to a policy of overthrowing the Taliban. From his point of view, once the United States made the commitment to arm the Northern Alliance, even covertly, it was taking action to initiate regime change, and it should give those opponents the strength to achieve complete victory.[213]

Pakistan.

The Bush administration immediately encountered the dilemmas that arose from the varied objectives the United States was trying to accomplish in its relationship with Pakistan. In February 2001, President Bush wrote General Musharraf on a number of matters. He emphasized that Bin Ladin and al Qaeda were "a direct threat to the United States and its interests that must be addressed." He urged Musharraf to use his influence with the Taliban on Bin Ladin and al Qaeda.[214] Powell and Armitage reviewed the possibility of acquiring more carrots to dangle in front of Pakistan. Given the generally negative view of Pakistan on Capitol Hill, the idea of lifting sanctions may have seemed far-fetched, but perhaps no more so than the idea of persuading Musharraf to antagonize the Islamists in his own government and nation.[215]

On June 18, Rice met with the visiting Pakistani foreign minister, Abdul Sattar. She "really let him have it" about al Qaeda, she told us.[216] Other evidence corroborates her account. But, as she was upbraiding Sattar, Rice recalled thinking that the Pakistani diplomat seemed to have heard it all before. Sattar urged senior U.S. policymakers to engage the Taliban, arguing that such a course would take time but would produce results. In late June, the deputies agreed to review U.S. objectives. Clarke urged Hadley to split off all other issues in U.S.-Pakistani relations and just focus on demanding that Pakistan move vigorously against terrorism—to push the Pakistanis to do *before* an al Qaeda attack what Washington would demand that they do after. He had made similar requests in the Clinton administration; he had no more success with Rice than he had with Berger.[217]

On August 4, President Bush wrote President Musharraf to request his support in dealing with terrorism and to urge Pakistan to engage actively against al Qaeda. The new administration was again registering its concerns, just as its predecessor had, but it was still searching for new incentives to open up diplomatic possibilities. For its part, Pakistan had done little. Assistant Secretary of State Christina Rocca described the administration's plan to break this logjam as a move from "half engagement" to "enhanced engagement." The administration was not ready to confront Islamabad and threaten to rupture relations. Deputy Secretary Armitage told us that before 9/11, the envisioned new approach to Pakistan had not yet been attempted.[218]

Saudi Arabia.

The Bush administration did not develop new diplomatic initiatives on al Qaeda with the Saudi government before 9/11. Vice President Cheney called Crown Prince Abdullah on July 5, 2001, to seek Saudi help in preventing threatened attacks on American facilities in the Kingdom. Secretary of State Powell met with the crown prince twice before 9/11. They discussed topics like Iraq, not al Qaeda. U.S.-Saudi relations in the summer of 2001 were marked by sometimes heated disagreements about ongoing Israeli-Palestinian violence, not about Bin Ladin.[219]

Military Plans

The confirmation of the Pentagon's new leadership was a lengthy process. Deputy Secretary Wolfowitz was confirmed in March 2001 and Under Secretary of Defense for Policy Douglas Feith in July. Though the new officials were briefed about terrorism and some of the earlier planning, including that for Operation Infinite Resolve, they were focused, as Secretary Rumsfeld told us, on creating a twenty-first-century military.[220]

At the Joint Chiefs of Staff, General Shelton did not recall much interest by the new administration in military options against al Qaeda in Afghanistan. He could not recall any specific guidance on the topic from the secretary. Brian Sheridan—the outgoing assistant secretary of defense for special operations and low-intensity conflict (SOLIC), the key counterterrorism policy office in the Pentagon—never briefed Rumsfeld. He departed on January 20; he had not been replaced by 9/11.[221]

Rumsfeld noted to us his own interest in terrorism, which came up often in his regular meetings with Tenet. He thought that the Defense Department, before 9/11, was not organized adequately or prepared to deal with new threats like terrorism. But his time was consumed with getting new officials in place and working on the foundation documents of a new defense policy, the quadrennial defense review, the defense planning guidance, and the existing contingency plans. He did not recall any particular counterterrorism issue that engaged his attention before 9/11, other than the development of the Predator unmanned aircraft system.[222]

The commander of Central Command, General Franks, told us that he did not regard the existing plans as serious. To him a real military plan to address al Qaeda would need to go all the way, following through the details of a full campaign (including the political-military issues of where operations would be based) and securing the rights to fly over neighboring countries.[223]

The draft presidential directive circulated in June 2001 began its discussion of the military by reiterating the Defense Department's lead role in protecting its forces abroad. The draft included a section directing Secretary Rumsfeld to "develop contingency plans" to attack both al Qaeda and Taliban targets in Afghanistan. The new section did not specifically order planning for the use of ground troops, or clarify how this guidance differed from the existing Infinite Resolve plans.[224]

Hadley told us that by circulating this section, a draft Annex B to the directive, the White House was putting the Pentagon on notice that it would need to produce new military plans to address this problem.[225] "The military didn't particularly want this mission," Rice told us.[226]

With this directive still awaiting President Bush's signature, Secretary Rumsfeld did not order his subordinates to begin preparing any new military plans against either al Qaeda or the Taliban before 9/11.

President Bush told us that before 9/11, he had not seen good options for special military operations against Bin Ladin. Suitable bases in neighboring countries were not available and, even if the U.S. forces were sent in, it was not clear where they would go to find Bin Ladin.[227]

President Bush told us that before 9/11 there was an appetite in the government for killing Bin Ladin, not for war. Looking back in 2004, he equated the presidential directive with a readiness to invade Afghanistan. The problem, he said, would have been how to do that if there had not been another attack on America. To many people, he said, it would have seemed like an ultimate act of unilateralism. But he said that he was prepared to take that on.[228]

Domestic Change and Continuity

During the transition, Bush had chosen John Ashcroft, a former senator from Missouri, as his attorney general. On his arrival at the Justice Department, Ashcroft told us, he faced a number of problems spotlighting the need for reform at the FBI.[229]

In February, Clarke briefed Attorney General Ashcroft on his directorate's issues. He reported that at the time, the attorney general acknowledged a "steep learning curve," and asked about the progress of the *Cole* investigation.[230] Neither Ashcroft nor his predecessors received the President's Daily Brief. His office did receive the daily intelligence report for senior officials that, during the spring and summer of 2001, was carrying much of the same threat information.

The FBI was struggling to build up its institutional capabilities to do more against terrorism, relying on a strategy called MAXCAP 05 that had been unveiled in the summer of 2000. The FBI's assistant director for counterterrorism, Dale Watson, told us that he felt the new Justice Department leadership was not supportive of the strategy. Watson had the sense that the Justice Department wanted the FBI to get back to the investigative basics: guns, drugs, and civil rights. The new administration did seek an 8 percent increase in overall FBI funding in its initial budget proposal for fiscal year 2002, including the largest proposed percentage increase in the FBI's counterterrorism program since fiscal year 1997. The additional funds included the FBI's support of the 2002 Winter Olympics in Salt Lake City, Utah (a onetime increase), enhanced security at FBI facilities, and improvements to the FBI's WMD incident response capability.[231]

In May, the Justice Department began shaping plans for building a budget for fiscal year 2003, the process that would usually culminate in an administration proposal at the beginning of 2002. On May 9, the attorney general testified at a congressional hearing concerning federal efforts to combat terrorism. He said that "one of the nation's most fundamental responsibilities is to protect its citizens . . . from terrorist attacks." The budget guidance issued the next day, however, highlighted gun crimes, narcotics trafficking, and civil rights as priorities. Watson told us that he almost fell out of his chair when he saw this memo, because it did not mention counterterrorism. Longtime FBI Director Louis Freeh left in June 2001, after announcing the indictment in the Khobar Towers case that he had worked so long to obtain. Thomas Pickard was the acting director during the summer. Freeh's successor, Robert Mueller, took office just before 9/11.[232]

The Justice Department prepared a draft fiscal year 2003 budget that maintained but did not increase the funding level for counterterrorism in its pending fiscal year 2002 proposal. Pickard appealed for more counterterrorism enhancements, an appeal the attorney general denied on September 10.[233]

Ashcroft had also inherited an ongoing debate on whether and how to modify the 1995 procedures governing intelligence sharing between the FBI and the Justice Department's Criminal Division. But in August 2001, Ashcroft's deputy, Larry Thompson, issued a memorandum reaffirming the 1995 procedures with the clarification that evidence of "any federal felony" was to be immediately reported by the FBI to the Criminal Division. The 1995 procedures remained in effect until after 9/11.[234]

Covert Action and the Predator

In March 2001, Rice asked the CIA to prepare a new series of authorities for covert action in Afghanistan. Rice's recollection was that the idea had come from Clarke and the NSC senior director for intelligence, Mary McCarthy, and had been linked to the proposal for aid to the Northern Alliance and the Uzbeks. Rice described the draft document as providing for "consolidation plus," superseding the various

Clinton administration documents. In fact, the CIA drafted two documents. One was a finding that did concern aid to opponents of the Taliban regime; the other was a draft Memorandum of Notification, which included more open-ended language authorizing possible lethal action in a variety of situations. Tenet delivered both to Hadley on March 28. The CIA's notes for Tenet advised him that "in response to the NSC request for drafts that will help the policymakers review their options, each of the documents has been crafted to provide the Agency with the broadest possible discretion permissible under the law." At the meeting, Tenet argued for deciding on a policy before deciding on the legal authorities to implement it. Hadley accepted this argument, and the draft MON was put on hold.[235]

As the policy review moved forward, the planned covert action program for Afghanistan was included in the draft presidential directive, as part of an "Annex A" on intelligence activities to "eliminate the al Qaeda threat."[236] The main debate during the summer of 2001 concentrated on the one new mechanism for a lethal attack on Bin Ladin—an armed version of the Predator drone.

In the first months of the new administration, questions concerning the Predator became more and more a central focus of dispute. Clarke favored resuming Predator flights over Afghanistan as soon as weather permitted, hoping that they still might provide the elusive "actionable intelligence" to target Bin Ladin with cruise missiles. Learning that the Air Force was thinking of equipping Predators with warheads, Clarke became even more enthusiastic about redeployment.[237]

The CTC chief, Cofer Black, argued against deploying the Predator for reconnaissance purposes. He recalled that the Taliban had spotted a Predator in the fall of 2000 and scrambled their MiG fighters. Black wanted to wait until the armed version was ready. "I do not believe the possible recon value outweighs the risk of possible program termination when the stakes are raised by the Taliban parading a charred Predator in front of CNN," he wrote. Military officers in the Joint Staff shared this concern.[238] There is some dispute as to whether or not the Deputies Committee endorsed resuming reconnaissance flights at its April 30, 2001, meeting. In any event, Rice and Hadley ultimately went along with the CIA and the Pentagon, holding off on reconnaissance flights until the armed Predator was ready.[239]

The CIA's senior management saw problems with the armed Predator as well, problems that Clarke and even Black and Allen were inclined to minimize. One (which also applied to reconnaissance flights) was money. A Predator cost about $3 million. If the CIA flew Predators for its own reconnaissance or covert action purposes, it might be able to borrow them from the Air Force, but it was not clear that the Air Force would bear the cost if a vehicle went down. Deputy Secretary of Defense Wolfowitz took the position that the CIA should have to pay for it; the CIA disagreed.[240]

Second, Tenet in particular questioned whether he, as Director of Central Intelligence, should operate an armed Predator. "This was new ground," he told us. Tenet ticked off key questions: What is the chain of command? Who takes the shot? Are America's leaders comfortable with the CIA doing this, going outside of normal military command and control? Charlie Allen told us that when these questions were discussed at the CIA, he and the Agency's executive director, A. B. "Buzzy" Krongard, had said that either one of them would be happy to pull the trigger, but Tenet was appalled, telling them that they had no authority to do it, nor did he.[241]

Third, the Hellfire warhead carried by the Predator needed work. It had been built to hit tanks, not people. It needed to be designed to explode in a different way, and even then had to be targeted with extreme precision. In the configuration planned by the Air Force through mid-2001, the Predator's missile would not be able to hit a moving vehicle.[242]

White House officials had seen the Predator video of the "man in white." On July 11, Hadley tried to hurry along preparation of the armed system. He directed McLaughlin,

Wolfowitz, and Joint Chiefs Vice Chairman Richard Myers to deploy Predators capable of being armed no later than September 1. He also directed that they have cost-sharing arrangements in place by August 1. Rice told us that this attempt by Hadley to dictate a solution had failed and that she eventually had to intervene herself.[243]

On August 1, the Deputies Committee met again to discuss the armed Predator. They concluded that it was legal for the CIA to kill Bin Ladin or one of his deputies with the Predator. Such strikes would be acts of self-defense that would not violate the ban on assassinations in Executive Order 12333. The big issues—who would pay for what, who would authorize strikes, and who would pull the trigger—were left for the principals to settle. The Defense Department representatives did not take positions on these issues.[244]

The CIA's McLaughlin had also been reticent. When Hadley circulated a memorandum attempting to prod the deputies to reach agreement, McLaughlin sent it back with a handwritten comment on the cost-sharing: "We question whether it is advisable to make such an investment *before* the decision is taken on flying an armed Predator." For Clarke, this came close to being a final straw. He angrily asked Rice to call Tenet. "Either al Qida is a threat worth acting against or it is not," Clarke wrote. "CIA leadership has to decide which it is and cease these bi-polar mood swings."[245]

These debates, though, had little impact in advancing or delaying efforts to make the Predator ready for combat. Those were in the hands of military officers and engineers. General John Jumper had commanded U.S. air forces in Europe and seen Predators used for reconnaissance in the Balkans. He started the program to develop an armed version and, after returning in 2000 to head the Air Combat Command, took direct charge of it.

There were numerous technical problems, especially with the Hellfire missiles. The Air Force tests conducted during the spring were inadequate, so missile testing needed to continue and modifications needed to be made during the summer. Even then, Jumper told us, problems with the equipment persisted. Nevertheless, the Air Force was moving at an extraordinary pace. "In the modern era, since the 1980s," Jumper said to us, "I would be shocked if you found anything that went faster than this."[246]

September 2001
The Principals Committee had its first meeting on al Qaeda on September 4. On the day of the meeting, Clarke sent Rice an impassioned personal note. He criticized U.S. counterterrorism efforts past and present. The "real question" before the principals, he wrote, was "are we serious about dealing with the al Qida threat? . . . Is al Qida a big deal? . . . *Decision makers should imagine themselves on a future day when the CSG has not succeeded in stopping al Qida attacks and hundreds of Americans lay dead in several countries, including the US*," Clarke wrote. "What would those decision makers wish that they had done earlier? That future day could happen at any time."[247]

Clarke then turned to the *Cole*. *"The fact that the USS Cole was attacked during the last Administration does not absolve us of responding for the attack,"* he wrote. "Many in al Qida and the Taliban may have drawn the wrong lesson from the Cole: that they can kill Americans without there being a US response, without there being a price. . . . One might have thought that with a $250m hole in a destroyer and 17 dead sailors, the Pentagon might have wanted to respond. Instead, they have often talked about the fact that there is 'nothing worth hitting in Afghanistan' and said 'the cruise missiles cost more than the jungle gyms and mud huts' at terrorist camps." Clarke could not understand *"why we continue to allow the existence of large scale al Qida bases where we know people are being trained to kill Americans."*[248]

Turning to the CIA, Clarke warned that its bureaucracy, which was "masterful at passive aggressive behavior," would resist funding the new national security presidential directive, leaving it a "hollow shell of words without deeds." The CIA would insist its other priorities were more important. Invoking President Bush's own language, Clarke wrote, *"You are left with a modest effort to swat flies,* to try to prevent specific al Qida attacks by using [intelligence] to detect them and friendly governments' police and intelligence officers to stop them. *You are left waiting for the big attack,* with lots of casualties, after which some major US retaliation will be in order[.]"[249]

Rice told us she took Clarke's memo as a warning not to get dragged down by bureaucratic inertia.[250] While his arguments have force, we also take Clarke's jeremiad as something more. After nine years on the NSC staff and more than three years as the president's national coordinator, he had often failed to persuade these agencies to adopt his views, or to persuade his superiors to set an agenda of the sort he wanted or that the whole government could support.

Meanwhile, another counterterrorism veteran, Cofer Black, was preparing his boss for the principals meeting. He advised Tenet that the draft presidential directive envisioned an ambitious covert action program, but that the authorities for it had not yet been approved and the funding still had not been found. If the CIA was reluctant to use the Predator, Black did not mention it. He wanted "a timely decision from the Principals," adding that the window for missions within 2001 was a short one. The principals would have to decide whether Rice, Tenet, Rumsfeld, or someone else would give the order to fire.[251]

At the September 4 meeting, the principals approved the draft presidential directive with little discussion.[252] Rice told us that she had, at some point, told President Bush that she and his other advisers thought it would take three years or so for their al Qaeda strategy to work.[253] They then discussed the armed Predator.

Hadley portrayed the Predator as a useful tool, although perhaps not for immediate use. Rice, who had been advised by her staff that the armed Predator was not ready for deployment, commented about the potential for using the armed Predator in the spring of 2002.[254]

The State Department supported the armed Predator, although Secretary Powell was not convinced that Bin Ladin was as easy to target as had been suggested. Treasury Secretary Paul O'Neill was skittish, cautioning about the implications of trying to kill an individual.[255]

The Defense Department favored strong action. Deputy Secretary Wolfowitz questioned the United States' ability to deliver Bin Ladin and bring him to justice. He favored going after Bin Ladin as part of a larger air strike, similar to what had been done in the 1986 U.S. strike against Libya. General Myers emphasized the Predator's value for surveillance, perhaps enabling broader air strikes that would go beyond Bin Ladin to attack al Qaeda's training infrastructure.[256]

The principals also discussed which agency—CIA or Defense—should have the authority to fire a missile from the armed Predator.[257]

At the end, Rice summarized the meeting's conclusions. The armed Predator capability was needed but not ready. The Predator would be available for the military to consider along with its other options. The CIA should consider flying reconnaissance-only missions. The principals—including the previously reluctant Tenet—thought that such reconnaissance flights were a good idea, combined with other efforts to get actionable intelligence. Tenet deferred an answer on the additional reconnaissance flights, conferred with his staff after the meeting, and then directed the CIA to press ahead with them.[258]

A few days later, a final version of the draft presidential directive was circulated, incorporating two minor changes made by the principals.[259]

On September 9, dramatic news arrived from Afghanistan. The leader of the Northern Alliance, Ahmed Shah Massoud, had granted an interview in his bungalow near the Tajikistan border with two men whom the Northern Alliance leader had been told were Arab journalists. The supposed reporter and cameraman—actually al Qaeda assassins—then set off a bomb, riddling Massoud's chest with shrapnel. He died minutes later.

On September 10, Hadley gathered the deputies to finalize their three-phase, multiyear plan to pressure and perhaps ultimately topple the Taliban leadership.[260]

That same day, Hadley instructed DCI Tenet to have the CIA prepare new draft legal authorities for the "broad covert action program" envisioned by the draft presidential directive. Hadley also directed Tenet to prepare a separate section "authorizing a broad range of other covert activities, including authority to capture or to use lethal force" against al Qaeda command-and-control elements. This section would supersede the Clinton-era documents. Hadley wanted the authorities to be flexible and broad enough "to cover any additional UBL-related covert actions contemplated."[261]

Funding still needed to be located. The military component remained unclear. Pakistan remained uncooperative. The domestic policy institutions were largely uninvolved. But the pieces were coming together for an integrated policy dealing with al Qaeda, the Taliban, and Pakistan.

CHAPTER SEVEN

The Attack Looms

7.1 FIRST ARRIVALS IN CALIFORNIA

In chapter 5 we described the Southeast Asia travels of Nawaf al Hazmi, Khalid al Mihdhar, and others in January 2000 on the first part of the "planes operation." In that chapter we also described how Mihdhar was spotted in Kuala Lumpur early in January 2000, along with associates who were not identified, and then was lost to sight when the group passed through Bangkok. On January 15, Hazmi and Mihdhar arrived in Los Angeles. They spent about two weeks there before moving on to San Diego.[1]

Two Weeks in Los Angeles

Why Hazmi and Mihdhar came to California, we do not know for certain. Khalid Sheikh Mohammed (KSM), the organizer of the planes operation, explains that California was a convenient point of entry from Asia and had the added benefit of being far away from the intended target area.[2]

Hazmi and Mihdhar were ill-prepared for a mission in the United States. Their only qualifications for this plot were their devotion to Usama Bin Ladin, their veteran service, and their ability to get valid U.S. visas. Neither had spent any substantial time in the West, and neither spoke much, if any, English.[3]

It would therefore be plausible that they or KSM would have tried to identify, in advance, a friendly contact for them in the United States. In detention, KSM denies that al Qaeda had any agents in Southern California. We do not credit this denial.[4] We believe it is unlikely that Hazmi and Mihdhar—neither of whom, in contrast to the Hamburg group, had any prior exposure to life in the West—would have come to the United States without arranging to receive assistance from one or more individuals informed in advance of their arrival.[5]

KSM says that though he told others involved in the conspiracy to stay away from mosques and to avoid establishing personal contacts, he made an exception in this case and instructed Hazmi and Mihdhar to pose as newly arrived Saudi students and seek assistance at local mosques. He counted on their breaking off any such relationships once they moved to the East Coast.[6] Our inability to ascertain the activities of Hazmi and Mihdhar during their first two weeks in the United States may reflect al Qaeda tradecraft designed to protect the identity of anyone who may have assisted them during that period.

Hazmi and Mihdhar were directed to enroll in English-language classes upon arriving in Southern California, so that they could begin pilot training as soon as possible. KSM claims to have steered the two to San Diego on the basis of his own research, which supposedly included thumbing through a San Diego phone book acquired at a Karachi flea market. Contradicting himself, he also says that, as instructed, they attempted to enroll in three language schools in Los Angeles.[7]

After the pair cleared Immigration and Customs at Los Angeles International Airport, we do not know where they went.[8] They appear to have obtained assistance from the Muslim community, specifically the community surrounding the King Fahd mosque in Culver City, one of the most prominent mosques in Southern California.

It is fairly certain that Hazmi and Mihdhar spent time at the King Fahd mosque and made some acquaintances there. One witness interviewed by the FBI after the September 11 attacks has said he first met the hijackers at the mosque in early 2000. Furthermore, one of the people who would be-

friend them—a man named Mohdar Abdullah—recalled a
trip with Hazmi and Mihdhar to Los Angeles in June when,
on their arrival, the three went to the King Fahd mosque.
There Hazmi and Mihdhar greeted various individuals
whom they appeared to have met previously, including a
man named "Khallam." In Abdullah's telling, when Khallam
visited the al Qaeda operatives at their motel that evening,
Abdullah was asked to leave the room so that Hazmi, Mihdhar, and Khallam could meet in private. The identity of
Khallam and his purpose in meeting with Hazmi and Mihdhar remain unknown.[9]

To understand what Hazmi and Mihdhar did in their first
weeks in the United States, evidently staying in Los Angeles, we have investigated whether anyone associated with the
King Fahd mosque assisted them. This subject has received
substantial attention in the media. Some have speculated
that Fahad al Thumairy—an imam at the mosque and an ac-
credited diplomat at the Saudi Arabian consulate from 1996
until 2003—may have played a role in helping the hijackers
establish themselves on their arrival in Los Angeles. This
speculation is based, at least in part, on Thumairy's reported
leadership of an extremist faction at the mosque.[10]

A well-known figure at the King Fahd mosque and within
the Los Angeles Muslim community, Thumairy was reputed
to be an Islamic fundamentalist and a strict adherent to or-
thodox Wahhabi doctrine. Some Muslims concerned about
his preaching have said he "injected non-Islamic themes into
his guidance/prayers at the [King Fahd] Mosque" and had
followers "supportive of the events of September 11,
2001."[11] Thumairy appears to have associated with a particularly radical faction within the community of local worshippers, and had a network of contacts in other cities in the
United States. After 9/11, Thumairy's conduct was a subject
of internal debate among some Saudi officials. He apparently lost his position at the King Fahd mosque, possibly because of his immoderate reputation. On May 6, 2003,
Thumairy attempted to reenter the United States from Saudi
Arabia but was refused entry, based on a determination by

the State Department that he might be connected with terrorist activity.[12]

When interviewed by both the FBI and the Commission staff, Thumairy has denied preaching anti-Western sermons, much less promoting violent jihad. More to the point, he claimed not to recognize either Hazmi or Mihdhar. Both denials are somewhat suspect. (He likewise denied knowing Omar al Bayoumi—a man from San Diego we will discuss shortly—even though witnesses and telephone records establish that the two men had contact with each other. Similarly, Thumairy's claim not to know Mohdar Abdullah is belied by Abdullah's contrary assertion.) On the other hand, Thumairy undoubtedly met with and provided religious counseling to countless individuals during his tenure at the King Fahd mosque, so he might not remember two transients like Hazmi and Mihdhar several years later.[13]

The circumstantial evidence makes Thumairy a logical person to consider as a possible contact for Hazmi and Mihdhar. Yet, after exploring the available leads, we have not found evidence that Thumairy provided assistance to the two operatives.[14]

We do not pick up their trail until February 1, 2000, when they encountered Omar al Bayoumi and Caysan Bin Don at a halal food restaurant on Venice Boulevard in Culver City, a few blocks away from the King Fahd mosque. Bayoumi and Bin Don have both told us that they had driven up from San Diego earlier that day so that Bayoumi could address a visa issue and collect some papers from the Saudi consulate. Bayoumi heard Hazmi and Mihdhar speaking in what he recognized to be Gulf Arabic and struck up a conversation. Since Bin Don knew only a little Arabic, he had to rely heavily on Bayoumi to translate for him.[15]

Mihdhar and Hazmi said they were students from Saudi Arabia who had just arrived in the United States to study English. They said they were living in an apartment near the restaurant but did not specify the address. They did not like Los Angeles and were having a hard time, especially because they did not know anyone. Bayoumi told them how pleasant San Diego was and offered to help them settle there. The two pairs then left the restaurant and went their separate ways.[16]

Bayoumi and Bin Don have been interviewed many times about the February 1, 2000, lunch. For the most part, their respective accounts corroborate each other. However, Bayoumi has said that he and Bin Don attempted to visit the King Fahd mosque after lunch but could not find it. Bin Don, on the other hand, recalls visiting the mosque twice that day for prayers, both before and after the meal. Bin Don's recollection is spotty and inconsistent. Bayoumi's version can be challenged as well, since the mosque is close to the restaurant and Bayoumi had visited it, and the surrounding area, on multiple occasions, including twice within six weeks of February 1. We do not know whether the lunch encounter occurred by chance or design. We know about it because Bayoumi told law enforcement that it happened.[17]

Bayoumi, then 42 years old, was in the United States as a business student, supported by a private contractor for the Saudi Civil Aviation Authority, where Bayoumi had worked for over 20 years.[18] The object of considerable media speculation following 9/11, he lives now in Saudi Arabia, well aware of his notoriety. Both we and the FBI have interviewed him and investigated evidence about him.

Bayoumi is a devout Muslim, obliging and gregarious. He spent much of his spare time involved in religious study and helping run a mosque in El Cajon, about 15 miles from San Diego. It is certainly possible that he has dissembled about some aspects of his story, perhaps to counter suspicion. On the other hand, we have seen no credible evidence that he believed in violent extremism or knowingly aided extremist groups.[19] Our investigators who have dealt directly with him and studied his background find him to be an unlikely candidate for clandestine involvement with Islamist extremists.

The Move to San Diego

By February 4, Hazmi and Mihdhar had come to San Diego from Los Angeles, possibly driven by Mohdar Abdullah.

Abdullah, a Yemeni university student in his early 20s, is fluent in both Arabic and English, and was perfectly suited to assist the hijackers in pursuing their mission.[20]

After 9/11, Abdullah was interviewed many times by the FBI. He admitted knowing of Hazmi and Mihdhar's extremist leanings and Mihdhar's involvement with the Islamic Army of Aden (a group with ties to al Qaeda) back in Yemen. Abdullah clearly was sympathetic to those extremist views. During a post-9/11 search of his possessions, the FBI found a notebook (belonging to someone else) with references to planes falling from the sky, mass killing, and hijacking. Further, when detained as a material witness following the 9/11 attacks, Abdullah expressed hatred for the U.S. government and "stated that the U.S. brought 'this' on themselves."[21]

When interviewed by the FBI after 9/11, Abdullah denied having advance knowledge of attacks. In May 2004, however, we learned of reports about Abdullah bragging to fellow inmates at a California prison in September–October 2003 that he had known Hazmi and Mihdhar were planning a terrorist attack. The stories attributed to Abdullah are not entirely consistent with each other. Specifically, according to one inmate, Abdullah claimed an unnamed individual had notified him that Hazmi and Mihdhar would be arriving in Los Angeles with plans to carry out an attack. Abdullah allegedly told the same inmate that he had driven the two al Qaeda operatives from Los Angeles to San Diego, but did not say when this occurred. We have been unable to corroborate this account.[22]

Another inmate has recalled Abdullah claiming he first heard about the hijackers' terrorist plans after they arrived in San Diego, when they told him they planned to fly an airplane into a building and invited him to join them on the plane. According to this inmate, Abdullah also claimed to have found out about the 9/11 attacks three weeks in advance, a claim that appears to dovetail with evidence that Abdullah may have received a phone call from Hazmi around that time, that he stopped making calls from his telephone after August 25, 2001, and that, according to his friends, he started acting strangely.[23]

Although boasts among prison inmates often tend to be unreliable, this evidence is obviously important. To date, neither we nor the FBI have been able to verify Abdullah's alleged jailhouse statements, despite investigative efforts.

We thus do not know when or how Hazmi and Mihdhar first came to San Diego. We do know that on February 4, they went to the Islamic Center of San Diego to find Omar al Bayoumi and take him up on his offer of help. Bayoumi obliged by not only locating an apartment but also helping them fill out the lease application, co-signing the lease and, when the real estate agent refused to take cash for a deposit, helping them open a bank account (which they did with a $9,900 deposit); he then provided a certified check from his own account for which the al Qaeda operatives reimbursed him on the spot for the deposit. Neither then nor later did Bayoumi give money to either Hazmi or Mihdhar, who had received money from KSM.[24]

Hazmi and Mihdhar moved in with no furniture and practically no possessions. Soon after the move, Bayoumi used their apartment for a party attended by some 20 male members of the Muslim community. At Bayoumi's request, Bin Don videotaped the gathering with Bayoumi's video camera. Hazmi and Mihdhar did not mingle with the other guests and reportedly spent most of the party by themselves off camera, in a back room.[25]

Hazmi and Mihdhar immediately started looking for a different place to stay. Based on their comment to Bayoumi about the first apartment being expensive, one might infer that they wanted to save money. They may also have been reconsidering the wisdom of living so close to the video camera–wielding Bayoumi, who Hazmi seemed to think was some sort of Saudi spy. Just over a week after moving in, Hazmi and Mihdhar filed a 30-day notice of intention to vacate. Bayoumi apparently loaned them his cell phone to help them check out possibilities for new accommodations.[26]

Their initial effort to move turned out poorly. An acquain-

tance arranged with his landlord to have Mihdhar take over
his apartment. Mihdhar put down a $650 deposit and signed
a lease for the apartment effective March 1. Several weeks
later, Mihdhar sought a refund of his deposit, claiming he no
longer intended to move in because the apartment was too
messy. When the landlord refused to refund the deposit, Mihdhar became belligerent. The landlord remembers him
"ranting and raving" as if he were "psychotic."[27]

Hazmi and Mihdhar finally found a room to rent in the
home of an individual they had met at a mosque in San
Diego. According to the homeowner, the future hijackers
moved in on May 10, 2000. Mihdhar moved out after only
about a month. On June 9, he left San Diego to return to
Yemen. Hazmi, on the other hand, stayed at this house for
the rest of his time in California, until mid-December; he
would then leave for Arizona with a newly arrived 9/11
hijacker-pilot, Hani Hanjour.[28]

While in San Diego, Hazmi and Mihdhar played the part
of recently arrived foreign students. They continued to reach
out to members of the Muslim community for help. At least
initially, they found well-meaning new acquaintances at the
Islamic Center of San Diego, which was only a stone's throw
from the apartment where they first lived. For example,
when they purchased a used car (with cash), they bought it
from a man who lived across the street from the Islamic
Center and who let them use his address in registering the
vehicle, an accommodation "to help a fellow Muslim
brother." Similarly, in April, when their cash supply may
have been dwindling, Hazmi persuaded the administrator of
the Islamic Center to let him use the administrator's bank
account to receive a $5,000 wire transfer from someone in
Dubai, in the United Arab Emirates (this was KSM's
nephew, Ali Abdul Aziz Ali).[29]

Hazmi and Mihdhar visited other mosques as well, mixing comfortably as devout worshippers. During the operatives' critical first weeks in San Diego, Mohdar Abdullah
helped them. Translating between English and Arabic, he assisted them in obtaining California driver's licenses and with

applying to language and flight schools. Abdullah also introduced them to his circle of friends; he shared an apartment with some of those friends near the Rabat mosque in La Mesa, a few miles from the hijackers' residence.[30]

Abdullah has emerged as a key associate of Hazmi and Mihdhar in San Diego. Detained after 9/11 (first as a material witness, then on immigration charges), he was deported to Yemen on May 21, 2004, after the U.S. Attorney for the Southern District of California declined to prosecute him on charges arising out of his alleged jailhouse admissions concerning the 9/11 operatives. The Department of Justice declined to delay his removal pending further investigation of this new information.[31]

Other friends of Abdullah also translated for Hazmi and Mihdhar and helped them adjust to life in San Diego. Some held extremist beliefs or were well acquainted with known extremists. For example, immediately after 9/11, Osama Awadallah, a Yemeni whose telephone number was found in Hazmi's Toyota at Washington Dulles International Airport, was found to possess photos, videos, and articles relating to Bin Ladin. Awadallah also had lived in a house where copies of Bin Ladin's fatwas and other similar materials were distributed to the residents. Omar Bakarbashat, a Saudi, also met Hazmi and Mihdhar at the Rabat mosque. He admitted helping Hazmi to learn English and taking over the operatives' first apartment in San Diego after they moved out. Bakarbashat apparently had downloaded stridently anti-American Web pages to his computer's hard drive.[32]

Another potentially significant San Diego contact for Hazmi and Mihdhar was Anwar Aulaqi, an imam at the Rabat mosque. Born in New Mexico and thus a U.S. citizen, Aulaqi grew up in Yemen and studied in the United States on a Yemeni government scholarship. We do not know how or when Hazmi and Mihdhar first met Aulaqi. The operatives may even have met or at least talked to him the same day they first moved to San Diego. Hazmi and Mihdhar reportedly respected Aulaqi as a religious figure and developed a close relationship with him.[33]

When interviewed after 9/11, Aulaqi said he did not recognize Hazmi's name but did identify his picture. Although Aulaqi admitted meeting with Hazmi several times, he claimed not to remember any specifics of what they discussed. He described Hazmi as a soft-spoken Saudi student who used to appear at the mosque with a companion but who did not have a large circle of friends.[34]

Aulaqi left San Diego in mid-2000, and by early 2001 had relocated to Virginia. As we will discuss later, Hazmi eventually showed up at Aulaqi's mosque in Virginia, an appearance that may not have been coincidental. We have been unable to learn enough about Aulaqi's relationship with Hazmi and Mihdhar to reach a conclusion.[35]

In sum, although the evidence is thin as to specific motivations, our overall impression is that soon after arriving in California, Hazmi and Mihdhar sought out and found a group of young and ideologically like-minded Muslims with roots in Yemen and Saudi Arabia, individuals mainly associated with Mohdar Abdullah and the Rabat mosque. The al Qaeda operatives lived openly in San Diego under their true names, listing Hazmi in the telephone directory. They managed to avoid attracting much attention.

Flight Training Fails; Mihdhar Bails Out

Hazmi and Mihdhar came to the United States to learn English, take flying lessons, and become pilots as quickly as possible. They turned out, however, to have no aptitude for English. Even with help and tutoring from Mohdar Abdullah and other bilingual friends, Hazmi and Mihdhar's efforts to learn proved futile. This lack of language skills in turn became an insurmountable barrier to learning how to fly.[36]

A pilot they consulted at one school, the Sorbi Flying Club in San Diego, spoke Arabic. He explained to them that their flight instruction would begin with small planes. Hazmi and Mihdhar emphasized their interest in learning to fly jets, Boeing aircraft in particular, and asked where they might enroll to train on jets right away. Convinced that the two were either joking or dreaming, the pilot responded that no such school existed. Other instructors who worked with Hazmi and Mihdhar remember them as poor students who focused on learning to control the aircraft in flight but took no interest in takeoffs or landings. By the end of May 2000, Hazmi and Mihdhar had given up on learning how to fly.[37]

Mihdhar's mind seems to have been with his family back in Yemen, as evidenced by calls he made from the apartment telephone. When news of the birth of his first child arrived, he could stand life in California no longer. In late May and early June of 2000, he closed his bank account, transferred the car registration to Hazmi, and arranged his return to Yemen. According to KSM, Mihdhar was bored in San Diego and foresaw no problem in coming back to the United States since he had not overstayed his visa. Hazmi and Mohdar Abdullah accompanied him to Los Angeles on June 9. After visiting the King Fahd mosque one last time with his friends, Mihdhar left the country the following day.[38]

KSM kept in fairly close touch with his operatives, using a variety of methods. When Bin Ladin called KSM back from Pakistan to Afghanistan in the spring of 2000, KSM asked Khallad (whom we introduced in chapter 5) to maintain email contact with Hazmi in the United States. Mihdhar's decision to strand Hazmi in San Diego enraged KSM, who had not authorized the departure and feared it would compromise the plan. KSM attempted to drop Mihdhar from the planes operation and would have done so, he says, had he not been overruled by Bin Ladin.[39]

Following Mihdhar's departure, Hazmi grew lonely and worried that he would have trouble managing by himself. He prayed with his housemate each morning at 5:00 A.M. and attended services at the Islamic Center. He borrowed his housemate's computer for Internet access, following news coverage of fighting in Chechnya and Bosnia. With his housemate's help, Hazmi also used the Internet to search for a wife (after obtaining KSM's approval to marry). This search did not succeed. Although he developed a close relationship with his housemate, Hazmi preferred not to use the house telephone, continuing the practice he and Mihdhar had adopted of going outside to make phone calls.[40]

After Mihdhar left, other students moved into the house. One of these, Yazeed al Salmi, stands out. In July 2000, Salmi purchased $4,000 in traveler's checks at a bank in Riyadh, Saudi Arabia. On September 5, Hazmi deposited $1,900 of the traveler's checks into his bank account, after withdrawing the same amount in cash. It is possible that Hazmi was simply cashing the traveler's checks for a friend. We do not know; Salmi claims not to remember the transaction. After 9/11, Salmi reportedly confided to Mohdar Abdullah that he had previously known terrorist pilot Hani Hanjour. After living in the same house with Hazmi for about a month, Salmi moved to the La Mesa apartment shared by Abdullah and others.[41]

By the fall of 2000, Hazmi no longer even pretended to study English or take flying lessons. Aware that his co-conspirators in Afghanistan and Pakistan would be sending him a new colleague shortly, he bided his time and worked for a few weeks at a gas station in La Mesa where some of his friends, including Abdullah, were employed. On one occasion, Hazmi told a fellow employee that he was planning to find a better job, and let slip a prediction that he would become famous.[42]

On December 8, 2000, Hani Hanjour arrived in San Diego, having traveled from Dubai via Paris and Cincinnati. Hazmi likely picked up Hanjour at the airport. We do not know where Hanjour stayed; a few days later, both men left San Diego. Before departing, they visited the gas station in La Mesa, where Hazmi reportedly introduced Hanjour as a "long time friend from Saudi Arabia." Hazmi told his housemate that he and his friend "Hani" were headed for San Jose to take flying lessons and told his friends that he would stay in touch. Hazmi promised to return to San Diego soon, and he and Hanjour drove off.[43]

Hazmi did not sever all contact with his friends in San Diego. According to Abdullah, after Hazmi left San Diego in December 2000, he telephoned Abdullah twice: in December 2000 or January 2001, Hazmi said he was in San Francisco and would be attending flight school there; about two weeks later, he said he was attending flight school in Arizona. Some evidence, which we will discuss later, indicates that Hazmi contacted Abdullah again, in August 2001. In addition, during the month following Hazmi's departure from San Diego, he emailed his housemate three times, including a January 2001 email that Hazmi signed "Smer," an apparent attempt to conceal his identity that struck the housemate as strange at the time. Hazmi also telephoned his housemate that he and his friend had decided to take flight lessons in Arizona, and that Mihdhar was now back in Yemen. That was their last contact. When the housemate emailed Hazmi in February and March of 2001 to find out how he was faring, Hazmi did not reply.[44]

The housemate who rented the room to Hazmi and Mihdhar during 2000 is an apparently law-abiding citizen with long-standing, friendly contacts among local police and FBI personnel. He did not see anything unusual enough in the behavior of Hazmi or Mihdhar to prompt him to report to his law enforcement contacts. Nor did those contacts ask him for information about his tenants/housemates.

7.2 THE 9/11 PILOTS IN THE UNITED STATES

The Hamburg Pilots Arrive in the United States

In the early summer of 2000, the Hamburg group arrived in the United States to begin flight training. Marwan al Shehhi came on May 29, arriving in Newark on a flight from Brussels. He went to New York City and waited there for Mohamed Atta to join him. On June 2, Atta traveled to the Czech Republic by bus from Germany and then flew from Prague to Newark the next day. According to Ramzi Binalshibh, Atta did not meet with anyone in Prague; he simply believed it would contribute to operational security to fly out of Prague rather than Hamburg, the departure point for much of his previous international travel.[45]

Atta and Shehhi had not settled on where they would obtain their flight training. In contrast, Ziad Jarrah had already arranged to attend the Florida Flight Training Center (FFTC) in Venice, Florida. Jarrah arrived in Newark on June 27 and then flew to Venice. He immediately began the private pilot program at FFTC, intending to get a multi-engine license. Jarrah moved in with some of the flight instructors affiliated with his school and bought a car.[46]

While Jarrah quickly settled into training in Florida, Atta and Shehhi kept searching for a flight school. After visiting the Airman Flight School in Norman, Oklahoma (where Zacarias Moussaoui would enroll several months later and where another al Qaeda operative, Ihab Ali, had taken lessons in the mid-1990s), Atta started flight instruction at Huffman Aviation in Venice, Florida, and both Atta and Shehhi subsequently enrolled in the Accelerated Pilot Program at that school. By the end of July, both of them took solo flights, and by mid-August they passed the private pilot airman test. They trained through the summer at Huffman, while Jarrah continued his training at FFTC.[47]

The Hamburg operatives paid for their flight training primarily with funds wired from Dubai by KSM's nephew, Ali Abdul Aziz Ali. Between June 29 and September 17, 2000, Ali sent Shehhi and Atta a total of $114,500 in five transfers ranging from $5,000 to $70,000. Ali relied on the unremarkable nature of his transactions, which were essentially invisible amid the billions of dollars flowing daily across the globe.[48] Ali was not required to provide identification in sending this money and the aliases he used were not questioned.[49]

In mid-September, Atta and Shehhi applied to change their immigration status from tourist to student, stating their intention to study at Huffman until September 1, 2001. In late September, they decided to enroll at Jones Aviation in Sarasota, Florida, about 20 miles north of Venice. According to the instructor at Jones, the two were aggressive, rude, and sometimes even fought with him to take over the controls during their training flights. In early October, they took the Stage I exam for instruments rating at Jones Aviation and failed. Very upset, they said they were in a hurry because jobs awaited them at home. Atta and Shehhi then returned to Huffman.[50]

In the meantime, Jarrah obtained a single-engine private pilot certificate in early August. Having reached that milestone, he departed on the first of five foreign trips he would take after first entering the United States. In October, he flew back to Germany to visit his girlfriend, Aysel Senguen. The two traveled to Paris before Jarrah returned to Florida on October 29. His relationship with her remained close throughout his time in the United States. In addition to his trips, Jarrah made hundreds of phone calls to her and communicated frequently by email.[51]

Jarrah was supposed to be joined at FFTC by Ramzi Binalshibh, who even sent the school a deposit. But Binalshibh could not obtain a U.S. visa. His first applications in May and June 2000 were denied because he lacked established ties in Germany ensuring his return from a trip to the United States. In September, he went home to Yemen to apply for a visa from there, but was denied on grounds that he also lacked sufficient ties to Yemen. In October, he tried one last time, in Berlin, applying for a student visa to attend "aviation language school," but the prior denials were noted and this application was denied as well, as incomplete.[52]

Unable to participate directly in the operation, Binalshibh instead took on the role of coordinating between KSM and the operatives in the United States. Apart from sending a total of about $10,000 in wire transfers to Atta and Shehhi during the summer of 2000, one of Binalshibh's first tasks in his new role as plot coordinator was to assist another possible pilot, Zacarias Moussaoui.[53]

In the fall of 2000, KSM had sent Moussaoui to Malaysia for flight training, but Moussaoui did not find a school he liked. He worked instead on other terrorist schemes, such as buying four tons of ammonium nitrate for bombs to be planted on cargo planes flying to the United States. When KSM found out, he recalled Moussaoui back to Pakistan and directed him to go to the United States for flight training. In early October, Moussaoui went to London. When Binalshibh visited London in December, he stayed at the same 16-room dormitory where Moussaoui was still residing. From London, Moussaoui sent inquiries to the Airman Flight School in Norman, Oklahoma.[54]

Confronting training or travel problems with Hazmi, Mihdhar, Binalshibh, and Moussaoui, al Qaeda was looking for another possible pilot candidate. A new recruit with just the right background conveniently presented himself in Afghanistan.

The Fourth Pilot: Hani Hanjour

Hani Hanjour, from Ta'if, Saudi Arabia, first came to the United States in 1991 to study at the Center for English as a Second Language at the University of Arizona. He seems to have been a rigorously observant Muslim. According to his older brother, Hani Hanjour went to Afghanistan for the first time in the late 1980s, as a teenager, to participate in the jihad and, because the Soviets had already withdrawn, worked for a relief agency there.[55]

In 1996, Hanjour returned to the United States to pursue flight training, after being rejected by a Saudi flight school. He checked out flight schools in Florida, California, and Arizona; and he briefly started at a couple of them before returning to Saudi Arabia. In 1997, he returned to Florida and then, along with two friends, went back to Arizona and began his flight training there in earnest. After about three months, Hanjour was able to obtain his private pilot's license. Several more months of training yielded him a commercial pilot certificate, issued by the Federal Aviation Administration (FAA) in April 1999. He then returned to Saudi Arabia.[56]

Hanjour reportedly applied to the civil aviation school in Jeddah after returning home, but was rejected. He stayed home for a while and then told his family he was going to the United Arab Emirates to work for an airline. Where Hanjour actually traveled during this time period is unknown. It is possible he went to the training camps in Afghanistan.[57]

The fact that Hanjour spent so much time in Arizona may be significant. A number of important al Qaeda figures attended the University of Arizona in Tucson or lived in Tucson in the 1980s and early 1990s.[58] Some of Hanjour's known Arizona associates from the time of his flight training in the late 1990s have also raised suspicion.[59] FBI investigators have speculated that al Qaeda may have directed other extremist Muslims in the Phoenix area to enroll in aviation training. It is clear that when Hanjour lived in Arizona in the 1990s, he associated with several individuals holding extremist beliefs who have been the subject of counterterrorism investigations. Some of them trained with Hanjour to be pilots. Others had apparent connections to al Qaeda, including training in Afghanistan.[60]

By the spring of 2000, Hanjour was back in Afghanistan. According to KSM, Hanjour was sent to him in Karachi for inclusion in the plot after Hanjour was identified in al Qaeda's al Faruq camp as a trained pilot, on the basis of background information he had provided. Hanjour had been at a camp in Afghanistan for a few weeks when Bin Ladin or Atef apparently realized that he was a trained pilot; he was told to report to KSM, who then trained Hanjour for a few days in the use of code words.[61]

On June 20, Hanjour returned home to Saudi Arabia. He obtained a U.S. student visa on September 25 and told his family he was returning to his job in the UAE. Hanjour did go to the UAE, but to meet facilitator Ali Abdul Aziz Ali.[62]

Ali opened a bank account in Dubai for Hanjour and providing the initial funds for his trip. On December 8, Hanjour traveled to San Diego. His supposed destination was an English as a second language program in Oakland, California, which he had scheduled before leaving Saudi Arabia but never attended. Instead, as mentioned earlier, he joined Nawaf al Hazmi in San Diego.[63]

Hazmi and Hanjour left San Diego almost immediately and drove to Arizona. Settling in Mesa, Hanjour began refresher training at his old school, Arizona Aviation. He wanted to train on multi-engine planes, but had difficulties because his English was not good enough. The instructor advised him to discontinue but Hanjour said he could not go home without completing the training. In early 2001, he started training on a Boeing 737 simulator at Pan Am International Flight Academy in Mesa. An instructor there found his work well below standard and discouraged him from continuing. Again, Hanjour persevered; he completed the initial training by the end of March 2001. At that point, Hanjour and Hazmi vacated their apartment and started driving east, anticipating the arrival of the "muscle hijackers"—the operatives who would storm the cockpits and control the passengers. By as early as April 4, Hanjour and Hazmi had arrived in Falls Church, Virginia.[64]

The three pilots in Florida continued with their training. Atta and Shehhi finished up at Huffman and earned their instrument certificates from the FAA in November. In mid-December 2000, they passed their commercial pilot tests and received their licenses. They then began training to fly large jets on a flight simulator. At about the same time, Jarrah began simulator training, also in Florida but at a different center. By the end of 2000, less than six months after their arrival, the three pilots on the East Coast were simulating flights on large jets.[65]

Travels in Early 2001

Jarrah, Atta, and Shehhi, having progressed in their training, all took foreign trips during the holiday period of 2000–2001. Jarrah flew through Germany to get home to Beirut. A few weeks later, he returned to Florida via Germany, with Aysel Senguen. She stayed with him in Florida for ten days, even accompanying him to a flight training session. We do not know whether Atta or al Qaeda leaders knew about Jarrah's trips and Senguen's visit. The other operatives had broken off regular contact with their families. At the end of January 2001, Jarrah again flew to Beirut, to visit his sick father. After staying there for several weeks, Jarrah visited Senguen in Germany for a few days before returning to the United States at the end of February.[66]

While Jarrah took his personal trips, Atta traveled to Germany in early January 2001 for a progress meeting with Ramzi Binalshibh. Binalshibh says Atta told him to report to the al Qaeda leadership in Afghanistan that the three Hamburg pilots had completed their flight training and were awaiting orders. Atta also disclosed that a fourth pilot, Hanjour, had joined Hazmi. Upon returning to Florida, Atta wired Binalshibh travel money. Binalshibh proceeded to Afghanistan, made his report, and spent the next several months there and in Pakistan.[67]

When Atta returned to Florida, Shehhi left for Morocco, traveling to Casablanca in mid-January. Shehhi's family, concerned about not having heard from him, reported him missing to the UAE government. The UAE embassy in turn contacted the Hamburg police and a UAE representative tried to find him in Germany, visiting mosques and Shehhi's last address in Hamburg. After learning that his family was looking for him, Shehhi telephoned them on January 20 and said he was still living and studying in Hamburg. The UAE government then told the Hamburg police they could call off the search.[68]

Atta and Shehhi both encountered some difficulty reentering the United States, on January 10 and January 18, respectively. Because neither presented a student visa, both of them had to persuade INS inspectors that they should be admitted so that they could continue their flight training. Neither operative had any problem clearing Customs.[71]

After returning to Florida from their trips, Atta and Shehhi visited Georgia, staying briefly in Norcross and Decatur, and renting a single-engine plane to fly with an instructor in Lawrenceville. By February 19, Atta and Shehhi were in Virginia. They rented a mailbox in Virginia Beach, cashed a check, and then promptly returned to Georgia, staying in Stone Mountain. We have found no explanation for these

Atta's Alleged Trip to Prague

Mohamed Atta is known to have been in Prague on two occasions: in December 1994, when he stayed one night at a transit hotel, and in June 2000, when he was en route to the United States. On the latter occasion, he arrived by bus from Germany, on June 2, and departed for Newark the following day.[69]

The allegation that Atta met with an Iraqi intelligence officer in Prague in April 2001 originates from the reporting of a single source of the Czech intelligence service. Shortly after 9/11, the source reported having seen Atta meet with Ahmad Khalil Ibrahim Samir al Ani, an Iraqi diplomat, at the Iraqi Embassy in Prague on April 9, 2001, at 11:00 A.M. This information was passed to CIA headquarters.

The U.S. legal attaché ("Legat") in Prague, the representative of the FBI, met with the Czech service's source. After the meeting, the assessment of the Legat and the Czech officers present was that they were 70 percent sure that the source was sincere and believed his own story of the meeting. Subsequently, the Czech intelligence service publicly stated that there was a 70 percent probability that the meeting between Atta and Ani had taken place. The Czech Interior Minister also made several statements to the press about his belief that the meeting had occurred, and the story was widely reported.

The FBI has gathered evidence indicating that Atta was in Virginia Beach on April 4 (as evidenced by a bank surveillance camera photo), and in Coral Springs, Florida on April 11, where he and Shehhi leased an apartment. On April 6, 9, 10, and 11, Atta's cellular telephone was used numerous times to call various lodging establishments in Florida from cell sites within Florida. We cannot confirm that he placed those calls. But there are no U.S. records indicating that Atta departed the country during this period. Czech officials have reviewed their flight and border records as well for any indication that Atta was in the Czech Republic in April 2001, including records of anyone crossing the border who even looked Arab. They have also reviewed pictures from the area near the Iraqi embassy and have not discovered photos of anyone who looked like Atta. No evidence has been found that Atta was in the Czech Republic in April 2001.

According to the Czech government, Ani, the Iraqi officer alleged to have met with Atta, was about 70 miles away from Prague on April 8–9 and did not return until the afternoon of the ninth, while the source was firm that the sighting occurred at 11:00 A.M. When questioned about the reported April 2001 meeting, Ani—now in custody—has denied ever meeting or having any contact with Atta. Ani says that shortly after 9/11, he became concerned that press stories about the alleged meeting might hurt his career. Hoping to clear his name, Ani asked his superiors to approach the Czech government about refuting the allegation. He also denies knowing of any other Iraqi official having contact with Atta.

These findings cannot absolutely rule out the possibility that Atta was in Prague on April 9, 2001. He could have used an alias to travel and a passport under that alias, but this would be an exception to his practice of using his true name while traveling (as he did in January and would in July when he took his next overseas trip). The FBI and CIA have uncovered no evidence that Atta held any fraudulent passports.

KSM and Binalshibh both deny that an Atta-Ani meeting occurred. There was no reason for such a meeting, especially considering the risk it would pose to the operation. By April 2001, all four pilots had completed most of their training, and the muscle hijackers were about to begin entering the United States.

The available evidence does not support the original Czech report of an Atta-Ani meeting.[70]

travels. In mid-March, Jarrah was in Georgia as well, staying in Decatur. There is no evidence that the three pilots met, although Jarrah and Atta apparently spoke on the phone. At the end of the month, Jarrah left the United States again and visited Senguen in Germany for two weeks. In early April, Atta and Shehhi returned to Virginia Beach and closed the mailbox they had opened in February.[72]

By the time Atta and Shehhi returned to Virginia Beach from their travels in Georgia, Hazmi and Hanjour had also arrived in Virginia, in Falls Church. They made their way to a large mosque there, the Dar al Hijra mosque, sometime in early April.[73]

As we mentioned earlier, one of the imams at this mosque was the same Anwar Aulaqi with whom Hazmi had spent time at the Rabat mosque in San Diego. Aulaqi had moved to Virginia in January 2001. He remembers Hazmi from San Diego but has denied having any contact with Hazmi or Hanjour in Virginia.[74]

At the Dar al Hijra mosque, Hazmi and Hanjour met a Jordanian named Eyad al Rababah. Rababah says he had gone to the mosque to speak to the imam, Aulaqi, about finding work. At the conclusion of services, which normally had 400 to 500 attendees, Rababah says he happened to meet Hazmi and Hanjour. They were looking for an apartment; Rababah referred them to a friend who had one to rent. Hazmi and Hanjour moved into the apartment, which was in Alexandria.[75]

Some FBI investigators doubt Rababah's story. Some agents suspect that Aulaqi may have tasked Rababah to help Hazmi and Hanjour. We share that suspicion, given the remarkable coincidence of Aulaqi's prior relationship with Hazmi. As noted above, the Commission was unable to locate and interview Aulaqi. Rababah has been deported to Jordan, having been convicted after 9/11 in a fraudulent driver's license scheme.[76]

Rababah, who had lived in Connecticut, New York, and New Jersey, told investigators that he had recommended Paterson, New Jersey, as a place with an Arabic-speaking community where Hazmi and Hanjour might want to settle. They asked for his help in getting them an apartment in Paterson. Rababah tried without success. He says he then suggested that Hazmi and Hanjour travel with him to Connecticut where they could look for a place to live.[77]

On May 8, Rababah went to Hazmi and Hanjour's apartment to pick them up for the trip to Connecticut. There he says he found them with new roommates—Ahmed al Ghamdi and Majed Moqed. These two men had been sent to America to serve as muscle hijackers and had arrived at Dulles Airport on May 2. Rababah drove Hanjour to Fairfield, Connecticut, followed by Hazmi, who had Moqed and Ghamdi in his car. After a short stay in Connecticut, where they apparently called area flight schools and real estate agents, Rababah drove the four to Paterson to have dinner and show them around. He says that they returned with him to Fairfield that night, and that he never saw them again.[78]

Within a few weeks, Hanjour, Hazmi, and several other operatives moved to Paterson and rented a one-room apartment. When their landlord later paid a visit, he found six men living there—Nawaf al Hazmi, now joined by his younger brother Salem, Hanjour, Moqed, probably Ahmed al Ghamdi, and Abdul Aziz al Omari; Hazmi's old friend Khalid al Mihdhar would soon join them.[79]

Atta and Shehhi had already returned to Florida. On April 11, they moved into an apartment in Coral Springs. Atta stayed in Florida, awaiting the arrival of the first muscle hijackers.[80]

Shehhi, on the other hand, bought a ticket to Cairo and flew there from Miami on April 18. We do not know much more about Shehhi's reason for traveling to Egypt in April than we know about his January trip to Morocco. Shehhi did meet with Atta's father, who stated in a post-9/11 interview that Shehhi just wanted to pick up Atta's international driver's license and some money. This story is not credible. Atta already had the license with him and presented it during a traffic stop on April 26 while Shehhi was still abroad. Shehhi spent about two weeks in Egypt, obviously more time than would have been needed just to meet with Atta's father. Shehhi could have traveled elsewhere during this time, but no records indicating additional travel have been discovered.[81]

Shehhi returned to Miami on May 2. That day, Atta and Jarrah were together, about 30 miles to the north, visiting a Department of Motor Vehicles office in Lauderdale Lakes, Florida, to get Florida driver's licenses. Back in Virginia, Hazmi and Hanjour were about to leave for Connecticut and New Jersey. As the summer approached, the lead operatives were settled in Florida and New Jersey, waiting for the rest of their contingent to join them.[82]

7.3 ASSEMBLING THE TEAMS

During the summer and early autumn of 2000, Bin Ladin and senior al Qaeda leaders in Afghanistan started selecting the muscle hijackers—the operatives who would storm the cockpits and control the passengers. Despite the phrase widely used to describe them, the so-called muscle hijackers were not at all physically imposing; most were between 5'5" and 5'7" in height.[83]

Recruitment and Selection for 9/11

Twelve of the 13 muscle hijackers (excluding Nawaf al Hazmi and Mihdhar) came from Saudi Arabia: Satam al Suqami, Wail al Shehri, Waleed al Shehri, Abdul Aziz al Omari, Ahmed al Ghamdi, Hamza al Ghamdi, Mohand al Shehri, Majed Moqed, Salem al Hazmi, Saeed al Ghamdi, Ahmad al Haznawi, and Ahmed al Nami. The remaining recruit, Fayez Banihammad, came from the UAE. He appears to have played a unique role among the muscle hijackers because of his work with one of the plot's financial facilitators, Mustafa al Hawsawi.[84]

Saudi authorities interviewed the relatives of these men and have briefed us on what they found. The muscle hijackers came from a variety of educational and societal backgrounds. All were between 20 and 28 years old; most were unemployed with no more than a high school education and were unmarried.[85]

Four of them—Ahmed al Ghamdi, Saeed al Ghamdi, Hamza al Ghamdi, and Ahmad al Haznawi—came from a cluster of three towns in the al Bahah region, an isolated and underdeveloped area of Saudi Arabia, and shared the same tribal affiliation. None had a university degree. Their travel patterns and information from family members suggest that the four may have been in contact with each other as early as the fall of 1999.[86]

Five more—Wail al Shehri, Waleed al Shehri, Abdul Aziz al Omari, Mohand al Shehri, and Ahmed al Nami—came from Asir Province, a poor region in southwestern Saudi Arabia that borders Yemen; this weakly policed area is sometimes called "the wild frontier." Wail and Waleed al Shehri were brothers. All five in this group had begun university studies. Omari had graduated with honors from high school, had attained a degree from the Imam Muhammad Ibn Saud Islamic University, was married, and had a daughter.[87]

The three remaining muscle hijackers from Saudi Arabia were Satam al Suqami, Majed Moqed, and Salem al Hazmi. Suqami came from Riyadh. Moqed hailed from a small town called Annakhil, west of Medina. Suqami had very little education, and Moqed had dropped out of university. Neither Suqami nor Moqed appears to have had ties to the other, or to any of the other operatives, before getting involved with extremists, probably by 1999.[88]

Salem al Hazmi, a younger brother of Nawaf, was born in Mecca. Salem's family recalled him as a quarrelsome teenager. His brother Nawaf probably recommended him for recruitment into al Qaeda. One al Qaeda member who knew them says that Nawaf pleaded with Bin Ladin to allow Salem to participate in the 9/11 operation.[89]

Detainees have offered varying reasons for the use of so many Saudi operatives. Binalshibh argues that al Qaeda wanted to send a message to the government of Saudi Arabia about its relationship with the United States. Several other al Qaeda figures, however, have stated that ethnicity generally was not a factor in the selection of operatives unless it was important for security or operational reasons.[90]

KSM, for instance, denies that Saudis were chosen for the 9/11 plot to drive a wedge between the United States and Saudi Arabia, and stresses practical reasons for considering ethnic background when selecting operatives. He says that so many were Saudi because Saudis comprised the largest portion of the pool of recruits in the al Qaeda training camps. KSM estimates that in any given camp, 70 percent of the mujahideen were Saudi, 20 percent were Yemeni, and 10 percent were from elsewhere. Although Saudi and Yemeni trainees were most often willing to volunteer for suicide operations, prior to 9/11 it was easier for Saudi operatives to get into the United States.[91]

Most of the Saudi muscle hijackers developed their ties to extremists two or three years before the attacks. Their families often did not consider these young men religious zealots. Some were perceived as devout, others as lacking in faith. For instance, although Ahmed al Ghamdi, Hamza al Ghamdi, and Saeed al Ghamdi attended prayer services regularly and Omari often served as an imam at his mosque in Saudi Arabia, Suqami and Salem al Hazmi appeared unconcerned with religion and, contrary to Islamic law, were known to drink alcohol.[92]

Like many other al Qaeda operatives, the Saudis who eventually became the muscle hijackers were targeted for recruitment outside Afghanistan—probably in Saudi Arabia itself. Al Qaeda recruiters, certain clerics, and—in a few cases—family members probably all played a role in spotting potential candidates. Several of the muscle hijackers seem to have been recruited through contacts at local universities and mosques.[93]

According to the head of one of the training camps in Afghanistan, some were chosen by unnamed Saudi sheikhs who had contacts with al Qaeda. Omari, for example, is believed to have been a student of a radical Saudi cleric named

Sulayman al Alwan. His mosque, which is located in al Qassim Province, is known among more moderate clerics as a "terrorist factory." The province is at the very heart of the strict Wahhabi movement in Saudi Arabia. Saeed al Ghamdi and Mohand al Shehri also spent time in al Qassim, both breaking with their families. According to his father, Mohand al Shehri's frequent visits to this area resulted in his failing exams at his university in Riyadh. Saeed al Ghamdi transferred to a university in al Qassim, but he soon stopped talking to his family and dropped out of school without informing them.[94]

The majority of these Saudi recruits began to break with their families in late 1999 and early 2000. According to relatives, some recruits began to make arrangements for extended absences. Others exhibited marked changes in behavior before disappearing. Salem al Hazmi's father recounted that Salem—who had had problems with alcohol and petty theft—stopped drinking and started attending mosque regularly three months before he disappeared.[95]

Several family members remembered that their relatives had expressed a desire to participate in jihad, particularly in Chechnya. None had mentioned going to Afghanistan. These statements might be true or cover stories. The four recruits from the al Ghamdi tribe, for example, all told their families that they were going to Chechnya. Only two—Ahmed al Ghamdi and Saeed al Ghamdi—had documentation suggesting travel to a Russian republic.[96]

Some aspiring Saudi mujahideen, intending to go to Chechnya, encountered difficulties along the way and diverted to Afghanistan. In 1999, Ibn al Khattab—the primary commander of Arab nationals in Chechnya—reportedly had started turning away most foreign mujahideen because of their inexperience and inability to adjust to the local conditions. KSM states that several of the 9/11 muscle hijackers faced problems traveling to Chechnya and so went to Afghanistan, where they were drawn into al Qaeda.[97]

Khallad has offered a more detailed story of how such diversions occurred. According to him, a number of Saudi mujahideen who tried to go to Chechnya in 1999 to fight the Russians were stopped at the Turkish-Georgian border. Upon arriving in Turkey, they received phone calls at guest-houses in places such as Istanbul and Ankara, informing them that the route to Chechnya via Georgia had been closed. These Saudis then decided to travel to Afghanistan, where they could train and wait to make another attempt to enter Chechnya during the summer of 2000. While training at al Qaeda camps, a dozen of them heard Bin Ladin's speeches, volunteered to become suicide operatives, and eventually were selected as muscle hijackers for the planes operation. Khallad says he met a number of them at the Kandahar airport, where they were helping to provide extra security. He encouraged Bin Ladin to use them. Khallad claims to have been closest with Saeed al Ghamdi, whom he convinced to become a martyr and whom he asked to recruit a friend, Ahmed al Ghamdi, to the same cause. Although Khallad claims not to recall everyone from this group who was later chosen for the 9/11 operation, he says they also included Suqami, Waleed and Wail al Shehri, Omari, Nami, Hamza al Ghamdi, Salem al Hazmi, and Moqed.[98]

According to KSM, operatives volunteered for suicide operations and, for the most part, were not pressured to martyr themselves. Upon arriving in Afghanistan, a recruit would fill out an application with standard questions, such as, What brought you to Afghanistan? How did you travel here? How did you hear about us? What attracted you to the cause? What is your educational background? Where have you worked before? Applications were valuable for determining the potential of new arrivals, for filtering out potential spies from among them, and for identifying recruits with special skills. For instance, as pointed out earlier, Hani Hanjour noted his pilot training. Prospective operatives also were asked whether they were prepared to serve as suicide operatives; those who answered in the affirmative were interviewed by senior al Qaeda lieutenant Muhammad Atef.[99]

KSM claims that the most important quality for any al Qaeda operative was willingness to martyr himself. Khallad agrees, and claims that this criterion had preeminence in selecting the planes operation participants. The second most important criterion was demonstrable patience, Khallad says, because the planning for such attacks could take years.[100]

Khallad claims it did not matter whether the hijackers had fought in jihad previously, since he believes that U.S. authorities were not looking for such operatives before 9/11. But KSM asserts that young mujahideen with clean records were chosen to avoid raising alerts during travel. The al Qaeda training camp head mentioned above adds that operatives with no prior involvement in activities likely to be known to international security agencies were purposefully selected for the 9/11 attacks.[101]

Most of the muscle hijackers first underwent basic training similar to that given other al Qaeda recruits. This included training in firearms, heavy weapons, explosives, and topography. Recruits learned discipline and military life. They were subjected to artificial stresses to measure their psychological fitness and commitment to jihad. At least seven of the Saudi muscle hijackers took this basic training regime at the al Faruq camp near Kandahar. This particular camp appears to have been the preferred location for vetting and training the potential muscle hijackers because of its proximity to Bin Ladin and senior al Qaeda leadership. Two others—Suqami and Moqed—trained at Khaldan, another large basic training facility located near Kabul, where Mihdhar had trained in the mid-1990s.[102]

By the time operatives for the planes operation were picked in mid-2000, some of them had been training in Afghanistan for months, others were just arriving for the first time, and still others may have been returning after prior visits to the camps. According to KSM, Bin Ladin would travel to the camps to deliver lectures and meet the trainees personally. If Bin Ladin believed a trainee held promise for a special operation, that trainee would be invited to the al Qaeda leader's compound at Tarnak Farms for further meetings.[103]

KSM claims that Bin Ladin could assess new trainees
very quickly, in about ten minutes, and that many of the 9/11
hijackers were selected in this manner. Bin Ladin, assisted
by Atef, personally chose all the future muscle hijackers for
the planes operation, primarily between the summer of 2000
and April 2001. Upon choosing a trainee, Bin Ladin would
ask him to swear loyalty for a suicide operation. After the selection and oath-swearing, the operative would be sent to
KSM for training and the filming of a martyrdom video, a
function KSM supervised as head of al Qaeda's media committee.[104]

KSM sent the muscle hijacker recruits on to Saudi Arabia
to obtain U.S. visas. He gave them money (about $2,000
each) and instructed them to return to Afghanistan for more
training after obtaining the visas. At this early stage, the operatives were not told details about the operation. The majority of the Saudi muscle hijackers obtained U.S. visas in
Jeddah or Riyadh between September and November of
2000.[105]

KSM told potential hijackers to acquire new "clean"
passports in their home countries before applying for a U.S.
visa. This was to avoid raising suspicion about previous
travel to countries where al Qaeda operated. Fourteen of the
19 hijackers, including nine Saudi muscle hijackers, obtained new passports. Some of these passports were then
likely doctored by the al Qaeda passport division in Kandahar, which would add or erase entry and exit stamps to create
"false trails" in the passports.[106]

In addition to the operatives who eventually participated
in the 9/11 attacks as muscle hijackers, Bin Ladin apparently
selected at least nine other Saudis who, for various reasons,
did not end up taking part in the operation: Mohamed Mani
Ahmad al Kahtani, Khalid Saeed Ahmad al Zahrani, Ali Abd
al Rahman al Faqasi al Ghamdi, Saeed al Baluchi, Qutaybah
al Najdi, Zuhair al Thubaiti, Saeed Abdullah Saeed al
Ghamdi, Saud al Rashid, and Mushabib al Hamlan. A tenth
individual, a Tunisian with Canadian citizenship named Ab-
derraouf Jdey, may have been a candidate to participate in

9/11, or he may have been a candidate for a later attack. These candidate hijackers either backed out, had trouble obtaining needed travel documents, or were removed from the operation by the al Qaeda leadership. Khallad believes KSM wanted between four and six operatives per plane. KSM states that al Qaeda had originally planned to use 25 or 26 hijackers but ended up with only the 19.[107]

Final Training and Deployment to the United States

Having acquired U.S. visas in Saudi Arabia, the muscle hijackers returned to Afghanistan for special training in late 2000 to early 2001. The training reportedly was conducted at the al Matar complex by Abu Turab al Jordani, one of only a handful of al Qaeda operatives who, according to KSM, was aware of the full details of the planned planes operation. Abu Turab taught the operatives how to conduct hijackings, disarm air marshals, and handle explosives. He also trained them in bodybuilding and provided them with a few basic English words and phrases.[108]

According to KSM, Abu Turab even had the trainees butcher a sheep and a camel with a knife to prepare to use knives during the hijackings. The recruits learned to focus on storming the cockpit at the earliest opportunity when the doors first opened, and to worry about seizing control over the rest of the plane later. The operatives were taught about other kinds of attack as well, such as truck bombing, so that they would not be able to disclose the exact nature of their operation if they were caught. According to KSM, the muscle did not learn the full details—including the plan to hijack planes and fly them into buildings—before reaching the United States.[109]

After training in Afghanistan, the operatives went to a safehouse maintained by KSM in Karachi and stayed there temporarily before being deployed to the United States via the UAE. The safehouse was run by al Qaeda operative Abd al Rahim Ghulum Rabbani, also known as Abu Rahmah, a close associate of KSM who assisted him for three years by

finding apartments and lending logistical support to operatives KSM would send.

According to an al Qaeda facilitator, operatives were
brought to the safehouse by a trusted Pakistani al Qaeda
courier named Abdullah Sindhi, who also worked for KSM.
The future hijackers usually arrived in groups of two or
three, staying at the safe house for as long as two weeks. The
facilitator has identified each operative whom he assisted at
KSM's direction in the spring of 2001. Before the operatives
left Pakistan, each of them received $10,000 from KSM for
future expenses.[110]

From Pakistan, the operatives transited through the UAE
en route to the United States. In the Emirates they were assisted primarily by al Qaeda operatives Ali Abdul Aziz Ali
and Mustafa al Hawsawi. Ali apparently assisted nine future
hijackers between April and June 2001 as they came through
Dubai. He helped them with plane tickets, traveler's checks,
and hotel reservations; he also taught them about everyday
aspects of life in the West, such as purchasing clothes and
ordering food. Dubai, a modern city with easy access to a
major airport, travel agencies, hotels, and Western commercial establishments, was an ideal transit point.[111]

Ali reportedly assumed the operatives he was helping
were involved in a big operation in the United States, he did
not know the details.[112] When he asked KSM to send him an
assistant, KSM dispatched Hawsawi, who had worked on al
Qaeda's media committee in Kandahar. Hawsawi helped
send the last four operatives (other than Mihdhar) to the
United States from the UAE. Hawsawi would consult with
Atta about the hijackers' travel schedules to the United
States and later check with Atta to confirm that each had arrived. Hawsawi told the muscle hijackers that they would be
met by Atta at the airport. Hawsawi also facilitated some of
the operation's financing.[113]

The muscle hijackers began arriving in the United States
in late April 2001. In most cases, they traveled in pairs on
tourist visas and entered the United States in Orlando or Miami, Florida; Washington, D.C.; or New York. Those arriv-

ing in Florida were assisted by Atta and Shehhi, while Hazmi and Hanjour took care of the rest. By the end of June, 14 of the 15 muscle hijackers had crossed the Atlantic.[114]

The muscle hijackers supplied an infusion of funds, which they carried as a mixture of cash and traveler's checks purchased in the UAE and Saudi Arabia. Seven muscle hijackers are known to have purchased a total of nearly $50,000 in traveler's checks that were used in the United States. Moreover, substantial deposits into operatives' U.S. bank accounts immediately followed the entry of other muscle hijackers, indicating that those newcomers brought money with them as well. In addition, muscle hijacker Banihammad came to the United States after opening bank accounts in the UAE into which were deposited the equivalent of approximately $30,000 on June 25, 2001. After his June 27 arrival in the United States, Banihammad made Visa and ATM withdrawals from his UAE accounts.[115]

The hijackers made extensive use of banks in the United States, choosing both branches of major international banks and smaller regional banks. All of the hijackers opened accounts in their own name, and used passports and other identification documents that appeared valid on their face. Contrary to numerous published reports, there is no evidence the hijackers ever used false Social Security numbers to open any bank accounts. While the hijackers were not experts on the use of the U.S. financial system, nothing they did would have led the banks to suspect criminal behavior, let alone a terrorist plot to commit mass murder.[116]

The last muscle hijacker to arrive was Khalid al Mihdhar. As mentioned earlier, he had abandoned Hazmi in San Diego in June 2000 and returned to his family in Yemen. Mihdhar reportedly stayed in Yemen for about a month before Khallad persuaded him to return to Afghanistan. Mihdhar complained about life in the United States. He met with KSM, who remained annoyed at his decision to go AWOL. But KSM's desire to drop him from the operation yielded to Bin Ladin's insistence to keep him.[117]

By late 2000, Mihdhar was in Mecca, staying with a

cousin until February 2001, when he went home to visit his family before returning to Afghanistan. In June 2001, Mihdhar returned once more to Mecca to stay with his cousin for another month. Mihdhar said that Bin Ladin was planning five attacks on the United States. Before leaving, Mihdhar asked his cousin to watch over his home and family because of a job he had to do.[118]

On July 4, 2001, Mihdhar left Saudi Arabia to return to the United States, arriving at John F. Kennedy International Airport in New York. Mihdhar gave his intended address as the Marriott Hotel, New York City, but instead spent one night at another New York hotel. He then joined the group of hijackers in Paterson, reuniting with Nawaf al Hazmi after more than a year. With two months remaining, all 19 hijackers were in the United States and ready to take the final steps toward carrying out the attacks.[119]

Assistance from Hezbollah and Iran to al Qaeda

As we mentioned in chapter 2, while in Sudan, senior managers in al Qaeda maintained contacts with Iran and the Iranian-supported worldwide terrorist organization Hezbollah, which is based mainly in southern Lebanon and Beirut. Al Qaeda members received advice and training from Hezbollah.

Intelligence indicates the persistence of contacts between Iranian security officials and senior al Qaeda figures after Bin Ladin's return to Afghanistan. Khallad has said that Iran made a concerted effort to strengthen relations with al Qaeda after the October 2000 attack on the USS *Cole*, but was rebuffed because Bin Ladin did not want to alienate his supporters in Saudi Arabia. Khallad and other detainees have described the willingness of Iranian officials to facilitate the travel of al Qaeda members through Iran, on their way to and from Afghanistan. For example, Iranian border inspectors would be told not to place telltale stamps in the passports of these travelers. Such arrangements were particularly beneficial to Saudi members of al Qaeda.[120]

Our knowledge of the international travels of the al

Qaeda operatives selected for the 9/11 operation remains fragmentary. But we now have evidence suggesting that 8 to 10 of the 14 Saudi "muscle" operatives traveled into or out of Iran between October 2000 and February 2001.[121]

In October 2000, a senior operative of Hezbollah visited Saudi Arabia to coordinate activities there. He also planned to assist individuals in Saudi Arabia in traveling to Iran during November. A top Hezbollah commander and Saudi Hezbollah contacts were involved.[122]

Also in October 2000, two future muscle hijackers, Mohand al Shehri and Hamza al Ghamdi, flew from Iran to Kuwait. In November, Ahmed al Ghamdi apparently flew to Beirut, traveling—perhaps by coincidence—on the same flight as a senior Hezbollah operative. Also in November, Salem al Hazmi apparently flew from Saudi Arabia to Beirut.[123]

In mid-November, we believe, three of the future muscle hijackers, Wail al Shehri, Waleed al Shehri, and Ahmed al Nami, all of whom had obtained their U.S. visas in late October, traveled in a group from Saudi Arabia to Beirut and then onward to Iran. An associate of a senior Hezbollah operative was on the same flight that took the future hijackers to Iran. Hezbollah officials in Beirut and Iran were expecting the arrival of a group during the same time period. The travel of this group was important enough to merit the attention of senior figures in Hezbollah.[124]

Later in November, two future muscle hijackers, Satam al Suqami and Majed Moqed, flew into Iran from Bahrain. In February 2001, Khalid al Mihdhar may have taken a flight from Syria to Iran, and then traveled further within Iran to a point near the Afghan border.[125]

KSM and Binalshibh have confirmed that several of the 9/11 hijackers (at least eight, according to Binalshibh) transited Iran on their way to or from Afghanistan, taking advantage of the Iranian practice of not stamping Saudi passports. They deny any other reason for the hijackers' travel to Iran. They also deny any relationship between the hijackers and Hezbollah.[126]

In sum, there is strong evidence that Iran facilitated the transit of al Qaeda members into and out of Afghanistan before 9/11, and that some of these were future 9/11 hijackers. There also is circumstantial evidence that senior Hezbollah operatives were closely tracking the travel of some of these future muscle hijackers into Iran in November 2000. However, we cannot rule out the possibility of a remarkable coincidence—that is, that Hezbollah was actually focusing on some other group of individuals traveling from Saudi Arabia during this same time frame, rather than the future hijackers.[127]

We have found no evidence that Iran or Hezbollah was aware of the planning for what later became the 9/11 attack. At the time of their travel through Iran, the al Qaeda operatives themselves were probably not aware of the specific details of their future operation.

After 9/11, Iran and Hezbollah wished to conceal any past evidence of cooperation with Sunni terrorists associated with al Qaeda. A senior Hezbollah official disclaimed any Hezbollah involvement in 9/11.[128]

We believe this topic requires further investigation by the U.S. government.

7.4 FINAL STRATEGIES AND TACTICS

Final Preparations in the United States

During the early summer of 2001, Atta, assisted by Shehhi, was busy coordinating the arrival of most of the muscle hijackers in southern Florida—picking them up at the airport, finding them places to stay, and helping them settle in the United States.[129]

The majority settled in Florida. Some opened bank accounts, acquired mailboxes, and rented cars. Several also joined local gyms, presumably to stay fit for the operation. Upon first arriving, most stayed in hotels and motels; but by mid-June, they settled in shared apartments relatively close to one another and Atta.[130] Though these muscle hijackers did not travel much after arriving in the United States, two of them, Waleed al Shehri and Satam al Suqami, took unusual trips.

On May 19, Shehri and Suqami flew from Fort Lauderdale to Freeport, the Bahamas, where they had reservations at the Bahamas Princess Resort. The two were turned away by Bahamian officials on arrival, however, because they lacked visas; they returned to Florida that same day. They likely took this trip to renew Suqami's immigration status, as Suqami's legal stay in the United States ended May 21.[131]

On July 30, Shehri traveled alone from Fort Lauderdale to Boston. He flew to San Francisco the next day, where he stayed one night before returning via Las Vegas. While this travel may have been a casing flight—Shehri traveled in first class on the same type of aircraft he would help hijack on September 11 (a Boeing 767) and the trip included a layover in Las Vegas—Shehri was neither a pilot nor a plot leader, as were the other hijackers who took surveillance flights.[132]

The three Hamburg pilots—Atta, Shehhi, and Jarrah—took the first of their cross-country surveillance flights early in the summer. Shehhi flew from New York to Las Vegas via San Francisco in late May. Jarrah flew from Baltimore to Las Vegas via Los Angeles in early June. Atta flew from Boston to Las Vegas via San Francisco at the end of June. Each traveled in first class, on United Airlines. For the east-west transcontinental leg, each operative flew on the same type of aircraft he would pilot on September 11 (Atta and Shehhi, a Boeing 767; Jarrah, a Boeing 757).[133] Hanjour and Hazmi, as noted below, took similar cross-country surveillance flights in August.

Jarrah and Hanjour also received additional training and practice flights in the early summer. A few days before departing on his cross-country test flight, Jarrah flew from Fort Lauderdale to Philadelphia, where he trained at Hortman Aviation and asked to fly the Hudson Corridor, a low-altitude "hallway" along the Hudson River that passes New York landmarks like the World Trade Center. Heavy traffic in the area can make the corridor a dangerous route for an inexperienced pilot. Because Hortman deemed Jarrah unfit to fly solo, he could fly this route only with an instructor.[134]

Hanjour, too, requested to fly the Hudson Corridor about this same time, at Air Fleet Training Systems in Teterboro, New Jersey, where he started receiving ground instruction soon after settling in the area with Hazmi. Hanjour flew the Hudson Corridor, but his instructor declined a second request because of what he considered Hanjour's poor piloting skills. Shortly thereafter, Hanjour switched to Caldwell Flight Academy in Fairfield, New Jersey, where he rented small aircraft on several occasions during June and July. In one such instance on July 20, Hanjour—likely accompanied by Hazmi—rented a plane from Caldwell and took a practice flight from Fairfield to Gaithersburg, Maryland, a route that would have allowed them to fly near Washington, D.C. Other evidence suggests that Hanjour may even have returned to Arizona for flight simulator training earlier in June.[135]

There is no indication that Atta or Shehhi received any additional flight training in June. Both were likely too busy organizing the newly arrived muscle hijackers and taking their cross-country surveillance flights. Atta, moreover, needed to coordinate with his second-in-command, Nawaf al Hazmi.[136]

Although Atta and Hazmi appear to have been in Virginia at about the same time in early April, they probably did not meet then. Analysis of late April communications associated with KSM indicates that they had wanted to get together in April but could not coordinate the meeting.[137] Atta and Hazmi probably first met in the United States only when Hazmi traveled round-trip from Newark to Miami between June 19 and June 25.

After he returned to New Jersey, Hazmi's behavior began to closely parallel that of the other hijackers. He and Hanjour, for instance, soon established new bank accounts, acquired a mailbox, rented cars, and started visiting a gym. So did the four other hijackers who evidently were staying with

them in New Jersey. Several also obtained new photo identification, first in New Jersey and then at the Virginia Department of Motor Vehicles, where Hazmi and Hanjour had
obtained such documents months earlier, likely with help
from their Jordanian friend, Rababah.[138]

Atta probably met again with Hazmi in early July. Re-
turning from his initial cross-country surveillance flight,
Atta flew into New York. Rather than return immediately to
Florida, he checked into a New Jersey hotel. He picked up
tickets to travel to Spain at a travel agency in Paterson on
July 4 before departing for Fort Lauderdale. Now that the
muscle hijackers had arrived, he was ready to meet with
Ramzi Binalshibh for the last time.[139]

The Meeting in Spain

After meeting with Atta in Berlin in January 2001, Binalshibh had spent much of the spring of 2001 in Afghanistan
and Pakistan, helping move the muscle hijackers as they
passed through Karachi. During the Berlin meeting, the two
had agreed to meet later in the year in Kuala Lumpur to discuss the operation in person again. In late May, Binalshibh
reported directly to Bin Ladin at an al Qaeda facility known
as "Compound Six" near Kandahar.[140]

Bin Ladin told Binalshibh to instruct Atta and the others
to focus on their security and that of the operation, and to
advise Atta to proceed as planned with the targets discussed
before Atta left Afghanistan in early 2000—the World Trade
Center, the Pentagon, the White House, and the Capitol. According to Binalshibh, Bin Ladin said he preferred the White
House over the Capitol, asking Binalshibh to confirm that
Atta understood this preference. Binalshibh says Bin Ladin
had given the same message to Waleed al Shehri for con-
veyance to Atta earlier that spring. Binalshibh also received
permission to meet Atta in Malaysia. Atef provided money
for the trip, which KSM would help Binalshibh arrange in
Karachi.[141]

In early June, Binalshibh traveled by taxi from Kandahar
to Quetta, Pakistan, where al Qaeda courier Abu Rahmah

took him to KSM. According to Binalshibh, KSM provided
a plane ticket to Malaysia and a fraudulent Saudi passport to
use for the trip. KSM told him to ask Atta to select a date for
the attacks. Binalshibh was to return to Germany and then
inform KSM of the date. KSM also gave Binalshibh the
email address of Zacarias Moussaoui for future contact. Binalshibh then left for Kuala Lumpur.[142]

Binalshibh contacted Atta upon arriving in Malaysia and
found a change in plan. Atta could not travel because he was
too busy helping the new arrivals settle in the United States.
After remaining in Malaysia for approximately three weeks,
Binalshibh went to Bangkok for a few days before returning
to Germany. He and Atta agreed to meet later at a location to
be determined.[143]

In early July, Atta called Binalshibh to suggest meeting in
Madrid, for reasons Binalshibh claims not to know. He says
he preferred Berlin, but that he and Atta knew too many people in Germany and feared being spotted together. Unable to
buy a ticket to Madrid at the height of the tourist season, Binalshibh booked a seat on a flight to Reus, near Barcelona,
the next day. Atta was already en route to Madrid, so Binalshibh phoned Shehhi in the United States to inform him of
the change in itinerary.[144]

Atta arrived in Madrid on July 8. He spent the night in a
hotel and made three calls from his room, most likely to coordinate with Binalshibh. The next day, Atta rented a car and
drove to Reus to pick up Binalshibh; the two then drove to
the nearby town of Cambrils. Hotel records show Atta renting rooms in the same area until July 19, when he returned
his rental car in Madrid and flew back to Fort Lauderdale. On
July 16, Binalshibh returned to Hamburg, using a ticket Atta
had purchased for him earlier that day. According to Binalshibh, they did not meet with anyone else while in Spain.[145]

Binalshibh says he told Atta that Bin Ladin wanted the attacks carried out as soon as possible. Bin Ladin, Binalshibh
conveyed, was worried about having so many operatives in
the United States. Atta replied that he could not yet provide
a date because he was too busy organizing the arriving hi-

jackers and still needed to coordinate the timing of the
flights so that the crashes would occur simultaneously. Atta
said he required about five to six weeks before he could provide an attack date. Binalshibh advised Atta that Bin Ladin
had directed that the other operatives not be informed of the
date until the last minute. Atta was to provide Binalshibh
with advance notice of at least a week or two so that Binalshibh could travel to Afghanistan and report the date personally to Bin Ladin.[146]

As to targets, Atta understood Bin Ladin's interest in
striking the White House. Atta said he thought this target too
difficult, but had tasked Hazmi and Hanjour to evaluate its
feasibility and was awaiting their answer. Atta said that those
two operatives had rented small aircraft and flown reconnaissance flights near the Pentagon. Atta explained that Hanjour was assigned to attack the Pentagon, Jarrah the Capitol,
and that both Atta and Shehhi would hit the World Trade
Center. If any pilot could not reach his intended target, he
was to crash the plane. If Atta could not strike the World
Trade Center, he planned to crash his aircraft directly into
the streets of New York. Atta told Binalshibh that each pilot
had volunteered for his assigned target, and that the assignments were subject to change.[147]

During the Spain meeting, Atta also mentioned that he
had considered targeting a nuclear facility he had seen during
familiarization flights near New York—a target they referred
to as "electrical engineering." According to Binalshibh, the
other pilots did not like the idea. They thought a nuclear target would be difficult because the airspace around it was restricted, making reconnaissance flights impossible and
increasing the likelihood that any plane would be shot down
before impact. Moreover, unlike the approved targets, this
alternative had not been discussed with senior al Qaeda
leaders and therefore did not have the requisite blessing. Nor
would a nuclear facility have particular symbolic value. Atta
did not ask Binalshibh to pass this idea on to Bin Ladin,
Atef, or KSM, and Binalshibh says he did not mention it to
them until after September 11.[148]

Binalshibh claims that during their time in Spain, he and Atta also discussed how the hijackings would be executed. Atta said he, Shehhi, and Jarrah had encountered no problems carrying box cutters on cross-country surveillance flights. The best time to storm the cockpit would be about 10–15 minutes after takeoff, when the cockpit doors typically were opened for the first time. Atta did not believe they would need any other weapons. He had no firm contingency plan in case the cockpit door was locked. While he mentioned general ideas such as using a hostage or claiming to have a bomb, he was confident the cockpit doors would be opened and did not consider breaking them down a viable idea. Atta told Binalshibh he wanted to select planes departing on long flights because they would be full of fuel, and that he wanted to hijack Boeing aircraft because he believed them easier to fly than Airbus aircraft, which he understood had an autopilot feature that did not allow them to be crashed into the ground.[149]

Finally, Atta confirmed that the muscle hijackers had arrived in the United States without incident. They would be divided into teams according to their English-speaking ability. That way they could assist each other before the operation and each team would be able to command the passengers in English. According to Binalshibh, Atta complained that some of the hijackers wanted to contact their families to say goodbye, something he had forbidden. Atta, moreover, was nervous about his future communications with Binalshibh, whom he instructed to obtain new telephones upon returning to Germany. Before Binalshibh left Spain, he gave Atta eight necklaces and eight bracelets that Atta had asked him to buy when he was recently in Bangkok, believing that if the hijackers were clean shaven and well dressed, others would think them wealthy Saudis and give them less notice.[150]

As directed, upon returning from Spain, Binalshibh obtained two new phones, one to communicate with Atta and another to communicate with KSM and others, such as Zacarias Moussaoui. Binalshibh soon contacted KSM and, using code words, reported the results of his meeting with Atta. This important exchange occurred in mid-July.[151]

The conversation covered various topics. For example, Jarrah was to send Binalshibh certain personal materials from the hijackers, including copies of their passports, which Binalshibh in turn would pass along to KSM, probably for subsequent use in al Qaeda propaganda.[152]

The most significant part of the mid-July conversation concerned Jarrah's troubled relationship with Atta. KSM and Binalshibh both acknowledge that Jarrah chafed under Atta's authority over him. Binalshibh believes the disagreement arose in part from Jarrah's family visits. Moreover, Jarrah had been on his own for most of his time in the United States because Binalshibh's visa difficulty had prevented the two of them from training together. Jarrah thus felt excluded from the decisionmaking. Binalshibh had to act as a broker between Jarrah and Atta.[153]

Concerned that Jarrah might withdraw from the operation at this late stage, KSM emphasized the importance of Atta and Jarrah's resolving their differences. Binalshibh claims that such concern was unwarranted, and in their mid-July discussion reassured KSM that Atta and Jarrah would reconcile and be ready to move forward in about a month, after Jarrah visited his family. Noting his concern and the potential for delay, KSM at one point instructed Binalshibh to send "the skirts" to "Sally"—a coded instruction to Binalshibh to send funds to Zacarias Moussaoui. While Binalshibh admits KSM did direct him to send Moussaoui money during the mid-July conversation, he denies knowing exactly why he received this instruction—though he thought the money was being provided "within the framework" of the 9/11 operation.[154]

KSM may have instructed Binalshibh to send money to Moussaoui in order to help prepare Moussaoui as a potential substitute pilot for Jarrah. On July 20, 2001, Aysel Senguen, Jarrah's girlfriend, purchased a one-way ticket for Jarrah from Miami to Dusseldorf. On Jarrah's previous four trips from the United States to see Senguen and his family in

Lebanon, he had always traveled with a round-trip ticket. When Jarrah departed Miami on July 25, Atta appears to have driven him to the airport, another unique circumstance.[155]

Binalshibh picked up Jarrah at the airport in Dusseldorf on July 25. Jarrah wanted to see Senguen as soon as possible, so he and Binalshibh arranged to meet a few days later. When they did, they had an emotional conversation during which Binalshibh encouraged Jarrah to see the plan through.[156]

While Jarrah was in Germany, Binalshibh and Moussaoui were in contact to arrange for the transfer of funds. Binalshibh received two wire transfers from Hawsawi in the UAE totaling $15,000 and, within days, relayed almost all of this money to Moussaoui in two installments.[157]

Moussaoui had been taking flight lessons at the Airman Flight School in Norman, Oklahoma, since February but stopped in late May. Although at that point he had only about 50 hours of flight time and no solo flights to his credit, Moussaoui began making inquiries about flight materials and simulator training for Boeing 747s. On July 10, he put down a $1,500 deposit for flight simulator training at Pan Am International Flight Academy in Eagan, Minnesota, and by the end of the month, he had received a simulator schedule to train from August 13 through August 20. Moussaoui also purchased two knives and inquired of two manufacturers of GPS equipment whether their products could be converted for aeronautical use—activities that closely resembled those of the 9/11 hijackers during their final preparations for the attacks.[158]

On August 10, shortly after getting the money from Binalshibh, Moussaoui left Oklahoma with a friend and drove to Minnesota. Three days later, Moussaoui paid the $6,800 balance owed for his flight simulator training at Pan Am in cash and began his training. His conduct, however, raised the suspicions of his flight instructor. It was unusual for a student with so little training to be learning to fly large jets without any intention of obtaining a pilot's license or other goal. On August 16, once the instructor reported his suspicion to the authorities, Moussaoui was arrested by the INS on immigration charges.[159]

KSM denies ever considering Moussaoui for the planes operation. Instead he claims that Moussaoui was slated to participate in a "second wave" of attacks. KSM also states that Moussaoui had no contact with Atta, and we are unaware of evidence contradicting this assertion.[160]

Yet KSM has also stated that by the summer of 2001, he was too busy with the planes operation to continue planning for any second-wave attacks. Moreover, he admits that only three potential pilots were ever recruited for the alleged second wave, Moussaoui plus two others who, by midsummer of 2001, had backed out of the plot.[161] We therefore believe that the effort to push Moussaoui forward in August 2001 lends credence to the suspicion that he was being primed as a possible pilot in the immediate planes operation.

Binalshibh says he assumed Moussaoui was to take his place as another pilot in the 9/11 operation. Recounting a post-9/11 discussion with KSM in Kandahar, Binalshibh claims KSM mentioned Moussaoui as being part of the 9/11 operation. Although KSM never referred to Moussaoui by name, Binalshibh understood he was speaking of the operative to whom Binalshibh had wired money. Binalshibh says KSM did not approve of Moussaoui but believes KSM did not remove him from the operation only because Moussaoui had been selected and assigned by Bin Ladin himself.[162]

KSM did not hear about Moussaoui's arrest until after September 11. According to Binalshibh, had Bin Ladin and KSM learned prior to 9/11 that Moussaoui had been detained, they might have canceled the operation. When Binalshibh discussed Moussaoui's arrest with KSM after September 11, KSM congratulated himself on not having Moussaoui contact the other operatives, which would have compromised the operation. Moussaoui had been in contact with Binalshibh, of course, but this was not discovered until after 9/11.[163]

As it turned out, Moussaoui was not needed to replace

Jarrah. By the time Moussaoui was arrested in mid-August, Jarrah had returned to the United States from his final trip to Germany, his disagreement with Atta apparently resolved. The operatives began their final preparations for the attacks.[164]

Readying the Attacks

A week after he returned from meeting Binalshibh in Spain, Atta traveled to Newark, probably to coordinate with Hazmi and give him additional funds. Atta spent a few days in the area before returning to Florida on July 30. The month of August was busy, as revealed by a set of contemporaneous Atta-Binalshibh communications that were recovered after September 11.[165]

On August 3, for example, Atta and Binalshibh discussed several matters, such as the best way for the operatives to purchase plane tickets and the assignment of muscle hijackers to individual teams. Atta and Binalshibh also revisited the question of whether to target the White House. They discussed targets in coded language, pretending to be students discussing various fields of study: "architecture" referred to the World Trade Center, "arts" the Pentagon, "law" the Capitol, and "politics" the White House.[166]

Binalshibh reminded Atta that Bin Ladin wanted to target the White House. Atta again cautioned that this would be difficult. When Binalshibh persisted, Atta agreed to include the White House but suggested they keep the Capitol as an alternate target in case the White House proved too difficult. Atta also suggested that the attacks would not happen until after the first week in September, when Congress reconvened.[167]

Atta and Binalshibh also discussed "the friend who is coming as a tourist"—a cryptic reference to candidate hijacker Mohamed al Kahtani (mentioned above), whom Hawsawi was sending the next day as "the last one" to "complete the group." On August 4, Atta drove to the Orlando airport to meet Kahtani. Upon arrival, however, Kahtani was denied entry by immigration officials because he had a one-way ticket and little money, could not speak English, and could not adequately explain what he intended to do in the United States. He was sent back to Dubai. Hawsawi contacted KSM, who told him to help Kahtani return to Pakistan.[168]

On August 7, Atta flew from Fort Lauderdale to Newark, probably to coordinate with Hazmi. Two days later, Ahmed al Ghamdi and Abdul Aziz al Omari, who had been living in New Jersey with Hazmi and Hanjour, flew to Miami—probably signifying that the four hijacking teams had finally been assigned. While Atta was in New Jersey, he, Hazmi, and Hanjour all purchased tickets for another set of surveillance flights. Like Shehhi, Jarrah, Atta, and Waleed al Shehri before them, Hazmi and Hanjour each flew in first class on the same type of aircraft they would hijack on 9/11 (a Boeing 757), and on transcontinental flights that connected to Las Vegas. This time, however, Atta himself also flew directly to Las Vegas, where all three stayed on August 13–14. Beyond Las Vegas's reputation for welcoming tourists, we have seen no credible evidence explaining why, on this occasion and others, the operatives flew to or met in Las Vegas.[169]

Through August, the hijackers kept busy with their gym training and the pilots took frequent practice flights on small rented aircraft. The operatives also began to make purchases suggesting that the planning was coming to an end. In mid-August, for example, they bought small knives that may actually have been used in the attacks. On August 22, moreover, Jarrah attempted to purchase four GPS units from a pilot shop in Miami. He was able to buy only one unit, which he picked up a few days later when he also purchased three aeronautical charts.[170]

Perhaps most significant, however, was the purchase of plane tickets for September 11. On August 23, Atta again flew to Newark, probably to meet with Hazmi and select flights. All 19 tickets were booked and purchased between August 25 and September 5.[171]

It therefore appears that the attack date was selected by the third week of August. This timing is confirmed by Binalshibh, who claims Atta called him with the date in mid-August. According to Binalshibh, Atta used a riddle to convey the date in code—a message of two branches, a slash, and a lollipop (to non-Americans, 11/9 would be interpreted as September 11). Binalshibh says he called Atta back to confirm the date before passing it to KSM.[172]

KSM apparently received the date from Binalshibh in a message sent through Binalshibh's old Hamburg associate, Zakariya Essabar. Both Binalshibh and KSM claim that Essabar was not privy to the meaning of the message and had no foreknowledge of the attacks. According to Binalshibh, shortly after the date was chosen, he advised Essabar and another Hamburg associate, Said Bahaji, that if they wanted to go to Afghanistan, now was the time because it would soon become more difficult. Essabar made reservations on August 22 and departed Hamburg for Karachi on August 30; Bahaji purchased his tickets on August 20 and departed Hamburg for Karachi on September 3.[173]

Binalshibh also made arrangements to leave for Pakistan during early September, before the attacks, as did Ali and Hawsawi, the plot facilitators in the UAE. During these final days, Binalshibh and Atta kept in contact by phone, email, and instant messaging. Although Atta had forbidden the hijackers to contact their families, he apparently placed one last call to his own father on September 9. Atta also asked Binalshibh to contact the family of one hijacker, pass along goodbyes from others, and give regards to KSM. Jarrah alone appears to have left a written farewell—a sentimental letter to Aysel Senguen.[174]

Hazmi, however, may not have been so discreet. He may have telephoned his former San Diego companion, Mohdar Abdullah, in late August. Several bits of evidence indicate that others in Abdullah's circle may have received word that something big would soon happen. As noted earlier, Abdullah's behavior reportedly changed noticeably. Prior to September 11, both he and Yazeed al Salmi suddenly became intent on proceeding with their planned marriages. One witness quotes Salmi as commenting after the 9/11 attacks, "I knew they were going to do something, that is why I got married." Moreover, as of August 2001, Iyad Kreiwesh and other employees at the Texaco station where Hazmi had worked suddenly were anticipating attention from law enforcement authorities in the near future. Finally, according to an uncorroborated witness account, early on the morning of September 10, Abdullah, Osama Awadallah, Omar Bakarbashat, and others behaved suspiciously at the gas station. According to the witness, after the group met, Awadallah said "it is finally going to happen" as the others celebrated by giving each other high fives.[175]

Dissent within the al Qaeda Leadership

While tactical preparations for the attack were nearing completion, the entire operation was being questioned at the top, as al Qaeda and the Taliban argued over strategy for 2001. Our focus has naturally been on the specifics of the planes operation. But from the perspective of Bin Ladin and Atef, this operation was only one, admittedly key, element of their unfolding plans for the year. Living in Afghanistan, interacting constantly with the Taliban, the al Qaeda leaders would never lose sight of the situation in that country.

Bin Ladin's consistent priority was to launch a major attack directly against the United States. He wanted the planes operation to proceed as soon as possible. Mihdhar reportedly told his cousin during the summer of 2001 that Bin Ladin was reputed to have remarked, "I will make it happen even if I do it by myself."[176]

According to KSM, Bin Ladin had been urging him to advance the date of the attacks. In 2000, for instance, KSM remembers Bin Ladin pushing him to launch the attacks amid the controversy after then-Israeli opposition party leader Ariel Sharon's visit to the Temple Mount in Jerusalem. KSM claims Bin Ladin told him it would be enough for the hijackers simply to down planes rather than crash them into specific targets. KSM says he resisted the pressure.[177]

KSM claims to have faced similar pressure twice more in

2001. According to him, Bin Ladin wanted the operation carried out on May 12, 2001, seven months to the day after the *Cole* bombing. KSM adds that the 9/11 attacks had originally been envisioned for May 2001. The second time he was urged to launch the attacks early was in June or July 2001, supposedly after Bin Ladin learned from the media that Sharon would be visiting the White House. On both occasions KSM resisted, asserting that the hijacking teams were not ready. Bin Ladin pressed particularly strongly for the latter date in two letters stressing the need to attack early. The second letter reportedly was delivered by Bin Ladin's son-in-law, Aws al Madani.[178]

Other evidence corroborates KSM's account. For instance, Mihdhar told his cousin that the attacks were to happen in May, but were postponed twice, first to July, then to September. Moreover, one candidate hijacker remembers a general warning being issued in the al Qaeda camps in July or early August, just like the warnings issued two weeks before the *Cole* bombing and ten days before the eventual 9/11 attacks. During the midsummer alert, al Qaeda members dispersed with their families, security was increased, and Bin Ladin disappeared for about 30 days, until the alert was canceled.[179]

While the details of the operation were strictly compartmented, by the time of the alert, word had begun to spread that an attack against the United States was coming. KSM notes that it was generally well known by the summer of 2001 that he was planning some kind of operation against the United States. Many were even aware that he had been preparing operatives to go to the United States, leading some to conclude that al Qaeda was planning a near-term attack on U.S. soil. Moreover, Bin Ladin had made several remarks that summer hinting at an upcoming attack and generating rumors throughout the worldwide jihadist community. Bin Ladin routinely told important visitors to expect significant attacks against U.S. interests soon and, during a speech at the al Faruq camp, exhorted trainees to pray for the success of an attack involving 20 martyrs. Others have confirmed hearing indications of an impending attack and have verified that such news, albeit without specific details, had spread across al Qaeda.[180]

Although Bin Ladin's top priority apparently was to attack the United States, others had a different view. The Taliban leaders put their main emphasis on the year's military offensive against the Northern Alliance, an offensive that ordinarily would begin in the late spring or summer. They certainly hoped that this year's offensive would finally finish off their old enemies, driving them from Afghanistan. From the Taliban's perspective, an attack against the United States might be counterproductive. It might draw the Americans into the war against them, just when final victory seemed within their grasp.[181]

There is evidence that Mullah Omar initially opposed a major al Qaeda operation directly against the United States in 2001. Furthermore, by July, with word spreading of a coming attack, a schism emerged among the senior leadership of al Qaeda. Several senior members reportedly agreed with Mullah Omar. Those who reportedly sided with Bin Ladin included Atef, Sulayman Abu Ghayth, and KSM. But those said to have opposed him were weighty figures in the organization—including Abu Hafs the Mauritanian, Sheikh Saeed al Masri, and Sayf al Adl. One senior al Qaeda operative claims to recall Bin Ladin arguing that attacks against the United States needed to be carried out immediately to support insurgency in the Israeli-occupied territories and protest the presence of U.S. forces in Saudi Arabia. Beyond these rhetorical appeals, Bin Ladin also reportedly thought an attack against the United States would benefit al Qaeda by attracting more suicide operatives, eliciting greater donations, and increasing the number of sympathizers willing to provide logistical assistance.[182]

Mullah Omar is reported to have opposed this course of action for ideological reasons rather than out of fear of U.S. retaliation. He is said to have preferred for al Qaeda to attack Jews, not necessarily the United States. KSM contends that Omar faced pressure from the Pakistani government to keep al Qaeda from engaging in operations outside Afghanistan. Al Qaeda's chief financial manager, Sheikh Saeed, argued that al Qaeda should defer to the Taliban's wishes. Another source says that Sheikh Saeed opposed the operation, both out of deference to Omar and because he feared the U.S. response to an attack. Abu Hafs the Mauritanian reportedly even wrote Bin Ladin a message basing opposition to the attacks on the Qur'an.[183]

According to KSM, in late August, when the operation was fully planned, Bin Ladin formally notified the al Qaeda Shura Council that a major attack against the United States would take place in the coming weeks. When some council members objected, Bin Ladin countered that Mullah Omar lacked authority to prevent al Qaeda from conducting jihad outside Afghanistan. Though most of the Shura Council reportedly disagreed, Bin Ladin persisted. The attacks went forward.[184]

The story of dissension within al Qaeda regarding the 9/11 attacks is probably incomplete. The information on which the account is based comes from sources who were not privy to the full scope of al Qaeda and Taliban planning. Bin Ladin and Atef, however, probably would have known, at least, that

- The general Taliban offensive against the Northern Alliance would rely on al Qaeda military support.
- Another significant al Qaeda operation was making progress during the summer—a plot to assassinate the Northern Alliance leader, Ahmed Shah Massoud. The operatives, disguised as journalists, were in Massoud's camp and prepared to kill him sometime in August. Their appointment to see him was delayed.[185]

But on September 9, the Massoud assassination took place. The delayed Taliban offensive against the Northern Alliance was apparently coordinated to begin as soon as he was killed, and it got under way on September 10.[186]

As they deliberated earlier in the year, Bin Ladin and

Atef would likely have remembered that Mullah Omar was dependent on them for the Massoud assassination and for vital support in the Taliban military operations. KSM remembers Atef telling him that al Qaeda had an agreement with the Taliban to eliminate Massoud, after which the Taliban would begin an offensive to take over Afghanistan. Atef hoped Massoud's death would also appease the Taliban when the 9/11 attacks happened. There are also some scant indications that Omar may have been reconciled to the 9/11 attacks by the time they occurred.[187]

Moving to Departure Positions
In the days just before 9/11, the hijackers returned leftover funds to al Qaeda and assembled in their departure cities. They sent the excess funds by wire transfer to Hawsawi in the UAE, about $26,000 altogether.[188]

The hijackers targeting American Airlines Flight 77, to depart from Dulles, migrated from New Jersey to Laurel, Maryland, about 20 miles from Washington, D.C. They stayed in a motel during the first week in September and spent time working out at a gym. On the final night before the attacks, they lodged at a hotel in Herndon, Virginia, close to the airport.[189]

Further north, the hijackers targeting United Airlines Flight 93, to depart from Newark, gathered in that city from their base in Florida on September 7. Just after midnight on September 8–9, Jarrah received a speeding ticket in Maryland as he headed north on I-95. He joined the rest of his team at their hotel.[190]

Atta was still busy coordinating the teams. On September 7, he flew from Fort Lauderdale to Baltimore, presumably to meet with the Flight 77 team in Laurel. On September 9, he flew from Baltimore to Boston. By then, Shehhi had arrived there, and Atta was seen with him at his hotel. The next day, Atta picked up Omari at another hotel, and the two drove to Portland, Maine, for reasons that remain unknown. In the early morning hours of September 11, they boarded a commuter flight to Boston to connect to American Airlines

Flight 11. The two spent their last night pursuing ordinary activities: making ATM withdrawals, eating pizza, and shopping at a convenience store. Their three fellow hijackers for Flight 11 stayed together in a hotel in Newton, Massachusetts, just outside of Boston.[191]

Shehhi and his team targeting United Airlines Flight 175 from Logan Airport spent their last hours at two Boston hotels.[192] The plan that started with a proposal by KSM in 1996 had evolved to overcome numerous obstacles. Now 19 men waited in nondescript hotel rooms to board four flights the next morning.

CHAPTER EIGHT

"The System Was Blinking Red"

8.1 THE SUMMER OF THREAT

As 2001 began, counterterrorism officials were receiving frequent but fragmentary reports about threats. Indeed, there appeared to be possible threats almost everywhere the United States had interests—including at home.

To understand how the escalation in threat reporting was handled in the summer of 2001, it is useful to understand how threat information in general is collected and conveyed. Information is collected through several methods, including signals intelligence and interviews of human sources, and gathered into intelligence reports. Depending on the source and nature of the reporting, these reports may be highly classified—and therefore tightly held—or less sensitive and widely disseminated to state and local law enforcement agencies. Threat reporting must be disseminated, either through individual reports or through threat advisories. Such advisories, intended to alert their recipients, may address a specific threat or be a general warning.

Because the amount of reporting is so voluminous, only a select fraction can be chosen for briefing the president and senior officials. During 2001, Director of Central Intelligence George Tenet was briefed regularly regarding threats and other operational information relating to Usama Bin Ladin.[1] He in turn met daily with President Bush, who was briefed by the CIA through what is known as the President's Daily Brief (PDB). Each PDB consists of a series of six to eight relatively short articles or briefs covering a broad array of topics; CIA staff decides which subjects are the most important on any given day. There were more than 40 intelligence articles in the PDBs from January 20 to September 10, 2001, that related to Bin Ladin. The PDB is considered highly sensitive and is distributed to only a handful of high-level officials.[2]

The Senior Executive Intelligence Brief (SEIB), distributed to a broader group of officials, has a similar format and generally covers the same subjects as the PDB. It usually contains less information so as to protect sources and methods. Like their predecessors, the Attorney General, the FBI Director, and Richard Clarke, the National Security Council (NSC) counterterrorism coordinator, all received the SEIB, not the PDB.[3] Clarke and his staff had extensive access to terrorism reporting, but they did not have access to internal, nondisseminated information at the National Security Agency (NSA), CIA, or FBI.

The Drumbeat Begins

In the spring of 2001, the level of reporting on terrorist threats and planned attacks increased dramatically to its highest level since the millennium alert. At the end of March, the intelligence community disseminated a terrorist threat advisory, indicating a heightened threat of Sunni extremist terrorist attacks against U.S. facilities, personnel, and other interests.[4]

On March 23, in connection with discussions about possibly reopening Pennsylvania Avenue in front of the White House, Clarke warned National Security Advisor Condoleezza Rice that domestic or foreign terrorists might use a truck bomb—their "weapon of choice"—on Pennsylvania Avenue. That would result, he said, in the destruction of the West Wing and parts of the residence.[5] He also told her that he thought there were terrorist cells within the United States, including al Qaeda.

The next week, Rice was briefed on the activities of Abu Zubaydah and on CIA efforts to locate him. As pointed out in chapter 6, Abu Zubaydah had been a major figure in the millennium plots. Over the next few weeks, the CIA repeatedly issued warnings—including calls from DCI Tenet to Clarke—that Abu Zubaydah was planning an operation in the near future. One report cited a source indicating that Abu Zubaydah was planning an attack in a country that CIA analysts thought might be Israel, or perhaps Saudi Arabia or India. Clarke relayed these reports to Rice.[6]

In response to these threats, the FBI sent a message to all its field offices on April 13, summarizing reporting to date. It asked the offices to task all resources, including human sources and electronic databases, for any information pertaining to "current operational activities relating to Sunni extremism." It did not suggest that there was a domestic threat.[7]

The interagency Counterterrorism Security Group (CSG) that Clarke chaired discussed the Abu Zubaydah reports on April 19. The next day, a briefing to top officials reported "Bin Ladin planning multiple operations." When the deputies discussed al Qaeda policy on April 30, they began with a briefing on the threat.[8]

In May 2001, the drumbeat of reporting grew louder with reports to top officials that "Bin Ladin public profile may presage attack" and "Bin Ladin network's plans advancing." In early May, a walk-in to the FBI claimed there was a plan to launch attacks on London, Boston, and New York. Attorney General John Ashcroft was briefed by the CIA on May 15 regarding al Qaeda generally and the current threat reporting specifically. The next day brought a report that a phone call to a U.S. embassy had warned that Bin Ladin supporters were planning an attack in the United States using "high explosives." On May 17, based on the previous day's report, the first item on the CSG's agenda was "UBL: Operation Planned in U.S."[9] The anonymous caller's tip could not be corroborated.

Late May brought reports of a possible hostage plot against Americans abroad to force the release of prisoners, including Sheikh Omar Abdel Rahman, the "Blind Sheikh," who was serving a life sentence for his role in the 1993 plot to blow up sites in New York City. The reporting noted that operatives might opt to hijack an aircraft or storm a U.S. embassy. This report led to a Federal Aviation Administration (FAA) information circular to airlines noting the potential for "an airline hijacking to free terrorists incarcerated in the United States." Other reporting mentioned that Abu Zubaydah was planning an attack, possibly against Israel, and expected to carry out several more if things went well. On May 24 alone, counterterrorism officials grappled with reports alleging plots in Yemen and Italy, as well as a report about a cell in Canada that an anonymous caller had claimed might be planning an attack against the United States.[10]

Reports similar to many of these were made available to President Bush in morning intelligence briefings with DCI Tenet, usually attended by Vice President Dick Cheney and National Security Advisor Rice. While these briefings discussed general threats to attack America and American interests, the specific threats mentioned in these briefings were all overseas.

On May 29, Clarke suggested that Rice ask DCI Tenet what more the United States could do to stop Abu Zubaydah from launching "a series of major terrorist attacks," probably on Israeli targets, but possibly on U.S. facilities. Clarke wrote to Rice and her deputy, Stephen Hadley, "When these attacks occur, as they likely will, we will wonder what more we could have done to stop them." In May, CIA Counterterrorist Center (CTC) Chief Cofer Black told Rice that the current threat level was a 7 on a scale of 1 to 10, as compared to an 8 during the millennium.[11]

High Probability of Near-Term "Spectacular" Attacks

Threat reports surged in June and July, reaching an even higher peak of urgency. The summer threats seemed to be focused on Saudi Arabia, Israel, Bahrain, Kuwait, Yemen, and possibly Rome, but the danger could be anywhere—including a possible attack on the G-8 summit in Genoa. A

June 12 CIA report passing along biographical background information on several terrorists mentioned, in commenting on Khalid Sheikh Mohammed, that he was recruiting people to travel to the United States to meet with colleagues already there so that they might conduct terrorist attacks on Bin Ladin's behalf. On June 22, the CIA notified all its station chiefs about intelligence suggesting a possible al Qaeda suicide attack on a U.S. target over the next few days. DCI Tenet asked that all U.S. ambassadors be briefed.[12]

That same day, the State Department notified all embassies of the terrorist threat and updated its worldwide public warning. In June, the State Department initiated the Visa Express program in Saudi Arabia as a security measure, in order to keep long lines of foreigners away from vulnerable embassy spaces. The program permitted visa applications to be made through travel agencies, instead of directly at the embassy or consulate.[13]

A terrorist threat advisory distributed in late June indicated a high probability of near-term "spectacular" terrorist attacks resulting in numerous casualties. Other reports' titles warned, "Bin Ladin Attacks May be Imminent" and "Bin Ladin and Associates Making Near-Term Threats." The latter reported multiple attacks planned over the coming days, including a "severe blow" against U.S. and Israeli "interests" during the next two weeks.[14]

On June 21, near the height of the threat reporting, U.S. Central Command raised the force protection condition level for U.S. troops in six countries to the highest possible level, Delta. The U.S. Fifth Fleet moved out of its port in Bahrain, and a U.S. Marine Corps exercise in Jordan was halted. U.S. embassies in the Persian Gulf conducted an emergency security review, and the embassy in Yemen was closed. The CSG had foreign emergency response teams, known as FESTs, ready to move on four hours' notice and kept up the terrorism alert posture on a "rolling 24 hour basis."[15]

On June 25, Clarke warned Rice and Hadley that six separate intelligence reports showed al Qaeda personnel warning of a pending attack. An Arabic television station reported Bin Ladin's pleasure with al Qaeda leaders who were saying that the next weeks "will witness important surprises" and that U.S. and Israeli interests will be targeted. Al Qaeda also released a new recruitment and fund-raising tape. Clarke wrote that this was all too sophisticated to be merely a psychological operation to keep the United States on edge, and the CIA agreed. The intelligence reporting consistently described the upcoming attacks as occurring on a calamitous level, indicating that they would cause the world to be in turmoil and that they would consist of possible multiple—but not necessarily simultaneous—attacks.[16]

On June 28, Clarke wrote Rice that the pattern of al Qaeda activity indicating attack planning over the past six weeks "had reached a crescendo." "A series of new reports continue to convince me and analysts at State, CIA, DIA [Defense Intelligence Agency], and NSA that a major terrorist attack or series of attacks is likely in July," he noted. One al Qaeda intelligence report warned that something "very, very very, very" big was about to happen, and most of Bin Ladin's network was reportedly anticipating the attack. In late June, the CIA ordered all its station chiefs to share information on al Qaeda with their host governments and to push for immediate disruptions of cells.[17]

The headline of a June 30 briefing to top officials was stark: "Bin Ladin Planning High-Profile Attacks." The report stated that Bin Ladin operatives expected near-term attacks to have dramatic consequences of catastrophic proportions. That same day, Saudi Arabia declared its highest level of terror alert. Despite evidence of delays possibly caused by heightened U.S. security, the planning for attacks was continuing.[18]

On July 2, the FBI Counterterrorism Division sent a message to federal agencies and state and local law enforcement agencies summarizing information regarding threats from Bin Ladin. It warned that there was an increased volume of threat reporting, indicating a potential for attacks against U.S. targets abroad from groups "aligned with or sympathetic to Usama Bin Ladin." Despite the general warnings, the message further stated, "The FBI has no information indicating a credible threat of terrorist attack in the United States." However, it went on to emphasize that the possibility of attack in the United States could not be discounted. It also noted that the July 4 holiday might heighten the threats. The report asked recipients to "exercise extreme vigilance" and "report suspicious activities" to the FBI. It did not suggest specific actions that they should take to prevent attacks.[19]

Disruption operations against al Qaeda-affiliated cells were launched involving 20 countries. Several terrorist operatives were detained by foreign governments, possibly disrupting operations in the Gulf and Italy and perhaps averting attacks against two or three U.S. embassies. Clarke and others told us of a particular concern about possible attacks on the Fourth of July. After it passed uneventfully, the CSG decided to maintain the alert.[20]

To enlist more international help, Vice President Cheney contacted Saudi Crown Prince Abdullah on July 5. Hadley apparently called European counterparts, while Clarke worked with senior officials in the Gulf. In late July, because of threats, Italy closed the airspace over Genoa and mounted antiaircraft batteries at the Genoa airport during the G-8 summit, which President Bush attended.[21]

At home, the CSG arranged for the CIA to brief intelligence and security officials from several domestic agencies. On July 5, representatives from the Immigration and Naturalization Service (INS), the FAA, the Coast Guard, the Secret Service, Customs, the CIA, and the FBI met with Clarke to discuss the current threat. Attendees report that they were told not to disseminate the threat information they received at the meeting. They interpreted this direction to mean that although they could brief their superiors, they could not send out advisories to the field. An NSC official recalls a somewhat different emphasis, saying that attendees were asked to take the information back to their home agencies and "do what you can" with it, subject to classification and distribution restrictions. A representative from the INS asked for a summary of the information that she could share with field offices. She never received one.[22]

That same day, the CIA briefed Attorney General Ashcroft on the al Qaeda threat, warning that a significant terrorist attack was imminent. Ashcroft was told that preparations for multiple attacks were in late stages or already complete and that little additional warning could be expected. The briefing addressed only threats outside the United States.[23]

The next day, the CIA representative told the CSG that al Qaeda members believed the upcoming attack would be "spectacular," qualitatively different from anything they had done to date.[24]

Apparently as a result of the July 5 meeting with Clarke, the interagency committee on federal building security was tasked to examine security measures. This committee met on July 9, when 37 officials from 27 agencies and organizations were briefed on the "current threat level" in the United States. They were told that not only the threat reports from abroad but also the recent convictions in the East Africa bombings trial, the conviction of Ahmed Ressam, and the just-returned Khobar Towers indictments reinforced the need to "exercise extreme vigilance." Attendees were expected to determine whether their respective agencies needed enhanced security measures.[25]

On July 18, 2001, the State Department provided a warning to the public regarding possible terrorist attacks in the Arabian Peninsula.[26]

Acting FBI Director Thomas Pickard told us he had one of his periodic conference calls with all special agents in charge on July 19. He said one of the items he mentioned was the need, in light of increased threat reporting, to have evidence response teams ready to move at a moment's notice, in case of an attack.[27] He did not task field offices to try to determine whether any plots were being considered within the United States or to take any action to disrupt any such plots.

In mid-July, reporting started to indicate that Bin Ladin's

plans had been delayed, maybe for as long as two months, but not abandoned. On July 23, the lead item for CSG discussion was still the al Qaeda threat, and it included mention of suspected terrorist travel to the United States.[28]

On July 31, an FAA circular appeared alerting the aviation community to "reports of possible near-term terrorist operations . . . particularly on the Arabian Peninsula and/or Israel." It stated that the FAA had no credible evidence of specific plans to attack U.S. civil aviation, though it noted that some of the "currently active" terrorist groups were known to "plan and train for hijackings" and were able to build and conceal sophisticated explosive devices in luggage and consumer products.[29]

Tenet told us that in his world "the system was blinking red." By late July, Tenet said, it could not "get any worse."[30] Not everyone was convinced. Some asked whether all these threats might just be deception. On June 30, the SEIB contained an article titled "Bin Ladin Threats Are Real." Yet Hadley told Tenet in July that Deputy Secretary of Defense Paul Wolfowitz questioned the reporting. Perhaps Bin Ladin was trying to study U.S. reactions. Tenet replied that he had already addressed the Defense Department's questions on this point; the reporting was convincing. To give a sense of his anxiety at the time, one senior official in the Counterterrorist Center told us that he and a colleague were considering resigning in order to go public with their concerns.[31]

The Calm Before the Storm

On July 27, Clarke informed Rice and Hadley that the spike in intelligence about a near-term al Qaeda attack had stopped. He urged keeping readiness high during the August vacation period, warning that another report suggested an attack had just been postponed for a few months "but will still happen."[32]

On August 1, the FBI issued an advisory that in light of the increased volume of threat reporting and the upcoming anniversary of the East Africa embassy bombings, increased attention should be paid to security planning. It noted that although most of the reporting indicated a potential for attacks on U.S. interests abroad, the possibility of an attack in the United States could not be discounted.[33]

On August 3, the intelligence community issued an advisory concluding that the threat of impending al Qaeda attacks would likely continue indefinitely. Citing threats in the Arabian Peninsula, Jordan, Israel, and Europe, the advisory suggested that al Qaeda was lying in wait and searching for gaps in security before moving forward with the planned attacks.[34]

During the spring and summer of 2001, President Bush had on several occasions asked his briefers whether any of the threats pointed to the United States. Reflecting on these questions, the CIA decided to write a briefing article summarizing its understanding of this danger. Two CIA analysts involved in preparing this briefing article believed it represented an opportunity to communicate their view that the threat of a Bin Ladin attack in the United States remained both current and serious.[35] The result was an article in the August 6 Presidential Daily Brief titled "Bin Ladin Determined to Strike in US." It was the 36th PDB item briefed so far that year that related to Bin Ladin or al Qaeda, and the first devoted to the possibility of an attack in the United States.

The President told us the August 6 report was historical in nature. President Bush said the article told him that al Qaeda was dangerous, which he said he had known since he had become President. The President said Bin Ladin had long been talking about his desire to attack America. He recalled some operational data on the FBI, and remembered thinking it was heartening that 70 investigations were under way. As best he could recollect, Rice had mentioned that the Yemenis' surveillance of a federal building in New York had been looked into in May and June, but there was no actionable intelligence.

He did not recall discussing the August 6 report with the Attorney General or whether Rice had done so. He said that if his advisers had told him there was a cell in the United States, they would have moved to take care of it. That never happened.[36]

The following is the text of an item from the Presidential Daily Brief received by President George W. Bush on August 6, 2001.[37] Redacted material is indicated by brackets.

Bin Ladin Determined To Strike in US

Clandestine, foreign government, and media reports indicate Bin Ladin since 1997 has wanted to conduct terrorist attacks in the US. Bin Ladin implied in US television interviews in 1997 and 1998 that his followers would follow the example of World Trade Center bomber Ramzi Yousef and "bring the fighting to America."

After US missile strikes on his base in Afghanistan in 1998, Bin Ladin told followers he wanted to retaliate in Washington, according to a [—] service.

An Egyptian Islamic Jihad (EIJ) operative told an [—] service at the same time that Bin Ladin was planning to exploit the operative's access to the US to mount a terrorist strike.

The millennium plotting in Canada in 1999 may have been part of Bin Ladin's first serious attempt to implement a terrorist strike in the US.
Convicted plotter Ahmed Ressam has told the FBI that he conceived the idea to attack Los Angeles International Airport himself, but that Bin Ladin lieutenant Abu Zubaydah encouraged him and helped facilitate the operation. Ressam also said that in 1998 Abu Zubaydah was planning his own US attack.

Ressam says Bin Ladin was aware of the Los Angeles operation.

Although Bin Ladin has not succeeded, his attacks against the US Embassies in Kenya and Tanzania in

1998 demonstrate that he prepares operations years in advance and is not deterred by setbacks. Bin Ladin associates surveilled our Embassies in Nairobi and Dar es Salaam as early as 1993, and some members of the Nairobi cell planning the bombings were arrested and deported in 1997.

Al-Qa'ida members—including some who are US citizens—have resided in or traveled to the US for years, and the group apparently maintains a support structure that could aid attacks. Two al-Qua' da members found guilty in the conspiracy to bomb our embassies in East Africa were US citizens, and a senior EIJ member lived in California in the mid-1990s.

A clandestine source said in 1998 that a Bin Ladin cell in New York was recruiting Muslim-American youth for attacks.

We have not been able to corroborate some of the more sensational threat reporting, such as that from a [—] service in 1998 saying that Bin Ladin wanted to hijack a US aircraft to gain the release of "Blind Shaykh" 'Umar 'Abd al-Rahman and other US-held extremists.

Nevertheless, FBI information since that time indicates patterns of suspicious activity in this country consistent with preparations for hijackings or other types of attacks, including recent surveillance of federal buildings in New York.

The FBI is conducting approximately 70 full field investigations throughout the US that it considers Bin Ladin-related. CIA and the FBI are investigating a call to our Embassy in the UAE in May saying that a group of Bin Ladin supporters was in the US planning attacks with explosives.

Although the following day's SEIB repeated the title of this PDB, it did not contain the reference to hijackings, the alert in New York, the alleged casing of buildings in New York, the threat phoned in to the embassy, or the fact that the FBI had approximately 70 ongoing bin Ladin–related investigations.[38] No CSG or other NSC meeting was held to discuss the possible threat of a strike in the United States as a result of this report.

Late in the month, a foreign service reported that Abu Zubaydah was considering mounting terrorist attacks in the United States, after postponing possible operations in Europe. No targets, timing, or method of attack were provided.[39]

We have found no indication of any further discussion before September 11 among the President and his top advisers of the possibility of a threat of an al Qaeda attack in the United States. DCI Tenet visited President Bush in Crawford, Texas, on August 17 and participated in PDB briefings of the President between August 31 (after the President had returned to Washington) and September 10. But Tenet does not recall any discussions with the President of the domestic threat during this period.[40]

Most of the intelligence community recognized in the summer of 2001 that the number and severity of threat reports were unprecedented. Many officials told us that they knew something terrible was planned, and they were desperate to stop it. Despite their large number, the threats received contained few specifics regarding time, place, method, or target. Most suggested that attacks were planned against targets overseas; others indicated threats against unspecified "U.S. interests." We cannot say for certain whether these reports, as dramatic as they were, related to the 9/11 attacks.

Government Response to the Threats

National Security Advisor Rice told us that the CSG was the "nerve center" for running the crisis, although other senior officials were involved over the course of the summer. In addition to his daily meetings with President Bush, and weekly meetings to go over other issues with Rice, Tenet was speaking regularly with Secretary of State Colin Powell and Secretary of Defense Donald Rumsfeld. The foreign policy principals routinely talked on the telephone every day on a variety of topics.[41]

Hadley told us that before 9/11, he and Rice did not feel they had the job of coordinating domestic agencies. They felt that Clarke and the CSG (part of the NSC) were the NSC's bridge between foreign and domestic threats.[42]

There was a clear disparity in the levels of response to foreign versus domestic threats. Numerous actions were taken overseas to disrupt possible attacks—enlisting foreign partners to upset terrorist plans, closing embassies, moving military assets out of the way of possible harm. Far less was done domestically—in part, surely, because to the extent that specifics did exist, they pertained to threats overseas. As noted earlier, a threat against the embassy in Yemen quickly resulted in its closing. Possible domestic threats were more vague. When reports did not specify where the attacks were to take place, officials presumed that they would again be overseas, though they did not rule out a target in the United States. Each of the FBI threat advisories made this point.[43]

Clarke mentioned to National Security Advisor Rice at least twice that al Qaeda sleeper cells were likely in the United States. In January 2001, Clarke forwarded a strategy paper to Rice warning that al Qaeda had a presence in the United States. He noted that two key al Qaeda members in the Jordanian cell involved in the millennium plot were naturalized U.S. citizens and that one jihadist suspected in the East Africa bombings had "informed the FBI that an extensive network of al Qida 'sleeper agents' currently exists in the US." He added that Ressam's abortive December 1999 attack revealed al Qaeda supporters in the United States.[44] His analysis, however, was based not on new threat reporting but on past experience.

The September 11 attacks fell into the void between the foreign and domestic threats. The foreign intelligence agencies were watching overseas, alert to foreign threats to U.S.

interests there. The domestic agencies were waiting for evidence of a domestic threat from sleeper cells within the United States. No one was looking for a foreign threat to domestic targets. The threat that was coming was not from sleeper cells. It was foreign—but from foreigners who had infiltrated into the United States.

A second cause of this disparity in response is that domestic agencies did not know what to do, and no one gave them direction. Cressey told us that the CSG did not tell the agencies how to respond to the threats. He noted that the agencies that were operating overseas did not need direction on how to respond; they had experience with such threats and had a "playbook." In contrast, the domestic agencies did not have a game plan. Neither the NSC (including the CSG) nor anyone else instructed them to create one.[45]

This lack of direction was evident in the July 5 meeting with representatives from the domestic agencies. The briefing focused on overseas threats. The domestic agencies were not questioned about how they planned to address the threat and were not told what was expected of them. Indeed, as noted earlier, they were specifically told they could not issue advisories based on the briefing.[46] The domestic agencies' limited response indicates that they did not perceive a call to action.

Clarke reflected a different perspective in an email to Rice on September 15, 2001. He summarized the steps taken by the CSG to alert domestic agencies to the possibility of an attack in the United States. Clarke concluded that domestic agencies, including the FAA, knew that the CSG believed a major al Qaeda attack was coming and could be in the United States.

Although the FAA had authority to issue security directives mandating new security procedures, none of the few that were released during the summer of 2001 increased security at checkpoints or on board aircraft. The information circulars mostly urged air carriers to "exercise prudence" and be alert. Prior to 9/11, the FAA did present a CD-ROM to air carriers and airport authorities describing the increased threat to civil aviation. The presentation mentioned the possibility of suicide hijackings but said that "fortunately, we have no indication that any group is currently thinking in that direction."[47] The FAA conducted 27 special security briefings for specific air carriers between May 1, 2001, and September 11, 2001. Two of these briefings discussed the hijacking threat overseas. None discussed the possibility of suicide hijackings or the use of aircraft as weapons. No new security measures were instituted.[48]

Rice told us she understood that the FBI had tasked its 56 U.S. field offices to increase surveillance of suspected terrorists and to reach out to informants who might have information about terrorist plots. An NSC staff document at the time describes such a tasking as having occurred in late June but does not indicate whether it was generated by the NSC or the FBI. Other than the previously described April 13 communication sent to all FBI field offices, however, the FBI could not find any record of having received such a directive. The April 13 document asking field offices to gather information on Sunni extremism did not mention any possible threat within the United States and did not order surveillance of suspected operatives. The NSC did not specify what the FBI's directives should contain and did not review what had been issued earlier.[49]

Acting FBI Director Pickard told us that in addition to his July 19 conference call, he mentioned the heightened terrorist threat in individual calls with the special agents in charge of field offices during their annual performance review discussions. In speaking with agents around the country, we found little evidence that any such concerns had reached FBI personnel beyond the New York Field Office.[50]

The head of counterterrorism at the FBI, Dale Watson, said he had many discussions about possible attacks with Cofer Black at the CIA. They had expected an attack on July 4. Watson said he felt deeply that something was going to happen. But he told us the threat information was "nebulous." He wished he had known more. He wished he had had

"500 analysts looking at Usama Bin Ladin threat information instead of two."[51]

Attorney General Ashcroft was briefed by the CIA in May and by Pickard in early July about the danger. Pickard said he met with Ashcroft once a week in late June, through July, and twice in August. There is a dispute regarding Ashcroft's interest in Pickard's briefings about the terrorist threat situation. Pickard told us that after two such briefings Ashcroft told him that he did not want to hear about the threats anymore. Ashcroft denies Pickard's charge. Pickard says he continued to present terrorism information during further briefings that summer, but nothing further on the "chatter" the U.S. government was receiving.[52]

The Attorney General told us he asked Pickard whether there was intelligence about attacks in the United States and that Pickard said no. Pickard said he replied that he could not assure Ashcroft that there would be no attacks in the United States, although the reports of threats were related to overseas targets. Ashcroft said he therefore assumed the FBI was doing what it needed to do. He acknowledged that in retrospect, this was a dangerous assumption. He did not ask the FBI what it was doing in response to the threats and did not task it to take any specific action. He also did not direct the INS, then still part of the Department of Justice, to take any specific action.[53]

In sum, the domestic agencies never mobilized in response to the threat. They did not have direction, and did not have a plan to institute. The borders were not hardened. Transportation systems were not fortified. Electronic surveillance was not targeted against a domestic threat.[54] State and local law enforcement were not marshaled to augment the FBI's efforts. The public was not warned.

The terrorists exploited deep institutional failings within our government. The question is whether extra vigilance might have turned up an opportunity to disrupt the plot. As seen in chapter 7, al Qaeda's operatives made mistakes. At least two such mistakes created opportunities during 2001, especially in late August.

8.2 LATE LEADS—MIHDHAR, MOUSSAOUI, AND KSM

In chapter 6 we discussed how intelligence agencies successfully detected some of the early travel in the planes operation, picking up the movements of Khalid al Mihdhar and identifying him, and seeing his travel converge with someone they perhaps could have identified but did not—Nawaf al Hazmi—as well as with less easily identifiable people such as Khallad and Abu Bara. These observations occurred in December 1999 and January 2000. The trail had been lost in January 2000 without a clear realization that it had been lost, and without much effort to pick it up again. Nor had the CIA placed Mihdhar on the State Department's watchlist for suspected terrorists, so that either an embassy or a port of entry might take note if Mihdhar showed up again.

On four occasions in 2001, the CIA, the FBI, or both had apparent opportunities to refocus on the significance of Hazmi and Mihdhar and reinvigorate the search for them. After reviewing those episodes we will turn to the handling of the Moussaoui case and some late leads regarding Khalid Sheikh Mohammed.

January 2001: Identification of Khallad

Almost one year after the original trail had been lost in Bangkok, the FBI and the CIA were working on the investigation of the *Cole* bombing. They learned of the link between a captured conspirator and a person called "Khallad." They also learned that Khallad was a senior security official for Bin Ladin who had helped direct the bombing (we introduced Khallad in chapter 5, and returned to his role in the *Cole* bombing in chapter 6).[55]

One of the members of the FBI's investigative team in Yemen realized that he had heard of Khallad before, from a joint FBI/CIA source four months earlier. The FBI agent obtained from a foreign government a photo of the person believed to have directed the *Cole* bombing. It was shown to the source, and he confirmed that the man in that photograph was the same Khallad he had described.[56]

In December 2000, on the basis of some links associated with Khalid al Mihdhar, the CIA's Bin Ladin unit speculated that Khallad and Khalid al Mihdhar might be one and the same.[57]

The CIA asked that a Kuala Lumpur surveillance photo of Mihdhar be shown to the joint source who had identified Khallad. In early January 2001, two photographs from the Kuala Lumpur meeting were shown to the source. One was a known photograph of Mihdhar, the other a photograph of a then unknown subject. The source did not recognize Mihdhar. But he indicated he was 90 percent certain that the other individual was Khallad.[58]

This meant that Khallad and Mihdhar were two different people. It also meant that there was a link between Khallad and Mihdhar, making Mihdhar seem even more suspicious.[59] Yet we found no effort by the CIA to renew the long-abandoned search for Mihdhar or his travel companions.

In addition, we found that the CIA did not notify the FBI of this identification. DCI Tenet and Cofer Black testified before Congress's Joint Inquiry into 9/11 that the FBI had access to this identification from the beginning. But drawing on an extensive record, including documents that were not available to the CIA personnel who drafted that testimony, we conclude this was not the case. The FBI's primary *Cole* investigators had no knowledge that Khallad had been in Kuala Lumpur with Mihdhar and others until after the September 11 attacks. Because the FBI had not been informed in January 2000 about Mihdhar's possession of a U.S. visa, it had not then started looking for him in the United States. Because it did not know of the links between Khallad and Mihdhar, it did not start looking for him in January 2001.[60]

This incident is an example of how day-to-day gaps in information sharing can emerge even when there is mutual goodwill. The information was from a joint FBI/CIA source who spoke essentially no English and whose languages were not understood by the FBI agent on the scene overseas. Is-

sues of travel and security necessarily kept short the amount
of time spent with the source. As a result, the CIA officer
usually did not translate either questions or answers for his
FBI colleague and friend.[61]

For interviews without simultaneous translation, the FBI
agent on the scene received copies of the reports that the
CIA disseminated to other agencies regarding the interviews. But he was not given access to the CIA's internal operational reports, which contained more detail. It was
there—in reporting to which FBI investigators did not have
access—that information regarding the January 2001 identification of Khallad appeared. The CIA officer does not recall this particular identification and thus cannot say why it
was not shared with his FBI colleague. He might not have
understood the possible significance of the new identification.[62]

In June 2000, Mihdhar left California and returned to
Yemen. It is possible that if, in January 2001, the CIA had
resumed its search for him, placed him on the State Department's TIPOFF watchlist, or provided the FBI with the information, he might have been found—either before or at
the time he applied for a new visa in June 2001, or when he
returned to the United States on July 4.

Spring 2001: Looking Again at Kuala Lumpur

By mid-May 2001, as the threat reports were surging, a CIA
official detailed to the International Terrorism Operations
Section at the FBI wondered where the attacks might occur.
We will call him "John." Recalling the episode about the
Kuala Lumpur travel of Mihdhar and his associates, "John"
searched the CIA's databases for information regarding the
travel. On May 15, he and an official at the CIA reexamined
many of the old cables from early 2000, including the information that Mihdhar had a U.S. visa, and that Hazmi had
come to Los Angeles on January 15, 2000.[63]

The CIA official who reviewed the cables took no action
regarding them. "John," however, began a lengthy exchange
with a CIA analyst, whom we will call "Dave," to figure out

what these cables meant. "John" was aware of how dangerous Khallad was—at one point calling him a "major league
killer." He concluded that "something bad was definitely
up." Despite the U.S. links evident in this traffic, "John"
made no effort to determine whether any of these individuals was in the United States. He did not raise that possibility
with his FBI counterpart. He was focused on Malaysia.[64]

"John" described the CIA as an agency that tended to
play a "zone defense." He was worrying solely about Southeast Asia, not the United States. In contrast, he told us, the
FBI tends to play "man-to-man."[65]

Desk officers at the CIA's Bin Ladin unit did not have
"cases" in the same sense as an FBI agent who works an investigation from beginning to end. Thus, when the trail went
cold after the Kuala Lumpur meeting in January 2000, the
desk officer moved on to different things. By the time the
March 2000 cable arrived with information that one of the
travelers had flown to Los Angeles, the case officer was no
longer responsible for follow-up. While several individuals
at the Bin Ladin unit opened the cable when it arrived in
March 2000, no action was taken.[66]

The CIA's zone defense concentrated on "where," not
"who." Had its information been shared with the FBI, a
combination of the CIA's zone defense and the FBI's man-
to-man approach might have been productive.

June 2001: The Meeting in New York

"John's" review of the Kuala Lumpur meeting did set off
some more sharing of information, getting the attention of an
FBI analyst whom we will call "Jane." "Jane" was assigned to
the FBI's *Cole* investigation. She knew that another terrorist
involved in that operation, Fahd al Quso, had traveled to
Bangkok in January 2000 to give money to Khallad.[67]

"Jane" and the CIA analyst, "Dave," had been working together on *Cole*-related issues. Chasing Quso's trail, "Dave"
suggested showing some photographs to FBI agents in New
York who were working on the *Cole* case and had interviewed Quso.[68]

"John" gave three Kuala Lumpur surveillance pictures to "Jane" to show to the New York agents. She was told that one of the individuals in the photographs was someone named Khalid al Mihdhar. She did not know why the photographs had been taken or why the Kuala Lumpur travel might be significant, and she was not told that someone had identified Khallad in the photographs. When "Jane" did some research in a database for intelligence reports, Intelink, she found the original NSA reports on the planning for the meeting. Because the CIA had not disseminated reports on its tracking of Mihdhar, "Jane" did not pull up any information about Mihdhar's U.S. visa or about travel to the United States by Hazmi or Mihdhar.[69]

"Jane," "Dave," and an FBI analyst who was on detail to the CIA's Bin Ladin unit went to New York on June 11 to meet with the agents about the *Cole* case. "Jane" brought the surveillance pictures. At some point in the meeting she showed the photographs to the agents and asked whether they recognized Quso in any of them. The agents asked questions about the photographs—Why were they taken? Why were these people being followed? Where are the rest of the photographs?[70]

The only information "Jane" had about the meeting—other than the photographs—were the NSA reports that she had found on Intelink. These reports, however, contained caveats that their contents could not be shared with criminal investigators without the permission of the Justice Department's Office of Intelligence Policy and Review (OIPR). Therefore "Jane" concluded that she could not pass on information from those reports to the agents. This decision was potentially significant, because the signals intelligence she did not share linked Mihdhar to a suspected terrorist facility in the Middle East. The agents would have established a link to the suspected facility from their work on the embassy bombings case. This link would have made them very interested in learning more about Mihdhar.[71] The sad irony is that the agents who found the source were being kept from obtaining the fruits of their own work.

"Dave," the CIA analyst, knew more about the Kuala Lumpur meeting. He knew that Mihdhar possessed a U.S. visa, that his visa application indicated that he intended to travel to New York, that Hazmi had traveled to Los Angeles, and that a source had put Mihdhar in the company of Khallad. No one at the meeting asked him what he knew; he did not volunteer anything. He told investigators that as a CIA analyst, he was not authorized to answer FBI questions regarding CIA information. "Jane" said she assumed that if "Dave" knew the answers to questions, he would have volunteered them. The New York agents left the meeting without obtaining information that might have started them looking for Mihdhar.[72]

Mihdhar had been a weak link in al Qaeda's operational planning. He had left the United States in June 2000, a mistake KSM realized could endanger the entire plan—for to continue with the operation, Mihdhar would have to travel to the United States again. And unlike other operatives, Mihdhar was not "clean": he had jihadist connections. It was just such connections that had brought him to the attention of U.S. officials.

Nevertheless, in this case KSM's fears were not realized. Mihdhar received a new U.S. visa two days after the CIA-FBI meeting in New York. He flew to New York City on July 4. No one was looking for him.

August 2001: The Search for Mihdhar and Hazmi Begins and Fails

During the summer of 2001 "John," following a good instinct but not as part of any formal assignment, asked "Mary," an FBI analyst detailed to the CIA's Bin Ladin unit, to review all the Kuala Lumpur materials one more time. She had been at the New York meeting with "Jane" and "Dave" but had not looked into the issues yet herself. "John" asked her to do the research in her free time.[73]

"Mary" began her work on July 24. That day, she found the cable reporting that Mihdhar had a visa to the United States. A week later, she found the cable reporting that Mihdhar's visa application—what was later discovered to be his first application—listed New York as his destination. On August 21, she located the March 2000 cable that "noted with interest" that Hazmi had flown to Los Angeles in January 2000. She immediately grasped the significance of this information.[74]

"Mary" and "Jane" promptly met with an INS representative at FBI headquarters. On August 22, the INS told them that Mihdhar had entered the United States on January 15, 2000, and again on July 4, 2001. "Jane" and "Mary" also learned that there was no record that Hazmi had left the country since January 2000, and they assumed he had left with Mihdhar in June 2000. They decided that if Mihdhar was in the United States, he should be found.[75]

They divided up the work. "Mary" asked the Bin Ladin unit to draft a cable requesting that Mihdhar and Hazmi be put on the TIPOFF watchlist. Both Hazmi and Mihdhar were added to this watchlist on August 24.[76]

"Jane" took responsibility for the search effort inside the United States. As the information indicated that Mihdhar had last arrived in New York, she began drafting what is known as a lead for the FBI's New York Field Office. A lead relays information from one part of the FBI to another and requests that a particular action be taken. She called an agent in New York to give him a "heads-up" on the matter, but her draft lead was not sent until August 28. Her email told the New York agent that she wanted him to get started as soon as possible, but she labeled the lead as "Routine"—a designation that informs the receiving office that it has 30 days to respond.[77]

The agent who received the lead forwarded it to his squad supervisor. That same day, the supervisor forwarded the lead to an intelligence agent to open an intelligence case—an agent who thus was behind "the wall" keeping FBI intelligence information from being shared with criminal prosecutors. He also sent it to the *Cole* case agents and an agent who had spent significant time in Malaysia searching for another Khalid: Khalid Sheikh Mohammad.[78]

The suggested goal of the investigation was to locate Mihdhar, determine his contacts and reasons for being in the United States, and possibly conduct an interview. Before sending the lead, "Jane" had discussed it with "John," the CIA official on detail to the FBI. She had also checked with the acting head of the FBI's Bin Ladin unit. The discussion seems to have been limited to whether the search should be classified as an intelligence investigation or as a criminal one. It appears that no one informed higher levels of management in either the FBI or CIA about the case.[79] There is no evidence that the lead, or the search for these terrorist suspects, was substantively discussed at any level above deputy chief of a section within the Counterterrorism Division at FBI headquarters.

One of the *Cole* case agents read the lead with interest, and contacted "Jane" to obtain more information. "Jane" argued, however, that because the agent was designated a "criminal" FBI agent, not an intelligence FBI agent, the wall kept him from participating in any search for Mihdhar. In fact, she felt he had to destroy his copy of the lead because it contained NSA information from reports that included caveats ordering that the information not be shared without OIPR's permission. The agent asked "Jane" to get an opinion from the FBI's National Security Law Unit (NSLU) on whether he could open a criminal case on Mihdhar.[80]

"Jane" sent an email to the *Cole* case agent explaining that according to the NSLU, the case could be opened only as an intelligence matter, and that if Mihdhar was found, only designated intelligence agents could conduct or even be present at any interview. She appears to have misunderstood the complex rules that could apply to this situation.[81]

The FBI agent angrily responded:

Whatever has happened to this—someday someone will die—and wall or not—the public will not understand why we were not more effective and throwing every resource we had at certain "problems."

Let's hope the National Security Law Unit will stand

behind their decisions then, especially since the biggest threat to us now, UBL, is getting the most "protection."

"Jane" replied that she was not making up the rules; she claimed that they were in the relevant manual and "ordered by the [FISA] Court and every office of the FBI is required to follow them including FBI NY."[82]

It is now clear that everyone involved was confused about the rules governing the sharing and use of information gathered in intelligence channels. Because Mihdhar was being sought for his possible connection to or knowledge of the *Cole* bombing, he could be investigated or tracked under the existing *Cole* criminal case. No new criminal case was needed for the criminal agent to begin searching for Mihdhar. And as NSA had approved the passage of its information to the criminal agent, he could have conducted a search using all available information. As a result of this confusion, the criminal agents who were knowledgeable about al Qaeda and experienced with criminal investigative techniques, including finding suspects and possible criminal charges, were thus excluded from the search.[83]

The search was assigned to one FBI agent, and it was his very first counterterrorism lead. Because the lead was "routine," he was given 30 days to open an intelligence case and make some unspecified efforts to locate Mihdhar. He started the process a few days later. He checked local New York databases for criminal record and driver's license information and checked the hotel listed on Mihdhar's U.S. entry form. Finally, on September 11, the agent sent a lead to Los Angeles, because Mihdhar had initially arrived in Los Angeles in January 2000.[84]

We believe that if more resources had been applied and a significantly different approach taken, Mihdhar and Hazmi might have been found. They had used their true names in the United States. Still, the investigators would have needed luck as well as skill to find them prior to September 11 even if such searches had begun as early as August 23, when the lead was first drafted.[85]

Many FBI witnesses have suggested that even if Mihdhar had been found, there was nothing the agents could have done except follow him onto the planes. We believe this is incorrect. Both Hazmi and Mihdhar could have been held for immigration violations or as material witnesses in the *Cole* bombing case. Investigation or interrogation of them, and investigation of their travel and financial activities, could have yielded evidence of connections to other participants in the 9/11 plot. The simple fact of their detention could have derailed the plan. In any case, the opportunity did not arise.

Phoenix Memo

The Phoenix memo was investigated thoroughly by the Joint Inquiry and the Department of Justice Inspector General.[86] We will recap it briefly here. In July 2001, an FBI agent in the Phoenix field office sent a memo to FBI headquarters and to two agents on international terrorism squads in the New York Field Office, advising of the "possibility of a co-ordinated effort by Usama Bin Ladin" to send students to the United States to attend civil aviation schools. The agent based his theory on the "inordinate number of individuals of investigative interest" attending such schools in Arizona.[87]

The agent made four recommendations to FBI headquarters: to compile a list of civil aviation schools, establish liaison with those schools, discuss his theories about Bin Ladin with the intelligence community, and seek authority to obtain visa information on persons applying to flight schools. His recommendations were not acted on. His memo was forwarded to one field office. Managers of the Usama Bin Ladin unit and the Radical Fundamentalist unit at FBI headquarters were addressees, but they did not even see the memo until after September 11. No managers at headquarters saw the memo before September 11, and the New York Field Office took no action.[88]

As its author told investigators, the Phoenix memo was not an alert about suicide pilots. His worry was more about a Pan Am Flight 103 scenario in which explosives were placed on an aircraft. The memo's references to aviation training were broad, including aeronautical engineering.[89] If the memo had been distributed in a timely fashion and its recommendations acted on promptly, we do not believe it would have uncovered the plot. It might well, however, have sensitized the FBI so that it might have taken the Moussaoui matter more seriously the next month.

Zacarias Moussaoui

On August 15, 2001, the Minneapolis FBI Field Office initiated an intelligence investigation on Zacarias Moussaoui. As mentioned in chapter 7, he had entered the United States in February 2001, and had begun flight lessons at Airman Flight School in Norman, Oklahoma. He resumed his training at the Pan Am International Flight Academy in Eagan, Minnesota, starting on August 13. He had none of the usual qualifications for flight training on Pan Am's Boeing 747 flight simulators. He said he did not intend to become a commercial pilot but wanted the training as an "ego boosting thing." Moussaoui stood out because, with little knowledge of flying, he wanted to learn how to "take off and land" a Boeing 747.[90]

The agent in Minneapolis quickly learned that Moussaoui possessed jihadist beliefs. Moreover, Moussaoui had $32,000 in a bank account but did not provide a plausible explanation for this sum of money. He had traveled to Pakistan but became agitated when asked if he had traveled to nearby countries while in Pakistan (Pakistan was the customary route to the training camps in Afghanistan). He planned to receive martial arts training, and intended to purchase a global positioning receiver. The agent also noted that Moussaoui became extremely agitated whenever he was questioned regarding his religious beliefs. The agent concluded that Moussaoui was "an Islamic extremist preparing for some future act in furtherance of radical fundamentalist goals." He also believed Moussaoui's plan was related to his flight training.[91]

Moussaoui can be seen as an al Qaeda mistake and a

missed opportunity. An apparently unreliable operative, he had fallen into the hands of the FBI. As discussed in chapter 7, Moussaoui had been in contact with and received money from Ramzi Binalshibh. If Moussaoui had been connected to al Qaeda, questions should instantly have arisen about a possible al Qaeda plot that involved piloting airliners, a possibility that had never been seriously analyzed by the intelligence community.

The FBI agent who handled the case in conjunction with the INS representative on the Minneapolis Joint Terrorism Task Force suspected that Moussaoui might be planning to hijack a plane. Minneapolis and FBI headquarters debated whether Moussaoui should be arrested immediately or surveilled to obtain additional information. Because it was not clear whether Moussaoui could be imprisoned, the FBI case agent decided the most important thing was to prevent Moussaoui from obtaining any further training that he could use to carry out a potential attack.[92]

As a French national who had overstayed his visa, Moussaoui could be detained immediately. The INS arrested Moussaoui on the immigration violation. A deportation order was signed on August 17, 2001.[93]

The agents in Minnesota were concerned that the U.S. Attorney's Office in Minneapolis would find insufficient probable cause of a crime to obtain a criminal warrant to search Moussaoui's laptop computer.[94] Agents at FBI headquarters believed there was insufficient probable cause. Minneapolis therefore sought a special warrant under the Foreign Intelligence Surveillance Act to conduct the search (we introduced FISA in chapter 3).

To do so, however, the FBI needed to demonstrate probable cause that Moussaoui was an agent of a foreign power, a demonstration that was not required to obtain a criminal warrant but was a statutory requirement for a FISA warrant.[95] The case agent did not have sufficient information to connect Moussaoui to a "foreign power," so he reached out for help, in the United States and overseas.

The FBI agent's August 18 message requested assistance

from the FBI legal attaché in Paris. Moussaoui had lived in London, so the Minneapolis agent sought assistance from the legal attaché there as well. By August 24, the Minneapolis agent had also contacted an FBI detailee and a CIA desk officer at the Counterterrorist Center about the case.[96]

The FBI legal attaché's office in Paris first contacted the French government on August 16 or 17, shortly after speaking to the Minneapolis case agent on the telephone. On August 22 and 27, the French provided information that made a connection between Moussaoui and a rebel leader in Chechnya, Ibn al Khattab. This set off a spirited debate between the Minneapolis Field Office, FBI headquarters, and the CIA as to whether the Chechen rebels and Khattab were sufficiently associated with a terrorist organization to constitute a "foreign power" for purposes of the FISA statute. FBI headquarters did not believe this was good enough, and its National Security Law Unit declined to submit a FISA application.[97]

After receiving the written request for assistance, the legal attaché in London had promptly forwarded it to his counterparts in the British government, hand-delivering the request on August 21. On August 24, the CIA also sent a cable to London and Paris regarding "subjects involved in suspicious 747 flight training" that described Moussaoui as a possible "suicide hijacker." On August 28, the CIA sent a request for information to a different service of the British government; this communication warned that Moussaoui might be expelled to Britain by the end of August. The FBI office in London raised the matter briefly with British officials as an aside, after a meeting about a more urgent matter on September 3, and sent the British service a written update on September 5. The case was not handled by the British as a priority amid a large number of other terrorist-related inquiries.[98]

On September 4, the FBI sent a teletype to the CIA, the FAA, the Customs Service, the State Department, the INS, and the Secret Service summarizing the known facts regarding Moussaoui. It did not report the case agent's personal assessment that Moussaoui planned to hijack an airplane. It did contain the FAA's comment that it was not unusual for Middle Easterners to attend flight training schools in the United States.[99]

Although the Minneapolis agents wanted to tell the FAA from the beginning about Moussaoui, FBI headquarters instructed Minneapolis that it could not share the more complete report the case agent had prepared for the FAA. The Minneapolis supervisor sent the case agent in person to the local FAA office to fill in what he thought were gaps in the FBI headquarters teletype.[100] No FAA actions seem to have been taken in response.

There was substantial disagreement between Minneapolis agents and FBI headquarters as to what Moussaoui was planning to do. In one conversation between a Minneapolis supervisor and a headquarters agent, the latter complained that Minneapolis's FISA request was couched in a manner intended to get people "spun up." The supervisor replied that was precisely his intent. He said he was "trying to keep someone from taking a plane and crashing into the World Trade Center." The headquarters agent replied that this was not going to happen and that they did not know if Moussaoui was a terrorist.[101]

There is no evidence that either FBI Acting Director Pickard or Assistant Director for Counterterrorism Dale Watson was briefed on the Moussaoui case prior to 9/11. Michael Rolince, the FBI assistant director heading the Bureau's International Terrorism Operations Section (ITOS), recalled being told about Moussaoui in two passing hallway conversations but only in the context that he might be receiving telephone calls from Minneapolis complaining about how headquarters was handling the matter. He never received such a call. Although the acting special agent in charge of Minneapolis called the ITOS supervisors to discuss the Moussaoui case on August 27, he declined to go up the chain of command at FBI headquarters and call Rolince.[102]

On August 23, DCI Tenet was briefed about the Moussaoui case in a briefing titled "Islamic Extremist Learns to Fly."[103] Tenet was also told that Moussaoui wanted to learn to fly a 747, paid for his training in cash, was interested to learn the doors do not open in flight, and wanted to fly a simulated flight from London to New York. He was told that the FBI had arrested Moussaoui because of a visa overstay and that the CIA was working the case with the FBI. Tenet told us that no connection to al Qaeda was apparent to him at the time. Seeing it as an FBI case, he did not discuss the matter with anyone at the White House or the FBI. No connection was made between Moussaoui's presence in the United States and the threat reporting during the summer of 2001.[104]

On September 11, after the attacks, the FBI office in London renewed their appeal for information about Moussaoui. In response to U.S. requests, the British government supplied some basic biographical information about Moussaoui. The British government informed us that it also immediately tasked intelligence collection facilities for information about Moussaoui. On September 13, the British government received new, sensitive intelligence that Moussaoui had attended an al Qaeda training camp in Afghanistan. It passed this intelligence to the United States on the same day. Had this information been available in late August 2001, the Moussaoui case would almost certainly have received intense, high-level attention.[105]

The FBI also learned after 9/11 that the millennium terrorist Ressam, who by 2001 was cooperating with investigators, recognized Moussaoui as someone who had been in the Afghan camps.[106] As mentioned above, before 9/11 the FBI agents in Minneapolis had failed to persuade supervisors at headquarters that there was enough evidence to seek a FISA warrant to search Moussaoui's computer hard drive and belongings. Either the British information or the Ressam identification would have broken the logjam.

A maximum U.S. effort to investigate Moussaoui conceivably could have unearthed his connections to Binalshibh. Those connections might have brought investigators to the core of the 9/11 plot. The Binalshibh connection was recognized shortly after 9/11, though it was not an easy trail to find. Discovering it would have required quick and very substantial cooperation from the German government, which might well have been difficult to obtain.

However, publicity about Moussaoui's arrest and a possible hijacking threat might have derailed the plot.[107] With time, the search for Mihdhar and Hazmi and the investigation of Moussaoui might also have led to a breakthrough that would have disrupted the plot.

Khalid Sheikh Mohammed
Another late opportunity was presented by a confluence of information regarding Khalid Sheikh Mohammed received by the intelligence community in the summer of 2001. The possible links between KSM, Moussaoui, and an individual only later identified as Ramzi Binalshibh would remain undiscovered, however.

Although we readily equate KSM with al Qaeda today, this was not the case before 9/11. KSM, who had been indicted in January 1996 for his role in the Manila air plot, was seen primarily as another freelance terrorist, associated with Ramzi Yousef. Because the links between KSM and Bin Ladin or al Qaeda were not recognized at the time, responsibility for KSM remained in the small Islamic Extremist Branch of the Counterterrorist Center, not in the Bin Ladin unit.

Moreover, because KSM had already been indicted, he became targeted for arrest. In 1997, the Counterterrorist Center added a Renditions Branch to help find wanted fugitives. Responsibility for KSM was transferred to this branch, which gave the CIA a "man-to-man" focus but was not an analytical unit. When subsequent information came, more critical for analysis than for tracking, no unit had the job of following up on what the information might mean.[108]

For example, in September 2000, a source had reported that an individual named Khalid al-Shaykh al-Ballushi was a key lieutenant in al Qaeda. Al-Ballushi means "from

Baluchistan," and KSM is from Baluchistan. Recognizing the possible significance of this information, the Bin Ladin unit sought more information. When no information was forthcoming, the Bin Ladin unit dropped the matter.[109] When additional pieces of the puzzle arrived in the spring and summer of 2001, they were not put together.

The first piece of the puzzle concerned some intriguing information associated with a person known as "Mukhtar" that the CIA had begun analyzing in April 2001. The CIA did not know who Mukhtar was at the time—only that he associated with al Qaeda lieutenant Abu Zubaydah and that, based on the nature of the information, he was evidently involved in planning possible terrorist activities.[110]

The second piece of the puzzle was some alarming information regarding KSM. On June 12, 2001, a CIA report said that "Khaled" was actively recruiting people to travel outside Afghanistan, including to the United States where colleagues were reportedly already in the country to meet them, to carry out terrorist-related activities for Bin Ladin. CIA headquarters presumed from the details of the reporting that this person was Khalid Sheikh Mohammed. In July, the same source was shown a series of photographs and identified a photograph of Khalid Sheikh Mohammed as the Khaled he had previously discussed.[111]

The final piece of the puzzle arrived at the CIA's Bin Ladin unit on August 28 in a cable reporting that KSM's nickname was Mukhtar. No one made the connection to the reports about Mukhtar that had been circulated in the spring. This connection might also have underscored concern about the June reporting that KSM was recruiting terrorists to travel, including to the United States. Only after 9/11 would it be discovered that Mukhtar/KSM had communicated with a phone that was used by Binalshibh, and that Binalshibh had used the same phone to communicate with Moussaoui, as discussed in chapter 7. As in the Moussaoui situation already described, the links to Binalshibh might not have been an easy trail to find and would have required substantial cooperation from the German government. But time was short, and running out.[112]

Time Runs Out

As Tenet told us, "the system was blinking red" during the summer of 2001. Officials were alerted across the world. Many were doing everything they possibly could to respond to the threats.

Yet no one working on these late leads in the summer of 2001 connected the case in his or her in-box to the threat reports agitating senior officials and being briefed to the President. Thus, these individual cases did not become national priorities. As the CIA supervisor "John" told us, no one looked at the bigger picture; no analytic work foresaw the lightning that could connect the thundercloud to the ground.[113]

We see little evidence that the progress of the plot was disturbed by any government action. The U.S. government was unable to capitalize on mistakes made by al Qaeda. Time ran out.

CHAPTER NINE

Heroism and Horror

9.1 PREPAREDNESS AS OF SEPTEMBER 11

Emergency response is a product of preparedness. On the morning of September 11, 2001, the last best hope for the community of people working in or visiting the World Trade Center rested not with national policymakers but with private firms and local public servants, especially the first responders: fire, police, emergency medical service, and building safety professionals.

Building Preparedness
The World Trade Center.
The World Trade Center (WTC) complex was built for the Port Authority of New York and New Jersey. Construction began in 1966, and tenants began to occupy its space in 1970. The Twin Towers came to occupy a unique and symbolic place in the culture of New York City and America.

The WTC actually consisted of seven buildings, including one hotel, spread across 16 acres of land. The buildings were connected by an underground mall (the concourse). The Twin Towers (1 WTC, or the North Tower, and 2 WTC, or the South Tower) were the signature structures, containing 10.4 million square feet of office space. Both towers had 110 stories, were about 1,350 feet high, and were square; each wall measured 208 feet in length. On any given workday, up to 50,000 office workers occupied the towers, and 40,000 people passed through the complex.[1]

Each tower contained three central stairwells, which ran essentially from top to bottom, and 99 elevators. Generally, elevators originating in the lobby ran to "sky lobbies" on higher floors, where additional elevators carried passengers to the tops of the buildings.[2]

Stairwells A and C ran from the 110th floor to the raised mezzanine level of the lobby. Stairwell B ran from the 107th floor to level B6, six floors below ground, and was accessible from the West Street lobby level, which was one floor below the mezzanine. All three stairwells ran essentially straight up and down, except for two deviations in stairwells A and C where the staircase jutted out toward the perimeter of the building. On the upper and lower boundaries of these deviations were transfer hallways contained within the stairwell proper. Each hallway contained smoke doors to prevent smoke from rising from lower to upper portions of the building; they were kept closed but not locked. Doors leading from tenant space into the stairwells were never kept locked; reentry from the stairwells was generally possible on at least every fourth floor.[3]

Doors leading to the roof were locked. There was no rooftop evacuation plan. The roofs of both the North Tower and the South Tower were sloped and cluttered surfaces with radiation hazards, making them impractical for helicopter landings and as staging areas for civilians. Although the South Tower roof had a helipad, it did not meet 1994 Federal Aviation Administration guidelines.[4]

The 1993 Terrorist Bombing of the WTC and the Port Authority's Response.

Unlike most of America, New York City and specifically the World Trade Center had been the target of terrorist attacks before 9/11. At 12:18 P.M. on February 26, 1993, a 1,500-pound bomb stashed in a rental van was detonated on a parking garage ramp beneath the Twin Towers. The explosion

*The World Trade Center
Complex as of 9/11*

Rendering by Marco Crupi

killed six people, injured about 1,000 more, and exposed vulnerabilities in the World Trade Center's and the city's emergency preparedness.[5]

The towers lost power and communications capability. Generators had to be shut down to ensure safety, and elevators stopped. The public-address system and emergency lighting systems failed. The unlit stairwells filled with smoke and were so dark as to be impassable. Rescue efforts by the Fire Department of New York (FDNY) were hampered by the inability of its radios to function in buildings as large as the Twin Towers. The 911 emergency call system was overwhelmed. The general evacuation of the towers' occupants via the stairwells took more than four hours.[6]

Several small groups of people who were physically unable to descend the stairs were evacuated from the roof of the South Tower by New York Police Department (NYPD) helicopters. At least one person was lifted from the North Tower roof by the NYPD in a dangerous helicopter rappel operation—15 hours after the bombing. General knowledge that these air rescues had occurred appears to have left a number of civilians who worked in the Twin Towers with the false impression that helicopter rescues were part of the WTC evacuation plan and that rescue from the roof was a viable, if not favored, option for those who worked on upper floors. Although they were considered after 1993, helicopter evacuations in fact were not incorporated into the WTC fire safety plan.[7]

To address the problems encountered during the response to the 1993 bombing, the Port Authority spent an initial $100 million to make physical, structural, and technological improvements to the WTC, as well as to enhance its fire safety plan and reorganize and bolster its fire safety and security staffs.[8]

Substantial enhancements were made to power sources and exits. Fluorescent signs and markings were added in and near stairwells. The Port Authority also installed a sophisticated computerized fire alarm system with redundant electronics and control panels, and state-of-the-art fire command stations were placed in the lobby of each tower.[9]

To manage fire emergency preparedness and operations, the Port Authority created the dedicated position of fire safety director. The director supervised a team of deputy fire safety directors, one of whom was on duty at the fire command station in the lobby of each tower at all times. He or she would be responsible for communicating with building occupants during an emergency.[10]

The Port Authority also sought to prepare civilians better for future emergencies. Deputy fire safety directors conducted fire drills at least twice a year, with advance notice to tenants. "Fire safety teams" were selected from among civilian employees on each floor and consisted of a fire warden, deputy fire wardens, and searchers. The standard procedure for fire drills was for fire wardens to lead co-workers in their respective areas to the center of the floor, where they would use the emergency intercom phone to obtain specific information on how to proceed. Some civilians have told us that their evacuation on September 11 was greatly aided by changes and training implemented by the Port Authority in response to the 1993 bombing.[11]

But during these drills, civilians were not directed into the stairwells, or provided with information about their configuration and about the existence of transfer hallways and smoke doors. Neither full nor partial evacuation drills were held. Moreover, participation in drills that were held varied greatly from tenant to tenant. In general, civilians were never told not to evacuate up. The standard fire drill announcement advised participants that in the event of an actual emergency, they would be directed to descend to at least three floors below the fire. Most civilians recall simply being taught to await the instructions that would be provided at the time of an emergency. Civilians were not informed that rooftop evacuations were not part of the evacuation plan, or that doors to the roof were kept locked. The Port Authority acknowledges that it had no protocol for rescuing people trapped above a fire in the towers.[12]

Six weeks before the September 11 attacks, control of the WTC was transferred by net lease to a private developer, Silverstein Properties. Select Port Authority employees were designated to assist with the transition. Others remained on-site but were no longer part of the official chain of command. However, on September 11, most Port Authority World Trade Department employees—including those not on the designated "transition team"—reported to their regular stations to provide assistance throughout the morning. Although Silverstein Properties was in charge of the WTC on September 11, the WTC fire safety plan remained essentially the same.[13]

Preparedness of First Responders

On 9/11, the principal first responders were from the Fire Department of New York, the New York Police Department, the Port Authority Police Department (PAPD), and the Mayor's Office of Emergency Management (OEM).

Port Authority Police Department.

On September 11, 2001, the Port Authority of New York and New Jersey Police Department consisted of 1,331 officers, many of whom were trained in fire suppression methods as well as in law enforcement. The PAPD was led by a superintendent. There was a separate PAPD command for each of the Port Authority's nine facilities, including the World Trade Center.[14]

Most Port Authority police commands used ultra-high-frequency radios. Although all the radios were capable of using more than one channel, most PAPD officers used one local channel. The local channels were low-wattage and worked only in the immediate vicinity of that command. The PAPD also had an agencywide channel, but not all commands could access it.[15]

As of September 11, the Port Authority lacked any standard operating procedures to govern how officers from multiple commands would respond to and then be staged and utilized at a major incident at the WTC. In particular, there were no standard operating procedures covering how different commands should communicate via radio during such an incident.

The New York Police Department.

The 40,000-officer NYPD was headed by a police commissioner, whose duties were not primarily operational but who retained operational authority. Much of the NYPD's operational activities were run by the chief of department. In the event of a major emergency, a leading role would be played by the Special Operations Division. This division included the Aviation Unit, which provided helicopters for surveys and rescues, and the Emergency Service Unit (ESU), which carried out specialized rescue missions. The NYPD had specific and detailed standard operating procedures for the dispatch of officers to an incident, depending on the incident's magnitude.[16]

The NYPD precincts were divided into 35 different radio zones, with a central radio dispatcher assigned to each. In addition, there were several radio channels for citywide operations. Officers had portable radios with 20 or more available channels, so that the user could respond outside his or her precinct. ESU teams also had these channels but at an operation would use a separate point-to-point channel (which was not monitored by a dispatcher).[17]

The NYPD also supervised the city's 911 emergency call system. Its approximately 1,200 operators, radio dispatchers, and supervisors were civilian employees of the NYPD. They were trained in the rudiments of emergency response. When a 911 call concerned a fire, it was transferred to FDNY dispatch.[18]

The Fire Department of New York.

The 11,000-member FDNY was headed by a fire commissioner who, unlike the police commissioner, lacked operational authority. Operations were headed by the chief of department—the sole five-star chief.[19]

The FDNY was organized in nine separate geographic divisions. Each division was further divided into between four to seven battalions. Each battalion contained typically between three and four engine companies and two to four ladder companies. In total, the FDNY had 205 engine companies and 133 ladder companies. On-duty ladder companies consisted of a captain or lieutenant and five firefighters; on-duty engine companies consisted of a captain or lieutenant and normally four firefighters. Ladder companies' primary function was to conduct rescues; engine companies focused on extinguishing fires.[20]

The FDNY's Specialized Operations Command (SOC) contained a limited number of units that were of particular importance in responding to a terrorist attack or other major incident. The department's five rescue companies and seven squad companies performed specialized and highly risky rescue operations.[21]

The logistics of fire operations were directed by Fire Dispatch Operations Division, which had a center in each of the five boroughs. All 911 calls concerning fire emergencies were transferred to FDNY dispatch.[22]

As of September 11, FDNY companies and chiefs responding to a fire used analog, point-to-point radios that had six normal operating channels. Typically, the companies would operate on the same tactical channel, which chiefs on the scene would monitor and use to communicate with the firefighters. Chiefs at a fire operation also would use a separate command channel. Because these point-to-point radios had weak signal strength, communications on them could be heard only by other FDNY personnel in the immediate vicinity. In addition, the FDNY had a dispatch frequency for each of the five boroughs; these were not point-to-point channels and could be monitored from around the city.[23]

The FDNY's radios performed poorly during the 1993 WTC bombing for two reasons. First, the radios signals often did not succeed in penetrating the numerous steel and concrete floors that separated companies attempting to communicate; and second, so many different companies were attempting to use the same point-to-point channel that communications became unintelligible.[24]

The Port Authority installed, at its own expense, a repeater system in 1994 to greatly enhance FDNY radio communications in the difficult high-rise environment of the Twin Towers. The Port Authority recommended leaving the repeater system on at all times. The FDNY requested, however, that the repeater be turned on only when it was actually needed because the channel could cause interference with other FDNY operations in Lower Manhattan. The repeater system was installed at the Port Authority police desk in 5 WTC, to be activated by members of the Port Authority police when the FDNY units responding to the WTC complex so requested. However, in the spring of 2000 the FDNY asked that an activation console for the repeater system be placed instead in the lobby fire safety desk of each of the towers, making FDNY personnel entirely responsible for its activation. The Port Authority complied.[25]

Between 1998 and 2000, fewer people died from fires in New York City than in any three-year period since accurate measurements began in 1946. Firefighter deaths—a total of 22 during the 1990s—compared favorably with the most tranquil periods in the department's history.[26]

Office of Emergency Management and Interagency Preparedness.

In 1996, Mayor Rudolph Giuliani created the Mayor's Office of Emergency Management, which had three basic functions. First, OEM's Watch Command was to monitor the city's key communications channels—including radio frequencies of FDNY dispatch and the NYPD—and other data. A second purpose of the OEM was to improve New York City's response to major incidents, including terrorist attacks, by planning and conducting exercises and drills that would involve multiple city agencies, particularly the NYPD and FDNY. Third, the OEM would play a crucial role in managing the city's overall response to an incident. After

The World Trade Center Radio Repeater System
Rendering by Marco Crupi

OEM's Emergency Operations Center was activated, designated liaisons from relevant agencies, as well as the mayor
and his or her senior staff, would respond there. In addition,
an OEM field responder would be sent to the scene to ensure
that the response was coordinated.[27]

The OEM's headquarters was located at 7 WTC. Some
questioned locating it both so close to a previous terrorist
target and on the 23rd floor of a building (difficult to access
should elevators become inoperable). There was no backup
site.[28]

In July 2001, Mayor Giuliani updated a directive titled

"Direction and Control of Emergencies in the City of New York." Its purpose was to eliminate "potential conflict among responding agencies which may have areas of over-lapping expertise and responsibility." The directive sought to accomplish this objective by designating, for different types of emergencies, an appropriate agency as "Incident Commander." This Incident Commander would be "responsible for the management of the City's response to the emergency," while the OEM was "designated the 'On Scene Interagency Coordinator.'"[29]

Nevertheless, the FDNY and NYPD each considered itself operationally autonomous. As of September 11, they were not prepared to comprehensively coordinate their efforts in responding to a major incident. The OEM had not overcome this problem.

9.2 SEPTEMBER 11, 2001

As we turn to the events of September 11, we are mindful of the unfair perspective afforded by hindsight. Nevertheless, we will try to describe what happened in the following 102 minutes:

- the 17 minutes from the crash of the hijacked American Airlines Flight 11 into 1 World Trade Center (the North Tower) at 8:46 until the South Tower was hit
- the 56 minutes from the crash of the hijacked United Airlines Flight 175 into 2 World Trade Center (the South Tower) at 9:03 until the collapse of the South Tower
- the 29 minutes from the collapse of the South Tower at 9:59 until the collapse of the North Tower at 10:28

From 8:46 until 9:03 A.M.

At 8:46:40, the hijacked American Airlines Flight 11 flew into the upper portion of the North Tower, cutting through floors 93 to 99. Evidence suggests that all three of the build-

ing's stairwells became impassable from the 92nd floor up.
Hundreds of civilians were killed instantly by the impact.
Hundreds more remained alive but trapped.[30]

Civilians, Fire Safety Personnel, and 911 Calls
North Tower.

A jet fuel fireball erupted upon impact and shot down at least
one bank of elevators. The fireball exploded onto numerous
lower floors, including the 77th and 22nd; the West Street
lobby level; and the B4 level, four stories below ground. The
burning jet fuel immediately created thick, black smoke that
enveloped the upper floors and roof of the North Tower. The
roof of the South Tower was also engulfed in smoke because
of prevailing light winds from the northwest.[31]

Within minutes, New York City's 911 system was flooded
with eyewitness accounts of the event. Most callers correctly
identified the target of the attack. Some identified the plane
as a commercial airliner.[32]

The first response came from private firms and individuals—the people and companies in the building. Everything
that would happen to them during the next few minutes
would turn on their circumstances and their preparedness,
assisted by building personnel on-site.

Hundreds of civilians trapped on or above the 92nd floor
gathered in large and small groups, primarily between the
103rd and 106th floors. A large group was reported on the
92nd floor, technically below the impact but unable to descend. Civilians were also trapped in elevators. Other civilians below the impact zone—mostly on floors in the 70s and
80s, but also on at least the 47th and 22nd floors—were either trapped or waiting for assistance.[33]

It is unclear when the first full building evacuation order
was attempted over the public-address system. The deputy
fire safety director in the lobby, while immediately aware
that a major incident had occurred, did not know for approximately ten minutes that a commercial jet had directly hit the
building. Following protocol, he initially gave announcements to those floors that had generated computerized

alarms, advising those tenants to descend to points of
safety—at least two floors below the smoke or fire—and to
wait there for further instructions. The deputy fire safety director has told us that he began instructing a full evacuation
within about ten minutes of the explosion. But the first
FDNY chiefs to arrive in the lobby were advised by the Port
Authority fire safety director—who had reported to the
lobby although he was no longer the designated fire safety
director—that the full building evacuation announcement
had been made within one minute of the building being hit.[34]

Because of damage to building systems caused by the impact of the plane, public-address announcements were not
heard in many locations. For the same reason, many civilians may have been unable to use the emergency intercom
phones, as they had been advised to do in fire drills. Many
called 911.[35]

The 911 system was not equipped to handle the enormous
volume of calls it received. Some callers were unable to connect with 911 operators, receiving an "all circuits busy"
message. Standard operating procedure was for calls relating to fire emergencies to be transferred from 911 operators
to FDNY dispatch operators in the appropriate borough (in
this case, Manhattan). Transfers were often plagued by delays and were in some cases unsuccessful. Many calls were
also prematurely disconnected.[36]

The 911 operators and FDNY dispatchers had no information about either the location or the magnitude of the impact zone and were therefore unable to provide information
as fundamental as whether callers were above or below the
fire. Because the operators were not informed of NYPD Aviation's determination of the impossibility of rooftop rescues
from the Twin Towers on that day, they could not knowl-
edgeably answer when callers asked whether to go up or
down. In most instances, therefore, the operators and the
FDNY dispatchers relied on standard operating procedures
for high-rise fires—that civilians should stay low, remain
where they are, and wait for emergency personnel to reach
them. This advice was given to callers from the North Tower

for locations both above and below the impact zone. Fire chiefs told us that the evacuation of tens of thousands of people from skyscrapers can create many new problems, especially for individuals who are disabled or in poor health. Many of the injuries after the 1993 bombing occurred during the evacuation.[37]

Although the guidance to stay in place may seem understandable in cases of conventional high-rise fires, FDNY chiefs in the North Tower lobby determined at once that all building occupants should attempt to evacuate immediately. By 8:57, FDNY chiefs had instructed the PAPD and building personnel to evacuate the South Tower as well, because of the magnitude of the damage caused by the first plane's impact.[38]

These critical decisions were not conveyed to 911 operators or to FDNY dispatchers. Departing from protocol, a number of operators told callers that they could break windows, and several operators advised callers to evacuate if they could.[39] Civilians who called the Port Authority police desk located at 5 WTC were advised to leave if they could.[40]

Most civilians who were not obstructed from proceeding began evacuating without waiting for instructions over the intercom system. Some remained to wait for help, as advised by 911 operators. Others simply continued to work or delayed to collect personal items, but in many cases were urged to leave by others. Some Port Authority civilian employees remained on various upper floors to help civilians who were trapped and to assist in the evacuation.[41]

While evacuating, some civilians had trouble reaching the exits because of damage caused by the impact. Some were confused by deviations in the increasingly crowded stairwells, and impeded by doors that appeared to be locked but actually were jammed by debris or shifting that resulted from the impact of the plane. Despite these obstacles, the evacuation was relatively calm and orderly.[42]

Within ten minutes of impact, smoke was beginning to rise to the upper floors in debilitating volumes and isolated fires were reported, although there were some pockets of refuge. Faced with insufferable heat, smoke, and fire, and with no prospect for relief, some jumped or fell from the building.[43]

South Tower.

Many civilians in the South Tower were initially unaware of what had happened in the other tower. Some believed an incident had occurred in their building; others were aware that a major explosion had occurred on the upper floors of the North Tower. Many people decided to leave, and some were advised to do so by fire wardens. In addition, Morgan Stanley, which occupied more than 20 floors of the South Tower, evacuated its employees by the decision of company security officials.[44]

Consistent with protocol, at 8:49 the deputy fire safety director in the South Tower told his counterpart in the North Tower that he would wait to hear from "the boss from the Fire Department or somebody" before ordering an evacuation.[45] At about this time, an announcement over the public-address system in the South Tower stated that the incident had occurred in the other building and advised tenants, generally, that their building was safe and that they should remain on or return to their offices or floors. A statement from the deputy fire safety director informing tenants that the incident had occurred in the other building was consistent with protocol; the expanded advice did not correspond to any existing written protocol, and did not reflect any instruction known to have been given to the deputy fire safety director that day. We do not know the reason for the announcement, as both the deputy fire safety director believed to have made it and the director of fire safety for the WTC complex perished in the South tower's collapse. Clearly, however, the prospect of another plane hitting the second building was beyond the contemplation of anyone giving advice. According to one of the first fire chiefs to arrive, such a scenario was unimaginable, "beyond our consciousness." As a result of the announcement, many civilians remained on their floors. Others reversed their evacuation and went back up.[46]

The World Trade Center North Tower Stairwell with Deviation
Rendering by Marco Crupi

Similar advice was given in person by security officials in both the ground floor lobby—where a group of 20 that had descended by the elevators was personally instructed to go back upstairs—and in the upper sky lobby, where many waited for express elevators to take them down. Security officials who gave this advice were not part of the fire safety staff.[47]

Several South Tower occupants called the Port Authority police desk in 5 WTC. Some were advised to stand by for further instructions; others were strongly advised to leave.[48]

It is not known whether the order by the FDNY to evacuate the South Tower was received by the deputy fire safety director making announcements there. However, at approximately 9:02—less than a minute before the building was hit—an instruction over the South Tower's public-address system advised civilians, generally, that they could begin an orderly evacuation if conditions warranted. Like the earlier advice to remain in place, it did not correspond to any prewritten emergency instruction.[49]

FDNY Initial Response
Mobilization.

The FDNY response began within five seconds of the crash. By 9:00, many senior FDNY leaders, including 7 of the 11 most highly ranked chiefs in the department, as well as the Commissioner and many of his deputies and assistants, had begun responding from headquarters in Brooklyn. While en route over the Brooklyn Bridge, the Chief of Department and the Chief of Operations had a clear view of the situation on the upper floors of the North Tower. They determined that because of the fire's magnitude and location near the top of the building, their mission would be primarily one of rescue. They called for a fifth alarm, which would bring additional engine and ladder companies, as well as for two more elite rescue units. The Chief of Department arrived at about 9:00; general FDNY Incident Command was transferred to his location on the West Side Highway. In all, 22 of the 32 senior chiefs and commissioners arrived at the WTC before 10:00.[50]

As of 9:00, the units that were dispatched (including senior chiefs responding to headquarters) included approximately 235 firefighters. These units consisted of 21 engine companies, nine ladder companies, four of the department's elite rescue teams, the department's single Hazmat team, two of the city's elite squad companies, and support staff. In addition, at 8:53 nine Brooklyn units were staged on the Brooklyn side of the Brooklyn-Battery Tunnel to await possible dispatch orders.[51]

Operations.

A battalion chief and two ladder and two engine companies arrived at the North Tower at approximately 8:52. As they entered the lobby, they encountered badly burned civilians who had been caught in the path of the fireball. Floor-to-ceiling windows in the northwest corner of the West Street level of the lobby had been blown out; some large marble tiles had been dislodged from the walls; one entire elevator bank was destroyed by the fireball. Lights were functioning, however, and the air was clear of smoke.[52]

As the highest-ranking officer on the scene, the battalion chief initially was the FDNY incident commander. Minutes later, the on-duty division chief for Lower Manhattan arrived and took over. Both chiefs immediately began speaking with the former fire safety director and other building personnel to learn whether building systems were working. They were advised that all 99 elevators in the North Tower appeared to be out, and there were no assurances that sprinklers or standpipes were working on upper floors. Chiefs also spoke with Port Authority police personnel and an OEM representative.[53]

After conferring with the chiefs in the lobby, one engine and one ladder company began climbing stairwell C at about 8:57, with the goal of approaching the impact zone as scouting units and reporting back to the chiefs in the lobby. The radio channel they used was tactical 1. Following FDNY high-rise fire protocols, other units did not begin climbing immediately, as the chiefs worked to formulate a plan before sending them up. Units began mobilizing in the lobby, lining up and awaiting their marching orders.[54]

Also by approximately 8:57, FDNY chiefs had asked both building personnel and a Port Authority police officer to evacuate the South Tower, because in their judgment the impact of the plane into the North Tower made the entire complex unsafe—not because of concerns about a possible second plane.[55]

The FDNY chiefs in the increasingly crowded North

Tower lobby were confronting critical choices with little to no information. They had ordered units up the stairs to report back on conditions, but did not know what the impact floors were; they did not know if any stairwells into the impact zone were clear; and they did not know whether water for firefighting would be available on the upper floors. They also did not know what the fire and impact zone looked like from the outside.[56]

They did know that the explosion had been large enough to send down a fireball that blew out elevators and windows in the lobby and that conditions were so dire that some civilians on upper floors were jumping or falling from the building. They also knew from building personnel that some civilians were trapped in elevators and on specific floors. According to Division Chief for Lower Manhattan Peter Hayden, "We had a very strong sense we would lose firefighters and that we were in deep trouble, but we had estimates of 25,000 to 50,000 civilians, and we had to try to rescue them."[57]

The chiefs concluded that this would be a rescue operation, not a firefighting operation. One of the chiefs present explained:

> We realized that, because of the impact of the plane, that there was some structural damage to the building, and most likely that the fire suppression systems within the building were probably damaged and possibly inoperable. . . . We knew that at the height of the day there were as many as 50,000 people in this building. We had a large volume of fire on the upper floors. Each floor was approximately an acre in size. Several floors of fire would have been beyond the fire-extinguishing capability of the forces that we had on hand. So we determined, very early on, that this was going to be strictly a rescue mission. We were going to vacate the building, get everybody out, and then we were going to get out.[58]

The specifics of the mission were harder to determine, as they had almost no information about the situation 80 or more stories above them. They also received advice from senior FDNY chiefs that while the building might eventually suffer a partial collapse on upper floors, such structural failure was not imminent. No one anticipated the possibility of a total collapse.[59]

Emergency medical services (EMS) personnel were directed to one of four triage areas being set up around the perimeter of the WTC. Some entered the lobby to respond to specific casualty reports. In addition, many ambulance paramedics from private hospitals were rushing to the WTC complex.[60]

NYPD Initial Response

Numerous NYPD officers saw the plane strike the North Tower and immediately reported it to NYPD communications dispatchers.[61]

At 8:58, while en route, the NYPD Chief of Department raised the NYPD's mobilization to level 4, thereby sending to the WTC approximately 22 lieutenants, 100 sergeants, and 800 police officers from all over the city. The Chief of Department arrived at Church and Vesey at 9:00.[62]

At 9:01, the NYPD patrol mobilization point was moved to West and Vesey in order to handle the greater number of patrol officers dispatched in the higher-level mobilization. These officers would be stationed around the perimeter of the complex to direct the evacuation of civilians. Many were diverted on the way to the scene by intervening emergencies related to the attack.[63]

At 8:50, the Aviation Unit of the NYPD dispatched two helicopters to the WTC to report on conditions and assess the feasibility of a rooftop landing or of special rescue operations. En route, the two helicopters communicated with air traffic controllers at the area's three major airports and informed them of the commercial airplane crash at the World Trade Center. The air traffic controllers had been unaware of the incident.[64]

At 8:56, an NYPD ESU team asked to be picked up at the Wall Street heliport to initiate rooftop rescues. At 8:58, however, after assessing the North Tower roof, a helicopter pilot advised the ESU team that they could not land on the roof, because "it is too engulfed in flames and heavy smoke condition."[65]

By 9:00, a third NYPD helicopter was responding to the WTC complex. NYPD helicopters and ESU officers remained on the scene throughout the morning, prepared to commence rescue operations on the roof if conditions improved. Both FDNY and NYPD protocols called for FDNY personnel to be placed in NYPD helicopters in the event of an attempted rooftop rescue at a high-rise fire. No FDNY personnel were placed in NYPD helicopters on September 11.[66]

The 911 operators and FDNY dispatchers were not advised that rooftop rescues were not being undertaken. They thus were not able to communicate this fact to callers, some of whom spoke of attempting to climb to the roof.[67]

Two on-duty NYPD officers were on the 20th floor of the North Tower at 8:46. They climbed to the 29th floor, urging civilians to evacuate, but did not locate a group of civilians trapped on the 22nd floor.[68]

Just before 9:00, an ESU team began to walk from Church and Vesey to the North Tower lobby, with the goal of climbing toward and setting up a triage center on the upper floors for the severely injured. A second ESU team would follow them to assist in removing those individuals.[69]

Numerous officers responded in order to help injured civilians and to urge those who could walk to vacate the area immediately. Putting themselves in danger of falling debris, several officers entered the plaza and successfully rescued at least one injured, nonambulatory civilian, and attempted to rescue others.[70]

Also by about 9:00, transit officers began shutting down subway stations in the vicinity of the World Trade Center and evacuating civilians from those stations.[71]

Around the city, the NYPD cleared major thoroughfares for emergency vehicles to access the WTC. The NYPD and

PAPD coordinated the closing of bridges and tunnels into Manhattan.[72]

PAPD Initial Response

The Port Authority's on-site commanding police officer was standing in the concourse when a fireball erupted out of elevator shafts and exploded onto the mall concourse, causing him to dive for cover. The on-duty sergeant initially instructed the officers in the WTC Command to meet at the police desk in 5 WTC. Soon thereafter, he instructed officers arriving from outside commands to meet him at the fire safety desk in the North Tower lobby. A few of these officers from outside commands were given WTC Command radios.[73]

One Port Authority police officer at the WTC immediately began climbing stairwell C in the North Tower.[74] Other officers began performing rescue and evacuation operations on the ground floors and in the PATH (Port Authority Trans-Hudson) station below the WTC complex.

Within minutes of impact, Port Authority police officers from the PATH, bridges, tunnels, and airport commands began responding to the WTC. The PAPD lacked written standard operating procedures for personnel responding from outside commands to the WTC during a major incident. In addition, officers from some PAPD commands lacked interoperable radio frequencies. As a result, there was no comprehensive coordination of PAPD's overall response.[75]

At 9:00, the PAPD commanding officer of the WTC ordered an evacuation of all civilians in the World Trade Center complex, because of the magnitude of the calamity in the North Tower. This order was given over WTC police radio channel W, which could not be heard by the deputy fire safety director in the South Tower.[76]

Also at 9:00, the PAPD Superintendent and Chief of Department arrived separately and made their way to the North Tower.[77]

OEM Initial Response

By 8:48, officials in OEM headquarters on the 23rd floor of 7 WTC—just to the north of the North Tower—began to activate the Emergency Operations Center by calling such agencies as the FDNY, NYPD, Department of Health, and the Greater Hospital Association and instructing them to send their designated representatives to the OEM. In addition, the Federal Emergency Management Agency (FEMA) was called and asked to send at least five federal Urban Search and Rescue Teams (such teams are located throughout the United States). At approximately 8:50, a senior representative from the OEM arrived in the lobby of the North Tower and began to act as the OEM field responder to the incident. He soon was joined by several other OEM officials, including the OEM Director.[78]

Summary

In the 17-minute period between 8:46 and 9:03 A.M. on September 11, New York City and the Port Authority of New York and New Jersey had mobilized the largest rescue operation in the city's history. Well over a thousand first responders had been deployed, an evacuation had begun, and the critical decision that the fire could not be fought had been made.

Then the second plane hit.

From 9:03 until 9:59 A.M.

At 9:03:11, the hijacked United Airlines Flight 175 hit 2 WTC (the South Tower) from the south, crashing through the 77th to 85th floors. What had been the largest and most complicated rescue operation in city history instantly doubled in magnitude. The plane banked as it hit the building, leaving portions of the building undamaged on impact floors. As a consequence—and in contrast to the situation in the North Tower—one of the stairwells (A) initially remained passable from at least the 91st floor down, and likely from top to bottom.[79]

Civilians, Fire Safety Personnel, and 911 Calls
South Tower.

At the lower end of the impact, the 78th-floor sky lobby, hundreds had been waiting to evacuate when the plane hit. Many had attempted but failed to squeeze into packed express elevators. Upon impact, many were killed or severely injured; others were relatively unharmed. We know of at least one civilian who seized the initiative and shouted that anyone who could walk should walk to the stairs, and anyone who could help should help others in need of assistance. As a result, at least two small groups of civilians descended from that floor. Others remained on the floor to help the injured and move victims who were unable to walk to the stairwell to aid their rescue.[80]

Still others remained alive in the impact zone above the 78th floor. Damage was extensive, and conditions were highly precarious. The only survivor known to have escaped from the heart of the impact zone described the 81st floor—where the wing of the plane had sliced through his office—as a "demolition" site in which everything was "broken up" and the smell of jet fuel was so strong that it was almost impossible to breathe. This person escaped by means of an unlikely rescue, aided by a civilian fire warden descending from a higher floor, who, critically, had been provided with a flashlight.[81]

At least four people were able to descend stairwell A from the 81st floor or above. One left the 84th floor immediately after the building was hit. Even at that point, the stairway was dark, smoky, and difficult to navigate; glow strips on the stairs and handrails were a significant help. Several flights down, however, the evacuee became confused when he reached a smoke door that caused him to believe the stairway had ended. He was able to exit that stairwell and switch to another.[82]

Many civilians in and above the impact zone ascended the stairs. One small group reversed its descent down stairwell A after being advised by another civilian that they were

approaching a floor "in flames." The only known survivor
has told us that their intention was to exit the stairwell in
search of clearer air. At the 91st floor, joined by others from
intervening floors, they perceived themselves to be trapped
in the stairwell and began descending again. By this time,
the stairwell was "pretty black," intensifying smoke caused
many to pass out, and fire had ignited in the 82nd-floor transfer hallway.[83]

Others ascended to attempt to reach the roof but were
thwarted by locked doors. At approximately 9:30 a "lock release" order—which would unlock all areas in the complex
controlled by the buildings' computerized security system,
including doors leading to the roofs—was transmitted to the
Security Command Center located on the 22nd floor of the
North Tower. Damage to the software controlling the system, resulting from the impact of the plane, prevented this
order from being executed.[84]

Others, attempting to descend, were frustrated by
jammed or locked doors in stairwells or confused by the
structure of the stairwell deviations. By the lower 70s, however, stairwells A and B were well-lit, and conditions were
generally normal.[85]

Some civilians remained on affected floors, and at least
one ascended from a lower point into the impact zone, to
help evacuate colleagues or assist the injured.[86]

Within 15 minutes after the impact, debilitating smoke
had reached at least one location on the 100th floor, and severe smoke conditions were reported throughout floors in
the 90s and 100s over the course of the following half hour.
By 9:30, a number of civilians who had failed to reach the
roof remained on the 105th floor, likely unable to descend
because of intensifying smoke in the stairwell. There were
reports of tremendous smoke on that floor, but at least one
area remained less affected until shortly before the building
collapsed. There were several areas between the impact zone
and the uppermost floors where conditions were better. At
least a hundred people remained alive on the 88th and 89th
floors, in some cases calling 911 for direction.[87]

The 911 system remained plagued by the operators' lack of awareness of what was occurring. Just as in the North Tower, callers from below and above the impact zone were advised to remain where they were and wait for help. The operators were not given any information about the inability to conduct rooftop rescues and therefore could not advise callers that they had essentially been ruled out. This lack of information, combined with the general advice to remain where they were, may have caused civilians above the impact not to attempt to descend, although stairwell A may have been passable.[88]

In addition, the 911 system struggled with the volume of calls and rigid standard operating procedures according to which calls conveying crucial information had to wait to be transferred to either EMS or FDNY dispatch.[89] According to one civilian who was evacuating down stairwell A from the heart of the impact zone and who stopped on the 31st floor in order to call 911,

> I told them when they answered the phone, where I was, that I had passed somebody on the 44th floor, injured— they need to get a medic and a stretcher to this floor, and described the situation in brief, and the person then asked for my phone number, or something, and they said—they put me on hold. "You gotta talk to one of my supervisors"—and suddenly I was on hold. And so I waited a considerable amount of time. Somebody else came back on the phone, I repeated the story. And then it happened again. I was on hold a second time, and needed to repeat the story for a third time. But I told the third person that I am only telling you once. I am getting out of the building, here are the details, write it down, and do what you should do.[90]

Very few 911 calls were received from floors below the impact, but at least one person was advised to remain on the 73rd floor despite the caller's protests that oxygen was running out. The last known 911 call from this location came at 9:52.[91]

Evidence suggests that the public-address system did not continue to function after the building was hit. A group of people trapped on the 97th floor, however, made repeated references in calls to 911 to having heard "announcements" to go down the stairs. Evacuation tones were heard in locations both above and below the impact zone.[92]

By 9:35, the West Street lobby level of the South Tower was becoming overwhelmed by injured people who had descended to the lobby but were having difficulty going on. Those who could continue were directed to exit north or east through the concourse and then out of the WTC complex.[93]

By 9:59, at least one person had descended from as high as the 91st floor of that tower, and stairwell A was reported to have been almost empty. Stairwell B was also reported to have contained only a handful of descending civilians at an earlier point in the morning. But just before the tower collapsed, a team of NYPD ESU officers encountered a stream of civilians descending an unidentified stairwell in the 20s. These civilians may have been descending from at or above the impact zone.[94]

North Tower.

In the North Tower, civilians continued their evacuation. On the 91st floor, the highest floor with stairway access, all civilians but one were uninjured and able to descend. While some complained of smoke, heat, fumes, and crowding in the stairwells, conditions were otherwise fairly normal on floors below the impact. At least one stairwell was reported to have been "clear and bright" from the upper 80s down.[95]

Those who called 911 from floors below the impact were generally advised to remain in place. One group trapped on the 83rd floor pleaded repeatedly to know whether the fire was above or below them, specifically asking if 911 operators had any information from the outside or from the news. The callers were transferred back and forth several times and advised to stay put. Evidence suggests that these callers died.[96]

At 8:59, the Port Authority police desk at Newark Airport

told a third party that a group of Port Authority civilian employees on the 64th floor should evacuate. (The third party was not at the WTC, but had been in phone contact with the group on the 64th floor.) At 9:10, in response to an inquiry from the employees themselves, the Port Authority police desk in Jersey City confirmed that employees on the 64th floor should "be careful, stay near the stairwells, and wait for the police to come up." When the third party inquired again at 9:31, the police desk at Newark Airport advised that they "absolutely" evacuate. The third party informed the police desk that the employees had previously received contrary advice from the FDNY, which could only have come via 911. These workers were not trapped, yet unlike most occupants on the upper floors, they had chosen not to descend immediately after impact. They eventually began to descend the stairs, but most of them died in the collapse of the North Tower.[97]

All civilians who reached the lobby were directed by NYPD and PAPD officers into the concourse, where other police officers guided them to exit the concourse and complex to the north and east so that they might avoid falling debris and victims.[98]

By 9:55, only a few civilians were descending above the 25th floor in stairwell B; these primarily were injured, handicapped, elderly, or severely overweight civilians, in some cases being assisted by other civilians.[99]

By 9:59, tenants from the 91st floor had already descended the stairs and exited the concourse. However, a number of civilians remained in at least stairwell C, approaching lower floors. Other evacuees were killed earlier by debris falling on the street.[100]

FDNY Response
Increased Mobilization.
Immediately after the second plane hit, the FDNY Chief of Department called a second fifth alarm.[101]

By 9:15, the number of FDNY personnel en route to or present at the scene was far greater than the commanding chiefs at the scene had requested. Five factors account for this disparity. First, while the second fifth alarm had called for 20 engine and 8 ladder companies, in fact 23 engine and 13 ladder companies were dispatched. Second, several other units self-dispatched. Third, because the attacks came so close to the 9:00 shift change, many firefighters just going off duty were given permission by company officers to "ride heavy" and became part of those on-duty teams, under the leadership of that unit's officer. Fourth, many off-duty fire-fighters responded from firehouses separately from the on-duty unit (in some cases when expressly told not to) or from home. The arrival of personnel in excess of that dispatched was particularly pronounced in the department's elite units. Fifth, numerous additional FDNY personnel—such as fire marshals and firefighters in administrative positions—who lacked a predetermined operating role also reported to the WTC.[102]

The Repeater System.

Almost immediately after the South Tower was hit, senior FDNY chiefs in the North Tower lobby huddled to discuss strategy for the operations in the two towers. Of particular concern to the chiefs—in light of FDNY difficulties in re-sponding to the 1993 bombing—was communications capa-bility. One of the chiefs recommended testing the repeater channel to see if it would work.[103]

Earlier, an FDNY chief had asked building personnel to activate the repeater channel, which would enable greatly-enhanced FDNY portable radio communications in the high-rises. One button on the repeater system activation con-sole in the North Tower was pressed at 8:54, though it is un-clear by whom. As a result of this activation, communication became possible between FDNY portable radios on the re-peater channel. In addition, the repeater's master handset at the fire safety desk could hear communications made by FDNY portable radios on the repeater channel. The activa-tion of *transmission* on the master handset required, however, that a second button be pressed. That second button was never activated on the morning of September 11.[104]

At 9:05, FDNY chiefs tested the WTC complex's repeater system. Because the second button had not been activated, the chief on the master handset could not transmit. He was also apparently unable to hear another chief who was attempting to communicate with him from a portable radio, either because of a technical problem or because the volume was turned down on the console (the normal setting when the system was not in use). Because the repeater channel seemed inoperable—the master handset appeared unable to transmit or receive communications—the chiefs in the North Tower lobby decided not to use it. The repeater system was working at least partially, however, on portable FDNY radios, and firefighters subsequently used repeater channel 7 in the South Tower.[105]

FDNY North Tower Operations.

Command and control decisions were affected by the lack of knowledge of what was happening 30, 60, 90, and 100 floors above. According to one of the chiefs in the lobby, "One of the most critical things in a major operation like this is to have information. We didn't have a lot of information coming in. We didn't receive any reports of what was seen from the [NYPD] helicopters. It was impossible to know how much damage was done on the upper floors, whether the stairwells were intact or not."[106] According to another chief present, "People watching on TV certainly had more knowledge of what was happening a hundred floors above us than we did in the lobby. . . . [W]ithout critical information coming in . . . it's very difficult to make informed, critical decisions[.]"[107]

As a result, chiefs in the lobby disagreed over whether anyone at or above the impact zone possibly could be rescued, or whether there should be even limited firefighting for the purpose of cutting exit routes through fire zones.[108]

Many units were simply instructed to ascend toward the impact zone and report back to the lobby via radio. Some units were directed to assist specific groups of individuals trapped in elevators or in offices well below the impact zone. One FDNY company successfully rescued some civilians who were trapped on the 22nd floor as a result of damage caused by the initial fireball.[109]

An attempt was made to track responding units' assignments on a magnetic board, but the number of units and individual firefighters arriving in the lobby made this an overwhelming task. As the fire companies were not advised to the contrary, they followed protocol and kept their radios on tactical channel 1, which would be monitored by the chiefs in the lobby. Those battalion chiefs who would climb would operate on a separate command channel, which also would be monitored by the chiefs in the lobby.[110]

Fire companies began to ascend stairwell B at approximately 9:07, laden with about 100 pounds of heavy protective clothing, self-contained breathing apparatuses, and other equipment (including hoses for engine companies and heavy tools for ladder companies).[111]

Firefighters found the stairways they entered intact, lit, and clear of smoke. Unbeknownst to the lobby command post, one battalion chief in the North Tower found a working elevator, which he took to the 16th floor before beginning to climb.[112]

In ascending stairwell B, firefighters were passing a steady and heavy stream of descending civilians. Firemen were impressed with the composure and total lack of panic shown by almost all civilians. Many civilians were in awe of the firefighters and found their mere presence to be calming.[113]

Firefighters periodically stopped on particular floors and searched to ensure that no civilians were still on it. In a few instances healthy civilians were found on floors, either because they still were collecting personal items or for no apparent reason; they were told to evacuate immediately. Firefighters deputized healthy civilians to be in charge of others who were struggling or injured.[114]

Climbing up the stairs with heavy protective clothing and

equipment was hard work even for physically fit firefighters. As firefighters began to suffer varying levels of fatigue, some became separated from others in their unit.[115]

At 9:32, a senior chief radioed all units in the North Tower to return to the lobby, either because of a false report of a third plane approaching or because of his judgment about the deteriorating condition of the building. Once the rumor of the third plane was debunked, other chiefs continued operations, and there is no evidence that any units actually returned to the lobby. At the same time, a chief in the lobby was asked to consider the possibility of a rooftop rescue but was unable to reach FDNY dispatch by radio or phone. Out on West Street, however, the FDNY Chief of Department had already dismissed any rooftop rescue as impossible.[116]

As units climbed higher, their ability to communicate with chiefs on tactical 1 became more limited and sporadic, both because of the limited effectiveness of FDNY radios in high-rises and because so many units on tactical 1 were trying to communicate at once. When attempting to reach a particular unit, chiefs in the lobby often heard nothing in response.[117]

Just prior to 10:00, in the North Tower one engine company had climbed to the 54th floor, at least two other companies of firefighters had reached the sky lobby on the 44th floor, and numerous units were located between the 5th and 37th floors.[118]

FDNY South Tower and Marriott Hotel Operations.

Immediately after the repeater test, a senior chief and a battalion chief commenced operations in the South Tower lobby. Almost at once they were joined by an OEM field responder. They were not, however, joined right away by a sizable number of fire companies, as units that had been in or en route to the North Tower lobby at 9:03 were not reallocated to the South Tower.[119]

A battalion chief and a ladder company found a working

elevator to the 40th floor and from there proceeded to climb
stairwell B. Another ladder company arrived soon thereafter,
and began to rescue civilians trapped in an elevator between
the first and second floors. The senior chief in the lobby expressed frustration about the lack of units he initially had at
his disposal for South Tower operations.[120]

Unlike the commanders in the North Tower, the senior
chief in the lobby and the ascending battalion chief kept
their radios on repeater channel 7. For the first 15 minutes of
the operations, communications among them and the ladder
company climbing with the battalion chief worked well.
Upon learning from a company security official that the impact zone began at the 78th floor, a ladder company transmitted this information, and the battalion chief directed an
engine company staged on the 40th floor to attempt to find
an elevator to reach that upper level.[121]

To our knowledge, no FDNY chiefs outside the South
Tower realized that the repeater channel was functioning and
being used by units in that tower. The senior chief in the
South Tower lobby was initially unable to communicate his
requests for more units to chiefs either in the North Tower
lobby or at the outdoor command post.[122]

From approximately 9:21 on, the ascending battalion
chief was unable to reach the South Tower lobby command
post because the senior chief in the lobby had ceased to
communicate on repeater channel 7. The vast majority of
units that entered the South Tower did not communicate on
the repeater channel.[123]

The first FDNY fatality of the day occurred at approximately 9:30, when a civilian landed on and killed a fireman
near the intersection of West and Liberty streets.[124]

By 9:30, chiefs in charge of the South Tower still were in
need of additional companies. Several factors account for
the lag in response. First, only two units that had been dispatched to the North Tower prior to 9:03 reported immediately to the South Tower. Second, units were not actually
sent until approximately five minutes after the FDNY Chief
of Department ordered their dispatch. Third, those units that

had been ordered at 8:53 to stage at the Brooklyn-Battery Tunnel—and thus very close to the WTC complex—were not dispatched after the plane hit the South Tower. Fourth, units parked further north on West Street, then proceeded south on foot and stopped at the overall FDNY command post on West Street, where in some cases they were told to wait. Fifth, some units responded directly to the North Tower. (Indeed, radio communications indicated that in certain cases some firemen believed that the South Tower was 1 WTC when in fact it was 2 WTC.) Sixth, some units couldn't find the staging area (at West Street south of Liberty) for the South Tower. Finally, the jumpers and debris that confronted units attempting to enter the South Tower from its main entrance on Liberty Street caused some units to search for indirect ways to enter that tower, most often through the Marriott Hotel, or simply to remain on West Street.[125]

A chief at the overall outdoor command post was under the impression that he was to assist in lobby operations of the South Tower, and in fact his aide already was in that lobby. But because of his lack of familiarity with the WTC complex and confusion over how to get to there, he instead ended up in the Marriott at about 9:35. Here he came across about 14 units, many of which had been trying to find safe access to the South Tower. He directed them to secure the elevators and conduct search-and-rescue operations on the upper floors of the Marriott. Four of these companies searched the spa on the hotel's top floor—the 22nd floor—for civilians, and found none.[126]

Feeling satisfied with the scope of the operation in the Marriott, the chief in the lobby there directed some units to proceed to what he thought was the South Tower. In fact, he pointed them to the North Tower. Three of the FDNY companies who had entered the North Tower from the Marriott found a working elevator in a bank at the south end of the lobby, which they took to the 23rd floor.[127]

In response to the shortage of units in the South Tower, at 9:37 an additional second alarm was requested by the chief at the West and Liberty streets staging area. At this time, the units that earlier had been staged on the Brooklyn side of the Brooklyn-Battery Tunnel were dispatched to the South Tower; some had gone through the tunnel already and had responded to the Marriott, not the South Tower.[128]

Between 9:45 and 9:58, the ascending battalion chief continued to lead FDNY operations on the upper floors of the South Tower. At 9:50, an FDNY ladder company encountered numerous seriously injured civilians on the 70th floor. With the assistance of a security guard, at 9:53 a group of civilians trapped in an elevator on the 78th-floor sky lobby were found by an FDNY company. They were freed from the elevator at 9:58. By that time the battalion chief had reached the 78th floor on stairwell A; he reported that it looked open to the 79th floor, well into the impact zone. He also reported numerous civilian fatalities in the area.[129]

FDNY Command and Control Outside the Towers.

The overall command post consisted of senior chiefs, commissioners, the field communications van (Field Comm), numerous units that began to arrive after the South Tower was hit, and EMS chiefs and personnel.[130]

Field Comm's two main functions were to relay information between the overall operations command post and FDNY dispatch and to track all units operating at the scene on a large magnetic board. Both of these missions were severely compromised by the magnitude of the disaster on September 11. First, the means of transmitting information were unreliable. For example, while FDNY dispatch advised Field Comm that 100 people were reported via 911 to be trapped on the 105th floor of the North Tower, and Field Comm then attempted to convey that report to chiefs at the outdoor command post, this information did not reach the North Tower lobby. Second, Field Comm's ability to keep track of which units were operating where was limited, because many units reported directly to the North Tower, the South Tower, or the Marriott. Third, efforts to track units by listening to tactical 1 were severely hampered by the number of units using that channel; as many people tried to speak at once, their transmissions overlapped and often became indecipherable. In the opinion of one of the members of the Field Comm. group, tactical 1 simply was not designed to handle the number of units operating on it that morning.[131]

The primary Field Comm van had access to the NYPD's Special Operations channel (used by NYPD Aviation), but it was in the garage for repairs on September 11. The backup van lacked that capability.[132]

The Chief of Department, along with civilian commissioners and senior EMS chiefs, organized ambulances on West Street to expedite the transport of injured civilians to hospitals.[133]

To our knowledge, none of the chiefs present believed that a total collapse of either tower was possible. One senior chief did articulate his concern that upper floors could begin to collapse in a few hours, and that firefighters thus should not ascend above floors in the 60s. That opinion was not conveyed to chiefs in the North Tower lobby, and there is no evidence that it was conveyed to chiefs in the South Tower lobby either.[134]

Although the Chief of Department had general authority over operations, tactical decisions remained the province of the lobby commanders. The highest-ranking officer in the North Tower was responsible for communicating with the Chief of Department. They had two brief conversations. In the first, the senior lobby chief gave the Chief of Department a status report and confirmed that this was a rescue, not firefighting, operation. In the second conversation, at about 9:45, the Chief of Department suggested that given how the North Tower appeared to him, the senior lobby chief might want to consider evacuating FDNY personnel.[135]

At 9:46, the Chief of Department called an additional fifth alarm, and at 9:54 an additional 20 engine and 6 ladder companies were sent to the WTC. As a result, more than one-third of all FDNY companies now had been dispatched to the WTC. At about 9:57, an EMS paramedic approached the FDNY Chief of Department and advised that an engineer in front of 7 WTC had just remarked that the Twin Towers in fact were in imminent danger of a total collapse.[136]

NYPD Response

Immediately after the second plane hit, the Chief of Department of the NYPD ordered a second Level 4 mobilization, bringing the total number of NYPD officers responding to close to 2,000.[137]

The NYPD Chief of Department called for Operation Omega, which required the protection of sensitive locations around the city. NYPD headquarters were secured and all other government buildings were evacuated.[138]

The ESU command post at Church and Vesey streets coordinated all NYPD ESU rescue teams. After the South Tower was hit, the ESU officer running this command post decided to send one ESU team (each with approximately six police officers) up each of the Twin Towers' stairwells. While he continued to monitor the citywide SOD channel, which NYPD helicopters were using, he also monitored the point-to-point tactical channel that the ESU teams climbing in the towers would use.[139]

The first NYPD ESU team entered the West Street—level lobby of the North Tower and prepared to begin climbing at about 9:15 A.M. They attempted to check in with the FDNY chiefs present, but were rebuffed. OEM personnel did not intervene. The ESU team began to climb the stairs. Shortly thereafter, a second NYPD ESU team entered the South Tower. The OEM field responder present ensured that they check in with the FDNY chief in charge of the lobby, and it was agreed that the ESU team would ascend and support FDNY personnel.[140]

A third ESU team subsequently entered the North Tower at its elevated mezzanine lobby level and made no effort to check in with the FDNY command post. A fourth ESU team entered the South Tower. By 9:59, a fifth ESU team was next to 6 WTC and preparing to enter the North Tower.[141]

By approximately 9:50, the lead ESU team had reached the 31st floor, observing that there appeared to be no more civilians still descending. This ESU team encountered a large group of firefighters and administered oxygen to some of them who were exhausted.[142]

At about 9:56, the officer running the ESU command post on Church and Vesey streets had a final radio communication with one of the ESU teams in the South Tower. The team then stated that it was ascending via stairs, was somewhere in the 20s, and was making slow progress because of the numerous descending civilians crowding the stairwell.[143]

Three plainclothes NYPD officers without radios or protective gear had begun ascending either stairwell A or C of the North Tower. They began checking every other floor above the 12th for civilians. Only occasionally did they find any, and in those few cases they ordered the civilians to evacuate immediately. While checking floors, they used office phones to call their superiors. In one phone call an NYPD chief instructed them to leave the North Tower, but they refused to do so. As they climbed higher, they encountered increasing smoke and heat. Shortly before 10:00 they arrived on the 54th floor.[144]

Throughout this period (9:03 to 9:59), a group of NYPD and Port Authority police officers, as well as two Secret Service agents, continued to assist civilians leaving the North Tower. They were positioned around the mezzanine lobby level of the North Tower, directing civilians leaving stairwells A and C to evacuate down an escalator to the concourse. The officers instructed those civilians who seemed composed to evacuate the complex calmly but rapidly. Other civilians exiting the stairs who were either injured or exhausted collapsed at the foot of these stairs; officers then assisted them out of the building.[145]

When civilians reached the concourse, another NYPD officer stationed at the bottom of the escalator directed them to exit through the concourse to the north and east and then out of the WTC complex. This exit route ensured that civilians would not be endangered by falling debris and people on West Street, on the plaza between the towers, and on Liberty Street.[146]

Some officers positioned themselves at the top of a flight of stairs by 5 WTC that led down into the concourse, going into the concourse when necessary to evacuate injured or disoriented civilians. Numerous other NYPD officers were stationed throughout the concourse, assisting burned, injured, and disoriented civilians, as well as directing all civilians to exit to the north and east. NYPD officers were also in the South Tower lobby to assist in civilian evacuation. NYPD officers stationed on Vesey Street between West Street and Church Street urged civilians not to remain in the area and instead to keep walking north.[147]

At 9:06, the NYPD Chief of Department instructed that no units were to land on the roof of either tower. At about 9:30, one of the helicopters present advised that a rooftop evacuation still would not be possible. One NYPD helicopter pilot believed one portion of the North Tower roof to be free enough of smoke that a hoist could be lowered in order to rescue people, but there was no one on the roof. This pilot's helicopter never attempted to hover directly over the tower. Another helicopter did attempt to do so, and its pilot stated that the severity of the heat from the jet fuel—laden fire in the North Tower would have made it impossible to hover low enough for a rescue, because the high temperature would have destabilized the helicopter.[148]

At 9:51, an aviation unit warned units of large pieces of debris hanging from the building. Prior to 9:59, no NYPD helicopter pilot predicted that either tower would collapse.[149]

Interaction of 911 Calls and NYPD Operations.

At 9:37, a civilian on the 106th floor of the South Tower reported to a 911 operator that a lower floor—the "90-something floor"—was collapsing. This information was conveyed inaccurately by the 911 operator to an NYPD dispatcher. The dispatcher further confused the substance of the 911 call by telling NYPD officers at the WTC complex that "the 106th floor is crumbling" at 9:52, 15 minutes after the 911 call was placed. The NYPD dispatcher conveyed this message on the radio frequency used in precincts in the vicinity of the WTC and subsequently on the Special Operations Division channel, but not on City Wide channel 1.[150]

PAPD Response

Initial responders from outside PAPD commands proceeded to the police desk in 5 WTC or to the fire safety desk in the North Tower lobby. Some officers were then assigned to assist in stairwell evacuations; others were assigned to expedite evacuation in the plaza, concourse, and PATH station. As information was received of civilians trapped above ground-level floors of the North Tower, other PAPD officers were instructed to climb to those floors for rescue efforts. Still others began climbing toward the impact zone.[151]

At 9:11, the PAPD Superintendent and an inspector began walking up stairwell B of the North Tower to assess damage near and in the impact zone. The PAPD Chief and several other PAPD officers began ascending a stairwell in order to reach the Windows on the World restaurant on the 106th floor, from which calls had been made to the PAPD police desk reporting at least 100 people trapped.[152]

Many PAPD officers from different commands responded on their own initiative. By 9:30, the PAPD central police desk requested that responding officers meet at West and Vesey and await further instructions. In the absence of a predetermined command structure to deal with an incident of this magnitude, a number of PAPD inspectors, captains, and lieutenants stepped forward at around 9:30 to formulate an on-site response plan. They were hampered by not knowing how many officers were responding to the site and where those officers were operating. Many of the officers who responded to this command post lacked suitable protective equipment to enter the complex.[153]

By 9:58, one PAPD officer had reached the 44th-floor sky lobby of the North Tower. Also in the North Tower, one team of PAPD officers was in the mid-20s and another was in the lower 20s. Numerous PAPD officers were also climbing in the South Tower, including the PAPD ESU team. Many PAPD officers were on the ground floors of the complex—some assisting in evacuation, others manning the PAPD desk in 5 WTC or assisting at lobby command posts.[154]

OEM Response
After the South Tower was hit, OEM senior leadership decided to remain in its "bunker" and continue conducting operations, even though all civilians had been evacuated from 7 WTC. At approximately 9:30, a senior OEM official ordered the evacuation of the facility, after a Secret Service agent in 7 WTC advised him that additional commercial planes were not accounted for. Prior to its evacuation, no outside agency liaisons had reached OEM. OEM field responders were stationed in each tower's lobby, at the FDNY overall command post, and, at least for some period of time, at the NYPD command post at Church and Vesey.[155]

Summary
The emergency response effort escalated with the crash of United 175 into the South Tower. With that escalation, communications as well as command and control became increasingly critical and increasingly difficult. First responders assisted thousands of civilians in evacuating the towers, even as incident commanders from responding agencies lacked knowledge of what other agencies and, in some cases, their own responders were doing.

From 9:59 until 10:28 A.M.
At 9:58:59, the South Tower collapsed in ten seconds, killing all civilians and emergency personnel inside, as well a number of individuals—both first responders and civilians—in the concourse, in the Marriott, and on neighboring streets. The building collapsed into itself, causing a ferocious windstorm and creating a massive debris cloud. The Marriott hotel suffered significant damage as a result of the collapse of the South Tower.[156]

Civilian Response in the North Tower

The 911 calls placed from most locations in the North Tower grew increasingly desperate as time went on. As late as 10:28, people remained alive in some locations, including on the 92nd and 79th floors. Below the impact zone, it is likely that most civilians who were physically and emotionally capable of descending had exited the tower. The civilians who were nearing the bottom of stairwell C were assisted out of the building by NYPD, FDNY, and PAPD personnel. Others, who experienced difficulty evacuating, were being helped by first responders on lower floors.[157]

FDNY Response
Immediate Impact of the Collapse of the South Tower.

The FDNY overall command post and posts in the North Tower lobby, the Marriott lobby, and the staging area on West Street south of Liberty all ceased to operate upon the collapse of the South Tower, as did EMS staging areas, because of their proximity to the building.[158]

Those who had been in the North Tower lobby had no way of knowing that the South Tower had suffered a complete collapse. Chiefs who had fled from the overall command post on the west side of West Street took shelter in the underground parking garage at 2 World Financial Center and were not available to influence FDNY operations for the next ten minutes or so.[159]

When the South Tower collapsed, firefighters on upper floors of the North Tower heard a violent roar, and many were knocked off their feet; they saw debris coming up the stairs and observed that the power was lost and emergency lights activated. Nevertheless, those firefighters not standing near windows facing south had no way of knowing that the South Tower had collapsed; many surmised that a bomb had exploded, or that the North Tower had suffered a partial collapse on its upper floors.[160]

We do not know whether the repeater channel continued to function after 9:59.[161]

Initial Evacuation Instructions and Communications.

The South Tower's total collapse was immediately communicated on the Manhattan dispatch channel by an FDNY boat on the Hudson River; but to our knowledge, no one at the site received this information, because every FDNY command post had been abandoned—including the overall command post, which included the Field Comm van. Despite his lack of knowledge of what had happened to the South Tower, a chief in the process of evacuating the North Tower lobby sent out an order within a minute of the collapse: "Command to all units in Tower 1, evacuate the building." Another chief from the North Tower lobby soon followed with an additional evacuation order issued on tactical 1.[162]

Evacuation orders did not follow the protocol for giving instructions when a building's collapse may be imminent—a protocol that includes constantly repeating "Mayday, Mayday, Mayday"—during the 29 minutes between the fall of the South Tower and that of the North Tower. In addition, most of the evacuation instructions did not mention that the South Tower had collapsed. However, at least three firefighters heard evacuation instructions which stated that the North Tower was in danger of "imminent collapse."[163]

FDNY Personnel above the Ground Floors of the North Tower.

Within minutes, some firefighters began to hear evacuation orders over tactical 1. At least one chief also gave the evacuation instruction on the command channel used only by chiefs in the North Tower, which was much less crowded.[164]

At least two battalion chiefs on upper floors of the North Tower—one on the 23rd floor and one on the 35th floor—heard the evacuation instruction on the command channel and repeated it to everyone they came across. The chief on the 23rd floor apparently aggressively took charge to ensure that all firefighters on the floors in the immediate area were evacuating. The chief on the 35th floor also heard a separate radio communication stating that the South Tower had collapsed (which the chief on the 23rd floor may have heard as well). He subsequently acted with a sense of urgency, and some firefighters heard the evacuation order for the first time when he repeated it on tactical 1. This chief also had a bullhorn and traveled to each of the stairwells and shouted the evacuation order: "All FDNY, get the fuck out!" As a result of his efforts, many firefighters who had not been in the process of evacuating began to do so.[165]

Other firefighters did not receive the evacuation transmissions, for one of four reasons: First, some FDNY radios did not pick up the transmission because of the difficulties of radio communications in high-rises. Second, the numbers trying to use tactical 1 after the South Tower collapsed may have drowned out some evacuation instructions. According to one FDNY lieutenant who was on the 31st floor of the North Tower at the time, "[Tactical] channel 1 just might have been so bogged down that it may have been impossible to get that order through."[166] Third, some firefighters in the North Tower were off-duty and did not have radios. Fourth, some firefighters in the North Tower had been dispatched to the South Tower and likely were on the different tactical channel assigned to that tower.[167]

FDNY personnel in the North Tower who received the evacuation orders did not respond uniformly. Some units—including one whose officer knew that the South Tower had collapsed—either delayed or stopped their evacuation in order to assist nonambulatory civilians. Some units whose members had become separated during the climb attempted to regroup so they could descend together. Some units began to evacuate but, according to eyewitnesses, did not hurry. At least several firefighters who survived believed that they and others would have evacuated more urgently had they known of the South Tower's complete collapse. Other firefighters continued to sit and rest on floors while other companies descended past them and reminded them that they were supposed to evacuate. Some firefighters were determined not to leave the building while other FDNY personnel remained inside and, in one case, convinced others to remain with them. In another case, firefighters had successfully descended to the lobby, where another firefighter then persuaded them to reascend in order to look for specific FDNY personnel.[168]

Other FDNY personnel did not hear the evacuation order on their radio but were advised orally to leave the building by other firefighters and police who were themselves evacuating.[169]

By 10:24, approximately five FDNY companies reached the bottom of stairwell B and entered the North Tower lobby. They stood in the lobby for more than a minute, not certain what to do, as no chiefs were present. Finally, one firefighter—who had earlier seen from a window that the South Tower had collapsed—urged that they all leave, as this tower could fall as well. The units then proceeded to exit onto West Street. While they were doing so, the North Tower began its pancake collapse, killing some of these men.[170]

Other FDNY Personnel.

The Marriott Hotel suffered significant damage in the collapse of the South Tower. Those in the lobby were knocked down and enveloped in the darkness of a debris cloud. Some were hurt but could walk. Others were more severely injured, and some were trapped. Several firefighters came across a group of about 50 civilians who had been taking shelter in the restaurant and assisted them in evacuating. Up above, at the time of the South Tower's collapse four companies were descending the stairs single file in a line of approximately 20 men. Four survived.[171]

At the time of the South Tower's collapse, two FDNY companies were either at the eastern side of the North Tower lobby, near the mall concourse, or actually in the mall concourse, trying to reach the South Tower. Many of these men were thrown off their feet by the collapse of the South

Tower; they then attempted to regroup in the darkness of the debris cloud and evacuate civilians and themselves, not knowing that the South Tower had collapsed. Several of these firefighters subsequently searched the PATH station below the concourse—unaware that the PAPD had cleared the area of all civilians by 9:19.[172]

At about 10:15, the FDNY Chief of Department and the Chief of Safety, who had returned to West Street from the parking garage, confirmed that the South Tower had collapsed. The Chief of Department issued a radio order for all units to evacuate the North Tower, repeating it about five times. He then directed that the FDNY command post be moved further north on West Street and told FDNY units in the area to proceed north on West Street toward Chambers Street. At approximately 10:25, he radioed for two ladder companies to respond to the Marriott, where he was aware that both FDNY personnel and civilians were trapped.[173]

Many chiefs, including several of those who had been in the North Tower lobby, did not learn that the South Tower had collapsed until 30 minutes or more after the event. According to two eyewitnesses, however, one senior FDNY chief who knew that the South Tower had collapsed strongly expressed the opinion that the North Tower would not collapse, because unlike the South Tower, it had not been hit on a corner.[174]

After the South Tower collapsed, some firefighters on the streets neighboring the North Tower remained where they were or came closer to the North Tower. Some of these firefighters did not know that the South Tower had collapsed, but many chose despite that knowledge to remain in an attempt to save additional lives. According to one such firefighter, a chief who was preparing to mount a search-and-rescue mission in the Marriott, "I would never think of myself as a leader of men if I had headed north on West Street after [the] South Tower collapsed." Just outside the North Tower on West Street one firefighter was directing others exiting the building, telling them when no jumpers were coming down and it was safe to run out. A senior chief had grabbed an

NYPD bullhorn and was urging firefighters exiting onto West Street to continue running north, well away from the WTC. Three of the most senior and respected members of the FDNY were involved in attempting to rescue civilians and firefighters from the Marriott.[175]

NYPD Response

A member of the NYPD Aviation Unit radioed that the South Tower had collapsed immediately after it happened, and further advised that all people in the WTC complex and nearby areas should be evacuated. At 10:04, NYPD aviation reported that the top 15 stories of the North Tower "were glowing red" and that they might collapse. At 10:08, a helicopter pilot warned that he did not believe the North Tower would last much longer.[176]

Immediately after the South Tower collapsed, many NYPD radio frequencies became overwhelmed with transmissions relating to injured, trapped, or missing officers. As a result, NYPD radio communications became strained on most channels. Nevertheless, they remained effective enough for the two closest NYPD mobilization points to be moved further from the WTC at 10:06.[177]

Just like most firefighters, the ESU rescue teams in the North Tower had no idea that the South Tower had collapsed. However, by 10:00 the ESU officer running the command post at Church and Vesey ordered the evacuation of all ESU units from the WTC complex. This officer, who had observed the South Tower collapse, reported it to ESU units in the North Tower in his evacuation instruction.[178]

This instruction was clearly heard by the two ESU units already in the North Tower and the other ESU unit preparing to enter the tower. The ESU team on the 31st floor found the full collapse of the South Tower so unfathomable that they radioed back to the ESU officer at the command post and asked him to repeat his communication. He reiterated his urgent message.[179]

The ESU team on the 31st floor conferred with the FDNY personnel there to ensure that they, too, knew that they had to evacuate, then proceeded down stairwell B. During the descent, they reported seeing many firefighters who were resting and did not seem to be in the process of evacuating. They further reported advising these firefighters to evacuate, but said that at times they were not acknowledged. In the opinion of one of the ESU officers, some of these firefighters essentially refused to take orders from cops. At least one firefighter who was in the North Tower has supported that assessment, stating that he was not going to take an evacuation instruction from a cop that morning. However, another firefighter reports that ESU officers ran past him without advising him to evacuate.[180]

The ESU team on the 11th floor began descending stairwell C after receiving the evacuation order. Once near the mezzanine level—where stairwell C ended—this team spread out in chain formation, stretching from several floors down to the mezzanine itself. They used their flashlights to provide a path of beacons through the darkness and debris for civilians climbing down the stairs. Eventually, when no one else appeared to be descending, the ESU team exited the North Tower and ran one at a time to 6 WTC, dodging those who still were jumping from the upper floors of the North Tower by acting as spotters for each other. They remained in the area, conducting additional searches for civilians; all but two of them died.[181]

After surviving the South Tower's collapse, the ESU team that had been preparing to enter the North Tower spread into chain formation and created a path for civilians (who had exited from the North Tower mezzanine) to evacuate the WTC complex by descending the stairs on the north side of 5 and 6 WTC, which led down to Vesey Street. They remained at this post until the North Tower collapsed, yet all survived.[182]

The three plainclothes NYPD officers who had made it up to the 54th floor of the North Tower felt the building shake violently at 9:59 as the South Tower collapsed (though they did not know the cause). Immediately thereafter, they were joined by three firefighters from an FDNY engine company. One of the firefighters apparently heard an evacuation order on his radio, but responded in a return radio communication, "We're not fucking coming out!" However, the firefighters urged the police officers to descend because they lacked the protective gear and equipment needed to handle the increasing smoke and heat. The police officers reluctantly began descending, checking that the lower floors were clear of civilians. They proceeded down stairwell B, poking their heads into every floor and briefly looking for civilians.[183]

Other NYPD officers helping evacuees on the mezzanine level of the North Tower were enveloped in the debris cloud that resulted from the South Tower's collapse. They struggled to regroup in the darkness and to evacuate both themselves and civilians they encountered. At least one of them died in the collapse of the North Tower. At least one NYPD officer from this area managed to evacuate out toward 5 WTC, where he teamed up with a Port Authority police officer and acted as a spotter in advising the civilians who were still exiting when they could safely run from 1 WTC to 5 WTC and avoid being struck by people and debris falling from the upper floors.[184]

At the time of the collapse of the South Tower, there were numerous NYPD officers in the concourse, some of whom are believed to have died there. Those who survived struggled to evacuate themselves in darkness, assisting civilians as they exited the concourse in all directions.[185]

Port Authority Response
The collapse of the South Tower forced the evacuation of the PAPD command post on West and Vesey, compelling PAPD officers to move north. There is no evidence that PAPD officers without WTC Command radios received an evacuation order by radio. Some of these officers in the North Tower decided to evacuate, either on their own or in consultation with other first responders they came across. Some greatly slowed their own descent in order to assist nonambulatory civilians.[186]

After 10:28 A.M.

The North Tower collapsed at 10:28:25 A.M., killing all civilians alive on upper floors, an undetermined number below, and scores of first responders. The FDNY Chief of Department, the Port Authority Police Department Superintendent, and many of their senior staff were killed. Incredibly, twelve firefighters, one PAPD officer, and three civilians who were descending stairwell B of the North Tower survived its collapse.[187]

On September 11, the nation suffered the largest loss of life—2,973—on its soil as a result of hostile attack in its history. The FDNY suffered 343 fatalities—the largest loss of life of any emergency response agency in history. The PAPD suffered 37 fatalities—the largest loss of life of any police force in history. The NYPD suffered 23 fatalities—the second largest loss of life of any police force in history, exceeded only by the number of PAPD officers lost the same day.[188]

Mayor Giuliani, along with the Police and Fire commissioners and the OEM director, moved quickly north and established an emergency operations command post at the Police Academy. Over the coming hours, weeks, and months, thousands of civilians and city, state, and federal employees devoted themselves around the clock to putting New York City back on its feet.[189]

9.3 EMERGENCY RESPONSE AT THE PENTAGON

If it had happened on any other day, the disaster at the Pentagon would be remembered as a singular challenge and an extraordinary national story. Yet the calamity at the World Trade Center that same morning included catastrophic damage 1,000 feet above the ground that instantly imperiled tens of thousands of people. The two experiences are not comparable. Nonetheless, broader lessons in integrating multiagency response efforts are apparent when we analyze the response at the Pentagon.

The emergency response at the Pentagon represented a mix of local, state, and federal jurisdictions and was generally effective. It overcame the inherent complications of a response across jurisdictions because the Incident Command System, a formalized management structure for emergency response, was in place in the National Capital Region on 9/11.[190]

Because of the nature of the event—a plane crash, fire, and partial building collapse—the Arlington County Fire Department served as incident commander. Different agencies had different roles. The incident required a major rescue, fire, and medical response from Arlington County at the U.S. military's headquarters—a facility under the control of the secretary of defense. Since it was a terrorist attack, the Department of Justice was the lead federal agency in charge (with authority delegated to the FBI for operational response). Additionally, the terrorist attack affected the daily operations and emergency management requirements of Arlington County and all bordering and surrounding jurisdictions.[191]

At 9:37, the west wall of the Pentagon was hit by hijacked American Airlines Flight 77, a Boeing 757. The crash caused immediate and catastrophic damage. All 64 people aboard the airliner were killed, as were 125 people inside the Pentagon (70 civilians and 55 military service members). One hundred six people were seriously injured and transported to area hospitals.[192]

While no emergency response is flawless, the response to the 9/11 terrorist attack on the Pentagon was mainly a success for three reasons: first, the strong professional relationships and trust established among emergency responders; second, the adoption of the Incident Command System; and third, the pursuit of a regional approach to response. Many fire and police agencies that responded had extensive prior experience working together on regional events and training exercises. Indeed, at the time preparations were under way at many of these agencies to ensure public safety at the annual meetings of the International Monetary Fund and the World Bank scheduled to be held later that month in Washington, D.C.[193]

Local, regional, state, and federal agencies immediately responded to the Pentagon attack. In addition to county fire, police, and sheriff's departments, the response was assisted by the Metropolitan Washington Airports Authority, Ronald Reagan Washington National Airport Fire Department, Fort Myer Fire Department, the Virginia State Police, the Virginia Department of Emergency Management, the FBI, FEMA, a National Medical Response Team, the Bureau of Alcohol, Tobacco, and Firearms, and numerous military personnel within the Military District of Washington.[194]

Command was established at 9:41. At the same time, the Arlington County Emergency Communications Center contacted the fire departments of Fairfax County, Alexandria, and the District of Columbia to request mutual aid. The incident command post provided a clear view of and access to the crash site, allowing the incident commander to assess the situation at all times.[195]

At 9:55, the incident commander ordered an evacuation of the Pentagon impact area because a partial collapse was imminent; it occurred at 9:57, and no first responder was injured.[196]

At 10:15, the incident commander ordered a full evacuation of the command post because of the warning of an approaching hijacked aircraft passed along by the FBI. This was the first of three evacuations caused by reports of incoming aircraft, and the evacuation order was well communicated and well coordinated.[197]

Several factors facilitated the response to this incident, and distinguish it from the far more difficult task in New York. There was a single incident, and it was not 1,000 feet above ground. The incident site was relatively easy to secure and contain, and there were no other buildings in the immediate area. There was no collateral damage beyond the Pentagon.[198]

Yet the Pentagon response encountered difficulties that echo those experienced in New York. As the "Arlington County: After-Action Report" notes, there were significant problems with both self-dispatching and communications: "Organizations, response units, and individuals proceeding on their own initiative directly to an incident site, without the knowledge and permission of the host jurisdiction and the Incident Commander, complicate the exercise of command, increase the risks faced by bonafide responders, and exacerbate the challenge of accountability." With respect to communications, the report concludes: "Almost all aspects of communications continue to be problematic, from initial notification to tactical operations. Cellular telephones were of little value. . . . Radio channels were initially oversaturated. . . . Pagers seemed to be the most reliable means of notification when available and used, but most firefighters are not issued pagers."[199]

It is a fair inference, given the differing situations in New York City and Northern Virginia, that the problems in command, control, and communications that occurred at both sites will likely recur in any emergency of similar scale. The task looking forward is to enable first responders to respond in a coordinated manner with the greatest possible awareness of the situation.

9.4 ANALYSIS

Like the national defense effort described in chapter 1, the emergency response to the attacks on 9/11 was necessarily improvised. In New York, the FDNY, NYPD, the Port Authority, WTC employees, and the building occupants themselves did their best to cope with the effects of an unimaginable catastrophe—unfolding furiously over a mere 102 minutes—for which they were unprepared in terms of both training and mindset. As a result of the efforts of first responders, assistance from each other, and their own good instincts and goodwill, the vast majority of civilians below the impact zone were able to evacuate the towers.

The National Institute of Standards and Technology has provided a preliminary estimation that between 16,400 and 18,800 civilians were in the WTC complex as of 8:46 A.M. on September 11. At most 2,152 individuals died at the WTC complex who were not (1) fire or police first responders, (2) security or fire safety personnel of the WTC or individual companies, (3) volunteer civilians who ran to the WTC after the planes' impact to help others, or (4) on the two planes that crashed into the Twin Towers. Out of this total number of fatalities, we can account for the workplace location of 2,052 individuals, or 95.35 percent. Of this number, 1,942 or 94.64 percent either worked or were supposed to attend a meeting at or above the respective impact zones of the Twin Towers; only 110, or 5.36 percent of those who died, worked below the impact zone. While a given person's office location at the WTC does not definitively indicate where that individual died that morning or whether he or she could have evacuated, these data strongly suggest that the evacuation was a success for civilians below the impact zone.[200]

Several factors influenced the evacuation on September 11. It was aided greatly by changes made by the Port Authority in response to the 1993 bombing and by the training of both Port Authority personnel and civilians after that time. Stairwells remained lit near unaffected floors; some tenants relied on procedures learned in fire drills to help them to safety; others were guided down the stairs by fire safety officials based in the lobby. Because of damage caused by the impact of the planes, the capability of the sophisticated building systems may have been impaired. Rudimentary improvements, however, such as the addition of glow strips to the handrails and stairs, were credited by some as the reason for their survival. The general evacuation time for the towers dropped from more than four hours in 1993 to under one hour on September 11 for most civilians who were not trapped or physically incapable of enduring a long descent.

First responders also played a significant role in the success of the evacuation. Some specific rescues are quantifiable, such as an FDNY company's rescue of civilians trapped on the 22d floor of the North Tower, or the success of FDNY, PAPD, and NYPD personnel in carrying nonambulatory civilians out of both the North and South Towers. In other instances, intangibles combined to reduce what could have been a much higher death total. It is impossible to measure how many more civilians who descended to the ground floors would have died but for the NYPD and PAPD personnel directing them—via safe exit routes that avoided jumpers and debris—to leave the complex urgently but calmly. It is impossible to measure how many more civilians would have died but for the determination of many members of the FDNY, PAPD, and NYPD to continue assisting civilians after the South Tower collapsed. It is impossible to measure the calming influence that ascending firefighters had on descending civilians or whether but for the firefighters' presence the poor behavior of a very few civilians could have caused a dangerous and panicked mob flight. But the positive impact of the first responders on the evacuation came at a tremendous cost of first responder lives lost.[201]

Civilian and Private-Sector Challenges

The "first" first responders on 9/11, as in most catastrophes, were private-sector civilians. Because 85 percent of our nation's critical infrastructure is controlled not by government but by the private sector, private-sector civilians are likely to be the first responders in any future catastrophes. For that reason, we have assessed the state of private sector and civilian preparedness in order to formulate recommendations to address this critical need. Our recommendations grow out of the experience of the civilians at the World Trade Center on 9/11.

THE 9/11 REPORT

Lack of Protocol for Rooftop Rescues.

Civilians at or above the impact zone in the North Tower had the smallest hope of survival. Once the plane struck, they were prevented from descending because of damage to or impassable conditions in the building's three stairwells. The only hope for those on the upper floors of the North Tower would have been a swift and extensive air rescue. Several factors made this impossible. Doors leading to the roof were kept locked for security reasons, and damage to software in the security command station prevented a lock release order from taking effect. Even if the doors had not been locked, structural and radiation hazards made the rooftops unsuitable staging areas for a large number of civilians; and even if conditions permitted general helicopter evacuations—which was not the case—only several people could be lifted at a time.

The WTC lacked any plan for evacuation of civilians on upper floors of the WTC in the event that all stairwells were impassable below.

Lack of Comprehensive Evacuation of South Tower Immediately after the North Tower Impact.

No decision has been criticized more than the decision of building personnel not to evacuate the South Tower immediately after the North Tower was hit. A firm and prompt evacuation order would likely have led many to safety. Even a strictly "advisory" announcement would not have dissuaded those who decided for themselves to evacuate. The advice to stay in place was understandable, however, when considered in its context. At that moment, no one appears to have thought a second plane could hit the South Tower. The evacuation of thousands of people was seen as inherently dangerous. Additionally, conditions were hazardous in some areas outside the towers.[202]

Less understandable, in our view, is the instruction given to some civilians who had reached the lobby to return to their offices. They could have been held in the lobby or perhaps directed through the underground concourse.

Despite the initial advice given over its public-address system, the South Tower was ordered to be evacuated by the FDNY and PAPD within 12 minutes of the North Tower's being hit. If not for a second, unanticipated attack, the evacuation presumably would have proceeded.

Impact of Fire Safety Plan and Fire Drills on Evacuation.

Once the South Tower was hit, civilians on upper floors wasted time ascending the stairs instead of searching for a clear path down, when stairwell A was at least initially passable. Although rooftop rescues had not been conclusively ruled out, civilians were not informed in fire drills that roof doors were locked, that rooftop areas were hazardous, and that no helicopter evacuation plan existed.

In both towers, civilians who were able to reach the stairs and descend were also stymied by the deviations in the stairways and by smoke doors. This confusion delayed the evacuation of some and may have obstructed that of others. The Port Authority has acknowledged that in the future, tenants should be made aware of what conditions they will encounter during descent.

Impact of 911 Calls on Evacuation.

The NYPD's 911 operators and FDNY dispatch were not adequately integrated into the emergency response. In several ways, the 911 system was not ready to cope with a major disaster. These operators and dispatchers were one of the only sources of information for individuals at and above the impact zone of the towers. The FDNY ordered both towers fully evacuated by 8:57, but this guidance was not conveyed to 911 operators and FDNY dispatchers, who for the next hour often continued to advise civilians not to self-evacuate, regardless of whether they were above or below the impact zones. Nor were 911 operators or FDNY dispatchers advised that rooftop rescues had been ruled out. This failure may have been harmful to civilians on the upper floors of the South Tower who called 911 and were not told that their only evacuation hope was to attempt to descend, not to ascend. In planning for future disasters, it is important to integrate those taking 911 calls into the emergency response team and to involve them in providing up-to-date information and assistance to the public.

Preparedness of Individual Civilians.

One clear lesson of September 11 is that individual civilians need to take responsibility for maximizing the probability that they will survive, should disaster strike. Clearly, many building occupants in the World Trade Center did not take preparedness seriously. Individuals should know the exact location of every stairwell in their work-place. In addition, they should have access at all times to flashlights, which were deemed invaluable by some civilians who managed to evacuate the WTC on September 11.

Challenges Experienced by First Responders
The Challenge of Incident Command.

As noted above, in July 2001, Mayor Giuliani updated a directive titled "Direction and Control of Emergencies in the City of New York." The directive designated, for different types of emergencies, an appropriate agency as "Incident Commander"; it would be "responsible for the management of the City's response to the emergency." The directive also provided that where incidents are "so multifaceted that no one agency immediately stands out as the Incident Commander, OEM will assign the role of Incident Commander to an agency as the situation demands."[203]

To some degree, the Mayor's directive for incident command was followed on 9/11. It was clear that the lead response agency was the FDNY, and that the other responding local, federal, bistate, and state agencies acted in a supporting role. There was a tacit understanding that FDNY personnel would have primary responsibility for evacuating civilians who were above the ground floors of the Twin Towers, while NYPD and

PAPD personnel would be in charge of evacuating civilians from the WTC complex once they reached ground level. The NYPD also greatly assisted responding FDNY units by clearing emergency lanes to the WTC.[204]

In addition, coordination occurred at high levels of command. For example, the Mayor and Police Commissioner consulted with the Chief of the Department of the FDNY at approximately 9:20. There were other instances of coordination at operational levels, and information was shared on an ad hoc basis. For example, an NYPD ESU team passed the news of their evacuation order to firefighters in the North Tower.[205]

It is also clear, however, that the response operations lacked the kind of integrated communications and unified command contemplated in the directive. These problems existed both within and among individual responding agencies.

Command and Control within First Responder Agencies.

For a unified incident management system to succeed, each participant must have command and control of its own units and adequate internal communications. This was not always the case at the WTC on 9/11.

Understandably lacking experience in responding to events of the magnitude of the World Trade Center attacks, the FDNY as an institution proved incapable of coordinating the numbers of units dispatched to different points within the 16-acre complex. As a result, numerous units were congregating in the undamaged Marriott Hotel and at the overall command post on West Street by 9:30, while chiefs in charge of the South Tower still were in desperate need of units. With better understanding of the resources already available, additional units might not have been dispatched to the South Tower at 9:37.

The task of accounting for and coordinating the units was rendered difficult, if not impossible, by internal communications breakdowns resulting from the limited capabilities of radios in the high-rise environment of the WTC and from confusion over which personnel were assigned to which frequency. Furthermore, when the South Tower collapsed the overall FDNY command post ceased to operate, which compromised the FDNY's ability to understand the situation; an FDNY marine unit's immediate radio communication to FDNY dispatch that the South Tower had fully collapsed was not conveyed to chiefs at the scene. The FDNY's inability to coordinate and account for the different radio channels that would be used in an emergency of this scale contributed to the early lack of units in the South Tower, whose lobby chief initially could not communicate with anyone outside that tower.[206]

Though almost no one at 9:50 on September 11 was contemplating an imminent total collapse of the Twin Towers, many first responders and civilians were contemplating the possibility of imminent additional terrorist attacks throughout New York City. Had any such attacks occurred, the FDNY's response would have been severely compromised by the concentration of so many of its off-duty personnel, particularly its elite personnel, at the WTC.

The Port Authority's response was hampered by the lack of both standard operating procedures and radios capable of enabling multiple commands to respond in unified fashion to an incident at the WTC. Many officers reporting from the tunnel and airport commands could not hear instructions being issued over the WTC Command frequency. In addition, command and control was complicated by senior Port Authority Police officials becoming directly involved in frontline rescue operations.

The NYPD experienced comparatively fewer internal command and control and communications issues. Because the department has a history of mobilizing thousands of officers for major events requiring crowd control, its technical radio capability and major incident protocols were more easily adapted to an incident of the magnitude of 9/11. In addition, its mission that day lay largely outside the towers themselves. Although there were ESU teams and a few individual police officers climbing in the towers, the vast majority of NYPD personnel were staged outside, assisting with crowd control and evacuation and securing other sites in the city. The NYPD ESU division had firm command and control over its units, in part because there were so few of them (in comparison to the number of FDNY companies) and all reported to the same ESU command post. It is unclear, however, whether non-ESU NYPD officers operating on the ground floors, and in a few cases on upper floors, of the WTC were as well coordinated.

Significant shortcomings within the FDNY's command and control capabilities were painfully exposed on September 11. To its great credit, the department has made a substantial effort in the past three years to address these. While significant problems in the command and control of the PAPD also were exposed on September 11, it is less clear that the Port Authority has adopted new training exercises or major incident protocols to address these shortcomings.[207]

Lack of Coordination among First Responder Agencies.

Any attempt to establish a unified command on 9/11 would have been further frustrated by the lack of communication and coordination among responding agencies. Certainly, the FDNY was not "responsible for the management of the City's response to the emergency," as the Mayor's directive would have required. The command posts were in different locations, and OEM headquarters, which could have served as a focal point for information sharing, did not play an integrating role in ensuring that information was shared among agencies on 9/11, even prior to its evacuation. There was a lack of comprehensive coordination between FDNY, NYPD, and PAPD personnel climbing above the ground floors in the Twin Towers.

Information that was critical to informed decision making was not shared among agencies. FDNY chiefs in leadership roles that morning have told us that their decision making capability was hampered by a lack of information from NYPD aviation. At 9:51 A.M., a helicopter pilot cautioned that "large pieces" of the South Tower appeared to be about to fall and could pose a danger to those below. Immediately after the tower's collapse, a helicopter pilot radioed that news. This transmission was followed by communications at 10:08, 10:15, and 10:22 that called into question the condition of the North Tower. The FDNY chiefs would have benefited greatly had they been able to communicate with personnel in a helicopter.

The consequence of the lack of real-time intelligence from NYPD aviation should not be overstated. Contrary to a widely held misperception, no NYPD helicopter predicted the fall of either tower before the South Tower collapsed, and no NYPD personnel began to evacuate the WTC complex prior to that time. Furthermore, the FDNY, as an institution, was in possession of the knowledge that the South Tower had collapsed as early as the NYPD, as its fall had been immediately reported by an FDNY boat on a dispatch channel. Because of internal breakdowns within the department, however, this information was not disseminated to FDNY personnel on the scene.

The FDNY, PAPD, and NYPD did not coordinate their units that were searching the WTC complex for civilians. In many cases, redundant searches of specific floors and areas were conducted. It is unclear whether fewer first responders in the aggregate would have been in the Twin Towers if there had been an integrated response, or what impact, if any, redundant searches had on the total number of first responder fatalities.

Whether the lack of coordination between the FDNY and NYPD on September 11 had a catastrophic effect has been the subject of controversy. We believe that there are too many variables for us to responsibly quantify those consequences. It is clear that the lack of coordination did not affect adversely the evacuation of civilians. It is equally clear, however, that the Incident Command System did not function to integrate awareness among agencies or to facilitate interagency response.[208]

If New York and other major cities are to be prepared for

future terrorist attacks, different first responder agencies within each city must be fully coordinated, just as different branches of the U.S. military are. Coordination entails a unified command that comprehensively deploys all dispatched police, fire, and other first responder resources.

In May 2004, New York City adopted an emergency response plan that expressly contemplates two or more agencies jointly being lead agency when responding to a terrorist attack but does not mandate a comprehensive and unified incident command that can deploy and monitor all first responder resources from one overall command post. In our judgment, this falls short of an optimal response plan, which requires clear command and control, common training, and the trust that such training creates. The experience of the military suggests that integrated into such a coordinated response should be a unified field intelligence unit, which should receive and combine information from all first responders—including 911 operators. Such a field intelligence unit could be valuable in large and complex incidents.

Radio Communication Challenges: The Effectiveness and Urgency of Evacuation Instructions.

As discussed above, the location of the NYPD ESU command post was crucial in making possible an urgent evacuation order explaining the South Tower's full collapse. Firefighters most certainly would have benefited from that information.

A separate matter is the varied success at conveying evacuation instructions to personnel in the North Tower after the South Tower's collapse. The success of NYPD ESU instruction is attributable to a combination of (1) the strength of the radios, (2) the relatively small numbers of individuals using them, and (3) use of the correct channel by all.

The same three factors worked against successful communication among FDNY personnel. First, the radios' effectiveness was drastically reduced in the high-rise environment. Second, tactical channel 1 was simply overwhelmed by the number of units attempting to communicate on it at 10:00. Third, some firefighters were on the wrong channel or simply lacked radios altogether.

It is impossible to know what difference it made that units in the North Tower were not using the repeater channel after 10:00. While the repeater channel was at least partially operational before the South Tower collapsed, we do not know whether it continued to be operational after 9:59.

Even without the repeater channel, *at least* 24 of the *at most* 32 companies who were dispatched to and actually in the North Tower received the evacuation instruction—either via radio or directly from other first responders. Nevertheless, many of these firefighters died, either because they delayed their evacuation to assist civilians, attempted to regroup their units, lacked urgency, or some combination of these factors. In addition, many other firefighters not dispatched to the North Tower also died in its collapse. Some had their radios on the wrong channel. Others were off-duty and lacked radios. In view of these considerations, we conclude that the technical failure of FDNY radios, while a contributing factor, was not the primary cause of the many firefighter fatalities in the North Tower.[209]

The FDNY has worked hard in the past several years to address its radio deficiencies. To improve radio capability in high-rises, the FDNY has internally developed a "post radio" that is small enough for a battalion chief to carry to the upper floors and that greatly repeats and enhances radio signal strength.[210]

The story with respect to Port Authority police officers in the North Tower is less complicated; most of them lacked access to the radio channel on which the Port Authority police evacuation order was given. Since September 11, the Port Authority has worked hard to integrate the radio systems of their different commands.

The lesson of 9/11 for civilians and first responders can be stated simply: in the new age of terror, they—we—are the primary targets. The losses America suffered that day demonstrated both the gravity of the terrorist threat and the commensurate need to prepare ourselves to meet it.

The first responders of today live in a world transformed by the attacks on 9/11. Because no one believes that every conceivable form of attack can be prevented, civilians and first responders will again find themselves on the front lines. We must plan for that eventuality. A rededication to preparedness is perhaps the best way to honor the memories of those we lost that day.

CHAPTER TEN

Wartime

After the attacks had occurred, while crisis managers were still sorting out a number of unnerving false alarms, Air Force One flew to Barksdale Air Force Base in Louisiana. One of these alarms was of a reported threat against Air Force One itself, a threat eventually run down to a misunderstood communication in the hectic White House Situation Room that morning.[1]

While the plan at the elementary school had been to return to Washington, by the time Air Force One was airborne at 9:55 A.M. the Secret Service, the President's advisers, and Vice President Cheney were strongly advising against it. President Bush reluctantly acceded to this advice and, at about 10:10, Air Force One changed course and began heading due west. The immediate objective was to find a safe location—not too far away—where the President could land and speak to the American people. The Secret Service was also interested in refueling the aircraft and paring down the size of the traveling party. The President's military aide, an Air Force officer, quickly researched the options and, sometime around 10:20, identified Barksdale Air Force Base as an appropriate interim destination.[2]

When Air Force One landed at Barksdale at about 11:45, personnel from the local Secret Service office were still en route to the airfield. The motorcade consisted of a military police lead vehicle and a van; the proposed briefing theater had no phones or electrical outlets. Staff scrambled to prepare another room for the President's remarks, while the lead Secret Service agent reviewed the security situation with superiors in Washington. The President completed his statement, which for security reasons was taped and not broadcast live, and the traveling party returned to Air Force One. The next destination was discussed: once again the Secret Service recommended against returning to Washington, and the Vice President agreed. Offutt Air Force Base in Nebraska was chosen because of its elaborate command and control facilities, and because it could accommodate overnight lodging for 50 persons. The Secret Service wanted a place where the President could spend several days, if necessary.[3]

Air Force One arrived at Offutt at 2:50 P.M. At about 3:15, President Bush met with his principal advisers through a secure video teleconference.[4] Rice said President Bush began the meeting with the words, "We're at war,"[5] and that Director of Central Intelligence George Tenet said the agency was still assessing who was responsible, but the early signs all pointed to al Qaeda.[6] That evening the Deputies Committee returned to the pending presidential directive they had labored over during the summer.[7]

The secretary of defense directed the nation's armed forces to Defense Condition 3, an increased state of military readiness.[8] For the first time in history, all nonemergency civilian aircraft in the United States were grounded, stranding tens of thousands of passengers across the country. Contingency plans for the continuity of government and the evacuation of leaders had been implemented.[9] The Pentagon had been struck; the White House or the Capitol had narrowly escaped direct attack. Extraordinary security precautions were put in place at the nation's borders and ports.

In the late afternoon, the President overruled his aides' continuing reluctance to have him return to Washington and ordered Air Force One back to Andrews Air Force Base. He was flown by helicopter back to the White House, passing over the still-smoldering Pentagon. At 8:30 that evening,

President Bush addressed the nation from the White House. After emphasizing that the first priority was to help the injured and protect against any further attacks, he said: "We will make no distinction between the terrorists who committed these acts and those who harbor them." He quoted Psalm 23—"though I walk through the valley of the shadow of death . . ." No American, he said, "will ever forget this day."[10]

Following his speech, President Bush met again with his National Security Council (NSC), expanded to include Secretary of Transportation Norman Mineta and Joseph Allbaugh, the director of the Federal Emergency Management Agency. Secretary of State Colin Powell, who had returned from Peru after hearing of the attacks, joined the discussion. They reviewed the day's events.[11]

10.1 IMMEDIATE RESPONSES AT HOME

As the urgent domestic issues accumulated, White House Deputy Chief of Staff Joshua Bolten chaired a temporary "domestic consequences" group.[12] The agenda in those first days is worth noting, partly as a checklist for future crisis planners. It began with problems of how to help victims and stanch the flowing losses to the American economy, such as

- Organizing federal emergency assistance. One question was what kind of public health advice to give about the air quality in Lower Manhattan in the vicinity of the fallen buildings.[13]
- Compensating victims. They evaluated legislative options, eventually setting up a federal compensation fund and defining the powers of a special master to run it.
- Determining federal assistance. On September 13, President Bush promised to provide $20 billion for New York City, in addition to the $20 billion his budget director had already guessed might be needed for the country as a whole.[14]

- Restoring civil aviation. On the morning of September 13, the national airspace reopened for use by airports that met newly improvised security standards.
- Reopening the financial markets. After extraordinary emergency efforts involving the White House, the Treasury Department, and the Securities and Exchange Commission, aided by unprecedented cooperation among the usually competitive firms of the financial industry, the markets reopened on Monday, September 17.[15]
- Deciding when and how to return border and port security to more normal operations.
- Evaluating legislative proposals to bail out the airline industry and cap its liability.

The very process of reviewing these issues underscored the absence of an effective government organization dedicated to assessing vulnerabilities and handling problems of protection and preparedness. Though a number of agencies had some part of the task, none had security as its primary mission.

By September 14, Vice President Cheney had decided to recommend, at least as a first step, a new White House entity to coordinate all the relevant agencies rather than tackle the challenge of combining them in a new department. This new White House entity would be a homeland security adviser and Homeland Security Council—paralleling the National Security Council system. Vice President Cheney reviewed the proposal with President Bush and other advisers. President Bush announced the new post and its first occupant— Pennsylvania governor Tom Ridge—in his address to a joint session of Congress on September 20.[16]

Beginning on September 11, Immigration and Naturalization Service agents working in cooperation with the FBI began arresting individuals for immigration violations whom they encountered while following up leads in the FBI's investigation of the 9/11 attacks. Eventually, 768 aliens were arrested as "special interest" detainees. Some (such as Zacarias Moussaoui) were actually in INS custody before 9/11; most were arrested after. Attorney General John Ashcroft told us that he saw his job in directing this effort as "risk minimization," both to find out who had committed the attacks and to prevent a subsequent attack. Ashcroft ordered all special interest immigration hearings closed to the public, family members, and press; directed government attorneys to seek denial of bond until such time as they were "cleared" of terrorist connections by the FBI and other agencies; and ordered the identity of the detainees kept secret. INS attorneys charged with prosecuting the immigration violations had trouble getting information about the detainees and any terrorist connections; in the chaos after the attacks, it was very difficult to reach law enforcement officials, who were following up on other leads. The clearance process approved by the Justice Department was time-consuming, lasting an average of about 80 days.[17]

We have assessed this effort to detain aliens of "special interest." The detainees were lawfully held on immigration charges. Records indicate that 531 were deported, 162 were released on bond, 24 received some kind of immigration benefits, 12 had their proceedings terminated, and 8—one of whom was Moussaoui—were remanded to the custody of the U.S. Marshals Service. The inspector general of the Justice Department found significant problems in the way the 9/11 detainees were treated.[18] In response to a request about the counterterrorism benefits of the 9/11 detainee program, the Justice Department cited six individuals on the special interest detainee list, noting that two (including Moussaoui) were linked directly to a terrorist organization and that it had obtained new leads helpful to the investigation of the 9/11 terrorist attacks.[19] A senior al Qaeda detainee has stated that U.S. government efforts after the 9/11 attacks to monitor the American homeland, including review of Muslims' immigration files and deportation of nonpermanent residents, forced al Qaeda to operate less freely in the United States.[20]

The government's ability to collect intelligence inside the United States, and the sharing of such information between the intelligence and law enforcement communities, was not a priority before 9/11. Guidelines on this subject issued in August 2001 by Deputy Attorney General Larry Thompson essentially recapitulated prior guidance. However, the attacks of 9/11 changed everything. Less than one week after September 11, an early version of what was to become the Patriot Act (officially, the USA PATRIOT Act) began to take shape.[21] A central provision of the proposal was the removal of "the wall" on information sharing between the intelligence and law enforcement communities (discussed in chapter 3). Ashcroft told us he was determined to take every conceivable action, within the limits of the Constitution, to identify potential terrorists and deter additional attacks.[22] The administration developed a proposal that eventually passed both houses of Congress by large majorities and was signed into law on October 26.[23]

10.2 PLANNING FOR WAR

By late in the evening of September 11, the President had addressed the nation on the terrible events of the day. Vice President Cheney described the President's mood as somber.[32] The long day was not yet over. When the larger meeting that included his domestic department heads broke up, President Bush chaired a smaller meeting of top advisers, a group he would later call his "war council."[33] This group usually included Vice President Cheney, Secretary of State Powell, Secretary of Defense Donald Rumsfeld, General Hugh Shelton, Vice Chairman of the Joint Chiefs (later to become chairman) General Myers, DCI Tenet, Attorney General Ashcroft, and FBI Director Robert Mueller. From the White House staff, National Security Advisor Condoleezza Rice and Chief of Staff Card were part of the core group, often joined by their deputies, Stephen Hadley and Joshua Bolten.

In this restricted National Security Council meeting, the President said it was a time for self-defense. The United

Flights of Saudi Nationals Leaving the United States

Three questions have arisen with respect to the departure of Saudi nationals from the United States in the immediate aftermath of 9/11: (1) Did any flights of Saudi nationals take place before national airspace reopened September 13, 2001? (2) Was there any political intervention to facilitate the departure of Saudi nationals? (3) Did the FBI screen Saudi nationals thoroughly before their departure?

First, we found no evidence that any flights of Saudi nationals, domestic or international, took place before the reopening of national airspace on the morning of September 13, 2001.[24] To the contrary, every flight we have identified occurred after national airspace reopened.[25]

Second, we found no evidence of political intervention. We found no evidence that anyone at the White House above the level of Richard Clarke participated in a decision on the departure of Saudi nationals. The issue came up in one of the many video teleconferences of the interagency group Clarke chaired, and Clarke said he approved of how the FBI was dealing with the matter when it came up for interagency discussion at his level. Clarke told us, "I asked the FBI, Dale Watson . . . to handle that, to check to see if that was all right with them, to see if they wanted access to any of these people, and to get back to me. And if they had no objections, it would be fine with me." Clarke added, "I have no recollection of clearing it with anybody at the White House."[26]

Although White House Chief of Staff Andrew Card remembered someone telling him about the Saudi request shortly after 9/11, he said he had not talked to the Saudis and did not ask anyone to do anything about it. The President and Vice President told us they were not aware of the issue at all until it surfaced much later in the media. None of the officials we interviewed recalled any

intervention or direction on this matter from any political
ppointee.[27]

Third, we believe that the FBI conducted a satisfac-
creening of Saudi nationals who left the United
charter flights.[28] The Saudi government was ad-
nd agreed to the FBI's requirements that passengers be identified and checked against various
databases before the flights departed.[29] The Federal Aviation Administration representative working in the FBI
operations center made sure that the FBI was aware of
the flights of Saudi nationals and was able to screen the
passengers before they were allowed to depart.[30]

The FBI interviewed all persons of interest on these
flights prior to their departures. They concluded that
none of the passengers was connected to the 9/11 attacks
and have since found no evidence to change that conclusion. Our own independent review of the Saudi nationals
involved confirms that no one with known links to terrorism departed on these flights.[31]

States would punish not just the perpetrators of the attacks,
but also those who harbored them. Secretary Powell said the
United States had to make it clear to Pakistan, Afghanistan,
and the Arab states that the time to act was now. He said we
would need to build a coalition. The President noted that the
attacks provided a great opportunity to engage Russia and
China. Secretary Rumsfeld urged the President and the principals to think broadly about who might have harbored the
attackers, including Iraq, Afghanistan, Libya, Sudan, and
Iran. He wondered aloud how much evidence the United
States would need in order to deal with these countries,
pointing out that major strikes could take up to 60 days to assemble.[34]

President Bush chaired two more meetings of the NSC on
September 12. In the first meeting, he stressed that the

United States was at war with a new and different kind of enemy. The President tasked principals to go beyond their pre-9/11 work and develop a strategy to eliminate terrorists and punish those who support them. As they worked on defining the goals and objectives of the upcoming campaign, they considered a paper that went beyond al Qaeda to propose the "elimination of terrorism as a threat to our way of life," an aim that would include pursuing other international terrorist organizations in the Middle East.[35]

Rice chaired a Principals Committee meeting on September 13 in the Situation Room to refine how the fight against al Qaeda would be conducted. The principals agreed that the overall message should be that anyone supporting al Qaeda would risk harm. The United States would need to integrate diplomacy, financial measures, intelligence, and military actions into an overarching strategy. The principals also focused on Pakistan and what it could do to turn the Taliban against al Qaeda. They concluded that if Pakistan decided not to help the United States, it too would be at risk.[36]

The same day, Deputy Secretary of State Richard Armitage met with the Pakistani ambassador to the United States, Maleeha Lodhi, and the visiting head of Pakistan's military intelligence service, Mahmud Ahmed. Armitage said that the United States wanted Pakistan to take seven steps:

- to stop al Qaeda operatives at its border and end all logistical support for Bin Ladin;
- to give the United States blanket overflight and landing rights for all necessary military and intelligence operations;
- to provide territorial access to U.S. and allied military intelligence and other personnel to conduct operations against al Qaeda;
- to provide the United States with intelligence information;
- to continue to publicly condemn the terrorist acts;
- to cut off all shipments of fuel to the Taliban and stop recruits from going to Afghanistan; and,

- if the evidence implicated bin Ladin and al Qaeda and the Taliban continued to harbor them, to break relations with the Taliban government.[37]

Pakistan made its decision swiftly. That afternoon, Secretary of State Powell announced at the beginning of an NSC meeting that Pakistani President Musharraf had agreed to every U.S. request for support in the war on terrorism. The next day, the U.S. embassy in Islamabad confirmed that Musharraf and his top military commanders had agreed to all seven demands. "Pakistan will need full US support as it proceeds with us," the embassy noted. "Musharraf said the GOP [government of Pakistan] was making substantial concessions in allowing use of its territory and that he would pay a domestic price. His standing in Pakistan was certain to suffer. To counterbalance that he needed to show that Pakistan was benefiting from his decisions."[38]

At the September 13 NSC meeting, when Secretary Powell described Pakistan's reply, President Bush led a discussion of an appropriate ultimatum to the Taliban. He also ordered Secretary Rumsfeld to develop a military plan against the Taliban. The President wanted the United States to strike the Taliban, step back, wait to see if they got the message, and hit them hard if they did not. He made clear that the military should focus on targets that would influence the Taliban's behavior.[39]

President Bush also tasked the State Department, which on the following day delivered to the White House a paper titled "Game Plan for a Political-Military Strategy for Pakistan and Afghanistan." The paper took it as a given that Bin Ladin would continue to act against the United States even while under Taliban control. It therefore detailed specific U.S. demands for the Taliban: surrender Bin Ladin and his chief lieutenants, including Ayman al Zawahiri; tell the United States what the Taliban knew about al Qaeda and its operations; close all terrorist camps; free all imprisoned foreigners; and comply with all UN Security Council resolutions.[40]

The State Department proposed delivering an ultimatum to the Taliban: produce Bin Ladin and his deputies and shut down al Qaeda camps within 24 to 48 hours, or the United States will use all necessary means to destroy the terrorist infrastructure. The State Department did not expect the Taliban to comply. Therefore, State and Defense would plan to build an international coalition to go into Afghanistan. Both departments would consult with NATO and other allies and request intelligence, basing, and other support from countries, according to their capabilities and resources. Finally, the plan detailed a public U.S. stance: America would use all its resources to eliminate terrorism as a threat, punish those responsible for the 9/11 attacks, hold states and other actors responsible for providing sanctuary to terrorists, work with a coalition to eliminate terrorist groups and networks, and avoid malice toward any people, religion, or culture.[41]

President Bush recalled that he quickly realized that the administration would have to invade Afghanistan with ground troops.[42] But the early briefings to the President and Secretary Rumsfeld on military options were disappointing.[43] Tommy Franks, the commanding general of Central Command (CENTCOM), told us that the President was dissatisfied. The U.S. military, Franks said, did not have an off-the-shelf plan to eliminate the al Qaeda threat in Afghanistan. The existing Infinite Resolve options did not, in his view, amount to such a plan.[44]

All these diplomatic and military plans were reviewed over the weekend of September 15–16, as President Bush convened his war council at Camp David.[45] Present were Vice President Cheney, Rice, Hadley, Powell, Armitage, Rumsfeld, Ashcroft, Mueller, Tenet, Deputy Secretary of Defense Paul Wolfowitz, and Cofer Black, chief of the DCI's Counterterrorist Center.

Tenet described a plan for collecting intelligence and mounting covert operations. He proposed inserting CIA teams into Afghanistan to work with Afghan warlords who would join the fight against al Qaeda.[46] These CIA teams would act jointly with the military's Special Operations units. President Bush later praised this proposal, saying it had been a turning point in his thinking.[47]

General Shelton briefed the principals on the preliminary plan for Afghanistan that the military had put together. It drew on the Infinite Resolve "phased campaign" plan the Pentagon had begun developing in November 2000 as an addition to the strike options it had been refining since 1998. But Shelton added a new element—the possible significant use of ground forces—and that is where President Bush reportedly focused his attention.[48]

After hearing from his senior advisers, President Bush discussed with Rice the contents of the directives he would issue to set all the plans into motion. Rice prepared a paper that President Bush then considered with principals on Monday morning, September 17. "The purpose of this meeting," he recalled saying, "is to assign tasks for the first wave of the war against terrorism. It starts today."[49]

In a written set of instructions slightly refined during the morning meeting, President Bush charged Ashcroft, Mueller, and Tenet to develop a plan for homeland defense. President Bush directed Secretary of State Powell to deliver an ultimatum to the Taliban along the lines that his department had originally proposed. The State Department was also tasked to develop a plan to stabilize Pakistan and to be prepared to notify Russia and countries near Afghanistan when hostilities were imminent.[50]

In addition, Bush and his advisers discussed new legal authorities for covert action in Afghanistan, including the administration's first Memorandum of Notification on Bin Ladin. Shortly thereafter, President Bush authorized broad new authorities for the CIA.[51]

President Bush instructed Rumsfeld and Shelton to develop further the Camp David military plan to attack the Taliban and al Qaeda if the Taliban rejected the ultimatum. The President also tasked Rumsfeld to ensure that robust measures to protect American military forces against terrorist attack were implemented worldwide. Finally, he directed Treasury Secretary Paul O'Neill to craft a plan to target al

Qaeda's funding and seize its assets.[52] NSC staff members had begun leading meetings on terrorist fund-raising by September 18.[53]

Also by September 18, Powell had contacted 58 of his foreign counterparts and received offers of general aid, search-and-rescue equipment and personnel, and medical assistance teams.[54] On the same day, Deputy Secretary of State Armitage was called by Mahmud Ahmed regarding a two-day visit to Afghanistan during which the Pakistani intelligence chief had met with Mullah Omar and conveyed the U.S. demands. Omar's response was "not negative on all these points."[55] But the administration knew that the Taliban was unlikely to turn over Bin Ladin.[56]

The pre-9/11 draft presidential directive on al Qaeda evolved into a new directive, National Security Presidential Directive 9, now titled "Defeating the Terrorist Threat to the United States." The directive would now extend to a global war on terrorism, not just on al Qaeda. It also incorporated the President's determination not to distinguish between terrorists and those who harbor them. It included a determination to use military force if necessary to end al Qaeda's sanctuary in Afghanistan. The new directive—formally signed on October 25, after the fighting in Afghanistan had already begun—included new material followed by annexes discussing each targeted terrorist group. The old draft directive on al Qaeda became, in effect, the first annex.[57] The United States would strive to eliminate all terrorist networks, dry up their financial support, and prevent them from acquiring weapons of mass destruction. The goal was the "elimination of terrorism as a threat to our way of life."[58]

10.3 "PHASE TWO" AND THE QUESTION OF IRAQ

President Bush had wondered immediately after the attack whether Saddam Hussein's regime might have had a hand in it. Iraq had been an enemy of the United States for 11 years, and was the only place in the world where the United States was engaged in ongoing combat operations. As a former pilot, the President was struck by the apparent sophistication of the operation and some of the piloting, especially Hanjour's high-speed dive into the Pentagon. He told us he recalled Iraqi support for Palestinian suicide terrorists as well. Speculating about other possible states that could be involved, the President told us he also thought about Iran.[59]

Clarke has written that on the evening of September 12, President Bush told him and some of his staff to explore possible Iraqi links to 9/11. "See if Saddam did this," Clarke recalls the President telling them. "See if he's linked in any way."[60] While he believed the details of Clarke's account to be incorrect, President Bush acknowledged that he might well have spoken to Clarke at some point, asking him about Iraq.[61]

Responding to a presidential tasking, Clarke's office sent a memo to Rice on September 18, titled "Survey of Intelligence Information on Any Iraq Involvement in the September 11 Attacks." Rice's chief staffer on Afghanistan, Zalmay Khalilzad, concurred in its conclusion that only some anecdotal evidence linked Iraq to al Qaeda. The memo found no "compelling case" that Iraq had either planned or perpetrated the attacks. It passed along a few foreign intelligence reports, including the Czech report alleging an April 2001 Prague meeting between Atta and an Iraqi intelligence officer (discussed in chapter 7) and a Polish report that personnel at the headquarters of Iraqi intelligence in Baghdad were told before September 11 to go on the streets to gauge crowd reaction to an unspecified event. Arguing that the case for links between Iraq and al Qaeda was weak, the memo pointed out that Bin Ladin resented the secularism of Saddam Hussein's regime. Finally, the memo said, there was no confirmed reporting on Saddam cooperating with Bin Ladin on unconventional weapons.[62]

On the afternoon of 9/11, according to contemporaneous notes, Secretary Rumsfeld instructed General Myers to obtain quickly as much information as possible. The notes indicate that he also told Myers that he was not simply interested in striking empty training sites. He thought the U.S. response should consider a wide range of options and possibilities. The secretary said his instinct was to hit Saddam Hussein at the same time—not only Bin Ladin. Secretary Rumsfeld later explained that at the time, he had been considering either one of them, or perhaps someone else, as the responsible party.[63]

According to Rice, the issue of what, if anything, to do about Iraq was really engaged at Camp David. Briefing papers on Iraq, along with many others, were in briefing materials for the participants. Rice told us the administration was concerned that Iraq would take advantage of the 9/11 attacks. She recalled that in the first Camp David session chaired by the President, Rumsfeld asked what the administration should do about Iraq. Deputy Secretary Wolfowitz made the case for striking Iraq during "this round" of the war on terrorism.[64]

A Defense Department paper for the Camp David briefing book on the strategic concept for the war on terrorism specified three priority targets for initial action: al Qaeda, the Taliban, and Iraq. It argued that of the three, al Qaeda and Iraq posed a strategic threat to the United States. Iraq's long-standing involvement in terrorism was cited, along with its interest in weapons of mass destruction.[65]

Secretary Powell recalled that Wolfowitz—not Rumsfeld—argued that Iraq was ultimately the source of the terrorist problem and should therefore be attacked.[66] Powell said that Wolfowitz was not able to justify his belief that Iraq was behind 9/11. "Paul was always of the view that Iraq was a problem that had to be dealt with," Powell told us. "And he saw this as one way of using this event as a way to deal with the Iraq problem." Powell said that President Bush did not give Wolfowitz's argument "much weight."[67] Though continuing to worry about Iraq in the following week, Powell said, President Bush saw Afghanistan as the priority.[68]

President Bush told Bob Woodward that the decision not to invade Iraq was made at the morning session on September 15. Iraq was not even on the table during the September 15 afternoon session, which dealt solely with Afghanistan.[69] Rice said that when President Bush called her on Sunday, September 16, he said the focus would be on Afghanistan, although he still wanted plans for Iraq should the country take some action or the administration eventually determine that it had been involved in the 9/11 attacks.[70]

At the September 17 NSC meeting, there was some further discussion of "phase two" of the war on terrorism.[71] President Bush ordered the Defense Department to be ready to deal with Iraq if Baghdad acted against U.S. interests, with plans to include possibly occupying Iraqi oil fields.[72]

Within the Pentagon, Deputy Secretary Wolfowitz continued to press the case for dealing with Iraq. Writing to Rumsfeld on September 17 in a memo headlined "Preventing More Events," he argued that if there was even a 10 percent chance that Saddam Hussein was behind the 9/11 attack, maximum priority should be placed on eliminating that threat. Wolfowitz contended that the odds were "far more" than 1 in 10, citing Saddam's praise for the attack, his long record of involvement in terrorism, and theories that Ramzi Yousef was an Iraqi agent and Iraq was behind the 1993 attack on the World Trade Center.[73] The next day, Wolfowitz renewed the argument, writing to Rumsfeld about the interest of Yousef's co-conspirator in the 1995 Manila air plot in crashing an explosives-laden plane into CIA headquarters, and about information from a foreign government regarding Iraqis' involvement in the attempted hijacking of a Gulf Air flight. Given this background, he wondered why so little thought had been devoted to the danger of suicide pilots, seeing a "failure of imagination" and a mind-set that dismissed possibilities.[74]

On September 19, Rumsfeld offered several thoughts for his commanders as they worked on their contingency plans. Though he emphasized the worldwide nature of the conflict, the references to specific enemies or regions named only the Taliban, al Qaeda, and Afghanistan.[75] Shelton told us the administration reviewed all the Pentagon's war plans and challenged certain assumptions underlying them, as any prudent organization or leader should do.[76]

General Tommy Franks, the commanding general of Central Command, recalled receiving Rumsfeld's guidance that each regional commander should assess what these plans meant for his area of responsibility. He knew he would soon be striking the Taliban and al Qaeda in Afghanistan. But, he told us, he now wondered how that action was connected to what might need to be done in Somalia, Yemen, or Iraq.[77]

On September 20, President Bush met with British Prime Minister Tony Blair, and the two leaders discussed the global conflict ahead. When Blair asked about Iraq, the President replied that Iraq was not the immediate problem. Some members of his administration, he commented, had expressed a different view, but he was the one responsible for making the decisions.[78]

Franks told us that he was pushing independently to do more robust planning on military responses in Iraq during the summer before 9/11—a request President Bush denied, arguing that the time was not right. (CENTCOM also began dusting off plans for a full invasion of Iraq during this period, Franks said.) The CENTCOM commander told us he renewed his appeal for further military planning to respond to Iraqi moves shortly after 9/11, both because he personally felt that Iraq and al Qaeda might be engaged in some form of collusion and because he worried that Saddam might take advantage of the attacks to move against his internal enemies in the northern or southern parts of Iraq, where the United States was flying regular missions to enforce Iraqi no-fly zones. Franks said that President Bush again turned down the request.[79]

Having issued directives to guide his administration's preparations for war, on Thursday, September 20, President Bush addressed the nation before a joint session of Congress. "Tonight," he said, "we are a country awakened to danger."[80] The President blamed al Qaeda for 9/11 and the 1998 embassy bombings and, for the first time, declared that al Qaeda was "responsible for bombing the USS *Cole*."[81] He reiterated the ultimatum that had already been conveyed privately. "The Taliban must act, and act immediately," he said. "They will hand over the terrorists, or they will share in their fate."[82] The President added that America's quarrel was not with Islam: "The enemy of America is not our many Muslim friends; it is not our many Arab friends. Our enemy is a radical network of terrorists, and every government that supports them." Other regimes faced hard choices, he pointed out: "Every nation, in every region, now has a decision to make: Either you are with us, or you are with the terrorists."[83]

President Bush argued that the new war went beyond Bin Ladin. "Our war on terror begins with al Qaeda, but it does not end there," he said. "It will not end until every terrorist group of global reach has been found, stopped, and defeated." The President had a message for the Pentagon: "The hour is coming when America will act, and you will make us proud." He also had a message for those outside the United States. "This is civilization's fight," he said. "We ask every nation to join us."[84]

President Bush approved military plans to attack Afghanistan in meetings with Central Command's General Franks and other advisers on September 21 and October 2. Originally titled "Infinite Justice," the operation's code word was changed—to avoid the sensibilities of Muslims who associate the power of infinite justice with God alone—to the operational name still used for operations in Afghanistan: "Enduring Freedom."[85]

The plan had four phases.

- In *Phase One*, the United States and its allies would move forces into the region and arrange to operate from or over neighboring countries such as Uzbekistan and Pakistan. This occurred in the weeks following 9/11, aided by overwhelming international sympathy for the United States.
- In *Phase Two*, air strikes and Special Operations attacks would hit key al Qaeda and Taliban targets. In an inno-

vative joint effort, CIA and Special Operations forces would be deployed to work together with each major Afghan faction opposed to the Taliban. The Phase Two strikes and raids began on October 7. The basing arrangements contemplated for Phase One were substantially secured—after arduous effort—by the end of that month.

- In *Phase Three*, the United States would carry out "decisive operations" using all elements of national power, including ground troops, to topple the Taliban regime and eliminate al Qaeda's sanctuary in Afghanistan. Mazar-e-Sharif, in northern Afghanistan, fell to a coalition assault by Afghan and U.S. forces on November 9. Four days later the Taliban had fled from Kabul. By early December, all major cities had fallen to the coalition. On December 22, Hamid Karzai, a Pashtun leader from Kandahar, was installed as the chairman of Afghanistan's interim administration. Afghanistan had been liberated from the rule of the Taliban.

In December 2001, Afghan forces, with limited U.S. support, engaged al Qaeda elements in a cave complex called Tora Bora. In March 2002, the largest engagement of the war was fought, in the mountainous Shah-i-Kot area south of Gardez, against a large force of al Qaeda jihadists. The three-week battle was substantially successful, and almost all remaining al Qaeda forces took refuge in Pakistan's equally mountainous and lightly governed frontier provinces. As of July 2004, Bin Ladin and Zawahiri are still believed to be at large.

- In *Phase Four*, civilian and military operations turned to the indefinite task of what the armed forces call "security and stability operations."

Within about two months of the start of combat operations, several hundred CIA operatives and Special Forces soldiers, backed by the striking power of U.S. aircraft and a much larger infrastructure of intelligence and support efforts, had combined with Afghan militias and a small number of other coalition soldiers to destroy the Taliban regime and disrupt al Qaeda. They had killed or captured about a quarter of the enemy's known leaders. Mohammed Atef, al Qaeda's military commander and a principal figure in the 9/11 plot, had been killed by a U.S. air strike. According to a senior CIA officer who helped devise the overall strategy, the CIA provided intelligence, experience, cash, covert action capabilities, and entrée to tribal allies. In turn, the U.S. military offered combat expertise, firepower, logistics, and communications.[86] With these initial victories won by the middle of 2002, the global conflict against Islamist terrorism became a different kind of struggle.

CHAPTER ELEVEN

Foresight—and Hindsight

In composing this narrative, we have tried to remember that we write with the benefit and the handicap of hindsight. Hindsight can sometimes see the past clearly—with 20/20 vision. But the path of what happened is so brightly lit that it places everything else more deeply into shadow. Commenting on Pearl Harbor, Roberta Wohlstetter found it "much easier *after* the event to sort the relevant from the irrelevant signals. After the event, of course, a signal is always crystal clear; we can now see what disaster it was signaling since the disaster has occurred. But before the event it is obscure and pregnant with conflicting meanings."[1]

As time passes, more documents become available, and the bare facts of what happened become still clearer. Yet the picture of *how* those things happened becomes harder to reimagine, as that past world, with its preoccupations and uncertainty, recedes and the remaining memories of it become colored by what happened and what was written about it later. With that caution in mind, we asked ourselves, before we judged others, whether the insights that seem apparent now would really have been meaningful at the time, given the limits of what people then could reasonably have known or done.

We believe the 9/11 attacks revealed four kinds of failures: in imagination, policy, capabilities, and management.

11.1 IMAGINATION

Historical Perspective

The 9/11 attack was an event of surpassing disproportion.
America had suffered surprise attacks before—Pearl Harbor
is one well-known case, the 1950 Chinese attack in Korea
another. But these were attacks by major powers.

While by no means as threatening as Japan's act of war,
the 9/11 attack was in some ways more devastating. It was
carried out by a tiny group of people, not enough to man a
full platoon. Measured on a governmental scale, the resources behind it were trivial. The group itself was dispatched by an organization based in one of the poorest, most
remote, and least industrialized countries on earth. This organization recruited a mixture of young fanatics and highly
educated zealots who could not find suitable places in their
home societies or were driven from them.

To understand these events, we attempted to reconstruct
some of the context of the 1990s. Americans celebrated the
end of the Cold War with a mixture of relief and satisfaction.
The people of the United States hoped to enjoy a peace dividend, as U.S. spending on national security was cut following the end of the Soviet military threat.

The United States emerged into the post–Cold War world
as the globe's preeminent military power. But the vacuum
created by the sudden demise of the Soviet Union created
fresh sources of instability and new challenges for the
United States. President George H. W. Bush dealt with the
first of these in 1990 and 1991 when he led an international
coalition to reverse Iraq's invasion of Kuwait. Other examples of U.S. leaders' handling new threats included the removal of nuclear weapons from Ukraine, Belarus, and
Kazakhstan; the Nunn-Lugar threat reduction program to
help contain new nuclear dangers; and international involvement in the wars in Bosnia and Kosovo.

America stood out as an object for admiration, envy, and
blame. This created a kind of cultural asymmetry. To us,

Afghanistan seemed very far away. To members of al Qaeda,
America seemed very close. In a sense, they were more
globalized than we were.

Understanding the Danger

If the government's leaders understood the gravity of the
threat they faced and understood at the same time that their
policies to eliminate it were not likely to succeed any time
soon, then history's judgment will be harsh. Did they understand the gravity of the threat?

The U.S. government responded vigorously when the attack was on our soil. Both Ramzi Yousef, who organized the
1993 bombing of the World Trade Center, and Mir Amal
Kansi, who in 1993 killed two CIA employees as they
waited to go to work in Langley, Virginia, were the objects
of relentless, uncompromising, and successful efforts to
bring them back to the United States to stand trial for their
crimes.

Before 9/11, al Qaeda and its affiliates had killed fewer
than 50 Americans, including the East Africa embassy
bombings and the *Cole* attack. The U.S. government took
the threat seriously, but not in the sense of mustering anything like the kind of effort that would be gathered to confront an enemy of the first, second, or even third rank. The
modest national effort exerted to contain Serbia and its
depredations in the Balkans between 1995 and 1999, for example, was orders of magnitude larger than that devoted to
al Qaeda.

As best we can determine, neither in 2000 nor in the first
eight months of 2001 did any polling organization in the
United States think the subject of terrorism sufficiently on
the minds of the public to warrant asking a question about it
in a major national survey. Bin Ladin, al Qaeda, or even terrorism was not an important topic in the 2000 presidential
campaign. Congress and the media called little attention to it.

If a president wanted to rally the American people to a
warlike effort, he would need to publicize an assessment of
the growing al Qaeda danger. Our government could spark a

full public discussion of who Usama Bin Ladin was, what kind of organization he led, what Bin Ladin or al Qaeda intended, what past attacks they had sponsored or encouraged, and what capabilities they were bringing together for future assaults. We believe American and international public opinion might have been different—and so might the range of options for a president—had they been informed of these details. Recent examples of such debates include calls to arms against such threats as Serbian ethnic cleansing, biological attacks, Iraqi weapons of mass destruction, global climate change, and the HIV/AIDS epidemic.

While we now know that al Qaeda was formed in 1988, at the end of the Soviet occupation of Afghanistan, the intelligence community did not describe this organization, at least in documents we have seen, until 1999. A National Intelligence Estimate distributed in July 1995 predicted future terrorist attacks against the United States—and *in* the United States. It warned that this danger would increase over the next several years. It specified as particular points of vulnerability the White House, the Capitol, symbols of capitalism such as Wall Street, critical infrastructure such as power grids, areas where people, congregate such as sports arenas, and civil aviation generally. It warned that the 1993 World Trade Center bombing had been intended to kill a lot of people, not to achieve any more traditional political goal.

This 1995 estimate described the greatest danger as "transient groupings of individuals" that lacked "strong organization but rather are loose affiliations." They operate "outside traditional circles but have access to a worldwide network of training facilities and safehavens."[2] This was an excellent summary of the emerging danger, based on what was then known.

In 1996–1997, the intelligence community received new information making clear that Bin Ladin headed his own terrorist group, with its own targeting agenda and operational commanders. Also revealed was the previously unknown involvement of Bin Ladin's organization in the 1992 attack on a Yemeni hotel quartering U.S. military personnel, the 1993 shootdown of U.S. Army Black Hawk helicopters in Somalia, and quite possibly the 1995 Riyadh bombing of the American training mission to the Saudi National Guard.

The 1997 update of the 1995 estimate did not discuss the new intelligence. It did state that the terrorist danger depicted in 1995 would persist. In the update's summary of key points, the only reference to Bin Ladin was this sentence: "Iran and its surrogates, as well as terrorist financier Usama Bin Ladin and his followers, have stepped up their threats and surveillance of US facilities abroad in what also may be a portent of possible additional attacks in the United States."[3] Bin Ladin was mentioned in only two other sentences in the six-page report. The al Qaeda organization was not mentioned. The 1997 update was the last national estimate on the terrorism danger completed before 9/11.[4]

From 1998 to 2001, a number of very good analytical papers were distributed on specific topics. These included Bin Ladin's political philosophy, his command of a global network, analysis of information from terrorists captured in Jordan in December 1999, al Qaeda's operational style, and the evolving goals of the Islamist extremist movement. Many classified articles for morning briefings were prepared for the highest officials in the government with titles such as "Bin Ladin Threatening to Attack US Aircraft [with antiaircraft missiles]" (June 1998), "Strains Surface Between Taliban and Bin Ladin" (January 1999), "Terrorist Threat to US Interests in Caucasus" (June 1999), "Bin Ladin to Exploit Looser Security During Holidays" (December 1999), "Bin Ladin Evading Sanctions" (March 2000), "Bin Ladin's Interest in Biological, Radiological Weapons" (February 2001), "Taliban Holding Firm on Bin Ladin for Now" (March 2001), "Terrorist Groups Said Cooperating on US Hostage Plot" (May 2001), and "Bin Ladin Determined to Strike in the US" (August 2001).[5]

Despite such reports and a 1999 paper on Bin Ladin's command structure for al Qaeda, there were no complete portraits of his strategy or of the extent of his organization's involvement in past terrorist attacks. Nor had the intelligence community provided an authoritative depiction of his organization's relationships with other governments, or the scale of the threat his organization posed to the United States.

Though Deputy DCI John McLaughlin said to us that the cumulative output of the Counterterrorist Center (CTC) "dramatically eclipsed" any analysis that could have appeared in a fresh National Intelligence Estimate, he conceded that most of the work of the Center's 30- to 40-person analytic group dealt with collection issues.[6] In late 2000, DCI George Tenet recognized the deficiency of strategic analysis against al Qaeda. To tackle the problem within the CTC he appointed a senior manager, who briefed him in March 2001 on "creating a strategic assessment capability." The CTC established a new strategic assessments branch during July 2001. The decision to add about ten analysts to this effort was seen as a major bureaucratic victory, but the CTC labored to find them. The new chief of this branch reported for duty on September 10, 2001.[7]

Whatever the weaknesses in the CIA's portraiture, both Presidents Bill Clinton and George Bush and their top advisers told us they got the picture—they understood Bin Ladin was a danger. But given the character and pace of their policy efforts, we do not believe they fully understood just how many people al Qaeda might kill, and how soon it might do it. At some level that is hard to define, we believe the threat had not yet become compelling.

It is hard now to recapture the conventional wisdom before 9/11. For example, a *New York Times* article in April 1999 sought to debunk claims that Bin Ladin was a terrorist leader, with the headline "U.S. Hard Put to Find Proof Bin Laden Directed Attacks."[8] The head of analysis at the CTC until 1999 discounted the alarms about a catastrophic threat as relating only to the danger of chemical, biological, or nuclear attack—and he downplayed even that, writing several months before 9/11: "It would be a mistake to redefine counterterrorism as a task of dealing with 'catastrophic,' 'grand,' or 'super' terrorism, when in fact these labels do not represent most of the terrorism that the United States is likely to face or most of the costs that terrorism imposes on U.S. interests."[9]

Beneath the acknowledgment that Bin Ladin and al Qaeda presented serious dangers, there was uncertainty among senior officials about whether this was just a new and especially venomous version of the ordinary terrorist threat America had lived with for decades, or was radically new, posing a threat beyond any yet experienced. Such differences affect calculations about whether or how to go to war.

Therefore, those government experts who saw Bin Ladin as an unprecedented new danger needed a way to win broad support for their views, or at least spotlight the areas of dispute, and perhaps prompt action across the government. The national estimate has often played this role, and is sometimes controversial for this very reason.[10] Such assessments, which provoke widespread thought and debate, have a major impact on their recipients, often in a wider circle of decisionmakers. The National Intelligence Estimate is noticed in the Congress, for example. But, as we have said, none was produced on terrorism between 1997 and 9/11.

By 2001 the government still needed a decision at the highest level as to whether al Qaeda was or was not "a first order threat," Richard Clarke wrote in his first memo to Condoleezza Rice on January 25, 2001. In his blistering protest about foot-dragging in the Pentagon and at the CIA, sent to Rice just a week before 9/11, he repeated that the "real question" for the principals was "are we serious about dealing with the al Qida threat? . . . Is al Qida a big deal?"

One school of thought, Clarke wrote in this September 4 note, implicitly argued that the terrorist network was a nuisance that killed a score of Americans every 18–24 months. If that view was credited, then current policies might be proportionate. Another school saw al Qaeda as the "point of the spear of radical Islam." But no one forced the argument into the open by calling for a national estimate or a broader discussion of the threat. The issue was never joined as a collective debate by the U.S. government, including the Congress, before 9/11.

We return to the issue of proportion—and imagination. Even Clarke's note challenging Rice to imagine the day after an attack posits a strike that kills "hundreds" of Americans. He did not write "thousands."

Institutionalizing Imagination: The Case of Aircraft as Weapons

Imagination is not a gift usually associated with bureaucracies. For example, before Pearl Harbor the U.S. government had excellent intelligence that a Japanese attack was coming, especially after peace talks stalemated at the end of November 1941. These were days, one historian notes, of "excruciating uncertainty." The most likely targets were judged to be in Southeast Asia. An attack was coming, "but officials were at a loss to know where the blow would fall or what more might be done to prevent it."[11] In retrospect, available intercepts pointed to Japanese examination of Hawaii as a possible target. But, another historian observes, "in the face of a clear warning, alert measures bowed to routine."[12]

It is therefore crucial to find a way of routinizing, even bureaucratizing, the exercise of imagination. Doing so requires more than finding an expert who can imagine that aircraft could be used as weapons. Indeed, since al Qaeda and other groups had already used suicide vehicles, namely truck bombs, the leap to the use of other vehicles such as boats (the *Cole* attack) or planes is not far-fetched.

Yet these scenarios were slow to work their way into the thinking of aviation security experts. In 1996, as a result of the TWA Flight 800 crash, President Clinton created a commission under Vice President Al Gore to report on shortcomings in aviation security in the United States. The Gore Commission's report, having thoroughly canvassed available expertise in and outside of government, did not mention suicide hijackings or the use of aircraft as weapons. It focused mainly on the danger of placing bombs onto aircraft—the approach of the Manila air plot. The Gore Commission did call attention, however, to lax screening of passengers and what they carried onto planes.

In late 1998, reports came in of a possible al Qaeda plan to hijack a plane. One, a December 4 Presidential Daily Briefing for President Clinton (reprinted in chapter 4), brought the focus back to more traditional hostage taking; it reported Bin Ladin's involvement in planning a hijack operation to free prisoners such as the "Blind Sheikh," Omar Abdel Rahman. Had the contents of this PDB been brought to the attention of a wider group, including key members of Congress, it might have brought much more attention to the need for permanent changes in domestic airport and airline security procedures.[13]

Threat reports also mentioned the possibility of using an aircraft filled with explosives. The most prominent of these mentioned a possible plot to fly an explosives-laden aircraft into a U.S. city. This report, circulated in September 1998, originated from a source who had walked into an American consulate in East Asia. In August of the same year, the intelligence community had received information that a group of Libyans hoped to crash a plane into the World Trade Center. In neither case could the information be corroborated. In addition, an Algerian group hijacked an airliner in 1994, most likely intending to blow it up over Paris, but possibly to crash it into the Eiffel Tower.[14]

In 1994, a private airplane had crashed onto the south lawn of the White House. In early 1995, Abdul Hakim Murad—Ramzi Yousef's accomplice in the Manila airlines bombing plot—told Philippine authorities that he and Yousef had discussed flying a plane into CIA headquarters.[15]

Clarke had been concerned about the danger posed by aircraft since at least the 1996 Atlanta Olympics. There he had tried to create an air defense plan using assets from the Treasury Department, after the Defense Department declined to contribute resources. The Secret Service continued to work on the problem of airborne threats to the Washington region. In 1998, Clarke chaired an exercise designed to highlight the inadequacy of the solution. This paper exercise involved a scenario in which a group of terrorists commandeered a Learjet on the ground in Atlanta, loaded it with explosives, and flew it toward a target in Washington, D.C. Clarke asked officials from the Pentagon, Federal Aviation Administration (FAA), and Secret Service what they could do about the situation. Officials from the Pentagon said they could scramble aircraft from Langley Air Force Base, but they would need to go to the President for rules of engagement, and there was no mechanism to do so. There was no clear resolution of the problem at the exercise.[16]

In late 1999, a great deal of discussion took place in the media about the crash off the coast of Massachusetts of EgyptAir Flight 990, a Boeing 767. The most plausible explanation that emerged was that one of the pilots had gone berserk, seized the controls, and flown the aircraft into the sea. After the 1999–2000 millennium alerts, when the nation had relaxed, Clarke held a meeting of his Counterterrorism Security Group devoted largely to the possibility of a possible airplane hijacking by al Qaeda.[17]

In his testimony, Clarke commented that he thought that warning about the possibility of a suicide hijacking would have been just one more speculative theory among many, hard to spot since the volume of warnings of "al Qaeda threats and other terrorist threats, was in the tens of thousands—probably hundreds of thousands."[18] Yet the possibility was imaginable, and imagined. In early August 1999, the FAA's Civil Aviation Security intelligence office summarized the Bin Ladin hijacking threat. After a solid recitation of all the information available on this topic, the paper identified a few principal scenarios, one of which was a "suicide hijacking operation." The FAA analysts judged such an operation unlikely, because "it does not offer an opportunity for dialogue to achieve the key goal of obtaining Rahman and other key captive extremists. . . . A suicide hijacking is assessed to be an option of last resort."[19]

Analysts could have shed some light on what kind of "opportunity for dialogue" al Qaeda desired.[20] The CIA did not write any analytical assessments of possible hijacking scenarios.

One prescient pre-9/11 analysis of an aircraft plot was written by a Justice Department trial attorney. The attorney had taken an interest, apparently on his own initiative, in the legal issues that would be involved in shooting down a U.S. aircraft in such a situation.[21]

The North American Aerospace Defense Command imagined the possible use of aircraft as weapons, too, and developed exercises to counter such a threat—from planes coming to the United States from overseas, perhaps carrying a weapon of mass destruction. None of this speculation was based on actual intelligence of such a threat. One idea, intended to test command and control plans and NORAD's readiness, postulated a hijacked airliner coming from overseas and crashing into the Pentagon. The idea was put aside in the early planning of the exercise as too much of a distraction from the main focus (war in Korea), and as too unrealistic. As we pointed out in chapter 1, the military planners assumed that since such aircraft would be coming from overseas; they would have time to identify the target and scramble interceptors.[22]

We can therefore establish that at least some government agencies were concerned about the hijacking danger and had speculated about various scenarios. The challenge was to flesh out and test those scenarios, then figure out a way to turn a scenario into constructive action.

Since the Pearl Harbor attack of 1941, the intelligence community has devoted generations of effort to understanding the problem of forestalling a surprise attack. Rigorous analytic methods were developed, focused in particular on the Soviet Union, and several leading practitioners within the intelligence community discussed them with us. These methods have been articulated in many ways, but almost all seem to have at least four elements in common: (1) think about how surprise attacks might be launched; (2) identify telltale indicators connected to the most dangerous possibilities; (3) where feasible, collect intelligence on these indicators; and (4) adopt defenses to deflect the most dangerous possibilities or at least trigger an earlier warning.

After the end of the Gulf War, concerns about lack of warning led to a major study conducted for DCI Robert Gates in 1992 that proposed several recommendations, among them strengthening the national intelligence officer for warning. We were told that these measures languished under Gates's successors. Responsibility for warning related to a terrorist attack passed from the national intelligence officer for warning to the CTC. An Intelligence Community Counterterrorism Board had the responsibility to issue threat advisories.[23]

With the important exception of analysis of al Qaeda efforts in chemical, biological, radiological, and nuclear weapons, we did not find evidence that the methods to avoid surprise attack that had been so laboriously developed over the years were regularly applied.

Considering what was not done suggests possible ways to institutionalize imagination. To return to the four elements of analysis just mentioned:

1. The CTC did not analyze how an aircraft, hijacked or explosives-laden, might be used as a weapon. It did not perform this kind of analysis from the enemy's perspective ("red team" analysis), even though suicide terrorism had become a principal tactic of Middle Eastern terrorists. If it had done so, we believe such an analysis would soon have spotlighted a critical constraint for the terrorists—finding a suicide operative able to fly large jet aircraft. They had never done so before 9/11.

2. The CTC did not develop a set of telltale indicators for this method of attack. For example, one such indicator might be the discovery of possible terrorists pursuing flight training to fly large jet aircraft, or seeking to buy advanced flight simulators.

3. The CTC did not propose, and the intelligence community collection management process did not set, requirements to monitor such telltale indicators. Therefore the warning system was not looking for information such as the July 2001 FBI report of potential terrorist interest in various kinds of aircraft training in Arizona, or the August 2001 arrest of Zacarias Moussaoui because of his suspicious behavior in a Minnesota flight school. In late August, the Moussaoui arrest was briefed to the DCI and other top CIA officials under the heading "Islamic Extremist Learns to Fly."[24] Because the system was not tuned to comprehend the potential significance of this information, the news had no effect on warning.

4. Neither the intelligence community nor aviation security experts analyzed systemic defenses within an aircraft or against terrorist-controlled aircraft, suicidal or otherwise. The many threat reports mentioning aircraft were passed to the FAA. While that agency continued to react to specific, credible threats, it did not try to perform the broader warning functions we describe here. No one in the government was taking on that role for domestic vulnerabilities.

Richard Clarke told us that he was concerned about the danger posed by aircraft in the context of protecting the Atlanta Olympics of 1996, the White House complex, and the 2001 G-8 summit in Genoa. But he attributed his awareness more to Tom Clancy novels than to warnings from the intelligence community. He did not, or could not, press the government to work on the systemic issues of how to strengthen the layered security defenses to protect aircraft against hijackings or put the adequacy of air defenses against suicide hijackers on the national policy agenda.

The methods for detecting and then warning of surprise attack that the U.S. government had so painstakingly developed in the decades after Pearl Harbor did not fail; instead, they were not really tried. They were not employed to analyze the enemy that, as the twentieth century closed, was most likely to launch a surprise attack directly against the United States.

11.2 POLICY

The road to 9/11 again illustrates how the large, unwieldy U.S. government tended to underestimate a threat that grew ever greater. The terrorism fostered by Bin Ladin and al Qaeda was different from anything the government had faced before. The existing mechanisms for handling terrorist acts had been trial and punishment for acts committed by individuals; sanction, reprisal, deterrence, or war for acts by hostile governments. The actions of al Qaeda fit neither category. Its crimes were on a scale approaching acts of war, but they were committed by a loose, far-flung, nebulous conspiracy with no territories or citizens or assets that could be readily threatened, overwhelmed, or destroyed.

Early in 2001, DCI Tenet and Deputy Director for Operations James Pavitt gave an intelligence briefing to President-elect Bush, Vice President-elect Cheney, and Rice; it included the topic of al Qaeda. Pavitt recalled conveying that Bin Ladin was one of the gravest threats to the country.[25]

Bush asked whether killing Bin Ladin would end the problem. Pavitt said he and the DCI had answered that killing Bin Ladin would have an impact, but would not stop the threat. The CIA later provided more formal assessments to the White House reiterating that conclusion. It added that in the long term, the only way to deal with the threat was to end al Qaeda's ability to use Afghanistan as a sanctuary for its operations.[26]

Perhaps the most incisive of the advisors on terrorism to the new administration was the holdover Richard Clarke. Yet he admits that his policy advice, even if it had been accepted immediately and turned into action, would not have prevented 9/11.[27]

We must then ask when the U.S. government had reasonable opportunities to mobilize the country for major action against al Qaeda and its Afghan sanctuary. The main opportunities came after the new information the U.S. government received in 1996–1997, after the embassy bombings of August 1998, after the discoveries of the Jordanian and Ressam plots in late 1999, and after the attack on the USS *Cole* in October 2000.

The U.S. policy response to al Qaeda before 9/11 was essentially defined following the embassy bombings of August 1998. We described those decisions in chapter 4. It is worth noting that they were made by the Clinton administration under extremely difficult domestic political circumstances. Opponents were seeking the President's impeachment. In addition, in 1998–99 President Clinton was preparing the government for possible war against Serbia, and he had authorized major air strikes against Iraq.

The tragedy of the embassy bombings provided an opportunity for a full examination, across the government, of the national security threat that Bin Ladin posed. Such an examination could have made clear to all that issues were at stake that were much larger than the domestic politics of the moment. But the major policy agencies of the government did not meet the threat.

The diplomatic efforts of the Department of State were largely ineffective. Al Qaeda and terrorism was just one more priority added to already-crowded agendas with countries like Pakistan and Saudi Arabia. After 9/11 that changed.

Policymakers turned principally to the CIA and covert action to implement policy. Before 9/11, no agency had more responsibility—or did more—to attack al Qaeda, working day and night, than the CIA. But there were limits to what the CIA was able to achieve in its energetic worldwide efforts to disrupt terrorist activities or use proxies to try to capture or kill Bin Ladin and his lieutenants. As early as mid-1997, one CIA officer wrote to his supervisor: "All we're doing is holding the ring until the cavalry gets here."[28]

Military measures failed or were not applied. Before 9/11 the Department of Defense was not given the mission of ending al Qaeda's sanctuary in Afghanistan.

Officials in both the Clinton and Bush administrations regarded a full U.S. invasion of Afghanistan as practically inconceivable before 9/11. It was never the subject of formal interagency deliberation.

Lesser forms of intervention could also have been considered. One would have been the deployment of U.S. military or intelligence personnel, or special strike forces, to Afghanistan itself or nearby—openly, clandestinely (secretly), or covertly (with their connection to the United States hidden). Then the United States would no longer have been dependent on proxies to gather actionable intelligence. However, it would have needed to secure basing and overflight support from neighboring countries. A significant political, military, and intelligence effort would have been required, extending over months and perhaps years, with associated costs and risks. Given how hard it has proved to locate Bin Ladin even today when there are substantial ground forces in Afghanistan, its odds of sucess are hard to calculate. We have found no indication that President Clinton was offered such an intermediate choice, or that this option was given any more consideration than the idea of invasion.

These policy challenges are linked to the problem of imagination we have already discussed. Since we believe that both President Clinton and President Bush were genuinely concerned about the danger posed by al Qaeda, approaches involving more direct intervention against the sanctuary in Afghanistan apparently must have seemed—if they were considered at all—to be disproportionate to the threat.

Insight for the future is thus not easy to apply in practice. It is hardest to mount a major effort while a problem still seems minor. Once the danger has fully materialized, evident to all, mobilizing action is easier—but it then may be too late.

Another possibility, short of putting U.S. personnel on the ground, was to issue a blunt ultimatum to the Taliban, backed by a readiness to at least launch an indefinite air campaign to disable that regime's limited military capabilities and tip the balance in Afghanistan's ongoing civil war. The United States had warned the Taliban that they would be held accountable for further attacks by Bin Ladin against Afghanistan's U.S. interests. The warning had been given in 1998, again in late 1999, once more in the fall of 2000, and again in the summer of 2001. Delivering it repeatedly did not make it more effective.

As evidence of al Qaeda's responsibility for the *Cole* attack came in during November 2000, National Security Advisor Samuel Berger asked the Pentagon to develop a plan for a sustained air campaign against the Taliban. Clarke developed a paper laying out a formal, specific ultimatum. But Clarke's plan apparently did not advance to formal consideration by the Small Group of principals. We have found no indication that the idea was briefed to the new administration or that Clarke passed his paper to them, although the same team of career officials spanned both administrations.

After 9/11, President Bush announced that al Qaeda was responsible for the attack on the USS *Cole*. Before 9/11, neither president took any action. Bin Ladin's inference may well have been that attacks, at least at the level of the *Cole*, were risk free.[29]

11.3 CAPABILITIES

Earlier chapters describe in detail the actions decided on by the Clinton and Bush administrations. Each president considered or authorized covert actions, a process that consumed considerable time—especially in the Clinton administration—and achieved little success beyond the collection of intelligence. After the August 1998 missile strikes in Afghanistan, naval vessels remained on station in or near the region, prepared to fire cruise missiles. General Hugh Shelton developed as many as 13 different strike options, and did not recommend any of them. The most extended debate on counterterrorism in the Bush administration before 9/11 had to do with missions for the unmanned Predator—whether to use it just to locate Bin Ladin or to wait until it was armed with a missile, so that it could find him and also attack him. Looking back, we are struck with the narrow and unimaginative menu of options for action offered to both President Clinton and President Bush.

Before 9/11, the United States tried to solve the al Qaeda problem with the same government institutions and capabilities it had used in the last stages of the Cold War and its immediate aftermath. These capabilities were insufficient, but little was done to expand or reform them.

For covert action, of course, the White House depended on the Counterterrorist Center and the CIA's Directorate of Operations. Though some officers, particularly in the Bin Ladin unit, were eager for the mission, most were not. The higher management of the directorate was unenthusiastic. The CIA's capacity to conduct paramilitary operations with its own personnel was not large, and the Agency did not seek a large-scale general expansion of these capabilities before 9/11. James Pavitt, the head of this directorate, remembered that covert action, promoted by the White House, had gotten the Clandestine Service into trouble in the past. He had no desire to see this happen again. He thought, not unreasonably, that a truly serious counterterrorism campaign against an enemy of this magnitude would be business primarily for the military, not the Clandestine Service.[30]

As for the Department of Defense, some officers in the Joint Staff were keen to help. Some in the Special Operations Command have told us that they worked on plans for using Special Operations Forces in Afghanistan and that they hoped for action orders. JCS Chairman General Shelton and General Anthony Zinni at Central Command had a dif-

ferent view. Shelton felt that the August 1998 attacks had
proved a waste of good ordnance and thereafter consistently
opposed firing expensive Tomahawk missiles merely at
"jungle gym" terrorist training infrastructure.[31] In this view,
he had complete support from Defense Secretary William
Cohen. Shelton was prepared to plan other options, but he
was also prepared to make perfectly clear his own strong
doubts about the wisdom of any military action that risked
U.S. lives unless the intelligence was "actionable."[32]

The high price of keeping counterterrorism policy within
the restricted circle of the Counterterrorism Security Group
and the highest-level principals was nowhere more apparent
than in the military establishment. After the August 1998
missile strike, other members of the JCS let the press know
their unhappiness that, in conformity with the Goldwater-
Nichols reforms, Shelton had been the only member of the
JCS to be consulted. Although follow-on military options
were briefed more widely, the vice director of operations on
the Joint Staff commented to us that intelligence and planning documents relating to al Qaeda arrived in a ziplock red
package and that many flag and general officers never had
the clearances to see its contents.[33]

At no point before 9/11 was the Department of Defense
fully engaged in the mission of countering al Qaeda, though
this was perhaps the most dangerous foreign enemy then
threatening the United States. The Clinton administration
effectively relied on the CIA to take the lead in preparing
long-term offensive plans against an enemy sanctuary. The
Bush administration adopted this approach, although its
emerging new strategy envisioned some yet undefined further role for the military in addressing the problem. Within
Defense, both Secretary Cohen and Secretary Donald
Rumsfeld gave their principal attention to other challenges.

America's homeland defenders faced outward. NORAD
itself was barely able to retain any alert bases. Its planning
scenarios occasionally considered the danger of hijacked
aircraft being guided to American targets, but only aircraft
that were coming from overseas. We recognize that a costly

change in NORAD's defense posture to deal with the danger of suicide hijackers, before such a threat had ever actually been realized, would have been a tough sell. But NORAD did not canvass available intelligence and try to make the case.

The most serious weaknesses in agency capabilities were in the domestic arena. In chapter 3 we discussed these institutions—the FBI, the Immigration and Naturalization Service, the FAA, and others. The major pre-9/11 effort to strengthen domestic agency capabilities came in 2000, as part of a millennium after-action review. President Clinton and his principal advisers paid considerable attention then to border security problems, but were not able to bring about significant improvements before leaving office. The NSC-led interagency process did not effectively bring along the leadership of the Justice and Transportation departments in an agenda for institutional change.

The FBI did not have the capability to link the collective knowledge of agents in the field to national priorities. The acting director of the FBI did not learn of his Bureau's hunt for two possible al Qaeda operatives in the United States or about his Bureau's arrest of an Islamic extremist taking flight training until September 11. The director of central intelligence knew about the FBI's Moussaoui investigation weeks before word of it made its way even to the FBI's own assistant director for counterterrorism.

Other agencies deferred to the FBI. In the August 6 PDB reporting to President Bush of 70 full-field investigations related to al Qaeda, news the President said he found heartening, the CIA had simply restated what the FBI had said. No one looked behind the curtain.

The FAA's capabilities to take aggressive, anticipatory security measures were especially weak. Any serious policy examination of a suicide hijacking scenario, critiquing each of the layers of the security system, could have suggested changes to fix glaring vulnerabilities—expanding no-fly lists, searching passengers identified by the CAPPS screening system, deploying Federal Air Marshals domestically,

hardening cockpit doors, alerting air crew to a different kind
of hijacking than what they had been trained to expect, or
adjusting the training of controllers and managers in the
FAA and NORAD.

Government agencies also sometimes display a tendency
to match capabilities to mission by defining away the hardest part of their job. They are often passive, accepting what
are viewed as givens, including that efforts to identify and
fix glaring vulnerabilities to dangerous threats would be too
costly, too controversial, or too disruptive.

11.4 MANAGEMENT

Operational Management

Earlier in this report we detailed various missed opportunities to thwart the 9/11 plot. Information was not shared,
sometimes inadvertently or because of legal misunderstandings. Analysis was not pooled. Effective operations were not
launched. Often the handoffs of information were lost across
the divide separating the foreign and domestic agencies of
the government.

However the specific problems are labeled, we believe
they are symptoms of the government's broader inability to
adapt how it manages problems to the new challenges of the
twenty-first century. The agencies are like a set of specialists
in a hospital, each ordering tests, looking for symptoms, and
prescribing medications. What is missing is the attending
physician who makes sure they work as a team.

One missing element was effective management of
transnational operations. Action officers should have drawn
on all available knowledge in the government. This management should have ensured that information was shared and
duties were clearly assigned across agencies, and across the
foreign-domestic divide.

Consider, for example, the case of Mihdhar, Hazmi, and
their January 2000 trip to Kuala Lumpur, detailed in chapter
6. In late 1999, the National Security Agency (NSA) ana-

lyzed communications associated with a man named Khalid, a man named Nawaf, and a man named Salem. Working-level officials in the intelligence community knew little more than this. But they correctly concluded that "Nawaf" and "Khalid" might be part of "an operational cadre" and that "something nefarious might be afoot."

The NSA did not think its job was to research these identities. It saw itself as an agency to support intelligence consumers, such as CIA. The NSA tried to respond energetically to any request made. But it waited to be asked.

If NSA had been asked to try to identify these people, the agency would have started by checking its own database of earlier information from these same sources. Some of this information had been reported; some had not. But it was all readily accessible in the database. NSA's analysts would promptly have discovered who Nawaf was, that his full name might be Nawaf al Hazmi, and that he was an old friend of Khalid.

With this information and more that was available, managers could have more effectively tracked the movement of these operatives in southeast Asia. With the name "Nawaf al Hazmi," a manager could then have asked the State Department also to check that name. State would promptly have found its own record on Nawaf al Hazmi, showing that he too had been issued a visa to visit the United States. Officials would have learned that the visa had been issued at the same place—Jeddah—and on almost the same day as the one given to Khalid al Mihdhar.

When the travelers left Kuala Lumpur for Bangkok, local officials were able to identify one of the travelers as Khalid al Mihdhar. After the flight left, they learned that one of his companions had the name Alhazmi. But the officials did not know what that name meant.

The information arrived at Bangkok too late to track these travelers as they came in. Had the authorities there already been keeping an eye out for Khalid al Mihdhar as part of a general regional or worldwide alert, they might have tracked him coming in. Had they been alerted to look for a possible companion named Nawaf al Hazmi, they might have noticed him too. Instead, they were notified only after Kuala Lumpur sounded the alarm. By that time, the travelers had already disappeared into the streets of Bangkok.

On January 12, the head of the CIA's al Qaeda unit told his bosses that surveillance in Kuala Lumpur was continuing. He may not have known that in fact Mihdhar and his companions had dispersed and the tracking was falling apart. U.S. officials in Bangkok regretfully reported the bad news on January 13. The names they had were put on a watchlist in Bangkok, so that Thai authorities might notice if the men left the country. On January 14, the head of the CIA's al Qaeda unit again updated his bosses, telling them that officials were continuing to track the suspicious individuals who had now dispersed to various countries.

Unfortunately, there is no evidence of any tracking efforts actually being undertaken by anyone after the Arabs disappeared into Bangkok. No other effort was made to create other opportunities to spot these Arab travelers in case the screen in Bangkok failed. Just from the evidence in Mihdhar's passport, one of the logical possible destinations and interdiction points would have been the United States. Yet no one alerted the INS or the FBI to look for these individuals. They arrived, unnoticed, in Los Angeles on January 15.

In early March 2000, Bangkok reported that Nawaf al Hazmi, now identified for the first time with his full name, had departed on January 15 on a United Airlines flight to Los Angeles. Since the CIA did not appreciate the significance of that name or notice the cable, we have found no evidence that this information was sent to the FBI.

Even if watchlisting had prevented or at least alerted U.S. officials to the entry of Hazmi and Mihdhar, we do not think it is likely that watchlisting, by itself, have prevented the 9/11 attacks. Al Qaeda adapted to the failure of some of its operatives to gain entry into the United States. None of these future hijackers was a pilot. Alternatively, had they been permitted entry and surveilled, some larger results might have been possible had the FBI been patient.

These are difficult what-ifs. The intelligence community might have judged that the risks of conducting such a prolonged intelligence operation were too high—potential terrorists might have been lost track of, for example. The pre-9/11 FBI might not have been judged capable of conducting such an operation. But surely the intelligence community would have preferred to have the chance to make these choices.

From the details of this case, or from the other opportunities we catalogue in the text box, one can see how hard it is for the intelligence community to assemble enough of the puzzle pieces gathered by different agencies to make some sense of them and then develop a fully informed joint plan. Accomplishing all this is especially difficult in a transnational case. We sympathize with the working-level officers, drowning in information and trying to decide what is important or what needs to be done when no particular action has been requested of them.

Who had the job of managing the case to make sure these things were done? One answer is that everyone had the job. The CIA's deputy director for operations, James Pavitt, stressed to us that the responsibility resided with all involved. Above all he emphasized the primacy of the field. The field had the lead in managing operations. The job of headquarters, he stressed, was to support the field, and do so without delay. If the field asked for information or other support, the job of headquarters was to get it—right away.[34]

This is a traditional perspective on operations and, traditionally, it has had great merit. It reminded us of the FBI's pre-9/11 emphasis on the primacy of its field offices. When asked about how this traditional structure would adapt to the challenge of managing a transnational case, one that hopped from place to place as this one did, the deputy director argued that all involved were responsible for making it work. Pavitt underscored the responsibility of the particular field location where the suspects were being tracked at any given time. On the other hand, he also said that the Counterterrorist Center was supposed to manage all the moving parts,

Operational Opportunities

1. January 2000: the CIA does not watchlist Khalid al Mihdhar or notify the FBI when it learned Mihdhar possessed a valid U.S. visa.

2. January 2000: the CIA does not develop a transnational plan for tracking Mihdhar and his associates so that they could be followed to Bangkok and onward, including the United States.

3. March 2000: the CIA does not watchlist Nawaf al Hazmi or notify the FBI when it learned that he possessed a U.S. visa and had flown to Los Angeles on January 15, 2000.

4. January 2001: the CIA does not inform the FBI that a source had identified Khallad, or Tawfiq bin Attash, a major figure in the October 2000 bombing of the USS *Cole*, as having attended the meeting in Kuala Lumpur with Khalid al Mihdhar.

5. May 2001: a CIA official does not notify the FBI about Mihdhar's U.S. visa, Hazmi's U.S. travel, or Khallad's having attended the Kuala Lumpur meeting (identified when he reviewed all of the relevant traffic because of the high level of threats).

6. June 2001: FBI and CIA officials do not ensure that all relevant information regarding the Kuala Lumpur meeting was shared with the *Cole* investigators at the June 11 meeting.

7. August 2001: the FBI does not recognize the significance of the information regarding Mihdhar and Hazmi's possible arrival in the United States and thus does not take adequate action to share information, assign resources, and give sufficient priority to the search.

8. August 2001: FBI headquarters does not recognize the significance of the information regarding Moussaoui's training and beliefs and thus does

> not take adequate action to share information, involve higher-level officials across agencies, obtain information regarding Moussaoui's ties to al Qaeda, and give sufficient priority to determining what Moussaoui might be planning.
>
> 9. August 2001: the CIA does not focus on information that Khalid Sheikh Mohammed is a key al Qaeda lieutenant or connect information identifying KSM as the "Mukhtar" mentioned in other reports to the analysis that could have linked "Mukhtar" with Ramzi Binalshibh and Moussaoui.
>
> 10. August 2001: the CIA and FBI do not connect the presence of Mihdhar, Hazmi, and Moussaoui to the general threat reporting about imminent attacks.

while what happened on the ground was the responsibility of managers in the field.[35]

Headquarters tended to support and facilitate, trying to make sure everyone was in the loop. From time to time a particular post would push one way, or headquarters would urge someone to do something. But headquarters never really took responsibility for the successful management of this case. Hence the managers at CIA headquarters did not realize that omissions in planning had occurred, and they scarcely knew that the case had fallen apart.

The director of the Counterterrorist Center at the time, Cofer Black, recalled to us that this operation was one among many and that, at the time, it was "considered interesting, but not heavy water yet." He recalled the failure to get the word to Bangkok fast enough, but has no evident recollection of why the case then dissolved, unnoticed.[36]

The next level down, the director of the al Qaeda unit in CIA at the time recalled that he did not think it was his job to direct what should or should not be done. He did not pay attention when the individuals dispersed and things fell apart. There was no conscious decision to stop the operation after the trail was temporarily lost in Bangkok. He acknowledged, however, that perhaps there had been a letdown for his overworked staff after the extreme tension and long hours in the period of the millennium alert.[37]

The details of this case illuminate real management challenges, past and future. The U.S. government must find a way of pooling intelligence and using it to guide the planning of and assignment of responsibilities for *joint operations* involving organizations as disparate as the CIA, the FBI, the State Department, the military, and the agencies involved in homeland security.

Institutional Management

Beyond those day-to-day tasks of bridging the foreign-domestic divide and matching intelligence with plans, the challenges include broader management issues pertaining to how the top leaders of the government set priorities and allocate resources. Once again it is useful to illustrate the problem by examining the CIA, since before 9/11 this agency's role was so central in the government's counterterrorism efforts.

On December 4, 1998, DCI Tenet issued a directive to several CIA officials and his deputy for community management, stating: "We are at war. I want no resources or people spared in this effort, either inside CIA or the Community."[38] The memorandum had little overall effect on mobilizing the CIA or the intelligence community.[39]

The memo was addressed only to CIA officials and the deputy for community management, Joan Dempsey. She faxed the memo to the heads of the major intelligence agencies after removing covert action sections. Only a handful of people received it. The NSA director at the time, Lieutenant General Kenneth Minihan, believed the memo applied only to the CIA and not the NSA, because no one had informed him of any NSA shortcomings. For their part, CIA officials thought the memorandum was intended for the rest of the intelligence community, given that they were already doing all they could and believed that the rest of the community needed to pull its weight.[40]

The episode indicates some of the limitations of the DCI's authority over the direction and priorities of the intelligence community, especially its elements within the Department of Defense. The DCI has to direct agencies without controlling them. He does not receive an appropriation for their activities, and therefore does not control their purse strings. He has little insight into how they spend their resources. Congress attempted to strengthen the DCI's authority in 1996 by creating the positions of deputy DCI for community management and assistant DCIs for collection, analysis and production, and administration. But the authority of these positions is limited, and the vision of central management clearly has not been realized.

The DCI did not develop a management strategy for a war against Islamist terrorism before 9/11. Such a management strategy would define the capabilities the intelligence community must acquire for such a war—from language training to collection systems to analysts. Such a management strategy would necessarily extend beyond the CTC to the components that feed its expertise and support its operations, linked transparently to counterterrorism objectives. It would then detail the proposed expenditures and organizational changes required to acquire and implement these capabilities.

DCI Tenet and his deputy director for operations told us they did have a management strategy for a war on terrorism. It was to rebuild the CIA. They said the CIA as a whole had been badly damaged by prior budget constraints and that capabilities needed to be restored across the board. Indeed, the CTC budget had not been cut while the budgets had been slashed in many other parts of the Agency. By restoring funding across the CIA, a rising tide would lift all boats. They also stressed the synergy between improvements of every part of the Agency and the capabilities that the CTC or stations overseas could draw on in the war on terror.[41]

As some officials pointed out to us, there is a tradeoff in this management approach. In an attempt to rebuild everything at once, the highest priority efforts might not get the maximum support that they need. Furthermore, this approach attempted to channel relatively strong outside support for combating terrorism into backing for across-the-board funding increases. Proponents of the counterterrorism agenda might respond by being less inclined to loosen the purse strings than they would have been if offered a convincing counterterrorism budget strategy. The DCI's management strategy was also focused mainly on the CIA.

Lacking a management strategy for the war on terrorism or ways to see how funds were being spent across the community, DCI Tenet and his aides found it difficult to develop an overall intelligence community budget for a war on terrorism.

Responsibility for domestic intelligence gathering on terrorism was vested solely in the FBI, yet during almost all of the Clinton administration the relationship between the FBI Director and the President was nearly nonexistent. The FBI Director would not communicate directly with the President. His key personnel shared very little information with the National Security Council and the rest of the national security community. As a consequence, one of the critical working relationships in the counterterrorism effort was broken.

The Millennium Exception

Before concluding our narrative, we offer a reminder, and an explanation, of the one period in which the government as a whole seemed to be acting in concert to deal with terrorism—the last weeks of December 1999 preceding the millennium.

In the period between December 1999 and early January 2000, information about terrorism flowed widely and abundantly. The flow from the FBI was particularly remarkable because the FBI at other times shared almost no information. That from the intelligence community was also remarkable, because some of it reached officials—local airport managers and local police departments—who had not seen such information before and would not see it again before 9/11, if then. And the terrorist threat, in the United States even more than abroad, engaged the frequent attention of high officials in the executive branch and leaders in both houses of Congress.

Why was this so? Most obviously, it was because everyone was already on edge with the millennium and possible computer programming glitches ("Y2K") that might obliterate records, shut down power and communication lines, or otherwise disrupt daily life. Then, Jordanian authorities arrested 16 al Qaeda terrorists planning a number of bombings in that country. Those in custody included two U.S. citizens. Soon after, an alert Customs agent caught Ahmed Ressam bringing explosives across the Canadian border with the apparent intention of blowing up Los Angeles airport. He was found to have confederates on both sides of the border.

These were not events whispered about in highly classified intelligence dailies or FBI interview memos. The information was in all major newspapers and highlighted in network television news. Though the Jordanian arrests only made page 13 of the *New York Times*, they were featured on every evening newscast. The arrest of Ressam was on front pages, and the original story and its follow-ups dominated television news for a week. FBI field offices around the country were swamped by calls from concerned citizens. Representatives of the Justice Department, the FAA, local police departments, and major airports had microphones in their faces whenever they showed themselves.[42]

After the millennium alert, the government relaxed. Counterterrorism went back to being a secret preserve for segments of the FBI, the Counterterrorist Center, and the Counterterrorism Security Group. But the experience showed that the government was capable of mobilizing itself for an alert against terrorism. While one factor was the pre-existence of widespread concern about Y2K, another, at least equally important, was simply shared information.

Everyone knew not only of an abstract threat but of at least one terrorist who had been arrested *in the United States*. Terrorism had a face—that of Ahmed Ressam—and Americans from Vermont to southern California went on the watch for his like.

In the summer of 2001, DCI Tenet, the Counterterrorist Center, and the Counterterrorism Security Group did their utmost to sound a loud alarm, its basis being intelligence indicating that al Qaeda planned something big. But the millennium phenomenon was not repeated. FBI field offices apparently saw no abnormal terrorist activity, and headquarters was not shaking them up.

Between May 2001 and September 11, there was very little in newspapers or on television to heighten anyone's concern about terrorism. Front-page stories touching on the subject dealt with the windup of trials dealing with the East Africa embassy bombings and Ressam. All this reportage looked backward, describing problems satisfactorily resolved. Back-page notices told of tightened security at embassies and military installations abroad and government cautions against travel to the Arabian Peninsula. All the rest was secret.

CHAPTER TWELVE

What To Do?
A Global Strategy

12.1 REFLECTING ON A GENERATIONAL CHALLENGE

Three years after 9/11, Americans are still thinking and talking about how to protect our nation in this new era. The national debate continues.

Countering terrorism has become, beyond any doubt, the top national security priority for the United States. This shift has occurred with the full support of the Congress, both major political parties, the media, and the American people.

The nation has committed enormous resources to national security and to countering terrorism. Between fiscal year 2001, the last budget adopted before 9/11, and the present fiscal year 2004, total federal spending on defense (including expenditures on both Iraq and Afghanistan), homeland security, and international affairs rose more than 50 percent, from $354 billion to about $547 billion. The United States has not experienced such a rapid surge in national security spending since the Korean War.[1]

This pattern has occurred before in American history. The United States faces a sudden crisis and summons a tremendous exertion of national energy. Then, as that surge transforms the landscape, comes a time for reflection and reevaluation. Some programs and even agencies are discarded; others are invented or redesigned. Private firms and engaged citizens redefine their relationships with government, working through the processes of the American republic.

Now is the time for that reflection and reevaluation. The United States should consider *what to do*—the shape and objectives of a strategy. Americans should also consider *how to do it*—organizing their government in a different way.

Defining the Threat

In the post-9/11 world, threats are defined more by the fault lines within societies than by the territorial boundaries between them. From terrorism to global disease or environmental degradation, the challenges have become transnational rather than international. That is the defining quality of world politics in the twenty-first century.

National security used to be considered by studying foreign frontiers, weighing opposing groups of states, and measuring industrial might. To be dangerous, an enemy had to muster large armies. Threats emerged slowly, often visibly, as weapons were forged, armies conscripted, and units trained and moved into place. Because large states were more powerful, they also had more to lose. They could be deterred.

Now threats can emerge quickly. An organization like al Qaeda, headquartered in a country on the other side of the earth, in a region so poor that electricity or telephones were scarce, could nonetheless scheme to wield weapons of unprecedented destructive power in the largest cities of the United States.

In this sense, 9/11 has taught us that terrorism against American interests "over there" should be regarded just as we regard terrorism against America "over here." In this same sense, the American homeland is the planet.

But the enemy is not just "terrorism," some generic evil.[2] This vagueness blurs the strategy. The catastrophic threat at this moment in history is more specific. It is the threat posed by *Islamist* terrorism—especially the al Qaeda network, its affiliates, and its ideology.[3]

As we mentioned in chapter 2, Usama Bin Ladin and other Islamist terrorist leaders draw on a long tradition of extreme intolerance within one stream of Islam (a minority tradition), from at least Ibn Taimiyyah, through the founders of Wahhabism, through the Muslim Brotherhood, to Sayyid Qutb. That stream is motivated by religion and does not distinguish politics from religion, thus distorting both. It is further fed by grievances stressed by Bin Ladin and widely felt throughout the Muslim world—against the U.S. military presence in the Middle East, policies perceived as anti-Arab and anti-Muslim, and support of Israel. Bin Ladin and Islamist terrorists mean exactly what they say: to them America is the font of all evil, the "head of the snake," and it must be converted or destroyed.

It is not a position with which Americans can bargain or negotiate. With it there is no common ground—not even respect for life—on which to begin a dialogue. It can only be destroyed or utterly isolated.

Because the Muslim world has fallen behind the West politically, economically, and militarily for the past three centuries, and because few tolerant or secular Muslim democracies provide alternative models for the future, Bin Ladin's message finds receptive ears. It has attracted active support from thousands of disaffected young Muslims and resonates powerfully with a far larger number who do not actively support his methods. The resentment of America and the West is deep, even among leaders of relatively successful Muslim states.[4]

Tolerance, the rule of law, political and economic openness, the extension of greater opportunities to women—these cures must come from within Muslim societies themselves. The United States must support such developments.

But this process is likely to be measured in decades, not years. It is a process that will be violently opposed by Islamist terrorist organizations, both inside Muslim countries and in attacks on the United States and other Western nations. The United States finds itself caught up in a clash *within* a civilization. That clash arises from particular conditions in the Muslim world, conditions that spill over into expatriate Muslim communities in non-Muslim countries.

Our enemy is twofold: al Qaeda, a stateless network of terrorists that struck us on 9/11; and a radical ideological movement in the Islamic world, inspired in part by al Qaeda, which has spawned terrorist groups and violence across the globe. The first enemy is weakened, but continues to pose a grave threat. The second enemy is gathering, and will menace Americans and American interests long after Usama Bin Ladin and his cohorts are killed or captured. Thus our strategy must match our means to two ends: dismantling the al Qaeda network and prevailing in the longer term over the ideology that gives rise to Islamist terrorism.

Islam is not the enemy. It is not synonymous with terror. Nor does Islam teach terror. America and its friends oppose a perversion of Islam, not the great world faith itself. Lives guided by religious faith, including literal beliefs in holy scriptures, are common to every religion, and represent no threat to us.

Other religions have experienced violent internal struggles. With so many diverse adherents, every major religion will spawn violent zealots. Yet understanding and tolerance among people of different faiths can and must prevail.

The present transnational danger is Islamist terrorism. What is needed is a broad political-military strategy that rests on a firm tripod of policies to

- attack terrorists and their organizations;
- prevent the continued growth of Islamist terrorism; and
- protect against and prepare for terrorist attacks.

More Than a War on Terrorism

Terrorism is a tactic used by individuals and organizations to kill and destroy. Our efforts should be directed at those individuals and organizations.

Calling this struggle a war accurately describes the use of American and allied armed forces to find and destroy terrorist groups and their allies in the field, notably in Afghanistan.

The language of war also evokes the mobilization for a national effort. Yet the strategy should be balanced.

The first phase of our post-9/11 efforts rightly included military action to topple the Taliban and pursue al Qaeda. This work continues. But long-term success demands the use of all elements of national power: diplomacy, intelligence, covert action, law enforcement, economic policy, foreign aid, public diplomacy, and homeland defense. If we favor one tool while neglecting others, we leave ourselves vulnerable and weaken our national effort.

Certainly the strategy should include offensive operations to counter terrorism. Terrorists should no longer find safe haven where their organizations can grow and flourish. America's strategy should be a coalition strategy, that includes Muslim nations as partners in its development and implementation.

Our effort should be accompanied by a preventive strategy that is as much, or more, political as it is military. The strategy must focus clearly on the Arab and Muslim world, in all its variety.

Our strategy should also include defenses. America can be attacked in many ways and has many vulnerabilities. No defenses are perfect. But risks must be calculated; hard choices must be made about allocating resources. Responsibilities for America's defense should be clearly defined. Planning does make a difference, identifying where a little money might have a large effect. Defenses also complicate the plans of attackers, increasing their risks of discovery and failure. Finally, the nation must prepare to deal with attacks that are not stopped.

Measuring Success

What should Americans expect from their government in the struggle against Islamist terrorism? The goals seem unlimited: Defeat terrorism anywhere in the world. But Americans have also been told to expect the worst: An attack is probably coming; it may be terrible.

With such benchmarks, the justifications for action and

spending seem limitless. Goals are good. Yet effective public policies also need concrete objectives. Agencies need to be able to measure success.

These measurements do not need to be quantitative: government cannot measure success in the ways that private firms can. But the targets should be specific enough so that reasonable observers—in the White House, the Congress, the media, or the general public—can judge whether or not the objectives have been attained.

Vague goals match an amorphous picture of the enemy. Al Qaeda and its affiliates are popularly described as being all over the world, adaptable, resilient, needing little higher-level organization, and capable of anything. The American people are thus given the picture of an omnipotent, unslayable hydra of destruction. This image lowers expectations for government effectiveness.

It should not lower them too far. Our report shows a determined and capable group of plotters. Yet the group was fragile, dependent on a few key personalities, and occasionally left vulnerable by the marginal, unstable people often attracted to such causes. The enemy made mistakes—like Khalid al Mihdhar's unauthorized departure from the United States that required him to enter the country again in July 2001, or the selection of Zacarias Moussaoui as a participant and Ramzi Binalshibh's transfer of money to him. The U.S. government was not able to capitalize on those mistakes in time to prevent 9/11.

We do not believe it is possible to defeat all terrorist attacks against Americans, every time and everywhere. A president should tell the American people:

- No president can promise that a catastrophic attack like that of 9/11 will not happen again. History has shown that even the most vigilant and expert agencies cannot always prevent determined, suicidal attackers from reaching a target.
- But the American people are entitled to expect their government to do its very best. They should expect that

officials will have realistic objectives, clear guidance,
and effective organization. They are entitled to see
some standards for performance so they can judge, with
the help of their elected representatives, whether the
objectives are being met.

12.2 ATTACK TERRORISTS AND THEIR ORGANIZATIONS

The U.S. government, joined by other governments around
the world, is working through intelligence, law enforcement,
military, financial, and diplomatic channels to identify, disrupt, capture, or kill individual terrorists. This effort was going on before 9/11 and it continues on a vastly enlarged
scale. But to catch terrorists, a U.S. or foreign agency needs
to be able to find and reach them.

No Sanctuaries

The 9/11 attack was a complex international operation, the
product of years of planning. Bombings like those in Bali in
2003 or Madrid in 2004, while able to take hundreds of
lives, can be mounted locally. Their requirements are far
more modest in size and complexity. They are more difficult
to thwart. But the U.S. government must build the capacities
to prevent a 9/11-scale plot from succeeding, and those capabilities will help greatly to cope with lesser but still devastating attacks.

A complex international terrorist operation aimed at
launching a catastrophic attack cannot be mounted by just
anyone in any place. Such operations appear to require

- time, space, and ability to perform competent planning
  and staff work;
- a command structure able to make necessary decisions
  and possessing the authority and contacts to assemble
  needed people, money, and materials;
- opportunity and space to recruit, train, and select opera-

tives with the needed skills and dedication, providing
the time and structure required to socialize them into
the terrorist cause, judge their trustworthiness, and hone
their skills;

- a logistics network able to securely manage the travel
  of operatives, move money, and transport resources
  (like explosives) where they need to go;
- access, in the case of certain weapons, to the special
  materials needed for a nuclear, chemical, radiological,
  or biological attack;
- reliable communications between coordinators and operatives; and
- opportunity to test the workability of the plan.

Many details in chapters 2, 5, and 7 illustrate the direct and
indirect value of the Afghan sanctuary to al Qaeda in preparing the 9/11 attack and other operations. The organization
cemented personal ties among veteran jihadists working together there for years. It had the operational space to gather
and sift recruits, indoctrinating them in isolated, desert
camps. It built up logistical networks, running through Pakistan and the United Arab Emirates.

Al Qaeda also exploited relatively lax internal security
environments in Western countries, especially Germany. It
considered the environment in the United States so hos-
pitable that the 9/11 operatives used America as their staging area for further training and exercises—traveling into,
out of, and around the country and complacently using their
real names with little fear of capture.

To find sanctuary, terrorist organizations have fled to
some of the least governed, most lawless places in the world.
The intelligence community has prepared a world map that
highlights possible terrorist havens, using no secret intelligence—just indicating areas that combine rugged terrain,
weak governance, room to hide or receive supplies, and low
population density with a town or city near enough to allow
necessary interaction with the outside world. Large areas
scattered around the world meet these criteria.[5]

In talking with American and foreign government officials and military officers on the front lines fighting terrorists today, we asked them: If you were a terrorist leader today, where would you locate your base? Some of the same places come up again and again on their lists:

- western Pakistan and the Pakistan-Afghanistan border region
- southern or western Afghanistan
- the Arabian Peninsula, especially Saudi Arabia and Yemen, and the nearby Horn of Africa, including Somalia and extending southwest into Kenya
- Southeast Asia, from Thailand to the southern Philippines to Indonesia
- West Africa, including Nigeria and Mali
- European cities with expatriate Muslim communities, especially cities in central and eastern Europe where security forces and border controls are less effective

In the twentieth century, strategists focused on the world's great industrial heartlands. In the twenty-first, the focus is in the opposite direction, toward remote regions and failing states. The United States has had to find ways to extend its reach, straining the limits of its influence.

Every policy decision we make needs to be seen through this lens. If, for example, Iraq becomes a failed state, it will go to the top of the list of places that are breeding grounds for attacks against Americans at home. Similarly, if we are paying insufficient attention to Afghanistan, the rule of the Taliban or warlords and narcotraffickers may reemerge and its countryside could once again offer refuge to al Qaeda, or its successor.

Recommendation: The U.S. government must identify and prioritize actual or potential terrorist sanctuaries. For each, it should have a realistic strategy to keep possible terrorists insecure and on the run, using all elements

of national power. We should reach out, listen to, and work with other countries that can help.

We offer three illustrations that are particularly applicable today, in 2004: Pakistan, Afghanistan, and Saudi Arabia.

Pakistan

Pakistan's endemic poverty, widespread corruption, and often ineffective government create opportunities for Islamist recruitment. Poor education is a particular concern. Millions of families, especially those with little money, send their children to religious schools, or madrassahs. Many of these schools are the only opportunity available for an education, but some have been used as incubators for violent extremism. According to Karachi's police commander, there are 859 madrassahs teaching more than 200,000 youngsters in his city alone.[6]

It is hard to overstate the importance of Pakistan in the struggle against Islamist terrorism. Within Pakistan's borders are 150 million Muslims, scores of al Qaeda terrorists, many Taliban fighters, and—perhaps—Usama Bin Ladin. Pakistan possesses nuclear weapons and has come frighteningly close to war with nuclear-armed India over the disputed territory of Kashmir. A political battle among anti-American Islamic fundamentalists, the Pakistani military, and more moderate mainstream political forces has already spilled over into violence, and there have been repeated recent attempts to kill Pakistan's president, Pervez Musharraf.

In recent years, the United States has had three basic problems in its relationship with Pakistan:

• On terrorism, Pakistan helped nurture the Taliban. The Pakistani army and intelligence services, especially below the top ranks, have long been ambivalent about confronting Islamist extremists. Many in the government have sympathized with or provided support to the extremists. Musharraf agreed that Bin Ladin was bad. But before 9/11, preserving good relations with the Taliban took precedence.

- On proliferation, Musharraf has repeatedly said that Pakistan does not barter with its nuclear technology. But proliferation concerns have been long-standing and very serious. Most recently, the Pakistani government has claimed not to have known that one of its nuclear weapons developers, a national figure, was leading the most dangerous nuclear smuggling ring ever disclosed.
- Finally, Pakistan has made little progress toward the return of democratic rule at the national level, although that turbulent process does continue to function at the provincial level and the Pakistani press remains relatively free.

Immediately after 9/11, confronted by the United States with a stark choice, Pakistan made a strategic decision. Its government stood aside and allowed the U.S.-led coalition to destroy the Taliban regime. In other ways, Pakistan actively assisted: its authorities arrested more than 500 al Qaeda operatives and Taliban members, and Pakistani forces played a leading part in tracking down KSM, Abu Zubaydah, and other key al Qaeda figures.[7]

In the following two years, the Pakistani government tried to walk the fence, helping against al Qaeda while seeking to avoid a larger confrontation with Taliban remnants and other Islamic extremists. When al Qaeda and its Pakistani allies repeatedly tried to assassinate Musharraf, almost succeeding, the battle came home.

The country's vast unpoliced regions make Pakistan attractive to extremists seeking refuge and recruits and also provide a base for operations against coalition forces in Afghanistan. Almost all the 9/11 attackers traveled the northsouth nexus of Kandahar–Quetta–Karachi. The Baluchistan region of Pakistan (KSM's ethnic home) and the sprawling city of Karachi remain centers of Islamist extremism where the U.S. and Pakistani security and intelligence presence has been weak. The U.S. consulate in Karachi is a makeshift fortress, reflecting the gravity of the surrounding threat.[8]

During the winter of 2003–2004, Musharraf made another strategic decision. He ordered the Pakistani army into the frontier provinces of northwest Pakistan along the Afghan border, where Bin Ladin and Ayman al Zawahiri have reportedly taken refuge. The army is confronting groups of al Qaeda fighters and their local allies in very difficult terrain. On the other side of the frontier, U.S. forces in Afghanistan have found it challenging to organize effective joint operations, given Pakistan's limited capabilities and reluctance to permit U.S. military operations on its soil. Yet in 2004, it is clear that the Pakistani government is trying harder than ever before in the battle against Islamist terrorists.[9]

Acknowledging these problems and Musharraf's own part in the story, we believe that Musharraf's government represents the best hope for stability in Pakistan and Afghanistan.

- In an extraordinary public essay asking how Muslims can "drag ourselves out of the pit we find ourselves in, to raise ourselves up," Musharraf has called for a strategy of "enlightened moderation." The Muslim world, he said, should shun militancy and extremism; the West—and the United States in particular—should seek to resolve disputes with justice and help better the Muslim world.[10]
- Having come close to war in 2002 and 2003, Pakistan and India have recently made significant progress in peacefully discussing their longstanding differences. The United States has been and should remain a key supporter of that process.
- The constant refrain of Pakistanis is that the United States long treated them as allies of convenience. As the United States makes fresh commitments now, it should make promises it is prepared to keep, for years to come.

Recommendation: If Musharraf stands for enlightened moderation in a fight for his life and for the life of his country, the United States should be willing to make hard choices too, and make the difficult long-term commitment to the future of Pakistan. Sustaining the current scale of aid to Pakistan, the United States should support Pakistan's government in its struggle against extremists with a comprehensive effort that extends from military aid to support for better education, so long as Pakistan's leaders remain willing to make difficult choices of their own.

Afghanistan

Afghanistan was the incubator for al Qaeda and for the 9/11 attacks. In the fall of 2001, the U.S.-led international coalition and its Afghan allies toppled the Taliban and ended the regime's protection of al Qaeda. Notable progress has been made. International cooperation has been strong, with a clear UN mandate and a NATO-led peacekeeping force (the International Security Assistance Force, or ISAF). More than 10,000 American soldiers are deployed today in Afghanistan, joined by soldiers from NATO allies and Muslim states. A central government has been established in Kabul, with a democratic constitution, new currency, and a new army. Most Afghans enjoy greater freedom, women and girls are emerging from subjugation, and 3 million children have returned to school. For the first time in many years, Afghans have reason to hope.[11]

But grave challenges remain. Taliban and al Qaeda fighters have regrouped in the south and southeast. Warlords control much of the country beyond Kabul, and the land is awash in weapons. Economic development remains a distant hope. The narcotics trade—long a massive sector of the Afghan economy—is again booming. Even the most hardened aid workers refuse to operate in many regions, and some warn that Afghanistan is near the brink of chaos.[12]

Battered Afghanistan has a chance. Elections are being prepared. It is revealing that in June 2004, Taliban fighters resorted to slaughtering 16 Afghans on a bus, apparently for no reason other than their boldness in carrying an unprecedented Afghan weapon: a voter registration card.

Afghanistan's president, Hamid Karzai, is brave and committed. He is trying to build genuinely national institutions that can overcome the tradition of allocating powers among ethnic communities. Yet even if his efforts are successful and elections bring a democratic government to Afghanistan, the United States faces some difficult choices.

After paying relatively little attention to rebuilding Afghanistan during the military campaign, U.S. policies changed noticeably during 2003. Greater consideration of the political dimension and congressional support for a substantial package of assistance signaled a longer-term commitment to Afghanistan's future. One Afghan regional official plaintively told us the country finally has a good government. He begged the United States to keep its promise and not abandon Afghanistan again, as it had in the 1990s. Another Afghan leader noted that if the United States leaves, "we will lose all that we have gained."[13]

Most difficult is to define the security mission in Afghanistan. There is continuing political controversy about whether military operations in Iraq have had any effect on the scale of America's commitment to the future of Afghanistan. The United States has largely stayed out of the central government's struggles with dissident warlords and it has largely avoided confronting the related problem of narcotrafficking.[14]

Recommendation: The President and the Congress deserve praise for their efforts in Afghanistan so far. Now the United States and the international community should make a long-term commitment to a secure and stable Afghanistan, in order to give the government a reasonable opportunity to improve the life of the Afghan people. Afghanistan must not again become a sanctuary for international crime and terrorism. The United States and the international community should help the Afghan

government extend its authority over the country, with a strategy and nation-by-nation commitments to achieve their objectives.

- This is an ambitious recommendation. It would mean a redoubled effort to secure the country, disarm militias, and curtail the age of warlord rule. But the United States and NATO have already committed themselves to the future of this region—wisely, as the 9/11 story shows—and failed half-measures could be worse than useless.

- NATO in particular has made Afghanistan a test of the Alliance's ability to adapt to current security challenges of the future. NATO must pass this test. Currently, the United States and the international community envision enough support so that the central government can build a truly national army and extend essential infrastructure and minimum public services to major towns and regions. The effort relies in part on foreign civil-military teams, arranged under various national flags. The institutional commitments of NATO and the United Nations to these enterprises are weak. NATO member states are not following through; some of the other states around the world that have pledged assistance to Afghanistan are not fulfilling their pledges.

- The U.S. presence in Afghanistan is overwhelmingly oriented toward military and security work. The State Department presence is woefully understaffed, and the military mission is narrowly focused on al Qaeda and Taliban remnants in the south and southeast. The U.S. government can do its part if the international community decides on a joint effort to restore the rule of law and contain rampant crime and narcotics trafficking in this crossroads of Central Asia.[15]

We heard again and again that the money for assistance is allocated so rigidly that, on the ground, one U.S. agency often cannot improvise or pitch in to help another agency, even in small ways when a few thousand dollars could make a great difference.

The U.S. government should allocate money so that lower-level officials have more flexibility to get the job done across agency lines, adjusting to the circumstances they find in the field. This should include discretionary funds for expenditures by military units that often encounter opportunities to help the local population.

Saudi Arabia

Saudi Arabia has been a problematic ally in combating Islamic extremism. At the level of high policy, Saudi Arabia's leaders cooperated with American diplomatic initiatives aimed at the Taliban or Pakistan before 9/11. At the same time, Saudi Arabia's society was a place where al Qaeda raised money directly from individuals and through charities. It was the society that produced 15 of the 19 hijackers.

The Kingdom is one of the world's most religiously conservative societies, and its identity is closely bound to its religious links, especially its position as the guardian of Islam's two holiest sites. Charitable giving, or *zakat*, is one of the five pillars of Islam. It is broader and more pervasive than Western ideas of charity—functioning also as a form of income tax, educational assistance, foreign aid, and a source of political influence. The Western notion of the separation of civic and religious duty does not exist in Islamic cultures. Funding charitable works is an integral function of the governments in the Islamic world. It is so ingrained in Islamic culture that in Saudi Arabia, for example, a department within the Saudi Ministry of Finance and National Economy collects zakat directly, much as the U.S. Internal Revenue Service collects payroll withholding tax. Closely tied to zakat is the dedication of the government to propagating the Islamic faith, particularly the Wahhabi sect that flourishes in Saudi Arabia.

Traditionally, throughout the Muslim world, there is no formal oversight mechanism for donations. As Saudi wealth increased, the amounts contributed by individuals and the state grew dramatically. Substantial sums went to finance Islamic charities of every kind.

While Saudi domestic charities are regulated by the Ministry of Labor and Social Welfare, charities and international relief agencies, such as the World Assembly of Muslim Youth (WAMY), are currently regulated by the Ministry of Islamic Affairs. This ministry uses zakat and government funds to spread Wahhabi beliefs throughout the world, including in mosques and schools. Often these schools provide the only education available; even in affluent countries, Saudi-funded Wahhabi schools are often the only Islamic schools. Some Wahhabi-funded organizations have been exploited by extremists to further their goal of violent jihad against non-Muslims. One such organization has been the al Haramain Islamic Foundation; the assets of some branch offices have been frozen by the U.S. and Saudi governments.

Until 9/11, few Saudis would have considered government oversight of charitable donations necessary; many would have perceived it as interference in the exercise of their faith. At the same time, the government's ability to finance most state expenditures with energy revenues has delayed the need for a modern income tax system. As a result, there have been strong religious, cultural, and administrative barriers to monitoring charitable spending. That appears to be changing, however, now that the goal of violent jihad also extends to overthrowing Sunni governments (such as the House of Saud) that are not living up to the ideals of the Islamist extremists.[16]

The leaders of the United States and the rulers of Saudi Arabia have long had friendly relations, rooted in fundamentally common interests against the Soviet Union during the Cold War, in American hopes that Saudi oil supplies would stabilize the supply and price of oil in world markets, and in Saudi hopes that America could help protect the Kingdom against foreign threats.

In 1990, the Kingdom hosted U.S. armed forces before the first U.S.-led war against Iraq. American soldiers and airmen have given their lives to help protect Saudi Arabia.

The Saudi government has difficulty acknowledging this. American military bases remained there until 2003, as part of an international commitment to contain Iraq.

For many years, leaders on both sides preferred to keep their ties quiet and behind the scenes. As a result, neither the U.S. nor the Saudi people appreciated all the dimensions of the bilateral relationship, including the Saudi role in U.S. strategies to promote the Middle East peace process. In each country, political figures find it difficult to publicly defend good relations with the other.

Today, mutual recriminations flow. Many Americans see Saudi Arabia as an enemy, not as an embattled ally. They perceive an autocratic government that oppresses women, dominated by a wealthy and indolent elite. Saudi contacts with American politicians are frequently invoked as accusations in partisan political arguments. Americans are often appalled by the intolerance, anti-Semitism, and anti-American arguments taught in schools and preached in mosques.

Saudis are angry too. Many educated Saudis who were sympathetic to America now perceive the United States as an unfriendly state. One Saudi reformer noted to us that the demonization of Saudi Arabia in the U.S. media gives ammunition to radicals, who accuse reformers of being U.S. lackeys. Tens of thousands of Saudis who once regularly traveled to (and often had homes in) the United States now go elsewhere.[17]

Among Saudis, the United States is seen as aligned with Israel in its conflict with the Palestinians, with whom Saudis ardently sympathize. Although Saudi Arabia's cooperation against terrorism improved to some extent after the September 11 attacks, significant problems remained. Many in the Kingdom initially reacted with disbelief and denial. In the following months, as the truth became clear, some leading Saudis quietly acknowledged the problem but still did not see their own regime as threatened, and thus often did not respond promptly to U.S. requests for help. Though Saddam Hussein was widely detested, many Saudis are sympathetic to the anti-U.S. insurgents in Iraq, although majorities also condemn jihadist attacks in the Kingdom.[18]

As in Pakistan, Yemen, and other countries, attitudes changed when the terrorism came home. Cooperation had already become significant, but after the bombings in Riyadh on May 12, 2003, it improved much more. The Kingdom openly discussed the problem of radicalism, criticized the terrorists as religiously deviant, reduced official support for religious activity overseas, closed suspect charitable foundations, and publicized arrests—very public moves for a government that has preferred to keep internal problems quiet.

The Kingdom of Saudi Arabia is now locked in mortal combat with al Qaeda. Saudi police are regularly being killed in shootouts with terrorists. In June 2004, the Saudi ambassador to the United States called publicly—in the Saudi press—for his government to wage a jihad of its own against the terrorists. "We must all, as a state and as a people, recognize the truth about these criminals," he declared, "[i]f we do not declare a general mobilization—we will lose this war on terrorism."[19]

Saudi Arabia is a troubled country. Although regarded as very wealthy, in fact per capita income has dropped from $28,000 at its height to the present level of about $8,000. Social and religious traditions complicate adjustment to modern economic activity and limit employment opportunities for young Saudis. Women find their education and employment sharply limited.

President Clinton offered us a perceptive analysis of Saudi Arabia, contending that fundamentally friendly rulers have been constrained by their desire to preserve the status quo. He, like others, made the case for pragmatic reform instead. He hopes the rulers will envision what they want their Kingdom to become in 10 or 20 years, and start a process in which their friends can help them change.[20]

There are signs that Saudi Arabia's royal family is trying to build a consensus for political reform, though uncertain about how fast and how far to go. Crown Prince Abdullah wants the Kingdom to join the World Trade Organization to accelerate economic liberalization. He has embraced the *Arab Human Development Report,* which was highly critical of the Arab world's political, economic, and social failings and called for greater economic and political reform.[21]

Cooperation with Saudi Arabia against Islamist terrorism is very much in the U.S. interest. Such cooperation can exist for a time largely in secret, as it does now, but it cannot grow and thrive there. Nor, on either side, can friendship be unconditional.

Recommendation: The problems in the U.S.-Saudi relationship must be confronted, openly. The United States and Saudi Arabia must determine if they can build a relationship that political leaders on both sides are prepared to publicly defend—a relationship about more than oil. It should include a shared commitment to political and economic reform, as Saudis make common cause with the outside world. It should include a shared interest in greater tolerance and cultural respect, translating into a commitment to fight the violent extremists who foment hatred.

12.3 PREVENT THE CONTINUED GROWTH OF ISLAMIST TERRORISM

In October 2003, reflecting on progress after two years of waging the global war on terrorism, Defense Secretary Donald Rumsfeld asked his advisers: "Are we capturing, killing or deterring and dissuading more terrorists every day than the madrassas and the radical clerics are recruiting, training and deploying against us? Does the US need to fashion a broad, integrated plan to stop the next generation of terrorists? The US is putting relatively little effort into a long-range plan, but we are putting a great deal of effort into trying to stop terrorists. The cost-benefit ratio is against us! Our cost is billions against the terrorists' costs of millions."[22]

These are the right questions. Our answer is that we need short-term action on a long-range strategy, one that invigorates our foreign policy with the attention that the President and Congress have given to the military and intelligence parts of the conflict against Islamist terrorism.

Engage the Struggle of Ideas

The United States is heavily engaged in the Muslim world and will be for many years to come. This American engagement is resented. Polls in 2002 found that among America's friends, like Egypt—the recipient of more U.S. aid for the past 20 years than any other Muslim country—only 15 percent of the population had a favorable opinion of the United States. In Saudi Arabia the number was 12 percent. And two-thirds of those surveyed in 2003 in countries from Indonesia to Turkey (a NATO ally) were very or somewhat fearful that the United States may attack them.[23]

Support for the United States has plummeted. Polls taken in Islamic countries after 9/11 suggested that many or most people thought the United States was doing the right thing in its fight against terrorism; few people saw popular support for al Qaeda; half of those surveyed said that ordinary people had a favorable view of the United States. By 2003, polls showed that "the bottom has fallen out of support for America in most of the Muslim world. Negative views of the U.S. among Muslims, which had been largely limited to countries in the Middle East, have spread. . . . Since last summer, favorable ratings for the U.S. have fallen from 61% to 15% in Indonesia and from 71% to 38% among Muslims in Nigeria."[24]

Many of these views are at best uninformed about the United States and, at worst, informed by cartoonish stereotypes, the coarse expression of a fashionable "Occidentalism" among intellectuals who caricature U.S. values and policies. Local newspapers and the few influential satellite broadcasters—like al Jazeera—often reinforce the jihadist theme that portrays the United States as anti-Muslim.[25]

The small percentage of Muslims who are fully committed to Usama Bin Ladin's version of Islam are impervious to persuasion. It is among the large majority of Arabs and Muslims that we must encourage reform, freedom, democracy, and opportunity, even though our own promotion of these messages is limited in its effectiveness simply because we are its carriers. Muslims themselves will have to reflect upon such basic issues as the concept of jihad, the position of women, and the place of non-Muslim minorities. The United States can promote moderation, but cannot ensure its ascendancy. Only Muslims can do this.

The setting is difficult. The combined gross domestic product of the 22 countries in the Arab League is less than the GDP of Spain. Forty percent of adult Arabs are illiterate, two-thirds of them women. One-third of the broader Middle East lives on less than two dollars a day. Less than 2 percent of the population has access to the Internet. The majority of older Arab youths have expressed a desire to emigrate to other countries, particularly those in Europe.[26]

In short, the United States has to help defeat an ideology, not just a group of people, and we must do so under difficult circumstances. How can the United States and its friends help moderate Muslims combat the extremist ideas?

Recommendation: The U.S. government must define what the message is, what it stands for. We should offer an example of moral leadership in the world, committed to treat people humanely, abide by the rule of law, and be generous and caring to our neighbors. America and Muslim friends can agree on respect for human dignity and opportunity. To Muslim parents, terrorists like Bin Ladin have nothing to offer their children but visions of violence and death. America and its friends have a crucial advantage—we can offer these parents a vision that might give their children a better future. If we heed the views of thoughtful leaders in the Arab and Muslim world, a moderate consensus can be found.

The vision of the future should stress life over death: individual educational and economic opportunity. This vision includes widespread political participation and contempt for indiscriminate violence. It includes respect for the rule of law, openness in discussing differences, and tolerance for opposing points of view.

Recommendation: Where Muslim governments, even those who are friends, do not respect these principles, the United States must stand for a better future. One of the lessons of the long Cold War was that short-term gains in cooperating with the most repressive and brutal governments were too often outweighed by long-term setbacks for America's stature and interests.

American foreign policy is part of the message. America's policy choices have consequences. Right or wrong, it is simply a fact that American policy regarding the Israeli-Palestinian conflict and American actions in Iraq are dominant staples of popular commentary across the Arab and Muslim world. That does not mean U.S. choices have been wrong. It means those choices must be integrated with America's message of opportunity to the Arab and Muslim world. Neither Israel nor the new Iraq will be safer if worldwide Islamist terrorism grows stronger.

The United States must do more to communicate its message. Reflecting on Bin Ladin's success in reaching Muslim audiences, Richard Holbrooke wondered, "How can a man in a cave outcommunicate the world's leading communications society?" Deputy Secretary of State Richard Armitage worried to us that Americans have been "exporting our fears and our anger," not our vision of opportunity and hope.[27]

Recommendation: Just as we did in the Cold War, we need to defend our ideals abroad vigorously. America does stand up for its values. The United States defended, and still defends, Muslims against tyrants and criminals in Somalia, Bosnia, Kosovo, Afghanistan, and Iraq. If the United

States does not act aggressively to define itself in the Islamic world, the extremists will gladly do the job for us.

- Recognizing that Arab and Muslim audiences rely on satellite television and radio, the government has begun some promising initiatives in television and radio broadcasting to the Arab world, Iran, and Afghanistan. These efforts are beginning to reach large audiences. The Broadcasting Board of Governors has asked for much larger resources. It should get them.
- The United States should rebuild the scholarship, exchange, and library programs that reach out to young people and offer them knowledge and hope. Where such assistance is provided, it should be identified as coming from the citizens of the United States.

An Agenda of Opportunity

The United States and its friends can stress educational and economic opportunity. The United Nations has rightly equated "literacy as freedom."

- The international community is moving toward setting a concrete goal—to cut the Middle East region's illiteracy rate in half by 2010, targeting women and girls and supporting programs for adult literacy.
- Unglamorous help is needed to support the basics, such as textbooks that translate more of the world's knowledge into local languages and libraries to house such materials. Education about the outside world, or other cultures, is weak.
- More vocational education is needed, too, in trades and business skills. The Middle East can also benefit from some of the programs to bridge the digital divide and increase Internet access that have already been developed for other regions of the world.

Education that teaches tolerance, the dignity and value of each individual, and respect for different beliefs is a key element in any global strategy to eliminate Islamist terrorism.

Recommendation: The U.S. government should offer to join with other nations in generously supporting a new International Youth Opportunity Fund. Funds will be spent directly for building and operating primary and secondary schools in those Muslim states that commit to sensibly investing their own money in public education.

Economic openness is essential. Terrorism is not caused by poverty. Indeed, many terrorists come from relatively well-off families. Yet when people lose hope, when societies break down, when countries fragment, the breeding grounds for terrorism are created. Backward economic policies and repressive political regimes slip into societies that are without hope, where ambition and passions have no constructive outlet.

The policies that support economic development and reform also have political implications. Economic and political liberties tend to be linked. Commerce, especially international commerce, requires ongoing cooperation and compromise, the exchange of ideas across cultures, and the peaceful resolution of differences through negotiation or the rule of law. Economic growth expands the middle class, a constituency for further reform. Successful economies rely on vibrant private sectors, which have an interest in curbing indiscriminate government power. Those who develop the practice of controlling their own economic destiny soon desire a voice in their communities and political societies.

The U.S. government has announced the goal of working toward a Middle East Free Trade Area, or MEFTA, by 2013. The United States has been seeking comprehensive free trade agreements (FTAs) with the Middle Eastern nations most firmly on the path to reform. The U.S.-Israeli FTA was enacted in 1985, and Congress implemented an FTA with Jordan in 2001. Both agreements have expanded trade and investment, thereby supporting domestic economic reform. In 2004, new FTAs were signed with Morocco and Bahrain, and are awaiting congressional approval. These models are drawing the interest of their neighbors. Muslim countries can become full participants in the rules-based global trading system, as the United States considers lowering its trade barriers with the poorest Arab nations.

Recommendation: A comprehensive U.S. strategy to counter terrorism should include economic policies that encourage development, more open societies, and opportunities for people to improve the lives of their families and to enhance prospects for their children's future.

Turning a National Strategy into a Coalition Strategy

Practically every aspect of U.S. counterterrorism strategy relies on international cooperation. Since 9/11, these contacts concerning military, law enforcement, intelligence, travel and customs, and financial matters have expanded so dramatically, and often in an ad hoc way, that it is difficult to track these efforts, much less integrate them.

Recommendation: The United States should engage other nations in developing a comprehensive coalition strategy against Islamist terrorism. There are several multilateral institutions in which such issues should be addressed. But the most important policies should be discussed and coordinated in a flexible contact group of leading coalition governments. This is a good place, for example, to develop joint strategies for targeting terrorist travel, or for hammering out a common strategy for the places where terrorists may be finding sanctuary.

Presently the Muslim and Arab states meet with each other, in organizations such as the Islamic Conference and the Arab League. The Western states meet with each other in organizations such as NATO and the Group of Eight summit of leading industrial nations. A recent G-8 summit initiative to begin a dialogue about reform may be a start toward finding a place where leading Muslim states can discuss—and be seen to discuss—critical policy issues with the leading

Western powers committed to the future of the Arab and Muslim world.

These new international efforts can create durable habits of visible cooperation, as states willing to step up to their responsibilities join together in constructive efforts to direct assistance and coordinate action.

Coalition warfare also requires coalition policies on what to do with enemy captives. Allegations that the United States abused prisoners in its custody make it harder to build the diplomatic, political, and military alliances the government will need. The United States should work with friends to develop mutually agreed—on principles for the detention and humane treatment of captured international terrorists who are not being held under a particular country's criminal laws. Countries such as Britain, Australia, and Muslim friends, are committed to fighting terrorists. America should be able to reconcile its views on how to balance humanity and security with our nation's commitment to these same goals.

The United States and some of its allies do not accept the application of full Geneva Convention treatment of prisoners of war to captured terrorists. Those Conventions establish a minimum set of standards for prisoners in internal conflicts. Since the international struggle against Islamist terrorism is not internal, those provisions do not formally apply, but they are commonly accepted as basic standards for humane treatment.

Recommendation: The United States should engage its friends to develop a common coalition approach toward the detention and humane treatment of captured terrorists. New principles might draw upon Article 3 of the Geneva Conventions on the law of armed conflict. That article was specifically designed for those cases in which the usual laws of war did not apply. Its minimum standards are generally accepted throughout the world as customary international law.

Proliferation of Weapons of Mass Destruction

The greatest danger of another catastrophic attack in the United States will materialize if the world's most dangerous terrorists acquire the world's most dangerous weapons. As we note in chapter 2, al Qaeda has tried to acquire or make nuclear weapons for at least ten years. In chapter 4, we mentioned officials worriedly discussing, in 1998, reports that Bin Ladin's associates thought their leader was intent on carrying out a "Hiroshima."

These ambitions continue. In the public portion of his February 2004 worldwide threat assessment to Congress, DCI Tenet noted that Bin Ladin considered the acquisition of weapons of mass destruction to be a "religious obligation." He warned that al Qaeda "continues to pursue its strategic goal of obtaining a nuclear capability." Tenet added that "more than two dozen other terrorist groups are pursuing CBRN [chemical, biological, radiological, and nuclear] materials."[28]

A nuclear bomb can be built with a relatively small amount of nuclear material. A trained nuclear engineer with an amount of highly enriched uranium or plutonium about the size of a grapefruit or an orange, together with commercially available material, could fashion a nuclear device that would fit in a van like the one Ramzi Yousef parked in the garage of the World Trade Center in 1993. Such a bomb would level Lower Manhattan.[29]

The coalition strategies we have discussed to combat Islamist terrorism should therefore be combined with a parallel, vital effort to prevent and counter the proliferation of weapons of mass destruction (WMD). We recommend several initiatives in this area.

Strengthen Counterproliferation Efforts.

While efforts to shut down Libya's illegal nuclear program have been generally successful, Pakistan's illicit trade and the nuclear smuggling networks of Pakistani scientist A. Q.

Khan have revealed that the spread of nuclear weapons is a problem of global dimensions. Attempts to deal with Iran's nuclear program are still underway. Therefore, the United States should work with the international community to develop laws and an international legal regime with universal jurisdiction to enable the capture, interdiction, and prosecution of such smugglers by any state in the world where they do not disclose their activities.

Expand the Proliferation Security Initiative.

In May 2003, the Bush administration announced the Proliferation Security Initiative (PSI): nations in a willing partnership combining their national capabilities to use military, economic, and diplomatic tools to interdict threatening shipments of WMD and missile-related technology.

The PSI can be more effective if it uses intelligence and planning resources of the NATO alliance. Moreover, PSI membership should be open to non-NATO countries. Russia and China should be encouraged to participate.

Support the Cooperative Threat Reduction Program.

Outside experts are deeply worried about the U.S. government's commitment and approach to securing the weapons and highly dangerous materials still scattered in Russia and other countries of the Soviet Union. The government's main instrument in this area, the Cooperative Threat Reduction Program (usually referred to as "Nunn-Lugar," after the senators who sponsored the legislation in 1991), is now in need of expansion, improvement, and resources. The U.S. government has recently redoubled its international commitments to support this program, and we recommend that the United States do all it can, if Russia and other countries will do their part. The government should weigh the value of this investment against the catastrophic cost America would face should such weapons find their way to the terrorists who are so anxious to acquire them.

Recommendation: Our report shows that al Qaeda has tried to acquire or make weapons of mass destruction for at least ten years. There is no doubt the United States would be a prime target. Preventing the proliferation of these weapons warrants a maximum effort—by strengthening counterproliferation efforts, expanding the Proliferation Security Initiative, and supporting the Cooperative Threat Reduction program.

Targeting Terrorist Money

The general public sees attacks on terrorist finance as a way to "starve the terrorists of money." So, initially, did the U.S. government. After 9/11, the United States took aggressive actions to designate terrorist financiers and freeze their money, in the United States and through resolutions of the United Nations. These actions appeared to have little effect and, when confronted by legal challenges, the United States and the United Nations were often forced to unfreeze assets.

The difficulty, understood later, was that even if the intelligence community might "link" someone to a terrorist group through acquaintances or communications, the task of tracing the money from that individual to the terrorist group, or otherwise showing complicity, was far more difficult. It was harder still to do so without disclosing secrets.

These early missteps made other countries unwilling to freeze assets or otherwise act merely on the basis of a U.S. action. Multilateral freezing mechanisms now require waiting periods before being put into effect, eliminating the element of surprise and thus virtually ensuring that little money is actually frozen. Worldwide asset freezes have not been adequately enforced and have been easily circumvented, often within weeks, by simple methods.

But trying to starve the terrorists of money is like trying to catch one kind of fish by draining the ocean. A better strategy has evolved since those early months, as the government learned more about how al Qaeda raises, moves, and spends money.

Recommendation: Vigorous efforts to track terrorist financing must remain front and center in U.S. counterterrorism efforts. The government has recognized that information about terrorist money helps us to understand their networks, search them out, and disrupt their operations. Intelligence and law enforcement have targeted the relatively small number of financial facilitators—individuals al Qaeda relied on for their ability to raise and deliver money—at the core of al Qaeda's revenue stream. These efforts have worked. The death or capture of several important facilitators has decreased the amount of money available to al Qaeda and has increased its costs and difficulty in raising and moving that money. Captures have additionally provided a windfall of intelligence that can be used to continue the cycle of disruption.

The U.S. financial community and some international financial institutions have generally provided law enforcement and intelligence agencies with extraordinary cooperation, particularly in supplying information to support quickly developing investigations. Obvious vulnerabilities in the U.S. financial system have been corrected. The United States has been less successful in persuading other countries to adopt financial regulations that would permit the tracing of financial transactions.

Public designation of terrorist financiers and organizations is still part of the fight, but it is not the primary weapon. Designations are instead a form of diplomacy, as governments join together to identify named individuals and groups as terrorists. They also prevent open fundraising. Some charities that have been identified as likely avenues for terrorist financing have seen their donations diminish and their activities come under more scrutiny, and others have been put out of business, although controlling overseas branches of Gulf-area charities remains a challenge. The Saudi crackdown after the May 2003 terrorist attacks in Riyadh has apparently reduced the funds available to al

Qaeda—perhaps drastically—but it is too soon to know if this reduction will last.

Though progress apparently has been made, terrorists have shown considerable creativity in their methods of moving money. If al Qaeda is replaced by smaller, decentralized terrorist groups, the premise behind the government's efforts—that terrorists need a financial support network—may become outdated. Moreover, some terrorist operations do not rely on outside sources of money and may now be self-funding, either through legitimate employment or low-level criminal activity.[30]

12.4 PROTECT AGAINST AND PREPARE FOR TERRORIST ATTACKS

In the nearly three years since 9/11, Americans have become better protected against terrorist attack. Some of the changes are due to government action, such as new precautions to protect aircraft. A portion can be attributed to the sheer scale of spending and effort. Publicity and the vigilance of ordinary Americans also make a difference.

But the President and other officials acknowledge that although Americans may be safer, they are not safe. Our report shows that the terrorists analyze defenses. They plan accordingly.

Defenses cannot achieve perfect safety. They make targets harder to attack successfully, and they deter attacks by making capture more likely. Just increasing the attacker's odds of failure may make the difference between a plan attempted, or a plan discarded. The enemy also may have to develop more elaborate plans, thereby increasing the danger of exposure or defeat.

Protective measures also prepare for the attacks that may get through, containing the damage and saving lives.

Terrorist Travel

More than 500 million people annually cross U.S. borders at legal entry points, about 330 million of them noncitizens. Another 500,000 or more enter illegally without inspection across America's thousands of miles of land borders or remain in the country past the expiration of their permitted stay. The challenge for national security in an age of terrorism is to prevent the very few people who may pose overwhelming risks from entering or remaining in the United States undetected.[31]

In the decade before September 11, 2001, border security—encompassing travel, entry, and immigration—was not seen as a national security matter. Public figures voiced concern about the "war on drugs," the right level and kind of immigration, problems along the southwest border, migration crises originating in the Caribbean and elsewhere, or the growing criminal traffic in humans. The immigration system as a whole was widely viewed as increasingly dysfunctional and badly in need of reform. In national security circles, however, only smuggling of weapons of mass destruction carried weight, not the entry of terrorists who might use such weapons or the presence of associated foreign-born terrorists.

For terrorists, travel documents are as important as weapons. Terrorists must travel clandestinely to meet, train, plan, case targets, and gain access to attack. To them, international travel presents great danger, because they must surface to pass through regulated channels, present themselves to border security officials, or attempt to circumvent inspection points.

In their travels, terrorists use evasive methods, such as altered and counterfeit passports and visas, specific travel methods and routes, liaisons with corrupt government officials, human smuggling networks, supportive travel agencies, and immigration and identity fraud. These can sometimes be detected.

Before 9/11, no agency of the U.S. government systematically analyzed terrorists' travel strategies. Had they done so, they could have discovered the ways in which the terrorist predecessors to al Qaeda had been systematically but detectably exploiting weaknesses in our border security since the early 1990s.

We found that as many as 15 of the 19 hijackers were potentially vulnerable to interception by border authorities. Analyzing their characteristic travel documents and travel patterns could have allowed authorities to intercept 4 to 15 hijackers and more effective use of information available in U.S. government databases could have identified up to 3 hijackers.[32]

Looking back, we can also see that the routine operations of our immigration laws—that is, aspects of those laws not specifically aimed at protecting against terrorism—inevitably shaped al Qaeda's planning and opportunities. Because they were deemed not to be bona fide tourists or students as they claimed, five conspirators that we know of tried to get visas and failed, and one was denied entry by an inspector. We also found that had the immigration system set a higher bar for determining whether individuals are who or what they claim to be—and ensuring routine consequences for violations—it could potentially have excluded, removed, or come into further contact with several hijackers who did not appear to meet the terms for admitting short-term visitors.[33]

Our investigation showed that two systemic weaknesses came together in our border system's inability to contribute to an effective defense against the 9/11 attacks: a lack of well-developed counterterrorism measures as a part of border security and an immigration system not able to deliver on its basic commitments, much less support counterterrorism. These weaknesses have been reduced but are far from being overcome.

Recommendation: Targeting travel is at least as powerful a weapon against terrorists as targeting their money. The United States should combine terrorist travel intelli-

gence, operations, and law enforcement in a strategy to intercept terrorists, find terrorist travel facilitators, and constrain terrorist mobility.

Since 9/11, significant improvements have been made to create an integrated watchlist that makes terrorist name information available to border and law enforcement authorities. However, in the already difficult process of merging border agencies in the new Department of Homeland Security—"changing the engine while flying" as one official put it[34]—new insights into terrorist travel have not yet been integrated into the front lines of border security.

The small terrorist travel intelligence collection and analysis program currently in place has produced disproportionately useful results. It should be expanded. Since officials at the borders encounter travelers and their documents first and investigate travel facilitators, they must work closely with intelligence officials.

Internationally and in the United States, constraining terrorist travel should become a vital part of counterterrorism strategy. Better technology and training to detect terrorist travel documents are the most important immediate steps to reduce America's vulnerability to clandestine entry. Every stage of our border and immigration system should have as a part of its operations the detection of terrorist indicators on travel documents. Information systems able to authenticate travel documents and detect potential terrorist indicators should be used at consulates, at primary border inspection lines, in immigration services offices, and in intelligence and enforcement units. All frontline personnel should receive some training. Dedicated specialists and ongoing linkages with the intelligence community are also required. The Homeland Security Department's Directorate of Information Analysis and Infrastructure Protection should receive more resources to accomplish its mission as the bridge between the frontline border agencies and the rest of the government counterterrorism community.

A Biometric Screening System

When people travel internationally, they usually move through defined channels, or portals. They may seek to acquire a passport. They may apply for a visa. They stop at ticket counters, gates, and exit controls at airports and seaports. Upon arrival, they pass through inspection points. They may transit to another gate to get on an airplane. Once inside the country, they may seek another form of identification and try to enter a government or private facility. They may seek to change immigration status in order to remain.

Each of these checkpoints or portals is a screening—a chance to establish that people are who they say they are and are seeking access for their stated purpose, to intercept identifiable suspects, and to take effective action.

The job of protection is shared among these many defined checkpoints. By taking advantage of them all, we need not depend on any one point in the system to do the whole job. The challenge is to see the common problem across agencies and functions and develop a conceptual framework—an architecture—for an effective screening system.[35]

Throughout government, and indeed in private enterprise, agencies and firms at these portals confront recurring judgments that balance security, efficiency, and civil liberties. These problems should be addressed systemically, not in an ad hoc, fragmented way. For example:

What information is an individual required to present and in what form?

A fundamental problem, now beginning to be addressed, is the lack of standardized information in "feeder" documents used in identifying individuals. Biometric identifiers that measure unique physical characteristics, such as facial features, fingerprints, or iris scans, and reduce them to digitized, numerical statements called algorithms, are just beginning to be used. Travel history, however, is still recorded in passports with entry-exit stamps called cachets, which al Qaeda has

trained its operatives to forge and use to conceal their terrorist activities.

How will the individual and the information be checked?

There are many databases just in the United States—for terrorist, criminal, and immigration history, as well as financial
information, for instance. Each is set up for different purposes and stores different kinds of data, under varying rules
of access. Nor is access always guaranteed. Acquiring information held by foreign governments may require painstaking negotiations, and records that are not yet digitized are
difficult to search or analyze. The development of terrorist
indicators has hardly begun, and behavioral cues remain important.

Who will screen individuals, and what will they be trained to do?

A wide range of border, immigration, and law enforcement
officials encounter visitors and immigrants and they are
given little training in terrorist travel intelligence. Fraudulent travel documents, for instance, are usually returned to
travelers who are denied entry without further examination
for terrorist trademarks, investigation as to their source, or
legal process.

What are the consequences of finding a suspicious indicator, and who will take action?

One risk is that responses may be ineffective or produce no
further information. Four of the 9/11 attackers were pulled
into secondary border inspection, but then admitted. More
than half of the 19 hijackers were flagged by the Federal Aviation Administration's profiling system when they arrived for
their flights, but the consequence was that bags, not people,
were checked. Competing risks include "false positives," or
the danger that rules may be applied with insufficient training
or judgment. Overreactions can impose high costs too—on
individuals, our economy, and our beliefs about justice.

- A special note on the importance of trusting subjective judgment: One potential hijacker was turned back by an immigration inspector as he tried to enter the United States. The inspector relied on intuitive experience to ask questions more than he relied on any objective factor that could be detected by "scores" or a machine. Good people who have worked in such jobs for a long time understand this phenomenon well. Other evidence we obtained confirmed the importance of letting experienced gate agents or security screeners ask questions and use their judgment. This is not an invitation to arbitrary exclusions. But any effective system has to grant some scope, perhaps in a little extra inspection or one more check, to the instincts and discretion of well trained human beings.

Recommendation: The U.S. border security system should be integrated into a larger network of screening points that includes our transportation system and access to vital facilities, such as nuclear reactors. The President should direct the Department of Homeland Security to lead the effort to design a comprehensive screening system, addressing common problems and setting common standards with systemwide goals in mind. Extending those standards among other governments could dramatically strengthen America and the world's collective ability to intercept individuals who pose catastrophic threats.

We advocate a system for screening, not categorical profiling. A screening system looks for particular, identifiable suspects or indicators of risk. It does not involve guesswork about who might be dangerous. It requires frontline border officials who have the tools and resources to establish that people are who they say they are, intercept identifiable suspects, and disrupt terrorist operations.

The U.S. Border Screening System

The border and immigration system of the United States must remain a visible manifestation of our belief in freedom, democracy, global economic growth, and the rule of law, yet serve equally well as a vital element of counterterrorism. Integrating terrorist travel information in the ways we have described is the most immediate need. But the underlying system must also be sound.

Since September 11, the United States has built the first phase of a biometric screening program, called US VISIT (the United States Visitor and Immigrant Status Indicator Technology program). It takes two biometric identifiers—digital photographs and prints of two index fingers—from travelers. False identities are used by terrorists to avoid being detected on a watchlist. These biometric identifiers make such evasions far more difficult.

So far, however, only visitors who acquire visas to travel to the United States are covered. While visitors from "visa waiver" countries will be added to the program, beginning this year, covered travelers will still constitute only about 12 percent of all noncitizens crossing U.S. borders. Moreover, exit data are not uniformly collected and entry data are not fully automated. It is not clear the system can be installed before 2010, but even this timetable may be too slow, given the possible security dangers.[36]

- Americans should not be exempt from carrying biometric passports or otherwise enabling their identities to be securely verified when they enter the United States; nor should Canadians or Mexicans. Currently U.S. persons are exempt from carrying passports when returning from Canada, Mexico, and the Caribbean. The current system enables non-U.S. citizens to gain entry by showing minimal identification. The 9/11 experience shows that terrorists study and exploit America's vulnerabilities.

- To balance this measure, programs to speed known travelers should be a higher priority, permitting inspectors to focus on greater risks. The daily commuter should not be subject to the same measures as first-time travelers. An individual should be able to preenroll, with his or her identity verified in passage. Updates of database information and other checks can ensure ongoing reliability. The solution, requiring more research and development, is likely to combine radio frequency technology with biometric identifiers.[37]
- The current patchwork of border screening systems, including several frequent traveler programs, should be consolidated with the USVISIT system to enable the development of an integrated system, which in turn can become part of the wider screening plan we suggest.
- The program allowing individuals to travel from foreign countries through the United States to a third country, without having to obtain a U.S. visa, has been suspended. Because "transit without visa" can be exploited by terrorists to enter the United States, the program should not be reinstated unless and until transit passage areas can be fully secured to prevent passengers from illegally exiting the airport.

Inspectors adjudicating entries of the 9/11 hijackers lacked adequate information and knowledge of the rules. All points in the border system—from consular offices to immigration services offices—will need appropriate electronic access to an individual's file. Scattered units at Homeland Security and the State Department perform screening and data mining: instead, a government-wide team of border and transportation officials should be working together. A modern border and immigration system should combine a biometric entry-exit system with accessible files on visitors and immigrants, along with intelligence on indicators of terrorist travel.

Our border screening system should check people efficiently and welcome friends. Admitting large numbers of students, scholars, businesspeople, and tourists fuels our economy, cultural vitality, and political reach. There is evidence that the present system is disrupting travel to the United States. Overall, visa applications in 2003 were down over 32 percent since 2001. In the Middle East, they declined about 46 percent. Training and the design of security measures should be continuously adjusted.[38]

Recommendation: The Department of Homeland Security, properly supported by the Congress, should complete, as quickly as possible, a biometric entry-exit screening system, including a single system for speeding qualified travelers. It should be integrated with the system that provides benefits to foreigners seeking to stay in the United States. Linking biometric passports to good data systems and decisionmaking is a fundamental goal. No one can hide his or her debt by acquiring a credit card with a slightly different name. Yet today, a terrorist can defeat the link to electronic records by tossing away an old passport and slightly altering the name in the new one.

Completion of the entry-exit system is a major and expensive challenge. Biometrics have been introduced into an antiquated computer environment. Replacement of these systems and improved biometric systems will be required. Nonetheless, funding and completing a biometrics-based entry-exit system is an essential investment in our national security.

Exchanging terrorist information with other countries, consistent with privacy requirements, along with listings of lost and stolen passports, will have immediate security benefits. We should move toward real-time verification of passports with issuing authorities. The further away from our borders that screening occurs, the more security benefits we gain. At least some screening should occur before a passenger departs on a flight destined for the United States. We should also work with other countries to ensure effective inspection regimes at all airports.[39]

The international community arrives at international standards for the design of passports through the International Civil Aviation Organization (ICAO). The global standard for identification is a digital photograph; fingerprints are optional. We must work with others to improve passport standards and provide foreign assistance to countries that need help in making the transition.[40]

Recommendation: The U.S. government cannot meet its own obligations to the American people to prevent the entry of terrorists without a major effort to collaborate with other governments. We should do more to exchange terrorist information with trusted allies, and raise U.S. and global border security standards for travel and border crossing over the medium and long term through extensive international cooperation.

Immigration Law and Enforcement

Our borders and immigration system, including law enforcement, ought to send a message of welcome, tolerance, and justice to members of immigrant communities in the United States and in their countries of origin. We should reach out to immigrant communities. Good immigration services are one way of doing so that is valuable in every way—including intelligence.

It is elemental to border security to know who is coming into the country. Today more than 9 million people are in the United States outside the legal immigration system. We must also be able to monitor and respond to entrances between our ports of entry, working with Canada and Mexico as much as possible.

There is a growing role for state and local law enforcement agencies. They need more training and work with federal agencies so that they can cooperate more effectively with those federal authorities in identifying terrorist suspects.

All but one of the 9/11 hijackers acquired some form of U.S. identification document, some by fraud. Acquisition of these forms of identification would have assisted them in boarding commercial flights, renting cars, and other necessary activities.

Recommendation: Secure identification should begin in the United States. The federal government should set standards for the issuance of birth certificates and sources of identification, such as drivers licenses. Fraud in identification documents is no longer just a problem of theft. At many entry points to vulnerable facilities, including gates for boarding aircraft, sources of identification are the last opportunity to ensure that people are who they say they are and to check whether they are terrorists.[41]

Strategies for Aviation and Transportation Security

The U.S. transportation system is vast and, in an open society, impossible to secure completely against terrorist attacks. There are hundreds of commercial airports, thousands of planes, and tens of thousands of daily flights carrying more than half a billion passengers a year. Millions of containers are imported annually through more than 300 sea and river ports served by more than 3,700 cargo and passenger terminals. About 6,000 agencies provide transit services through buses, subways, ferries, and light-rail service to about 14 million Americans each weekday.[42]

In November 2001, Congress passed and the President signed the Aviation and Transportation Security Act. This act created the Transportation Security Administration (TSA), which is now part of the Homeland Security Department. In November 2002, both the Homeland Security Act and the Maritime Transportation Security Act followed. These laws required the development of strategic plans to describe how the new department and TSA would provide security for critical parts of the U.S. transportation sector.

Over 90 percent of the nation's $5.3 billion annual investment in the TSA goes to aviation—to fight the last war. The money has been spent mainly to meet congressional mandates to federalize the security checkpoint screeners and to deploy existing security methods and technologies at airports. The current efforts do not yet reflect a forward-looking strategic plan systematically analyzing assets, risks, costs, and benefits. Lacking such a plan, we are not convinced that our transportation security resources are being allocated to the greatest risks in a cost-effective way.

- Major vulnerabilities still exist in cargo and general aviation security. These, together with inadequate screening and access controls, continue to present aviation security challenges.
- While commercial aviation remains a possible target, terrorists may turn their attention to other modes. Opportunities to do harm are as great, or greater, in maritime or surface transportation. Initiatives to secure shipping containers have just begun. Surface transportation systems such as railroads and mass transit remain hard to protect because they are so accessible and extensive.

Despite congressional deadlines, the TSA has developed neither an integrated strategic plan for the transportation sector nor specific plans for the various modes—air, sea, and ground.

Recommendation: Hard choices must be made in allocating limited resources. The U.S. government should identify and evaluate the transportation assets that need to be protected, set risk-based priorities for defending them, select the most practical and cost-effective ways of doing so, and then develop a plan, budget, and funding to implement the effort. The plan should assign roles and missions to the relevant authorities (federal, state, regional, and local) and to private stakeholders. In measuring ef-

fectiveness, perfection is unattainable. But terrorists should perceive that potential targets are defended. They may be deterred by a significant chance of failure.

Congress should set a specific date for the completion of these plans and hold the Department of Homeland Security and TSA accountable for achieving them.

The most powerful investments may be for improvements in technologies with applications across the transportation modes, such as scanning technologies designed to screen containers that can be transported by plane, ship, truck, or rail. Though such technologies are becoming available now, widespread deployment is still years away.

In the meantime, the best protective measures may be to combine improved methods of identifying and tracking the high-risk containers, operators, and facilities that require added scrutiny with further efforts to integrate intelligence analysis, effective procedures for transmitting threat information to transportation authorities, and vigilance by transportation authorities and the public.

A Layered Security System

No single security measure is foolproof. Accordingly, the TSA must have multiple layers of security in place to defeat the more plausible and dangerous forms of attack against public transportation.

- The plan must take into consideration the full array of possible enemy tactics, such as use of insiders, suicide terrorism, or standoff attack. Each layer must be effective in its own right. Each must be supported by other layers that are redundant and coordinated.
- The TSA should be able to identify for Congress the array of potential terrorist attacks, the layers of security in place, and the reliability provided by each layer. TSA must develop a plan as described above to improve weak individual layers and the effectiveness of the layered systems it deploys.

On 9/11, the 19 hijackers were screened by a computer-assisted screening system called CAPPS. More than half were identified for further inspection, which applied only to their checked luggage.

Under current practices, air carriers enforce government orders to stop certain known and suspected terrorists from boarding commercial flights and to apply secondary screening procedures to others. The "no-fly" and "automatic selectee" lists include only those individuals who the U.S. government believes pose a direct threat of attacking aviation.

Because air carriers implement the program, concerns about sharing intelligence information with private firms and foreign countries keep the U.S. government from listing all terrorist and terrorist suspects who should be included. The TSA has planned to take over this function when it deploys a new screening system to take the place of CAPPS. The deployment of this system has been delayed because of claims it may violate civil liberties.

Recommendation: Improved use of "no-fly" and "automatic selectee" lists should not be delayed while the argument about a successor to CAPPS continues. This screening function should be performed by the TSA, and it should utilize the larger set of watchlists maintained by the federal government. Air carriers should be required to supply the information needed to test and implement this new system.

CAPPS is still part of the screening process, still profiling passengers, with the consequences of selection now including personal searches of the individual and carry-on bags. The TSA is dealing with the kind of screening issues that are being encountered by other agencies. As we mentioned earlier, these screening issues need to be elevated for high-level attention and addressed promptly by the government. Working through these problems can help clear the way for the TSA's screening improvements and would help many other agencies too.

The next layer is the screening checkpoint itself. As the screening system tries to stop dangerous people, the checkpoint needs to be able to find dangerous items. Two reforms are needed soon: (1) screening people for explosives, not just their carry-on bags, and (2) improving screener performance.

Recommendation: The TSA and the Congress must give priority attention to improving the ability of screening checkpoints to detect explosives on passengers. As a start, each individual selected for special screening should be screened for explosives. Further, the TSA should conduct a human factors study, a method often used in the private sector, to understand problems in screener performance and set attainable objectives for individual screeners and for the checkpoints where screening takes place.

Concerns also remain regarding the screening and transport of checked bags and cargo. More attention and resources should be directed to reducing or mitigating the threat posed by explosives in vessels' cargo holds. The TSA should expedite the installation of advanced (in-line) baggage-screening equipment. Because the aviation industry will derive substantial benefits from this deployment, it should pay a fair share of the costs. The TSA should require that every passenger aircraft carrying cargo must deploy at least one hardened container to carry any suspect cargo. TSA also needs to intensify its efforts to identify, track, and appropriately screen potentially dangerous cargo in both the aviation and maritime sectors.

The Protection of Civil Liberties

Many of our recommendations call for the government to increase its presence in our lives—for example, by creating standards for the issuance of forms of identification, by better securing our borders, by sharing information gathered by many different agencies. We also recommend the consolidation of authority over the now far-flung entities constituting the intelligence community. The Patriot Act vests substantial powers in our federal government. We have seen the government use the immigration laws as a tool in its counterterrorism effort. Even without the changes we recommend, the American public has vested enormous authority in the U.S. government.

At our first public hearing on March 31, 2003, we noted the need for balance as our government responds to the real and ongoing threat of terrorist attacks. The terrorists have used our open society against us. In wartime, government calls for greater powers, and then the need for those powers recedes after the war ends. This struggle will go on. Therefore, while protecting our homeland, Americans should be mindful of threats to vital personal and civil liberties. This balancing is no easy task, but we must constantly strive to keep it right.

This shift of power and authority to the government calls for an enhanced system of checks and balances to protect the precious liberties that are vital to our way of life. We therefore make three recommendations.

First, as we will discuss in chapter 13, to open up the sharing of information across so many agencies and with the private sector, the President should take responsibility for determining what information can be shared by which agencies and under what conditions. Protection of privacy rights should be one key element of this determination.

Recommendation: As the President determines the guidelines for information sharing among government agencies and by those agencies with the private sector, he should safeguard the privacy of individuals about whom information is shared.

Second, Congress responded, in the immediate aftermath of 9/11, with the Patriot Act, which vested substantial new powers in the investigative agencies of the government. Some of the most controversial provisions of the Patriot Act are to "sunset" at the end of 2005. Many of the act's provisions are relatively noncontroversial, updating America's surveillance laws to reflect technological developments in a digital age. Some executive actions that have been criticized are unrelated to the Patriot Act. The provisions in the act that facilitate the sharing of information among intelligence agencies and between law enforcement and intelligence appear, on balance, to be beneficial. Because of concerns regarding the shifting balance of power to the government, we think that a full and informed debate on the Patriot Act would be healthy.

Recommendation: The burden of proof for retaining a particular governmental power should be on the executive, to explain (a) that the power actually materially enhances security and (b) that there is adequate supervision of the executive's use of the powers to ensure protection of civil liberties. If the power is granted, there must be adequate guidelines and oversight to properly confine its use.

Third, during the course of our inquiry, we were told that there is no office within the government whose job it is to look across the government at the actions we are taking to protect ourselves to ensure that liberty concerns are appropriately considered. If, as we recommend, there is substantial change in the way we collect and share intelligence, there should be a voice within the executive branch for those concerns. Many agencies have privacy offices, albeit of limited scope. The Intelligence Oversight Board of the President's Foreign Intelligence Advisory Board has, in the past, had the job of overseeing certain activities of the intelligence community.

Recommendation: At this time of increased and consolidated government authority, there should be a board within the executive branch to oversee adherence to the guidelines we recommend and the commitment the government makes to defend our civil liberties.

We must find ways of reconciling security with liberty, since the success of one helps protect the other. The choice between security and liberty is a false choice, as nothing is more likely to endanger America's liberties than the success of a terrorist attack at home. Our history has shown us that insecurity threatens liberty. Yet, if our liberties are curtailed, we lose the values that we are struggling to defend.

Setting Priorities for National Preparedness

Before 9/11, no executive department had, as its first priority, the job of defending America from domestic attack. That changed with the 2002 creation of the Department of Homeland Security. This department now has the lead responsibility for problems that feature so prominently in the 9/11 story, such as protecting borders, securing transportation and other parts of our critical infrastructure, organizing emergency assistance, and working with the private sector to assess vulnerabilities.

Throughout the government, nothing has been harder for officials—executive or legislative—than to set priorities, making hard choices in allocating limited resources. These difficulties have certainly afflicted the Department of Homeland Security, hamstrung by its many congressional overseers. In delivering assistance to state and local governments, we heard—especially in New York—about imbalances in the allocation of money. The argument concentrates on two questions.

First, how much money should be set aside for criteria not directly related to risk? Currently a major portion of the billions of dollars appropriated for state and local assistance is allocated so that each state gets a certain amount, or an allocation based on its population—wherever they live.

Recommendation: Homeland security assistance should be based strictly on an assessment of risks and vulnerabilities. Now, in 2004, Washington, D.C., and New York City are certainly at the top of any such list. We understand the contention that every state and city needs to

have some minimum infrastructure for emergency response. But federal homeland security assistance should not remain a program for general revenue sharing. It should supplement state and local resources based on the risks or vulnerabilities that merit additional support. Congress should not use this money as a pork barrel.

The second question is, Can useful criteria to measure risk and vulnerability be developed that assess all the many variables? The allocation of funds should be based on an assessment of threats and vulnerabilities. That assessment should consider such factors as population, population density, vulnerability, and the presence of critical infrastructure within each state. In addition, the federal government should require each state receiving federal emergency preparedness funds to provide an analysis based on the same criteria to justify the distribution of funds in that state.

In a free-for-all over money, it is understandable that representatives will work to protect the interests of their home states or districts. But this issue is too important for politics as usual to prevail. Resources must be allocated according to vulnerabilities. We recommend that a panel of security experts be convened to develop written benchmarks for evaluating community needs. We further recommend that federal homeland security funds be allocated in accordance with those benchmarks, and that states be required to abide by those benchmarks in disbursing the federal funds. The benchmarks will be imperfect and subjective; they will continually evolve. But hard choices must be made. Those who would allocate money on a different basis should then defend their view of the national interest.

Command, Control, and Communications

The attacks on 9/11 demonstrated that even the most robust emergency response capabilities can be overwhelmed if an attack is large enough. Teamwork, collaboration, and cooperation at an incident site are critical to a successful response. Key decisionmakers who are represented at the incident command level help to ensure an effective response, the efficient use of resources, and responder safety. Regular joint training at all levels is, moreover, essential to ensuring close coordination during an actual incident.

Recommendation: Emergency response agencies nation-wide should adopt the Incident Command System (ICS). When multiple agencies or multiple jurisdictions are involved, they should adopt a unified command. Both are proven frameworks for emergency response. We strongly support the decision that federal homeland security funding will be contingent, as of October 1, 2004, upon the adoption and regular use of ICS and unified command procedures. In the future, the Department of Homeland Security should consider making funding contingent on aggressive and realistic training in accordance with ICS and unified command procedures.

The attacks of September 11, 2001 overwhelmed the response capacity of most of the local jurisdictions where the hijacked airliners crashed. While many jurisdictions have established mutual aid compacts, a serious obstacle to multi-jurisdictional response has been the lack of indemnification for mutual-aid responders in areas such as the National Capital Region.

Public safety organizations, chief administrative officers, state emergency management agencies, and the Department of Homeland Security should develop a regional focus within the emergency responder community and promote multi-jurisdictional mutual assistance compacts. Where such compacts already exist, training in accordance with their terms should be required. Congress should pass legislation to remedy the long-standing indemnification and liability impediments to the provision of public safety mutual aid in the National Capital Region and where applicable throughout the nation.

The inability to communicate was a critical element at

the World Trade Center, Pentagon, and Somerset County, Pennsylvania, crash sites, where multiple agencies and multiple jurisdictions responded. The occurrence of this problem at three very different sites is strong evidence that compatible and adequate communications among public safety organizations at the local, state, and federal levels remains an important problem.

Recommendation: Congress should support pending legislation which provides for the expedited and increased assignment of radio spectrum for public safety purposes. Furthermore, high-risk urban areas such as New York City and Washington, D.C., should establish signal corps units to ensure communications connectivity between and among civilian authorities, local first responders, and the National Guard. Federal funding of such units should be given high priority by Congress.

Private-Sector Preparedness

The mandate of the Department of Homeland Security does not end with government; the department is also responsible for working with the private sector to ensure preparedness. This is entirely appropriate, for the private sector controls 85 percent of the critical infrastructure in the nation. Indeed, unless a terrorist's target is a military or other secure government facility, the "first" first responders will almost certainly be civilians. Homeland security and national preparedness therefore often begins with the private sector.

Preparedness in the private sector and public sector for rescue, restart, and recovery of operations should include (1) a plan for evacuation, (2) adequate communications capabilities, and (3) a plan for continuity of operations. As we examined the emergency response to 9/11, witness after witness told us that despite 9/11, the private sector remains largely unprepared for a terrorist attack. We were also advised that the lack of a widely embraced private-sector preparedness standard was a principal contributing factor to this lack of preparedness.

We responded by asking the American National Standards Institute (ANSI) to develop a consensus on a "National Standard for Preparedness" for the private sector. ANSI convened safety, security, and business continuity experts from a wide range of industries and associations, as well as from federal, state, and local government stakeholders, to consider the need for standards for private sector emergency preparedness and business continuity.

The result of these sessions was ANSI's recommendation that the Commission endorse a voluntary National Preparedness Standard. Based on the existing American National Standard on Disaster/Emergency Management and Business Continuity Programs (NFPA 1600), the proposed National Preparedness Standard establishes a common set of criteria and terminology for preparedness, disaster management, emergency management, and business continuity programs. The experience of the private sector in the World Trade Center emergency demonstrated the need for these standards.

Recommendation: We endorse the American National Standards Institute's recommended standard for private preparedness. We were encouraged by Secretary Tom Ridge's praise of the standard, and urge the Department of Homeland Security to promote its adoption. We also encourage the insurance and credit-rating industries to look closely at a company's compliance with the ANSI standard in assessing its insurability and creditworthiness. We believe that compliance with the standard should define the standard of care owed by a company to its employees and the public for legal purposes. Private-sector preparedness is not a luxury; it is a cost of doing business in the post-9/11 world. It is ignored at a tremendous potential cost in lives, money, and national security.

CHAPTER THIRTEEN

How to Do It? A Different Way of Organizing the Government

As presently configured, the national security institutions of the U.S. government are still the institutions constructed to win the Cold War. The United States confronts a very different world today. Instead of facing a few very dangerous adversaries, the United States confronts a number of less visible challenges that surpass the boundaries of traditional nation-states and call for quick, imaginative, and agile responses.

The men and women of the World War II generation rose to the challenges of the 1940s and 1950s. They restructured the government so that it could protect the country. That is now the job of the generation that experienced 9/11. Those attacks showed, emphatically, that ways of doing business rooted in a different era are just not good enough. Americans should not settle for incremental, ad hoc adjustments to a system designed generations ago for a world that no longer exists.

We recommend significant changes in the organization of the government. We know that the quality of the people is more important than the quality of the wiring diagrams. Some of the saddest aspects of the 9/11 story are the outstanding efforts of so many individual officials straining, often without success, against the boundaries of the possible. Good people can overcome bad structures. They should not have to.

The United States has the resources and the people. The government should combine them more effectively, achieving unity of effort. We offer five major recommendations to do that:

- unifying strategic intelligence and operational planning against Islamist terrorists across the foreign-domestic divide with a National Counterterrorism Center;
- unifying the intelligence community with a new National Intelligence Director;
- unifying the many participants in the counterterrorism effort and their knowledge in a network-based information-sharing system that transcends traditional governmental boundaries;
- unifying and strengthening congressional oversight to improve quality and accountability; and
- strengthening the FBI and homeland defenders.

13.1 UNITY OF EFFORT ACROSS THE FOREIGN-DOMESTIC DIVIDE

Joint Action

Much of the public commentary about the 9/11 attacks has dealt with "lost opportunities," some of which we reviewed in chapter 11. These are often characterized as problems of "watchlisting," of "information sharing," or of "connecting the dots." In chapter 11 we explained that these labels are too narrow. They describe the symptoms, not the disease.

In each of our examples, no one was firmly in charge of managing the case and able to draw relevant intelligence from anywhere in the government, assign responsibilities across the agencies (foreign or domestic), track progress, and quickly bring obstacles up to the level where they could be resolved. Responsibility and accountability were diffuse.

The agencies cooperated, some of the time. But even such cooperation as there was is not the same thing as joint action. When agencies cooperate, one defines the problem and seeks help with it. When they act jointly, the problem and options for action are defined differently from the start. Individuals from different backgrounds come together in analyzing a case and planning how to manage it.

In our hearings we regularly asked witnesses: Who is the

quarterback? The other players are in their positions, doing their jobs. But who is calling the play that assigns roles to help them execute as a team?

Since 9/11, those issues have not been resolved. In some ways joint work has gotten better, and in some ways worse. The effort of fighting terrorism has flooded over many of the usual agency boundaries because of its sheer quantity and energy. Attitudes have changed. Officials are keenly conscious of trying to avoid the mistakes of 9/11. They try to share information. They circulate—even to the President— practically every reported threat, however dubious.

Partly because of all this effort, the challenge of coordinating it has multiplied. Before 9/11, the CIA was plainly the lead agency confronting al Qaeda. The FBI played a very secondary role. The engagement of the departments of Defense and State was more episodic.

- Today the CIA is still central. But the FBI is much more active, along with other parts of the Justice Department.
- The Defense Department effort is now enormous. Three of its unified commands, each headed by a four-star general, have counterterrorism as a primary mission: Special Operations Command, Central Command (both headquartered in Florida), and Northern Command (headquartered in Colorado).
- A new Department of Homeland Security combines formidable resources in border and transportation security, along with analysis of domestic vulnerability and other tasks.
- The State Department has the lead on many of the foreign policy tasks we described in chapter 12.
- At the White House, the National Security Council (NSC) now is joined by a parallel presidential advisory structure, the Homeland Security Council.

So far we have mentioned two reasons for joint action—the virtue of joint planning and the advantage of having someone in charge to ensure a unified effort. There is a third: the simple shortage of experts with sufficient skills. The limited pool of critical experts—for example, skilled counterterrorism analysts and linguists—is being depleted. Expanding these capabilities will require not just money, but time.

Primary responsibility for terrorism analysis has been assigned to the Terrorist Threat Integration Center (TTIC), created in 2003, based at the CIA headquarters but staffed with representatives of many agencies, reporting directly to the Director of Central Intelligence. Yet the CIA houses another intelligence "fusion" center: the Counterterrorist Center that played such a key role before 9/11. A third major analytic unit is at Defense, in the Defense Intelligence Agency. A fourth, concentrating more on homeland vulnerabilities, is at the Department of Homeland Security. The FBI is in the process of building the analytic capability it has long lacked, and it also has the Terrorist Screening Center.[1]

The U.S. government cannot afford so much duplication of effort. There are not enough experienced experts to go around. The duplication also places extra demands on already hard-pressed single-source national technical intelligence collectors like the National Security Agency.

Combining Joint Intelligence and Joint Action

A "smart" government would *integrate* all sources of information to see the enemy as a whole. Integrated all-source analysis should also inform and shape strategies to collect more intelligence. Yet the Terrorist Threat Integration Center, while it has primary responsibility for terrorism analysis, is formally proscribed from having any oversight or operational authority and is not part of any operational entity, other than reporting to the director of central intelligence.[2]

The government now tries to handle the problem of joint management, informed by analysis of intelligence from all sources, in two ways.

- First, agencies with lead responsibility for certain problems have constructed their own interagency entities and task forces in order to get cooperation. The Counterterrorist Center at CIA, for example, recruits liaison officers from throughout the intelligence community. The military's Central Command has its own interagency center, recruiting liaison officers from all the agencies from which it might need help. The FBI has Joint Terrorism Task Forces in 84 locations to coordinate the activities of other agencies when action may be required.

- Second, the problem of joint operational planning is often passed to the White House, where the NSC staff tries to play this role. The national security staff at the White House (both NSC and new Homeland Security Council staff) has already become 50 percent larger since 9/11. But our impression, after talking to serving officials, is that even this enlarged staff is consumed by meetings on day-to-day issues, sifting each day's threat information and trying to coordinate everyday operations.

Even as it crowds into every square inch of available office space, the NSC staff is still not sized or funded to be an executive agency. In chapter 3 we described some of the problems that arose in the 1980s when a White House staff, constitutionally insulated from the usual mechanisms of oversight, became involved in direct operations. During the 1990s Richard Clarke occasionally tried to exercise such authority, sometimes successfully, but often causing friction.

Yet a subtler and more serious danger is that as the NSC staff is consumed by these day-to-day tasks, it has less capacity to find the time and detachment needed to advise a president on larger policy issues. That means less time to work on major new initiatives, help with legislative management to steer needed bills through Congress, and track the design and implementation of the strategic plans for regions, countries, and issues that we discuss in chapter 12.

Much of the job of operational coordination remains with the agencies, especially the CIA. There DCI Tenet and his chief aides ran interagency meetings nearly every day to coordinate much of the government's day-to-day work. The DCI insisted he did not make policy and only oversaw its implementation. In the struggle against terrorism these distinctions seem increasingly artificial. Also, as the DCI becomes a lead coordinator of the government's operations, it becomes harder to play all the position's other roles, including that of analyst in chief.

The problem is nearly intractable because of the way the government is currently structured. Lines of operational authority run to the expanding executive departments, and they are guarded for understandable reasons: the DCI commands the CIA's personnel overseas; the secretary of defense will not yield to others in conveying commands to military forces; the Justice Department will not give up the responsibility of deciding whether to seek arrest warrants. But the result is that each agency or department needs its own intelligence apparatus to support the performance of its duties. It is hard to "break down stovepipes" when there are so many stoves that are legally and politically entitled to have cast-iron pipes of their own.

Recalling the Goldwater-Nichols legislation of 1986, Secretary Rumsfeld reminded us that to achieve better joint capability, each of the armed services had to "give up some of their turf and authorities and prerogatives." Today, he said, the executive branch is "stove-piped much like the four services were nearly 20 years ago." He wondered if it might be appropriate to ask agencies to "give up some of their existing turf and authority in exchange for a stronger, faster, more efficient government wide joint effort."[3] Privately, other key officials have made the same point to us.

We therefore propose a new institution: a civilian-led unified joint command for counterterrorism. It should combine strategic intelligence and joint operational planning.

In the Pentagon's Joint Staff, which serves the chairman of the joint Chiefs of Staff, intelligence is handled by the J-2 directorate, operational planning by J-3, and overall policy by J-5. Our concept combines the J-2 and J-3 functions (intelligence and operational planning) in one agency, keeping overall policy coordination where it belongs, in the National Security Council.

Recommendation: We recommend the establishment of a National Counterterrorism Center (NCTC), built on the foundation of the existing Terrorist Threat Integration Center (TTIC). Breaking the older mold of national government organization, this NCTC should be a center for joint operational planning *and* joint intelligence, staffed by personnel from the various agencies. The head of the NCTC should have authority to evaluate the performance of the people assigned to the Center.

- Such a joint center should be developed in the same spirit that guided the military's creation of unified joint commands, or the shaping of earlier national agencies like the National Reconnaissance Office, which was formed to organize the work of the CIA and several defense agencies in space.

NCTC—Intelligence. The NCTC should lead strategic analysis, pooling all-source intelligence, foreign and domestic, about transnational terrorist organizations with global reach. It should develop *net* assessments (comparing enemy capabilities and intentions against U.S. defenses and countermeasures). It should also provide warning. It should do this work by drawing on the efforts of the CIA, FBI, Homeland Security, and other departments and agencies. It should task collection requirements both inside and outside the United States.

- The intelligence function (J-2) should build on the existing TTIC structure and remain distinct, as a national intelligence center, within the NCTC. As the government's principal knowledge bank on Islamist terrorism, with the main responsibility for strategic analysis and net assessment, it should absorb a significant portion of the analytical talent now residing in the CIA's Counterterrorist Center and the DIA's Joint Intelligence Task Force—Combatting Terrorism (JITF-CT).

NCTC—Operations. The NCTC should perform joint planning. The plans would assign operational responsibilities to lead agencies, such as State, the CIA, the FBI, Defense and its combatant commands, Homeland Security, and other agencies. The NCTC should *not* direct the actual execution of these operations, leaving that job to the agencies. The NCTC would then track implementation; it would look across the foreign-domestic divide and across agency boundaries, updating plans to follow through on cases.[4]

- The joint operational planning function (J-3) will be new to the TTIC structure. The NCTC can draw on analogous work now being done in the CIA and every other involved department of the government, as well as reaching out to knowledgeable officials in state and local agencies throughout the United States.
- The NCTC should *not* be a policy making body. Its operations and planning should follow the policy direction of the president and the National Security Council.

NCTC—Authorities. The head of the NCTC should be appointed by the president, and should be equivalent in rank to a deputy head of a cabinet department. The head of the NCTC would report to the national intelligence director, an office whose creation we recommend below, placed in the Executive Office of the President. The head of the NCTC would thus also report indirectly to the president. This official's nomination should be confirmed by the Senate and he or she should testify to the Congress, as is the case now with other statutory presidential offices, like the U.S. trade representative.

- To avoid the fate of other entities with great nominal authority and little real power, the head of the NCTC must have the right to concur in the choices of personnel to lead the operating entities of the departments and agencies focused on counterterrorism, specifically including the head of the Counterterrorist Center, the head of the FBI's Counterterrorism Division, the commanders of the Defense Department's Special Operations Command and Northern Command, and the State Department's coordinator for counterterrorism.[5] The head of the NCTC should also work with the director of the Office of Management and Budget in developing the president's counterterrorism budget.

Consider this hypothetical case. The NSA discovers that a suspected terrorist is traveling to Bangkok and Kuala Lumpur. The NCTC should draw on joint intelligence resources, including its own NSA counterterrorism experts, to analyze the identities and possible destinations of these individuals. Informed by this analysis, the NCTC would then organize and plan the management of the case, drawing on the talents and differing kinds of experience among the several agency representatives assigned to it—assigning tasks to the CIA overseas, to Homeland Security watching entry points into the United States, and to the FBI. If military assistance might be needed, the Special Operations Command could be asked to develop an appropriate concept for such an operation. The NCTC would be accountable for tracking the progress of the case, ensuring that the plan evolved with it, and integrating the information into a warning. The NCTC would be responsible for being sure that intelligence gathered from the activities in the field became part of the government's institutional memory about Islamist terrorist personalities, organizations, and possible means of attack.

In each case the involved agency would make its own senior managers aware of what it was being asked to do. If those agency heads objected, and the issue could not easily be resolved, then the disagreement about roles and missions could be brought before the National Security Council and the president.

- There are precedents for surrendering authority for joint planning while preserving an agency's operational control. In the international context, NATO commanders may get line authority over forces assigned by other nations. In U.S. unified commands, commanders plan operations that may involve units belonging to one of the services. In each case, procedures are worked out, formal and informal, to define the limits of the joint commander's authority.

The most serious disadvantage of the NCTC is the reverse of its greatest virtue. The struggle against Islamist terrorism is so important that any clear-cut centralization of authority to manage and be accountable for it may concentrate too much power in one place. The proposed NCTC would be given the authority of planning the activities of other agencies. Law or executive order must define the scope of such line authority.

The NCTC would not eliminate interagency policy disputes. These would still go to the National Security Council. To improve coordination at the White House, we believe the existing Homeland Security Council should soon be merged into a single National Security Council. The creation of the NCTC should help the NSC staff concentrate on its core duties of assisting the president and supporting interdepartmental policymaking.

We recognize that this is a new and difficult idea precisely because the authorities we recommend for the NCTC really would, as Secretary Rumsfeld foresaw, ask strong agencies to "give up some of their turf and authority in exchange for a stronger, faster, more efficient government wide joint effort." Countering transnational Islamist terrorism will test whether the U.S. government can fashion more flexible models of management needed to deal with the twenty-first-century world.

An argument against change is that the nation is at war, and cannot afford to recognize in midstream. But some of the main innovations of the 1940s and 1950s, including the creation of the Joint Chiefs of Staff and even the construction of the Pentagon itself, were undertaken in the midst of war. Surely the country cannot wait until the struggle against Islamist terrorism is over.

"Surprise, when it happens to a government, is likely to be a complicated, diffuse, bureaucratic thing. It includes neglect of responsibility, but also responsibility so poorly defined or so ambiguously delegated that action gets lost."[6] That comment was made more than 40 years ago, about Pearl Harbor. We hope another commission, writing in the future about another attack, does not again find this quotation to be so apt.

13.2 UNITY OF EFFORT IN THE INTELLIGENCE COMMUNITY

In our first section, we concentrated on counterterrorism, discussing how to combine the analysis of information from all sources of intelligence with the joint planning of operations that draw on that analysis. In this section, we step back from looking just at the counterterrorism problem. We reflect on whether the government is organized adequately to direct resources and build the intelligence capabilities it will need not just for countering terrorism, but for the broader range of national security challenges in the decades ahead.

The Need for a Change
During the Cold War, intelligence agencies did not depend on seamless integration to track and count the thousands of military targets—such as tanks and missiles—fielded by the Soviet Union and other adversary states. Each agency concentrated on its specialized mission, acquiring its own information and then sharing it via formal, finished reports. The Department of Defense had given birth to and dominated the main agencies for technical collection of intelligence. Resources were shifted at an incremental pace, coping with challenges that arose over years, even decades.

We summarized the resulting organization of the intelligence community in chapter 3. It is outlined below.

Members of the U.S. Intelligence Community

Office of the Director of Central Intelligence, which includes the Office of the Deputy Director of Central Intelligence for Community Management, the Community Management Staff, the Terrorism Threat Integration Center, the National Intelligence Council, and other community offices

The Central Intelligence Agency (CIA), which performs human source collection, all-source analysis, and advanced science and technology

National intelligence agencies:
- National Security Agency (NSA), which performs signals collection and analysis
- National Geospatial-Intelligence Agency (NGA), which performs imagery collection and analysis
- National Reconnaissance Office (NRO), which develops, acquires, and launches space systems for intelligence collection
- Other national reconnaissance programs

Departmental intelligence agencies:
- Defense Intelligence Agency (DIA) of the Department of Defense
- Intelligence entities of the Army, Navy, Air Force, and Marines
- Bureau of Intelligence and Research (INR) of the Department of State
- Office of Terrorism and Finance Intelligence of the Department of Treasury
- Office of Intelligence and the Counterterrorism and Counterintelligence Divisions of the Federal Bureau of Investigation of the Department of Justice
- Office of Intelligence of the Department of Energy
- Directorate of Information Analysis and Infrastructure Protection (IAIP) and Directorate of Coast Guard Intelligence of the Department of Homeland Security

---

The need to restructure the intelligence community grows out of six problems that have become apparent before and after 9/11:

- *Structural barriers to performing joint intelligence work.* National intelligence is still organized around the collection disciplines of the home agencies, not the joint mission. The importance of integrated, all-source analysis cannot be overstated. Without it, it is not possible to "connect the dots." No one component holds all the relevant information.

  By contrast, in organizing national defense, the Goldwater-Nichols legislation of 1986 created joint commands for operations in the field, the Unified Command Plan. The services—the Army, Navy, Air Force, and Marine Corps—organize, train, and equip their people and units to perform their missions. Then they assign personnel and units to the joint combatant commander, like the commanding general of the Central Command (CENTCOM). The Goldwater-Nichols Act required officers to serve tours outside their service in order to win promotion. The culture of the Defense Department was transformed, its collective mind-set moved from service-specific to "joint," and its operations became more integrated.[7]

- *Lack of common standards and practices across the foreign-domestic divide.* The leadership of the intelligence community should be able to pool information gathered overseas with information gathered in the United States, holding the work—wherever it is done—to a common standard of quality in how it is collected, processed (e.g., translated), reported, shared, and analyzed. A common set of personnel standards for intelligence can create a group of professionals better able to operate in joint activities, transcending their own service-specific mind-sets.

- *Divided management of national intelligence capabilities.* While the CIA was once "central" to our national intelligence capabilities, following the end of the Cold War it has been less able to influence the use of the nation's imagery and signals intelligence capabilities in three national agencies housed within the Department of Defense: the National Security Agency, the National Geospatial-Intelligence Agency, and the National Reconnaissance Office. One of the lessons learned from the 1991 Gulf War was the value of national intelligence systems (satellites in particular) in precision warfare. Since that war, the department has appropriately drawn these agencies into its transformation of the military. Helping to orchestrate this transformation is the under secretary of defense for intelligence, a position established by Congress after 9/11. An unintended consequence of these developments has been the far greater demand made by Defense on technical systems, leaving the DCI less able to influence how these technical resources are allocated and used.

- *Weak capacity to set priorities and move resources.* The agencies are mainly organized around what they collect or the way they collect it. But the priorities for collection are national. As the DCI makes hard choices about moving resources, he or she must have the power to reach across agencies and reallocate effort.

- *Too many jobs.* The DCI now has at least three jobs. He is expected to run a particular agency, the CIA. He is expected to manage the loose confederation of agencies that is the intelligence community. He is expected to be the analyst in chief for the government, sifting evidence and directly briefing the President as his principal intelligence adviser. No recent DCI has been able to do all three effectively. Usually what loses out is management of the intelligence community, a difficult task even in the best case because the DCI's current authorities are weak. With so much to do, the DCI often has not used even the authority he has.

- *Too complex and secret.* Over the decades, the agencies and the rules surrounding the intelligence community

have accumulated to a depth that practically defies public comprehension. There are now 15 agencies or parts
of agencies in the intelligence community. The community and the DCI's authorities have become arcane matters, understood only by initiates after long study. Even
the most basic information about how much money is
actually allocated to or within the intelligence community and most of its key components is shrouded from
public view.

The current DCI is responsible for community performance
but lacks the three authorities critical for any agency head or
chief executive officer: (1) control over purse strings, (2) the
ability to hire or fire senior managers, and (3) the ability
to set standards for the information infrastructure and personnel.[8]

The only budget power of the DCI over agencies other
than the CIA lies in coordinating the budget requests of the
various intelligence agencies into a single program for submission to Congress. The overall funding request of the 15
intelligence entities in this program is then presented to the
president and Congress in 15 separate volumes.

When Congress passes an appropriations bill to allocate
money to intelligence agencies, most of their funding is hidden in the Defense Department in order to keep intelligence spending secret. Therefore, although the House and
Senate Intelligence committees are the authorizing committees for funding of the intelligence community, the final budget review is handled in the Defense Subcommittee
of the Appropriations committees. Those committees have
no subcommittees just for intelligence, and only a few members and staff review the requests.

The appropriations for the CIA and the national intelligence agencies—NSA, NGA, and NRO—are then given
to the secretary of defense. The secretary transfers the
CIA's money to the DCI but disburses the national agencies' money directly. Money for the FBI's national security components falls within the appropriations for

Commerce, Justice, and State and goes to the attorney general.[9]

In addition, the DCI lacks hire-and-fire authority over most of the intelligence community's senior managers. For the national intelligence agencies housed in the Defense Department, the secretary of defense must seek the DCI's concurrence regarding the nomination of these directors, who are presidentially appointed. But the secretary may submit recommendations to the president without receiving this concurrence. The DCI cannot fire these officials. The DCI has even less influence over the head of the FBI's national security component, who is appointed by the attorney general in consultation with the DCI.[10]

Combining Joint Work with Stronger Management

We have received recommendations on the topic of intelligence reform from many sources. Other commissions have been over this same ground. Thoughtful bills have been introduced, most recently a bill by the chairman of the House Intelligence Committee Porter Goss (R-Fla.), and another by the ranking minority member, Jane Harman (D-Calif.). In the Senate, Senators Bob Graham (D-Fla.) and Dianne Feinstein (D-Calif.) have introduced reform proposals as well. Past efforts have foundered, because the president did not support them; because the DCI, the secretary of defense, or both opposed them; and because some proposals lacked merit. We have tried to take stock of these experiences, and borrow from strong elements in many of the ideas that have already been developed by others.

Recommendation: The current position of Director of Central Intelligence should be replaced by a National Intelligence Director with two main areas of responsibility: (1) to oversee national intelligence centers on specific subjects of interest across the U.S. government and (2) to manage the national intelligence program and oversee the agencies that contribute to it.

First, the National Intelligence Director should oversee *national intelligence centers* to provide all-source analysis and plan intelligence operations for the whole government on major problems.

- One such problem is counterterrorism. In this case, we believe that the center should be the intelligence entity (formerly TTIC) inside the National Counterterrorism Center we have proposed. It would sit there alongside the operations management unit we described earlier, with both making up the NCTC, in the Executive Office of the President. Other national intelligence centers—for instance, on counterproliferation, crime and narcotics, and China—would be housed in whatever department or agency is best suited for them.
- The National Intelligence Director would retain the present DCI's role as the principal intelligence adviser to the president. We hope the president will come to look directly to the directors of the national intelligence centers to provide all-source analysis in their areas of responsibility, balancing the advice of these intelligence chiefs against the contrasting viewpoints that may be offered by department heads at State, Defense, Homeland Security, Justice, and other agencies.

Second, the National Intelligence Director should manage the national intelligence program and oversee the component agencies of the intelligence community. (See diagram.)[11]

- The National Intelligence Director would submit a unified budget for national intelligence that reflects priorities chosen by the National Security Council, an appropriate balance among the varieties of technical and human intelligence collection, and analysis. He or she would receive an appropriation for national intelligence and apportion the funds to the appropriate agencies, in line with that budget, and with authority to reprogram funds among the national intelligence agencies to meet any new priority (as counterterrorism was in the 1990s). The National Intelligence Director should approve and submit nominations to the president of the individuals who would lead the CIA, DIA, FBI Intelligence Office, NSA, NGA, NRO, Information Analysis and Infrastructure Protection Directorate of the Department of Homeland Security, and other national intelligence capabilities.[12]

- The National Intelligence Director would manage this national effort with the help of three deputies, each of whom would also hold a key position in one of the component agencies.[13]
- foreign intelligence (the head of the CIA)
- defense intelligence (the under secretary of defense for intelligence)[14]
- homeland intelligence (the FBI's executive assistant director for intelligence or the under secretary of homeland security for information analysis and infrastructure protection)

Other agencies in the intelligence community would coordinate their work within each of these three areas, largely staying housed in the same departments or agencies that support them now.

Returning to the analogy of the Defense Department's organization, these three deputies—like the leaders of the Army, Navy, Air Force, or Marines—would have the job of acquiring the systems, training the people, and executing the operations planned by the national intelligence centers.

And, just as the combatant commanders also report to the secretary of defense, the directors of the national intelligence centers—e.g., for counterproliferation, crime and narcotics, and the rest—also would report to the National Intelligence Director.

- The Defense Department's military intelligence programs—the joint military intelligence program (JMIP) and the tactical intelligence and related activities program (TIARA)—would remain part of that department's responsibility.

- The National Intelligence Director would set personnel policies to establish standards for education and training and facilitate assignments at the national intelligence centers and across agency lines. The National Intelligence Director also would set information sharing and information technology policies to maximize data sharing, as well as policies to protect the security of information.

- Too many agencies now have an opportunity to say no to change. The National Intelligence Director should participate in an NSC executive committee that can resolve differences in priorities among the agencies and bring the major disputes to the president for decision.

The National Intelligence Director should be located in the Executive Office of the President. This official, who would be confirmed by the Senate and would testify before Congress, would have a relatively small staff of several hundred people, taking the place of the existing community management offices housed at the CIA.

In managing the whole community, the National Intelligence Director is still providing a service function. With the partial exception of his or her responsibilities for overseeing the NCTC, the National Intelligence Director should support the consumers of national intelligence—the president and policymaking advisers such as the secretaries of state, defense, and homeland security and the attorney general.

We are wary of too easily equating government management problems with those of the private sector. But we have noticed that some very large private firms rely on a powerful CEO who has significant control over how money is spent and can hire or fire leaders of the major divisions, assisted by a relatively modest staff, while leaving responsibility for execution in the operating divisions.

There are disadvantages to separating the position of National Intelligence Director from the job of heading the CIA. For example, the National Intelligence Director will not head a major agency of his or her own and may have a

Unity of Effort in Managing Intelligence

Executive Office of the President

POTUS

National Intelligence Director

Staff

National Counterterrorism Center

National Intelligence Centers
(conduct "joint" collection and analysis – *illustrative*)

WMD Proliferation

Int'l Crime & Narcotics

China / East Asia

Middle East

Russia / Eurasia

Hire, Train, Acquire, Equip & Field
(agencies support / staff the Nat'l Intel Centers)

Deputy NID Foreign Intelligence (CIA Dir.)
- CIA
  - Clandestine Services
  - All-Source Analysis
  - Open Source Agency (new)

Deputy NID Defense Intelligence (USD Intelligence)
- DIA
- NSA
- NGA
- NRO
- Other

Deputy NID Homeland Intelligence (FBI/Intel Dir.)
- FBI
  - Intel & CT / CI
- DHS / IAIP
  - Other DHS (e.g., CBP, TSA, Nat'l Labs, Coast Guard, etc.)

weaker base of support. But we believe that these disadvantages are outweighed by several other considerations:

- The National Intelligence Director must be able to directly oversee intelligence collection inside the United States. Yet law and custom has counseled against giving such a plain domestic role to the head of the CIA.
- The CIA will be one among several claimants for funds in setting national priorities. The National Intelligence Director should not be both one of the advocates and the judge of them all.
- Covert operations tend to be highly tactical, requiring close attention. The National Intelligence Director should rely on the relevant joint mission center to oversee these details, helping to coordinate closely with the White House. The CIA will be able to concentrate on building the capabilities to carry out such operations and on providing the personnel who will be directing and executing such operations in the field.
- Rebuilding the analytic and human intelligence collection capabilities of the CIA should be a full-time effort, and the director of the CIA should focus on extending its comparative advantages.

Recommendation: The CIA Director should emphasize (a) rebuilding the CIA's analytic capabilities; (b) transforming the clandestine service by building its human intelligence capabilities; (c) developing a stronger language program, with high standards and sufficient financial incentives; (d) renewing emphasis on recruiting diversity among operations officers so they can blend more easily in foreign cities; (e) ensuring a seamless relationship between human source collection and signals collection at the operational level; and (f) stressing a better balance between unilateral and liaison operations.

The CIA should retain responsibility for the direction and execution of clandestine and covert operations, as assigned

by the relevant national intelligence center and authorized
by the National Intelligence Director and the president. This
would include propaganda, renditions, and nonmilitary disruption. We believe, however, that one important area of responsibility should change.

**Recommendation: Lead responsibility for directing and
executing paramilitary operations, whether clandestine
or covert, should shift to the Defense Department. There
it should be consolidated with the capabilities for training, direction, and execution of such operations already
being developed in the Special Operations Command.**

- Before 9/11, the CIA did not invest in developing a robust capability to conduct paramilitary operations with
  U.S. personnel. It relied on proxies instead, organized
  by CIA operatives without the requisite military training. The results were unsatisfactory.
- Whether the price is measured in either money or people, the United States cannot afford to build two separate capabilities for carrying out secret military
  operations, secretly operating standoff missiles, and secretly training foreign military or paramilitary forces.
  The United States should concentrate responsibility and
  necessary legal authorities in one entity.
- The post-9/11 Afghanistan precedent of using joint
  CIA-military teams for covert and clandestine operations was a good one. We believe this proposal to be
  consistent with it. Each agency would concentrate on its
  comparative advantages in building capabilities for
  joint missions. The operation itself would be planned in
  common.
- The CIA has a reputation for agility in operations. The
  military has a reputation for being methodical and cumbersome. We do not know if these stereotypes match
  current reality; they may also be one more symptom of
  the civil-military misunderstandings we described in
  chapter 4. It is a problem to be resolved in policy guid-

ance and agency management, not in the creation of redundant, overlapping capabilities and authorities in
such sensitive work. The CIA's experts should be integrated into the military's training, exercises, and planning. To quote a CIA official now serving in the field:
"One fight, one team."

**Recommendation: Finally, to combat the secrecy and
complexity we have described, the overall amounts of
money being appropriated for national intelligence and
to its component agencies should no longer be kept secret. Congress should pass a separate appropriations act
for intelligence, defending the broad allocation of how
these tens of billions of dollars have been assigned among
the varieties of intelligence work.**

The specifics of the intelligence appropriation would remain classified, as they are today. Opponents of declassifica-
tion argue that America's enemies could learn about
intelligence capabilities by tracking the top-line appropriations
figure. Yet the top-line figure by itself provides little insight
into U.S. intelligence sources and methods. The U.S. government readily provides copious information about spending on
its military forces, including military intelligence. The intelligence community should not be subject to that much disclosure. But when even aggregate categorical numbers remain
hidden, it is hard to judge priorities and foster accountability.

13.3 UNITY OF EFFORT IN SHARING INFORMATION

Information Sharing

We have already stressed the importance of intelligence
analysis that can draw on all relevant sources of information.
The biggest impediment to all-source analysis—to a greater
likelihood of connecting the dots—is the human or systemic
resistance to sharing information.

The U.S. government has access to a vast amount of information. When databases not usually thought of as "intelligence," such as customs or immigration information, are included, the storehouse is immense. But the U.S. government has a weak system for processing and using what it has. In interviews around the government, official after official urged us to call attention to frustrations with the unglamorous "back office" side of government operations.

In the 9/11 story, for example, we sometimes see examples of information that could be accessed—like the undistributed NSA information that would have helped identify Nawaf al Hazmi in January 2000. But someone had to ask for it. In that case, no one did. Or, as in the episodes we describe in chapter 8, the information is distributed, but in a compartmented channel. Or the information is available, and someone does ask, but it cannot be shared.

What all these stories have in common is a system that requires a demonstrated "need to know" before sharing. This approach assumes it is possible to know, in advance, who will need to use the information. Such a system implicitly assumes that the risk of inadvertent disclosure outweighs the benefits of wider sharing. Those Cold War assumptions are no longer appropriate. The culture of agencies feeling they own the information they gathered at taxpayer expense must be replaced by a culture in which the agencies instead feel they have a duty to the information—to repay the taxpayers' investment by making that information available.

Each intelligence agency has its own security practices, outgrowths of the Cold War. We certainly understand the reason for these practices. Counterintelligence concerns are still real, even if the old Soviet enemy has been replaced by other spies.

But the security concerns need to be weighed against the costs. Current security requirements nurture overclassification and excessive compartmentation of information among agencies. Each agency's incentive structure opposes sharing, with risks (criminal, civil, and internal administrative sanctions) but few rewards for sharing information. No one

has to pay the long-term costs of overclassifying information, though these costs—even in literal financial terms—are
substantial. There are no punishments for *not* sharing information. Agencies uphold a "need-to-know" culture of information protection rather than promoting a "need-to-share"
culture of integration.[15]

**Recommendation: Information procedures should pro-
vide incentives for sharing, to restore a better balance between security and shared knowledge.**

Intelligence gathered about transnational terrorism
should be processed, turned into reports, and distributed according to the same quality standards, whether it is collected
in Pakistan or in Texas.

The logical objection is that sources and methods may vary
greatly in different locations. We therefore propose that when a
report is first created, its data be separated from the sources
and methods by which they are obtained. The report should
begin with the information in its most shareable, but still meaningful, form. Therefore the maximum number of recipients
can access some form of that information. If knowledge of further details becomes important, any user can query further,
with access granted or denied according to the rules set for the
network—and with queries leaving an audit trail in order to determine who accessed the information. But the questions may
not come at all unless experts at the "edge" of the network can
readily discover the clues that prompt to them.[16]

We propose that information be shared horizontally,
across new networks that transcend individual agencies.

- The current system is structured on an old mainframe,
  or hub-and-spoke, concept. In this older approach, each
  agency has its own database. Agency users send information to the database and then can retrieve it from the
  database.
- A decentralized network model, the concept behind
  much of the information revolution, shares data horizon-

tally too. Agencies would still have their own databases, but those databases would be searchable across agency lines. In this system, secrets are protected through the design of the network and an "information rights management" approach that controls access to the data, not access to the whole network. An outstanding conceptual framework for this kind of "trusted information network" has been developed by a task force of leading professionals in national security, information technology, and law assembled by the Markle Foundation. Its report has been widely discussed throughout the U.S. government, but has not yet been converted into action.[17]

Recommendation: The president should lead the government-wide effort to bring the major national security institutions into the information revolution. He should coordinate the resolution of the legal, policy, and technical issues across agencies to create a "trusted information network."

- No one agency can do it alone. Well-meaning agency officials are under tremendous pressure to update their systems. Alone, they may only be able to modernize the stovepipes, not replace them.
- Only presidential leadership can develop government-wide concepts and standards. Currently, no one is doing this job. Backed by the Office of Management and Budget, a new National Intelligence Director empowered to set common standards for information use throughout the community, and a secretary of homeland security who helps extend the system to public agencies and relevant private-sector data-bases, a government-wide initiative can succeed.
- White House leadership is also needed because the policy and legal issues are harder than the technical ones. The necessary technology already exists. What does not are the rules for acquiring, accessing, sharing, and using the vast stores of public and private data that may be available. When information sharing works, it is a pow-

erful tool. Therefore the sharing and uses of information must be guided by a set of practical policy guidelines that simultaneously empower and constrain officials, telling them clearly what is and is not permitted.

"This is government acting in new ways, to face new threats," the most recent Markle report explains. "And while such change is necessary, it must be accomplished while engendering the people's trust that privacy and other civil liberties are being protected, that businesses are not being unduly burdened with requests for extraneous or useless information, that taxpayer money is being well spent, and that, ultimately, the network will be effective in protecting our security." The authors add: "Leadership is emerging from all levels of government and from many places in the private sector. What is needed now is a plan to accelerate these efforts, and public debate and consensus on the goals."[18]

13.4 UNITY OF EFFORT IN THE CONGRESS

Strengthen Congressional Oversight of Intelligence and Homeland Security

Of all our recommendations, strengthening congressional oversight may be among the most difficult and important. So long as oversight is governed by current congressional rules and resolutions, we believe the American people will not get the security they want and need. The United States needs a strong, stable, and capable congressional committee structure to give America's national intelligence agencies oversight, support, and leadership.

Few things are more difficult to change in Washington than congressional committee jurisdiction and prerogatives. To a member, these assignments are almost as important as the map of his or her congressional district. The American people may have to insist that these changes occur, or they may well not happen. Having interviewed numerous members of Congress from both parties, as well as congressional staff members, we found that dissatisfaction with congressional oversight remains widespread.

The future challenges of America's intelligence agencies are daunting. They include the need to develop leading-edge technologies that give our policy-makers and warfighters a decisive edge in any conflict where the interests of the United States are vital. Not only does good intelligence win wars, but the best intelligence enables us to prevent them from happening altogether.

Under the terms of existing rules and resolutions the House and Senate intelligence committees lack the power, influence, and sustained capability to meet this challenge. While few members of Congress have the broad knowledge of intelligence activities or the know-how about the technologies employed, all members need to feel assured that good oversight is happening. When their unfamiliarity with the subject is combined with the need to preserve security, a mandate emerges for substantial change.

Tinkering with the existing structure is not sufficient. Either Congress should create a joint committee for intelligence, using the Joint Atomic Energy Committee as its model, or it should create House and Senate committees with combined authorizing and appropriations powers.

Whichever of these two forms are chosen, the goal should be a structure—codified by resolution with powers expressly granted and carefully limited—allowing a relatively small group of members of Congress, given time and reason to master the subject and the agencies, to conduct oversight of the intelligence establishment and be clearly accountable for their work. The staff of this committee should be nonpartisan and work for the entire committee and not for individual members.

The other reforms we have suggested—for a National Counterterrorism Center and a National Intelligence Director—will not work if congressional oversight does not change too. Unity of effort in executive management can be lost if it is fractured by divided congressional oversight.

Recommendation: Congressional oversight for intelligence—and counterterrorism—is now dysfunctional. Congress should address this problem. We have considered various alternatives: A joint committee on the old model of the Joint Committee on Atomic Energy is one. A single committee in each house of Congress, combining authorizing and appropriating authorities, is another.

- The new committee or committees should conduct continuing studies of the activities of the intelligence agencies and report problems relating to the development and use of intelligence to all members of the House and Senate.
- We have already recommended that the total level of funding for intelligence be made public, and that the national intelligence program be appropriated to the National Intelligence Director, not to the secretary of defense.[19]
- We also recommend that the intelligence committee should have a subcommittee specifically dedicated to oversight, freed from the consuming responsibility of working on the budget.
- The resolution creating the new intelligence committee structure should grant subpoena authority to the committee or committees. The majority party's representation on this committee should never exceed the minority's representation by more than one.
- Four of the members appointed to this committee or committees should be a member who also serves on each of the following additional committees: Armed Services, Judiciary, Foreign Affairs, and the Defense Appropriations subcommittee. In this way the other major congressional interests can be brought together in the new committee's work.
- Members should serve indefinitely on the intelligence committees, without set terms, thereby letting them accumulate expertise.
- The committees should be smaller—perhaps seven or nine members in each house—so that each member

feels a greater sense of responsibility, and accountability, for the quality of the committee's work.

The leaders of the Department of Homeland Security now appear before 88 committees and subcommittees of Congress. One expert witness (not a member of the administration) told us that this is perhaps the single largest obstacle impeding the department's successful development. The one attempt to consolidate such committee authority, the House Select Committee on Homeland Security, may be eliminated. The Senate does not have even this.

Congress needs to establish for the Department of Homeland Security the kind of clear authority and responsibility that exist to enable the Justice Department to deal with crime and the Defense Department to deal with threats to national security. Through not more than one authorizing committee and one appropriating subcommittee in each house, Congress should be able to ask the secretary of homeland security whether he or she has the resources to provide reasonable security against major terrorist acts within the United States and to hold the secretary accountable for the department's performance.

Recommendation: Congress should create a single, principal point of oversight and review for homeland security. Congressional leaders are best able to judge what committee should have jurisdiction over this department and its duties. But we believe that Congress does have the obligation to choose one in the House and one in the Senate, and that this committee should be a permanent standing committee with a nonpartisan staff.

Improve the Transitions between Administrations

In chapter 6, we described the transition of 2000–2001. Beyond the policy issues we described, the new administration did not have its deputy cabinet officers in place until the spring of 2001, and the critical subcabinet officials were not confirmed until the summer—if then. In other words, the new administration—like others before it—did not have its team on the job until at least six months after it took office.

Recommendation: Since a catastrophic attack could occur with little or no notice, we should minimize as much as possible the disruption of national security policymaking during the change of administrations by accelerating the process for national security appointments. We think the process could be improved significantly so transitions can work more effectively and allow new officials to assume their new responsibilities as quickly as possible.

- Before the election, candidates should submit the names of selected members of their prospective transition teams to the FBI so that, if necessary, those team members can obtain security clearances immediately after the election is over.
- A president-elect should submit lists of possible candidates for national security positions to begin obtaining security clearances immediately after the election, so that their background investigations can be complete before January 20.
- A single federal agency should be responsible for providing and maintaining security clearances, ensuring uniform standards-including uniform security questionnaires and financial report requirements, and maintaining a single database. This agency can also be responsible for administering polygraph tests on behalf of organizations that require them.
- A president-elect should submit the nominations of the entire new national security team, through the level of under secretary of cabinet departments, not later than January 20. The Senate, in return, should adopt special rules requiring hearings and votes to confirm or reject national security nominees within 30 days of their submission. The Senate should not require confirmation of such executive appointees below Executive Level 3.

- The outgoing administration should provide the president-elect, as soon as possible after election day, with a classified, compartmented list that catalogues specific, operational threats to national security; major military or covert operations; and pending decisions on the possible use of force. Such a document could provide both notice and a checklist, inviting a president-elect to inquire and learn more.

13.5 ORGANIZING AMERICA'S DEFENSES IN THE UNITED STATES

The Future Role of the FBI

We have considered proposals for a new agency dedicated to intelligence collection in the United States. Some call this a proposal for an "American MI-5," although the analogy is weak—the actual British Security Service is a relatively small worldwide agency that combines duties assigned in the U.S. government to the Terrorist Threat Integration Center, the CIA, the FBI, and the Department of Homeland Security.

The concern about the FBI is that it has long favored its criminal justice mission over its national security mission. Part of the reason for this is the demand around the country for FBI help on criminal matters. The FBI was criticized, rightly, for the overzealous domestic intelligence investigations disclosed during the 1970s. The pendulum swung away from those types of investigations during the 1980s and 1990s, though the FBI maintained an active counterintelligence function and was the lead agency for the investigation of foreign terrorist groups operating inside the United States.

We do not recommend the creation of a new domestic intelligence agency. It is not needed if our other recommendations are adopted—to establish a strong national intelligence center, part of the NCTC, that will oversee counterterrorism intelligence work, foreign and domestic, and to create a National Intelligence Director who can set and enforce standards for the collection, processing, and reporting of information.

Under the structures we recommend, the FBI's role is focused, but still vital. The FBI does need to be able to direct its thousands of agents and other employees to collect intelligence in America's cities and towns—interviewing informants, conducting surveillance and searches, tracking individuals, working collaboratively with local authorities, and doing so with meticulous attention to detail and compliance with the law. The FBI's job in the streets of the United States would thus be a domestic equivalent, operating under the U.S. Constitution and quite different laws and rules, to the job of the CIA's operations officers abroad.

Creating a new domestic intelligence agency has other drawbacks.

- The FBI is accustomed to carrying out sensitive intelligence collection operations in compliance with the law. If a new domestic intelligence agency were outside of the Department of Justice, the process of legal oversight—never easy—could become even more difficult. Abuses of civil liberties could create a backlash that would impair the collection of needed intelligence.
- Creating a new domestic intelligence agency would divert attention of the officials most responsible for current counterterrorism efforts while the threat remains high. Putting a new player into the mix of federal agencies with counterterrorism responsibilities would exacerbate existing information-sharing problems.
- A new domestic intelligence agency would need to acquire assets and personnel. The FBI already has 28,000 employees; 56 field offices, 400 satellite offices, and 47 legal attaché offices; a laboratory, operations center, and training facility; an existing network of informants, cooperating defendants, and other sources; and relationships with state and local law enforcement, the CIA, and foreign intelligence and law enforcement agencies.

- Counterterrorism investigations in the United States very quickly become matters that involve violations of criminal law and possible law enforcement action. Because the FBI can have agents working criminal matters and agents working intelligence investigations concerning the same international terrorism target, the full range of investigative tools against a suspected terrorist can be considered within one agency. The removal of "the wall" that existed before 9/11 between intelligence and law enforcement has opened up new opportunities for cooperative action within the FBI.
- Counterterrorism investigations often overlap or are cued by other criminal investigations, such as money laundering or the smuggling of contraband. In the field, the close connection to criminal work has many benefits.

Our recommendation to leave counterterrorism intelligence collection in the United States with the FBI still depends on an assessment that the FBI—if it makes an all-out effort to institutionalize change—can do the job. As we mentioned in chapter 3, we have been impressed by the determination that agents display in tracking down details, patiently going the extra mile and working the extra month, to put facts in the place of speculation. In our report we have shown how agents in Phoenix, Minneapolis, and New York displayed initiative in pressing their investigations.

FBI agents and analysts in the field need to have sustained support and dedicated resources to become stronger intelligence officers. They need to be rewarded for acquiring informants and for gathering and disseminating information differently and more broadly than usual in a traditional criminal investigation. FBI employees need to report and analyze what they have learned in ways the Bureau has never done before.

Under Director Robert Mueller, the Bureau has made significant progress in improving its intelligence capabilities. It now has an Office of Intelligence, overseen by the top tier of FBI management. Field intelligence groups have been created in all field offices to put FBI priorities and the emphasis on intelligence into practice. Advances have been made in improving the Bureau's information technology systems and in increasing connectivity and information sharing with intelligence community agencies.

Director Mueller has also recognized that the FBI's reforms are far from complete. He has outlined a number of areas where added measures may be necessary. Specifically, he has recognized that the FBI needs to recruit from a broader pool of candidates, that agents and analysts working on national security matters require specialized training, and that agents should specialize within programs after obtaining a generalist foundation. The FBI is developing career tracks for agents to specialize in counterterrorism/counterintelligence, cyber crimes, criminal investigations, or intelligence. It is establishing a program for certifying agents as intelligence officers, a certification that will be a prerequisite for promotion to the senior ranks of the Bureau. New training programs have been instituted for intelligence-related subjects.

The Director of the FBI has proposed creating an Intelligence Directorate as a further refinement of the FBI intelligence program. This directorate would include units for intelligence planning and policy and for the direction of analysts and linguists.

We want to ensure that the Bureau's shift to a preventive counterterrorism posture is more fully institutionalized so that it survives beyond Director Mueller's tenure. We have found that in the past the Bureau has announced its willingness to reform and restructure itself to address transnational security threats, but has fallen short—failing to effect the necessary institutional and cultural changes organization-wide. We want to ensure that this does not happen again. Despite having found acceptance of the Director's clear message that counterterrorism is now the FBI's top priority, two years after 9/11 we also found gaps between some of the announced reforms and the reality in the field. We are concerned that management in the field offices still can allocate people and resources to local concerns that diverge from the national security mission. This system could revert to a focus on lower-priority criminal justice cases over national security requirements.

Recommendation: A specialized and integrated national security workforce should be established at the FBI consisting of agents, analysts, linguists, and surveillance specialists who are recruited, trained, rewarded, and retained to ensure the development of an institutional culture imbued with a deep expertise in intelligence and national security.

- The president, by executive order or directive, should direct the FBI to develop this intelligence cadre.
- Recognizing that cross-fertilization between the criminal justice and national security disciplines is vital to the success of both missions, all new agents should receive basic training in both areas. Furthermore, new agents should begin their careers with meaningful assignments in both areas.
- Agents and analysts should then specialize in one of these disciplines and have the option to work such matters for their entire career with the Bureau. Certain advanced training courses and assignments to other intelligence agencies should be required to advance within the national security discipline.
- In the interest of cross-fertilization, all senior FBI managers, including those working on law enforcement matters, should be certified intelligence officers.
- The FBI should fully implement a recruiting, hiring, and selection process for agents and analysts that enhances its ability to target and attract individuals with educational and professional backgrounds in intelligence, international relations, language, technology, and other relevant skills.
- The FBI should institute the integration of analysts, agents, linguists, and surveillance personnel in the field

so that a dedicated team approach is brought to bear on national security intelligence operations.

- Each field office should have an official at the field office's deputy level for national security matters. This individual would have management oversight and ensure that the national priorities are carried out in the field.

- The FBI should align its budget structure according to its four main programs—intelligence, counterterrorism and counterintelligence, criminal, and criminal justice services—to ensure better transparency on program costs, management of resources, and protection of the intelligence program.[20]

- The FBI should report regularly to Congress in its semiannual program reviews designed to identify whether each field office is appropriately addressing FBI and national program priorities.

- The FBI should report regularly to Congress in detail on the qualifications, status, and roles of analysts in the field and at headquarters. Congress should ensure that analysts are afforded training and career opportunities on a par with those offered analysts in other intelligence community agencies.

- The Congress should make sure funding is available to accelerate the expansion of secure facilities in FBI field offices so as to increase their ability to use secure email systems and classified intelligence product exchanges. The Congress should monitor whether the FBI's information-sharing principles are implemented in practice.

The FBI is just a small fraction of the national law enforcement community in the United States, a community comprised mainly of state and local agencies. The network designed for sharing information, and the work of the FBI through local Joint Terrorism Task Forces, should build a reciprocal relationship, in which state and local agents understand what information they are looking for and, in return, receive some of the information being developed about what is happening, or may happen, in their communities. In this relationship, the Department of Homeland Security also will play an important part.

The Homeland Security Act of 2002 gave the under secretary for information analysis and infrastructure protection broad responsibilities. In practice, this directorate has the job to map "terrorist threats to the homeland against our assessed vulnerabilities in order to drive our efforts to protect against terrorist threats."[21] These capabilities are still embryonic. The directorate has not yet developed the capacity to perform one of its assigned jobs, which is to assimilate and analyze information from Homeland Security's own component agencies, such as the Coast Guard, Secret Service, Transportation Security Administration, Immigration and Customs Enforcement, and Customs and Border Protection. The secretary of homeland security must ensure that these components work with the Information Analysis and Infrastructure Protection Directorate so that this office can perform its mission.[22]

Homeland Defense

At several points in our inquiry, we asked, "Who is responsible for defending us at home?" Our national defense at home is the responsibility, first, of the Department of Defense and, second, of the Department of Homeland Security. They must have clear delineations of responsibility and authority.

We found that NORAD, which had been given the responsibility for defending U.S. airspace, had construed that mission to focus on threats coming from outside America's borders. It did not adjust its focus even though the intelligence community had gathered intelligence on the possibility that terrorists might turn to hijacking and even use of planes as missiles. We have been assured that NORAD has now embraced the full mission. Northern Command has been established to assume responsibility for the defense of the domestic United States.

Recommendation: The Department of Defense and its oversight committees should regularly assess the ade-

quacy of Northern Command's strategies and planning to defend the United States against military threats to the homeland.

The Department of Homeland Security was established to consolidate all of the domestic agencies responsible for securing America's borders and national infrastructure, most of which is in private hands. It should identify those elements of our transportation, energy, communications, financial, and other institutions that need to be protected, develop plans to protect that infrastructure, and exercise the mechanisms to enhance preparedness. This means going well beyond the preexisting jobs of the agencies that have been brought together inside the department.

Recommendation: The Department of Homeland Security and its oversight committees should regularly assess the types of threats the country faces to determine (a) the adequacy of the government's plans—and the progress against those plans—to protect America's critical infrastructure and (b) the readiness of the government to respond to the threats that the United States might face.

We look forward to a national debate on the merits of what we have recommended, and we will participate vigorously in that debate.

Appendix A
Common Abbreviations

CAP	combat air patrol
CAPPS	Computer Assisted Passenger Prescreening System
CENTCOM	Central Command
CIA	Central Intelligence Agency
CONR	Continental U.S. NORAD Region
CSG	Counterterrorism Security Group
CTC	Counterterrorist Center
DIA	Defense Intelligence Agency
DCI	Director of Central Intelligence
ESU	Emergency Service Unit (NYPD)
FAA	Federal Aviation Administration
FBI	Federal Bureau of Investigation
FDNY	Fire Department of New York
FFTC	Florida Flight Training Center
FISA	Foreign Intelligence Surveillance Act
FISC	Foreign Intelligence Surveillance Court
INS	Immigration and Naturalization Service
ISID	Inter-Services Intelligence Directorate (Pakistan)
JCS	Joint Chiefs of Staff
JI	Jemaah Islamiah
JTTF	Joint Terrorism Task Force
KSM	Khalid Sheikh Mohammed
Legat	legal attaché

MAK	Mektab al Khidmat
MON	memorandum of notification
NEADS	Northeast Air Defense Sector
NCTC	National Counterterrorism Center
NGO	nongovernmental organization
NMCC	National Military Command Center
NORAD	North American Aerospace Defense Command
NTSB	National Transportation Safety Board
NSA	National Security Agency
NSC	National Security Council
NSPD	national security policy directive
NYPD	New York Police Department
OEM	Office of Emergency Management (New York City)
OFAC	Office of Foreign Assets Control
OIPR	Office of Intelligence Policy and Review
OMB	Office of Management and Budget
PAPD	Port Authority Police Department
PDD	presidential decision directive
PEOC	Presidential Emergency Operations Center
SEC	Securities and Exchange Commission
TSA	Transportation Security Administration
TTIC	Terrorist Threat Integration Center
UBL	Usama Bin Ladin
WMD	weapons of mass destruction
WTC	World Trade Center
WTO	World Trade Organization

Appendix B
Table of Names

U.S. OFFICIALS

Madeleine Albright	Secretary of State, 1997–2001
Charles Allen	Assistant Director of Central Intelligence for Collection, 1998–
Richard Armitage	Deputy Secretary of State, 2001–
Larry Arnold	Commander, First Air Force and Commander of the Continental U.S. North American Aerospace Defense Command (NORAD) Region, 1997–2002
John Ashcroft	Attorney General, 2001–
Monte Belger	Acting Deputy Administrator, Federal Aviation Administration 1997–2002
Samuel "Sandy" Berger	National Security Advisor, 1997–2001; Deputy National Security Advisor 1993–1997
J. Cofer Black	Director, DCI Counterterrorist Center, 1999–2002
Joshua Bolten	White House Deputy Chief of Staff, 2001–2003

Robert "Bear" Bryant	Deputy Director, Federal Bureau of Investigation, 1997–1999
George H. W. Bush	41st President of the United States, 1989–1993; Vice President, 1981–1989
George W. Bush	43rd President of the United States, 2001–
Andrew Card, Jr.	White House Chief of Staff, 2001–
Richard B. Cheney	Vice President of the United States, 2001–
Richard Clarke	National Counterterrorism Coordinator, NSC, 1997–2001
William J. Clinton	42nd President of the United States, 1993–2001
William Cohen	Secretary of Defense, 1997–2001
Roger Cressey	NSC counterterrorism official, 1999–2001
Ralph Eberhart	Commander in Chief, NORAD and U.S. Space Command, 2000–
Tommy Franks	Commander, U.S. Central Command (CENTCOM), 2001–2003
Louis Freeh	Director, Federal Bureau of Investigation, 1993–2001
Scott Fry	Director of Operations for the Joint Chiefs of Staff, 1998–2000
Jane Garvey	Administrator, Federal Aviation Administration, 1997–2002
Newt Gingrich	Speaker of the House, 1995–1999
Rudolph Giuliani	Mayor, City of New York, 1994–2001
John Gordon	Deputy Director of Central Intelligence, 1997–2000

Al Gore, Jr.	Vice President of the United States, 1993–2001
Scott Gration	Fry's Chief Information Operations Officer, 2000–2001
Stephen Hadley	Deputy National Security Advisor, 2001–
Dennis Hastert	Speaker of the House, 1999–
Karl Inderfurth	Assistant Secretary of State for South Asia, 1997–2001
Donald Kerrick	Deputy National Security Advisor, 2000–2001
Zalmay Khalilzad	NSC Senior Director for Near East and South Asia and Special Envoy to Afghanistan, 2001–2003
Anthony Lake	National Security Advisor, 1993–1997
Trent Lott	Senate Majority Leader, 1996–2001
Mary McCarthy	NSC senior director for intelligence, 1998–2001
John McLaughlin	Deputy Director of Central Intelligence, 2000–2004
William Milam	U.S. Ambassador to Pakistan, 1998–2001
Norman Mineta	Secretary of Transportation, 2001–
Robert Mueller	Director, Federal Bureau of Investigation, 2001–
Richard Myers	Chairman of the Joint Chiefs, September 2001–; Joint Chiefs Vice Chairman, 2000–2001
John O'Neill	FBI Special Agent in Charge for National Security, New York Field Office, 1997–2001; Chief of Security of the World Trade Center, killed on 9/11

Paul O'Neill	Secretary of the Treasury, 2001–2002
James Pavitt	Deputy Director of Operations, CIA, 1999–2004
Thomas Pickard	Acting Director, Federal Bureau of Investigation, June 25, 2001–September 4, 2001
Thomas Pickering	Under Secretary of State, 1997–2000
Colin Powell	Secretary of State, 2001–
Ronald Reagan	40th President of the United States, 1981–1989
Janet Reno	Attorney General, 1993–2001
Condoleezza Rice	National Security Advisor, 2001–
Bill Richardson	Ambassador to the United Nations, 1997–1998
Thomas Ridge	First Secretary of Homeland Security, 2003–; Homeland Security Advisor, 2001–2003
Bruce Riedel	Senior Director for Near East and South Asia, NSC, 1997–2001
Christina Rocca	Assistant Secretary of State for South Asia, 2001–
Michael Rolince	FBI Section Chief, International Terrorism Operations Section, 1998–2002
Donald Rumsfeld	Secretary of Defense, 2001–
Peter Schoomaker	Commander, Special Operations Command, 1997–2000
Gary Schroen	CIA Station Chief, Islamabad, 1996–1999
Michael Sheehan	Counterterrorism Coordinator, U.S. Department of State, 1998–2000
Hugh Shelton	Chairman of the Joint Chiefs of Staff, 1997–2001

Walter Slocombe	Under Secretary of Defense for Policy, 1994–2001
James Steinberg	Deputy National Security Advisor, 1996–2000
Strobe Talbott	Deputy Secretary of State, 1994–2001
George Tenet	Director of Central Intelligence, 1997–2004
Larry Thompson	Deputy Attorney General, 2001–2003
Dale Watson	Executive Assistant Director for Counterterrorism and Counterintelligence, FBI, 2001–2002
Paul Wolfowitz	Deputy Secretary of Defense, 2001–
Anthony Zinni	Commander, U.S. Central Command (CENTCOM), 1997–2000

OTHERS

Abdullah bin Abdul Aziz	Crown Prince and de facto regent of Saudi Arabia, 1995–
Mohdar Abdullah	Yemeni; student in San Diego who assisted two 9/11 hijackers
Sayf al Adl	Egyptian; high-ranking member of al Qaeda military committee
Mahmud Ahmed	Director General of Pakistan's Inter-Services Intelligence Directorate, 1999–2001
Mohammed Farrah Aidid	Somali warlord who challenged U.S. presence in Somalia in the early 1990s (deceased)
Ali Abdul Aziz Ali	(a.k.a. Ammar al Baluchi) Pakistani; KSM's nephew; financial and travel facilitator for 9/11 plot

Ahmad Khalil Ibrahim Samir al Ani	Iraqi intelligence officer who allegedly met with Atta in Prague, Czech Republic; currently in U.S. custody
Mohamed Atta	Egyptian; tactical leader of 9/11 plot; pilot/hijacker (AA 11) (deceased)
Mohammed Atef	(a.k.a. Abu Hafs al Masri) Egyptian; al Qaeda military commander (deceased)
Tawfiq bin Attash	(a.k.a. Khallad, Waleed bin Attash) Yemeni; senior al Qaeda operative connected to the U.S. embassy bombings, the USS *Cole* attack, and the 9/11 attacks; currently in U.S. custody
Anwar Aulaqi	U.S. citizen; Imam at Rabat mosque (San Diego, CA) and later at Dar al Hijra mosque (Falls Church, VA), who associated with two 9/11 hijackers
Abdullah Azzam	Palestinian; founder of the Maktab al Khidmat, which provided logistical support to mujahideen in Afghanistan (deceased)
Jamal al Badawi	Yemeni; co-conspirator arrested in Yemen for the USS *Cole* attack
Said Bahaji	German son of Moroccan immigrant; Hamburg cell associate
Saeed al Baluchi	Saudi; candidate 9/11 hijacker
Fayez Banihammad	Emirati; 9/11 hijacker (UA 175) (deceased)
Abu Ubaidah al Banshiri	Egyptian; al Qaeda military commander until 1996 (deceased)

Abu Bara al Yemeni	(a.k.a. Abu al Bara al Ta'izi, Suhail Shurabi, and Barakat) Yemeni; potential suicide bomber in original 9/11 plot
Ramzi Binalshibh	Yemeni; Hamburg cell member; coordinator for 9/11 plot; currently in U.S. custody
Omar Hassan Ahmed al Bashir	President of Sudan, 1989–
Abu Bakar Bashir	Indonesian; spiritual leader and founder of Jemaah Islamiya, al Qaeda–affiliated terrorist group in Southeast Asia
Omar al Bayoumi	Saudi; assisted two 9/11 hijackers in San Diego, CA
Khalil Deek	U.S. citizen; created electronic version of *Encyclopedia of Jihad*; believed to be involved in millennium plot to destroy tourist landmarks in Jordan
Caysan Bin Don	(a.k.a Isamu Dyson, a.k.a Clayton Morgan) U.S. citizen; met two 9/11 hijackers in Los Angeles and San Diego, CA
Zakariya Essabar	Moroccan; Hamburg cell associate
Jamal Ahmed Mohamed al Fadl	Sudanese; al Qaeda member who defected to the United States in 1996
Ahmed al Ghamdi	Saudi; 9/11 hijacker (UA 175) (deceased)
Ali Abd al Rahman al Faqasi al Ghamdi	(a.k.a. Abu Bakr al Azdi) Saudi; candidate 9/11 hijacker; currently in U.S. custody
Hamza al Ghamdi	Saudi; 9/11 hijacker (UA 175) (deceased)
Saeed al Ghamdi	Saudi; 9/11 hijacker (UA 93) (deceased)

Saeed ("Jihad") al Ghamdi	Saudi; candidate 9/11 hijacker
Hassan Ghul	Pakistani; al Qaeda facilitator; currently in U.S. custody
Abu Hafs al Masri	*see* Mohammed Atef
Abu Hafs al Mauritani	Mauritanian; senior al Qaeda theologian
Wadi al Hage	U.S. citizen; al Qaeda operative; Bin Ladin's personal assistant; convicted in embassy bombings trial
Mushabib al Hamlan	Saudi; candidate 9/11 hijacker
Hani Hanjour	Saudi; 9/11 pilot/hijacker (AA 77) (deceased)
Mustafa al Hawsawi	Saudi; al Qaeda media committee member; financial and travel facilitator for 9/11 plot
Nawaf al Hazmi	Saudi; 9/11 hijacker (AA 77) (deceased)
Salem al Hazmi	Saudi; 9/11 hijacker (AA 77) (deceased)
Ahmad al Haznawi	Saudi; 9/11 hijacker (UA 93) (deceased)
Gulbuddin Hekmatyar	Afghani; founder and leader of the Hizb-e-Islami, a Taliban opposition group; Prime Minister of Afghanistan, 1993–1994; 1996
Saddam Hussein	President of Iraq, 1979–2003
Zein al Abideen Mohamed Hussein	(a.k.a. Abu Zubaydah) Palestinian; al Qaeda associate; currently in U.S. custody
Abu Hajer al Iraqi	*see* Mamdouh Mahmud Salim
Riduan Isamuddin	(a.k.a. Hambali) Indonesian; operational leader of Jemaah Islamiya; currently in U.S. custody

Ziad Jarrah	Lebanese; 9/11 pilot/hijacker (UA 93) (deceased)
Abderraouf Jdey	(a.k.a. Faruq al Tunisi) Tunisian/Canadian; candidate 9/11 hijacker
Mohamed al Kahtani	Saudi; candidate 9/11 hijacker; currently in U.S. custody
Mir Amal Kansi	Pakistani; extremist who killed two CIA employees at CIA headquarters in Virginia in 1993 (executed)
Hamid Karzai	Interim Leader and later President of Afghanistan, Dec. 2001–
Younis Khalis	Afghani; leader of Hizbe-e-Islami; hosted UBL upon his return to Afghanistan in 1996
Khallad	*see* Tawfiq bin Attash
Wali Khan Amin Shah	(a.k.a. Osama Asmurai) Turkmen; early associate of Usama Bin Ladin; convicted in Manila air (Bojinka) plot
Ibn al Khattab	Saudi; mujahid leader in Chechnya
L'Houssaine Kherchtou	(a.k.a. Joe the Moroccan, Abu Talal) Moroccan; former al Qaeda member who broke with Bin Ladin and became a U.S. government informant
Usama Bin Ladin	(UBL) Saudi; head of al Qaeda
Ibn al Shaykh al Libi	Libyan; head of jihadist training camp in Afghanistan
Ahmed al Nami	Saudi; 9/11 hijacker (UA 93) (deceased)
Sheikh Saeed al Masri	Egyptian; head of al Qaeda finance committee
Ahmed Shah Massoud	Leader of Afghanistan's Northern Alliance, a Taliban

	opposition group (assassinated Sept. 9, 2001)
Khalid al Mihdhar	Saudi; 9/11 hijacker (AA 77) (deceased)
Khalid Sheikh Mohammed	(KSM) (a.k.a. Mukhtar) Pakistani; mastermind of 9/11 attacks; currently in U.S. custody
Majed Moqed	Saudi; 9/11 hijacker (AA 77) (deceased)
Mounir el Motassadeq	Moroccan; Hamburg cell associate
Zacarias Moussaoui	French; arrested in the U.S. in connection with the 9/11 attacks
Hosni Mubarak	President of Egypt, 1981–
Pervez Musharraf	Leader of Pakistan, 1999–
Abdelghani Mzoudi	Moroccan; Hamburg cell associate
Qutaybah al Najdi	Saudi; candidate 9/11 hijacker
Abd al Rahim al Nashiri	(a.k.a. Mullah Bilal) Saudi; mastermind of USS *Cole* attack; currently in U.S. custody
Mullah Mohammed Omar	Leader of Afghanistan's Taliban, which ruled most of the country from 1996 to 2001
Abdul Aziz al Omari	Saudi; 9/11 hijacker (AA 11) (deceased)
Muammar Qadhafi	Leader of Libya, 1970–
Fahd al Quso	Yemeni; al Qaeda co-conspirator arrested in Yemen for the USS *Cole* attack
Sayyid Qutb	Egyptian writer; member of Muslim Brotherhood (deceased)
Eyad al Rababah	Jordanian; Virginia resident who helped Hazmi and Hanjour
Abd al Rahim Ghulum Rabbani	(a.k.a. Abu Rahmah) Saudi; al Qaeda member who worked closely with KSM in Karachi

	and assisted many of the 9/11 hijackers
Sheikh Omar Abdel Rahman	(a.k.a. the Blind Sheikh) Egyptian cleric; convicted for crimes related to 1993 World Trade Center bombing and 1995 plots against other NY landmarks
Saud al Rashid	Saudi; candidate 9/11 hijacker
Ahmed Ressam	(a.k.a. Benni Antoine Noris) Algerian; convicted in millennium plot to bomb Los Angeles International Airport
Mamdouh Mahmud Salim	(a.k.a. Abu Hajer al Iraqi) Iraqi; chief procurement officer for al Qaeda in Sudan; arrested in connection with 1998 embassy bombings
Yazeed al Salmi	Saudi; briefly a housemate of a 9/11 hijacker in San Diego
Abdul Rasul Sayyaf	Afghani; head of the Hizbul-Ittihad El-Islami, and KSM's mentor
Aysel Senguen	German; fiancée of 9/11 hijacker Jarrah
Nawaz Sharif	Pakistani Prime Minister, 1990–1993, 1997–1999
Marwan al Shehhi	Emirati; 9/11 pilot/hijacker (UA 175) (deceased)
Mohand al Shehri	Saudi; 9/11 hijacker (UA 175) (deceased)
Wail al Shehri	Saudi; 9/11 hijacker (AA 11) (deceased)
Waleed al Shehri	Saudi; 9/11 hijacker (AA 11) (deceased)
Mohamedou Ould Slahi	(a.k.a. Abu Musab) Mauritanian; recruited 9/11 hijackers in Germany

Yazid Sufaat	Malaysian; member of Jemaah Islamiya
Satam al Suqami	Saudi; 9/11 hijacker (AA 11) (deceased)
Madani al Tayyib	Saudi; former head of al Qaeda finance committee
Zuhair al Thubaiti	Saudi; candidate 9/11 hijacker
Fahad al Thumairy	Saudi; Imam of King Fahd mosque in Los Angeles; accredited diplomat at Saudi Consulate in Los Angeles
Hassan al Turabi	Sudan's longtime hard-line ideological leader and Speaker of the country's National Assembly during the 1990s
Prince Turki bin Faisal	Saudi intelligence chief prior to 9/11
Ramzi Yousef	(a.k.a. Abdul Basit) Pakistani; convicted mastermind of and co-conspirator in 1993 WTC bombing and Manila air (Bojinka) plots
Khalid Saeed Ahmad al Zahrani	Saudi; candidate 9/11 hijacker
Mohammed Haydar Zammar	German citizen from Syria; jihadist; possible recruiter of Hamburg cell members
Ayman al Zawahiri	Egyptian; UBL's deputy and leader of Egyptian Islamic Jihad terrorist group
Hamdan Bin Zayid	Emirati; Minister of State for Foreign Affairs of the United Arab Emirates
Abu Zubaydah	*see* Zein al Abideen Mohamed Hussein

Appendix C
Commission Hearings

The Commission held 12 public hearings during the course of its investigation, convening for a total of 19 days and receiving testimony from 160 witnesses. The following is a list of hearings and witnesses in order of their appearance. All witnesses appearing during the 2004 calendar year testified under oath.

FIRST PUBLIC HEARING
Alexander Hamilton Customs House, New York, N.Y.
March 31–April 1, 2003

The Honorable George Pataki, Governor, State of New York
The Honorable Michael R. Bloomberg, Mayor, City of New York

The Experience of the Attack
Harry Waizer, survivor, Cantor Fitzgerald, LP
David Lim, Police Department, Port Authority of New York and New Jersey
Lee Ielpi, Fire Department of New York (retired)
Lieutenant Colonel Brian Birdwell, United States Army
Craig Sincock, United States Army (retired)

Representatives of the Victims
Stephen Push, Families of September 11
Mary Fetchet, Voices of September 11
Mindy Kleinberg, September 11 Advocates
Allison Vadhan, Families of Flight 93

The Attackers, Intelligence, and Counterterrorism Policy
Daniel Byman, Georgetown University
Abraham D. Sofaer, Hoover Institution
Brian Jenkins, RAND Corporation
Magnus Ranstorp, University of St. Andrews

Borders, Money, and Transportation Security
Glenn Fine, Inspector General, U.S. Department of Justice
Lee Wolosky, Boies, Schiller & Flexner LLP
Gerald Dillingham, Director, Civil Aviation Issues, General
   Accounting Office

Law Enforcement, Domestic Intelligence, and Homeland Security
Michael Wermuth, RAND Corporation
Steven Brill, Author, *After: How America Confronted the
   September 12 Era*
Zoë Baird, Markle Foundation
Randy Larsen, ANSER Institute for Homeland Security

Immediate Response to the Attacks
Shawn Kelley, Assistant Chief, Arlington County Fire
   Department
William Baker, American Society of Civil Engineers
Ken Holden, Commissioner, New York City Department of
   Design and Construction

SECOND PUBLIC HEARING
Congress and Civil Aviation Security
Hart Senate Office Building, Washington, D.C.
May 22–23, 2003

Congressional Oversight
Representative Nancy Pelosi (D-Calif.)
Senator John McCain (R-Az.)
Senator Joseph Lieberman (D-Conn.)

Intelligence Oversight and the Joint Inquiry
Senator Bob Graham (D-Fla.)
Senator Richard Shelby (R-Ala.)
Representative Porter Goss (R-Fla.)
Representative Jane Harman (D-Calif.)

Affected Constituencies
Senator Charles Schumer (D-N.Y.)
Senator Hillary Rodham Clinton (D-N.Y.)
Senator Jon Corzine (D-N.J.)
Senator Frank Lautenberg (D-N.J.)
Representative Jerrold Nadler (D-N.Y.)
Representative Christopher Shays (R-Conn.)

State of the System: Civil Aviation Security on September 11
Jane Garvey, former Administrator, Federal Aviation Administration
Kenneth Mead, Inspector General, Department of Transportation
James May, Air Transport Association of America
Bogdan Dzakovic, Civil Aviation Security Inspector, Transportation Security Agency

September 11, 2001: The Attacks and the Response

The Honorable Norman Mineta, Secretary of Transportation

Major General Craig McKinley, Commander, 1st Air Force and the Continental United States NORAD Region (CONR)

Lieutenant General Mike Canavan (retired), former Associate Administrator for Civil Aviation Security, Federal Aviation Administrator

Reforming Civil Aviation Security: Next Steps

Stephen McHale, Deputy Administrator, Transportation Security Agency

Major General O.K. Steele (retired), former Associate Administrator for Civil Aviation Security, Federal Aviation Administration

Mary Schiavo, former Inspector General, Department of Transportation

THIRD PUBLIC HEARING

Terrorism, al Qaeda, and the Muslim World
Russell Senate Office Building, Washington, D.C.
July 9, 2003

Al Qaeda

Rohan Gunaratna, Institute for Defence and Strategic Studies

Mamoun Fandy, United States Institute of Peace

Marc Sageman, University of Pennsylvania

States and Terrorism

Laurie Mylroie, American Enterprise Institute

Judith Yaphe, National Defense University

Murhaf Jouejati, Middle East Institute and George Washington University

Mark Gasiorowski, Louisiana State University

The Challenge within the Muslim World
Rachel Bronson, Council on Foreign Relations
Steven Emerson, The Investigative Project
Gilles Kepel, Institute of Political Studies, Paris
Dennis Ross, Washington Institute for Near East Policy

FOURTH PUBLIC HEARING
Intelligence and the War on Terrorism
Russell Senate Office Building, Washington, D.C.
October 14, 2003

Leadership of U.S. Intelligence
James R. Schlesinger, former Director of Central
    Intelligence and Secretary of Defense
John M. Deutch, former Director of Central Intelligence
    and Deputy Secretary of Defense

Intelligence and National Security Policy
James B. Steinberg, The Brookings Institution and former
    Deputy National Security Advisor

Warning of Transnational Threats
Richard Kerr, former Deputy Director of Central
    Intelligence
Mary O. McCarthy, former National Intelligence Officer
    for Warning, Central Intelligence Agency
John Gannon, Staff Director, House Select Committee on
    Homeland Security

FIFTH PUBLIC HEARING
Private/Public Sector Partnerships for
Emergency Preparedness
Drew University, Madison, N.J.
November 19, 2003

Highlights of New Jersey's Public/Private Sector Partnerships
The Honorable James E. McGreevey, Governor, State of
   New Jersey

The Challenge of Private Sector Preparedness
John Degnan, The Chubb Corporation

Skyscraper Safety Issues from 9/11 Family Members
Monica Gabrielle, Skyscraper Safety Campaign
Sally Regenhard, Skyscraper Safety Campaign

Public/Private Initiatives Since 9/11
Michael F. Byrne, Director, Office of National Capital
   Region Coordination, Department of Homeland Security
Dennis J. Reimer, Oklahoma National Memorial Institute
   for Prevention of Terrorism
Richard A. Andrews, National Center for Crisis and
   Continuity Coordination

Private Sector Experience on 9/11
William Y. Yun, Fiduciary Trust Company International

Standards for Emergency Management and Business Continuity
Glenn Corbett, John Jay College of Criminal Justice
Randall Yim, Director, National Preparedness Team,
   General Accounting Office

Future Strategies for Private Sector Preparedness

William G. Raisch, Greater New York Safety Council

Peter R. Orszag, The Brookings Institution

James Haviaris, Rockefeller Group Development Corporation

Thomas Susman, Ropes & Gray

SIXTH PUBLIC HEARING

Security and Liberty
Russell Senate Office Building, Washington, D.C.
December 8, 2003

Intelligence Collection within the United States

Larry D. Thompson, former Deputy Attorney General of the United States

Philip B. Heymann, former Deputy Attorney General of the United States

Stephen J. Schulhofer, New York University, School of Law

Protecting Privacy, Preventing Terrorism

Judith A. Miller, former General Counsel, Department of Defense

Stewart A. Baker, former General Counsel, National Security Agency

Marc Rotenberg, Electronic Privacy Information Center

Preventive Detention: Use of Immigration Laws and Enemy Combatant Designations to Combat Terrorism

Jan Ting, Temple University

Khaled Medhat Abou El Fadl, UCLA School of Law

David Martin, University of Virginia School of Law and former General Counsel, Immigration and Naturalization Service, Department of Justice

Government Organization and Domestic Intelligence

The Honorable William P. Barr, former Attorney General of the United States

John J. Hamre, former Deputy Secretary of Defense

John MacGaffin, former Associate Deputy Director for Operations, Central Intelligence Agency

SEVENTH PUBLIC HEARING

Borders, Transportation, and Managing Risk
Hart Senate Office Building, Washington, D.C.
January 26–27, 2004

The Border Security System Prior to September 11

Mary A. Ryan, former Assistant Secretary for Consular Affairs, Department of State

Doris Meissner, former Commissioner, Immigration and Naturalization Service, Department of Justice

An Incident in Florida

Jose E. Melendez-Perez, Inspector, Customs and Border Protection, Department of Homeland Security

Visas and Watchlisting Today

Maura Harty, Assistant Secretary for Consular Affairs, Department of State

Russell E. Travers, Deputy Director, Information Sharing and Knowledge

Management Department, Terrorist Threat Integration Center, Central Intelligence Agency

Donna A. Bucella, Director, Terrorist Screening Center, Federal Bureau of Investigation

The Response to September 11 on the Borders
James Ziglar, former Commissioner, Immigration and
  Naturalization Service, Department of Justice
Robert C. Bonner, Commissioner, Customs and Border
  Protection, Department of Homeland Security
Peter F. Verga, Principal Deputy Assistant Secretary for
  Homeland Defense, Department of Defense

Aviation Security on 9/11: The Regulators
Jane F. Garvey, former Administrator, Federal Aviation
  Administration
Cathal L. "Irish" Flynn, former Associate Administrator of
  Civil Aviation Security, Federal Aviation Administration
Claudio Manno, Assistant Administrator for Intelligence,
  Transportation Security Administration

Aviation Security on 9/11: The Airlines
Edmond L. Soliday, former Vice President of Safety,
  Quality Assurance, and Security, United Airlines
Andrew P. Studdert, former Chief Operating Officer,
  United Airlines
Gerard J. Arpey, Chief Executive Officer, American
  Airlines
Timothy J. Ahern, Vice President-DFW Hub, and former
  Vice President of Safety, Security, and Environmental,
  American Airlines

Acts of Courage in the Sky
Nydia Gonzalez, Manager, Southeast Reservations Center,
  American Airlines

Risk Management after September 11
James M. Loy, Deputy Secretary, Department of Homeland
  Security

EIGHTH PUBLIC HEARING
Counterterrorism Policy
Hart Senate Office Building, Washington, D.C.
March 23–24, 2004

Diplomacy
The Honorable Madeleine K. Albright, former Secretary of
State
The Honorable Colin L. Powell, Secretary of State

The Military
The Honorable William S. Cohen, former Secretary of
Defense
The Honorable Donald H. Rumsfeld, Secretary of Defense

Intelligence Policy
The Honorable George J. Tenet, Director of Central
Intelligence

National Policy Coordination
The Honorable Samuel R. Berger, former Assistant to the
President for National Security Affairs
Richard A. Clarke, former National Coordinator for
Counterterrorism, National Security Council
Richard L. Armitage, Deputy Secretary of State

NINTH PUBLIC HEARING
Hart Senate Office Building, Washington, D.C.
April 8, 2004

The Honorable Condoleezza Rice, Assistant to the
President for National Security Affairs

TENTH PUBLIC HEARING
Law Enforcement and Intelligence
Hart Senate Office Building, Washington, D.C.
April 13–14, 2004

Law Enforcement, Counterterrorism, and Intelligence Collection in the United States Prior to 9/11

The Honorable Louis J. Freeh, former Director, Federal Bureau of Investigation

The Honorable Janet Reno, former Attorney General of the United States

Threats and Responses in 2001

Thomas J. Pickard, former Acting Director, Federal Bureau of Investigation

Ambassador J. Cofer Black, former Director, Counterterrorism Center, Central Intelligence Agency

The Honorable John Ashcroft, Attorney General of the United States

The Performance of the Intelligence Community

The Honorable George J. Tenet, Director of Central Intelligence

Preventing Future Attacks Inside the United States

John O. Brennan, Director, Terrorist Threat Integration Center, Central Intelligence Agency

Lieutenant General Patrick M. Hughes, Assistant Secretary for Information Analysis, Department of Homeland Security

John S. Pistole, Executive Assistant Director for Counterterrorism and Counterintelligence, Federal Bureau of Investigation

James L. Pavitt, Deputy Director of Operations, Central Intelligence Agency

FBI Leadership and Initiatives Post-9/11

The Honorable Robert S. Mueller III, Director, Federal
  Bureau of Investigation
Maureen Baginski, Executive Assistant Director for
  Intelligence, Federal Bureau of Investigation

ELEVENTH PUBLIC HEARING

Emergency Response
New School University, New York, N.Y.
May 18–19, 2004

Alan Reiss, former Director, World Trade Center, Port
  Authority of New York and New Jersey
Joseph Morris, former Chief, Port Authority of New York
  and New Jersey Police Department
Bernard B. Kerik, former Commissioner, New York Police
  Department
Thomas Von Essen, former Commissioner, Fire Department
  of New York
Richard Sheirer, former Director, New York City Office of
  Emergency Management
Raymond W. Kelly, Commissioner, New York Police
  Department
Nicholas Scoppetta, Commissioner, Fire Department of
  New York
Joseph F. Bruno, Director, New York City Office of
  Emergency Management
The Honorable Rudolph W. Giuliani, former Mayor, City of
  New York
Dennis Smith, Author, *Report from Ground Zero*
Jerome M. Hauer, former Commissioner, New York City
  Office of Emergency Management
Edward P. Plaugher, Chief, Arlington County Fire
  Department
The Honorable Michael R. Bloomberg, Mayor, City of New
  York

The Honorable Thomas J. Ridge, Secretary of Homeland
Security

TWELFTH PUBLIC HEARING
The 9/11 Plot and National Crisis Management
National Transportation Safety Board Conference Center,
Washington, D.C.
June 16–17, 2004

Al Qaeda
Mary Deborah Doran, Special Agent, Federal Bureau of
Investigation
Patrick J. Fitzgerald, U.S. Attorney for the Northern
District of Illinois CIA Officials

Outline of the 9/11 Plot
Jacqueline Maguire, Special Agent, Federal Bureau of
Investigation
James N. Fitzgerald, Special Agent, Federal Bureau of
Investigation
Adam B. Drucker, Supervisory Special Agent, Federal
Bureau of Investigation
CIA Officials

Military Response on 9/11
General Richard B. Myers, United States Air Force,
Chairman, Joint Chiefs of Staff
Admiral (select) Charles Joseph Leidig, United States
Navy, Deputy Director for Operations, National Military
Command Center
General Ralph E. Eberhart, United States Air Force,
Commander, North American Aerospace Defense
Command (NORAD) and United States Northern
Command
Major General Larry Arnold, United States Air Force
(retired), former Commander, Continental United States
NORAD Region (CONR)

FAA Response on 9/11

Monte R. Belger, former Acting Deputy Administrator, Federal Aviation Administration

Jeff Griffith, former Deputy Director, Air Traffic Control, Federal Aviation Administration

John S. White, former Facility Manager, Air Traffic Control Systems Command Center, Federal Aviation Administration

Benedict Sliney, Operations Manager, New York Terminal Radar Approach Control, Federal Aviation Administration

Due to length and time constraints with the publication of this edition of *The 9/11 Report*, the publisher was unable to include the notes section. However, this edition of the report does maintain the numerical superscripts that correspond to the notes section.

The notes for *The 9/11 Report* are available on the internet at the following sites:

http://www.gpoaccess.gov/911/index.html

and

www.9-11commission.gov